# MyFinanceLab

# The Key to Your Success in Three Easy Steps!

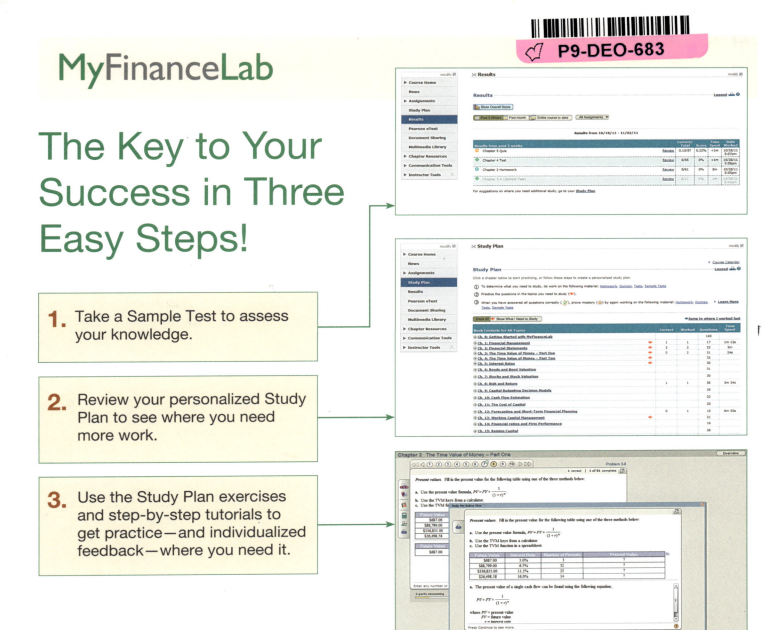

**1.** Take a Sample Test to assess your knowledge.

**2.** Review your personalized Study Plan to see where you need more work.

**3.** Use the Study Plan exercises and step-by-step tutorials to get practice—and individualized feedback—where you need it.

## If your instructor assigns homework and tests using MyFinanceLab

The MyFinanceLab Course Home page uses graphs to let students know their current progress in the course and it has a detailed calendar that not only displays due dates, but allows instructors to add entries.

Did your textbook come with a MyFinanceLab Student Access Kit? If so, go to www.pearsonmylab.com to register using the code. If not, you can purchase access to MyFinanceLab online at www.myfinancelab.com.

# Foundations of Finance

## The Logic and Practice of Financial Management

**Eighth Edition**

# The Pearson Series in Finance

**Bekaert/Hodrick**
*International Financial Management*

**Berk/DeMarzo**
*Corporate Finance\**

**Berk/DeMarzo**
*Corporate Finance: The Core\**

**Berk/DeMarzo/Harford**
*Fundamentals of Corporate Finance\**

**Brooks**
*Financial Management: Core Concepts\**

**Copeland/Weston/Shastri**
*Financial Theory and Corporate Policy*

**Dorfman/Cather**
*Introduction to Risk Management and Insurance*

**Eiteman/Stonehill/Moffett**
*Multinational Business Finance*

**Fabozzi**
*Bond Markets: Analysis and Strategies*

**Fabozzi/Modigliani**
*Capital Markets: Institutions and Instruments*

**Fabozzi/Modigliani/Jones**
*Foundations of Financial Markets and Institutions*

**Finkler**
*Financial Management for Public, Health, and Not-for-Profit Organizations*

**Frasca**
*Personal Finance*

**Gitman/Zutter**
*Principles of Managerial Finance\**

**Gitman/Zutter**
*Principles of Managerial Finance—Brief Edition\**

**Haugen**
*The Inefficient Stock Market: What Pays Off and Why*

**Haugen**
*The New Finance: Overreaction, Complexity, and Uniqueness*

**Holden**
*Excel Modeling in Corporate Finance*

**Holden**
*Excel Modeling in Investments*

**Hughes/MacDonald**
*International Banking: Text and Cases*

**Hull**
*Fundamentals of Futures and Options Markets*

**Hull**
*Options, Futures, and Other Derivatives*

**Keown**
*Personal Finance: Turning Money into Wealth\**

**Keown/Martin/Petty**
*Foundations of Finance: The Logic and Practice of Financial Management\**

**Kim/Nofsinger**
*Corporate Governance*

**Madura**
*Personal Finance\**

**Marthinsen**
*Risk Takers: Uses and Abuses of Financial Derivatives*

**McDonald**
*Derivatives Markets*

**McDonald**
*Fundamentals of Derivatives Markets*

**Mishkin/Eakins**
*Financial Markets and Institutions*

**Moffett/Stonehill/Eiteman**
*Fundamentals of Multinational Finance*

**Nofsinger**
*Psychology of Investing*

**Ormiston/Fraser**
*Understanding Financial Statements*

**Pennacchi**
*Theory of Asset Pricing*

**Rejda**
*Principles of Risk Management and Insurance*

**Seiler**
*Performing Financial Studies: A Methodological Cookbook*

**Smart/Gitman/Joehnk**
*Fundamentals of Investing\**

**Solnik/McLeavey**
*Global Investments*

**Stretcher/Michael**
*Cases in Financial Management*

**Titman/Keown/Martin**
*Financial Management: Principles and Applications\**

**Titman/Martin**
*Valuation: The Art and Science of Corporate Investment Decisions*

**Weston/Mitchel/Mulherin**
*Takeovers, Restructuring, and Corporate Governance*

# Foundations of Finance
## The Logic and Practice of Financial Management

**Eighth Edition**

### Arthur J. Keown

Virginia Polytechnic Institute and State University
R. B. Pamplin Professor of Finance

### John D. Martin

Baylor University
Professor of Finance
Carr P. Collins Chair in Finance

### J. William Petty

Baylor University
Professor of Finance
W. W. Caruth Chair in Entrepreneurship

**PEARSON**

Boston   Columbus   Indianapolis   New York   San Francisco   Upper Saddle River
Amsterdam   Cape Town   Dubai   London   Madrid   Milan   Munich   Paris   Montreal   Toronto
Delhi   Mexico City   Sao Paulo   Sydney   Hong Kong   Seoul   Singapore   Taipei   Tokyo

**Editor in Chief:** Donna Battista
**Acquisitions Editor:** Katie Rowland
**Editorial Project Manager:** Emily Biberger
**Editorial Assistant:** Elissa Senra-Sargent
**Managing Editor:** Jeff Holcomb
**Senior Production Project Manager:** Meredith Gertz
**Senior Marketing Manager:** Jami Minard
**Director of Media:** Susan Schoenberg
**Media Producer:** Melissa Honig
**MyFinanceLab Content Lead:** Miguel Leonarte
**Permissions Project Manager:** Jill C. Dougan
**Senior Manufacturing Buyer:** Carol Melville

**Art Director:** Jonathan Boylan
**Cover Designer:** RHDG | Riezebos Holzbaur
Design Group
**Cover Illustration:** mmaxer/Shutterstock.com
**Image Manager:** Rachel Youdelman
**Photo Research:** Integra
**Project Coordination, Composition, Text Design,
Illustrations, and Alterations:** Cenveo Publisher Services/
Nesbitt Graphics, Inc.
**Printer/Binder:** Courier Kendallville
**Cover Printer:** Lehigh Phoenix
**Text Font:** 9.75/12pt Janson

Credits and acknowledgments borrowed from other sources and reproduced, with permission, in this textbook appear on appropriate page within text.

Photo Credits: p. 3: Stanca Sanda/Alamy; p. 21: Paul Sakuma/AP Images; p. 51: Courtesy of Home Depot; p. 103: Kristoffer Tripplaar/Alamy; p. 143: Jorge Salcedo/Shutterstock; p. 183: Zef Nikolla/HO/EPA/Newscom; p. 221: Peter Carroll/Alamy; p. 251: M4OS Photos/Alamy; p. 275: PSL Images/Alamy; p. 305: Imaginechina/AP Images; p. 345: Larry W. Smith/EPA/Newscom; p. 381: Stuwdamdorp/Alamy; p. 417: Daniele Salvatori/Alamy; p. 437: DPD ImageStock/Alamy; p. 457: Paul Sakuma/AP Images; p. 485: Hemis/Alamy.

**Library of Congress Cataloging-in-Publication Data**

Keown, Arthur J.
  Foundations of finance : the logic and practice of financial management / Arthur J. Keown, John D. Martin, J. William Petty. — 8th ed.
    p. cm. — (The Pearson series in finance)
  Includes index.
  ISBN 978-0-13-299487-3
  1. Corporations—Finance. I. Martin, John D., II. Petty, J. William, III. Title.
  HG4026.F67 2014
  658.15--dc23

2012041146

www.pearsonhighered.com

ISBN-13: 978-0-13-301965-0
ISBN-10: 0-13-301965-9

*To my parents, from whom I learned the most.*
Arthur J. Keown

*To the Martin women—wife Sally and daughter-in-law Mel,
the Martin men—sons Dave and Jess, and
Martin boys—grandsons Luke and Burke.*
John D. Martin

*To my wife, Donna, who has been my friend,
encourager, and supporter for more years than
we care to admit. How quickly time has passed
since we first met all the way back in high school.*
J. William Petty

# About the Authors

**Arthur J. Keown** is the Department Head and R. B. Pamplin Professor of Finance at Virginia Polytechnic Institute and State University. He received his bachelor's degree from Ohio Wesleyan University, his M.B.A. from the University of Michigan, and his doctorate from Indiana University. An award-winning teacher, he is a member of the Academy of Teaching Excellence; has received five Certificates of Teaching Excellence at Virginia Tech, the W. E. Wine Award for Teaching Excellence, and the Alumni Teaching Excellence Award; and in 1999 received the Outstanding Faculty Award from the State of Virginia. Professor Keown is widely published in academic journals. His work has appeared in the *Journal of Finance*, the *Journal of Financial Economics*, the *Journal of Financial and Quantitative Analysis*, the *Journal of Financial Research*, the *Journal of Banking and Finance*, *Financial Management*, the *Journal of Portfolio Management*, and many others. In addition to *Foundations of Finance*, two other of his books are widely used in college finance classes all over the country—*Basic Financial Management* and *Personal Finance: Turning Money into Wealth*. Professor Keown is a Fellow of the Decision Sciences Institute, was a member of the Board of Directors of the Financial Management Association, and is the head of the finance department at Virginia Tech. In addition, he recently served as the co-editor of the *Journal of Financial Research* for 6½ years and as the co-editor of the Financial Management Association's *Survey and Synthesis* series for 6 years. He lives with his wife and two children in Blacksburg, Virginia, where he collects original art from *Mad Magazine*.

**John D. Martin** holds the Carr P. Collins Chair in Finance in the Hankamer School of Business at Baylor University, where he teaches in the Baylor EMBA programs and has three times been selected as the outstanding teacher. John joined the Baylor faculty in 1998 after spending 17 years on the faculty of the University of Texas at Austin. Over his career he has published over 50 articles in the leading finance journals, including papers in the *Journal of Finance, Journal of Financial Economics, Journal of Financial and Quantitative Analysis, Journal of Monetary Economics*, and *Management Science*. His recent research has spanned issues related to the economics of unconventional energy sources (both wind and shale gas), the hidden cost of venture capital, and managed versus unmanaged changes in capital structures. He is also co-author of several books, including *Financial Management: Principles and Practice* (11th ed., Prentice Hall), *Foundations of Finance* (8th ed., Prentice Hall), *Theory of Finance* (Dryden Press), *Financial Analysis* (3rd ed., McGraw Hill), *Valuation: The Art & Science of Corporate Investment Decisions* (2nd ed., Prentice Hall), and *Value Based Management with Social Responsibility* (2nd ed., Oxford University Press).

**J. William Petty, PhD,** University of Texas at Austin, is Professor of Finance and W. W. Caruth Chair of Entrepreneurship. Dr. Petty teaches entrepreneurial finance, both at the undergraduate and graduate levels. He is a University Master Teacher. In 2008, the Acton Foundation for Entrepreneurship Excellence selected him as the National Entrepreneurship Teacher of the Year. His research interests include the financing of entrepreneurial firms and shareholder value-based management. He has served as the co-editor for the *Journal of Financial Research* and the editor of the *Journal of Entrepreneurial Finance*. He has published articles in various academic and professional journals including *Journal of Financial and Quantitative Analysis, Financial Management, Journal of Portfolio Management, Journal of Applied Corporate Finance*, and *Accounting Review*. Dr. Petty is co-author of a leading textbook in small business and entrepreneurship, *Small Business Management: Launching and Growing Entrepreneurial Ventures*. He also co-authored *Value-Based Management: Corporate America's Response to the Shareholder Revolution* (2010). He serves on the Board of Directors of a publicly traded oil and gas firm. Finally, he has served as the Executive Director of the Baylor Angel Network, a network of private investors who provide capital to startups and early-stage companies.

# Brief Contents

# Contents

**Ethics in Financial Management:** The Financial Downside of Poor Ethical
Behavior   332

## 11   Cash Flows and Other Topics in Capital Budgeting   344

## Appendix 11A: The Modified Accelerated Cost of Recovery System   378

## PART 4   Capital Structure and Dividend Policy   380

## 12   Determining the Financing Mix   380

# Preface

The study of finance focuses on making decisions that enhance the value of the firm. This is done by providing customers with the best products and services in a cost-effective way. In a sense we, the authors of *Foundations of Finance*, are trying to do the same thing. That is, we have tried to present financial management to students in a way that makes their studies as easy and productive as possible by using a step-by-step approach to walking them through each new concept or problem.

We are very proud of the history of this volume, as it was the first "shortened book" of financial management when it was published in its first edition. The book broke new ground by reducing the number of chapters down to the foundational materials and by trying to present the subject in understandable terms. We continue our quest for readability with the Eighth Edition.

## Pedagogy That Works

This book provides students with a conceptual understanding of the financial decision-making process, rather than just an introduction to the tools and techniques of finance. For the student, it is all too easy to lose sight of the logic that drives finance and to focus instead on memorizing formulas and procedures. As a result, students have a difficult time understanding the interrelationships among the topics covered. Moreover, later in life when the problems encountered do not match the textbook presentation, students may find themselves unprepared to abstract from what they learned. To overcome this problem, the opening chapter presents five underlying principles of finance, which serve as a springboard for the chapters and topics that follow. In essence, the student is presented with a cohesive, interrelated perspective from which future problems can be approached.

With a focus on the big picture, we provide an introduction to financial decision making rooted in current financial theory and in the current state of world economic conditions. This focus is perhaps most apparent in the attention given to the capital markets and their influence on corporate financial decisions. What results is an introductory treatment of a discipline rather than the treatment of a series of isolated problems that face the financial manager. The goal of this text is not merely to teach the tools of a discipline or trade but also to enable students to abstract what is learned to new and yet unforeseen problems—in short, to educate the student in finance.

 **2** Understand the basic principles of finance, their importance, and the importance of ethics and trust.

### Five Principles That Form the Foundations of Finance

To the first-time student of finance, the subject matter may seem like a collection of unrelated decision rules. This could not be further from the truth. In fact, our decision rules, and the logic that underlies them, spring from five simple principles that do not require knowledge of finance to understand. These five principles guide the financial manager in the creation of value for the firm's owners (the stockholders).

As you will see, while it is not necessary to understand finance to understand these principles, it is necessary to understand these principles in order to understand finance. Although these principles may at first appear simple or even trivial, they provide the driving force behind all that follows, weaving together the concepts and techniques presented in this text, and thereby allowing us to focus on the logic underlying the practice of financial management. Now let's introduce the five principles.

 **Principle 1: Cash Flow Is What Matters**

You probably recall from your accounting classes that a company's profits can differ dramatically from its cash flows, which we will review in Chapter 3. But for now understand that cash flows, not profits, represent money that can be spent. Consequently, it is cash flow, not profits, that determines the value of a business. For this reason when we analyze the consequences of a managerial decision we focus on the resulting cash flows, not profits. In the movie industry, there is a big difference between accounting profits and cash

## Innovations and Distinctive Features in the Eighth Edition

### NEW! A Multistep Approach to Problem Solving and Analysis

As anyone who has taught the core undergraduate finance course knows, there is a wide range of math comprehension and skill. Students who do not have the math skills needed to master the subject sometimes end up memorizing formulas rather than focusing on the analysis of business decisions using math as a tool. We address this problem both in terms of text content and pedagogy.

- First, we present math only as a tool to help us analyze problems, and only when necessary. We do not present math for its own sake.
- Second, finance is an analytical subject and requires that students be able to solve problems. To help with this process, numbered chapter examples appear throughout the book. Each of these examples follows a very detailed and multistep approach to problem solving that helps students develop their problem-solving skills.

*Step 1: Formulate a Solution Strategy.* For example, what is the appropriate formula to apply? How can a calculator or spreadsheet be used to "crunch the numbers"?

*Step 2: Crunch the Numbers.* Here we provide a completely worked out step-by-step solution. We first present a description of the solution in prose and then a corresponding mathematical implementation.

*Step 3: Analyze Your Results.* We end each solution with an analysis of what the solution means. This stresses the point that problem solving is about analysis and decision making. Moreover, in this step we emphasize that decisions are often based on incomplete information, which requires the exercise of managerial judgment, a fact of life that is often learned on the job.

## NEW! Financial Decision Tools

This feature recaps keys equations shortly after their application in the chapter.

| FINANCIAL DECISION TOOLS | | |
|---|---|---|
| **Name of Tool** | **Formula** | **What It Tells You** |
| Current ratio | $\dfrac{\text{current assets}}{\text{current liabilities}}$ | Measures a firm's liquidity. A higher ratio means greater liquidity. |
| Acid-test ratio | $\dfrac{\text{cash} + \text{accounts receivable}}{\text{current liabilities}}$ | Gives a more stringent measure of liquidity than the current ratio in that it excludes inventories and other current assets from the numerator. A higher ratio means greater liquidity. |

## NEW! Chapter Summaries

These have been rewritten to make it easier for students to connect the summary with each of the in-chapter sections and learning objectives.

## NEW! Key Terms List for Each Chapter

New terminology introduced in the chapter is listed along with a brief definition.

## NEW! Study Problems

The end-of-chapter study problems have been improved and dramatically expanded to allow for a wider range of student practice. In addition, the study problems are now organized according to learning objective so that both the instructor and student can readily align text and problem materials.

## NEW! A Focus on Valuation

Although many professors and instructors make valuation the central theme of their course, students often lose sight of this focus when reading their text. We have revised this edition to reinforce this focus in the content and organization of our text in some very concrete ways:

- We build our discussion around five finance principles that provide the foundation for the valuation of any investment.
- New topics are introduced in the context of "what is the value proposition?" and "how is the value of the enterprise affected?"

## "Cautionary Tale" Boxes

These give students insights into how the core concepts of finance apply in the real world. Each "Cautionary Tale" box goes behind the headlines of finance pitfalls in the news to show how one of the five principles was forgotten or violated.

## Real-World Opening Vignettes

Each chapter begins with a story about a current, real-world company faced with a financial decision related to the chapter material that follows. These vignettes have been carefully prepared to stimulate student interest in the topic to come and can be used as a lecture tool to provoke class discussion.

## Use of an Integrated Learning System

The text is organized around the learning objectives that appear at the beginning of each chapter to provide the instructor and student with an easy-to-use integrated learning system. Numbered icons identifying each objective appear next to the related material throughout the text and in the summary, allowing easy location of material related to each objective.

## "Can You Do It?" and "Did You Get It?"

The text provides examples for the students to work at the conclusion of each major section of a chapter, which we call "Can You Do It?" followed by "Did You Get It?" a few pages later in the chapter. This tool provides an essential ingredient to the building-block approach to the material that we use.

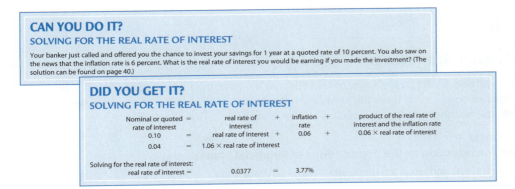

**CAN YOU DO IT?**

**SOLVING FOR THE REAL RATE OF INTEREST**

Your banker just called and offered you the chance to invest your savings for 1 year at a quoted rate of 10 percent. You also saw on the news that the inflation rate is 6 percent. What is the real rate of interest you would be earning if you made the investment? (The solution can be found on page 40.)

**DID YOU GET IT?**

**SOLVING FOR THE REAL RATE OF INTEREST**

| Nominal or quoted rate of interest | = | real rate of interest | + | inflation rate | + | product of the real rate of interest and the inflation rate |
|---|---|---|---|---|---|---|
| 0.10 | = | real rate of interest + | | 0.06 | + | 0.06 × real rate of interest |
| 0.04 | = | 1.06 × real rate of interest | | | | |

Solving for the real rate of interest:
real rate of interest = 0.0377 = 3.77%

## Concept Check

**Concept Check** _____

1. According to Principle 3, how do investors decide where to invest their money?
2. What is an efficient market?
3. What is the agency problem and why does it occur?
4. Why are ethics and trust important in business?

At the end of most major sections, this tool highlights the key ideas just presented and allows students to test their understanding of the material.

## Remember Your Principles

**REMEMBER YOUR PRINCIPLES**

Two principles are especially important in this chapter. **Principle 1** tells us that **Cash Flow Is What Matters**. At times, cash is more important than profits. Thus, considerable time is devoted to measuring cash flows. **Principle 5** warns us that there may be a conflict when managers and owners have different incentives. That is, **Conflicts of Interest Cause Agency Problems**. Because managers' incentives are at times different from those of owners, the firm's common stockholders, as well as other providers of capital (such as bankers), need information that can be used to monitor the managers' actions. Because the owners of large companies do not have access to internal information about the firm's operations, they must rely on public information from any and all sources. One of the main sources of such information comes from the company's financial statements provided by the firm's accountants. Although this information is by no means perfect, it is an important source used by outsiders to assess a company's activities. In this chapter, we learn how to use data from the firm's public financial statements to monitor management's actions.

These in-text inserts appear throughout to allow the student to take time out and reflect on the meaning of the material just presented. The use of these inserts, coupled with the use of the five principles, keeps the student focused on the interrelationships and motivating factors behind the concepts.

## Mini Case

*This Mini Case is available in* MyFinanceLab.

On the first day of your summer internship, you've been assigned to work with the chief financial officer (CFO) of SanBlas Jewels Inc. Not knowing how well trained you are, the CFO has decided to test your understanding of interest rates. Specifically, she asked you to provide a reasonable estimate of the nominal interest rate for a new issue of Aaa-rated bonds to be offered by SanBlas Jewels Inc. The final format that the chief financial officer of SanBlas Jewels has requested is that of equation (2-1) in the text. Your assignment also requires that you consult the data in Table 2-2.

Some agreed-upon procedures related to generating estimates for key variables in equation (2-1) follow.

a. The current 3-month Treasury bill rate is 2.96 percent, the 30-year Treasury bond rate is 5.43 percent, the 30-year Aaa-rated corporate bond rate is 6.71 percent, and the inflation rate is 2.33 percent.
b. The real risk-free rate of interest is the difference between the calculated average yield on 3-month Treasury bills and the inflation rate.
c. The default-risk premium is estimated by the difference between the average yield on Aaa-rated bonds and 30-year Treasury bonds.
d. The maturity-risk premium is estimated by the difference between the average yield on 30-year Treasury bonds and 3-month Treasury bills.
e. SanBlas Jewels' bonds will be traded on the New York Bond Exchange, so the liquidity-risk premium will be slight. It will be greater than zero, however, because the secondary market for the firm's bonds is more uncertain than that of some other jewel sellers. It is estimated at 4 basis points. A basis point is one one-hundredth of 1 percent.

Now place your output into the format of equation (2-1) so that the nominal interest rate can be estimated and the size of each variable can also be inspected for reasonableness and discussion with the CFO.

| CALCULATOR SOLUTION | |
|---|---|
| Data Input | Function Key |
| 10 | N |
| 6 | I/Y |
| −500 | FV |
| 0 | PMT |
| Function Key | Answer |
| CPT | |
| PV | 279.20 |

## Comprehensive Mini Cases

A comprehensive Mini Case appears at the end of almost every chapter, covering all the major topics included in that chapter. This Mini Case can be used as a lecture or review tool by the professor. For the students, it provides an opportunity to apply all the concepts presented within the chapter in a realistic setting, thereby strengthening their understanding of the material.

## Financial Calculators

The use of financial calculators has been integrated throughout this text, especially with respect to the presentation of the time value of money. Where appropriate, calculator solutions appear in the margin.

## Content Updates

In addition to the innovations of this edition, we have made some chapter-by-chapter updates in response to both the continued development of financial thought, reviewer comments, and the recent economic crisis. Some of these changes include:

### Chapter 1
### An Introduction to the Foundations of Financial Management
- Revised and updated discussion of the five principles
- New section on the current global financial crisis

### Chapter 2
### The Financial Markets and Interest Rates
- Revised to reflect recent changes in financial markets
- Simplified to make it livelier and more relevant to students
- Revised coverage of securities markets, reflecting recent technological advances coupled with deregulation and increased competition, which have blurred the difference between an organized exchange and the over-the-counter market
- Updated investment banking coverage, reflecting the dramatic impact of the recent financial crisis on investment banking firms
- Simplified, more intuitive discussion on interest rate determinants
- Additional problems on the determination of interest rates

### Chapter 3
### Understanding Financial Statements and Cash Flows
- Presents a live company, The Home Depot, instead of a hypothetical company, to illustrate financial statements
- Expanded coverage of balance sheets, focusing on what can be learned from them
- More comprehensive and intuitive presentation of cash flows
- New explanation of fixed and variable costs as part of presenting an income statement
- New appendix that presents free cash flows

## Chapter 4
### Evaluating a Firm's Financial Performance

- Continues the use of The Home Depot's financial data to illustrate how we evaluate a firm's financial performance, compared to industry norms or a peer group. In this case, we compare Home Depot's financial performance to that of Lowe's, a major competitor
- Includes comments from Home Depot's management regarding the firm's financial performance
- Revised presentation of evaluating a company's liquidity to align more closely with how business managers talk about liquidity

## Chapter 5
### The Time Value of Money

- Revised to appeal to students regardless of level of numerical skills
- Increased emphasis on the intuition behind the time value of money, stressing visualizing and setting up the problem
- Additional problems emphasizing complex streams of cash flows

## Chapter 6
### The Meaning and Measurement of Risk and Return

- Updated information on the rates of return that investors have earned over the long term with different types of security investments
- Updated examples of rates of return earned from investing in individual companies

## Chapter 7
### The Valuation and Characteristics of Bonds

- Expanded explanation of efficient markets
- New example of a company's credit rating being lowered, which has been a more frequent occurrence in recent times

## Chapter 8
### The Valuation and Characteristics of Stock

- More current explanation of options for getting stock quotes from the *Wall Street Journal*

## Chapter 9
### The Cost of Capital

- Streamlined exposition and reduced quantity of learning objectives
- Rewritten discussion of the divisional cost of capital

## Chapter 10
### Capital-Budgeting Techniques and Practice

- New introduction looks at Disney's decision to build the Shanghai Disney Resort
- Simplified presentation of the payback period and discounted payback period

## Chapter 11
### Cash Flows and Other Topics in Capital Budgeting

- New introduction examines the complications Toyota faced in estimating future cash flows when it introduced the Prius
- New discussion of the iPad as an example of synergistic effects
- New appendix that presents the modified accelerated cost recovery system

## Chapter 12
### Determining the Financing Mix

- Simplified presentation of chapter materials, including a reduced number of learning objectives

### Chapter 13
### Dividend Policy and Internal Financing

- Simplified presentation of chapter materials, including a reduced number of learning objectives
- Rewritten introduction focuses on Apple Computer, Inc.'s decision to re-initiate its cash dividend
- Problem set extensively revised with the addition of 13 new exercises

### Chapter 14
### Short-Term Financial Planning

- New study problem added, focusing on the limitations of the percent of sales forecast method
- New discussion of the regression method of forecasting financial variables in conjunction with the percent of sales method

### Chapter 15
### Working-Capital Management

- Simplified presentation of chapter materials, including reducing the number of learning objectives

### Chapter 16
### International Business Finance

- Comprehensively revised and updated to reflect changes in exchange rates and global financial markets in general
- Simplified and streamlined coverage in the section on interest rate parity, discussion of purchasing-power parity and the law of one price, and international capital budgeting

### Web Chapter 17
### Cash, Receivables, and Inventory Management

- Simplified presentation of chapter materials, including reducing the number of learning objectives

## A Complete Support Package for the Student and Instructor

### MyFinanceLab

This fully integrated online homework system gives students the hands-on practice and tutorial help they need to learn finance efficiently. Ample opportunities for online practice and assessment in MyFinanceLab are seamlessly integrated into each chapter. For more details, see the inside front cover.

### Instructor's Resource Center

This password-protected site, accessible at www.pearsonhighered.com/irc, hosts all of the instructor resources that follow. Instructors should click on the "IRC Help Center" link for easy-to-follow instructions on getting access or may contact their sales representative for further information.

### Test Bank

This online Test Bank, prepared by Curtis Bacon of Southern Oregon University, provides more than 1,600 multiple-choice, true/false, and short-answer questions with complete and detailed answers. The online Test Bank is designed for use with the TestGen-EQ test-generating software. This computerized package allows instructors to custom design, save, and generate classroom tests. The test program permits instructors to edit, add, or delete questions from the test bank; analyze test results; and organize a database of tests and student results. This software allows for greater flexibility and ease of use. It provides many options for organizing and displaying tests, along with a search and sort feature.

## Instructor's Manual with Solutions

Written by the authors, the Instructor's Manual follows the textbook's organization and represents a continued effort to serve the teacher's goal of being effective in the classroom. Each chapter contains a chapter orientation, an outline of each chapter (also suitable for lecture notes), answers to end-of-chapter review questions, and solutions to end-of-chapter study problems.

The Instructor's Manual is available electronically and instructors can download this file from the Instructor's Resource Center by visiting www.pearsonhighered.com/irc.

## The PowerPoint Lecture Presentation

This lecture presentation tool, prepared by Philip Samuel Russel of Philadelphia University, provides the instructor with individual lecture outlines to accompany the text. The slides include many of the figures and tables from the text. These lecture notes can be used as is or instructors can easily modify them to reflect specific presentation needs.

## Companion Web Site

(www.pearsonhighered.com/keown) The Web site contains various resources related specifically to the Eighth Edition of *Foundations of Finance: The Logic and Practice of Financial Management*, including Web Chapter 17 and Appendix A.

## Excel Spreadsheets

Created by the authors, these spreadsheets correspond to end-of-chapter problems from the text. This student resource is available on both the companion Web site and MyFinanceLab.

## CourseSmart for Instructors

CourseSmart goes beyond traditional teaching resources to provide instant, online access to the textbooks and course materials you need at a lower cost to students. And while students save money, you can save time and hassle with a digital textbook that allows you to search the most relevant content at the very moment you need it. Whether it's for evaluating textbooks or creating lecture notes to help students with difficult concepts, CourseSmart can make life a little easier. See how by visiting the CourseSmart Web site at www.coursesmart.com/instructors.

## CourseSmart for Students

CourseSmart goes beyond traditional expectations providing instant, online access to the textbooks and course materials students need at a lower cost. Students can also search, highlight, and take notes anywhere at any time. See all the benefits to students at www.coursesmart.com/students.

# Acknowledgments

We gratefully acknowledge the assistance, support, and encouragement of those individuals who have contributed to *Foundations of Finance*. Specifically, we wish to recognize the very helpful insights provided by many of our colleagues. For their careful comments and helpful reviews of the text, we are indebted to:

Haseeb Ahmed, Johnson C. Smith University

Joan Anderssen, Arapahoe Community College

Chris Armstrong, Draughons Junior College

Curtis Bacon, Southern Oregon University

Deb Bauer, University of Oregon

Pat Bernson, County College of Morris

Ed Boyer, Temple University

Joe Brocato, Tarleton State University

Joseph Brum, Fayetteville Technical Community College

Lawrence Byerly, Thomas More College

Juan R. Castro, LeTourneau University

Janice Caudill, Auburn University

Ting-Heng Chu, East Tennessee State University

David Daglio, Newbury College

Julie Dahlquist, University of Texas at San Antonio

David Darst, Central Ohio Technical College

Maria de Boyrie, New Mexico State University

Kate Demarest, Carroll Community College

Khaled Elkhal, University of Southern Indiana

Cheri Etling, University of Tampa

Robert W. Everett, Lock Haven University

Cheryl Fetterman, Cape Fear Community College

David R. Fewings, Western Washington University

Dr. Charles Gahala, Benedictine University

Harry Gallatin, Indiana State University

Deborah Giarusso, University of Northern Iowa

Gregory Goussak, University of Nevada, Las Vegas

Lori Grady, Bucks County Community College

Ed Graham, University of North Carolina Wilmington

Barry Greenberg, Webster University

Gary Greer, University of Houston Downtown

Indra Guertler, Simmons College

Bruce Hadburg, University of Tampa

Thomas Hiebert, University of North Carolina, Charlotte

Marlin Jensen, Auburn University

John Kachurick, Misericordia University

Okan Kavuncu, University of California at Santa Cruz

Gary Kayakachoian, Rbode Island College

David F. Kern, Arkansas State University

Brian Kluger, University of Cincinnati

Lynn Phillips Kugele, University of Mississippi

Mary LaPann, Adirondack Community College

Carlos Liard-Muriente, Central Connecticut State University

Christopher Liberty, College of St Rose, Empire State College

Lynda Livingston, University of Puget Sound

Y. Lal Mahajan, Monmouth University

Edmund Mantell, Pace University

Peter Marks, Rhode Island College

Mario Mastrandrea, Cleveland State University

Anna McAleer, Arcadia University

Robert Meyer, Parkland College

Ronald Moy, St. John's University

Elisa Muresan, Long Island University

Michael Nugent, Stony Brook University

Tony Plath, University of North Carolina at Charlotte

Anthony Pondillo, Siena College

Walter Purvis, Coastal Carolina Community College

Emil Radosevich, Central New Mexico Community College

Deana Ray, Forsyth Technical Community College

Clarence Rose, Radford University

Ahmad Salam, Widener University

Jeffrey Schultz, Christian Brothers University

Thomas W. Secrest, Coastal Carolina University

Ken Shakoori, California State University, Bakersfield

Michael Slates, Bowling Green State University

Suresh Srivastava, University of Alaska Anchorage

Maurry Tamarkin, Clark University

Fang Wang, West Virginia University

Paul Warrick, Westwood College

Jill Wetmore, Saginaw Valley State University

Kevin Yost, Auburn University

Jingxue Yuan, Texas Tech University

Mengxin Zhao, Bentley College

We also thank our friends at Pearson. They are a great group of folks. We offer our personal expression of appreciation to our editor-in-chief Donna Battista, who provided the leadership and direction to this project. She is the best, and she settles for nothing less than perfection—thanks Donna. We would also like to thank Katie Rowland, our finance editor. Katie is new to Pearson and full of energy and drive with amazing insights and intuition about what makes up a great book. We would also like to thank Emily Biberger, our editorial project manager, for her administrative deftness. She was superb. With Emily watching over us, there was no way the ball could be dropped. On top of this, Emily is just a great person—our hats are off to you Emily. We would also like to extend our thanks to Meredith Gertz, who served as our production supervisor and guided the book through a very complex production process. Meredith kept us on schedule while maintaining extremely high quality. Our thanks also go to Mary Sanger of Cenveo Publisher Services, who served as the project manager and did a superb job. Even more, she was fun to work with, always keeping us on task. It seemed that a day did not go by when we didn't call Mary to ask her advice or help on something, and she was always able and willing to help out. Miguel Leonarte, who worked on MyFinanceLab, also deserves a word of thanks for making My-FinanceLab flow so seamlessly with the book. He has continued to refine and improve MyFinanceLab, and as a result of his efforts, it has become a learning tool without equal. We also thank Melissa Honig, our media producer, who did a great job of making sure we are on the cutting edge in terms of Web applications and offerings.

As a final word, we express our sincere thanks to those who are using *Foundations of Finance* in the classroom. We thank you for making us a part of your teaching-learning team. Please feel free to contact any member of the author team should you have questions or needs.

—A.J.K. / J.D.M. / J.W.P.

# An Introduction to the Foundations of Financial Management

## Learning Objectives

**After reading this chapter, you should be able to:**

**1 Identify** the goal of the firm.
The Goal of the Firm

**2 Understand** the basic principles of finance, their importance, and the importance of ethics and trust.
Five Principles That Form the Foundations of Finance

**3 Describe** the role of finance in business.
The Role of Finance in Business

**4 Distinguish** between the different legal forms of business.
The Legal Forms of Business Organization

**5 Explain** what has led to the era of the multinational corporation.
Finance and the Multinational Firm: The New Role

Apple Computer (AAPL) ignited the personal computer revolution in the 1970s with the Apple II and reinvented the personal computer in the 1980s with the Macintosh. But by 1997, it looked like it might be nearing the end for Apple. Mac users were on the decline, and the company didn't seem to be headed in any real direction. It was at that point that Steve Jobs reappeared, taking back his old job as CEO of Apple, the company he cofounded in 1976. To say the least, things began to change. In fact, between then and April 2012, the price of Apple's common stock climbed by over one hundred and sixteen-fold!

How did Apple accomplish this? The company did it by going back to what it does best, which is to produce products that make the optimal trade-off between ease of use, complexity, and features. Apple took its special skills and applied them to more than just computers, introducing new products such as the iPod, iTunes, the sleek iMac, the MacBook Air, iPod Touch, and the iPhone along with its unlimited "apps." Although all these products have done well, the success of the iPod has been truly amazing. Between the introduction of the iPod in October 2001 and the beginning of 2005, Apple sold more than 6 million of the devices. Then, in 2004, it came out with the iPod Mini, about the length and width of a business card, which has also been a huge success, particularly among women. How successful has this new product been? By 2004, Apple was selling more iPods than its signature Macintosh desktop and notebook computers.

How do you follow up on the success of the iPod? You keep improving your products and you keep developing and introducing new products that consumers want. With this in mind, in October 2011, Apple unveiled its iPhone 4S, selling over 4 million phones in the first week. Then, in March 2012, during the same week that Apple's App Store downloads topped 25 billion, Apple introduced the New iPad, selling over 3 million units in the first week. In effect, Apple seems to have a never-ending supply of new, exciting products that we all want.

How did Apple make a decision to introduce the original iPod and now the iPad? The answer is by identifying a customer need, combined with sound financial management. Financial management deals with the maintenance and creation of economic value or wealth by focusing on decision making with an eye toward creating wealth. As such, this text deals with financial decisions such as when to introduce a new product, when to invest in new assets, when to replace existing assets, when to borrow from banks, when to sell stocks or bonds, when to extend credit to a customer, and how much cash and inventory to maintain. All of these aspects of financial management were factors in Apple's decision to introduce and continuously improve the iPod, Apple TV, iPhone, and iPad, and the end result is having a major financial impact on Apple.

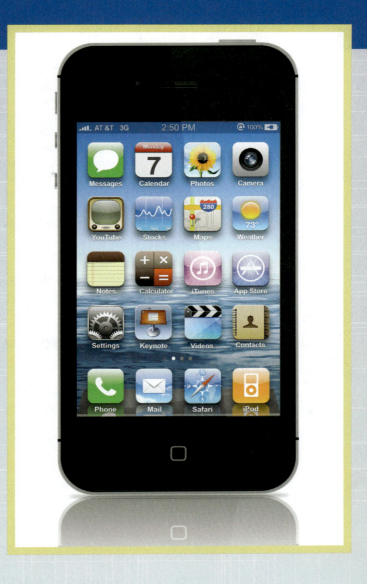

In this chapter, we lay the foundation for the entire book by explaining the key goal that guides financial decision making: maximizing shareholder wealth. From there we introduce the thread that ties everything together: the five basic principles of finance. Finally, we discuss the legal forms of business. We close the chapter with a brief look at what has led to the rise in multinational corporations.

## The Goal of the Firm

 Identify the goal of the firm.

The fundamental goal of a business is to create value for the company's owners (that is, its shareholders). This goal is frequently stated as "maximization of shareholder wealth." Thus, the goal of the financial manager is to create wealth for the shareholders, by making decisions that will maximize the price of the existing common stock. Not only does this goal directly benefit the shareholders of the company but it also provides benefits to society as scarce resources are directed to their most productive use by businesses competing to create wealth.

We have chosen maximization of shareholder wealth—that is, maximizing the market value of the existing shareholders' common stock—because all financial decisions ultimately affect the firm's stock price. Investors react to poor investment or dividend decisions by causing the total value of the firm's stock to fall, and they react to good decisions by pushing up the price of the stock. In effect, under this goal, good decisions are those that create wealth for the shareholder.

Obviously, there are some serious practical problems in using changes in the firm's stock to evaluate financial decisions. Many things affect stock prices; to attempt to identify a reaction to a particular financial decision would simply be impossible, but fortunately that is unnecessary. To employ this goal, we need not consider every stock price change to be a market interpretation of the worth of our decisions. Other factors, such as changes in the economy, also affect stock prices. What we do focus on is the effect that our decision *should have* on the stock price if everything else were held constant. The market price of the firm's stock reflects the value of the firm as seen by its owners and takes into account the complexities and complications of the real-world risk. As we follow this goal throughout our discussions, we must keep in mind one more question: Who exactly are the shareholders? The answer: Shareholders are the legal owners of the firm.

## Concept Check

1. What is the goal of the firm?
2. How would you apply this goal in practice?

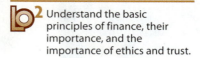

Understand the basic principles of finance, their importance, and the importance of ethics and trust.

# Five Principles That Form the Foundations of Finance

To the first-time student of finance, the subject matter may seem like a collection of unrelated decision rules. This could not be further from the truth. In fact, our decision rules, and the logic that underlies them, spring from five simple principles that do not require knowledge of finance to understand. These five principles guide the financial manager in the creation of value for the firm's owners (the stockholders).

As you will see, while it is not necessary to understand finance to understand these principles, it is necessary to understand these principles in order to understand finance. Although these principles may at first appear simple or even trivial, they provide the driving force behind all that follows, weaving together the concepts and techniques presented in this text, and thereby allowing us to focus on the logic underlying the practice of financial management. Now let's introduce the five principles.

### Principle 1: Cash Flow Is What Matters

You probably recall from your accounting classes that a company's profits can differ dramatically from its cash flows, which we will review in Chapter 3. But for now understand that cash flows, not profits, represent money that can be spent. Consequently, it is cash flow, not profits, that determines the value of a business. For this reason when we analyze the consequences of a managerial decision we focus on the resulting cash flows, not profits.

In the movie industry, there is a big difference between accounting profits and cash flow. Many a movie is crowned a success and brings in plenty of cash flow for the studio but doesn't produce a profit. Even some of the most successful box office hits—*Forrest Gump, Coming to America, Batman, My Big Fat Greek Wedding*, and the TV series *Babylon 5*—realized no accounting profits at all after accounting for various movie studio costs. That's because "Hollywood Accounting" allows for overhead costs not associated with the movie to be added on to the true cost of the movie. In fact, the movie *Harry Potter and the Order of the Phoenix*, which grossed almost $1 billion worldwide, actually lost $167 million according to the accountants. Was *Harry Potter and the Order of the Phoenix* a successful movie? It sure was—in fact it was the 16th highest grossing film of all time. Without question, it produced cash, but it didn't make any profits.

There is another important point we need to make about cash flows. Recall from your economics classes that we should always look at marginal, or **incremental, cash flows** when making a financial decision. The incremental cash flow to the company as a whole is *the difference between the cash flows the company will produce both with and without the investment it's thinking about making.* To understand this concept, let's think about the incremental cash flows of the *Pirates of the Caribbean* movies. Not only did Disney make money on the

**incremental cash flow** the difference between the cash flows a company will produce both with and without the investment it is thinking about making.

movies, but it also increased the number of people attracted to Disney theme parks to go on the "Pirates of the Caribbean" ride. So, if you were to evaluate a *Pirates of the Caribbean* movie, you'd want to include its impact on sales throughout the entire company.

## Principle 2: Money Has a Time Value

Perhaps the most fundamental principle of finance is that money has a "time" value. Very simply, a dollar received today is more valuable than a dollar received one year from now because we can invest the dollar we have today to earn interest so that at the end of one year we will have more than one dollar.

For example, suppose you have a choice of receiving $1,000 either today or one year from now. If you decide to receive it a year from now, you will have passed up the opportunity to earn a year's interest on the money. Economists would say you suffered an "opportunity loss" or an "opportunity cost." The cost is the interest you could have earned on the $1,000 if you invested it for one year. The concept of opportunity costs is fundamental to the study of finance and economics. Very simply, the **opportunity cost** of any choice you make *is the highest-valued alternative that you had to give up when you made the choice.* So if you loan money to your brother at no interest, money that otherwise would have been loaned to a friend for 8 percent interest (who is equally likely to repay you), then the opportunity cost of making the loan to your brother is 8 percent.

**opportunity cost** the cost of making a choice in terms of the next best alternative that must be foregone.

In the study of finance, we focus on the creation and measurement of value. To measure value, we use the concept of the time value of money to bring the future benefits and costs of a project, measured by its cash flows, back to the present. Then, if the benefits or cash inflows outweigh the costs, the project creates wealth and should be accepted; if the costs or cash outflows outweigh the benefits or cash inflows, the project destroys wealth and should be rejected. Without recognizing the existence of the time value of money, it is impossible to evaluate projects with future benefits and costs in a meaningful way.

## Principle 3: Risk Requires a Reward

Even the novice investor knows there are an unlimited number of investment alternatives to consider. But without exception, investors will not invest if they do not expect to receive a return on their investment. They will want a return that satisfies two requirements:

◆ *A return for delaying consumption.* Why would anyone make an investment that would not at least pay them something for delaying consumption? They won't—even if there is no risk. In fact, investors will want to receive at least the same return that is available for risk-free investments, such as the rate of return being earned on U.S. government securities.

◆ *An additional return for taking on risk.* Investors generally don't like risk. Thus, risky investments are less attractive—*unless* they offer the prospect of higher returns. That said, the more unsure people are about how an investment will perform, the higher the return they will demand for making that investment. So, if you are trying to persuade investors to put money into a risky venture you are pursuing, you will have to offer them a higher expected rate of return.

Figure 1-1 (on page 6) depicts the basic notion that an investor's rate of return should equal a rate of return for delaying consumption plus an additional return for assuming risk. For example, if you have $5,000 to invest and are considering either buying stock in International Business Machines (IBM) or investing in a new bio-tech startup firm that has no past record of success, you would want the startup investment to offer the prospect of a higher expected rate of return than the investment in an established company like IBM.

Notice that we keep referring to the *expected* return rather than the *actual* return. As investors, we have expectations about what returns our investments will earn. However, we can't know for certain what they *will* be. For example, if investors could have seen into the future, no one would have bought stock in AEterna Zentaris, Inc. (AEZS), the late-stage drug development company, on April 2, 2012. Why? Because on that day AEterna Zentaris

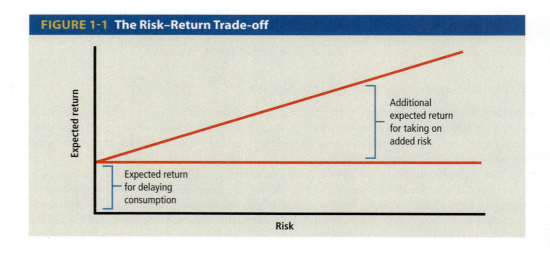

**FIGURE 1-1    The Risk–Return Trade-off**

reported its colon cancer treatment failed to improve survival rates in a late-stage clinical trial. The result was that within minutes of the announcement, the company's stock price dropped by a whopping 66 percent.

The risk–return relationship will be a key concept as we value stocks, bonds, and proposed new investment projects throughout this text. We will also spend some time determining how to measure risk. Interestingly, much of the work for which the 1990 Nobel Prize for economics was awarded centered on the graph in Figure 1-1 and how to measure risk. Both the graph and the risk–return relationship it depicts will reappear often in our study of finance.

## Principle 4: Market Prices Are Generally Right

To understand how securities such as bonds and stocks are valued or priced in the financial markets, it is necessary to have an understanding of the concept of an efficient market. An **efficient market** is *one where the prices of the assets traded in that market fully reflect all available information at any instant in time.*

> **efficient market** a market in which the prices of securities at any instant in time fully reflect all publicly available information about the securities and their actual public values.

Security markets such as the stock and bond markets are particularly important to our study of finance since these markets are the place where firms can go to raise money to finance their investments. Whether a security market such as the New York Stock Exchange (NYSE) is efficient depends on the speed with which newly released information is impounded into prices. Specifically, an efficient stock market is characterized by a large number of profit-driven individuals who act very quickly by buying (or selling) shares of stock in response to the release of new information.

If you are wondering just how vigilant investors in the stock market are in watching for good and bad news, consider the following set of events. While Nike (NKE) CEO William Perez flew aboard the company's Gulfstream jet one day in November 2005, traders on the ground sold off a significant amount of Nike's stock. Why? Because the plane's landing gear was malfunctioning, and they were watching TV coverage of the event! Before Perez landed safely, Nike's stock dropped 1.4 percent. Once Perez's plane landed, Nike's stock price immediately bounced back. This example illustrates that in the financial market there are ever-vigilant investors who are looking to act even *in the anticipation* of the release of new information.

Another example of the speed with which stock prices react to new information deals with Disney. Beginning with *Toy Story* in 1995, Disney (DIS) and Pixar (PIXR) were on a roll, making animated hits one after another, including *A Bug's Life, Toy Story 2, Monsters, Inc., Finding Nemo,* and *The Incredibles*. So in 2006, the hopes for the animated movie *Cars* were very high. However, in the movie's opening weekend, it grossed only $60 million, or about $10 million less than investors expected. How did the stock market respond? On the Monday following the opening weekend, Disney stock opened over 2 percent lower.

Apparently, the news of the disappointing box office receipts was reflected in Disney's opening stock price, even before it traded!

The key learning point here is the following: Stock market prices are a useful barometer of the value of a firm. Specifically, managers can expect their company's share prices to respond quickly to investors' assessment of their decisions. If investors on the whole agree that the decision is a good one that creates value, then they will push up the price of the firm's stock to reflect that added value. On the other hand, if investors feel that a decision is bad for share prices, then the firm's share value will be driven down.

Unfortunately, this principle doesn't always work perfectly in the real world. You just need to look at the housing price bubble that helped bring on the economic downturn in 2008–2009 to realize that prices and value don't always move in lockstep. Like it or not, the psychological biases of individuals impact decision making, and as a result, our decision-making process is not always rational. Behavioral finance considers this type of behavior and takes what we already know about financial decision making and adds in human behavior with all its apparent irrationality.

We'll try and point out the impact of human behavior on decisions throughout our study. But understand that the field of behavioral finance is a work in progress—we understand only a small portion of what may be going on. We can say, however, that behavioral biases have an impact on our financial decisions. As an example, people tend to be overconfident and many times mistake skill for luck. As Robert Shiller, a well-known economics professor at Yale put it, "people think they know more than they do."[1] This overconfidence applies to their abilities, their knowledge and understanding, and forecasting the future. Since they have confidence in their valuation estimates, they may take on more risk than they should. These behavioral biases impact everything in finance, from investment analysis, to analyzing new projects, to forecasting the future.

## Principle 5: Conflicts of Interest Cause Agency Problems

Throughout this book we will describe how to make financial decisions that increase the value of a firm's shares. However, managers do not always follow through with these decisions. Often they make decisions that actually lead to a decrease in the value of the firm's shares. When this happens, it is frequently because the managers' own interests are best served by ignoring shareholder interests. In other words, there is a conflict of interest between what is best for the managers and the stockholders. For example, it may be the case that shutting down an unprofitable plant is in the best interests of the firm's stockholders, but in so doing the managers will find themselves out of a job or having to transfer to a different job. This very clear conflict of interest might lead the management of the plant to continue running the plant at a loss.

Conflicts of interest lead to what are referred to by economists as an agency cost or **agency problem**. That is, managers are the agents of the firm's stockholders (the owners) and if the agents do not act in the best interests of their principal, this leads to an agency cost. Although the goal of the firm is to maximize shareholder value, in reality the agency problem may interfere with the implementation of this goal. *The agency problem results from the separation of management and the ownership of the firm.* For example, a large firm may be run by professional managers or agents who have little or no ownership in the firm. Because of this separation of the decision makers and owners, managers may make decisions that are not in line with the goal of maximizing shareholder wealth. They may approach work less energetically and attempt to benefit themselves in terms of salary and perquisites at the expense of shareholders.

**agency problem** problems and conflicts resulting from the separation of the management and ownership of the firm.

Managers might also avoid any projects that have risk associated with them—even if they are great projects with huge potential returns and a small chance of failure. Why is this so? Because if the project doesn't turn out, these agents of the shareholders may lose their jobs.

The costs associated with the agency problem are difficult to measure, but occasionally we see the problem's effect in the marketplace. If the market feels management is damaging

[1]See Robert J. Shiller, *Irrational Exuberance*, Broadway Books, 2000, page 142.

shareholder wealth, there may be a positive reaction in stock price to the removal of that management. For example, on the announcement of the death of Roy Farmer, the CEO of Farmer Brothers (FARM), a seller of coffee-related products, Farmer Brothers' stock price rose about 28 percent. Generally, the tragic loss of a company's top executive raises concerns over a leadership void, causing the share price to drop, but in the case of Farmer Brothers, investors thought a change in management would have a positive impact on the company.

If the firm's management works for the owners, who are the shareholders, why doesn't the management get fired if it doesn't act in the shareholders' best interest? In theory, the shareholders pick the corporate board of directors and the board of directors in turn picks the management. Unfortunately, in reality the system frequently works the other way around. Management selects the board of director nominees and then distributes the ballots. In effect, shareholders are offered a slate of nominees selected by the management. The end result is that management effectively selects the directors, who then may have more allegiance to managers than to shareholders. This, in turn, sets up the potential for agency problems, with the board of directors not monitoring managers on behalf of the shareholders as it should.

The root cause of agency problems is conflicts of interest. Whenever they exist in business, there is a chance that individuals will do what is in their best interests rather than the best interests of the organization. For example, in 2000 Edgerrin James was a running back for the Indianapolis Colts and was told by his coach to get a first down and then fall down. That way the Colts wouldn't be accused of running up the score against a team they were already beating badly. However, since James' contract included incentive payments associated with rushing yards and touchdowns, he acted in his own self-interest and ran for a touchdown on the very next play.

We will spend considerable time discussing monitoring managers and trying to align their interests with those of shareholders. As an example, managers can be monitored by rating agencies and by auditing financial statements, and compensation packages may be used to align the interests of managers and shareholders. Additionally, the interests of managers and shareholders can be aligned by establishing management stock options, bonuses, and perquisites that are directly tied to how closely managers' decisions coincide with the interest of shareholders. In other words, what is good for shareholders must also be good for managers. If that is not the case, managers will make decisions in their best interest rather than maximizing shareholder wealth.

## The Current Global Financial Crisis

Beginning in 2007 the United States experienced its most severe financial crisis since the Great Depression of the 1930s. As a result, some financial institutions collapsed while the government bailed others out, unemployment skyrocketed, the stock market plummeted, and the United States entered into a recession. Although the recession is now officially over, the economy still faces the lingering effects of the financial crisis that continue in the form of both a high rate of unemployment and a dramatic rise in our country's debt. Europe continues to face a financial crisis of its own. Many members of the European Union (EU) are experiencing severe budget problems, including Greece, Italy, Ireland, Portugal, and Spain. These nations are all unable to balance their budgets and face a very real prospect of defaulting on payments tied to government loans.

While many factors contributed to the financial crisis, the most immediate cause has been attributed to the collapse of the real estate market in the United States and the resulting real estate loan (mortgage) defaults. The focus of the loan defaults has been on what are commonly referred to as subprime loans. These are loans made to borrowers whose ability to repay them is highly doubtful. When the market for real estate began to falter in 2006, many of the homebuyers with subprime mortgages began to default. As the economy contracted during the recession, people lost their jobs and could no longer make their mortgage loan payments, resulting in even more defaults.

To complicate the problem, most real estate mortgages were packaged in portfolios and resold to investors around the world. This process of packaging mortgages is called *securitization*. Basically, securitization is a very useful tool for increasing the supply of new money that can be lent to new homebuyers. Here's how mortgages are securitized: First, homebuyers borrow money by taking out a mortgage to finance a home purchase. The lender, generally a bank, savings and loan, or mortgage broker that made the loan, then sells the mortgage to another firm or financial institution that pools together a portfolio of many different mortgages. The purchase of the pool of mortgages is financed through the sale of securities (called *mortgage-backed securities*, or MBS) that are sold to investors who can hold them as an investment or resell them to other investors. This process allows the mortgage bank or other financial institution that made the original mortgage loan to get its money back out of the loan and lend it to someone else. Thus, securitization provides liquidity to the mortgage market and makes it possible for banks to loan more money to homebuyers.

Ok, so what's the catch? As long as lenders properly screen the mortgages to make sure the borrowers are willing and able to repay their home loans and real estate values remain higher than the amount owed, everything works fine. However, if lenders make loans to individuals who really cannot afford to make the payments and real estate prices drop precipitously as they began to do in 2006, there will be problems and many mortgages (especially those where the amount of the loan was a very high percentage of the property value) will be "under water." That is, the homeowner will owe more than the home is worth. When this occurs homeowners may start to default on their mortgage loans. This is especially true when the economy goes into a recession and people lose their jobs and, correspondingly, the ability to make their mortgage payments. This was the scenario in 2006. In essence, this was a perfect storm of bad loans, falling housing prices, and a contracting economy.

Where are we now? As of this writing, in 2012, the recession is officially over, having ended in 2009; however, despite this pronouncement there is evidence that the economy is still not back to normal. Unemployment numbers are still higher than historical norms for nonrecession years. Moreover, these unemployment numbers do not accurately reflect what has become known as underemployment, whereby individuals are taking jobs but these jobs do not take advantage of the individuals' employment credentials (for example, college professors driving taxi cabs). Finally, the risk of financial crisis in many European countries remains at a very high level. Despite a series of financial "fixes" to the imbalances in the budgets of Greece, Spain, and several other European countries, for example, the budgetary woes in Europe continue into 2012.

## Avoiding Financial Crisis—Back to the Principles

Four significant economic events that have occurred during the last decade all point to the importance of keeping our eye closely affixed to the five principles of finance: the dot.com bubble; the accounting scandals headlined by Enron, WorldCom, and Bernie Madoff; the housing bubble; and, finally, the recent economic crisis. Specifically, the problems that firms encounter in times of crisis are often brought on by, and made worse as a result of, not paying close attention to the foundational principles of finance. To illustrate, consider the following:

◆ **Forgetting Principle 1: Cash Flow Is What Matters** (*Focusing on earnings instead of cash flow*). The financial fraud committed by Bernie Madoff, WorldCom, and others at the turn of the 21st century was a direct result of managerial efforts to manage the firm's reported earnings to the detriment of the firm's cash flows. The belief in the importance of current period earnings as the most critical determinant of the market valuation of the firm's shares led some firms to sacrifice future cash flows in order to maintain the illusion of high and growing earnings.

◆ **Forgetting Principle 2: Money Has a Time Value** (*Focusing on the short run*). When trying to put in place a system that would align the interests of managers and shareholders, many firms tied managerial compensation to short-run performance. Consequently, the focus shifted in many firms from what was best in the long run to what was best in the short run.

◆ **Forgetting Principle 3: Risk Requires a Reward** (*Excessive risk taking due to underestimation of risk*). Relying on historical evidence, managers often underestimated the real risks that their decisions entailed. This underestimation of the underlying riskiness of their decisions led managers to borrow excessively. This excessive use of borrowed money (or financial leverage) led to financial disaster and bankruptcy for many firms as the economy slipped into recession. Moreover, the financial crisis was exacerbated by the fact that many times companies simply didn't understand how much risk they were taking on. For example, AIG (AIG), the giant insurance company that the government bailed out, was involved in investments whose value is based on the price of oil in 50 years. Let's face it, no one knows what the price of oil will be in a half a century—being involved in this type of investment is blind risk.

◆ **Forgetting Principle 4: Market Prices Are Generally Right** (*Ignoring the efficiency of financial markets*). Huge numbers of so-called hedge funds sprang up over the last decade and entered into investment strategies that presupposed that security prices could be predicted. Many of these same firms borrowed heavily in an effort to boost their returns and later discovered that security markets were a lot smarter than they thought and consequently realized huge losses on their highly leveraged portfolios.

◆ **Forgetting Principle 5: Conflicts of Interest Cause Agency Problems** (*Executive compensation is out of control*). Executive compensation in the United States is dominated by performance-based compensation in the form of stock options and grants. The use of these forms of compensation over the last decade in the face of one of the longest bull markets in history has resulted in tremendous growth in executive compensation. The motivations behind these methods of compensation are primarily tied to a desire to make managers behave like stockholders (owners). Unfortunately, this practice has resulted in pay for nonperformance in many cases and a feeling among the general public that executive compensation is excessive. We are reminded again that solving the principal–agent problem is not easy to do, but it has to be done!

In this edition of *Foundations of Finance* we believe that now, perhaps more than at any time in our memory, adhering to the fundamental principles of finance is critical. In addition, to further emphasize the "back to principles theme" we include a feature called "Cautionary Tales" that highlights specific examples where a failure to adhere to one or more of the five principles led to problems.

## The Essential Elements of Ethics and Trust

While not one of the five principles of finance, ethics and trust are essential elements of the business world. In fact, without ethics and trust nothing works. This statement could be applied to almost everything in life. Virtually everything we do involves some dependence on others. Although businesses frequently try to describe the rights and obligations of their dealings with others using contracts, it is impossible to write a perfect contract. Consequently, business dealings between people and firms ultimately depend on the willingness of the parties to trust one another.

Ethics or, rather, a lack of ethics in finance is a recurring theme in the news. Financial scandals at Enron, WorldCom, Arthur Andersen, and Bernard L. Madoff Investment Securities demonstrate the fact that ethical lapses are not forgiven in the business world. Not only is acting in an ethical manner morally correct, it is a necessary ingredient to long-term business and personal success.

Ethical behavior is easily defined. It's simply "doing the right thing." But what is the right thing? For example, Bristol-Myers Squibb (BMY) gives away heart medication to people who can't afford it. Clearly, the firm's management feels this is socially responsible and the right thing to do. But is it? Should companies give away money and products or should they leave such acts of benevolence to the firm's shareholders? Perhaps the shareholders should decide if they personally want to donate some of their wealth to worthy causes.

Like most ethical questions, there is no clear-cut answer to the dilemma posited above. We acknowledge that people have a right to disagree about what "doing the right thing" means and that each of us has his or her personal set of values. These values form the basis for what we think is right and wrong. Moreover, every society adopts a set of rules or laws that prescribe what it believes constitutes "doing the right thing." In a sense, we can think of laws as a set of rules that reflect the values of a society as a whole.

You might ask yourself, "As long as I'm not breaking society's laws, why should I care about ethics?" The answer to this question lies in consequences. Everyone makes errors of judgment in business, which is to be expected in an uncertain world. But ethical errors are different. Even if they don't result in anyone going to jail, they tend to end careers and thereby terminate future opportunities. Why? Because unethical behavior destroys trust, and businesses cannot function without a certain degree of trust. Throughout this book, we will point out some of the ethical pitfalls that have tripped up managers.

## Concept Check

1. According to Principle 3, how do investors decide where to invest their money?
2. What is an efficient market?
3. What is the agency problem and why does it occur?
4. Why are ethics and trust important in business?

# The Role of Finance in Business

 **3** Describe the role of finance in business.

Finance is the study of how people and businesses evaluate investments and raise capital to fund them. Our interpretation of an investment is quite broad. When Apple designed its Apple TV, it was clearly making a long-term investment. The firm had to devote considerable expenses to designing, producing, and marketing the device with the hope that it would eventually become an essential living room companion. Similarly, Apple is making an investment decision whenever it hires a fresh new graduate, knowing that it will be paying a salary for at least 6 months before the employee will have much to contribute.

Thus, there are three basic types of issues that are addressed by the study of finance:

1. What long-term investments should the firm undertake? This area of finance is generally referred to as **capital budgeting**.
2. How should the firm raise money to fund these investments? The firm's funding choices are generally referred to as **capital structure decisions**.
3. How can the firm best manage its cash flows as they arise in its day-to-day operations? This area of finance is generally referred to as **working capital management**.

We'll be looking at each of these three areas of business finance—capital budgeting, capital structure, and working capital management—in the chapters ahead.

**capital budgeting** the decision-making process with respect to investment in fixed assets.

**capital structure decision** the decision-making process with funding choices and the mix of long-term sources of funds.

**working capital management** the management of the firm's current assets and short-term financing.

## Why Study Finance?

Even if you're not planning a career in finance, a working knowledge of finance will take you far in both your personal and professional life.

Those interested in management will need to study topics like strategic planning, personnel, organizational behavior, and human relations, all of which involve spending money today in the hopes of generating more money in the future. For example, GM made a strategic decision to introduce an electric car and invested $740 million to produce the Chevy Volt, only to find car buyers balk at the $40,000 sticker price. Similarly, marketing majors need to understand and decide how aggressively to price products and the amount to spend on advertising. Since aggressive marketing today costs money but allows firms to reap rewards in the future, it should be viewed as an investment that the firm needs to finance. Production and operations management majors need to understand how best to manage a firm's production and control its inventory and supply chain. These are all topics that involve risky choices that relate to the management of money over time, which is the central focus of finance. *While finance is primarily about the management of money, a key component of finance is the management and interpretation of information.* Indeed, if you pursue a career in management information systems or accounting, the finance managers are likely to be your most important clients. For the student with entrepreneurial aspirations, an understanding of finance is essential—after all, if you can't manage your finances, you won't be in business very long.

Finally, an understanding of finance is important to you as an individual. The fact that you are reading this book indicates that you understand the importance of investing in yourself. By obtaining a higher education degree, you are clearly making sacrifices in the hopes of making yourself more employable and improving your chances of having a rewarding and challenging career. Some of you are relying on your own earnings and the earnings of your parents to finance your education, whereas others are raising money or borrowing it from the **financial markets**, or *institutions and procedures that facilitate financial transactions.*

Although the primary focus of this book is on developing corporate finance tools that are used in business, much of the logic and tools we develop apply to the decisions you will have to make regarding your own personal finances. Financial decisions are everywhere, both for you and the firm you work for. In the future, both your business and personal life will be spent in the world of finance. Since you're going to be living in that world, it's time to learn the basics about it.

**financial markets** those institutions and procedures that facilitate transactions in all types of financial claims.

## The Role of the Financial Manager

A firm can assume many different organizational structures. Figure 1-2 shows a typical presentation of how the finance area fits into a firm. The vice president for finance, also called the chief financial officer (CFO), serves under the firm's chief executive officer (CEO) and is responsible for overseeing financial planning, strategic planning, and controlling the firm's cash flow. Typically, a treasurer and controller serve under the CFO. In a smaller

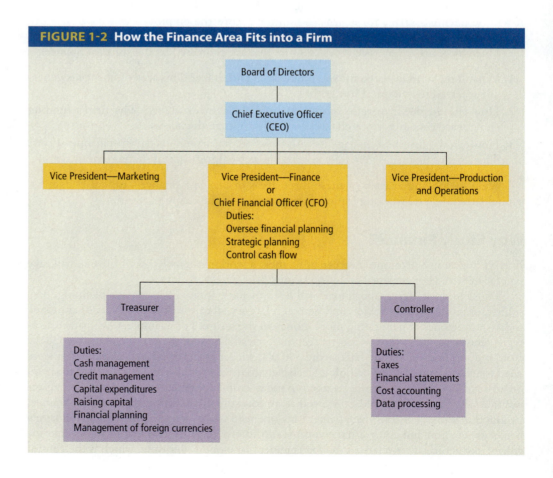

**FIGURE 1-2  How the Finance Area Fits into a Firm**

firm, the same person may fill both roles, with just one office handling all the duties. The treasurer generally handles the firm's financial activities, including cash and credit management, making capital expenditure decisions, raising funds, financial planning, and managing any foreign currency received by the firm. The controller is responsible for managing the firm's accounting duties, including producing financial statements, cost accounting, paying taxes, and gathering and monitoring the data necessary to oversee the firm's financial well-being. In this textbook, we focus on the duties generally associated with the treasurer and on how investment decisions are made.

## Concept Check

1. What are the basic types of issues that are addressed by the study of finance?
2. What are the duties of a treasurer? Of a controller?

# The Legal Forms of Business Organization

**4** Distinguish between the different legal forms of business.

In the chapters ahead we focus on financial decisions for corporations because, although the corporation is not the only legal form of business available, it is the most logical choice for a firm that is large or growing. It is also the dominant business form in terms of sales in this country. In this section we explain why this is so.

Although numerous and diverse, the legal forms of business organization fall into three categories: the sole proprietorship, the partnership, and the corporation. To understand the basic differences between each form, we need to define each one and understand its advantages and disadvantages. As the firm grows, the advantages of the corporation begin to dominate. As a result, most large firms take on the corporate form.

## Sole Proprietorships

A **sole proprietorship** is *a business owned by an individual*. The owner retains the title to the business's assets and is responsible, generally without limitation, for the liabilities incurred. The proprietor is entitled to the profits from the business but must also absorb any losses. This form of business is initiated by the mere act of beginning the business operations. Typically, no legal requirement must be met in starting the operation, particularly if the proprietor is conducting the business in his or her own name. If a special name is used, an assumed-name certificate should be filed, requiring a small registration fee. Termination of the sole proprietorship occurs on the owner's death or by the owner's choice. Briefly stated, the sole proprietorship is for all practical purposes the absence of any formal *legal* business structure.

**sole proprietorship** a business owned by a single individual.

## Partnerships

The primary difference between a partnership and a sole proprietorship is that the partnership has more than one owner. A **partnership** is *an association of two or more persons coming together as co-owners for the purpose of operating a business for profit*. Partnerships fall into two types: (1) general partnerships and (2) limited partnerships.

**partnership** an association of two or more individuals joining together as co-owners to operate a business for profit.

**General Partnerships** In a **general partnership** *each partner is fully responsible for the liabilities incurred by the partnership*. Thus, any partner's faulty conduct, even having the appearance of relating to the firm's business, renders the remaining partners liable as well. The relationship among partners is dictated entirely by the partnership agreement, which may be an oral commitment or a formal document.

**general partnership** a partnership in which all partners are fully liable for the indebtedness incurred by the partnership.

**Limited Partnerships** In addition to the general partnership, in which all partners are jointly liable without limitation, many states provide for **limited partnerships**. The state statutes permit *one or more of the partners to have limited liability, restricted to the amount of capital invested in the partnership*. Several conditions must be met to qualify as a limited partner. First, at least one general partner must have unlimited liability. Second, the names of the limited partners may not appear in the name of the firm. Third, the limited partners may

**limited partnership** a partnership in which one or more of the partners has limited liability, restricted to the amount of capital he or she invests in the partnership.

not participate in the management of the business. Thus, a limited partnership provides limited liability for a partner who is purely an investor.

## Corporations

**corporation** an entity that legally functions separate and apart from its owners.

The **corporation** has been a significant factor in the economic development of the United States. As early as 1819, U.S. Supreme Court Chief Justice John Marshall set forth the legal definition of a corporation as "an artificial being, invisible, intangible, and existing only in the contemplation of law."[2] This entity *legally functions separate and apart from its owners*. As such, the corporation can individually sue and be sued and purchase, sell, or own property, and its personnel are subject to criminal punishment for crimes. However, despite this legal separation, the corporation is composed of owners who dictate its direction and policies. The owners elect a board of directors, whose members in turn select individuals to serve as corporate officers, including the company's president, vice president, secretary, and treasurer. Ownership is reflected in common stock certificates, each designating the number of shares owned by its holder. The number of shares owned relative to the total number of shares outstanding determines the stockholder's proportionate ownership in the business. Because the shares are transferable, ownership in a corporation may be changed by a shareholder simply remitting the shares to a new shareholder. The shareholder's liability is confined to the amount of the investment in the company, thereby preventing creditors from confiscating stockholders' personal assets in settlement of unresolved claims. This is an extremely important advantage of a corporation. After all, would you be willing to invest in USAirways if you would be held liable if one of its planes crashed? Finally, the life of a corporation is not dependent on the status of the investors. The death or withdrawal of an investor does not affect the continuity of the corporation. Its managers continue to run the corporation when stock is sold or when it is passed on through inheritance.

## Organizational Form and Taxes: The Double Taxation on Dividends

Historically, one of the drawbacks of the corporate form was the double taxation of dividends. This occurs when a corporation earns a profit, pays taxes on those profits (the first taxation of earnings), and pays some of those profits back to the shareholders in the form of dividends, and then the shareholders pay personal income taxes on those dividends (the second taxation of those earnings). This double taxation of earnings does not take place with proprietorships and partnerships. Needless to say, that had been a major disadvantage of corporations. However, in an attempt to stimulate the economy, the tax rate on dividends was cut with the passage of the Tax Act of 2003.

Before the 2003 tax changes, you paid your regular, personal income tax rate on your dividend income, which could be as high as 35 percent. However, with the new law, qualified dividends from domestic corporations and qualified foreign corporations are now taxed at a maximum rate of 15 percent. Moreover, if your personal income puts you in the 10 percent or 15 percent income rate bracket, your dividends will be taxed at only 5 percent, and in 2008, this rate dropped to 0 percent. Unless Congress takes further action, this tax break on dividends will end after 2012 and individuals will once again be taxed at their regular personal tax rate.

## S-Corporations and Limited Liability Companies (LLCs)

One of the problems that entrepreneurs and small business owners face is that they need the benefits of the corporate form to expand, but the double taxation of earnings that comes with the corporate form makes it difficult to accumulate the necessary wealth for expansion. Fortunately, the government recognizes this problem and has provided two business forms

---

[2]*The Trustees of Dartmouth College* v. *Woodard*, 4 Wheaton 636 (1819).

that are, in effect, crosses between a partnership and a corporation with the tax benefits of partnerships (no double taxation of earnings) and the limited liability benefit of corporations (your liability is limited to what you invest).

The first is the **S-corporation**, which *provides limited liability while allowing the business's owners to be taxed as if they were a partnership*—that is, distributions back to the owners are not taxed twice as is the case with dividends distributed by regular corporations. Unfortunately, a number of restrictions accompany the S-corporation that detract from the desirability of this business form. Thus, an S-corporation cannot be used for a joint venture between two corporations. As a result, this business form has been losing ground in recent years in favor of the limited liability company.

The **limited liability company (LLC)** is also *a cross between a partnership and a corporation*. Just as with the S-corporation, the LLC retains limited liability for its owners but runs and is taxed like a partnership. In general, it provides more flexibility than the S-corporation. For example, corporations can be owners in an LLC. However, because LLCs operate under state laws, both states and the IRS have rules for what qualifies as an LLC, and different states have different rules. But the bottom line in all this is that the LLC must not look too much like a corporation or it will be taxed as one.

**S-corporation** a corporation that, because of specific qualifications, is taxed as though it were a partnership.

**limited liability company (LLC)** a cross between a partnership and a corporation under which the owners retain limited liability but the company is run and is taxed like a partnership.

## Which Organizational Form Should Be Chosen?

Owners of new businesses have some important decisions to make in choosing an organizational form. Whereas each business form seems to have some advantages over the others, the advantages of the corporation begin to dominate as the firm grows and needs access to the capital markets to raise funds.

Because of the limited liability, the ease of transferring ownership through the sale of common shares, and the flexibility in dividing the shares, the corporation is the ideal business entity in terms of attracting new capital. In contrast, the unlimited liabilities of the sole proprietorship and the general partnership are deterrents to raising equity capital. Between the extremes, the limited partnership does provide limited liability for limited partners, which has a tendency to attract wealthy investors. However, the impracticality of having a large number of partners and the restricted marketability of an interest in a partnership prevent this form of organization from competing effectively with the corporation. Therefore, when developing our decision models we assume we are dealing with the corporate form and corporate tax codes.

## Concept Check

1. What are the primary differences between a sole proprietorship, a partnership, and a corporation?
2. Explain why large and growing firms tend to choose the corporate form.
3. What is an LLC?

# Finance and the Multinational Firm: The New Role

 **5** Explain what has led to the era of the multinational corporation.

In the search for profits, U.S. corporations have been forced to look beyond our country's borders. This movement has been spurred on by the collapse of communism and the acceptance of the free market system in third-world countries. All this has taken place at a time when information technology has experienced a revolution brought on by the personal computer and the Internet. Concurrently, the United States went through an unprecedented period of deregulation of industries. These changes resulted in the opening of new international markets, and U.S. firms experienced a period of price competition here at home that made it imperative that businesses look across borders for investment opportunities. The end result is that many U.S. companies, including General Electric, IBM, Walt Disney, and American Express, have restructured their operations to expand internationally.

The bottom line is what you think of as a U.S. firm may be much more of a multinational firm than you would expect. For example, Coca-Cola earns over 80 percent of its profits from overseas sales and more money from its sales in Japan than it does from all its domestic sales. This is not uncommon. In fact, in 2011, close to 50 percent of the sales of S&P 500 listed companies came from outside the United States.

In addition to U.S. firms venturing abroad, foreign firms have also made their mark in the United States. You need only look to the auto industry to see what effects the entrance of Toyota, Honda, Nissan, BMW, and other foreign car manufacturers have had on the industry. In addition, foreigners have bought and now own such companies as Brooks Brothers, RCA, Pillsbury, A&P, 20th Century Fox, Columbia Pictures, and Firestone Tire & Rubber. Consequently, even if we wanted to, we couldn't keep all our attention focused on the United States, and even more important, we wouldn't want to ignore the opportunities that are available across international borders.

## Concept Check

1. What has brought on the era of the multinational corporation?
2. Has looking beyond U.S. borders been a profitable experience for U.S. corporations?

# Chapter Summaries

### Identify the goal of the firm.   (pgs. 3–4)

**SUMMARY:**  This chapter outlines the framework for the maintenance and creation of shareholder wealth, which should be the goal of the firm and its managers. The goal of maximization of shareholder wealth is chosen because it deals well with uncertainty and time in a real-world environment. As a result, the maximization of shareholder wealth is found to be the proper goal for the firm.

### Understand the basic principles of finance, their importance, and the importance of ethics and trust.   (pgs. 4–11)

**SUMMARY:**  The five basic principles of finance are:

1. **Cash Flow Is What Matters**—Incremental cash received and not accounting profits drives value.
2. **Money Has a Time Value**—A dollar received today is more valuable to the recipient than a dollar received in the future.
3. **Risk Requires a Reward**—The greater the risk of an investment, the higher will be the investor's required rate of return, and, other things remaining the same, the lower will be its value.
4. **Market Prices Are Generally Right**—For example, product market prices are often slower to react to important news than are prices in financial markets, which tend to be very efficient and quick to respond to news.
5. **Conflicts of Interest Cause Agency Problems**—Large firms are typically run by professional managers who own a small fraction of the firms' equity. The individual actions of these managers are often motivated by self-interest, which may result in managers not acting in the best interests of the firm's owners. When this happens, the firm's owners will lose value.

While not one of the five principles of finance, ethics and trust are also essential elements of the business world, and without them, nothing works.

**KEY TERMS**

**Incremental cash flow, page 4** The difference between the cash flows a company will produce both with and without the investment it is thinking about making.

**Opportunity cost, page 5** The cost of making a choice in terms of the next best alternative that must be foregone.

**Efficient market, page 6** A market in which the prices of securities at any instant in time fully reflect all publicly available information about the securities and their actual public values.

**Agency problem, page 7** Problems and conflicts resulting from the separation of the management and ownership of the firm.

---

## Describe the role of finance in business. (pgs. 11–13)

**SUMMARY:** Finance is the study of how people and businesses evaluate investments and raise capital to fund them. There are three basic types of issues that are addressed by the study of finance: (1) What long-term investments should the firm undertake? This area of finance is generally referred to as capital budgeting. (2) How should the firm raise money to fund these investments? The firm's funding choices are generally referred to as capital structure decisions. (3) How can the firm best manage its cash flows as they arise in its day-to-day operations? This area of finance is generally referred to as working capital management.

**KEY TERMS**

**Capital budgeting, page 11** The decision-making process with respect to investment in fixed assets.

**Capital structure decision, page 11** The decision-making process with funding choices and the mix of long-term sources of funds.

**Working capital management, page 11** The management of the firm's current assets and short-term financing.

**Financial markets, page 12** Those institutions and procedures that facilitate transactions in all types of financial claims.

---

## Distinguish between the different legal forms of business. (pgs. 13–15)

**SUMMARY:** The legal forms of business are examined. The sole proprietorship is a business operation owned and managed by an individual. Initiating this form of business is simple and generally does not involve any substantial organizational costs. The proprietor has complete control of the firm but must be willing to assume full responsibility for its outcomes.

The general partnership, which is simply a coming together of two or more individuals, is similar to the sole proprietorship. The limited partnership is another form of partnership sanctioned by states to permit all but one of the partners to have limited liability if this is agreeable to all partners.

The corporation increases the flow of capital from public investors to the business community. Although larger organizational costs and regulations are imposed on this legal entity, the corporation is more conducive to raising large amounts of capital. Limited liability, continuity of life, and ease of transfer in ownership, which increase the marketability of the investment, have contributed greatly in attracting large numbers of investors to the corporate environment. The formal control of the corporation is vested in the parties who own the greatest number of shares. However, day-to-day operations are managed by the corporate officers, who theoretically serve on behalf of the firm's stockholders.

**KEY TERMS**

**Sole proprietorship, page 13** A business owned by a single individual.

**Partnership, page 13** An association of two or more individuals joining together as co-owners to operate a business for profit.

**General partnership, page 13** A partnership in which all partners are fully liable for the indebtedness incurred by the partnership.

**Limited partnership, page 13** A partnership in which one or more of the partners has limited liability, restricted to the amount of capital he or she invests in the partnership.

**Corporation, page 14** An entity that legally functions separate and apart from its owners.

**S-corporation, page 15** A corporation that, because of specific qualifications, is taxed as though it were a partnership.

**Limited liability company (LLC), page 15** A cross between a partnership and a corporation under which the owners retain limited liability but the company is run and is taxed like a partnership.

### Explain what has led to the era of the multinational corporation.    (pg. 15)

**SUMMARY:** With the collapse of communism and the acceptance of the free market system in third-world countries, U.S. firms have been spurred on to look beyond their own boundaries for new business. The end result has been that it is not uncommon for major U.S. companies to earn over half their income from sales abroad. Foreign firms are also increasingly investing in the United States.

## Review Questions

*All Review Questions are available in* MyFinanceLab.

**1-1.** What are some of the problems involved in implementing the goal of maximization of shareholder wealth?

**1-2.** Firms often involve themselves in projects that do not result directly in profits. For example, Apple, which we featured in the chapter introduction, donated $50 million to Stanford University hospitals and another $50 million to the African aid organization (Product) RED, a charity fighting against AIDS, tuberculosis, and malaria. Do these projects contradict the goal of maximization of shareholder wealth? Why or why not?

**1-3.** What is the relationship between financial decision making and risk and return? Would all financial managers view risk–return trade-offs similarly?

**1-4.** What is the agency problem and how might it impact the goal of maximization of shareholder wealth?

**1-5.** Define (a) sole proprietorship, (b) partnership, and (c) corporation.

**1-6.** Identify the primary characteristics of each form of legal organization.

**1-7.** Using the following criteria, specify the legal form of business that is favored: (a) organizational requirements and costs, (b) liability of the owners, (c) the continuity of the business, (d) the transferability of ownership, (e) management control and regulations, (f) the ability to raise capital, and (g) income taxes.

**1-8.** There are a lot of great business majors. Check out the Careers in Business Web site at www.careers-in-business.com. It covers not only finance but also marketing, accounting, and management. Find out about and provide a short write-up describing the opportunities investment banking and financial planning offer.

**1-9.** Like it or not, ethical problems seem to crop up all the time in finance. Some of the worst financial scandals are examined at http://projects.exeter.ac.uk/RDavies/arian/scandals/classic. html. Take a look at the write-ups dealing with "The Credit Crunch," "The Dot-Com Bubble and Investment Banks," and "Bernard L. Madoff Investment Securities." Provide a short write-up on these events.

**1-10.** We know that if a corporation is to maximize shareholder wealth, the interests of the managers and the shareholders must be aligned. The simplest way to align these interests is to structure executive compensation packages appropriately to encourage managers to act in the best interests of shareholders through stock and option awards. However, has executive compensation gotten out of control? Take a look at the Executive Pay Watch Web site at www.aflcio.org/corporate-watch/paywatch to see to whom top salaries have gone (click on "100 Highest-paid CEOs" on the right-hand side of the page). What are the most recent total compensation packages for the head of Oracle (ORCL), Home Depot (HD), Disney (DIS), and ExxonMobil (XOM)? (Hint: you'll want to look in the CEO Pay Database in the Executive Pay Watch.)

## Mini Case

*This Mini Case is available in* MyFinanceLab.

The final stage in the interview process for an assistant financial analyst at Caledonia Products involves a test of your understanding of basic financial concepts. You are given the following memorandum and asked to respond to the questions. Whether you are offered a position at Caledonia will depend on the accuracy of your response.

> To: Applicants for the position of Financial Analyst
> From: Mr. V. Morrison, CEO, Caledonia Products
> Re: A test of your understanding of basic financial concepts and of the corporate tax code

Please respond to the following questions:

a. What is the appropriate goal for the firm and why?
b. What does the risk–return trade-off mean?
c. Why are we interested in cash flows rather than accounting profits in determining the value of an asset?
d. What is an efficient market and what are the implications of efficient markets for us?
e. What is the cause of the agency problem and how do we try to solve it?
f. What do ethics and ethical behavior have to do with finance?
g. Define (1) sole proprietorship, (2) partnership, and (3) corporation.

# The Financial Markets and Interest Rates

## Learning Objectives

| | | |
|---|---|---|
| **1** | **Describe** key components of the U.S. financial market system and the financing of business. | **Financing of Business: The Movement of Funds Through the Economy** |
| **2** | **Understand** how funds are raised in the capital markets. | **Selling Securities to the Public** |
| **3** | **Be acquainted** with recent rates of return. | **Rates of Return in the Financial Markets** |
| **4** | **Explain** the fundamentals of interest rate determination and the popular theories of the term structure of interest rates. | **Interest Rate Determinants in a Nutshell** |

Back in 1995, when they first met, Larry Page and Sergey Brin were not particularly fond of one another. Larry was on a weekend visit to Stanford University, and Sergey was in a group of students assigned to show him around. Nonetheless, in short time the two began to collaborate and even built their own computer housings in Larry's dorm room. That computer housing later became Google's first data center. From there things didn't move as smoothly as one might expect, there just wasn't the interest from the search-engine players of the day, so Larry and Sergey decided to go it alone. Stuck in a dorm room with maxed-out credit cards, the problem they faced was money—they didn't have any. So they put together a business plan and went looking for money. Fortunately for all of us who use Google today, they met up with one of the founders of Sun Microsystems, and after a short demo he had to run off somewhere and upon leaving said, "Instead of us discussing all the details, why don't I just write you a check?" It was made out to Google Inc. and was for $100,000.

With that, Google Inc. (GOOG) was founded, and over the next 10 years it became anything but a conventional company, with an official motto of "don't be evil"; a goal to make the world a better place; on-site meals prepared by a former caterer for the Grateful Dead; lava lamps; and a fleet of Segways to move employees about the Google campus to roller-hockey games in the parking lot and to other on-site diversions. It was not unexpected that when Google needed more money in 2004 it would raise that money in an unusual way—through a "Dutch auction." With a Dutch auction investors submit bids, saying how many shares they'd like and at what price. Next, Google used these bids to calculate an issue price that was just low enough to ensure that all the shares were sold, and everyone who bid at least that price got to buy shares at the issue price.

Eventually, Google settled on an issue price of $85 per share, and on August 19, 2004, it raised $1.76 billion dollars. How did those initial investors do? On the first day of trading Google's shares rose by 18 percent, and by mid-March

2005 the price of Google stock had risen to about $340 per share! In September 2005, Google went back to the financial markets and sold another 14.18 million shares at $295 per share, and by August 2012 it was selling at around $641 per share.

As you read this chapter you will learn about how funds are raised in the financial markets. This will help you, as an emerging business executive specializing in accounting, finance, marketing, or strategy, understand the basics of acquiring financial capital in the funds marketplace.

Long-term sources of financing, such as bonds and common stock, are raised in the capital markets. By the term **capital markets**, we mean *all the financial institutions that help a business raise long-term capital*, where "long term" is defined as a security with a maturity date of more than one year. After all, most companies are in the business of selling products and services to their customers and do not have the expertise on their own to raise money to finance the business. Examples of these financial institutions that you may have heard of would include Bank of America (BAC), Goldman Sachs (GS), Citigroup (C), Morgan Stanley (MS), UBS AG (UBS), and Deutsche Bank (DB).

> **capital markets** all institutions and procedures that facilitate transactions in long-term financial instruments.

This chapter focuses on the procedures by which businesses raise money in the capital markets. It helps us understand how the capital markets work. We will introduce the logic of how investors determine their required rate of return for making an investment. In addition, we will study the historical rates of returns in the capital markets so that we have a perspective on what to expect. This knowledge of financial market history will permit you as both a financial manager and an investor to realize that earning, say, a 40 percent annual return on a common stock investment does not occur very often.

As you work through this chapter, be on the lookout for direct applications of several of our principles from Chapter 1 that form the basics of business financial management. Specifically, your attention will be directed to: Principle 3: Risk Requires a Reward and Principle 4: Market Prices Are Generally Right.

# Financing of Business: The Movement of Funds Through the Economy

 Describe key components of the U.S. financial market system and the financing of business.

Financial markets play a critical role in a capitalist economy. In fact, when money quit flowing through the financial markets in 2008, our economy ground to a halt. When our economy is healthy, funds move from saving-surplus units—that is, those who spend less money than they take in—to savings-deficit units—that is, those who have a need for additional funding. What are some examples of savings-deficit units? Our federal government, which is running a huge deficit, takes much less in from taxes than it is spending. Hulu, the online video service, would like to build new facilities but does not have the $50 million it needs to fund the expansion. Rebecca Swank, the sole proprietor of the Sip and Stitch, a yarn and coffee shop, would like to open a second store but needs $100,000 to finance a second shop. Emily and Michael Dimmick would like to buy a house for $240,000 but have only $50,000

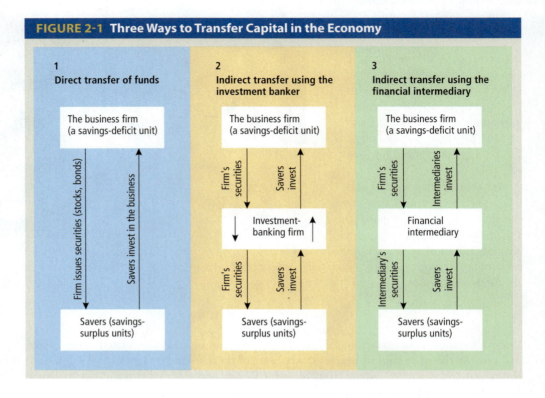

**FIGURE 2-1    Three Ways to Transfer Capital in the Economy**

saved up. In each case, our government, a large company, a small business owner, and a family are all in the same boat—they would like to spend more than they take in.

Where will this money come from? It will come from savings-surplus units in the economy—that is, from those who spend less than they take in. Examples of savings surplus units might include individuals, companies, and governments. For example, John and Sandy Randolph have been saving for retirement and earn $10,000 more each year than they spend. In addition, the firm John works for contributes $5,000 every year to his retirement plan. Likewise, ExxonMobil (XOM) generates about $50 billion in cash annually from its operations and invests about half of that on new exploration—the rest is available to invest. Also, there are a number of governments around the world that bring in more money than they spend—countries like China, the United Arab Emirates, and Saudi Arabia.

Now let's take a look at how savings are transferred to those who need the money. Actually, there are three ways that savings can be transferred through the financial markets to those in need of funds. These are displayed in Figure 2-1.

Let's take a closer look at these three methods:

1. **Direct transfer of funds**  Here the firm seeking cash sells its securities directly to savers (investors) who are willing to purchase them in hopes of earning a large return. A startup company is a good example of this process at work. The new business may go directly to *a wealthy private investor* called an **angel investor** or business angel for funds or it may go to a **venture capitalist** for early funding. That's how Koofers.com got up and running. The founders of Koofers were students at Virginia Tech who put together an interactive Web site that provides a place for students to share class notes and course and instructor ratings/grade distributions, along with study guides and past exams. The Web site proved to be wildly popular, and in 2009 received $2 million of funding from two venture capitalists to expand, who, in return, received part ownership of Koofers.

2. **Indirect transfer using an investment-banking firm**  An investment-banking firm is a financial institution that helps companies raise capital, trades in securities, and provides advice on transactions such as mergers and acquisitions. In helping

**angel investor** a wealthy private investor who provides capital for a business start-up.

**venture capitalist** an investment firm (or individual investor) that provides money to business start-ups.

firms raise capital, an investment banker frequently works together with other investment bankers in what is called a syndicate. The syndicate will buy the entire issue of securities from the firm that is in need of financial capital. The syndicate will then sell the securities at a higher price to the investing public (the savers) than it paid for them. Morgan Stanley and Goldman Sachs are examples of banks that perform investment-banking duties. Notice that under this second method of transferring savings, the securities being issued just pass through the investment-banking firm. They are not transformed into a different type of security.

3. **Indirect transfer using the financial intermediary** This is the type of system life insurance companies, mutual funds, and pension funds operate within. The financial intermediary collects the savings of individuals and issues its own (indirect) securities in exchange for these savings. The intermediary then uses the funds collected from the individual savers to acquire the business firm's (direct) securities, such as stocks and bonds.

A good financial system is one that efficiently takes money from savers and gets it to the individuals who can best put that money to use, and that's exactly what our system does. This may seem like common sense, but it is not necessarily common across the world. In spite of the fact that the U.S. financial system recently experienced some problems, it provides more choices for both borrowers and savers than most other financial systems, and as a result, it does a better job of allocating capital to those who can more productively use it. As a result, we all benefit from the three transfer mechanisms displayed in Figure 2-1, and capital formation and economic wealth are greater than they would be in the absence of this financial market system.

There are numerous ways to classify the financial markets. These markets can take the form of anything from an actual building on Wall Street in New York City to an electronic hookup among security dealers all over the world. Let's take a look at five sets of dichotomous terms that are used to describe the financial markets.

## Public Offerings Versus Private Placements

When a corporation decides to raise external capital, those funds can be obtained by making a public offering or a private placement. In a **public offering**, both *individual and institutional investors have the opportunity to purchase the securities.* The securities are usually made available to the public at large by an investment-banking firm, which is a firm that specializes in helping other firms raise money. This process of acting as an intermediary between an issuer of a security and the investing public is called underwriting, and the investment firm that does this is referred to as an underwriter. This is a very impersonal market, and the issuing firm never actually meets the ultimate purchasers of the securities.

> **public offering** a security offering where all investors have the opportunity to acquire a portion of the financial claims being sold.

In a **private placement**, also called a direct placement, the *securities are offered and sold directly to a limited number of investors.* The firm will usually hammer out, on a face-to-face basis with the prospective buyers, the details of the offering. In this setting, the investment-banking firm may act as a finder by bringing together potential lenders and borrowers. The private placement market is a more personal market than its public counterpart.

> **private placement** a security offering limited to a small number of potential investors.

A venture capital firm is an example of investors who are active in the private placement market. A venture capital firm first *raises money from institutional investors and high net worth individuals, to then pool the funds and invest in start-ups and early-stage companies* that have high-return potential but are also very risky investments. These companies are not appealing to the broader public markets owing to their (1) small absolute size, (2) very limited or no historical track record of operating results, (3) obscure growth prospects, and (4) their inability to sell the stock easily or quickly. Most venture capitalists invest for 5 to 7 years, in the hopes of selling the firms or taking them public through an IPO.

Due to the high risk, the venture capitalist will occupy a seat or seats on the young firm's board of directors and will take an active part in monitoring the company's management activities. *This situation should remind you of* **Principle 3: Risk Requires a Reward.**

## Primary Markets Versus Secondary Markets

A **primary market** is a *market in which new, as opposed to previously issued, securities are traded.* For example, if Google issues a new batch of stock, this issue would be considered a primary

> **primary market** a market in which securities are offered for the first time for sale to potential investors.

market transaction. In this case, Google would issue new shares of stock and receive money from investors. The primary market is akin to the new car market. For example, the only time that Ford ever gets money for selling a car is the first time the car is sold to the public. The same is true with securities in the primary market. That's the only time the issuing firm ever gets any money for the securities, and it is the type of transaction that introduces new financial assets—for example, stocks and bonds—into the economy. The *first time a company issues stock to the public* is referred to as an **initial public offering** or **IPO**. This is what happened with Google on August 19, 2004, when it first sold its common stock to the public at $85 per share and raised $1.76 billion dollars. When Google went back to the primary market in September 2005 and sold more Google stock, worth an additional $4.18 billion, it was considered a **seasoned equity offering,** or **SEO**. A seasoned equity offering is *the sale of additional shares by a company whose shares are already publicly traded* and is also called a secondary share offering.

The **secondary market** is *where currently outstanding securities are traded*. You can think of it as akin to the used car market. If a person who bought some shares of the Google stock subsequently sells them, he or she does so in the secondary market. Those shares can go from investor to investor, and Google never receives any money when they are traded. In effect, all transactions after the initial purchase in the primary market take place in the secondary market. These sales do not affect the total amount of financial assets that exists in the economy.

The job of regulation of the primary and secondary markets falls on the Security and Exchange Commission, or SEC. For example, before a firm can offer its securities for sale in the primary markets, it must register them with the SEC, and it is the job of the SEC to make sure that the information provided to investors is adequate and accurate. The SEC also regulates the secondary markets, making sure that investors are provided with enough accurate information to make intelligent decisions when buying and selling in the secondary markets.

**initial public offering, IPO** the first time a company issues its stock to the public.

**seasoned equity offering, SEO** the sale of additional stock by a company whose shares are already publicly traded.

**secondary market** a market in which currently outstanding securities are traded.

**money market** all institutions and procedures that facilitate transactions for short-term instruments issued by borrowers with very high credit ratings.

---

### REMEMBER YOUR PRINCIPLES

**P**rinciple   In this chapter, we cover material that introduces the financial manager to the process involved in raising funds in the nation's capital markets and how interest rates in those markets are determined.

Without question the United States has a highly developed, complex, and competitive system of financial markets that allows for the quick transfer of savings from people and organizations with a surplus of savings to those with a savings deficit. Such a system of highly developed financial markets allows great ideas (such as the personal computer) to be financed and increases the overall wealth of the economy. Consider your wealth, for example, compared to that of the average family in Russia. Russia lacks the complex system of financial markets to facilitate securities transactions. As a result, real capital formation there has suffered.

Thus, we return now to **Principle 4: Market Prices Are Generally Right.** Financial managers like the U.S. system of capital markets because they trust it. This trust stems from the fact that the markets are efficient, and so prices quickly and accurately reflect all available information about the value of the underlying securities. This means that the expected risks and expected cash flows matter more to market participants than do simpler things such as accounting changes and the sequence of past price changes in a specific security. With security prices and returns (such as interest rates) competitively determined, more financial managers (rather than fewer) participate in the markets and help ensure the basic concept of efficiency.

## The Money Market Versus the Capital Market

The key distinguishing feature between the money and capital markets is the maturity period of the securities traded in them. The **money market** refers to *transactions in short-term debt instruments*, with short-term meaning maturity periods of 1 year or less. Short-term securities are generally issued by borrowers with very high credit ratings. The major instruments issued and traded in the money market are U.S. Treasury bills, various federal agency securities, bankers' acceptances, negotiable certificates of deposit, and commercial paper. Stocks, either common or preferred, are not traded in the money market. Keep in mind that the money market isn't a physical place. You do not walk into a building on Wall Street that has the words "Money Market" etched in stone over its arches. Rather, the money market is primarily a telephone and computer market.

As we explained, the capital market refers to the market for long-term financial instruments. Long-term here means having maturity periods that extend beyond 1 year. In the broad sense, this encompasses term loans, financial leases, and corporate stocks and bonds.

## Spot Markets Versus Futures Markets

**spot market** cash market.

**futures markets** markets where you can buy or sell something at a future date.

Cash markets are where something sells today, right now, on the spot—in fact, *cash markets are often called **spot markets**. **Futures markets** are where you can *buy or sell something* *at some future date*—in effect, you sign a contract that states what you're buying, how much of it you're buying, at what price you're buying it, and when you will actually make the purchase. The difference between purchasing something in the spot market and purchasing it in the futures market is when it is delivered and when you pay for it. For example, say it is May right now and you need 250,000 euros in December. You could purchase 125,000 euros today in the spot market and another 125,000 euros in the futures market for delivery in December. You get the euros you purchased in the spot market today, and you get the euros you purchased in the futures market seven months later.

## Stock Exchanges: Organized Security Exchanges Versus Over-the-Counter Markets, a Blurring Difference

Many times markets are differentiated as being organized security exchanges or over-the-counter markets. Because of the technological advances over the past 10 years coupled with deregulation and increased competition, the difference between an organized exchange and the over-the-counter market has been blurred. Still, these remain important elements of the capital markets. **Organized security exchanges** are tangible entities; that is, they physically occupy space (such as a building or part of a building), and financial instruments are traded on their premises. The **over-the-counter markets** include all security markets except the organized exchanges. The money market, then, is an over-the-counter market because it doesn't occupy a physical location. Because both markets are important to financial officers concerned with raising long-term capital, some additional discussion is warranted.

Today, the mechanics of trading have changed dramatically and 80 to 90 percent of all trades are done electronically, blurring the difference between trading on an organized exchange versus trading on the over-the-counter market. Even if your stock is listed on the New York Stock Exchange (NYSE), the odds are that it won't be executed on the floor of the exchange, but rather will be executed electronically in the maze of computers that make up the global trading network. In effect, today there is little difference between how a security is traded on an organized security exchange versus the over-the-counter market.

**organized security exchanges** formal organizations that facilitate the trading of securities.

**over-the-counter markets** all security markets except organized exchanges. The money market is an over-the-counter market. Most corporate bonds also are traded in the over-the-counter market.

**Organized Security Exchanges**  The New York Stock Exchange is consider a national stock exchange, and in addition to it there are several others generally termed regional stock exchanges. If a firm's stock trades on a particular exchange, it is said to be listed on that exchange. Securities can be listed on more than one exchange. All of these active exchanges are registered with the Securities and Exchange Commission. Firms whose securities are traded on the registered exchanges must comply with reporting requirements of both the specific exchange and the SEC.

The NYSE, also called the "Big Board," is the oldest of all the organized exchanges. Without question, the NYSE is the big player, with the total value of the shares of stock listed in 2012 at over $14 trillion. Today, the NYSE is a hybrid market, allowing for face-to-face trading between individuals on the floor of the stock exchange in addition to automated, electronic trading. As a result, during times of extreme flux in the market, at the opening or close of the market, or on large trades, human judgment can be called on to make sure that the trade is executed appropriately.

**Over-the-Counter Markets**  Many publicly held firms either don't meet the listing requirements of the organized stock exchanges or simply would rather be listed on NASDAQ, which is an electronic stock exchange. In effect, NASDAQ is a computerized system that provides price quotes on over 5,000 over-the-counter stocks and also facilitates trades by matching up buyers and sellers. Recently, Facebook decided to list its stock on NASDAQ rather than the NYSE because of its lower fees and expertise with technology companies.

**Stock Exchange Benefits**  Both corporations and investors enjoy several benefits provided by the existence of organized security exchanges. These include

1. **Providing a continuous market**  This may be the most important function of an organized security exchange. A continuous market provides a series of continuous

security prices. Price changes from trade to trade tend to be smaller than they would be in the absence of organized markets. The reasons are that there is a relatively large sales volume of each security traded, trading orders are executed quickly, and the range between the price asked for a security and the offered price tends to be narrow. The result is that price volatility is reduced.

2. **Establishing and publicizing fair security prices** An organized exchange permits security prices to be set by competitive forces. They are not set by negotiations off the floor of the exchange, where one party might have a bargaining advantage. The bidding process flows from the supply and demand underlying each security. This means the specific price of a security is determined in the manner of an auction. In addition, the security prices determined at each exchange are widely publicized.

3. **Helping business raise new capital** Because a continuous secondary market exists, it is easier for firms to float, or issue, new security offerings at competitively determined prices. This means that the comparative values of securities offered in these markets are easily observed.

## Concept Check

1. Explain the difference between (a) public offerings and private placements, (b) primary markets and secondary markets, (c) the money market and the capital market, and (d) organized security exchanges and over-the-counter markets.

2. Name the benefits derived from the existence of stock exchanges.

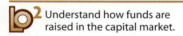 **2** Understand how funds are raised in the capital market.

**investment banker** a financial specialist who underwrites and distributes new securities and advises corporate clients about raising new funds.

**underwriting** the purchase and subsequent resale of a new security issue. The risk of selling the new issue at a satisfactory (profitable) price is assumed (underwritten) by the investment banker.

**underwriter's spread** the difference between the price the corporation raising money gets and the public offering price of a security.

# Selling Securities to the Public

Most corporations do not raise long-term capital frequently. The activities of working-capital management go on daily, but attracting long-term capital is, by comparison, episodic. The sums involved can be huge, so these situations are considered of great importance to financial managers. Because most managers are unfamiliar with the subtleties of raising long-term funds, they enlist the help of an expert, an investment banker. It is with the help of an **investment banker** serving as the underwriter that stocks and bonds are generally sold in the primary markets. The **underwriting** process involves the purchase and subsequent resale of a new security issue with the risk of selling the new issue at a satisfactory price being assumed by the investment banker. The *difference between the price the corporation gets and the public offering price* is called the **underwriter's spread**.

Table 2-1 gives us some idea of who the major players are within the investment-banking industry. It lists the top 10 houses in 2011 based on the dollar volume of security issues that were managed. Today, there are no very large, stand-alone investment-banking firms;

| TABLE 2-1 Underwriter Rankings for 2011 | | |
|---|---|---|
| **Rank** | **Underwriter** | **Proceeds (Millions)** |
| 1 | Morgan Stanley | $9,656.2 |
| 2 | Bank of America Merrill Lynch | 8,262.1 |
| 3 | Goldman Sachs | 6,054.6 |
| 4 | J. P. Morgan | 3,757.4 |
| 5 | Citi | 3,192.0 |
| 6 | Barclays Capital | 1,191.0 |
| 7 | Credit Suisse | 966.5 |
| 8 | Deutsche Bank Securities | 746.2 |
| 9 | Raymond James | 601.2 |
| 10 | UBS Investment Bank | 597.4 |

Source: "Underwriter Rankings for 2011." Copyright © 2011 Renaissance Capital, Greenwhich, CT. Reprinted by permission. www.renaissancecapital.com.

they are all banks that are also investment bankers. You'll notice that only six bankers had over $1 trillion in proceeds in 2011.

Actually, we use the term "investment banker" to describe both the firm itself and the individuals who work for it in that capacity. Just what does this intermediary role involve? The easiest way to understand it is to look at the basic investment-banking functions.

## Functions

The investment banker performs three basic functions: (1) underwriting, (2) distributing, and (3) advising.

**Underwriting**  The term underwriting is borrowed from the field of insurance. It means *assuming a risk*. The investment banker assumes the risk of selling a security issued at a satisfactory price. A satisfactory price is one that generates a profit for the investment-banking house.

The procedure goes like this. The managing investment banker and its syndicate will buy the security issue from the corporation in need of funds. The **syndicate** is *a group of other investment bankers that is invited to help buy and resell the issue*. The managing house is the investment-banking firm that originated the business because its corporate client decided to raise external funds. On a specific day, the client that is raising capital is presented with a check from the managing house in exchange for the securities being issued. At this point the investment-banking syndicate owns the securities. The client has its cash, so it is immune from the possibility that the security markets might turn sour. That is, if the price of the newly issued security falls below that paid to the firm by the syndicate, the syndicate will suffer a loss. The syndicate, of course, hopes that the opposite situation will result. Its objective is to sell the new issue to the investing public at a price per security greater than its cost.

**syndicate** a group of investment bankers who contractually assist in the buying and selling of a new security issue.

**Distributing**  Once the syndicate owns the new securities, it must get them into the hands of the ultimate investors. This is the distribution or selling function of investment banking. The investment banker may have branch offices across the United States, or it may have an informal arrangement with several security dealers who regularly buy a portion of each new offering for final sale. It is not unusual to have 300 to 400 dealers involved in the selling effort. The syndicate can properly be viewed as the security wholesaler, and the dealer organization can be viewed as the security retailer.

**Advising**  The investment banker is an expert in the issuance and marketing of securities. A sound investment-banking house will be aware of prevailing market conditions and can relate those conditions to the particular type of security and the price at which it should be sold at a given time. For example, business conditions may be pointing to a future increase in interest rates, so the investment banker might advise the firm to issue its bonds in a timely fashion to avoid the higher interest rates that are forthcoming. The banker can analyze the firm's capital structure and make recommendations about what general source of capital should be issued. In many instances the firm will invite its investment banker to sit on the board of directors. This permits the banker to observe corporate activity and make recommendations on a regular basis.

## The Demise of the Stand-Alone Investment-Banking Industry

From the time of George Washington until the Great Depression that occurred in the 1930s, the U.S. economy experienced a recurring financial panic and banking crisis about every 15 years. During the Great Depression and the banking failures of 1933, some 4,004 banks closed their doors and Congress enacted a series of reforms that were designed to put an end to these recurring financial crises. The lynchpin of this reform was the Glass-Steagall Act, or the Banking Act of 1933. An important component of the Glass-Steagall Act was the creation of the Federal Deposit Insurance Corporation (FDIC), which provides deposit insurance for bank deposits in member banks of up to $250,000[1] per depositor per bank. The creation of the FDIC,

---

[1]On December 31, 2013, the standard coverage limit will return to $100,000 for all deposit categories except IRAs and certain retirement accounts, which will continue to be insured up to $250,000 per owner, unless Congress takes action to extend the limits beyond the end of 2013.

was an effort to provide assurance to depositors that their deposits were secure, thereby preventing runs on banks. Another key element of Glass-Steagall was the separation of the commercial-banking and investment-banking industries. The purpose of this was to keep banks safe by prohibiting them from entering the securities industry, where it is possible to incur large losses, and as a result, a strong "stand-alone" investment-banking industry emerged with names like Lehman Brothers, Bear Stearns, and J.P. Morgan.

With the repeal of Glass-Steagall in 1999, many commercial banks merged with large investment-banking firms; for example, Chase Manhattan Bank merged with J.P. Morgan, forming JPMorgan-Chase & Co. (JPM). The advantage of this to the investment banks was the access to stable funding through bank deposits along with the ability to borrow from the Fed in the case of an emergency, while the commercial bank gained access to the more lucrative, albeit more risky, securities industry. Then in 2008 as a result of the financial crisis and banking meltdown, the remaining stand-alone investment-banking firms that did not fail in the crisis, including Morgan Stanley and Goldman Sachs, quickly found commercial bank partners. At the end of the day, there were no stand-alone investment-banking firms left. Today, the investment-banking function is provided by "universal banks," that is, commercial banks that also provide investment-banking services.

## Distribution Methods

Several methods are available to the corporation for placing new security offerings in the hands of investment bankers followed by final investors. The investment banker's role is different in each of these. (Sometimes, in fact, it is possible to bypass the investment banker.) These methods are described in this section. Private placements, because of their importance, are treated later in the chapter.

**A Negotiated Purchase**    In a negotiated underwriting, the firm that needs funds makes contact with an investment banker, and deliberations concerning the new issue begin. If all goes well, a *method* is negotiated for determining the price the investment banker and the syndicate will pay for the securities. For example, the agreement might state that the syndicate will pay $2 less than the closing price of the firm's common stock on the day before the offering date of a new stock issue. The negotiated purchase is the most prevalent method of securities distribution in the private sector. It is generally thought to be the most profitable technique as far as investment bankers are concerned.

**A Competitive Bid Purchase**    The method by which the underwriting group is determined distinguishes the competitive bid purchase from the negotiated purchase. In a competitive underwriting, several underwriting groups bid for the right to purchase the new issue from the corporation that is raising funds. The firm does not directly select the investment banker. Instead, the investment banker that underwrites and distributes the issue is chosen by an auction process. The one willing to pay the greatest dollar amount per new security will win the competitive bid.

Most competitive bid purchases are confined to three situations, compelled by legal regulations: (1) railroad issues, (2) public utility issues, and (3) state and municipal bond issues. The argument in favor of competitive bids is that any undue influence of an investment banker over the firm is mitigated and the price received by the firm for each security should be higher. Thus, we would intuitively suspect that the cost of capital in a competitive bidding situation would be less than in a negotiated purchase situation. Evidence on this question, however, is mixed. One problem with the competitive bidding purchase as far as the fund-raising firm is concerned is that the benefits gained from the advisory function of the investment banker are lost. It may be necessary to use an investment banker for advisory purposes and then by law exclude the banker from the competitive bid process.

**A Commission or Best-Efforts Basis**    Here, the investment banker acts as an agent rather than as a principal in the distribution process. The securities are *not* underwritten. The investment banker attempts to sell the issue in return for a fixed commission on each security actually sold. Unsold securities are then returned to the corporation. This arrangement is typically used for more speculative issues. The issuing firm may be smaller or less established than the banker would like. Because the underwriting risk is not passed on to the investment banker, this distribution method is less costly to the issuer than a negotiated or competitive bid purchase. On the other hand, the investment banker only has to give it his or her "best effort." A successful sale is not guaranteed.

**A Privileged Subscription**    Occasionally, the firm may feel that a distinct market already exists for its new securities. When a *new issue is marketed to a definite and select group of investors*, it is called a **privileged subscription**. Three target markets are typically involved: (1) current stockholders, (2) employees, or (3) customers of the firm. Of these, distributions directed at current stockholders are the most prevalent. Such offerings are called *rights offerings*. In a privileged subscription the investment banker may act only as a selling agent. It is also possible that the issuing firm and the investment banker might sign a *standby agreement*, which obligates the investment banker to underwrite the securities that are not purchased by the privileged investors.

**privileged subscription** the process of marketing a new security issue to a select group of investors.

**Dutch Auction**    As we explained at the beginning of the chapter, with a **Dutch auction**, investors first bid on the number of shares they would like to buy and the price they are willing to pay for them. Once all the bids are in, the prices that were bid along with the number of shares are ranked from the highest price to the lowest price. The selling price for the stock is then calculated as the highest price that allows for all the stock to be sold. Although Google really brought this method to the public's eye, it has been used by a number of other companies, including Overstock.com (OSTK) and Salon (SLNM). Figure 2-2 explains in more detail how a Dutch auction works.

**Dutch auction** a method of issuing securities (common stock) by which investors place bids indicating how many shares they are willing to buy and at what price. The price the stock is then sold for becomes the lowest price at which the issuing company can sell all the available shares.

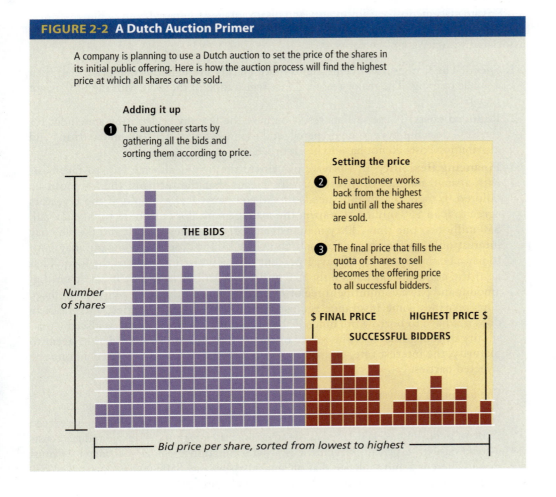

**FIGURE 2-2  A Dutch Auction Primer**

A company is planning to use a Dutch auction to set the price of the shares in its initial public offering. Here is how the auction process will find the highest price at which all shares can be sold.

**Adding it up**

❶ The auctioneer starts by gathering all the bids and sorting them according to price.

THE BIDS

Number of shares

**Setting the price**

❷ The auctioneer works back from the highest bid until all the shares are sold.

❸ The final price that fills the quota of shares to sell becomes the offering price to all successful bidders.

$ FINAL PRICE          HIGHEST PRICE $

SUCCESSFUL BIDDERS

— Bid price per share, sorted from lowest to highest —

**direct sale** the sale of securities by a corporation to the investing public without the services of an investment-banking firm.

**A Direct Sale** In a **direct sale** *the issuing firm sells the securities directly to the investing public without involving an investment banker.* Even among established corporate giants, this procedure is relatively rare. A variation of the direct sale involves the private placement of a new issue by the fund-raising corporation *without* the use of an investment banker as an intermediary. Texaco (now Chevron (CVX)), Mobil Oil (now ExxonMobil (XOM)), and International Harvester (now Navistar (NAV)) are examples of large firms that have followed this procedure.

## Private Debt Placements

Earlier in this chapter we discussed the private placement market. Here we take a closer look at the debt side of the private placement market and how it is used by seasoned corporations as distinct from start-ups. Thus, when we talk of private placements in this section, we are focusing on debt contracts rather than stock offerings. This debt side of the private placement market makes up a significant portion of the total private market.

Private placements are an alternative to the sale of securities to the public or to a restricted group of investors through a privileged subscription. Any type of security can be privately placed (directly placed). The major investors in private placements are large financial institutions. Based on the volume of securities purchased, the three most important investor groups are (1) life insurance companies, (2) state and local retirement funds, and (3) private pension funds.

In arranging a private placement, the firm may (1) avoid the use of an investment banker and work directly with the investing institutions or (2) engage the services of an investment banker. If the firm does not use an investment banker, of course, it does not have to pay a fee. However, investment bankers can provide valuable advice in the private placement process. They are usually in contact with several major institutional investors; thus, they will know who the major buyers able to invest in the proposed offering are, and they can help the firm evaluate the terms of the new issue.

Private placements have advantages and disadvantages compared with public offerings. The financial manager must carefully evaluate both sides of the question. The advantages associated with private placements are:

1. **Speed** The firm usually obtains funds more quickly through a private placement than a public offering. The major reason is that registration of the issue with the SEC is not required.

2. **Reduced costs** These savings result because the lengthy registration statement for the SEC does not have to be prepared, and the investment-banking underwriting and distribution costs do not have to be absorbed.

3. **Financing flexibility** In a private placement the firm deals on a face-to-face basis with a small number of investors. This means that the terms of the issue can be tailored to meet the specific needs of the company. For example, if the investors agree to loan $50 million to a firm, the management does not have to take the full $50 million at one time. They may instead borrow as they need it and thereby pay interest only on the amount actually borrowed. However, the company may have to pay a commitment fee of, say, 1 percent on the unused portion of the loan. That is, if the company borrows only $35 million, it will have to pay interest on that amount and pay a commitment fee of 1 percent or so on the remaining $15 million. This provides some insurance against capital market uncertainties, and the firm does not have to borrow the funds if the need does not arise. There is also the possibility of renegotiation. The terms of the debt issue can be altered. The term to maturity, the interest rate, or any restrictive covenants can be discussed among the affected parties.

The following disadvantages of private placements must be evaluated.

1. **Interest costs** It is generally conceded that interest costs on private placements exceed those of public issues. Whether this disadvantage is enough to offset the reduced costs associated with a private placement is a determination the financial manager must make. There is some evidence that on smaller issues, say $500,000 as opposed to $30 million, the private placement alternative would be preferable.

2. **Restrictive covenants** A firm's dividend policy, working-capital levels, and the raising of additional debt capital may all be affected by provisions in the private placement debt contract. This is not to say that such restrictions are always absent in public debt contracts. Rather, the firm's financial officer must be alert to the tendency for these covenants to be especially burdensome in private contracts.

3. **The possibility of future SEC registration** If the lender (investor) should decide to sell the issue to a public buyer before maturity, the issue must be registered with the SEC. Some lenders, then, require that the issuing firm agree to a future registration at their option.

## Flotation Costs

The firm raising long-term capital incurs two types of **flotation costs**: (1) the underwriter's spread and (2) issuing costs. Of these two costs, the underwriter's spread is the larger. The *underwriter's spread* is simply the difference between the gross and net proceeds from a given security issue expressed as a percent of the gross proceeds. The *issue costs* include (1) the printing and engraving of the security certificates, (2) legal fees, (3) accounting fees, (4) trustee fees, and (5) several other miscellaneous components. The two most significant issue costs are printing and engraving and legal fees.

**flotation costs** the transaction cost incurred when a firm raises funds by issuing a particular type of security.

Data published by the SEC have consistently revealed two relationships about flotation costs. First, the costs associated with issuing common stock are notably greater than the costs associated with preferred stock offerings. In turn, preferred stock costs exceed those of bonds. Second, flotation costs (expressed as a percentage of gross proceeds) decrease as the size of the security issue increases.

In the first instance, the stated relationship reflects the fact that issue costs are sensitive to the risks involved in successfully distributing a security issue. Common stock is riskier to own than corporate bonds. Underwriting risk is, therefore, greater with common stock than with bonds. Thus, flotation costs just mirror these risk relationships as identified in **Principle 3: Risk Requires a Reward**. In the second case, a portion of the issue costs is

## CAUTIONARY TALE

### FORGETTING PRINCIPLE 5: CONFLICTS OF INTEREST CAUSE AGENCY PROBLEMS

In 2004, America found itself in the midst of a housing boom. Fueled by low interest rates and government legislation aimed at allowing more people to qualify for housing loans, including those who wouldn't ordinarily qualify, new home construction rates were at a 20-year high. Homeownership was on the rise. And before long, even more first-time homebuyers would realize the American dream.

That was good news for investment bankers like Michael Francis, whose business entailed working with lenders on the West Coast who supplied him with mortgages he could package up as securities and sell to investors who, in turn, collected the interest monthly. For Francis, it didn't matter if the mortgages defaulted; after all, he collected his fees as soon as the mortgages were packaged up and sold as securities. If the mortgages went bad, it wasn't the bank that experienced a loss, it was the last one holding them.

But Francis could only sell the mortgages to big investors once they had been approved by a credit rating agency. The agency's appraisal signaled to investors that the securities were "safe" investments. However, the rating agencies were paid by the people selling the securities, and the more securities that were issued, the more they got paid, and that created a huge temptation to go easy.

Michael Francis admits he had doubts about the risk level of these securities, but the economy was booming and housing prices continued to climb. At the time, the mortgages seemed like safe enough investments to earn the "safe" rating from credit rating agencies. Besides, the investment bank Francis worked for (which he declined to name) was making oodles of money.

If this is starting to sound like one too many conflicts of interest, it should. The acts (or failures to act) of these investment banks and rating agencies are prime examples of how conflicts of interest can lead to agency problems and unethical behavior. Looking back, Francis says the judgment of many in the financial institutions was cloudy. He summed up the way lenders failed to adequately qualify borrowers as, "we removed the litmus test. No income, no asset. Not verifying income . . . breathe on a mirror and if there's fog you sort of get a loan."

Many players had a hand in the eventual housing bust that followed, but the credit rating agencies that gave risky securities a "safe" rating, investment banks that failed to question those ratings, and lenders who offered bad loans to homebuyers in the first place are all key players. The appeal of short-term profits and a massive failure to self-regulate caused these institutions to lose sight of the long-term interests of their clients. Many think these conflicts of interest and failure of self-governance all led to the financial crisis of 2009 and the economic downturn that followed.

Source: "House of Cards," directed by David Faber, CNBC Original Production (2009).

fixed. Legal fees and accounting costs are good examples. So, as the size of the security issue rises, the fixed component is spread over a larger gross proceeds base. As a consequence, average flotation costs vary inversely with the size of the issue.

### Regulation Aimed at Making the Goal of the Firm Work: The Sarbanes-Oxley Act

Because of growing concerns about both agency and ethical issues, in 2002 Congress passed the Sarbanes-Oxley Act, or SOX as it is commonly called. One of the primary inspirations for this new law was Enron, which failed financially in December 2001. Prior to bankruptcy, Enron's board of directors actually voted on two occasions to temporarily suspend its own "code of ethics" to permit its CFO to engage in risky financial ventures that benefited the CFO personally while exposing the corporation to substantial risk.

SOX holds corporate advisors who have access to or influence on company decisions (such as a firm's accountants, lawyers, company officers, and boards of directors) legally accountable for any instances of misconduct. The act very simply and directly identifies its purpose as being "to protect investors by improving the accuracy and reliability of corporate disclosures made pursuant to the securities laws, and for other purposes" and mandates that senior executives take individual responsibility for the accuracy and completeness of the firm's financial reports.[2]

SOX safeguards the interests of the shareholders by providing greater protection against accounting fraud and financial misconduct. Unfortunately, all this has not come without a price. While SOX has received praise from the likes of the former Federal Reserve Chairman Alan Greenspan and has increased investor confidence in financial reporting, it has also been criticized. The demanding reporting requirements are quite costly and, as a result, may inhibit firms listing on U.S. stock markets.

### Concept Check

1. What is the main difference between an investment banker and a commercial banker?
2. What are the three major functions that an investment banker performs?
3. What are the five key methods by which securities are distributed to final investors?
4. Within the financial markets, explain what we mean by "private placements" and what the advantages and disadvantages are.

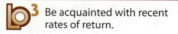 Be acquainted with recent rates of return.

# Rates of Return in the Financial Markets

In this chapter we've discussed the process of raising funds to finance new projects. As you might expect, to raise those funds a firm must offer a rate of return *competitive* with the next-best investment alternative available to that saver (investor).

**opportunity cost of funds** the next-best rate of return available to the investor for a given level of risk.

This *rate of return on the next-best investment alternative to the saver* is known as the investor's **opportunity cost of funds**. The opportunity cost concept is crucial in financial management and is referred to often.

Next we review the levels and variability in rates of return. This review focuses on returns from a wide array of financial instruments. In Chapter 6, we will explain the relationship of rates of return and risk more completely. Then in Chapter 9 we discuss at length the concept of an *overall* cost of capital. Part of that overall cost of capital is attributed to interest rate levels at given points in time. So we follow this initial broad look at interest rate levels with a discussion of the more recent period of 1981 through 2011.

### Rates of Return over Long Periods

History can tell us a great deal about the returns that investors earn in the financial markets. First, what should we expect in terms of return and risk? From **Principle 3: Risk Requires a Reward** we know that with higher returns we should expect to see higher risk, and that's

[2]Sarbanes-Okley Act, Pub.L.107-204, 116 Stat. 745, enacted July 29, 2002.

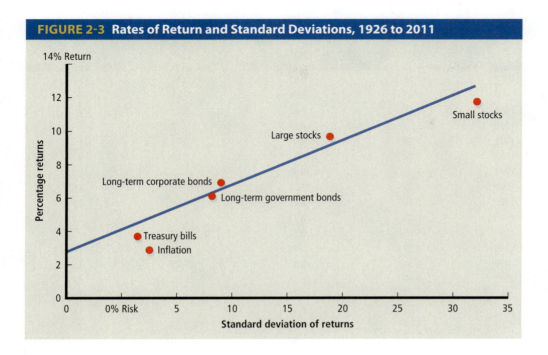

**FIGURE 2-3  Rates of Return and Standard Deviations, 1926 to 2011**

exactly the case. Common stocks of small firms have more risk and produce higher average annual returns than large stock, with the annual return on small-company stocks averaging 11.9 percent and the annual return on large-company stocks averaging 9.8 percent.

The data are summarized visually in Figure 2-3, which presents the relationship between the average annual observed rates of return for different types of securities along with the average annual rate of inflation. Over this period, the average inflation rate was 3.0 percent. We refer to this rate as the "inflation-risk premium." The investor who earns only the rate of inflation has earned no "real return." That is, the *real* return is the return earned above the rate of increase in the general price level for goods and services in the economy, which is the inflation rate. In addition to the danger of not earning above the inflation rate, investors are concerned about the risk of the borrower defaulting, or failing to repay the loan when due. Thus, we would expect investors to earn a default-risk premium for investing in long-term corporate bonds versus long-term government bonds because corporate bonds are considered more risky. The premium for 1926 to 2011, as shown in Figure 2-3, was 0.4 percent, or what is called 40 basis points (6.1 percent on long-term corporate bonds minus 5.7 percent on long-term government bonds). We would also expect an even greater risk premium for common stocks vis-à-vis long-term corporate bonds, because the variability in average returns is greater for common stocks. The results show such a risk premium: Common stocks earned 3.7 percent more than long-term corporate bonds (9.8 percent for common stocks minus 6.1 percent for long-term corporate bonds).

Remember that these returns are "averages" across many securities and over an extended period of time. However, these averages reflect the conventional wisdom regarding risk premiums: The greater the risk, the greater will be the expected returns. Such a relationship is shown in Figure 2-3, where the average returns are plotted against their standard deviations; note that higher average returns have historically been associated with higher dispersion in these returns.

## Interest Rate Levels in Recent Periods

The *nominal* interest rates on some key fixed-income securities are displayed within both Table 2-2 (on page 34) and Figure 2-4 (on page 34) for the 1987–2011 time frame. The rate of inflation at the consumer level is also presented in those two exhibits. This allows us to observe quite easily several concepts that were mentioned in the previous section. Specifically, we can observe (1) the inflation-risk premium, (2) the default-risk premium across the

| TABLE 2-2 Interest Rate Levels and Inflation Rates, 1987 through 2011 | | | | |
|---|---|---|---|---|
| Year | 3-month Treasury Bills % | 30-yr Treasury Bonds % | 30-yr Corporate Bonds % | Inflation Rate % |
| 1987 | 5.78 | 8.59 | 9.38 | 3.7 |
| 1988 | 6.67 | 8.96 | 9.71 | 4.1 |
| 1989 | 8.11 | 8.45 | 9.26 | 4.8 |
| 1990 | 7.5 | 8.61 | 9.32 | 5.4 |
| 1991 | 5.38 | 8.14 | 8.77 | 4.2 |
| 1992 | 3.43 | 7.67 | 8.14 | 3 |
| 1993 | 3 | 6.59 | 7.22 | 3 |
| 1994 | 4.25 | 7.37 | 7.97 | 2.6 |
| 1995 | 5.49 | 6.88 | 7.59 | 2.8 |
| 1996 | 5.01 | 6.71 | 7.37 | 2.9 |
| 1997 | 5.06 | 6.61 | 7.27 | 2.3 |
| 1998 | 4.78 | 5.58 | 6.53 | 1.6 |
| 1999 | 4.64 | 5.87 | 7.05 | 2.2 |
| 2000 | 5.82 | 5.94 | 7.62 | 3.4 |
| 2001 | 3.4 | 5.49 | 7.08 | 2.8 |
| 2002 | 1.61 | 5.43 | 6.49 | 1.6 |
| 2003 | 1.01 | 4.93 | 5.66 | 2.3 |
| 2004 | 1.37 | 4.86 | 5.63 | 2.7 |
| 2005 | 3.15 | 4.51 | 5.23 | 3.4 |
| 2006 | 4.73 | 4.91 | 5.59 | 3.2 |
| 2007 | 4.36 | 4.84 | 5.56 | 2.9 |
| 2008 | 1.37 | 4.28 | 5.63 | 3.8 |
| 2009 | 0.15 | 4.08 | 5.31 | −0.4 |
| 2010 | 0.14 | 4.25 | 4.94 | 1.6 |
| 2011 | 0.05 | 3.91 | 4.64 | 3.2 |
| Mean | 3.85 | 6.14 | 7.00 | 2.92 |

Source: Federal Reserve System, Release H-15, Selected Interest Rates.

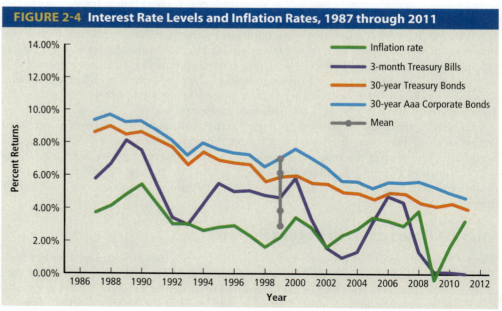

FIGURE 2-4 Interest Rate Levels and Inflation Rates, 1987 through 2011

Source: Federal Reserve System, Release H-15, Selected Interest Rates.

several instruments, and (3) the approximate real return for each instrument. Looking at the mean (average) values for each security and the inflation rate at the bottom of Table 2-2 will facilitate the discussion.

While inflation appears to have dropped a bit between 1987 and 2011, it was much higher just before this period. In fact, from 1979 through 1981 it averaged over 10 percent each year, peaking at 13.5 percent in 1980. As a result of this drop in the rate of inflation, interest rates have come down. This only makes sense according to the logic of the financial markets. Investors *require* a **nominal (or quoted) rate of interest** that exceeds the inflation rate or else their realized *real* return will be negative.

Table 2-2 indicates that between 1987 and 2011, on average, investor rationality prevailed. For example, the average return premium demanded on U.S. Treasury bills with a 3-month maturity was 0.93 percent (or 93 basis points, where a basis point is one one-hundredth of 1 percent) in excess of the inferred **inflation premium** of 2.92 percent. That is, an average 3.85 percent yield on Treasury bills over the period *minus* the average inflation rate of 2.92 percent over the same period produces a premium of 0.93 percent. This 0.93 percent can be thought of as the real risk-free short-term interest rate that prevailed over the 1987–2011 period. You'll notice that this rate becomes negative between 2009 and 2011. That's because the Federal Reserve took action to keep short-term interest rates artificially low in an attempt to stimulate the economy.

The **default-risk premium** is also evident in Table 2-2 and Figure 2-4:

| SECURITY | AVERAGE YIELD |
|---|---|
| 30-year Treasury bonds | 6.14% |
| 30-year Aaa corporate bonds | 7.00% |

Again, the basic rationale of the financial markets prevailed. The default-risk premium on 30-year high-rated (Aaa) corporate bonds relative to long-term Treasury bonds of 30-year maturity was 0.86 percent (7.00 percent minus 6.14 percent), or 86 basis points.

The preceding array of numbers can also be used to identify another factor that affects interest rate levels. It is referred to as the **maturity-risk premium**. The maturity-risk premium can be defined as *the additional return required by investors in longer-term securities (bonds in this case) to compensate them for the greater risk of price fluctuations on those securities caused by interest rate changes.* This maturity-risk premium arises even if securities possess equal (or approximately equal) odds of default. Notice that Treasury bonds with a 30-year maturity commanded a 2.29 percent yield differential over the shorter, 3-month-to-maturity Treasury bonds. (Both types of bonds are considered risk-free because they are issued and backed by the U.S. government.) This provides an estimate of the maturity premium demanded by all investors over this specific 1987–2011 period.

When you study the basic mathematics of financial decisions and the characteristics of fixed-income securities in later chapters, you will learn how to quantify this maturity premium that is imbedded in nominal interest rates.

One other type of risk premium that helps determine interest rate levels needs to be identified and defined. It is known as the "liquidity-risk premium." The **liquidity-risk premium** is defined as *the additional return required by investors in securities that cannot be quickly converted into cash at a reasonably predictable price.* The secondary markets for small-bank stocks, especially community banks, provide a good example of the liquidity premium. A bank holding company that trades on the New York Stock Exchange, such as Wells Fargo, will be more liquid to investors than, say, the common stock of Century National Bank of Orlando, Florida. Such a liquidity premium is reflected across the spectrum of financial assets, from bonds to stocks.

**nominal (or quoted) rate of interest** the interest rate paid on debt securities without an adjustment for any loss in purchasing power.

**inflation premium** a premium to compensate for anticipated inflation that is equal to the price change expected to occur over the life of the bond or investment instrument.

**default-risk premium** the additional return required by investors to compensate them for the risk of default. It is calculated as the difference in rates between a U.S. Treasury bond and a corporate bond of the same maturity and marketability.

**maturity-risk premium** the additional return required by investors in longer-term securities to compensate them for the greater risk of price fluctuations on those securities caused by interest rate changes.

**liquidity-risk premium** the additional return required by investors for securities that cannot be quickly converted into cash at a reasonably predictable price.

> **P**rinciple  **REMEMBER YOUR PRINCIPLES**
> *Our third principle,* **Principle 3: Risk Requires a Reward,** established the fundamental risk–return relationship that governs the financial markets. We are now trying to provide you with an understanding of the kinds of risks that are rewarded in the risk–return relationship presented in **Principle 3**.

## Concept Check

1. What is the "opportunity cost of funds"?
2. Over long periods of time is the "real rate of return" higher on 30-year Treasury bonds or 30-year Aaa corporate bonds?
3. Distinguish between the concepts of the "inflation premium" and the "default-risk premium."
4. Distinguish between the concepts of the "maturity-risk premium" and the "liquidity-risk premium."

 **4** Explain the fundamentals of interest rate determination and the popular theories of the term structure of interest rates.

**real risk-free interest rate** the required rate of return on a fixed-income security that has no risk in an economic environment of zero inflation.

# Interest Rate Determinants in a Nutshell

Using the logic from **Principle 3: Risk Requires a Reward,** we can deconstruct the interest rate paid on a security into a simple equation with the nominal interest rate equal to the sum of the real risk-free interest rate plus compensation for taking on several different types of risk and several risk premiums, where the **real risk-free interest rate** is *a required rate of return on a fixed-income security that has no risk in an economic environment of zero inflation.* The real risk-free interest rate can be thought of as the return demanded by investors in U.S. Treasury securities during periods of no inflation. The equation for the nominal interest rate is

$$
\begin{aligned}
\text{Nominal interest rate} = \ & \text{real risk-free interest rate} \\
& + \text{inflation premium} \\
& + \text{default-risk premium} \\
& + \text{maturity-risk premium} \\
& + \text{liquidity-risk premium}
\end{aligned}
\tag{2-1}
$$

where

| | |
|---|---|
| Nominal interest rate = | the quoted interest rate and is the interest rate paid on debt securities without an adjustment for any loss in purchasing power. |
| Real risk-free interest rate = | the interest rate on a fixed-income security that has no risk in an economic environment of zero inflation. It could also be stated as the nominal interest rate less the inflation, default-risk, maturity-risk, and liquidity-risk premium. |
| Inflation premium = | a premium to compensate for anticipated inflation that is equal to the price change expected to occur over the life of the bond or investment instrument. |
| Default-risk premium = | the additional return required by investors to compensate for the risk of default. It is calculated as the difference in rates between a U.S. Treasury bond and a corporate bond of the same maturity and marketability. |
| Maturity-risk premium = | the additional return required by investors in longer-term securities to compensate them for the greater risk of price fluctuation on those securities caused by interest rate changes. |
| Liquidity-risk premium = | the additional return required by investors for securities that cannot quickly be converted into cash at a reasonably predictable price. |

## Estimating Specific Interest Rates Using Risk Premiums

By using knowledge of various risk premiums as contained in equation (2-1), the financial manager can generate useful information for the firm's financial planning process. For instance, if the firm is about to offer a new issue of corporate bonds to the investing marketplace, it is possible for the financial manager or analyst to estimate and better understand what interest rate (yield) would satisfy the market to help ensure that the bonds are actually bought by investors. To make sense out of the different interest rate terminology—nominal, risk-free, and real—let's take a closer look at the difference between them.

## Real Risk-Free Interest Rate and the Risk-Free Interest Rate

What's the difference between the real risk-free interest rate and the risk-free interest rate? The answer is that the risk-free interest rate includes compensation for inflation while the real risk-free interest rate is the risk-free rate after inflation. As a result,

risk-free interest rate = real risk-free interest rate + inflation premium

or

real risk-free interest rate = risk-free interest rate − inflation premium

In effect, when you see the term "real" in front of an interest rate, that interest rate is referring to an "after inflation adjusted" return, that is, the impact of inflation has been subtracted from the interest rate. Furthermore, the term "risk-free" indicates there is no compensation for default risk, maturity risk, or liquidity risk. As a result, the term "real risk-free" indicates that the interest rate does not include compensation for the inflation, default-risk, maturity-risk, and liquidity-risk premiums. That is, it is the return if there was no risk and no inflation.

## Real and Nominal Rates of Interest

When a rate of interest is quoted, it is generally the nominal, or observed, rate. The nominal rate of interest tells you how much more money you will have. As we just learned, **real rate of interest,** in contrast, represents *the rate of increase in your actual purchasing power, after adjusting for inflation*. In effect, the real rate of interest tells you how much more purchasing power you will have. Keep in mind that the real rate of interest is not a risk-free rate, that is, the real rate of interest includes both the real risk-free rate of interest along with compensation for the default-risk, maturity-risk, and liquidity-risk premiums. The nominal interest rate can be calculated to be

**real rate of interest** the nominal (quoted) rate of interest less any loss in purchasing power of the dollar during the time of the investment.

Nominal interest rate ≅ (approximately equals) real rate of interest + inflation premium

(2-2)

---

## CAN YOU DO IT?

You have been asked to provide a reasonable estimate of the nominal interest rate for a new issue of 30-year Aaa-rated bonds (that is, very high quality corporate bonds) to be offered by Big Truck Producers Inc. The final format that the CFO of Big Truck has requested is that of equation (2-1) in the text.

After some thought, you decided to estimate the different premiums in equation (2-1) as follows:

1. The real risk-free rate of interest is the difference between the calculated average yield on 3-month Treasury bills and the inflation rate.

2. The inflation premium is the rate of inflation expected to occur over the life of the bond under consideration.

3. The default-risk premium is estimated by the difference between the average yield on 30-year Aaa-rated corporate bonds and 30-year Treasury bonds.

4. The maturity-risk premium is estimated by the difference between the calculated average yield on 30-year Treasury bonds and 3-month Treasury bills.

You next conducted research and found the following: The current 3-month Treasury bill rate is 4.89 percent, the 30-year Treasury bond rate is 5.38 percent, the 30-year Aaa-rated corporate bond rate is 6.24 percent, and the inflation rate is 3.60 percent. Finally, you have estimated that Big Truck's bonds will have a slight liquidity-risk premium of 0.03 percent because of the infrequency with which they are traded.

Now place your output into the format of equation (2-1) so that the nominal interest rate can be estimated and the size of each variable can also be inspected for reasonableness and discussion with the chief financial officer. (Solution can be found on page 38.)

# DID YOU GET IT?

Let's now look at the building blocks that will comprise our forecast of the nominal interest rate on Big Truck's new issue of bonds. The nominal rate that is forecast to satisfy the market turns out be 6.27 percent. The following tables illustrate how we obtained this estimate.

| (1) 3-month Treasury Bills % | (2) 30-year Treasury Bonds % | (3) 30-year Aaa-Rated Corporate Bonds % | (4) Inflation Rate % |
|---|---|---|---|
| 4.89 | 5.38 | 6.24 | 3.60 |

| Table Columns Shown Above | Equation (2-1) | |
|---|---|---|
| (1) – (4) | real risk-free interest rate | 1.29 |
|  | + | + |
| (4) | inflation premium | 3.60 |
|  | + | + |
| (3) – (2) | default-risk premium | 0.86 |
|  | + | + |
| (2) – (1) | maturity-risk premium | 0.49 |
|  | + | + |
| Given | liquidity-risk premium | 0.03 |
|  | = | = |
|  | nominal interest rate | 6.27 |

Thus, we see that:

1. The real risk-free rate of interest is 1.29 percent, which is the difference between the average yield on a 3-month Treasury bill and the inflation rate (column 1 less column 4).

2. The inflation premium of 3.60 percent is the inflation rate (column 4).

3. The default-risk premium of 0.86 is the difference in the average rate available to investors in the least risky (30-year Aaa-rated) corporate bonds that mature in 30 years and the average return for a Treasury bond that matures in 30 years (column 3 minus column 2).

4. The maturity-risk premium of 0.49 percent is the rate earned by investors on 30-year Treasury bonds less the rate on 3-month Treasury bills (column 2 minus column 1).

5. The liquidity-risk premium is 0.03 percent, based on your earlier assumption.

When we put this all together as an estimate of the nominal interest rate needed to satisfy the financial markets on Big Truck's new bond issue, we have

Nominal rate on Big Truck's bonds = 1.29 + 3.60 + 0.86 + 0.49 + 0.03 = 6.27%

Understanding this analysis will help you deal with the Mini Case at the end of this chapter. We move now to an examination of the relationship between real and nominal interest rates.

Equation 2-2 just says that the nominal rate of interest is approximately equal to the real interest rate plus the inflation premium and provides a quick and *approximate* way of estimating the real rate of interest by solving directly for this rate. You'll notice it is very similar to equation (2-1), except it lumps all the different risk premiums in with the real risk-free rate of interest to come up with the real rate of interest. This basic relationship in equation (2-2) contains important information for the financial decision maker. It has also been for years the subject of fascinating and lengthy discussions among financial economists.

As we saw in equation (2-2), a quick approximation for the nominal rate of interest is the real interest rate plus the inflation premium. Let's take a closer look at this relationship. Let's begin by assuming that you have $100 today and lend it to someone for 1 year at a nominal rate of interest of 11.3 percent. This means you will get back $111.30 in 1 year. But if during the year, the prices of goods and services rise by 5 percent, it will take $105 at year-end to purchase the same goods and services that $100 purchased at the beginning of the year. What was your increase in purchasing power over the year? The quick and dirty answer is found by subtracting the inflation rate from the nominal rate, 11.3% − 5% = 6.3%, but this is not exactly correct. We can also express the relationship among the nominal interest rate, the rate of inflation (that is, the inflation premium), and the real rate of interest as follows:

$$1 + \text{nominal interest rate} = (1 + \text{real rate of interest})(1 + \text{rate of inflation}) \quad (2\text{-}3)$$

Solving for the nominal rate of interest,

Nominal interest rate
= real rate of interest + rate of inflation + (real rate of interest) (rate of inflation)

Consequently, the nominal rate of interest is equal to the sum of the real rate of interest, the inflation rate, and the product of the real rate and the inflation rate. This relationship among nominal rates, real rates, and the rate of inflation has come to be called the *Fisher effect*.[3] What does the product of the real rate of interest and the inflation rate represent? It represents the fact that the money you earn on your investment is worth less because of inflation. All this demonstrates that the observed nominal rate of interest includes both the real rate and an *inflation premium*.

Substituting into equation (2-3) using a nominal rate of 11.3 percent and an inflation rate of 5 percent, we can calculate the real rate of interest as follows:

Nominal or quoted = real rate of interest   + inflation +   product of the real rate of
rate of interest                                 rate        interest and the inflation rate

0.113       = real rate of interest   +   0.05   +   0.05 × real rate of interest

0.063       = 1.05 × real rate of interest

0.063/1.05  = real rate of interest

Solving for the real rate of interest:

Real rate of interest = 0.06 = 6%

Thus, at the new higher prices, your purchasing power will have increased by only 6 percent, although you have $11.30 more than you had at the start of the year. To see why, let's assume that at the outset of the year, one unit of the market basket of goods and services costs $1, so you could purchase 100 units with your $100. At the end of the year, you have $11.30 more, but each unit now costs $1.05 (remember the 5 percent rate of inflation). How many units can you buy at the end of the year? The answer is $111.30 ÷ $1.05 = 106, which represents a 6 percent increase in real purchasing power.[4]

## Inflation and Real Rates of Return: The Financial Analyst's Approach

Although the algebraic methodology presented in the previous section is strictly correct, few practicing analysts or executives use it. Rather, they employ some version of the

## CAN YOU DO IT?

### SOLVING FOR THE REAL RATE OF INTEREST

Your banker just called and offered you the chance to invest your savings for 1 year at a quoted rate of 10 percent. You also saw on the news that the inflation rate is 6 percent. What is the real rate of interest you would be earning if you made the investment? (The solution can be found on page 40.)

[3]This relationship was analyzed many years ago by Irving Fisher. For those who want to explore Fisher's theory of interest in more detail, a fine overview is contained in Peter N. Ireland, "Long-Term Interest Rate and Inflation: A Fisherian Approach," Federal Reserve Bank of Richmond, *Economic Quarterly*, 82 (Winter 1996), pp. 22–26.
[4]In Chapter 5, we will study more about the time value of money.

## DID YOU GET IT?

### SOLVING FOR THE REAL RATE OF INTEREST

| Nominal or quoted rate of interest | = | real rate of interest | + inflation rate + | product of the real rate of interest and the inflation rate |
|---|---|---|---|---|

$$0.10 = \text{real rate of interest} + 0.06 + 0.06 \times \text{real rate of interest}$$

$$0.04 = 1.06 \times \text{real rate of interest}$$

Solving for the real rate of interest:

$$\text{real rate of interest} = 0.0377 = 3.77\%$$

following relationship (which comes from equation (2-2)), an approximation method, to estimate the real rate of interest over a selected past time frame.

Nominal interest rate − inflation rate ≅ real interest rate

The concept is straightforward, but its implementation requires that several judgments be made. For example, suppose we want to use this relationship to determine the real risk-free interest rate, which interest rate series and maturity period should be used? Suppose we settle for using some U.S. Treasury security as a surrogate for a nominal risk-free interest rate. Then, should we use the yield on 3-month U.S. Treasury bills or, perhaps, the yield on 30-year Treasury bonds? There is no absolute answer to the question.

So, we can have a real risk-free short-term interest rate, as well as a real risk-free long-term interest rate, and several variations in between. In essence, it just depends on what the analyst wants to accomplish. Of course we could also calculate the real rate of interest on some rating class of 30-year corporate bonds (such as Aaa-rated bonds) and have a risky real rate of interest as opposed to a real risk-free interest rate.

Furthermore, the choice of a proper inflation index is equally challenging. Again, we have several choices. We could use the consumer price index, the producer price index for finished goods, or some price index out of the national income accounts, such as the gross domestic product chain price index. Again, there is no precise scientific answer as to which specific price index to use. Logic and consistency do narrow the boundaries of the ultimate choice.

Let's tackle a very basic (simple) example. Suppose that an analyst wants to estimate the approximate real interest rate on (1) 3-month Treasury bills, (2) 30-year Treasury bonds, and (3) 30-year Aaa-rated corporate bonds over the 1987–2011 time frame. Furthermore, the annual rate of change in the consumer price index (measured from December to December) is considered a logical measure of past inflation experience. Most of our work is already done for us in Table 2-2. Some of the data from Table 2-2 are displayed here.

| SECURITY | MEAN NOMINAL YIELD (%) | MEAN INFLATION RATE (%) | INFERRED REAL RATE (%) |
|---|---|---|---|
| 3-month Treasury bills | 3.85 | 2.92 | 0.93 |
| 30-year Treasury bonds | 6.14 | 2.92 | 3.22 |
| 30-year Aaa-rated corporate bonds | 7.00 | 2.92 | 4.08 |

Notice that the mean yield over the 25 years from 1987 to 2011 on all three classes of securities has been used. Likewise, the mean inflation rate over the same time period has been used as an estimate of the inflation premium. The last column provides the approximation for the real interest rate on each class of securities.

Thus, over the 25-year examination period the real rate of interest on 3-month Treasury bills was 0.93 percent versus 3.22 percent on 30-year Treasury bonds, versus 4.08 percent on 30-year Aaa-rated corporate bonds. These three estimates (approximations) of the real interest rate provide a rough guide to the increase in real purchasing power associated with an in-

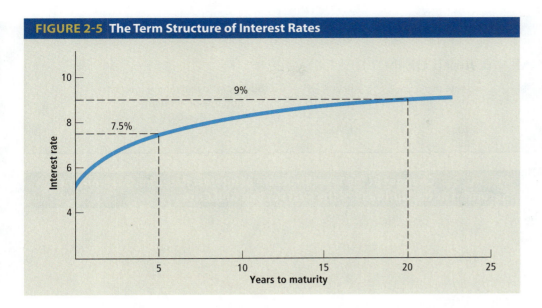

**FIGURE 2-5** The Term Structure of Interest Rates

vestment position in each security. Remember that the real rate on the corporate bonds is expected to be greater than that on long-term government bonds because of the default-risk premium placed on the corporate securities. We move in the next section to a more detailed discussion of the maturity-risk premium—specifically looking at the relationship between interest rates and the number of years to maturity.

## The Term Structure of Interest Rates

*The relationship between a debt security's rate of return and the length of time until the debt matures* is known as the **term structure of interest rates** or the **yield to maturity**. For the relationship to be meaningful to us, all the factors other than maturity, meaning factors such as the chance of the bond defaulting, must be held constant. Thus, *the term structure reflects observed rates or yields on similar securities, except for the length of time until maturity, at a particular moment in time.*

Figure 2-5 shows an example of the term structure of interest rates. The curve is upward sloping, indicating that longer terms to maturity command higher returns, or yields. In this hypothetical term structure, the rate of interest on a 5-year note or bond is 7.5 percent, whereas the comparable rate on a 20-year bond is 9 percent.

**term structure of interest rates** the relationship between interest rates and the term to maturity, where the risk of default is held constant.

**yield to maturity** the rate of return a bondholder will receive if the bond is held to maturity.

## Observing the Historical Term Structures of Interest Rates

As we might expect, the term structure of interest rates changes over time, depending on the environment. The particular term structure observed today may be quite different from the term structure 1 month ago and different still from the term structure 1 month from now. A perfect example of the changing term structure, or yield curve, was witnessed during the early days of the first Persian Gulf Crisis, which occurred in August 1990. Figure 2-6 (on page 42) shows the yield curves 1 day before the Iraqi invasion of Kuwait and then again just 3 weeks later. The change is noticeable, particularly for long-term interest rates. Investors quickly developed new fears about the prospect of increased inflation to be caused

## CAN YOU DO IT?
### SOLVING FOR THE NOMINAL RATE OF INTEREST

If you would like to earn a real rate of interest of 6 percent while the inflation rate is 4 percent, what nominal rate of interest would you have? (The solution can be found on page 42.)

## DID YOU GET IT?
### SOLVING FOR THE NOMINAL RATE OF INTEREST

| Nominal or quoted rate of interest | = | real rate of interest | + | inflation rate | + | product of the real rate of interest and the inflation rate |
|---|---|---|---|---|---|---|
| | = | 0.06 | + | 0.04 | + | (0.06 × 0.04) |
| | = | 0.1024 | = | 10.24% | | |

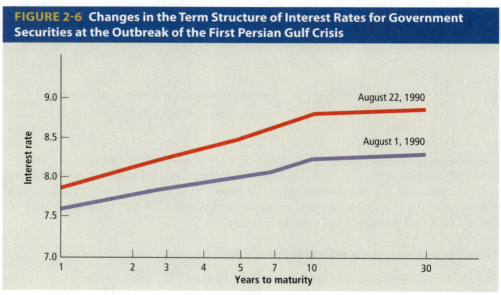

**FIGURE 2-6** Changes in the Term Structure of Interest Rates for Government Securities at the Outbreak of the First Persian Gulf Crisis

Source: Federal Reserve System, Release H-15.

by the crisis and, consequently, increased their required rates of return. Although the upward-sloping term-structure curves in Figures 2-5 and 2-6 are the ones most commonly observed, yield curves can assume several shapes. Sometimes the term structure is downward sloping; at other times it rises and then falls (is humpbacked); and at still other times it may be relatively flat. Figure 2-7 shows some yield curves at different points in time.

As you can see in Figure 2-7, the yield curve in April 2012 was very low, with short-term rates close to zero and historically low long-term rates at 3.13 percent. In response to the

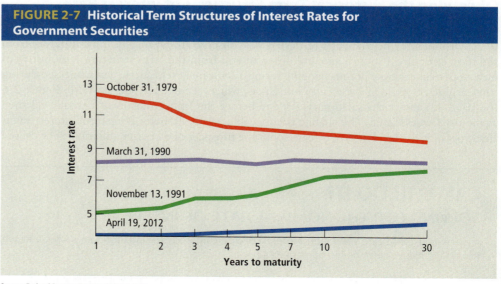

**FIGURE 2-7** Historical Term Structures of Interest Rates for Government Securities

Source: Federal Reserve System, Release H-15.

banking crisis and economic collapse, the government moved to reduce interest rates. In addition, interest rates came down as the economy slowed, while investors further pushed interest rates on Treasury securities as they moved money into Treasuries to escape the risk of the stock market. The reason the government worked to keep interest rates down was to help restart the economy by making borrowing inexpensive—hoping to help individuals buy new homes or refinance their mortgages and allow businesses to borrow money at low rates to invest.

## What Explains the Shape of the Term Structure?

A number of theories may explain the shape of the term structure of interest rates at any point in time. Three possible explanations are prominent: (1) the unbiased expectations theory, (2) the liquidity preference theory, and (3) the market segmentation theory.[5] Let's look at each in turn.

**The Unbiased Expectations Theory**  The **unbiased expectations theory** says that *the term structure is determined by an investor's expectations about future interest rates.*[6] To see how this works, consider the following investment problem faced by Mary Maxell. Mary has $10,000 that she wants to invest for 2 years, at which time she plans to use her savings to make a down payment on a new home. Wanting not to take any risk of losing her savings, she decides to invest in U.S. government securities. She has two choices. First, she can purchase a government security that matures in 2 years, which offers her an interest rate of 9 percent per year. If she does this, she will have $11,881 in 2 years, calculated as follows:[7]

**unbiased expectations theory** the theory that the shape of the term structure of interest rates is determined by an investor's expectations about future interest rates.

| | |
|---|---|
| Principal amount | $10,000 |
| Plus year 1 interest (0.09 × $10,000) | 900 |
| Principal plus interest at the end of year 1 | $10,900 |
| Plus year 2 interest (0.09 × $10,900) | 981 |
| Principal plus interest at the end of year 2 | $ 11,881 |

Alternatively, Mary could buy a government security maturing in 1 year that pays an 8 percent rate of interest. She would then need to purchase another 1-year security at the end of the first year. Which alternative Mary chooses obviously depends in part on the rate of interest she expects to receive on the government security she will purchase a year from now. We cannot tell Mary what the interest rate will be in a year; however, we can at least calculate the rate that will give her the same 2-year total savings she would get from her first choice, or $11,881. The interest rate can be calculated as follows:

| | |
|---|---|
| Savings needed in 2 years | $ 11,881 |
| Savings at the end of year 1 [$10,000(1 + 0.08)] | $10,800 |
| Interest needed in year 2 | $ 1,081 |

For Mary to receive $1,081 in the second year, she would have to earn about 10 percent on her second-year investment, computed as follows:

$$\frac{\text{Interest received in year 2}}{\text{Investment made at beginning of year 2}} = \frac{\$1,081}{\$10,800} = 10\%$$

---

[5] See Richard Roll, *The Behavior of Interest Rates: An Application of the Efficient Market Model to U.S. Treasury Bills* (New York: Basic Books, 1970).

[6] Irving Fisher thought of this idea in 1896. The theory was later refined by J. R. Hicks in *Value and Capital* (London: Oxford University Press, 1946) and F. A. Lutz and V. C. Lutz in *The Theory of Investment in the Firm* (Princeton, NJ: Princeton University Press, 1951).

[7] We could also calculate the principal plus interest for Mary's investment using the following compound interest equation: $10,000 (1 + 0.09)^2 = $11,881. We study the mathematics of compound interest in Chapter 5.

So the term structure of interest rates for our example consists of the 1-year interest rate of 8 percent and the 2-year rate of 9 percent. This exercise also gives us information about the *expected* 1-year rate for investments made 1 year hence. In a sense, the term structure contains implications about investors' expectations of future interest rates; thus, this explains the unbiased expectations theory of the term structure of interest rates.

Although we can see a relationship between current interest rates with different maturities and investors' expectations about future interest rates, is this the whole story? Are there other influences? Probably, so let's continue to think about Mary's dilemma.

### The Liquidity Preference Theory

**The Liquidity Preference Theory**    In presenting Mary's choices, we have suggested that she would be indifferent to a choice between the 2-year government security offering a 9 percent return and two consecutive 1-year investments offering 8 and 10 percent, respectively. However, that would be so only if she is unconcerned about the risk associated with not knowing the rate of interest on the second 1-year security as of today. If Mary is risk averse (that is, she dislikes risk), she might not be satisfied with expectations of a 10 percent return on the second 1-year government security. She might require some additional expected return to be truly indifferent. Mary might in fact decide that she will expose herself to the uncertainty of future interest rates only if she can reasonably *expect* to earn an additional 0.5 percent in interest, or 10.5 percent, on the second 1-year investment. This *risk premium* (additional required interest rate) to compensate for the risk of changing future interest rates is nothing more than the maturity premium introduced earlier, and this concept underlies the liquidity preference theory of the term structure.[8] According to the **liquidity preference theory**, *investors require maturity-risk premiums to compensate them for buying securities that expose them to the risks of fluctuating interest rates.*

> **liquidity preference theory** the theory that the shape of the term structure of interest rates is determined by an investor's additional required interest rate in compensation for additional risks.

### The Market Segmentation Theory

**The Market Segmentation Theory**    The **market segmentation theory** of the term structure of interest rates is built on the notion that legal restrictions and personal preferences limit choices for investors to certain ranges of maturities. For example, commercial banks prefer short- to medium-term maturities as a result of the short-term nature of their deposit liabilities. They prefer not to invest in long-term securities. Life insurance companies, on the other hand, have long-term liabilities, so they prefer longer maturities in investments. At the extreme, the market segmentation theory implies that *the rate of interest for a particular maturity is determined solely by demand and supply for a given maturity and that it is independent of the demand and supply for securities having different maturities.* A more moderate version of the theory allows investors to have strong maturity preferences, but it also allows them to modify their feelings and preferences if significant yield changes occur.

> **market segmentation theory** the theory that the shape of the term structure of interest rates implies that the rate of interest for a particular maturity is determined solely by demand and supply for a given maturity. This rate is independent of the demand and supply for securities having different maturities.

## Concept Check

1. What is the "nominal rate of interest"? Explain how it differs from the "real rate of interest."
2. Write an equation that includes the building blocks of the nominal rate of interest.
3. Identify three prominent theories that attempt to explain the term structure of interest rates.
4. Which shape of the yield curve is considered to be the most typical?

## Chapter Summaries

### Describe key components of the U.S. financial market system and the financing of business.    (pgs. 21–26)

**SUMMARY:** This chapter centers on the market environment in which corporations raise long-term funds, including the structure of the U.S. financial markets, the institution of investment

---

[8]This theory was first presented by John R. Hicks in *Value and Capital* (London: Oxford University Press, 1946), pp. 141–145, with the risk premium referred to as the liquidity premium. For our purposes we use the term *maturity-risk premium* to describe this risk premium, thereby keeping our terminology consistent within this chapter.

banking, and the various methods for distributing securities. It also discusses the role interest rates play in allocating savings to ultimate investment.

Corporations can raise funds through public offerings or private placements. The public market is impersonal in that the security issuer does not meet the ultimate investors in the financial instruments. In a private placement, the securities are sold directly to a limited number of institutional investors.

The primary market is the market for new issues. The secondary market represents transactions in currently outstanding securities. Both the money and capital markets have primary and secondary sides. The money market refers to transactions in short-term debt instruments. The capital market, on the other hand, refers to transactions in long-term financial instruments. Trading in the capital markets can occur in either the organized security exchanges or the over-the-counter market. The money market is exclusively an over-the-counter market.

### KEY TERMS

**Capital markets, page 21** All institutions and procedures that facilitate transactions in long-term financial instruments.

**Angel investor, page 22** A wealthy private investor who provides capital for a business start-up.

**Venture capitalist, page 22** An investment firm (or individual investor) that provides money to business start-ups.

**Public offering, page 23** A security offering where all investors have the opportunity to acquire a portion of the financial claims being sold.

**Private placement, page 23** A security offering limited to a small number of potential investors.

**Primary market, page 23** A market in which securities are offered for the first time for sale to potential investors.

**Initial public offering, IPO, page 24** The first time a company sells its stock to the public.

**Seasoned equity offering, SEO, page 24** The sale of additional stock by a company whose shares are already publically traded.

**Secondary market, page 24** A market in which currently outstanding securities are traded.

**Money market, page 24** All institutions and procedures that facilitate transactions in short-term instruments issued by borrowers with very high credit ratings.

**Spot market, page 24** Cash market.

**Futures market, page 24** Markets where you can buy or sell something at a future date.

**Organized security exchanges, page 25** Formal organizations that facilitate the trading of securities.

**Over-the-counter markets, page 25** All security markets except the organized exchanges. The money market is an over-the-counter market. Most corporate bonds also are traded in the over-the-counter market.

## Understand how funds are raised in the capital markets.    (pgs. 26–32)

**SUMMARY:** The investment banker is a financial specialist involved as an intermediary in the merchandising of securities. He or she performs the functions of (1) underwriting, (2) distributing, and (3) advising. Major methods for the public distribution of securities include (1) the negotiated purchase, (2) the competitive bid purchase, (3) the commission or best-efforts basis, (4) privileged subscriptions, and (5) direct sales. The direct sale bypasses the use of an investment banker. The negotiated purchase is the most profitable distribution method to the investment banker. It also provides the greatest amount of investment-banking services to the corporate client. Today, there are no major stand-alone investment bankers.

Privately placed debt provides an important market outlet for corporate bonds. Major investors in this market are (1) life insurance firms, (2) state and local retirement funds, and (3) private pension funds. Several advantages and disadvantages are associated with private placements. The financial officer must weigh these attributes and decide if a private placement is preferable to a public offering.

Flotation costs consist of the underwriter's spread and issuing costs. The flotation costs of common stock exceed those of preferred stock, which, in turn, exceed those of debt. Moreover, flotation costs as a percent of gross proceeds are inversely related to the size of the security issue.

### KEY TERMS

**Investment banker, page 26** A financial specialist who underwrites and distributes new securities and advises corporate clients about raising new funds.

**Underwriting, page 26** The purchase and subsequent resale of a new security issue. The risk of selling the new issue at a satisfactory (profitable) price is assumed (underwritten) by the investment banker.

**Underwriter's spread, page 26**  The difference between the price the corporation raising the money gets and the public offering price of a security.

**Syndicate, page 27**  A group of investment bankers who contractually assist in the buying and selling of a new security issue.

**Privileged subscription, page 29**  The process of marketing a new security to a select group of investors.

**Dutch auction, page 29**  A method of issuing securities (common stock) by which investors

place bids indicating how many shares they are willing to buy and at what price. The price the stock is then sold for becomes the lowest price at which the issuing company can sell all the available shares.

**Direct sale, page 30**  The sale of securities by a corporation to the investing public without the services of an investment-banking firm.

**Flotation costs, page 31**  The transaction cost incurred when a firm raises funds by issuing a particular type of security.

---

 **Be acquainted with recent rates of return.**    (pgs. 32–36)

**SUMMARY:** From Principle 3: Risk Requires a Reward, we know that with higher returns we should expect to see higher risk, and that's exactly the case. Common stocks of small firms have more risk and produce higher average annual returns than large-company stock. In recent years interest rates have fallen dramatically, with the rate on 3-month Treasury bills approaching zero and the rate on 30-year Treasury bonds dropping under 4 percent for 2011— down from close to 9 percent 25 years prior.

### KEY TERMS

**Opportunity cost of funds, page 32**  The next-best rate of return available to the investor for a given level of risk.

**Nominal (or quoted) rate of interest, page 35**  The interest rate paid on debt securities without an adjustment for any loss in purchasing power.

**Inflation premium, page 35**  A premium to compensate for anticipated inflation that is equal to the price change expected to occur over the life of the bond or investment instrument.

**Default-risk premium, page 35**  The additional return required by investors to

compensate them for the risk of default. It is calculated as the difference between a U.S. Treasury bond and a corporate bond of the same maturity and marketability.

**Maturity-risk premium, page 35**  The additional return required by investors in longer-term securities to compensate them for greater risk of price fluctuations on those securities caused by interest rate changes.

**Liquidity-risk premium, page 35**  The additional return required by investors for securities that cannot be quickly converted into cash at a reasonably predictable price.

---

 **Explain the fundamentals of interest rate determination and the popular theories of the term structure of interest rates.**    (pgs. 36–44)

**SUMMARY:** When lenders loan money they must take into account the anticipated loss in purchasing power that results during a period of price inflation. Consequently, nominal or observed rates of interest incorporate an inflation premium that reflects the anticipated rate of inflation over the period of the loan.

The term structure of interest rates (also called the yield curve) defines the relationship between rates of return for similar securities that differ only with respect to their time to maturity. For instance, if long-term government bonds offer a higher rate of return than do U.S. Treasury bills, then the yield curve is upward sloping. But if the Treasury bill is paying a higher rate of interest than its long-term counterparts, then the yield curve is downward sloping.

### KEY TERMS

**Real risk-free interest rate, page 36**  The required rate of return on a fixed-income security that has no risk in an economic environment of zero inflation.

**Real rate of interest, page 37**  The nominal (quoted) rate of interest less any loss in

purchasing power of the dollar during the time of the investment.

**Term structure of interest rates, page 41**  The relationship between interest rates and the term to maturity, where the risk of default is held constant.

**Yield to maturity, page 41** The rate of return a bondholder will receive if the bond is held to maturity.

**Unbiased expectations theory, page 43** The theory that the shape of the term structure of interest rates is determined by an investor's expectations about future interest rates.

**Liquidity preference theory, page 44** The theory that the shape of the term structure of interest rates is determined by an investor's additional required interest rate in compensation for additional risks.

**Market segmentation theory, page 44** The theory that the shape of the term structure of interest rates implies that the rate of interest for a particular maturity is determined solely by demand and supply for a given maturity. This rate is independent of the demand and supply for securities having different maturities.

## KEY EQUATIONS

$$
\begin{aligned}
\text{Nominal interest rate} = {}& \text{real risk-free interest rate} \\
&+ \text{inflation premium} \\
&+ \text{default-risk premium} \\
&+ \text{maturity-risk premium} \\
&+ \text{liquidity-risk premium}
\end{aligned}
$$

Nominal interest rate $\cong$ (approximately equals) real rate of interest + inflation-risk premium

$1 +$ nominal interest rate $= (1 + $ real rate of interest$)(1 + $ rate of inflation$)$

OR

$$
\begin{aligned}
\text{Nominal or quoted} = {}& \text{real rate of} + \text{inflation} + \text{product of the real rate of interest} \\
\text{rate of interest} \quad & \text{interest} \qquad \text{rate} \qquad\quad \text{and the inflation rate}
\end{aligned}
$$

# Review Questions

*All Review Questions are available in* MyFinanceLab.

**2-1.** Distinguish between the money and capital markets.

**2-2.** What major benefits do corporations and investors enjoy because of the existence of organized security exchanges?

**2-3.** What general criteria does an organized exchange examine to determine whether a firm's securities can be listed on the exchange? (Specific numbers are not needed here but rather areas of investigation.)

**2-4.** Why do you think most secondary-market trading in bonds takes place over the counter?

**2-5.** What is an investment banker, and what major functions does he or she perform?

**2-6.** What is the major difference between a negotiated purchase and a competitive bid purchase?

**2-7.** Why is an investment-banking syndicate formed?

**2-8.** Why might a large corporation want to raise long-term capital through a private placement rather than a public offering?

**2-9.** As a recent business school graduate, you work directly for the corporate treasurer. Your corporation is going to issue a new security and is concerned with the probable flotation costs. What tendencies about flotation costs can you relate to the treasurer?

**2-10.** Identify three distinct ways that savings are ultimately transferred to business firms in need of cash.

**2-11.** Explain the term *opportunity cost* with respect to the cost of funds to the firm.

**2-12.** Compare and explain the historical rates of return for different types of securities.

**2-13.** Explain the impact of inflation on rates of return.

**2-14.** Define the *term structure of interest rates*.

**2-15.** Explain the popular theories for the rationale of the term structure of interest rates.

# Study Problems

*All Study Problems are available in* MyFinanceLab.

**2-1.** (*Calculating the default-risk premium*) At present, 10-year Treasury bonds are yielding 4% while a 10-year corporate bond is yielding 6.8%. If the liquidity-risk premium on the corporate bond is 0.4%, what is the corporate bond's default-risk premium?

**2-2.** (*Calculating the maturity-risk premium*) At present, the real risk-free rate of interest is 2%, while inflation is expected to be 2% for the next 2 years. If a 2-year Treasury note yields 4.5%, what is the maturity-risk premium for this 2-year Treasury note?

**2-3.** (Inflation and interest rates) You're considering an investment that you expect will produce an 8 percent return next year, and you expect that your real rate of return on this investment will be 6 percent. What do you expect inflation to be next year?

**2-4.** (*Inflation and interest rates*) What would you expect the nominal rate of interest to be if the real rate is 4 percent and the expected inflation rate is 7 percent?

**2-5.** (*Inflation and interest rates*) Assume the expected inflation rate to be 4 percent. If the current real rate of interest is 6 percent, what ought the nominal rate of interest to be?

**2-6.** (*Real interest rates: approximation method*) The CFO of your firm has asked you for an approximate answer to this question: What was the increase in real purchasing power associated with both 3-month Treasury bills and 30-year Treasury bonds? Assume that the current 3-month Treasury bill rate is 4.34 percent, the 30-year Treasury bond rate is 7.33 percent, and the inflation rate is 2.78 percent. Also, the chief financial officer wants a short explanation should the 3-month real rate turn out to be less than the 30-year real rate.

**2-7.** (*Real interest rates: approximation method*) You are considering investing money in Treasury bills and wondering what the real risk-free rate of interest is. Currently, Treasury bills are yielding 4.5% and the future inflation rate is expected to be 2.1% per year. Ignoring the cross product between the real rate of interest and the inflation rate, what is the real risk-free rate of interest?

**2-8.** (*Real interest rates: approximation method*) If the real risk-free rate of interest is 4.8% and the rate of inflation is expected to be constant at a level of 3.1%, what would you expect 1-year Treasury bills to return if you ignore the cross product between the real rate of interest and the inflation rate?

**2-9.** (*Default risk premium*) At present, 20-year Treasury bonds are yielding 5.1% while some 20-year corporate bonds that you are interested in are yielding 9.1%. Assuming that the maturity-risk premium on both bonds is the same and that the liquidity-risk premium on the corporate bonds is 0.25% while it is 0.0% on the Treasury bonds, what is the default-risk premium on the corporate bonds?

**2-10.** (*Interest rate determination*) If the 10-year Treasury bond rate is 4.9%, the inflation premium is 2.1%, and the maturity-risk premium on 10-year Treasury bonds is 0.3%, assuming that there is no liquidity-risk premium on these bonds, what is the real risk-free interest rate?

**2-11.** (*Interest rate determination*) You've just taken a job at a investment banking firm and been given the job of calculating the appropriate nominal interest rate for a number of different Treasury bonds with different maturity dates. The real risk-free interest rate that you have been told to use is 2.5%, and this rate is expected to continue on into the future without any change. Inflation is expected to be constant over the future at a rate of 2.0%. Since these are bonds that are issued by the U.S. Treasury, they do not have any default risk or any liquidity risk (that is, there is no liquidity-risk premium). The maturity-risk premium is dependent upon how many years the bond has to maturity. The maturity-risk premiums are as follows:

| BOND MATURES IN: | MATURITY-RISK PREMIUM: |
|---|---|
| 0–1 year | 0.05% |
| 1–2 years | 0.30% |
| 2–3 years | 0.60% |
| 3–4 years | 0.90% |

Given this information, what should the nominal rate of interest on Treasury bonds maturing in 0–1 year, 1–2 years, 2–3 years, and 3–4 years be?

**2-12.** (*Interest rate determination*) You're looking at some corporate bonds issued by Ford, and you are trying to determine what the nominal interest rate should be on them. You have determined that the real risk-free interest rate is 3.0%, and this rate is expected to continue on into the future without any change. In addition, inflation is expected to be constant over the future at a rate of 3.0%. The default-risk premium is also expected to remain constant at a rate of 1.5%, and the liquidity-risk premium is very small for Ford bonds, only about 0.02%. The maturity-risk premium is dependent upon how many years the bond has to maturity. The maturity-risk premiums are as follows:

| BOND MATURES IN: | MATURITY-RISK PREMIUM: |
|---|---|
| 0–1 year | 0.07% |
| 1–2 years | 0.35% |
| 2–3 years | 0.70% |
| 3–4 years | 1.00% |

Given this information, what should the nominal rate of interest on Ford bonds maturing in 0–1 year, 1–2 years, 2–3 years, and 3–4 years be?

**2-13.** (*Term structure of interest rates*) You want to invest your savings of $20,000 in government securities for the next 2 years. Currently, you can invest either in a security that pays interest of 8 percent per year for the next 2 years or in a security that matures in 1 year but pays only 6 percent interest. If you make the latter choice, you would then reinvest your savings at the end of the first year for another year.

a. Why might you choose to make the investment in the 1-year security that pays an interest rate of only 6 percent, as opposed to investing in the 2-year security paying 8 percent? Provide numerical support for your answer. Which theory of term structure have you supported in your answer?

b. Assume your required rate of return on the second-year investment is 11 percent; otherwise, you will choose to go with the 2-year security. What rationale could you offer for your preference?

**2-14.** (*Yield curve*) If yields on Treasury securities were currently as follows:

| TERM | YIELD |
| --- | --- |
| 6 months | 1.0% |
| 1 year | 1.7% |
| 2 years | 2.1% |
| 3 years | 2.4% |
| 4 years | 2.7% |
| 5 years | 2.9% |
| 10 years | 3.5% |
| 15 years | 3.9% |
| 20 years | 4.0% |
| 30 years | 4.1% |

a. Plot the yield curve.
b. Explain this yield curve using the unbiased expectations theory and the liquidity preference theory.

# Mini Case

*This Mini Case is available in* MyFinanceLab.

On the first day of your summer internship, you've been assigned to work with the chief financial officer (CFO) of SanBlas Jewels Inc. Not knowing how well trained you are, the CFO has decided to test your understanding of interest rates. Specifically, she asked you to provide a reasonable estimate of the nominal interest rate for a new issue of Aaa-rated bonds to be offered by SanBlas Jewels Inc. The final format that the chief financial officer of SanBlas Jewels has requested is that of equation (2-1) in the text. Your assignment also requires that you consult the data in Table 2-2.

Some agreed-upon procedures related to generating estimates for key variables in equation (2-1) follow.

   a. The current 3-month Treasury bill rate is 2.96 percent, the 30-year Treasury bond rate is 5.43 percent, the 30-year Aaa-rated corporate bond rate is 6.71 percent, and the inflation rate is 2.33 percent.

   b. The real risk-free rate of interest is the difference between the calculated average yield on 3-month Treasury bills and the inflation rate.

   c. The default-risk premium is estimated by the difference between the average yield on Aaa-rated bonds and 30-year Treasury bonds.

   d. The maturity-risk premium is estimated by the difference between the average yield on 30-year Treasury bonds and 3-month Treasury bills.

   e. SanBlas Jewels' bonds will be traded on the New York Bond Exchange, so the liquidity-risk premium will be slight. It will be greater than zero, however, because the secondary market for the firm's bonds is more uncertain than that of some other jewel sellers. It is estimated at 4 basis points. A basis point is one one-hundredth of 1 percent.

Now place your output into the format of equation (2-1) so that the nominal interest rate can be estimated and the size of each variable can also be inspected for reasonableness and discussion with the CFO.

# Understanding Financial Statements and Cash Flows

## Learning Objectives

**1**    **Compute** a company's profits, as reflected by its income statement.      **The Income Statement**

**2**    **Determine** a firm's financial position at a point in time based on its balance sheet.      **The Balance Sheet**

**3**    **Measure** a company's cash flows.      **Measuring Cash Flows**

**4**    **Explain** the differences between GAAP and IFRS.      **GAAP and IFRS**

**5**    **Compute** taxable income and income taxes owed.      **Income Taxes and Finance**

**6**    **Describe** the limitations of financial statements.      **Accounting Malpractice and Limitations of Financial Statements**

**7**    **Calculate** a firm's free cash flows and financing cash flows.      **Free Cash Flows**

You have been offered a marketing position at Home Depot. In trying to decide whether or not to accept the offer, you have been searching the Internet for information about the company. Your Uncle Harry told you that he had read in the local newspaper that the firm has been having some financial problems. He could not remember for certain, but thought the article mentioned that the company's problems were tied to the downturn in the economy, particularly from being in the home-improvement industry. He suggested that you acquire a copy of the firm's 10-K. Not wanting to look uninformed, you responded, "great idea," but thought to yourself, "What is a 10-K?"

At your first opportunity, you went to the Home Depot Web site (www.homedepot.com), clicked on the *investor relations* link and then selected the Financial Reports link to find both the firm's annual report and the **10-K** that your Uncle Harry mentioned. You quickly discovered that the 10-K is an annual report that all publicly traded firms must file with the Securities and Exchange Commission (SEC). Among other things, the report presents the company's financial results, along with commentary about the company's financial performance, in the section entitled "Management Discussion and Analysis." As you peruse the annual report for the fiscal year ended January 30, 2011,[1] you read the letter to the shareholders written by Frank S. Blake, the firm's chairman and CEO, where he comments on the firm's recent performance (as shown below).

Finally, you begin looking at the firm's financial statements, where you see an income statement, a balance sheet, and a statement of cash flows. You are not certain exactly how to read these statements, so you try to remember what you learned in your finance course in college. Fortunately, you had saved your finance textbook and began reading the chapter on financial statements.

This chapter and the next chapter provide you with exactly what you need to understand Home Depot's financial statements, as well as any company's financial statements. Understanding financial statements is vital for any manager, since in some ways accounting is the "language" of business. To begin, we examine the three basic financial statements that are used to understand how a firm is doing financially: (1) the income statement, or what is sometimes called the profit and loss statement, (2) the balance sheet, which provides a snapshot on a particular date of a firm's financial position, and (3) the statement of cash flows, which identifies the sources and uses of a company's cash. In the appendix at the end of the chapter we present another important measure of cash flows called *free cash flows*.

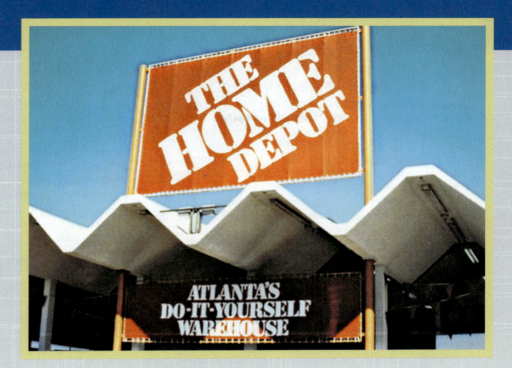

Dear Shareholders:

In 2010, we achieved our first year of positive sales growth since fiscal year 2006....

Our sales growth occurred against a backdrop of continued weakness in the housing market. In the U.S., private fixed residential investment as a percent of GDP reached a new 60 plus year low of 2.24 percent in the third quarter of 2010. Despite this, we had positive comp sales for all four quarters of 2010, and by the end of 2010, we were seeing strength across the U.S., as 49 of the 50 states had positive "same-store" sales for the fourth quarter. We view this as an indicator that our business can stabilize and improve even as the housing market remains under stress.

Over the course of 2010, we made significant improvements in our merchandising systems, with foundational work on our data warehouse and improved tools for forecasting and replenishment. We will continue on that path in 2011, and we are also continuing our investments in multi-channel—or interconnected—retailing. Through our mobile applications, website and social media presence, we are creating the capability to serve our customers "when, where and how" they want to be served.

At The Home Depot, our goal is to provide the best customer service and the best product values in our market, with an underlying principle of disciplined capital allocation. Our approach to capital allocation is straightforward: after making the necessary investments in our business, we will return excess cash to our shareholders through dividends and share repurchases. We have a goal of achieving a 15 percent return on invested capital, and we have a plan to reach that goal by the end of 2013.

I hope as you spend time in our stores or on our web site or on our mobile applications, you will see continued improvement in our service and our commitment to our customers.

*Frank*

**Frank S. Blake**
Chairman & Chief Executive Officer
March 24, 2011

[1]The Home Depot, Inc.'s fiscal year is a 52- or 53-week period ending on the Sunday nearest to January 31. Fiscal year 2010 ended January 30, 2011, and fiscal year 2009 ended January 31, 2010.

Our goal is not to make you an accountant, but instead to provide you with the tools to understand a firm's financial situation. With this knowledge, you will be able to understand the financial consequences of a company's decisions and actions—as well as your own.

The financial performance of a firm matters to a lot of groups—the company's management, its employees, and its investors, just to name a few. If you are an employee, the firm's performance is important to you because it may determine your annual bonus, your job security, and your opportunity to advance your professional career. This is true whether you are in the firm's marketing, finance, or human resources department. Moreover, an employee who can see how decisions affect a firm's finances has a competitive advantage. So regardless of your position in the firm, it is in your own best interest to know the basics of financial statements—even if accounting is not your greatest love.

Let's begin our review of financial statements by looking at the format and content of the income statement.

## The Income Statement

 Compute a company's profits, as reflected by its income statement.

**Form 10-K** an annual report required by the Securities and Exchange Commission (SEC) that provides such information as the firm's history, audited financial statements, management's analysis of the company's performance, and executive compensation.

**income statement (profit and loss statement)** a basic accounting statement that measures the results of a firm's operations over a specified period, commonly 1 year. The bottom line of the income statement, net profits (net income), shows the profit or loss for the period that is available for a company's owners (shareholders).

**cost of goods sold** the cost of producing or acquiring a product or service to be sold in the ordinary course of business.

**gross profit** sales or revenue minus the cost of goods sold.

**operating expenses** marketing and selling expenses, general and administrative expenses, and depreciation expense.

**operating income (earnings before interest and taxes)** sales less the cost of goods sold less operating expenses.

An **income statement**, or **profit and loss statement**, indicates the amount of profits generated by a firm over a given time period, such as 1 year. In its most basic form, the income statement may be represented as follows:

$$\text{Sales} - \text{expenses} = \text{profits} \tag{3-1}$$

The format for an income statement is shown in Figure 3-1. The income statement begins with sales or revenue, from which we subtract the **cost of goods sold** (the cost of producing or acquiring the product or service to be sold) to yield **gross profits**. Next, **operating expenses** are deducted to determine **operating income** (also called **operating profits** or **earnings before interest and taxes** or **EBIT**), where operating expenses consist of:

1. Marketing and selling expenses—the cost of promoting the firm's products or services to customers.
2. General and administrative expenses—the firm's overhead expenses, such as executive salaries and rent expense.
3. Depreciation expense—a noncash expense to allocate the cost of depreciable assets, such as plant and equipment, over the life of the asset.

Take another look at Figure 3-1, and notice something important: In the left margin of the figure we see that operating income is the result of management's decisions relating only to the *operations* of the business and is not affected at all by how much debt the company owes. In other words, the firm's *financing* expenses, its interest expense resulting from borrowing money, have no effect on operating income. Rather, the operating income of a firm reports the results of the following important activities:

1. **Sales (revenues),** which is equal to the selling price of the products or services to be sold times the number of units sold (selling price × units sold = total sales).
2. **Cost of goods sold,** which is the cost of producing or acquiring the goods or services that were sold.
3. **Operating expenses,** which include:
   a. Marketing and selling expenses (the expenses related to marketing, selling, and distributing the products or services).
   b. The firm's overhead expenses (general and administrative expenses, and depreciation expenses).

## FIGURE 3-1 The Income Statement: An Overview

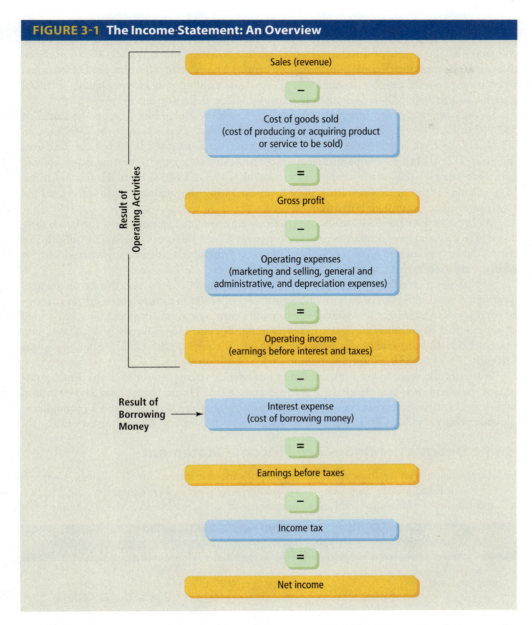

We next determine the **earnings before taxes**, or **taxable income**, by deducting the interest expense paid on the firm's debt. Next, the firm's income taxes are calculated based on its earnings before taxes and the applicable tax rate for the amount of income reported. For instance, if a firm had earnings before taxes of $100,000, and its tax rate is 28 percent, then it would owe $28,000 in taxes ($0.28 \times \$100,000 = \$28,000$).

The next and final number in the income statement is the **net income**, or **earnings available to common stockholders**, which represents income that may be reinvested in the firm or distributed to its owners—provided, of course, the cash is available to do so. As you will come to understand, a positive net income on an income statement does not necessarily mean that a firm has generated positive cash flows.

**earnings before taxes (taxable income)** operating income minus interest expense.

**net income (net profit, or earnings available to common stockholders)** the earnings available to the firm's common and preferred stockholders.

## Income Statement Illustrated: The Home Depot, Inc.

Let's apply what we have learned by looking at the income statement for Home Depot[2] for the 12 months ended January 30, 2011, as presented in Table 3-1(on page 54). When reading

[2]Publicly traded companies make their financial statements available online. Go to Yahoo! Finance and you can obtain the latest financial statements of most publicly traded businesses. You can also find annual reports (which include financial statements) of publicly traded companies on www.annualreports.com, or you can go to a specific company's Web site to see its financial statements.

Home Depot's financial statements, understand that they are expressed in millions. For example, look at the first line in Home Depot's income statement, which reads $67,997. That is, the company's sales were $67,997 million. But realize that $67,997 million is really $67.997 billion. (Notice that we use the decimal point when we express a number in billion, instead of a comma when we express the number in millions.) So any time a number in Home Depot's financial statements is $1,000 million or more, it is actually a billion dollars or more.

So let's begin. In the first line of Table 3-1, we see that Home Depot had *sales* of $67,997 million for the year, but we understand that the sales were actually $67.997 billion. The *cost of goods sold* was $44.693 billion, resulting in *gross profits* of $23.304 billion. The firm then had $17.501 billion of operating expenses. After deducting the operating expenses, the firm's *operating income* (*earnings before interest and taxes*) was $5.803 billion. To this point, we have calculated the profits resulting only from operating the business, without regard for any interest paid on money borrowed.

We next deduct the $530 million in interest expense (the amount paid for borrowing money) to arrive at the company's *earnings before taxes* (*taxable income*) of $5.273 billion. We then subtract the income taxes of $1.935 billion to determine the company's *net income*, or *earnings available to common stockholders*, of $3.338 billion.

At this point, we have completed the income statement. However, the firm's owners (common stockholders) like to know how much income the firm made on a *per share* basis, or what is called **earnings per share**. We calculate earnings per share as net income divided by the number of common stock shares outstanding. Because Home Depot had 1,623 million shares (1.623 billion) outstanding for the year (see Table 3-1), its earnings per share was $2.06 ($2.06 = $3.338 billion net income ÷ 1.623 billion shares).

Investors also want to know the amount of dividends a firm pays for each share outstanding, or the **dividends per share**. In Table 3-1 we see that Home Depot paid $1.569 billion in dividends during the year. We can then determine that the firm paid $0.97 in dividends per share ($0.97 = $1.569 billion total dividends ÷ 1.623 billion shares outstanding).

> **earnings per share** net income on a per share basis.

> **dividends per share** the amount of dividends a firm pays for each share outstanding.

## Home Depot's Common-Sized Income Statement

> **common-sized income statement** an income statement in which a firm's expenses and profits are expressed as a percentage of its sales.

What conclusions can we draw from Home Depot's income statement? To answer this question, it is helpful to look at each item in the income statement as a percentage of sales. Such a revision is called a **common-sized income statement** and is presented in the right column of

| TABLE 3.1 The Home Depot, Inc.: Income Statement (expressed in millions, except per share data, and as a percentage of sales) for the Year Ended January 30, 2011[3] | | |
|---|---|---|
| Sales | $67,977 | 100.0% |
| Cost of goods sold | (44,693) | 65.7% |
| Gross profits | $23,304 | 34.3% ← gross profit margin |
| Operating expenses: | | |
| Marketing, general and administrative expenses | ($15,885) | 23.4% |
| Depreciation expenses | (1,616) | 2.4% |
| Total operating expenses | ($17,501) | 25.7% |
| Operating income (earnings before interest and taxes) | $ 5,803 | 8.5% ← operating profit margin |
| Interest expense | (530) | 0.8% |
| Earnings before taxes (taxable income) | $ 5,273 | 7.8% |
| Income taxes | (1,935) | 2.8% |
| Net income (earnings available to common stockholders) | $ 3,338 | 4.9% ← net profit margin |
| Additional information: | | |
| Number of common shares outstanding | 1,623 | |
| Earnings per share (net income ÷ number of shares) | $ 2.06 | |
| Dividends paid to stockholders | $ 1,569 | |
| Dividends per share (total dividends ÷ number of shares) | $ 0.97 | |

Income from operating activities. Also called operating profits, or earnings before interest and taxes (EBIT).

Cost of debt financing

Income from operating and financing activities. Also called net profits or earnings available to common shareholders.

[3]This presentation of Home Depot's income statement and later its balance sheet have been simplified for learning purposes. The original statements can be found in Home Depot's annual report at www.homedepot.com. Also, the percentages shown in the right column are subject to rounding errors and may not add up precisely. Data from The Home Depot, Inc., Fiscal Year 2010 Form 10-K.

Table 3-1. The common-sized income statement allows us to express expenses and profits on a relative basis, so that we can more easily compare a firm's income performance across time and with competitors. The profits-to-sales relationships are defined as **profit margins**. In the right-hand margin of Home Depot's income statement (Table 3-1), we see that the firm earned

1. A 34.3 percent **gross profit margin** (34.3% = $23.304 billion of gross profits ÷ $67.997 billion of sales)

2. An 8.5 percent **operating profit margin** (8.5% = $5.803 billion of operating income ÷ $67.997 billion of sales)

3. A 4.9 percent **net profit margin** (4.9% = $3.338 billion of net income ÷ $67.997 billion of sales)

In practice, managers pay close attention to the firm's profit margins. Profit margins are considered to be an important measurement of how well the firm is doing financially. Managers carefully watch for any changes in margins, up or down. They also compare the firm's margins with those of competitors—something we will discuss in Chapter 4. For the time being, simply remember that profit-to-sales relationships, or *profit margins*, are important in assessing a firm's performance.

Finally, in Home Depot's income statement, no mention was made about which expenses are fixed and which are variable. This distinction is extremely important to a manager wanting to know what will happen to profits when sales change. **Fixed costs** are costs and expenses that do not vary at all with sales volume. Examples include property taxes and rent expenses, which must be paid no matter how much a company's sales change, particularly in the short term, such as a year. **Variable costs** are costs and expenses that vary directly and proportionately with changes in sales volume, such as the costs of material used in production and sales commissions. Finally, there are also **semivariable costs** that vary in the direction of, but not proportionately with, changes in the volume of sales. Examples include certain types of payrolls that change as a firm becomes larger but do not change proportionally with sales changes.

Much more will be said in Chapter 12 about the effect that fixed and variable costs and expenses have on a company's income as sales change.

**profit margins** financial ratios (sometimes simply referred to as margins) that reflect the level of the firm's profits relative to its sales. Examples include the gross profit margin (gross profit divided by sales), operating profit margin (operating income divided by sales), and the net profit margin (net income ÷ sales).

**gross profit margin** gross profit divided by net sales. It is a ratio denoting the gross profit earned by the firm as a percentage of its net sales.

**operating profit margin** operating income divided by sales. This ratio serves as an overall measure of the company's operating effectiveness.

**net profit margin** net income divided by sales. A ratio that measures the net income of the firm as a percent of sales.

**fixed costs** costs that remain constant, regardless of any change in a firm's activity.

**variable costs** costs that change in proportion to changes in a firm's activity.

**semivariable costs** costs composed of a mixture of fixed and variable components.

---

| EXAMPLE 3.1 | Constructing an income statement |

Menielle, Inc. is a wholesale distributor of electronics. It sells laptops, cameras, and other electronic gadgets. Use the scrambled information below to construct an income statement, along with a common-sized income statement. Also calculate the firm's earnings per share and dividends per share.

| Interest expense | $ 35,000 | Sales | $400,000 |
|---|---|---|---|
| Cost of goods sold | $150,000 | Common stock dividends | $ 15,000 |
| Selling and marketing expenses | $ 40,000 | Income taxes | $ 40,000 |
| Administrative expenses | $ 30,000 | Depreciation expense | $ 20,000 |
| Number of shares outstanding | 20,000 | | |

**STEP 1: FORMULATE A SOLUTION STRATEGY**

The following template provides the format of the income statement:

| | Sales |
|---|---|
| Less: | Cost of goods sold |
| Equals: | Gross profits |
| Less: | Operating expenses (selling and marketing expenses + Depreciation expense + Administrative expenses) |
| Equals: | Operating income |
| Less: | Interest expense |
| Equals: | Earnings before taxes |
| Less: | Income taxes |
| Equals: | Net income |

## STEP 2: CRUNCH THE NUMBERS
Your results should be as follows:

|  | Dollars | Percentage of Sales |
|---|---|---|
| Sales | $400,000 | 100.0% |
| Cost of goods sold | (150,000) | 37.5% |
| Gross profit | $250,000 | 62.5% |
| Operating expenses: | | |
|    Selling and marketing expenses | ($ 40,000) | 10.0% |
|    Administrative expenses | (30,000) | 7.5% |
|    Depreciation expense | (20,000) | 5.0% |
| Total operating expenses | ($ 90,000) | 22.5% |
| Operating income | $160,000 | 40.0% |
| Interest expense | (35,000) | 8.8% |
| Earnings before taxes | $125,000 | 31.3% |
| Income taxes | (40,000) | 10.0% |
| Net income | $ 85,000 | 21.3% |
| Earnings per share ($85,000 net income ÷ 20,000 shares) | $4.25 | |
| Dividends per share ($15,000 dividends ÷ 20,000 shares) | $0.75 | |

## STEP 3: ANALYZE YOUR RESULTS

There are some important observations we can make about Menielle's income statement. First, the firm is profitable, earning a net income of $85,000, or $4.25 on a per share basis, and then paying $15,000 in dividends to the shareholders, or $0.75 per share. Also, for every $100 of sales, Menielle earned $62.50 in gross profits, $40 in operating income, and $21.30 in net income. Finally, the rate of dividends to earnings, or what is called the **dividend payout ratio**, is $15,000 ÷ $85,000 = 17.6%, indicating that the firm is retaining most of its earnings to grow the business.

**dividend-payout ratio** percentage of earnings paid out in dividends to the shareholders.

## Concept Check

1. What can we learn by reviewing a firm's income statement?
2. What basic relationship can we see in an income statement?
3. How are gross profits, operating income, and net income different as they relate to the areas of business activity reported in the income statement?
4. What are earnings per share and dividends per share?
5. What is a profit margin? What are the different types of profit margins?

 **LO2** Determine a firm's financial position at a point in time based on its balance sheet.

**balance sheet** a statement that shows a firm's assets, liabilities, and shareholder equity at a given point in time. It is a snapshot of the firm's financial position on a particular date.

# The Balance Sheet

We have observed that a firm's income statement reports the results from operating a business *for a period of time*, such as 1 year. A firm's **balance sheet**, on the other hand, provides a snapshot of the firm's financial position *at a specific point in time*, presenting its asset holdings, liabilities, and owner-supplied capital (stockholders' equity).

In its simplest form, a balance sheet is represented by the following balance sheet equation:

Total assets = total debt (liabilities) + total shareholders' equity          (3-2)

where *total assets* represent the resources owned by the firm, and *total liabilities (debt)* and *total shareholders' equity* indicate how those resources were financed.

The conventional practice is to report the amount of a firm's various assets in the balance sheet by using the actual cost of acquiring them. Thus, the balance sheet does not

**FIGURE 3-2  The Balance Sheet: An Overview**

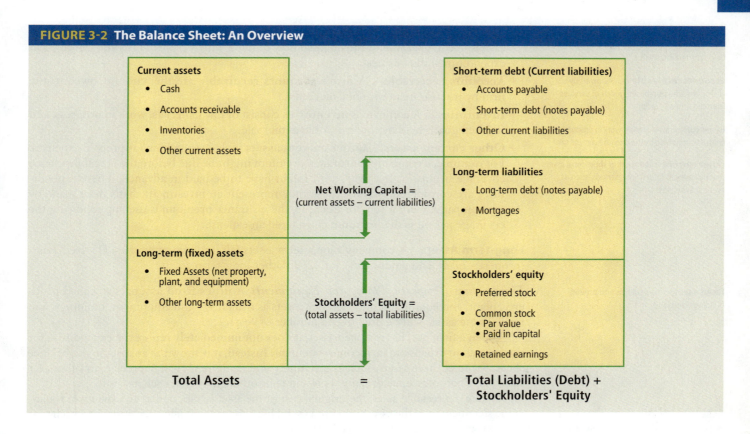

represent the current market value of a company's assets and consequently does not reflect the value of the company itself. Rather, *it reports historical transactions at their cost.*[4]

Therefore, the balance sheet reports a company's **accounting book value**, which is simply equal to a firm's total assets as listed in its balance sheet.

Figure 3-2 shows us the basic components of a balance sheet. On the left side of Figure 3-2, assets are listed according to their type; on the right side, we see the different sources of financing that companies frequently use to finance their assets.

## Types of Assets

On the balance sheet, assets are listed from the most liquid to the least liquid, that is, in the order of decreasing liquidity. **Liquidity** refers to the ability to quickly convert an asset into cash without lowering the selling price. A highly liquid asset can be sold quickly without causing a decrease in the value of the asset, whereas an illiquid asset either cannot be easily converted to cash or can only be sold quickly at a significant discount. For example, government securities are much more liquid than a building.

Liquidity is important because holding liquid assets reduces the chance that a firm will experience financial distress. However, liquid assets usually generate less return than illiquid assets. For example, holding cash would earn no return at all. Therefore, financial managers have to choose a reasonable percentage of liquid assets so that the company can enjoy the benefits of liquidity without significantly hurting a firm's profitability.

As shown in Figure 3-2, a company's assets fall into two basic categories: (1) current assets and (2) long-term assets, which include fixed assets (property, plant and equipment) and other long-term assets.

**Current Assets**    A company's **current assets,** or **gross working capital** as it is sometimes called, are those assets that are expected to be converted into cash within 12 months. Current assets include a firm's cash, accounts receivable, inventories, and other current assets.

**accounting book value** the value of an asset as shown on a firm's balance sheet. It represents the depreciated historical cost of the asset rather than its current market value or replacement cost.

**liquidity** the ability to convert an asset into cash quickly without a significant loss of its value.

**current assets (gross working capital)** current assets consist primarily of cash, marketable securities, accounts receivable, inventories, and other current assets.

[4]There are exceptions to showing all assets at their historical cost. For example, investments held to be sold will be reported at their current market value.

**cash** cash on hand, demand deposits, and short-term marketable securities that can quickly be converted into cash.

**accounts receivable** money owed by customers who purchased goods or services from the firm on credit.

**inventories** raw materials, work in progress, and finished goods held by the firm for eventual sale.

**other current assets** other short-term assets that will benefit future time periods, such as prepaid expenses.

**fixed assets** assets such as equipment, buildings, and land.

**depreciation expense** a noncash expense to allocate the cost of depreciable assets, such as plant and equipment, over the life of the asset.

**accumulated depreciation** the sum of all depreciation taken over the entire life of a depreciable asset.

**gross fixed assets** the original cost of a firm's fixed assets.

**net fixed assets** gross fixed assets minus the accumulated depreciation taken over the life of the assets.

◆ **Cash.**   Every firm must have **cash** to conduct its business operations. A reservoir of cash is needed because of the unequal flow of funds into (cash receipts) and out of (cash expenditures) the business.

◆ **Accounts receivable.**   A firm's **accounts receivable** are the amounts owed to the firm by its customers who buy on credit.

◆ **Inventories.**   A company's **inventories** consist of raw materials, work in progress, and finished goods held by the firm for eventual sale.

◆ **Other current assets.**   **Other current assets** include such items as prepaid expenses. For example, a company's insurance premium might be due before the actual insurance coverage begins; or the firm's rent might have to be paid in advance. These expenditures are considered assets because they represent an investment that's been made by the company. Only when, for example, the insurance premium is used up following the coverage period is the premium considered an expense.

**Long-term Assets**   A company's long-term assets fall into two categories: (1) fixed assets (property, plant, and equipment) and (2) all other long-term assets.

*Fixed Assets (Property, Plant, and Equipment)*   A firm's **fixed assets**, also called property, plant, and equipment, include such assets as machinery and equipment, buildings, and land. These assets will be used over a number of years.

When a firm purchases a fixed asset, it does not immediately report the expenditure for the asset as an expense in its income statement. Instead, it is shown as an asset in the balance sheet. Some of these assets, such as machinery and equipment, will depreciate in value over time due to obsolescence or daily wear and tear; others may not, such as land.

With a depreciable asset, the original cost of the asset is allocated as an expense in the income statement over the asset's expected useful life. The amount allocated as the cost each year is shown as a **depreciation expense** in the income statement. The sum of all depreciation taken over the life of the asset to date is shown as **accumulated depreciation** in the balance sheet.

To illustrate, assume that a truck purchased for $20,000 is to be evenly depreciated over a 4-year life.[5] The depreciation expense to be reported in the income statement for each year would be $5,000 ($20,000 asset cost ÷ 4 years). When a firm buys the truck, the $20,000 original cost of the asset is added to the balance sheet as a **gross fixed asset**. The cumulative depreciation taken over the asset's life is reported as *accumulated depreciation*. We subtract the accumulated depreciation each year from the gross fixed assets to determine **net fixed assets**. In this example, the income statements for each year and balance sheets over time would appear as follows:

**Depreciation Expense in the Income Statement**

| | FOR THE YEAR ENDED | | | |
| --- | --- | --- | --- | --- |
| | 1 | 2 | 3 | 4 |
| Depreciation expense | $5,000 | $5,000 | $5,000 | $5,000 |

**Accumulated Depreciation in the Balance Sheet**

| | END OF YEAR | | | |
| --- | --- | --- | --- | --- |
| | 1 | 2 | 3 | 4 |
| Gross fixed assets | $20,000 | $20,000 | $20,000 | $20,000 |
| Accumulated depreciation | (5,000) | (10,000) | (15,000) | (20,000) |
| Net fixed assets | $15,000 | $10,000 | $ 5,000 | $ 0 |

It is important to understand the distinction between gross fixed assets and net fixed assets and how depreciation expense in the income statement relates to accumulated depreciation in the balance sheet.

*Other Long-Term Assets*   Other long-term assets are all of the firm's assets that are not current assets or fixed assets. They include, for example, long-term investments and intangible assets such as the company's patents, copyrights, and goodwill.

[5]In this instance, we are using a straight-line depreciation method. Other methods allow a firm to accelerate the depreciation expenses in the early years of the asset's life and report less in the later years.

# Types of Financing

We now turn to the right side of the balance sheet in Figure 3-2 labeled "Total Liabilities (Debt) + Stockholders' Equity," which indicates how the firm finances its assets. **Debt** (liabilities) is money that has been borrowed and must be repaid at some predetermined date.[6] **Equity**, on the other hand, represents the shareholders' (owners') investment in the company.

**debt** liabilities consisting of such sources as credit extended by suppliers or a loan from a bank.

**equity** stockholders' investment in the firm and the cumulative profits retained in the business up to the date of the balance sheet.

**Debt (Liabilities)**    Debt capital is financing provided by a creditor. As shown in Figure 3-2, it is divided into (1) current or short-term debt and (2) long-term debt.

***Short-Term Debt (Current Liabilities)***    A firm's **short-term debt**, or **current liabilities**, includes borrowed money that must be repaid within the next 12 months. The sources of a firm's current debt include the following:

**current debt (short-term liabilities)** debt due to be paid within 12 months.

◆ **Accounts payable.**    The firm's **accounts payable** represent the credit that suppliers have extended to the firm when it purchased inventories. The purchasing firm may have 30, 60, or even 90 days to pay for the inventory. This form of credit extension is also called **trade credit**.

**accounts payable (trade credit)** credit provided by suppliers when a firm purchases inventory on credit.

◆ **Accrued expenses.**    **Accrued expenses** are short-term liabilities that have been incurred in the firm's operations but not yet paid. For example, the company's employees might have done work for which they will not be paid until the following week or month, and these are recorded as accrued wages.

**accrued expenses** expenses that have been incurred but not yet paid in cash.

◆ **Short-term notes.**    **Short-term notes** represent amounts borrowed from a bank or other lending source that are due and payable within 12 months.

**short-term notes (debt)** amounts borrowed from lenders, mostly financial institutions such as banks, where the loan is to be repaid within 12 months.

***Long-Term Debt***    The firm's **long-term debt** includes loans from banks or other sources for longer than 12 months.[7]

A firm might borrow money for 5 years to buy equipment, or it might borrow money for as long as 25 or 30 years to purchase real estate, such as land and buildings. Usually a loan to finance real estate is called a **mortgage**, where the lender has first claim on the property in the event the borrower is unable to repay the loan.

**long-term debt** loans from banks or other sources that lend money for longer than 12 months.

**mortgage** a loan to finance real estate where the lender has first claim on the property in the event the borrower is unable to repay the loan.

**Equity**    Equity includes the shareholders' investment—both preferred stockholders and common stockholders—in the firm.

◆ **Preferred stockholders**    generally receive a dividend that is fixed in amount. In the event of the firm being liquidated, these stockholders are paid after the firm's creditors but before the common stockholders.

**preferred stockholders** stockholders who have claims on the firm's income and assets after creditors, but before common stockholders.

◆ **Common stockholders**    are the residual owners of a business. They "own" whatever income is left over after paying all expenses. In the event the firm is liquidated, the common stockholders receive only what is left over—good or bad—after the creditors and preferred stockholders are paid. The amount of a firm's common equity is equal to the sum of two items:

**common stockholders** investors who own the firm's common stock. Common stockholders are the residual owners of the firm.

1. **The amount a company receives from selling stock to investors.**    This amount may simply be shown as **common stock** in the balance sheet or it may be divided into **par value** (an arbitrary amount a firm puts on each share of stock when it is sold, frequently a penny or a dollar) and **paid-in capital** above par (also called capital surplus). Paid-in capital is the amount of money above par value a firm receives when it issues new shares to investors. For instance, if a company sells a new issue of common stock for $50 per share and sets the par value of the stock at $1 per share, then the $49 ($50−$1) would be shown as paid-in capital. So if it sold 1 million shares, the total

**common stock** shares that represent ownership in a corporation.

**par value** the arbitrary value a firm puts on each share of stock prior to its being offered for sale.

**paid-in capital** the amount a company receives above par value from selling stock to investors.

---

[6]Just for simplicity, we will use the terms *debt* and *liabilities* interchangeably, which is not always done in practice. *Debt* is frequently used to refer to loans that require the borrower to pay interest, such as a bank loan, while *liabilities* may refer to non-interest-bearing liabilities, such as accounts-payable (credit provided by a company's suppliers.)

[7]Note that any part of long-term debt that must be repaid within 12 months will be shown as short-term debt. For example, if you borrow $5,000 to be repaid in equal principal payments of $1,000 per year, the first year's payment of $1,000 will be considered to be short-term debt with the remaining $4,000 reported as long-term debt.

**treasury stock** the firm's stock that has been issued and then repurchased by the firm.

paid-in capital would be $49 million ($49 × 1 million shares). Finally, the amount of common stock issued will be offset by any stock that has been repurchased by the company from its shareholders, which is shown as **treasury stock**.

To illustrate how a company might record an issuance of common stock, assume that a firm issues 1,000 shares of common stock for $100 per share. The company has a policy of assigning a $1 par value to each share of stock. (It could just as easily have chosen a par value of a penny a share. The decision is totally arbitrary.) The remaining $99 per share would be added to paid-in capital. Thus, the total increase in the common equity in the balance sheet would appear as follows:

| | |
|---|---:|
| Par value ($1 × 1,000 shares) | $ 1,000 |
| Paid-in capital ($99 × 1,000 shares) | 99,000 |
| Total increase in common stock | $100,000 |

**retained earnings** cumulative profits retained in a business up to the date of the balance sheet.

2. **The amount of a firm's retained earnings.** **Retained earnings** is the net income that has been retained in the business rather than being distributed to the shareholders over the life of the company; in other words, the *cumulative total of all the net income over the firm's life less the common stock dividends that have been paid over these years.* More simply, retained earnings at the end of a given year is determined as follows:[8]

$$\begin{array}{ccccc} \text{Beginning} & & \text{net} & & \text{dividends} & & \text{ending} \\ \text{retained} & + & \text{income} & - & \text{paid during} & = & \text{retained} \\ \text{earnings} & & \text{for the year} & & \text{the year} & & \text{earnings} \end{array} \quad (3\text{-}3)$$

But remember, profits and cash are not the same; *do not think of retained earnings as a big bucket of cash.* It is not!

To conclude, the common stockholders' equity can be represented as follows:

$$\begin{array}{ccc} & & \overbrace{\phantom{XXXXXXXXXXXXXXXXXXX}}^{\substack{\text{earnings retained} \\ \text{within the busniess}}} \\ \text{Common} & \text{common} & \\ \text{Common} = & \text{shareholders'} + & \text{cumulative} - \text{cumulative dividends paid} \\ \text{equity} & \text{investment} & \text{profits} \quad\quad \text{to common stockholders} \end{array} \quad (3\text{-}4)$$

## Balance Sheet Illustrated: The Home Depot, Inc.

Let's return to Home Depot to see a live firm's balance sheet. Balance sheets for the company are presented in Table 3-2 as of January 31, 2010 and January 30, 2011. In addition to reporting the two individual balance sheets in columns 1 and 2, we also show in column 3 the changes in the balance sheets between the two years. By looking at these changes, we learn something about what happened to the company during the year that can be observed in no other way. Finally, in columns 4 and 5, we restate the balance sheets for both years on a relative basis by restating all the dollar numbers to percentages of total assets, or what we call a common-sized balance sheet. This restatement allows us to compare the firm's balance sheets across time and against other companies more easily. We will consider both in turn.

**Changes in Home Depot's Balance Sheet** Looking at the changes in the balance sheets for Home Depot, as presented in column 3 of Table 3-2, we observe the following:

1. The firm's total assets decreased $752 million, going from $40.877 billion in assets to $40.125 billion. Why the decrease? Two primary reasons: the reduction in current assets and in net fixed assets.

 a. **Decrease in current assets.** The most significant reduction in current assets by far came from the company's decrease in cash in the amount of $876 million. Later

[8]Sometimes retained earnings will be affected by some unusual or extraordinary accounting transactions in addition to the reported net income and the dividends paid to stockholders. However, we are ignoring this possibility when explaining retained earnings.

**TABLE 3-2** The Home Depot, Inc. Balance Sheets ($ millions) for Years Ended January 31, 2010 and January 30, 2011

| Year ended | (Col. 1) Jan 31, 2010 | (Col. 2) Jan 30, 2011 | (Col. 3) 2010–2011 Changes (Col. 2 − Col. 1) | (Col. 4) Jan 31, 2010 (Col. 1 ÷ Total Assets) | (Col. 5) Jan 30, 2011 (Col. 2 ÷ Total Assets) |
|---|---|---|---|---|---|
| **ASSETS** | | | | | |
| Cash | $ 1,421 | $ 545 | ($ 876) | 3.5% | 1.4% |
| Accounts receivable | 964 | 1,085 | 121 | 2.4% | 2.7% |
| Inventories | 10,188 | 10,625 | 437 | 24.9% | 26.5% |
| Other current assets | 1,327 | 1,224 | (103) | 3.2% | 3.1% |
| Total current assets | $13,900 | $13,479 | ($ 421) | 34.0% | 33.6% |
| Gross fixed assets | $37,345 | $ 38,471 | $1,126 | 91.4% | 95.9% |
| Accumulated depreciation | (11,795) | (13,411) | (1,616) | −28.9% | −33.4% |
| Net fixed assets | $25,550 | $25,060 | ($ 490) | 62.5% | 62.5% |
| Other assets | 1,427 | 1,586 | 159 | 3.5% | 4.0% |
| Total assets | $40,877 | $40,125 | ($ 752) | 100.0% | 100.0% |
| **LIABILITIES (DEBT) AND EQUITY** | | | | | |
| Accounts payable | $ 9,343 | $ 9,080 | ($ 263) | 22.9% | 22.6% |
| Short-term notes payable | 1,020 | 1,042 | 22 | 2.5% | 2.6% |
| Total current liabilities | $10,363 | $10,122 | ($ 241) | 25.4% | 25.2% |
| Long-term debt | 11,121 | 11,114 | (7) | 27.2% | 27.7% |
| Total liabilities | $21,484 | $21,236 | ($ 248) | 52.6% | 52.9% |
| Common stock: | | | | | |
| Par value[9] | $ 86 | $ 86 | $ 0 | 0.2% | 0.2% |
| Additional paid-in capital (capital surplus) | 6,666 | 7,001 | 335 | 16.3% | 17.4% |
| Total common stock sold | $ 6,752 | $ 7,087 | $ 335 | 16.5% | 17.7% |
| Treasury stock (stock repurchased) | (585) | (3,193) | (2,608) | −1.4% | −8.0% |
| Total common stock | $ 6,167 | $ 3,894 | ($2,273) | 15.1% | 9.7% |
| Retained earnings | 13,226 | 14,995 | 1,769 | 32.4% | 37.4% |
| Total common equity | $19,393 | $18,889 | ($ 504) | 47.4% | 47.1% |
| Total liabilities and equity | $40,877 | $40,125 | ($ 752) | 100.0% | 100.0% |

Source: Data from The Home Depot, Inc., Fiscal Year 2010 and 2011 Form 10-K.

in this chapter, we will see specifically why this happened, but for now know that it would have been something the lenders and shareholders alike would want to understand. The decrease in cash was offset in part by the increases in accounts receivable, and especially inventories.

**b. Decrease in fixed assets.** The reduction in the *net* fixed assets in the amount of $490 million came from two offsetting changes: purchasing new fixed assets (increase in gross fixed assets) in the amount of $1.126 billion, but taking $1.616 billion in depreciation of the fixed assets. So we see that the change in a firm's *net* fixed assets is driven by (1) how much the firm spends on new fixed assets and (2) how much depreciation expense it takes on the fixed assets in place.

2. We next review the changes in the firm's debt and equity, which amounts to a $752 million decrease, exactly the amount of the decrease in total assets—as it must be. (Remember, total assets = total debt + total equity.) Primarily this change is the consequence of the following actions:

  **a.** Paying off $263 million owed to suppliers (reduction in accounts payable).

  **b.** Repurchasing stock from its shareholders in the amount of $2.608 billion (increase in treasury stock) less $335 million the firm received from issuing new stock.

  **c.** Retaining $1.769 billion of the firm's profits within the business (increase in retained earnings).

[9]Par value of common stock increased from $85.8 million on January 31, 2010 to $86.1 million on January 31, 2011. The balance sheet didn't show the change because the amount was negligible when expressed in millions.

Much of what we notice from looking at the changes in the balance sheet will appear again when we study Home Depot's statement of cash flows in the next section of the chapter.

**Home Depot's Common-Sized Balance Sheet**    Finally, we can gain additional perspective on a company's financial position by looking at each item on the balance sheet as a percentage of total assets (and total debt and equity). A balance sheet expressed this way is called a **common-sized balance sheet**. The last two columns (columns 4 and 5) of Table 3-2 show common-sized balance sheets for Home Depot.

> **common-sized balance sheet** a balance sheet in which a firm's assets and sources of debt and equity are expressed as a percentage of its total assets.

Based on the percentages, we can observe that:

1. Inventories make up most of the current assets, amounting to about one-fourth of all the assets owned by the company.

2. The company's total assets consist of about one-third current assets and two-thirds fixed assets.

3. Approximately one-half of Home Depot's financing comes from debt, with the remaining half coming from equity. To be more precise, we can calculate the **debt ratio**, which is the *percentage of a company's assets financed by debt*. For Home Depot, the debt ratios on January 31, 2010 and January 30, 2011, respectively, were 52.6 percent and 52.9 percent:

> **debt ratio** a firm's total liabilities divided by its total assets. It is a ratio that measures the extent to which a firm has been financed with debt.

| | | FISCAL YEAR ENDED | |
|---|---|---|---|
| | | JANUARY 31, 2010 | JANUARY 30, 2011 |
| Debt ratio = | $\dfrac{\text{total debt}}{\text{total assets}}$ | $\dfrac{\$21{,}484M}{\$40{,}877M} = 52.6\%$ | $\dfrac{\$21{,}236M}{\$40{,}125M} = 52.9\%$ |

The debt ratio is an important measure to lenders and investors because it indicates the amount of financial risk the company is bearing—the more debt a company uses to finance its assets, the greater is its financial risk. We will discuss this topic in detail in Chapter 12.

## Working Capital

Earlier we noted that the term *current assets* is also referred to as *gross working capital*. These two terms are used interchangeably. By contrast, **net working capital** is equal to a company's current assets *less* its current liabilities. That is,

> **net working capital** the difference between a firm's current assets and its current liabilities. When the term *working capital* is used, it is frequently intended to mean net working capital.

$$\text{Net working capital} = \text{current asset} - \text{current liabilities} \qquad (3\text{-}5)$$

Thus, net working capital compares the amount of current assets (assets that should convert into cash within the next 12 months) to the current liabilities (debt that must be paid within 12 months). The larger the net working capital a firm has, the more able the firm will be to pay its debt as it comes due. Thus, the amount of net working capital is important to a company's lenders, who are always concerned about a company's ability to repay its loans. For Home Depot, net working capital is computed as follows:

Gross working capital is the same as current assets

| | FISCAL YEAR ENDED | |
|---|---|---|
| | JANUARY 31, 2010 | JANUARY 30, 2011 |
| Gross working capital | $13,900 | $13,479 |
| Current liabilities | (10,363) | (10,122) |
| Net working capital | $ 3,537 | $ 3,357 |

Most firms have a positive amount of net working capital because their current assets are greater than their current debts. There are a few exceptions. For example, Disney actually has almost as much in current liabilities as in current assets. How do you think this could happen? Very simply, a big part of Disney's sales are cash generated in the theme parks, collecting cash immediately from its customers. However, Disney's suppliers have probably granted Disney 30 days or more to pay its bills. In other words, Disney collects early and pays late.

**EXAMPLE 3.2**    **Constructing a balance sheet**

Given the information below for Menielle, Inc., construct a balance sheet and a common-sized balance sheet. As a percent of assets, what are the firm's largest investments and sources of financing?

| | | | |
|---|---|---|---|
| Gross fixed assets | $75,000 | Accounts receivable | $ 50,000 |
| Cash | $10,000 | Long-term bank note | $ 5,000 |
| Other assets | $15,000 | Mortgage | $ 20,000 |
| Accounts payable | $40,000 | Common stock | $100,000 |
| Retained earnings | $15,000 | Inventories | $ 70,000 |
| Accumulated depreciation | $20,000 | Short-term notes | $ 20,000 |

## STEP 1: FORMULATE A SOLUTION STRATEGY
The balance sheet can be visualized as follows:

| | |
|---|---|
| Current assets | Current liabilities |
| + Long-term (fixed) assets | + Long-term liabilities |
| | + Shareholders' equity |
| **= Total assets** | **= Total liabilities + Shareholders' equity** |

## STEP 2: CRUNCH THE NUMBERS
Your results should be as follows:

**Balance Sheet**

| Assets: | | Liabilities and Equities: | |
|---|---|---|---|
| Cash | $ 10,000 | Accounts payable | $ 40,000 |
| Accounts receivable | 50,000 | Short-term notes | 20,000 |
| Inventories | 70,000 | Total short-term debt | $ 60,000 |
| Total current assets | $130,000 | Long-term bank note | $ 5,000 |
| Gross fixed assets | $ 75,000 | Mortgage | 20,000 |
| Accumulated depreciation | (20,000) | Total long-term debt | $ 25,000 |
| Net fixed assets | $ 55,000 | Total debt | $ 85,000 |
| Other assets | 15,000 | Common stock | 100,000 |
| Total assets | $200,000 | Retained earnings | 15,000 |
| | | Total equity | $115,000 |
| | | Total debt and equity | $200,000 |

**Common-Sized Balance Sheet**

| Assets: | | Liabilities and Equities: | |
|---|---|---|---|
| Cash | 5.0% | Accounts payable | 20.0% |
| Accounts receivable | 25.0% | Short-term notes | 10.0% |
| Inventories | 35.0% | Total short-term debt | 30.0% |
| Total current assets | 65.0% | Long-term bank note | 2.5% |
| Gross fixed assets | 37.5% | Mortgage | 10.0% |
| Accumulated depreciation | (10.0%) | Total long-term debt | 12.5% |
| Net fixed assets | 27.5% | Total debt | 42.5% |
| Other assets | 7.5% | Common stock | 50.0% |
| Total assets | 100.0% | Retained earnings | 7.5% |
| | | Total equity | 57.5% |
| | | Total debt and equity | 100.0% |

**STEP 3: ANALYZE YOUR RESULTS**

We see that the firm has invested a total of $200,000 in its assets, comprised of $130,000 in current assets (65% of total assets), $55,000 in fixed assets (27.5% of total assets), and $15,000 in other assets (7.5% of total assets). Second, the firm has $130,000 tied up in current assets and $60,000 in current liabilities, leaving the firm with a net working capital position of $130,000 − $60,000 = $70,000. Third, the firm uses more equity (57.5% of total assets) than debt (42.5% of total assets) to finance its business.

## The Balance Sheet and Income Statement—as One Picture

We have already stated that an income statement is for a period of time while a balance sheet is prepared at a specific date in time. Now that we have looked at both an income statement and a balance sheet, let's return to the difference in time perspectives between an income statement and a balance sheet. By examining two balance sheets, one at the beginning of a year and one at the end of the year, along with the income statement for the year, we have a better picture of a firm's operations. For instance, we could see what a company looked like at the beginning of 2013 (by looking at its balance sheet on December 31, 2012), what happened during the year (by looking at its income statement for 2013), and the final outcome at the end of 2013 (by looking at its balance sheet on December 31, 2013). The distinction between an income statement and a balance sheet is represented graphically as Figure 3-3.

## Concept Check

1. What does the basic balance sheet equation state, and what does it mean?
2. What is a firm's "accounting book value"?
3. What are a firm's two principal sources of financing? Of what do these sources consist?
4. What is gross working capital? Net working capital?
5. What is a debt ratio?
6. What is the difference between the time frame of the income statement and the balance sheet?

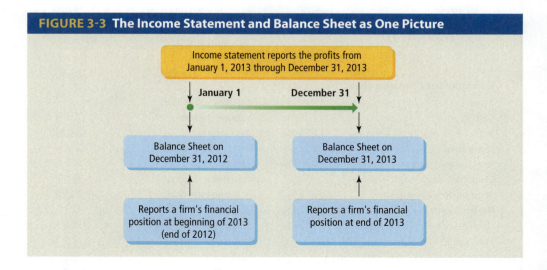

**FIGURE 3-3  The Income Statement and Balance Sheet as One Picture**

Income statement reports the profits from January 1, 2013 through December 31, 2013

January 1            December 31

Balance Sheet on December 31, 2012            Balance Sheet on December 31, 2013

Reports a firm's financial position at beginning of 2013 (end of 2012)            Reports a firm's financial position at end of 2013

# CAN YOU DO IT?

## PREPARING AN INCOME STATEMENT AND A BALANCE SHEET

Below is a scrambled list of accounts of Zhong, Inc., an energy company (in $ thousands). Complete the firm's income statement and balance sheet. Also calculate the earnings per share and dividends per share.

| | |
|---|---|
| Accounts payable | $ 4,400 |
| Account receivable | $ 2,500 |
| Accumulated depreciation | $ 4,200 |
| Cash | $ 3,300 |
| Cost of goods sold | $17,000 |
| Common stock | $13,800 |
| Depreciation expense | $ 1,500 |
| Dividends | $    40 |
| Gross fixed assets | $24,500 |
| Income taxes | $   150 |
| Interest expense | $ 1,000 |
| Long-term debt | $10,000 |
| Number of shares outstanding | $   800 |
| Other assets | $15,600 |
| Inventories | $ 1,500 |
| Retained earnings | $ 8,000 |
| Sales | $30,000 |
| Selling, marketing, and administrative expenses | $10,000 |
| Short-term notes | $ 7,000 |

(The solution to this problem can be found on page 66.)

# Measuring Cash Flows

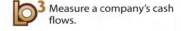
**3** Measure a company's cash flows.

Despite the fact that cash is the lifeblood of a business—the fuel that keeps the engine running—some managers do not fully understand what drives a firm's cash flows. Poor cash-flow management, especially for smaller firms, can result in a business failing. Managers must understand that profits and cash flows are not the same thing.

## Profits Versus Cash Flows

*You need to be aware that the profits shown on a company's income statement are not the same as its cash flows!* In the words of author Jan Norman, "Even profitable companies can go broke. That's a difficult truth for start-up business owners to swallow. But the sooner you learn that when you're out of cash, you're out of business, the better your chances for survival will be."[10] Many a profitable business on paper has had to file bankruptcy because the amount of cash coming in did not compare with the amount of cash going out. Without adequate cash flow, little problems become major problems!

An income statement is not a measure of cash flows because it is calculated on an *accrual* basis rather than a *cash* basis. Let's say it again for emphasis: *An income statement is not a measure of cash flows because it is calculated on an accrual basis rather than a cash basis.* This is an important point to understand. In **accrual basis accounting**, profits are recorded when earned—whether or not the profits have been received in cash—and expenses are recorded when they are incurred—even if money has not actually been paid out. In **cash basis accounting**, profits are reported when cash is received and expenses are recorded when they are paid.

**accrual basis accounting** a method of accounting whereby revenue is recorded when it is earned, whether or not the revenue has been received in cash. Likewise, expenses are recorded when they are incurred, even if the money has not actually been paid out.

**cash basis accounting** a method of accounting whereby revenue is recorded when physical cash is actually received. Likewise, expenses are recorded when physical cash is paid out.

[10]"How To Manage Your Cash Flow: You're making sales, but are you making money?" by Jan Norman from *Entrepreneur*, June 1, 1998.

For a number of reasons, profits based on an accrual accounting system will differ from the firm's cash flows. These reasons include the following:

1. Sales reported in an income statement include both *cash* sales and *credit* sales. Thus, total sales do not correspond to the actual cash collected. A company may have had sales of $1 million for the year but not collected all these sales. If accounts receivable increased $80,000 from the beginning of the year to the end of the year, then we would know that only $920,000 of the sales had been collected ($920,000 = $1,000,000 sales − $80,000 increase in accounts receivable).

2. Some inventory purchases are financed by credit, so inventory purchases do not exactly equal cash spent for inventory. Consider a business that purchased $500,000 in inventories during the year, but the supplier extended credit of $100,000 for the purchases. The actual cash paid for inventories would only be $400,000 ($400,000 = $500,000 total inventory purchases − $100,000 additional credit granted by the supplier).

3. The depreciation expense shown in the income statement is a noncash expense. It reflects the costs associated with using an asset that benefits the firm's operations over a period of multiple years, such as a piece of equipment used over 5 years. Thus, if a business had profits of $250,000 that included depreciation expenses of $40,000, then the cash flows would be $290,000 ($250,000 profits + $40,000 depreciation expense).

We could give you more examples to show why a firm's profits differ from its cash flows, but the point should be clear: Profits and cash flows are not the same thing. In fact, a business could be profitable but have negative cash flows, even to the point of going

## DID YOU GET IT?
### PREPARING AN INCOME STATEMENT AND A BALANCE SHEET

On page 65, we provided data for Zhong, Inc. and asked you to prepare an income statement and a balance sheet and to calculate the earnings per share and dividends per share based on the information. Your results should be as follows:

**Income statement:**

| | |
|---|---:|
| Sales | $30,000 |
| Cost of goods sold | (17,000) |
| Gross profit | $13,000 |
| Operating expenses: | |
|   Selling, marketing, and administrative expenses | ($10,000) |
|   Depreciation expense | (1,500) |
| Total operating expenses | $11,500 |
| Operating income | $ 1,500 |
| Interest expense | (1,000) |
| Earnings before tax | $    500 |
| Income taxes | (150) |
| Net income | $    350 |
| Earnings per share ($350 net income ÷ 800 shares) | $   0.44 |
| Dividends per share ($40 dividends ÷ 800 shares) | $   0.05 |

**Balance sheet:**

| | | | |
|---|---:|---|---:|
| Cash | $ 3,300 | Accounts payable | $ 4,400 |
| Accounts receivable | 2,500 | Short-term notes | 7,000 |
| Inventories | 1,500 | Total short-term debt | $11,400 |
| Total current assets | $ 7,300 | Long-term debt | 10,000 |
| Gross fixed assets | $24,500 | Total debt | $21,400 |
| Accumulated depreciation | (4,200) | Common stock | 13,800 |
| Net fixed assets | $20,300 | Retained earnings | 8,000 |
| Other assets | 15,600 | Total equity | $21,800 |
| Total assets | $43,200 | Total debt and equity | $43,200 |

Source: Data from The Home Depot, Inc. Fiscal Year 2010 Form 10-K.

bankrupt. So, understanding a firm's cash flows is very important to its managers. Cash flows are also important when applying for a loan. A banker will not make a loan without a clear indication that the firm's cash flows will adequately service the proposed loan. Revenue growth and profits are all fine, but only historical cash flows can demonstrate the ability to collect accounts receivable and properly manage inventory and accounts payable. So you had better understand the ins and outs of your firm's cash flows.

## A Beginning Look: Determining Sources and Uses of Cash

To begin, we need to understand that changes in a firm's balance sheets have implications for its cash flows. To determine whether a change in a balance sheet account is a source or a use of cash, you need to understand the following relationships:

| Sources of Cash | Uses of Cash |
| --- | --- |
| **Decrease in an Asset** | **Increase in an Asset** |
| *Example:* Selling inventories or collecting receivables provides cash. | *Example:* Investing in fixed assets or buying more inventories uses cash. |
| **Increase in Liability or Equity** | **Decrease in a Liability or Equity** |
| *Example:* Borrowing funds or selling stock provides the firm with cash. | *Example:* Paying off a loan or buying back stock uses cash. |

To illustrate the above relationships, return to Home Depot's balance sheets in Table 3-2. Earlier we studied the changes in the balance sheet, but this time we want to determine whether these changes result in sources or uses of cash. In Table 3-3, we list some of the changes in Home Depot's balance sheet and indicate whether the changes are sources or uses of cash. This information is then used in the next section to prepare the company's statement of cash flows. So keep in mind the relationships between changes in the balance sheet and the firm's cash flows, as shown in Table 3-3.

## Statement of Cash Flows

There are two common approaches to measuring a firm's cash flows. First, we can use the conventional accountant's presentation called a **statement of cash flows**, which is always included in the financial section of a firm's annual report. This method for presenting cash flows focuses on identifying the sources and uses of cash that explain the change in a firm's cash balance reported in the balance sheet. Alternatively, we can calculate a company's **free cash flows** and **financing cash flows**, which are measurements that managers and investors alike consider critically important. Once a firm has paid all of its operating expenses and taxes and made all of its investments, any remaining cash is free to be distributed to the creditors and shareholders. Alternatively, if the free cash flows are negative, management will have to acquire financing from creditors or shareholders. Understanding and calculating a company's free cash flows is

**statement of cash flows** a statement that shows how changes in balance sheet accounts and income affect cash and cash equivalents, and breaks the analysis down to operating, investing, and financing activities.

**free cash flows** the amount of cash available from operations after the firm pays for the investments it has made in operating working capital and fixed assets. This cash is available to distribute to the firm's creditors and owners.

**financing cash flows** the amount of cash received from or distributed to the firm's investors, usually in the form of interest, dividends, issuance of debt, or issuance or repurchase of stocks.

**TABLE 3-3  The Home Depot, Inc.: Sources and Uses of Cash for Year Ending January 30, 2011 ($ millions)**

| | Account Balance as of: | | | | |
| --- | --- | --- | --- | --- | --- |
| | Jan 31, 2010 | Jan 30, 2011 | Change | Sources | Use |
| Balance Sheet Changes | | | | | |
| Accounts receivable | $   964 | $ 1,085 | $   121 | | $   121 |
| Inventories | 10,188 | 10,625 | 437 | | 437 |
| Other current assets | 1,327 | 1,224 | (103) | 103 | |
| Gross fixed assets | 37,345 | 38,471 | 1,126 | | 1,126 |
| Other assets | 1,427 | 1,586 | 159 | | 159 |
| Accounts payable | 9,343 | 9,080 | (263) | | 263 |
| Short-term notes payable | 1,020 | 1,042 | 22 | 22 | |
| Long-term debt | 11,121 | 11,114 | (7) | | 7 |
| Common stock sold | 6,752 | 7,087 | 335 | 335 | |
| Stock repurchased (treasury stock) | (585) | (3,193) | (2,608) | | 2,608 |

Source: Data from The Home Depot, Inc. Fiscal Year 2010 Form 10-K.

## FIGURE 3-4  Statement of Cash Flows: An Overview

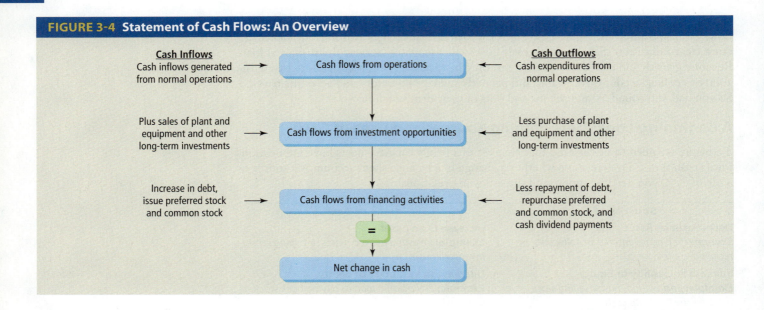

explained in the appendix to this chapter. But for now we will focus on the statement of cash flows that all publicly traded firms must provide for their lenders and investors.

As shown in Figure 3-4, there are three key activities that determine the cash inflows and outflows of a business:

1. **Generating cash flows from day-to-day business operations.** It is informative to know how much cash is being generated in the normal course of operating a business, beginning with purchasing inventories on credit, selling on credit, paying for the inventories, and finally collecting on the sales made on credit.
2. **Investing in fixed assets and other long-term investments.** When a company purchases or sells fixed assets, like equipment and buildings, there can be significant cash inflows from selling these assets and outflows from purchasing these assets.
3. **Financing the business.** Cash inflows and outflows occur from borrowing or repaying debt, paying dividends, and from issuing stock (equity) or repurchasing stock from the shareholders.

If we know the cash flows from the activities above, we can combine them to determine a company's change in cash and prepare a statement of cash flows. To understand how this is done, we will once again return to Home Depot's income statement (Table 3-1 on page 54) and balance sheets (Table 3-2 on page 61).

## FINANCE AT WORK

### MANAGING YOUR CASH FLOWS

If you want to improve cash flows, take a close look at your most recent financial statements. Watch out for:

- Money tied up in excess inventory that could be used to grow your business.
- Expensive office space. Don't spend for a prime location if you don't need it.
- Unpaid invoices from customers. Collect payments promptly.

- Not asking suppliers to extend credit terms. They might give you an extra 15 or even 30 days before you have to pay for purchases, if you simply ask.
- Not closely monitoring cash flows, which can take away money to grow your business.

Source: Adapted from Edward Marram, "6 Weeks to a Better Bottom Line," *Entrepreneur Magazine*, January 2010, http://www.entrepreneur.com/magazine/entrepreneur/2010/january/204390.html, accessed June 4, 2012.

**Cash Flow Activity 1: Cash Flows from Day-to-Day Operations**   Here we want to convert the company's income statement from an accrual basis to a cash basis. This conversion can be accomplished in five steps. We begin with the firm's net income and then we:

1. Add back depreciation expense since it is not a cash expense;
2. Subtract (add) any increase (decrease) in accounts receivable;
3. Subtract (add) any increase (decrease) in inventory;
4. Subtract (add) any increase (decrease) in other current assets;
5. Add (subtract) any increase (decrease) in accounts payable and other accrued expenses.

Why we add back depreciation should be clear; it simply is not a cash expense. The changes in accounts receivable, inventories, other current assets, and accounts payable may be less intuitive. Four comments are helpful:

1. A firm's sales are either cash sales or credit sales. If accounts receivable increase, that means customers did not pay for everything they purchased during the year. Thus, any increase in accounts receivable needs to be subtracted from sales to determine the cash that has not been collected from customers. On the other hand, if accounts receivable decrease, then a firm has collected more than it has sold, which indicates a cash inflow. In equation form, we can compute the cash collected from sales as follows:

$$\begin{array}{c}\text{Cash collections}\\\text{from sales}\end{array} = \text{sales} - \begin{array}{c}\text{change in}\\\text{accounts receivable}\end{array} \qquad (3\text{-}6)$$

2. An increase in inventories shows that we bought inventories, and a decrease in inventories shows that we sold inventories.
3. Other current assets include prepaid expenses, like prepaid insurance and prepaid rent. If other current assets increase (decrease), that means there has been a cash outflow (inflow).
4. While an increase in inventories indicates a cash outflow occurred, if accounts payable (credit extended by a supplier) increase as well, then we know that the firm's suppliers provided credit to the firm, which is a source of cash. The firm did not pay for all the inventories purchased. Thus, the net payment for inventories is equal to the change in inventories less the change in accounts payable. If, on the other hand, accounts payable decreased, there has been a cash outflow.

Figure 3-5 (on page 70) shows a graphical presentation of the procedure for computing a firm's cash flows from operations.

***Cash Flows from Operations Illustrated: Home Depot***   Given the basic framework for a statement of cash flows just explained, we can now prepare this section of the cash flow statement for Home Depot. Referring back to the company's income statement and balance sheets, we can compute the cash flows from operations (expressed in $ millions) as follows:

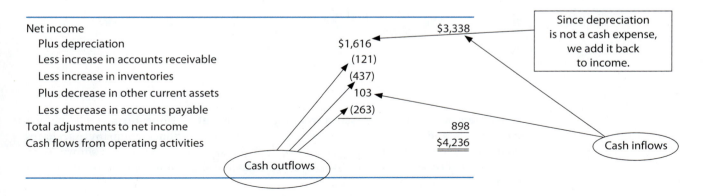

| | | |
|---|---|---|
| Net income | | $3,338 |
| Plus depreciation | $1,616 | |
| Less increase in accounts receivable | (121) | |
| Less increase in inventories | (437) | |
| Plus decrease in other current assets | 103 | |
| Less decrease in accounts payable | (263) | |
| Total adjustments to net income | | 898 |
| Cash flows from operating activities | | $4,236 |

Since depreciation is not a cash expense, we add it back to income.

Cash inflows

Cash outflows

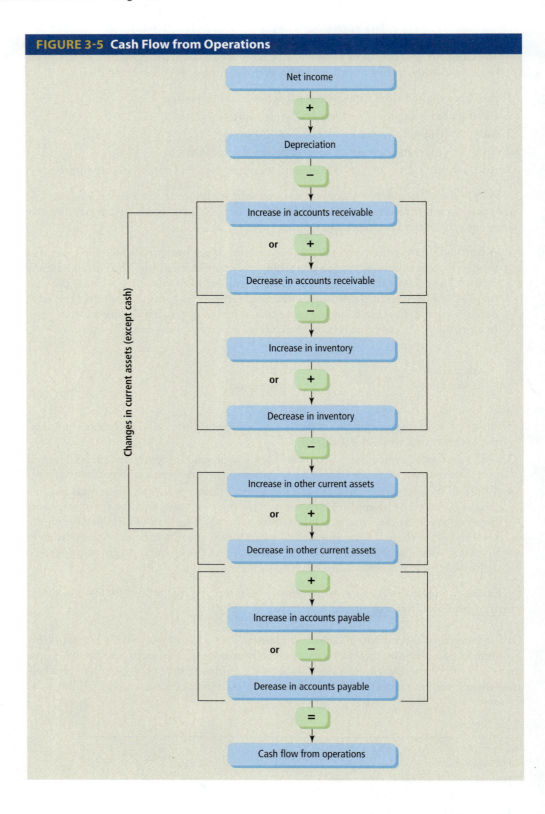

**FIGURE 3-5  Cash Flow from Operations**

**Cash Flow Activity 2: Investing in Long-Term Assets**    Long-term assets include fixed assets and other long-term assets. For example, when a company purchases (sells) fixed assets, such as equipment or buildings, these activities are shown as an increase (decrease) in *gross fixed assets* in the balance sheet and are cash outflows and cash inflows, respectively.

***Investing in Long-Term Assets Illustrated: Home Depot*** As shown in their balance sheets (Table 3-2), Home Depot spent $1.126 billion on new plant and equipment for the year ended January 30, 2011, based on the change in *gross fixed assets* from $37.345 billion to $38.471 billion. It also spent $159 million on other assets.

**Cash Flow Activity 3: Financing the Business** Cash flows associated with financing a business are as follows:

| Cash Inflow: | Cash Outflow: |
|---|---|
| The firm borrows more money (an increase in short-term and/or long-term debt) | The firm repays debt (a decrease in short-term and/ or long-term debt) |
| Owner(s) invest in the business (an increase in stockholders' equity) | The firm pays dividends to the owner(s) or repurchases the owners' stocks (a decrease in equity) |

When we talk about borrowing or repaying debt in financing activities, we do not include accounts payable and any accrued operating expenses. These items were included in cash-flow activity 1 when we computed cash flows from operations. Here in activity 3, we include only debt from such sources as banks in the form of short-term notes and long-term debt.

***Financing the Business Illustrated: Home Depot*** Continuing with Home Depot, we see from the income statement (Table 3-1) that it paid $1.569 billion in dividends to the shareholders. Then from their balance sheets (Table 3-2), we see that short-term notes increased $22 million (a source of cash), and long-term debt decreased $7 million (a use of cash). Also, the firm issued $335 million in common stock. This increase is reflected in the balance sheets in the combined changes in common stock par value and paid-in capital, which was $335 million.[11] Finally, it repurchased $2.608 billion in common stock. Thus, in net, Home Depot had $3.827 billion cash outflows in financing activities, shown as follows:

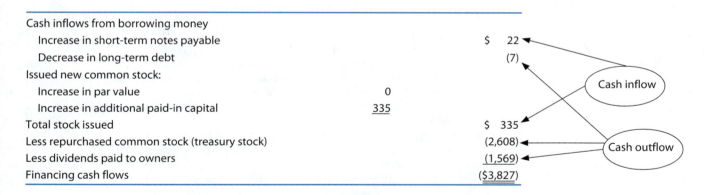

| | | |
|---|---|---|
| Cash inflows from borrowing money | | |
| Increase in short-term notes payable | | $ 22 |
| Decrease in long-term debt | | (7) |
| Issued new common stock: | | |
| Increase in par value | 0 | |
| Increase in additional paid-in capital | 335 | |
| Total stock issued | | $ 335 |
| Less repurchased common stock (treasury stock) | | (2,608) |
| Less dividends paid to owners | | (1,569) |
| Financing cash flows | | ($3,827) |

Using the computations to this point, we can now complete a statement of cash flows for Home Depot, which is shown in Table 3-4 (on page 72). From the table we see that the firm generated $4.236 billion in cash flows from operations; invested $1.285 billion in plant and equipment and other assets; and paid out $3.827 billion in financing activities, for a net decrease in cash of $876 million. This can be verified from the balance sheets (see Table 3-2), which show that Home Depot's cash decreased $876 million from January 31, 2010 to January 30, 2011 (from $1.421 billion to $545 million). Earlier in the chapter, we commented on the large decrease in cash and wondered about the cause. Now we know: The company generated positive cash flows from operations but used these cash flows and more to purchase fixed assets and make large distributions to creditors and stockholders in the form of interest, dividends, and share repurchases.

[11]Par value of common stock increased from $85.8 million on January 31, 2010 to $86.1 million on January 31, 2011. The balance sheet didn't show the change because the amount rounds to zero when expressed in whole millions.

**TABLE 3-4   The Home Depot, Inc. Statement of Cash Flows ($ millions) Year Ended January 30, 2011**

**Operating activities:**

| | | | |
|---|---|---|---|
| a. | Net income | | $3,338 |
| b. | Adjustments to net income to compute cash flow from operating activities | | |
| | 1.  Add depreciation expense (Source of cash) | $1,616 | |
| | 2.  Increased accounts receivable (Use of cash) | (121) | |
| | 3.  Increased inventories (Use of cash) | (437) | |
| | 4.  Decreased other current assets (Source of cash) | 103 | |
| | 5.  Decreased accounts payable (Use of cash) | (263) | |
| | Total adjustments to net income | | $  898 |
| | **Cash flows from operating activities** | | $4,236 |

**Investing activities:**

| | | | |
|---|---|---|---|
| c. | Increased gross fixed assets (Use of cash) | ($1,126) | |
| d. | Increased other assets (Use of cash) | (159) | |
| | **Cash flows from investing activities** | | ($1,285) |

**Financing activities:**

| | | | |
|---|---|---|---|
| e. | Increased short-term notes payable (Source of cash) | $    22 | |
| f. | Decreased long-term debt (Use of cash) | (7) | |
| g. | Increased (issued) new common stock (increase in par value and paid-in capital) (Source of cash) | 335 | |
| h. | Repurchased common stock (increased treasury stock) (Use of cash) | (2,608) | |
| i. | Dividends paid to shareholders (Use of cash) | (1,569) | |
| | **Cash flows from financing activities** | | ($3,827) |

**Summary:**

| | | |
|---|---|---|
| j. | Change in cash and cash equivalents | ($  876) |
| k. | Beginning cash (January 31, 2010) | 1,421 |
| l. | Ending cash (January 30, 2011) | $  545 |

*(Annotation: Same as the cash balances in Home Depot's balance sheets)*

**Legend:**

**Operating Activities**

a.  Home Depot had net income of $3,338.

b.  *Adjustments to net income to compute cash flows from operations:*

1.  *Depreciation.*  Since Home Depot's depreciation expense is a noncash charge, we add back $1,616 in depreciation to net income when calculating Home Depot's cash flow.

2.  *Increase in accounts receivable.*  Home Depot's accounts receivable rose by $121 million, which is a use of cash.

3.  *Increase in inventories.*  Home Depot increased its inventories by $437 million, which is a use of cash.

4.  *Decrease in other current assets.*  Home Depot's other current assets decreased by $103 million, which represents a cash inflow.

5.  *Decrease in accounts payable.*  Home Depot's accounts payable decreased by $263 million, which is a cash outflow.

   *Cash flows from operating activities* add up to a $4.236 billion net inflow of cash.

**Investing Activities**

c.  *Increase in gross fixed assets.*  Home Depot spent $1.126 billion on fixed assets during the current year, resulting in a cash outflow.

d.  *Increase in other assets.*  Home Depot spent $159 million on its other assets, resulting in a cash outflow.

   *Cash flows from investment activities.*  The total on this line is the sum of the investments listed above, $1.285 billion.

**Financing Activities**

e.  *Increase in short-term notes payable.*  Home Depot borrowed an additional $22 million from its bank, which was a cash inflow.

f.  *Decrease in long-term debt.*  Home depot repaid a net $7 million of its long-term debt, which is a cash outflow.

g.  *Issued new common stock.*  Home Depot issued new common stock of $335 million. Common stock includes both par value and additional paid-in capital. This increase is a cash inflow.

h.  *Repurchased common stock.*  Home Depot repurchased $2.608 billion of its common stock, which is a cash outflow.

i.  *Dividends paid to shareholders.*  Home Depot paid out $1.569 billion in dividends, which is a cash outflow.

   *Cash flows from financing activities.*  The sum of the five financing entries equals a negative $3.827 billion.

**Summary:**

j. *Change in cash and cash equivalents.* The net sum of the operating activities, investing activities, and financing activities resulted in an $876 million net decrease in cash during the fiscal year, mainly caused by stock repurchases, dividends paid, and investments in fixed assets.

k. *Beginning cash.* Home Depot began the fiscal year with $1.421 billion of cash.

l. *Ending cash.* Home Depot ended the 2011 fiscal year with $545 million of cash, the $1.421 billion it started with minus the $876 million net decrease in cash during 2011.

---

**EXAMPLE 3.3**    **Measuring cash flows**

Given the following information for Menielle, Inc., prepare a statement of cash flows.

| | | | |
|---|---|---|---|
| Increase in accounts receivable | $13 | Dividends | $ 5 |
| Increase in inventories | 25 | Change in common stock | 0 |
| Net income | 33 | Increase in gross fixed assets | 55 |
| Beginning cash | 15 | Depreciation expense | 7 |
| Increase in accounts payable | 20 | | |
| Increase in accrued expenses | 5 | | |
| Increase in long-term notes payable | 28 | | |

### STEP 1: FORMULATE A SOLUTION STRATEGY

The cash flow statement uses information from the firm's balance sheets and income statement to identify the net sources and uses of cash for a specific period of time. Moreover, the sources and uses are organized into cash from operating activities, from investing activities, and from financing activities.

| | |
|---|---|
| | Cash flow from operating activities |
| Plus/Minus: | Cash flow from investing activities |
| Plus/Minus: | Cash flow from financing activities |
| Equals: | Change in cash |
| Plus: | Beginning cash balance |
| Equals: | Ending cash balance |

### STEP 2: CRUNCH THE NUMBERS

Your results should be as follows:

| | | |
|---|---|---|
| Net income | | $33 |
| Adjustments: | | |
| Depreciation expense | $ 7 | |
| Less increase in accounts receivable | (13) | |
| Less increase in inventories | (25) | |
| Plus increase in accounts payable | 20 | |
| Plus increase in accrued expense | 5 | |
| Total adjustments | | ($ 6) |
| Cash flow from operating activities | | $27 |
| Investing activity: | | |
| Increase in gross fixed assets | | ($55) |
| Financing activities: | | |
| Increase in long-term notes payable | $28 | |
| Change in common stock | 0 | |
| Common stock dividends | (5) | |
| Total financing activities | | $23 |
| Change in cash | | ($ 5) |
| Beginning cash | | 15 |
| Ending cash | | $10 |

**STEP 3: ANALYZE YOUR RESULTS**

Menielle's cash decreased $5 from $15 to $10 because of (1) a $27 cash inflow from operations, (2) less a $55 cash outflow in investing, and (3) plus a $23 cash inflow from financing activities. The cash-flow statement portrays a firm that is investing in fixed assets at a pace that is roughly twice the firm's operating cash flows, which requires the firm to finance the difference.

## Concluding Suggestions for Computing Cash Flows

When calculating cash flows, there are some little things to remember, which, while small, can be very frustrating if not understood. They are:

1. Don't look at the cash-flow statement as a whole. It can be intimidating. Just work on the three parts of the statement individually, then put it all together to get to the whole. That just helps you focus on what needs to be done without being overwhelmed. After some time, it becomes much more intuitive, especially when it is your money!

2. Depreciation expense and net profits are the only two numbers you need from the income statement.

3. You need to be certain that you have used every change in the company's balance sheet, with two exceptions:

   a. Ignore accumulated depreciation and net fixed assets since they involve the noncash item of depreciation. Use only the change in *gross* fixed assets.

   b. Ignore the change in retained earnings since it equals the net profits less dividends paid, two items that are captured elsewhere.

## Conclusions About Home Depot's Financial Position

To conclude our discussion on financial statements, consider some of the main things we learned about Home Depot:

- Home Depot's inventories made up 79 percent of the current assets. Home Depot's total assets consisted of about one-third current assets and two-thirds fixed assets.
- For every $1 of sales, Home Depot earned 34 cents in gross profits, 9 cents in operating income, and 5 cents in net income.
- The firm financed its assets with slightly more debt than equity. It had a debt ratio of 52.9 percent.
- The firm had $4.236 billion in cash flows from operations.
- Management invested $1.285 billion in long-term assets and paid out $3.827 billion to lenders and shareholders.
- The firm's primary investments in 2010 were in additional long-term assets, mostly fixed assets, in the amount of $1.285 billion, and an increase in inventories amounting to $437 million.
- The cash flows received from investors came in the form of newly issued stock for $335 million.
- The primary cash flows going to investors were dividends ($1.569 billion) and stock repurchases ($2.608 billion). However, the firm also paid $530 million in interest expense, which can only be seen in the income statement. Since the statement of cash flows as prepared by the accountants begins with net income, interest expense was deducted when computing cash flows from operations. But from a pure finance perspective, it is very much a financing activity and should be recognized as such.

# FINANCE AT WORK

## WHAT DID HOME DEPOT'S MANAGEMENT HAVE TO SAY?

We have studied Home Depot's financial statements and drawn some conclusions about what we believe the statements told us. Let's now see what the firm's management concluded. Below are a few of management's comments that appeared in the firm's annual report.

### About profits?

Our U.S. stores experienced gross profit margin increase in fiscal 2010 as we realized benefits from better product assortment management through our portfolio approach and leveraging of our newly developed merchandising tools. Lower levels of clearance inventory in our stores for fiscal 2010 compared to last year also contributed to this increase. Additionally, we realized gross profit margin increase from our non-U.S. businesses, primarily Canada, due primarily to a change in the mix of products sold.

### About the firm's cash position?

As of January 30, 2011, we had $545 million in cash and cash equivalents. We believe that our current cash position, access to the debt capital markets and cash flow generated from operations should be sufficient to enable us to complete our capital expenditure programs and fund dividend payments, share repurchases and any required long-term debt payments through the next several fiscal years.

### About cash flows from operations?

Cash flow generated from operations provides us with a significant source of liquidity. For fiscal 2010, Net Cash Provided by Operating Activities was approximately $4.6 billion compared to approximately $5.1 billion for fiscal 2009. This decrease was primarily a result of changes in inventory levels and other net working capital items partially offset by increased earnings.*

### About cash flows from investing?

Net Cash Used in Investing Activities for fiscal 2010 was $1.0 billion compared to $755 million for fiscal 2009. This change was primarily due to increased Capital Expenditures and lower Proceeds from Sales of Property and Equipment.

### And about cash flows from financing?

Net cash used in financing activities for fiscal 2010 was $4.5 billion compared to $3.5 billion for fiscal 2009. This increase was primarily due to $2.4 billion more in Repurchases of Common Stock than in fiscal 2009, and was partially offset by a $998 million increase in Proceeds from Long-Term Borrowings and a $745 million decrease in Repayments of Long-Term Debt in fiscal 2010.

*Because we simplified Home Depot's financial statements for learning purposes, all cash-flow activities (cash flow from operations, cash flow from investing, and cash flow from financing) presented in our example are slightly different from the actual amount given in Home Depot's 10-K.

# CAN YOU DO IT?

## MEASURING CASH FLOWS

Given the following information for an electronics company, prepare a statement of cash flows.

| | | | |
|---|---|---|---|
| Increase in accounts receivable | $ 300 | Common stock dividends | $ 40 |
| Increase in inventories | 80 | Increase in common stock | 10 |
| Increase in long-term debts | 80 | Increase in gross fixed assets | 50 |
| Beginning cash | 1,785 | Depreciation expense | 1,500 |
| Increase in accounts payable | 60 | Net income | 485 |
| Increase in other current assets | 150 | | |

(The solution can be found on page 76.)

# Concept Check

1. Why doesn't an income statement provide a measure of a firm's cash flows?
2. What are three main parts of a statement of cash flows?
3. What does each part tell us about a company?

**4** Explain the differences between GAAP and IFRS.

**Generally Accepted Accounting Principles (GAAP)** rule-based set of accounting principles, standards, and procedures that companies use to compile their financial statements. These principles are issued by the Financial Accounting Standards Board.

**International Financial Reporting Standards (IFRS)** a principle-based set of international accounting standards stating how particular types of transactions and other events should be reported in financial statements. The principles are issued by the International Accounting Standards Board.

# GAAP and IFRS

The United States follows **Generally Accepted Accounting Principles (GAAP)**. GAAP is a set of rule-based accounting standards established by the Financial Accounting Standards Board (FASB). It sets out the standards, conventions, and rules that accountants must follow when preparing audited financial statements. It is complex, providing more than 150 "pronouncements" as to how to account for different types of transactions.

Most other countries follow the **International Financial Reporting Standards (IFRS)**. IFRS is a set of principle-based accounting standards that were established by the International Accounting Standards Board (IASB). IFRS sets out broad and general principles that accountants should follow when preparing financial statements. It leaves more room for discretion than GAAP does, permitting managers to exercise their own judgment when deciding how to report their financial statements, as long as they follow the spirit of the standards. Thus, IFRS offers simplicity but also possibly more leeway for accounting malpractice than does GAAP.

In 2008, the Securities and Exchange Commission (SEC) announced its plan to convert U.S. companies from GAAP to IFRS, by as early as 2014, even though there is considerable controversy about the switch. The U.S. accounting standard is going to undergo significant changes in the future.

## Concept Check

1. What are the differences between GAAP and IFRS?

---

# DID YOU GET IT?
## MEASURING CASH FLOWS

On page 75 we asked you to calculate an electronics company's cash flows. Your results should be as follows:

| | |
|---|---:|
| Net income | $ 485 |
| Plus depreciation | 1,500 |
| Less increase in accounts receivable | (300) |
| Less increase in inventories | (80) |
| Less increase in other current assets | (150) |
| Plus increase in accounts payable | 60 |
| Cash flow from operating activities | $1,515 |
| Investment activity | |
| Increase in gross fixed assets | ($ 50) |
| Financing activity | |
| Increase in long-term debts | $ 80 |
| Increase in common stock | 10 |
| Common stock dividends | (40) |
| Total financing activities | $ 50 |
| Change in cash | $1,515 |
| Beginning cash | 1,785 |
| Ending cash | $3,300 |

---

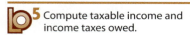

**5** Compute taxable income and income taxes owed.

# Income Taxes and Finance

Income tax is one of the largest expenses that a business encounters, and as a result, it must be considered in making investment and financing decisions. But understanding income taxes is a profession unto itself. Tax accountants spend a lifetime attempting to

## TABLE 3-5    J and S Corporation Taxable Income

| | | |
|---|---:|---:|
| Sales | | $50,000,000 |
| Cost of goods sold | | 23,000,000 |
| Gross profits | | $27,000,000 |
| Operating expenses | | |
|    Administrative expenses | $4,000,000 | |
|    Depreciation expenses | 1,500,000 | |
|    Marketing expenses | 4,500,000 | |
| Total operating expenses | | $10,000,000 |
| Operating income (earnings before interest and taxes) | | $17,000,000 |
| Other income | | 0 |
| Interest expense | | 1,000,000 |
| Taxable Income | | $16,000,000 |

Dividends paid to common stockholders ($1,000,000) are not tax-deductible expenses.

remain current with the tax laws. So we will limit our discussion to the basic issue of computing a corporation's income taxes and let the tax accountants provide us counsel on the rest.

For our purposes, we simply need to know that **taxable income** for a corporation consists of two basic components: operating income and capital gains. Operating income, as we have already defined, is essentially gross profits less any operating expenses, such as marketing expenses, administrative expenses, and so forth. We should also remember that while interest expense is a tax-deductible expense, dividends paid to shareholders are not.

**Capital gains** occur when a firm sells a capital asset, which is any asset that is not part of its ordinary operations. For example, when a company sells a piece of equipment or land, any gain or loss (sales price less the cost of the asset) is treated as a capital gain or loss.

**taxable income** gross income from all sources, except for allowable exclusions, less any tax-deductible expenses.

**capital gains** gains from selling any asset that is not part of the ordinary operations.

### Computing Taxable Income

To demonstrate how to compute a corporation's taxable income, consider the J and S Corporation, a manufacturer of home accessories. The firm, originally established by Kelly Stites, had sales of $50 million for the year. The cost of producing the accessories totaled $23 million. Operating expenses were $10 million. The corporation has $12.5 million in debt outstanding, with an 8 percent interest rate, which resulted in $1 million interest expense ($12,500,000 × 0.08 = $1,000,000). Management paid $1 million in dividends to the firm's common stockholders. No other income, such as interest or dividend income, was received. The taxable income for the J and S Corporation would be $16 million, as shown in Table 3-5.

Once we know J and S Corporation's taxable income, we can determine the amount of taxes the firm owes.

### Computing the Taxes Owed

The taxes to be paid by the corporation on its taxable income are based on the corporate tax rate structure. The specific rates for corporations, as of 2012, are given in Table 3-6.

## TABLE 3-6    Corporate Tax Rates

| | |
|---|---:|
| 15% | $0–$50,000 |
| 25% | $50,001–$75,000 |
| 34% | $75,001–$10,000,000 |
| 35% | over $10,000,000 |
| Additional surtax: | |
| • 5% on income between $100,000 and $335,000 | |
| • 3% on income between $15,000,000 and $18,333,333 | |

**marginal tax rate** the tax rate that would be applied to the next dollar of income.

The tax rates shown in Table 3-6 are the **marginal tax rates**, or *rates applicable to the next dollar of income.* For instance, if a firm has earnings of $60,000 and is contemplating an investment that would yield $10,000 in additional profits, the tax rate to be used in calculating the taxes on this added income is 25 percent; that is, the marginal tax rate is 25 percent.

The rates in Table 3-6 go up to a top marginal corporate tax rate of 35 percent for taxable income in excess of $10 million, and a surtax of 3 percent on taxable income between $15 million and $18,333,333. This means the corporation's marginal tax rate on income between $15 million and $18,333,333 is 38 percent (the 35 percent rate plus the 3 percent surtax). There is also a 5-percent surtax on taxable income between $100,000 and $335,000, which means the marginal rate on income between $100,000 and $335,000 is 39 percent (the 34 percent rate plus the 5 percent surtax). For example, the tax liability for J and S Corporation, which had $16 million in taxable earnings, would be $5,530,000, calculated as follows:

| EARNINGS | × | MARGINAL TAX RATE | = | TAXES |
|---|---|---|---|---|
| $    50,000 | × | 15% | = | $    7,500 |
| 25,000 | × | 25% | = | 6,250 |
| 9,925,000 | × | 34% | = | 3,374,500 |
| 6,000,000 | × | 35% | = | 2,100,000 |

Total income $16,000,000                                                                    $5,488,250

Additional surtaxes:

• Add 5% surtax on income between $100,000 and $335,000 (5% × [$335,000 − $100,000])                                                11,750

• Add 3% surtax on income between $15,000,000 and $18,333,333 (3% × [$16,000,000 − $15,000,000])                              30,000

Total tax liability                                                                                    $5,530,000

**average tax rate** the tax rate on average that a company pays on its total taxable income.

Given that the J and S Corporation owes $5,530,000 in taxes on $16 million taxable income, the firm's **average tax rate**, computed as taxes owed divided by taxable income, is 34.56 percent (34.56% = $5,530,000 ÷ $16,000,000). However, J and S Corporation's marginal tax rate is 38 percent (this is because $16 million falls into the 35 percent tax bracket with a 3 percent surtax); that is, the next dollar of any income will be taxed at a rate of 38 percent. However, after taxable income exceeds $18,333,333, the marginal tax rate declines to 35 percent, since the 3 percent surtax no longer applies.

For financial decision making, it's the marginal tax rate rather than the average tax rate that we are concerned with. Why? Because, generally speaking, the marginal rate is the rate that a corporation pays on the next dollar that is earned. We always want to consider the tax consequences of any financial decision. The marginal tax rate is the rate that will be applicable for any changes in earnings that occur as a result of the decision being made. Thus, when making financial decisions involving taxes, always use the marginal tax rate in your calculations.[12]

---

[12]On taxable income between $335,000 and $10 million, both the marginal and average tax rates equal 34 percent because of the imposition of the 5 percent surtax that applies to taxable income between $100,000 and $335,000. This surtax eliminates the benefit of having the first $75,000 of taxable income taxed at the rates lower than 34 percent. After the company's taxable income exceeds $18,333,333, both the marginal and average tax rates equal 35 percent because the 3 percent surtax on income between $15 million and $18,333,333 eliminates the benefits of having the first $10 million of income taxed at 34 percent rather than 35 percent.

| EXAMPLE 3.3 | Computing a corporation's income taxes |

Assume that the Griggs Corporation had sales during the past year of $5 million; its cost of goods sold was $3 million; and it incurred operating expenses of $950,000. In addition, it received $185,000 in interest income. In turn, it paid $40,000 in interest and $75,000 in common stock dividends. Compute the tax due for the Griggs Corporation.

### STEP 1: FORMULATE A SOLUTION STRATEGY

The following template provides us a useful guide for computing the taxable income:

|         | Sales |
|---------|-------|
| Less:   | Cost of goods sold |
| Equals: | Gross profits |
| Less:   | Operating expenses |
| Equals: | Operating income |
| Less:   | Interest expense |
| Plus:   | Interest income |
| Equals: | Taxable income |

Use Table 3-6 to find the appropriate tax rate. Don't forget the additional surtax.

### STEP 2: CRUNCH THE NUMBERS

| | | |
|---|---|---:|
| Sales | | $ 5,000,000 |
| Cost of goods sold | | ($ 3,000,000) |
| Gross profit | | $ 2,000,000 |
| Operating expenses | | ($ 950,000) |
| Operating income | | $ 1,050,000 |
| Other taxable income and expenses: | | |
|   Interest income | $185,000 | |
|   Interest expense | (40,000) | $ 145,000 |
| Taxable income | | $ 1,195,000 |

| Tax computation | | | | |
|---|---|---|---|---:|
| | 15% × | $ 50,000 = | | $ 7,500 |
| | 25% × | 25,000 = | | 6,250 |
| | 34% × | 1,120,000 = | | 380,800 |
| | | $1,195,000 | | $394,550 |
| Add 5% surtax for income between $100,000 and $335,000 | | | | 11,750 |
| Tax liability | | | | $406,300 |

### STEP 3: ANALYZE YOUR RESULTS

Note that the $75,000 Griggs paid in common stock dividends is not tax deductible. The marginal tax rate and the average tax rate both equal 34 percent; thus, we could have computed Griggs's tax liability as 34 percent of $1,195,000, or $406,300.

## Concept Check

1. How is taxable income computed?
2. How are taxes owed computed?
3. Why should we be more concerned with the marginal tax rate rather than the average tax rate?

## CAN YOU DO IT?

### COMPUTING A CORPORATION'S INCOME TAXES

A manufacturing company had sales during the past year of $32 million; its cost of goods sold was $17 million; and it incurred operating expenses of $12 million. In addition, it received $0.8 million in interest income. In turn, it paid $1 million in interest and $0.5 million in common stock dividends. Compute the company's taxes.
(The solution can be found on page 80.)

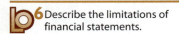

**6** Describe the limitations of financial statements.

# Accounting Malpractice and Limitations of Financial Statements

Financial statements are prepared following the Financial Accounting Standards Board's generally accepted accounting principles (GAAP). When reviewing financial statements, keep in mind that accounting rules give managers discretion; thus they may take advantage of the leeway, as long as it doesn't violate GAAP to produce the high or stable earnings that investors are looking for. In other words, if two companies have the same financial performance, their financial statements can be different, depending on how and when the managers choose to report certain transactions.

Sometimes, managers may even break the rules, which results in accounting malpractice/accounting fraud. There have been many cases of accounting fraud, and the managers involved have faced criminal charges for their illegal acts. In 2010, it was revealed in a report by the bankruptcy court examiner that Lehman Brothers used Repo 105 three times and didn't disclose it to investors. Repo 105 is a repurchase agreement that results in an "accounting gimmick" where a short-term loan is classified as a sale. The cash obtained through this "sale" is then used to pay down debt, allowing the company to appear to be paying down liabilities—just long enough to reflect on the company's published balance sheet. After the company's financial reports are published, the company borrows cash and repurchases its original assets.

## Concept Check

1. What are the limitations of financial statements?

This chapter has provided a basic understanding of financial statements, as demonstrated using Home Depot's financial data. In the next chapter, we will dig even deeper by conducting what is called *financial analysis*. We will continue using Home Depot to illustrate the use of this financial tool.

## DID YOU GET IT?
### COMPUTING A CORPORATION'S INCOME TAXES

| | | | |
|---|---|---|---|
| Sales | | | $32,000,000 |
| Cost of goods sold | | | (17,000,000) |
| Gross profit | | | $15,000,000 |
| Operating expenses | | | (12,000,000) |
| Operating income | | | $ 3,000,000 |
| Other taxable income and expenses: | | | |
|   Interest income | | $ 800,000 | |
|   Interest expense | | (1,000,000) | ($ 200,000) |
| Taxable income | | | $ 2,800,000 |
| Tax computation | | | |
| | 15% × $ 50,000 = | $ 7,500 | |
| | 25% × 25,000 = | 6,250 | |
| | 34% × 2,725,000 = | 926,500 | |
| | $2,800,000 | $ 940,250 | |
| Add 5% surtax for income between $100,000 | | | |
|     and $335,000 | | 11,750 | |
| Tax liability | | $ 952,000 | |

# Chapter Summaries

**Compute a company's profits, as reflected by its income statement.**
(pgs. 52–56)

**SUMMARY:**

1. A firm's profits may be viewed as follows:

   Gross profit = sales − cost of goods sold

   Earnings before interest and taxes (operating profits) = gross profit − operating expenses

   Net profit (net income) = earnings before interest and taxes (operating profits) − interest expense − taxes

2. The following five activities determine a company's net income:
   a. The revenue derived from selling the company's product or service
   b. The cost of producing or acquiring the goods or services to be sold
   c. The operating expenses related to (1) marketing and distributing the product or service to the customer and (2) administering the business
   d. The financing costs of doing business—namely, the interest paid to the firm's creditors
   e. The payment of taxes

**KEY TERMS**

**Income statement (profit and loss statement), page 52** a basic accounting statement that measures the results of a firm's operations over a specified period, commonly 1 year. The bottom line of the income statement, net profits (net income), shows the profit or loss for the period that is available for a company's owners (shareholders).

**Cost of goods sold, page 52** the cost of producing or acquiring a product or service to be sold in the ordinary course of business.

**Gross profit, page 52** sales or revenue minus the cost of goods sold.

**Operating expenses, page 52** marketing and selling expenses, general and administrative expenses, and depreciation expense.

**Operating income (earnings before interest and taxes), page 52** sales less the cost of goods sold less operating expenses.

**Earnings before taxes (taxable income), page 53** operating income minus interest expense.

**Net income (net profit, or earnings available to common stockholders), page 53** the earnings available to the firm's common and preferred stockholders.

**Earnings per share, page 54** net income on a per share basis.

**Dividends per share, page 54** the amount of dividends a firm pays for each share outstanding.

**Common-sized income statement, page 55** an income statement in which a firm's expenses and profits are expressed as a percentage of its sales.

**Profit margins, page 55** financial ratios (sometimes simply referred to as margins) that reflect the level of the firm's profits relative to its sales. Examples include the gross profit margin (gross profit divided by sales), operating profit margin (operating income divided by sales), and the net profit margin (net income divided by sales).

**Gross profit margin, page 55** gross profit divided by net sales. It is a ratio denoting the gross profit earned by the firm as a percentage of its net sales.

**Operating profit margin, page 55** operating income divided by sales. This ratio serves as an overall measure of the company's operating effectiveness.

**Net profit margin, page 55** net income divided by sales. A ratio that measures the net income of the firm as a percent of sales.

**Fixed costs, page 55** costs that remain constant, regardless of any change in a firm's activity.

**Variable costs, page 55** costs that change in proportion to changes in a firm's activity.

**Semivariable costs, page 55** costs composed of a mixture of fixed and variable components.

**KEY EQUATION**
Sales − expenses = profits

## Determine a firm's financial position at a point in time based on its balance sheet. (pgs. 56–64)

**SUMMARY:** The balance sheet presents a company's assets, liabilities, and equity on a specific date. Its total assets represent all the investments that the firm has made in the business. The total assets must equal the firm's total debt and equity because every dollar of assets has been financed by the firm's lenders or stockholders. The firm's assets include its current assets, fixed assets, and other assets. Its debt includes both its short-term and long-term debt. The firm's equity includes (1) common stock, which may be shown as par value plus paid-in capital, and (2) retained earnings. All the numbers in a balance sheet are based on historical costs, rather than current market values.

### KEY TERMS

**Balance sheet, page 56** a statement that shows a firm's assets, liabilities, and shareholder equity at a given point in time. It is a snapshot of the firm's financial position on a particular date.

**Accounting book value, page 57** the value of an asset as shown on a firm's balance sheet. It represents the depreciated historical cost of the asset rather than its current market value or replacement cost.

**Liquidity, page 57** the ability to convert an asset into cash quickly without a significant loss of its value.

**Current assets (gross working capital), page 57** current assets consist primarily of cash, marketable securities, accounts receivable, inventories, and prepaid expenses.

**Cash, page 58** cash on hand, demand deposits, and short-term marketable securities that can quickly be converted into cash.

**Accounts receivable, page 58** money owed by customers who purchased goods or services from the firm on credit.

**Inventories, page 58** raw materials, work in progress, and finished goods held by the firm for eventual sale.

**Other current assets, page 58** other short-term assets that will benefit future time periods, such as prepaid expenses.

**Fixed assets, page 58** assets such as equipment, buildings, and land.

**Depreciation expense, page 58** a noncash expense to allocate the cost of depreciable assets, such as plant and equipment, over the life of the asset.

**Accumulated depreciation, page 58** the sum of all depreciation taken over the entire life of a depreciable asset.

**Gross fixed assets, page 58** the original cost of a firm's fixed assets.

**Net fixed assets, page 58** gross fixed assets minus the accumulated depreciation taken over the life to date of the assets.

**Debt, page 59** liabilities consisting of such sources as credit extended by suppliers or a loan from a bank.

**Equity, page 59** stockholders' investment in the firm and the cumulative profits retained in the business up to the date of the balance sheet.

**Current debt (short-term liabilities), page 59** debt due to be paid within 12 months.

**Accounts payable (trade credit), page 59** credit provided by suppliers when a firm purchases inventory on credit.

**Accrued expenses, page 59** expenses that have been incurred but not yet paid in cash.

**Short-term notes (debt), page 59** amounts borrowed from lenders, mostly financial institutions such as banks, where the loan is to be repaid within 12 months.

**Long-term debt, page 59** loans from banks or other sources that lend money for longer than 12 months.

**Mortgage, page 59** a loan to finance real estate where the lender has first claim on the property in the event the borrower is unable to repay the loan.

**Preferred stockholders, page 59** stockholders who have claims on the firm's income and assets after creditors, but before common stockholders.

**Common stockholders, page 59** investors who own the firm's common stock. Common stockholders are the residual owners of the firm.

**Common stock, page 59** shares that represent ownership in a corporation.

**Par value, page 59** the arbitrary value a firm puts on each share of stock prior to its being offered for sale.

**Paid-in capital, page 59** the amount a company receives above par value from selling stock to investors.

**Treasury stock, page 60** the firm's stock that has been issued and then repurchased by the firm.

**Retained earnings, page 60** cumulative profits retained in a business up to the date of the balance sheet.

**Common-sized balance sheet, page 62** a balance sheet in which a firm's assets and sources of debt and equity are expressed as a percentage of its total assets.

**Debt ratio, page 62** a firm's total liabilities divided by its total assets. It is a ratio that measures the extent to which a firm has been financed with debt.

**Net working capital, page 62** the difference between a firm's current assets and its current liabilities. When the term *working capital* is used, it is frequently intended to mean net working capital.

### KEY EQUATIONS

Total assets = total liabilities (debt) + total shareholders' equity

Beginning retained earnings + net income for the year − dividends paid during the year = ending retained earnings

Common equity = common shareholders' investment + cumulative profits − cumulative dividends paid to common stockholders

Net working capital = current assets − current liabilities

---

## Measure a company's cash flows. (pgs. 65–75)

**SUMMARY:** A firm's profits are not an adequate measure of its cash flows. To measure a company's cash flows requires that we look both at the income statement and the changes in the balance sheet. There are three main parts of a statement of cash flows: cash flows from operations, investment cash flows, and financing cash flows. Examining these three parts of the statement of cash flows helps us understand where cash came from and how it was used.

### KEY TERMS

**Accrual basis accounting, page 65** a method of accounting whereby revenue is recorded when it is earned, whether or not the revenue has been received in cash. Likewise, expenses are recorded when they are incurred, even if the money has not actually been paid out.

**Cash basis accounting, page 65** a method of accounting whereby revenue is recorded when cash is actually received. Likewise, expenses are recorded when physical cash is paid out.

**Statement of cash flows, page 67** a statement that shows how changes in balance sheet accounts and income affect cash and cash equivalents, and breaks the analysis down to operating, investing, and financing activities.

**Free cash flows, page 67** the amount of cash available from operations after the firm pays for the investments it has made in operating working capital and fixed assets. This cash is available to distribute to the firm's creditors and owners.

**Financing cash flows, page 67** the amount of cash received from or distributed to the firm's investors, usually in the form of interest, dividends, issuance of debt, or issuance or repurchase of stocks.

### KEY EQUATIONS

$$\text{Cash collections from sales} = \text{sales} - \text{change in accounts receivable}$$

---

## Explain the differences between GAAP and IFRS. (pg. 76)

**SUMMARY:** GAAP is rules-based and sets out rules that accountants must follow when preparing financial statements. IFRS is principles-based and sets out general principles. IFRS leaves more room for discretion than GAAP does, permitting managers to exercise their own judgment when deciding how to report in their financial statements, as long as they follow the spirit of the standards.

**KEY TERMS**

**Generally Accepted Accounting Principles (GAAP), page 76** rules-based accounting principles, standards, and procedures that companies use to compile their financial statements. These principles are issued by the Financial Accounting Standards Board (FASB).

**International Financial Reporting Standards (IFRS), page 76** principles-based set of international accounting standards stating how particular types of transactions and other events should be reported in financial statements. IFRS are issued by the International Accounting Standards Board (IASB).

---

 **5    Compute taxable income and income taxes owed.** (pgs. 76–79)

**SUMMARY:** For the most part, taxable income for the corporation is equal to the firm's operating income plus capital gains less any interest expense. Tax consequences, particularly marginal tax rates, have a direct bearing on the decisions of the financial manager.

**KEY TERMS**

**Taxable income, page 77** income from all sources, except for allowable exclusions, less any tax-deductible expenses.

**Capital gains, page 77** gains from selling any asset that is not part of the ordinary operations.

**Marginal tax rate, page 78** the tax rate that would be applied to the next dollar of income.

**Average tax rate, page 78** the tax rate on average that a company pays on its total taxable income.

---

 **6    Describe the limitations of financial statements.** (pg. 80)

**SUMMARY:** Accounting rules give managers discretion. Therefore what we see in financial statements may not exactly reflect the company's financial situation. Sometimes, managers may even break the rules, which results in accounting malpractice/accounting fraud.

# Review Questions

*All Review Questions are available in* MyFinanceLab.

**3-1.** A company's financial statements consist of the balance sheet, income statement, and statement of cash flows. Describe what each statement tells us.

**3-2.** How do gross profits, operating profits, and net income differ?

**3-3.** How do dividends and interest expense differ?

**3-4.** Why is it that the preferred stockholders' equity section of the balance sheet changes only when new shares are sold or repurchased, whereas the common stockholders' equity section changes from year to year regardless of whether new shares are bought or sold?

**3-5.** What is net working capital?

**3-6.** Why might one firm have positive cash flows and be headed for financial trouble, whereas another firm with negative cash flows could actually be in a good financial position?

**3-7.** Why is the examination of only the balance sheet and income statement not adequate in evaluating a firm?

**3-8.** What are the differences between GAAP and IFRS?

**3-9.** Why are dividends paid to a firm's owners not a tax-deductible expense?

**3-10.** What are the limitations of financial statements?

**3-11.** See the annual report for the Dell Corporation by going to www.dell.com. Scroll to the bottom of the page, click, "About Dell," then "Investors," then "Financial Reporting," and finally the link "Annual Reports." Scan the list to determine which year you would like to review. Alternatively, select one of the other links (such as "Financial History") to learn additional financial information about Dell, Inc.

**3-12.** Go to www.homedepot.com for the home page of the Home Depot Corporation. Scroll to the bottom of the page and select "Investor Relations," and then "Financial Reports." Look for keywords in the income statement that appear in this chapter, such as sales, gross profits, and net income. What do you learn about the firm from its financial statements that you find interesting?

**3-13.** Go to the *Wall Street Journal* home page at www.wsj.com. Search for Barnes & Noble (ticker symbol BKS). Find the firm's earnings announcements. What did you learn about the company from the announcements? Also, search www.barnesandnoble.com to find the same information.

# Study Problems

*All Study Problems are available in MyFinanceLab.*

**3-1.** (*Computing earnings per share*) If ABC Company earned $280,000 in net income and paid cash dividends of $40,000, what are ABC's earnings per share if it has 80,000 shares outstanding?

**3-2.** (*Preparing an income statement*) Prepare an income statement and a common-sized income statement from the following information.

| | |
|---|---|
| Sales | $525,000 |
| Cost of goods sold | 200,000 |
| General and administrative expenses | 62,000 |
| Depreciation expenses | 8,000 |
| Interest expense | 12,000 |
| Income taxes | 97,200 |

**3-3.** (*Preparing a balance sheet*) Prepare a balance sheet from the following information. What is the net working capital and debt ratio?

| | |
|---|---|
| Cash | $ 50,000 |
| Accounts receivable | 42,700 |
| Accounts payable | 23,000 |
| Short-term notes payable | 10,500 |
| Inventories | 40,000 |
| Gross fixed assets | 1,280,000 |
| Other current assets | 5,000 |
| Long-term debt | 200,000 |
| Common stock | 490,000 |
| Other assets | 15,000 |
| Accumulated depreciation | 312,000 |
| Retained earnings | ? |

**3-4.** (*Preparing a balance sheet*) Prepare a balance sheet and a common-sized balance sheet from the following information.

| | |
|---|---|
| Cash | $ 30,000 |
| Accounts receivable | 63,800 |
| Accounts payable | 52,500 |
| Short-term notes payable | 11,000 |
| Inventories | 66,000 |
| Gross fixed assets | 1,061,000 |
| Accumulated depreciation | 86,000 |
| Long-term debt | 210,000 |
| Common stock | 480,000 |
| Other assets | 25,000 |
| Retained earnings | ? |

**3-5.** *(Working with an income statement and balance sheet)* Prepare a balance sheet and income statement for Belmond, Inc. from the following information.

| | |
|---|---:|
| Inventory | $ 6,500 |
| Common stock | 45,000 |
| Cash | 16,550 |
| Operating expenses | 1,350 |
| Short-term notes payable | 600 |
| Interest expense | 900 |
| Depreciation expense | 500 |
| Sales | 12,800 |
| Accounts receivable | 9,600 |
| Accounts payable | 4,800 |
| Long-term debt | 55,000 |
| Cost of goods sold | 5,750 |
| Buildings and equipment | 122,000 |
| Accumulated depreciation | 34,000 |
| Taxes | 1,440 |
| General and administrative expenses | 850 |
| Retained earnings | ? |

**3-6.** *(Working with an income statement and balance sheet)* Prepare a balance sheet and income statement for the Warner Company from the following scrambled list of items.

a. What is the firm's net working capital and debt ratio?
b. Complete a common-sized income statement and a common-sized balance sheet.
c. Interpret your findings.

| | |
|---|---:|
| Depreciation expense | $ 66,000 |
| Cash | 225,000 |
| Long-term debt | 334,000 |
| Sales | 573,000 |
| Accounts payable | 102,000 |
| General and administrative expenses | 79,000 |
| Buildings and equipment | 895,000 |
| Notes payable | 75,000 |
| Accounts receivable | 153,000 |
| Interest expense | 4,750 |
| Accrued operating expenses | 7,900 |
| Common stock | 289,000 |
| Cost of goods sold | 297,000 |
| Inventory | 99,300 |
| Taxes | 50,500 |
| Accumulated depreciation | 263,000 |
| Prepaid expenses | 14,500 |
| Taxes payable | 53,000 |
| Retained earnings | 262,900 |

**3-7.** *(Working with an income statement and balance sheet)* Prepare an income statement and a balance sheet from the following scrambled list of items. What is the firm's net working capital and debt ratio?

| | |
|---|---:|
| Sales | $550,000 |
| Accumulated depreciation 累积折旧 ✓ | 190,000 |
| Cash | ? |
| Cost of goods sold ✓ | 320,000 |
| Accounts receivable 应收账款 ✓ | 73,000 ✓ |
| Depreciation expenses 折旧费用 ✓ | 38,000 |
| Accounts payable 应付账款 ✓ | 65,000 |
| Interest expense 利息费用 ✓ | 26,000 |
| Short-term notes payable 应付票据 ✓ | 29,000 |
| Income taxes 收入税 ✓ | 59,850 |
| Inventories 存货 ✓ | 47,000 |
| Marketing, general, and administrative expenses ✓ | 45,000 |
| Gross fixed assets 总固定资产 ✓ | 648,000 |
| Long-term debt 债券 ✓ | 360,000 |
| Common stock 普通股 ✓ | 120,000 |
| Other assets 资产 ✓ | 15,000 |
| Retained earnings 留存利润 | 138,500 |

In addition, the firm has 10,000 shares outstanding and paid $15,000 in common stock dividends during the year.

股息

**3-8.** (*Working with a statement of cash flows*) Given the following information, prepare a statement of cash flows.

| | |
|---|---:|
| Increase in accounts receivable | $25 |
| Increase in inventories | 30 |
| Operating income | 75 |
| Interest expense | 25 |
| Increase in accounts payable | 25 |
| Dividends | 15 |
| Increase in common stock | 20 |
| Increase in net fixed assets | 23 |
| Depreciation expense | 12 |
| Income taxes | 17 |
| Beginning cash | 20 |

**3-9.** (*Analyzing a statement of cash flows*) Interpret the following information regarding Westlake Corporation's cash flows.

| | | |
|---|---:|---:|
| Net income | $ | 680 |
| Depreciation expense | | 125 |
| Profits before depreciation | | 805 |
| Increase in accounts receivable | | (200) |
| Increase in inventories | | (240) |
| Increase in accounts payable | | 120 |
| Increase in accrued expenses | | 81 |
| Cash flow from operations | $ | 566 |
| Investment activity | | |
| Change in fixed assets | | (1,064) |
| Financing activity | | |
| Increase in long-term debt | $ | 640 |
| Common stock dividends | | (120) |
| Total financing activities | $ | 520 |
| Change in cash | $ | 22 |
| Beginning cash | | 500 |
| Ending cash | $ | 522 |

**3-10.** (*Working with a statement of cash flows*) Given the following information, prepare a statement of cash flows.

| | |
|---|---:|
| Beginning Cash | $ 20 |
| Dividends | 25 |
| Increase in common stock | 27 |
| Increase in accounts receivable | 65 |
| Increase in inventories | 5 |
| Operating income | 215 |
| Increase in accounts payable | 40 |
| Interest expense | 50 |
| Depreciation expense | 20 |
| Increase in bank debt | 48 |
| Increase in accrued expenses | 15 |
| Increase in gross fixed assets | 55 |
| Income taxes | 45 |

**3-11.** (*Analyzing a statement of cash flows*) Interpret the following information regarding Maness Corporation's statement of cash flows.

| | |
|---|---:|
| Net income | $ 370 |
| Depreciation expense | 60 |
| Profits before depreciation | 430 |
| Increase in accounts receivable | (300) |
| Increase in inventories | (400) |
| Increase in accounts payable | 200 |
| Increase in accrued expenses | 40 |
| Cash flow from operations | ($   30) |
| Investment activity | |
| Change in fixed assets | ($1,500) |
| Financing activity | |
| Increase in short-term notes | $  100 |
| Repayment of long-term debt | (250) |
| Repurchase common stock | (125) |
| Common stock dividends | (75) |
| Total financing activities | ($  350) |
| Change in cash | ($1,880) |
| Beginning cash | 3,750 |
| Ending cash | $1,870 |

**3-12.** (*Working with a statement of cash flows*) Prepare a statement of cash flows for Abrahams Manufacturing Company for the year ended December 31, 2012. Interpret your results.

**Abrahams Manufacturing Company Balance Sheet for 12/31/2011 and 12/31/2012**

| | 2011 | 2012 |
|---|---:|---:|
| Cash | $ 89,000 | $100,000 |
| Accounts receivable | 64,000 | 70,000 |
| Inventory | 112,000 | 100,000 |
| Prepaid expenses | 10,000 | 10,000 |
| Total current assets | 275,000 | 280,000 |
| Gross plant and equipment | 238,000 | 311,000 |
| Accumulated depreciation | (40,000) | (66,000) |
| Total assets | $473,000 | $525,000 |
| Accounts payable | $ 85,000 | $ 90,000 |
| Accrued liabilities | 68,000 | 63,000 |

| Total current debt | 153,000 | 153,000 |
|---|---|---|
| Mortgage payable | 70,000 | 0 |
| Preferred stock | 0 | 120,000 |
| Common stock | 205,000 | 205,000 |
| Retained earnings | 45,000 | 47,000 |
| Total debt and equity | $473,000 | $525,000 |

**Abrahams Manufacturing Company Income Statement for the Year Ended 12/31/2012**

| | 2012 |
|---|---|
| Sales | $184,000 |
| Cost of goods sold | 60,000 |
| Gross profit | $124,000 |
| Selling, general, and administrative expenses | 44,000 |
| Depreciation expense | 26,000 |
| Operating income | $ 54,000 |
| Interest expense | 4,000 |
| Earnings before taxes | $ 50,000 |
| Taxes | 16,000 |
| Preferred stock dividends | 10,000 |
| Earnings available to common shareholders | $ 24,000 |

*Additional Information*

1. The only entry in the accumulated depreciation account is for 2012 depreciation.
2. The firm paid $22,000 in common stock dividends during 2012.

**3-13.** (*Working with a statement of cash flows*) Prepare a statement of cash flows from the following scrambled list of items.

| | |
|---|---|
| Increase in inventories | $ 7,000 |
| Operating income | 219,000 |
| Dividends | 29,000 |
| Increase in accounts payable | 43,000 |
| Interest expense | 45,000 |
| Increase in common stock (par) | 5,000 |
| Depreciation expense | 17,000 |
| Increase in accounts receivable | 69,000 |
| Increase in long-term debt | 53,000 |
| Increase in short-term notes payable | 15,000 |
| Increase in gross fixed assets | 54,000 |
| Increase in paid in capital | 20,000 |
| Income taxes | 45,000 |
| Beginning cash | 250,000 |

**3-14.** (*Working with financial statements*) Given the information on page 90 for Pamplin Inc.:
   **a.** How much is the firm's net working capital and what is the debt ratio?
   **b.** Complete a common-sized income statement, a common-sized balance sheet, and a statement of cash flows for 2012. Interpret your results.

**Pamplin Inc. Balance Sheet at 12/31/2011 and 12/31/2012**

| ASSETS | | |
|---|---|---|
| | 2011 | 2012 |
| Cash | $ 200 | $ 150 |
| Accounts receivable | 450 | 425 |
| Inventory | 550 | 625 |
| Current assets | $1,200 | $1,200 |
| Plant and equipment | $2,200 | $2,600 |
| Less accumulated depreciation | (1,000) | (1,200) |
| Net plant and equipment | $1,200 | $1,400 |
| Total assets | $2,400 | $2,600 |

| LIABILITIES AND OWNERS' EQUITY | | |
|---|---|---|
| | 2011 | 2012 |
| Accounts payable | $ 200 | $ 150 |
| Notes payable—current (9%) | 0 | 150 |
| Current liabilities | $ 200 | $ 300 |
| Bonds | $ 600 | $ 600 |
| Owners' equity | | |
| Common stock | $ 900 | $ 900 |
| Retained earnings | 700 | 800 |
| Total owners' equity | $1,600 | $1,700 |
| Total liabilities and owners' equity | $2,400 | $2,600 |

**Pamplin Inc. Income Statement for Years Ended 12/31/2011 and 12/31/2012**

| | 2011 | | 2012 | |
|---|---|---|---|---|
| Sales | | $1,200 | | $1,450 |
| Cost of goods sold | | 700 | | 850 |
| Gross profit | | $ 500 | | $ 600 |
| Selling, general, and administrative expenses | $ 30 | | $ 40 | |
| Depreciation | 220 | 250 | 200 | 240 |
| Operating income | | $ 250 | | $ 360 |
| Interest expense | | $ 50 | | 64 |
| Net income before taxes | | $ 200 | | $ 296 |
| Taxes (40%) | | 80 | | 118 |
| Net income | | $ 120 | | $ 178 |

**3-15.** (*Working with financial statements*) Based on the information for T. P. Jarmon Company for the year ended December 31, 2012:

    a. How much is the firm's net working capital and what is the debt ratio?

    b. Complete a statement of cash flows for the period. Interpret your results.

    c. Compute the changes in the balance sheets from 2011 to 2012. What do you learn about T. P. Jarmon from these computations? How do these numbers relate to the statement of cash flows?

**T. P. Jarmon Company Balance Sheet for 12/31/2011 and 12/31/2012**

| ASSETS | 2011 | 2012 |
| --- | --- | --- |
| Cash | $ 15,000 | $ 14,000 |
| Marketable securities | 6,000 | 6,200 |
| Accounts receivable | 42,000 | 33,000 |
| Inventory | 51,000 | 84,000 |
| Prepaid rent | $ 1,200 | $ 1,100 |
| Total current assets | $115,200 | $138,300 |
| Net plant and equipment | 286,000 | 270,000 |
| Total assets | $401,200 | $408,300 |

| LIABILITIES AND EQUITY | 2011 | 2012 |
| --- | --- | --- |
| Accounts payable | $ 48,000 | $ 57,000 |
| Accruals | 6,000 | 5,000 |
| Notes payable | 15,000 | 13,000 |
| Total current liabilities | $ 69,000 | $ 75,000 |
| Long-term debt | $160,000 | $150,000 |
| Common stockholders' equity | $172,200 | $183,300 |
| Total liabilities and equity | $401,200 | $408,300 |

**T. P. Jarmon Company Income Statement for the Year Ended 12/31/2012**

| | | |
| --- | --- | --- |
| Sales | | $600,000 |
| Less cost of goods sold | | 460,000 |
| Gross profit | | $140,000 |
| Operating and interest expenses | | |
| General and administrative | $30,000 | |
| Interest | 10,000 | |
| Depreciation | 30,000 | |
| Total operating and interest expenses | | $ 70,000 |
| Earnings before taxes | | $ 70,000 |
| Taxes | | 27,100 |
| Net income available to common stockholders | | $ 42,900 |
| Cash dividends | | 31,800 |
| Change in retained earnings | | $ 11,100 |

**3-16.** (*Computing income taxes*) The William B. Waugh Corporation is a regional Toyota dealer. The firm sells new and used trucks and is actively involved in the parts business. During the most recent year, the company generated sales of $3 million. The combined cost of goods sold and the operating expenses were $2.1 million. Also, $400,000 in interest expense was paid during the year. Calculate the corporation's tax liability.

**3-17.** (*Computing income taxes*) Sales for L. B. Menielle Inc. during the past year amounted to $5 million. The firm provides parts and supplies for oil field service companies. Gross profits for the year were $3 million. Operating expenses totaled $1 million. The interest income from the securities it owned was $20,000. The firm's interest expense was $100,000. Compute the corporation's tax liability.

**3-18.** (*Computing income taxes*) Sandersen Inc. sells minicomputers. During the past year, the company's sales were $3 million. The cost of its merchandise sold came to $2 million, and cash operating expenses were $400,000; depreciation expense was $100,000, and the firm paid $150,000 in interest on its bank loans. Also, the corporation paid $25,000 in the form of dividends to its own common stockholders. Calculate the corporation's tax liability.

# Mini Case

*This Mini Case is available in MyFinanceLab.*

In July 2011, the finale to the Harry Potter movie series, *Harry Potter and the Deathly Hallows— Part 2*, from Time Warner Inc.'s Warner Bros. Pictures, earned an estimated $307 million in 59 countries overseas for the opening week, topping the previous best international debut of $260.4 million set in May 2011 by Disney's *Pirates of the Caribbean: On Stranger Tides*. Time Warner Inc. and Walt Disney Co. both run diversified lines of entertainment and are major competitors with each other in many areas. According to Disney's annual report of fiscal 2010: "The Walt Disney Company, together with its subsidiaries, is a diversified worldwide entertainment company with operations in five business segments: Media Networks, Parks and Resorts, Studio Entertainment, Consumer Products and Interactive Media." And in the annual report of Time Warner: "Time Warner Inc., a Delaware corporation, is a leading media and entertainment company. The Company classifies its businesses into the following three reporting segments: Networks, Filmed Entertainment, and Publishing." Except for parks and resorts, Time Warner runs almost the same business lines as Disney.[13]

Below are the financial statements for the two firms. Time Warner's fiscal year ends on December 31; thus, the statements are for end-of-year 2009 and 2010. Disney, on the other hand, has a fiscal year ending on the Saturday closest to September 30; fiscal year 2009 ended on October 3, 2009, and fiscal year 2010 ended on October 2, 2010. As a result, Disney's financials are 3 months earlier than the financials for Time Warner.

a. How did Time Warner's profit margins change from 2009 to 2010? To what would you attribute the differences? Answer the same questions for Disney.
b. Compare the profit margins between Time Warner and Disney. How are they different? How would you explain these differences?
c. What differences do you notice in the common-sized balance sheets that might indicate that one of the firms is doing better than the other?
d. Conduct an Internet search on the two firms to gain additional insights as to causes of the financial differences between the firms in 2010 and continuing into 2011.
e. How are the two companies doing financially today?

**Time Warner Inc. Annual Income Statement and Common-Sized Income Statement for Years Ending December 31, 2009 and 2010 (in $ millions except earnings per share)**

|  | 2009 | | 2010 | |
|---|---|---|---|---|
|  | Dollar value | Percentage of sales | Dollar value | Percentage of sales |
| Sales | $25,388 | 100.0% | $26,888 | 100.0% |
| Cost of goods sold | 14,235 | 56.1% | 15,023 | 55.9% |
| Gross profits | $11,153 | 43.9% | $11,865 | 44.1% |
| Selling, general, and administrative expenses | 6,073 | 23.9% | 6,126 | 22.8% |
| Depreciation and amortization | 280 | 1.1% | 264 | 1.0% |
| Other operating expenses | 330 | 1.3% | 47 | 0.2% |
| Operating income | $ 4,470 | 17.6% | $ 5,428 | 20.2% |
| Interest expense | 1,166 | 4.6% | 1,178 | 4.4% |
| Nonoperating income (expenses) | (67) | −0.3% | (331) | −1.2% |
| Earnings before tax | $ 3,237 | 12.8% | $ 3,919 | 14.6% |
| Income taxes | 1,153 | 4.5% | 1,348 | 5.0% |
| Net income (loss) | $ 2,084 | 8.2% | $ 2,571 | 9.6% |
| | | | | |
| Common shares outstanding | 1,184.0 | | 1,128.4 | |
| Earnings per share | $ 1.76 | | $ 2.28 | |

Source: The Time Warner Cable 2010 Annual Report.

[13]Time Warner classifies its interactive media business as a part of the "Filmed Entertainment," and for Disney, publishing is a part of its "Consumer Products." Source: The Walt Disney Co. Fiscal Year 2010 Form 10-K.

**Time Warner Inc. Balance Sheet and Common-Sized Balance Sheet for Years Ending December 31, 2009 and 2010 ($ millions)**

| | DECEMBER 31, 2009 | | DECEMBER 31, 2010 | |
|---|---|---|---|---|
| ASSETS | Dollar value | Percentage of total assets | Dollar value | Percentage of total assets |
| Cash and short-term investments | $ 4,733 | 7.2% | $ 3,663 | 5.5% |
| Receivables | 5,875 | 8.9% | 6,413 | 9.6% |
| Inventories | 1,769 | 2.7% | 1,920 | 2.9% |
| Other current assets | 1,315 | 2.0% | 1,142 | 1.7% |
| Total current assets | $ 13,692 | 20.7% | $ 13,138 | 19.7% |
| Gross fixed assets | $ 14,950 | 22.6% | $ 15,824 | 23.8% |
| Accumulated depreciation and amortization | (3,732) | −5.6% | (4,169) | −6.3% |
| Net fixed assets | $ 11,218 | 17.0% | $ 11,655 | 17.5% |
| Other assets | 41,149 | 62.3% | 41,731 | 62.7% |
| TOTAL ASSETS | $ 66,059 | 100.0% | $ 66,524 | 100.0% |
| | | | | |
| LIABILITIES | | | | |
| Accounts payable and accruals | $ 7,807 | 11.8% | $ 7,733 | 11.6% |
| Short-term notes payable | 862 | 1.3% | 26 | 0.0% |
| Other current liabilities | 804 | 1.2% | 884 | 1.3% |
| Total current liabilities | $ 9,473 | 14.3% | $ 8,643 | 13.0% |
| Long-term debt | 15,346 | 23.2% | 16,523 | 24.8% |
| Deferred taxes | 1,607 | 2.4% | 1,950 | 2.9% |
| Other liabilities | 6,236 | 9.4% | 6,463 | 9.7% |
| TOTAL LIABILITIES | $ 32,662 | 49.4% | $ 33,579 | 50.5% |
| | | | | |
| EQUITY | | | | |
| Common equity: | | | | |
| Common stock: | | | | |
| Par value | $ 16 | 0.0% | $ 16 | 0.0% |
| Capital surplus | 158,129 | 239.4% | 157,146 | 236.2% |
| Total common stock sold | $158,145 | 239.4% | $157,162 | 236.2% |
| Less: Treasury stock—total dollar amount | (27,034) | −40.9% | (29,033) | −43.6% |
| Total common stock | $131,111 | 198.5% | $128,129 | 192.6% |
| Retained earnings | (97,714) | (147.9%) | (95,184) | (143.1%) |
| Total common equity | $ 33,397 | 50.6% | $ 32,945 | 49.5% |
| TOTAL LIABILITIES AND STOCKHOLDERS' EQUITY | $ 66,059 | 100.0% | $ 66,524 | 100.0% |

Source: The Time Warner Cable 2010 Annual Report.

**Walt Disney Co. Annual Income Statement and Common-Sized Income Statement for Years Ending October 3, 2009 and October 2, 2010 (in $ millions except earnings per share)**

|  | 2009 | | 2010 | |
|---|---|---|---|---|
|  | Dollar value | Percentage of sales | Dollar value | Percentage of sales |
| Sales | $36,149 | 100.0% | $38,063 | 100.0% |
| Cost of goods sold | 28,821 | 79.7% | 29,624 | 77.8% |
| Gross profits | $ 7,328 | 20.3% | $ 8,439 | 22.2% |
| Selling, general, and administrative expenses | 2,123 | 5.9% | 1,983 | 5.2% |
| Operating income | $ 5,205 | 14.4% | $ 6,456 | 17.0% |
| Interest expense | 466 | 1.3% | 409 | 1.1% |
| Nonoperating income (expenses) | 919 | 2.5% | 580 | 1.5% |
| Earnings before tax | $ 5,658 | 15.7% | $ 6,627 | 17.4% |
| Income taxes | 2,049 | 5.7% | 2,314 | 6.1% |
| Net income (loss) | $ 3,609 | 10.0% | $ 4,313 | 11.3% |
| Common shares outstanding | 1,875 | | 1,948 | |
| Earnings per share | $ 1.92 | | $ 2.21 | |

Source: Data from The Walt Disney Company's 2010 Annual Financial Report.

**Walt Disney Co. Balance Sheet and Common-Sized Balance Sheet for Years Ending October 3, 2009 and October 2, 2010 ($ millions)**

| ASSETS | OCTOBER 3, 2009 | | OCTOBER 2, 2010 | |
|---|---|---|---|---|
|  | Dollar value | Percentage of total assets | Dollar value | Percentage of total assets |
| Cash and cash equivalents | $ 3,417 | 5.4% | $ 2,722 | 3.9% |
| Receivables | 4,854 | 7.7% | 5,784 | 8.4% |
| Inventories | 1,271 | 2.0% | 1,442 | 2.1% |
| Other current assets | 2,347 | 3.7% | 2,277 | 3.3% |
| Total current assets | $11,889 | 18.8% | $12,225 | 17.7% |
| Gross fixed assets | $32,475 | 51.5% | $32,875 | 47.5% |
| Accumulated depreciation and amortization | (17,395) | −27.6% | (18,373) | −26.5% |
| Net fixed assets | $15,080 | 23.9% | $14,502 | 21.0% |
| Other assets | 36,148 | 57.3% | 42,479 | 61.4% |
| TOTAL ASSETS | $63,117 | 100.0% | $69,206 | 100.0% |
| | | | | |
| **LIABILITIES** | | | | |
| Accounts payable and accruals | $ 5,616 | 8.9% | $ 6,109 | 8.8% |
| Short-term notes payable | 1,206 | 1.9% | 2,350 | 3.4% |
| Other current liabilities | 2,112 | 3.3% | 2,541 | 3.7% |
| Total current liabilities | $ 8,934 | 14.2% | $11,000 | 15.9% |
| Long-term debt | 11,495 | 18.2% | 10,130 | 14.6% |
| Deferred taxes | 1,819 | 2.9% | 2,630 | 3.8% |
| Other liabilities | 5,444 | 8.6% | 6,104 | 8.8% |
| TOTAL LIABILITIES | $27,692 | 43.9% | $29,864 | 43.2% |
| | | | | |
| **EQUITY** | | | | |
| Common equity: | | | | |
| Total common stock sold | $27,038 | 42.8% | $28,736 | 41.5% |
| Less: Treasury stock—total dollar amount | (22,693) | −36.0% | (23,663) | −34.2% |
| Total common stock | $ 4,345 | 6.9% | $ 5,073 | 7.3% |
| Retained earnings | 31,033 | 49.2% | 34,327 | 49.6% |
| Other equity | 47 | 0.1% | (58) | −0.1% |
| Total common equity | $35,425 | 56.1% | $39,342 | 56.8% |
| TOTAL LIABILITIES AND STOCKHOLDERS' EQUITY | $63,117 | 100.0% | $69,206 | 100.0% |

Source: Data from The Walt Disney Company's 2010 Annual Financial Report.

## Appendix 3A

LO7 Calculate a firm's free cash flows and financing cash flows.

# Free Cash Flows

During recent years, free cash flow has come to be viewed by many executives as an important measure of a firm's performance. Jack Welch, the former CEO of General Electric, explains the importance of free cash flows to management in these words:

> [T]here's cash flow, which is valuable because it just does not lie. All your other profit-and-loss numbers, like net income, have some art to them. They've been massaged through the accounting process, which is filled with assumptions. But free cash flow tells you the true condition of the business.[14]

## What Is a Free Cash Flow?

We can think of a firm as a group of assets that produce cash flow. Once the firm has paid all its operating expenses and made all its investments, the remaining cash flows are *free* to be distributed to the firm's creditors and shareholders—thus, the term *free cash flows*. Being more specific, a company's *free* cash flows result from two activities:

1. *After-tax cash flows from operations* are the cash flows a firm generates from day-to-day operations after taxes are paid but before any investments in working capital or long-term assets are made. While not exactly true, you may think of it as the cash flows of a business if it were not getting larger or smaller in size. (You should note that when computing free cash flows, the term *cash flows from operations* is not the same as in the statement of cash flows presented earlier in the chapter.)

2. *Asset investments*, which include investments in (1) a company's *net operating working capital* and (2) its long-term assets. For the first item, *net operating working capital*, understand that this term is not exactly the same as *net working capital* described earlier in the chapter. The insertion of the word *operating* will change the meaning of the term. So watch for the subtle difference as you learn to compute free cash flows.

## Computing Free Cash Flow

Simply stated, free cash flows are calculated as follows:

$$
\begin{array}{c}
\text{Free cash} \\
\text{flow}
\end{array}
=
\left[
\begin{array}{c}
\text{after-tax} \\
\text{cash flows from operations}
\end{array}
\right]
$$

$$
less
\left[
\begin{array}{c}
\text{increase in} \\
\text{net operating} \\
\text{working capital}
\end{array}
\right]
or\ plus
\left[
\begin{array}{c}
\text{decrease in} \\
\text{net operating} \\
\text{working capital}
\end{array}
\right]
\qquad (3\text{-}1A)
$$

and

$$
less
\left[
\begin{array}{c}
\text{increase in} \\
\text{long-term assets}
\end{array}
\right]
or\ plus
\left[
\begin{array}{c}
\text{decrease in} \\
\text{long-term assets}
\end{array}
\right]
$$

[14]Source: "How Healthy Is Your Company?" by Jack and Suzy Welch from *Bloomberg Businessweek*, May 8, 2006.

So the procedure for computing a firm's free cash flows involves three steps:

1. Compute the after-tax cash flows from operations by converting the income statement from an accrual basis to a cash basis. But be aware that when computing free cash flows, the term *cash flows from operations* is not the same as in the statement of cash flows.
2. Calculate the increase or decrease in the firm's investment in **net operating working capital**. As already mentioned, net working capital is now called *net operating working capital*, which we will explain shortly.
3. Compute the increase or decrease in investments made in long-term assets, including fixed assets and other long-term assets (such as intangible assets).

Let's look at each of the steps involved in calculating free cash flows.

**STEP 1** *Determine the after-tax cash flows from operations*, computed as follows:

| |
|---|
| Operating income (earnings before interest and taxes, or EBIT) |
| + depreciation expense<br>− income tax expense[15]<br>= after-tax cash flows from operations |

Thus, we compute after-tax cash flows from operations by adding back depreciation expense to operating income, because depreciation expense is not a cash expense, and then subtracting taxes to get the cash flows on an after-tax basis.

To illustrate how to compute a firm's after-tax cash flows from operations, return to the Home Depot's income statement in Table 3-1 on page 54, where we find the following information expressed in $ millions:

| | |
|---|---|
| Operating income (EBIT) | $ 5,803 |
| Depreciation expense | 1,616 |
| Income tax expense | 1,935 |

Given this information, we find Home Depot's after-tax cash flows from operations to be $5.484 billion, computed as follows:

| | |
|---|---|
| Operating income (EBIT) | $ 5,803 |
| Plus depreciation | 1,616 |
| Less income tax expense | (1,935) |
| After-tax cash flows from operations | $ 5,484 |

**STEP 2** *Calculate the change in the net operating working capital.* For the second step, the change in net operating working capital is equal to the:

$$\begin{bmatrix} \text{change in} \\ \text{current assets} \end{bmatrix} - \begin{bmatrix} \text{change in} \\ \text{non-interest-bearing} \\ \text{current liabilities} \end{bmatrix}$$

[15]We should be subtracting actual taxes paid, which is frequently different from the income-tax expense shown in the income statement. But let's just keep things simple and assume they are the same for Home Depot.

where non-interest-bearing current liabilities are any short-term liabilities that do not require the firm to pay interest. This typically includes accounts payable (credit provided by the firm's suppliers) and any accrued operating expenses, such as accrued wages.

For Home Depot, the increase or decrease in *net operating working capital* is found by looking at the firm's balance sheets on January 31, 2010 and January 30, 2011 in Table 3-2, where we see that:

|  | JAN 31, 2010 | JAN 30, 2011 | CHANGES |
|---|---|---|---|
| Current assets | $13,900 | $13,479 | ($421) |
| Accounts payable* | 9,343 | 9,080 | (263) |
| Net operating working capital | $ 4,557 | $ 4,399 | ($158) |

*Accounts payable is Home Depot's non-interest-bearing debt.

Thus, Home Depot reduced its investments in current assets by $421 million and decreased (paid off) $263 million in accounts payable. *It is important to remember that a decrease in an asset is a cash inflow and a decrease in a liability is a cash outflow*. So, in net, there was a reduction in net operating working capital, resulting in a cash inflow of $158 million ($158 million net cash inflow = $421 million cash inflow from reducing current assets − $263 million outflow from payments to creditors).

**STEP 3** *Compute the change in long-term assets*. The final step involves computing the change in *gross* fixed assets (not *net* fixed assets) and other long-term assets. Again returning to the Home Depot's balance sheets, we see that there was an increase in gross fixed assets of $1.126 billion from $37.345 to $38.471 billion and an increase in other assets of $159 million from $1.427 to $1.586 billion. So Home Depot invested a total of $1.285 billion in long-term assets, the total of $1.126 billion and $159 million.

*Wrapping up*. We now have the three pieces to compute Home Depot's free cash flows: (1) after-tax cash flows from operations, (2) changes (investments) in net operating working capital, and (3) changes (investments) in long-term assets. As shown below (expressed in millions), the firm's free cash flows are $4.357 billion.

|  |  | $ MILLIONS |
|---|---|---|
| After-tax cash flows from operations |  | $5,484 |
| Less investments in net operating working capital |  | (158) |
| Investment in long-term assets: |  |  |
| Investment in fixed assets | ($1,126) |  |
| Investment in other assets | (159) |  |
| Total investments in long-term assets |  | ($1,285) |
| Free cash flows |  | $4,357 |

Given these computations, we see that the firm's free cash flows were *positive* in the amount of $4.357 billion, as a result of:

1. Generating $5.484 billion in after-tax cash flows from operations,
2. Reducing its investments in net working capital by $158 million, and
3. Investing $1.285 billion in plant and equipment and other long-term assets.

# The Other Side of the Coin: Financing Cash Flows

In the previous section, we saw that Home Depot's operations generated more than enough to finance its growth. So the question becomes, "What did Home Depot do with all the extra cash?" The answer: Positive free cash flows are distributed to the firm's investors. Negative free cash flows require that investors infuse money into the business. As we explain in the next section, any money coming from or paid to investors is called financing cash flows.

## Financing Cash Flows

A firm can either receive money from or distribute money to its investors, or some of both. In general, cash flows between investors and the firm, which we will call *financing cash flows*, occur in one of four ways. The firm can:

1. Pay interest to lenders.
2. Pay dividends to stockholders.
3. Increase or decrease interest-bearing debt.
4. Issue new stock to shareholders or repurchase stock from current investors.

When we speak of *investors* in this context, we include both lenders and shareholders. However, we do *not* include financing provided by non-interest-bearing current liabilities, such as accounts payable, which were recognized earlier as part of the firm's net operating working capital.

We will now return to Home Depot to illustrate the process for calculating the firm's financing cash flows, which will also let us determine how the $4.357 billion free cash flows that Home Depot experienced were distributed.

To compute the financing cash flows for Home Depot, we first determine the interest expense paid to lenders and the dividends paid to shareholders, which are provided in the firm's income statement (Table 3-1). We then refer to the balance sheet (Table 3-2) to see the changes in interest-bearing debt (both short-term and long-term) and common stock. The results are as follows:

| | | |
|---|---:|---|
| Interest paid to lenders | $ (530) | Use of cash |
| Common stock dividends | (1,569) | Use of cash |
| Change in interest-bearing debt: | | |
| Increase in short-term debt | 22 | Source of cash |
| Decrease in long-term debt | (7) | Use of cash |
| Change in equity: | | |
| Increase in common stock (par value + paid-in capital) | 335 | Source of cash |
| Repurchased common stock (treasury stock) | (2,608) | Use of cash |
| Financing cash flows | $(4,357) | |

So, the firm:

◆ Paid $530 million in interest and $1.569 billion in dividends.
◆ Spent $2.608 billion to repurchase outstanding common stock.
◆ Borrowed (increased) $22 million in short-term interest-bearing debt and paid back (reduced) $7 million of its long-term interest-bearing debt.
◆ Received $335 million by issuing new common stock.

Add it all up and Home Depot distributed a net amount of $4.357 billion to its creditors and shareholders. You should take a minute to compare this amount with the $3.827 billion shown as financing activities in Home Depot's statement of cash flows on page 72. By doing so, you will see that the difference is $530 million, which is exactly the amount of interest paid to lenders. Again, in the statement of cash flows, interest expense is included in operating cash flows, which is not the case here.

# A Concluding Thought

It is not a coincidence that Home Depot's free cash flows exactly equal its financing cash flows. They will always be equal. The firm's free cash flows, if positive, will be the amount distributed to the investors; and if the free cash flow is negative, it will be the amount that the investors provide to the firm to cover the shortage in free cash flows.

Based on our review of Home Depot's free cash flows and financing cash flows, we know that the company had significant positive cash flows from operations, more than enough to cover its investments and distribute large sums of money to its investors.

# Appendix Summary

## Calculate a firm's free cash flows and financing cash flows.  (pgs. 95–101)

**SUMMARY:** Free cash flows and financing cash flows are important measurements in making financial decisions. Only by understanding these cash flows can managers truly know how well a company is doing.

### KEY EQUATION

$$\text{Free cash flow} = \left[\begin{array}{c}\text{after-tax} \\ \text{cash flows from operations}\end{array}\right]$$

$$\textit{less} \left[\begin{array}{c}\text{increase in} \\ \text{net operating} \\ \text{working capital}\end{array}\right] \textit{or plus} \left[\begin{array}{c}\text{decrease in} \\ \text{net operating} \\ \text{working capital}\end{array}\right] \text{ and}$$

$$\textit{less} \left[\begin{array}{c}\text{increase in} \\ \text{long-term assets}\end{array}\right] \textit{or plus} \left[\begin{array}{c}\text{decrease in} \\ \text{long-term assets}\end{array}\right]$$

# Study Problems

*All Study Problems are available in* MyFinanceLab.

**3A-1** (*Computing free cash flows*) Given the following information, compute the firm's free cash flows and the financing cash flows.

| | |
|---|---|
| Dividends | $ 25 |
| Change in common stock | $ 27 |
| Change in inventories | $ 32 |
| Change in accounts receivable | $ 78 |
| Change in other current assets | $ 25 |
| Operating income | $215 |
| Interest expense | $ 50 |
| Depreciation expense | $ 20 |
| Increase in accounts payable | $ 48 |
| Increase in gross fixed assets | $ 55 |
| Income taxes | $ 45 |

**3A-2** (*Free cash flow analysis*) Interpret the following information regarding Bates Corporation's free cash flows and financing cash flows.

**Maness Corporation Free Cash Flows and Financing Cash Flows**

| FREE CASH FLOWS | | |
|---|---|---|
| Operating income (EBIT) | | $ 954 |
| Depreciation expense | | 60 |
| Tax expense | | (320) |
| After-tax cash flows from operations | | $ 694 |
| Increase in net working capital: | | |
|   Increase in current assets | ($899) | |
|   Increase in accounts payable | 175 | |
|   Increase in net working capital | | ($ 724) |
| Change in long-term assets: | | |
|   Decrease in fixed assets | | 2,161 |
| Free cash flows | | $2,131 |

| FINANCING CASH FLOWS | |
|---|---|
| Interest paid to lenders | ($ 364) |
| Repayment of long-term debt | (850) |
| Repurchase of common stock | (1,024) |
| Common stock dividends | (1,341) |
| Financing cash flows | ($3,579) |

**3A-3** (*Computing free cash flows and financing cash flows*) In Problem 3-12, you were asked to prepare a statement of cash flows for Abrahams Manufacturing Company. Use the information given in the problem to compute the firm's free cash flows and the financing cash flows, and interpret your results.

**3A-4** (*Computing free cash flows and financing cash flows*) In Problem 3-14, you were asked to prepare a statement of cash flows for Pamplin Inc. Pamplin's financial statements are provided again below. Using this information, compute the firm's free cash flows and the financing cash flows, and interpret your results.

**Pamplin Inc. Balance Sheet at 12/31/2011 and 12/31/2012**

| ASSETS | | |
|---|---|---|
| | 2011 | 2012 |
| Cash | $ 200 | $ 150 |
| Accounts receivable | 450 | 425 |
| Inventory | 550 | 625 |
| Current assets | $1,200 | $1,200 |
| Plant and equipment | $2,200 | $2,600 |
|   Less accumulated depreciation | (1,000) | (1,200) |
| Net plant and equipment | $1,200 | $1,400 |
| Total assets | $2,400 | $2,600 |

| LIABILITIES AND OWNERS' EQUITY | | |
|---|---|---|
| | 2011 | 2012 |
| Accounts payable | $ 200 | $ 150 |
| Notes payable—current (9%) | 0 | 150 |
| Current liabilities | $ 200 | $ 300 |
| Bonds | $ 600 | $ 600 |
| Owners' equity | | |
| Common stock | $ 900 | $ 900 |
| Retained earnings | 700 | 800 |
| Total owners' equity | $1,600 | $1,700 |
| Total liabilities and owners' equity | $2,400 | $2,600 |

**Pamplin Inc. Income Statement for Years Ended 12/31/2011 and 12/31/2012**

| | | 2011 | | 2012 |
|---|---|---|---|---|
| Sales | | $1,200 | | $1,450 |
| Cost of goods sold | | 700 | | 850 |
| Gross profit | | $ 500 | | $ 600 |
| Selling, general, and administrative expenses | $ 30 | | $ 40 | |
| Depreciation | 220 | 250 | 200 | 240 |
| Operating income | | $ 250 | | $ 360 |
| Interest expense | | $ 50 | | 64 |
| Net income before taxes | | $ 200 | | $ 296 |
| Taxes (40%) | | 80 | | 118 |
| Net income | | $ 120 | | $ 178 |

# 4

# Evaluating a Firm's Financial Performance

## Learning Objectives

 **1** **Explain** the purpose and importance of financial analysis.　　**The Purpose of Financial Analysis**

 **2** **Calculate** and use a comprehensive set of measurements to evaluate a company's performance.　　**Measuring Key Financial Relationships**

 **3** **Describe** the limitations of financial ratio analysis.　　**The Limitations of Financial Ratio Analysis**

As introduced in Chapter 3, you are giving serious consideration to joining the Home Depot, Inc. after graduation. You have been offered a position in marketing that you believe fits both your educational background and interests. Your Uncle Harry suggested that you learn more about the company's financial position by studying the firm's 10-K filed with the Securities and Exchange Commission, which you have done. You have studied the three financial statements provided by Home Depot but now want to dig deeper to interpret the information in the statements. You wonder how else you can use Home Depot's financial statements to evaluate the firm's financial strengths and weaknesses. Also, you wonder how you might compare Home Depot's financial performance with that of Lowe's, Inc., a major competitor.

As it turns out, this chapter is a natural extension of Chapter 3. It will help you evaluate a firm's financial performance in the same way as is done by any group having a financial interest in a business, including managers, employees, lenders, and shareholders. Specifically, we will look at key financial relationships, in the form of ratios, as a way to gain a better understanding of a company's financial performance—what we might call *financial analysis*. Before presenting the specific methods, let's start by first understanding the basic purpose and intent of conducting financial analysis.

 **1** Explain the purpose and importance of financial analysis.

## The Purpose of Financial Analysis

As explained in Chapter 1, the fundamental objective of financial management is not to focus on accounting numbers like earnings, but to create shareholder value. In a perfect world, we would rely totally on market values of a firm's assets to guide decision-making, rather than on its accounting data. However, since we rarely have market values for all of a firm's assets, accounting information can be a very useful substitute.

To begin, realize that financial analysis is about more than reviewing financial statements; it can be used both to evaluate historical performance and to serve as the basis for making projections about and improving future financial performance. The analysis helps us see critical relationships that might not otherwise be readily identifiable. Ratios are used to standardize financial information so that we can make comparisons. Otherwise, it is really difficult to compare the financial statements of two firms of different sizes or even of the same firm at different times.

**Financial ratios** give us two ways of making meaningful comparisons of a firm's financial data: (1) We can examine the ratios across time (say, for the past 5 years) to compare a firm's current and past performance; and (2) we can compare the firm's ratios with those of other firms. In comparing a firm with other companies, we could select a peer group of companies or we could use industry norms published by firms such as Dun & Bradstreet, Risk Management Association (RMA), Standard & Poor's, Value Line, and Prentice Hall. Dun & Bradstreet, for instance, annually publishes a set of 14 key ratios for each of 125 lines of business. The Risk Management Association (the association of bank loan and credit officers) publishes a set of 16 key ratios for more than 350 lines of business. The firms are grouped according to the North American Industrial Classification System (NAICS) codes. They are also segmented by firm size to provide the basis for more meaningful comparisons.

Figure 4-1 (on page 104) shows the financial statement information as reported by Risk Management Association for Software Publishers. The report shows the information by two asset-size and sales-size categories. The complete report (not provided here) presents other size categories. The balance sheet data in the report are provided as a percentage of total assets, or as what we called in Chapter 3 a *common-sized balance sheet*. Likewise, the income statement data are reported as a percentage of sales as a *common-sized income statement*.[1] In presenting the financial ratios in the bottom portion of the report, RMA gives three results for each ratio, representing the firms at the 75th, 50th, and 25th percentiles, respectively.

Financial analysis is not a tool just for financial managers; it can also be used effectively by investors, lenders, suppliers, employees, and customers. Within the firm, managers use financial ratios to:

◆ Identify deficiencies in the firm's performance and take corrective action.

◆ Evaluate employee performance and determine incentive compensation.

**financial ratios** accounting data restated in relative terms in order to help people identify some of the financial strengths and weaknesses of a company.

### REMEMBER YOUR PRINCIPLES

**Principle** As in Chapter 3 when we talked about financial statements, a primary rationale for evaluating a company's financial performance relates to **Principle 5: Conflicts of Interest Cause Agency Problems**. Thus, the firm's common stockholders need information that can be used to monitor managers' actions. Interpreting the firm's financial statements through the use of financial ratios is a key monitoring tool. Of course, the firm's managers also need metrics to monitor the company's performance so that corrective actions can be taken when necessary.

**Principle 4: Market Prices Are Generally Right** is also relevant when it comes to evaluating a firm's financial performance. Only if there are exceptionally profitable markets, where investments earn rates of return that exceed the opportunity cost of the money invested, can managers create shareholder value. Furthermore, financial ratios can help us have a sense of whether managers have indeed made exceptionally good investments or bad ones.

Finally, **Principle 3: Risk Requires a Reward** is also at work in this chapter. As we will see, how managers choose to finance the business affects the company's risk and, as a result, the rate of return stockholders receive on their investments.

[1] In Chapter 3, we presented a common-sized income statement and common-sized balance sheet for Home Depot. (See pages 54 and 61.)

## FIGURE 4-1   Financial Statement Data by Industry: Norms for Software Publishers

### INFORMATION—SOFTWARE PUBLISHERS NAICS 511210

| CURRENT DATA SORTED BY ASSETS 50-100MM % | 100-250MM % | ASSETS | CURRENT DATA SORTED BY SALES 10-25MM % | 25MM and OVER % |
|---|---|---|---|---|
| 23.3 | 14.6 | Cash and Equivalents | 24.6 | 23.0 |
| 17.3 | 13.8 | Trade Receivables (net) | 32.3 | 20.0 |
| 2.7 | 0.6 | Inventory | 1.3 | 1.9 |
| 8.1 | 5.4 | All Other Current | 7.0 | 6.9 |
| 51.3 | 34.4 | Total Current | 65.3 | 51.8 |
| 7.6 | 5.0 | Fixed Assets (net) | 9.1 | 7.2 |
| 34.9 | 51.8 | Intangibles (net) | 16.1 | 34.1 |
| 6.2 | 8.8 | All Other Non-current | 9.6 | 6.9 |
| 100.0 | 100.0 | Total | 100.0 | 100.0 |
| | | **LIABILITIES** | | |
| 0.2 | 0.5 | Notes Payable Short Term | 3.9 | 1.9 |
| 4.4 | 2.0 | Cur. Mat.-L/T/D | 11.9 | 2.9 |
| 5.1 | 5.4 | Trade Payables | 11.9 | 7.8 |
| 0.4 | 0.5 | Income Taxes Payable | 0.9 | 1.0 |
| 29.9 | 23.5 | All Other Current | 34.6 | 30.3 |
| 40.0 | 31.9 | Total Current | 63.3 | 46.9 |
| 20.7 | 24.6 | Long Term Debt | 8.3 | 21.7 |
| 1.1 | 3.4 | Deferred Taxes | 0.4 | 2.0 |
| 14.1 | 15.1 | All Other Non-current | 12.3 | 12.5 |
| 24.1 | 25.0 | Net Worth | 15.8 | 19.9 |
| | | Total Liabilities | | |
| 100.0 | 100.0 | and Net Worth | 100.0 | 100.0 |
| | | **INCOME DATA** | | |
| 100.0 | 100.0 | Net Sales | 100.0 | 100.0 |
| 89.3 | 93.1 | Operating Expenses | 95.9 | 92.1 |
| 10.7 | 6.9 | Operating Profit | 4.1 | 7.9 |
| | | All Other | | |
| 6.4 | 6.5 | Expenses (net) | 2.3 | 5.0 |
| 4.4 | 0.4 | Profit Before Taxes | 1.7 | 2.9 |
| | | **RATIOS** | | |
| 1.8 | 1.5 | | 2.1 | 1.8 |
| 1.2 | 1.1 | Current | 1.1 | 1.2 |
| 0.9 | 0.8 | | 0.8 | 0.8 |
| 1.5 | 1.2 | | 1.9 | 1.4 |
| 1.0 | 0.9 | Quick | (768) 0.9 | (1302) 1.0 |
| 0.6 | 0.6 | | 0.6 | 0.6 |

| CURRENT DATA SORTED BY ASSETS 50-100MM | | 100-250MM | | RATIOS | CURRENT DATA SORTED BY SALES 10-25MM | | 25MM and OVER | |
|---|---|---|---|---|---|---|---|---|
| | % | | % | | | % | | % |
| 45 | 8.1 | 47 | 7.7 | | 47 | 7.8 | 42 | 8.6 |
| 61 | 6.0 | 62 | 5.9 | Sales/Receivables | 61 | 6.0 | 58 | 6.3 |
| 97 | 3.8 | 82 | 4.5 | | 83 | 4.4 | 71 | 4.7 |
| | 3.0 | | 6.7 | | | 4.4 | | 5.5 |
| | 13.2 | | 30.2 | Sales/Working Capital | | 27.2 | | 18.1 |
| | −15.6 | | −8.2 | | | −18.2 | | −12.7 |
| | 7.0 | | 2.7 | | | 14.0 | | 6.9 |
| (31) | 4.0 | (49) | 10.9 | EBIT/Interest | (31) | 2.7 | (118) | 1.4 |
| | −0.9 | | −1.8 | | | −4.6 | | −1.2 |
| | 2.8 | | | | | 18.9 | | 3.8 |
| (14) | 1.3 | | | Net Profit+Depr., Dep., Amort./Cur. Mat. L/T/D | (10) | 2.3 | (34) | 1.5 |
| | 0.2 | | | | | 0.3 | | 0.2 |
| | −0.4 | | 0.3 | | | 0.1 | | 0.2 |
| | −0.4 | | −0.1 | Fixed Assets/Net Worth | | 1.0 | | −2.6 |
| | −0.1 | | 0.0 | | | −0.1 | | −0.1 |
| | 2.6 | | 4.0 | | | 1.4 | | 1.9 |
| | −7.4 | | −2.0 | Debt/Net Worth | | 7.8 | | −8.0 |
| | −1.8 | | −1.4 | | | −3.3 | | −1.7 |
| | 111.4 | | 33.1 | % Profit Before | | 133.4 | | 71.0 |
| (17) | 23.2 | (25) | 22.2 | Taxes/Tangible | (28) | 21.9 | (68) | 22.0 |
| | 0.7 | | −8.5 | Net Worth | | 4.4 | | −6.3 |
| | 12.4 | | 5.5 | | | 14.8 | | 10.3 |
| | 4.9 | | −0.3 | % Profit Before Taxes/ Total Assets | | 7.1 | | 1.4 |
| | −4.1 | | −7.5 | | | −7.2 | | −5.2 |
| | 34.5 | | 37.2 | | | 53.7 | | 42.0 |
| | 16.4 | | 22.7 | Sales/Net Fixed Assets | | 30.4 | | 22.5 |
| | 9.3 | | 12.5 | | | 16.7 | | 11.6 |
| | 1.1 | | 1.0 | | | 2.5 | | 1.8 |
| | 0.8 | | 0.6 | Sales/Total Assets | | 1.4 | | 1.0 |
| | 0.6 | | 0.4 | | | 1.1 | | 0.6 |
| | 1.9 | | 2.7 | % Depr., Dep., Amort./Sales | | 1.0 | | 1.5 |
| (23) | 4.3 | (13) | 3.6 | | (31) | 2.4 | (70) | 3.1 |
| | 7.2 | | 4.2 | | | 4.2 | | 6.1 |
| 2548082M | | 6738043M | | Net Sales ($) | 728430M | | 12099435M | |
| 2604550M | | 9439953M | | Total Assets ($) | 551806M | | 13514540M | |

M = $ thousand      MM = $ million

◆ Compare the financial performance of the firm's different divisions.
◆ Prepare, at both the firm and division levels, financial projections, such as those associated with the launch of a new product.
◆ Understand the financial performance of the firm's competitors.
◆ Evaluate the financial condition of a major supplier.

Outside the company, financial ratios can be used by:

◆ Lenders to decide whether or not to make a loan to the company.
◆ Credit-rating agencies to determine the firm's creditworthiness.

◆ Investors to decide whether or not to invest in a company.

◆ Major suppliers to decide whether or not to grant credit terms to a company.

The conclusion: Financial analysis tools can help a wide group of individuals in a variety of purposes. However, in this chapter we will focus on how the firm itself uses financial ratios to evaluate its performance. But remember that personnel in marketing, human

## FINANCE AT WORK

### HOME DEPOT AND LOWE'S: THE HISTORIES

We are spending a lot of time with Home Depot and to a lesser extent Lowe's as we draw on them to understand financial statements. We thought you might enjoy knowing a little about their histories.

**The Home Depot's History[2]**

The Home Depot was founded in 1978 by Bernie Marcus, Arthur Blank, Ron Brill, and Pat Farrah. The Home Depot's proposition was to build home-improvement warehouses that were larger than any of their competitors' facilities. The first two stores were opened on June 22, 1979 in Atlanta, Georgia, creating a new concept of do-it-yourself retail. With 60,000 square feet of product and floor space each, these two stores were the first megastores in the home-improvement industry.

The founders wanted to provide customers the knowledge they needed to undertake do-it-yourself projects. Employees were trained to advise customers on buying tools, selecting materials, and completing projects on their own.

In 1981, only 3 years after the first stores opened, the company went public on the NASDAQ, and in 1984, moved to the New York Stock Exchange. In 1989, 10 years after the founding of the company, Home Depot celebrated the opening of the 100th store.

In 2000, after the retirement of the company's founders, Robert Nardelli became the CEO and chairman of the board of directors. Nardelli was credited with improving gross revenue and lowering costs, almost doubling the company's net income over the course of his tenure. But according to some, his bottom-line management style negatively affected employee morale, which in turn hurt customer service. In 2007, Nardelli resigned amid complaints regarding his relatively high compensation and the company's stagnant stock price. Frank Blake followed Nardelli as Home Depot's CEO.

By 2012, Home Depot had over 2,200 stores, with almost 300 stores outside the United States. For the fiscal year ending on January 9, 2012, Home Depot had $70.4 billion in sales and $3.9 billion in profits—up 18 percent from the prior year.

**Lowe's History[3]**

In 1921, Lucius S. Lowe opened Lowe's North Wilkesboro Hardware in North Wilkesboro, North Carolina. When Lucius died in 1940, his daughter, Ruth, inherited the business. She later sold the company to her brother, Jim, who then added Carl Buchan as a partner.

Under Buchan's management, the store focused on hardware and building materials. In 1946, at the start of the post–World War II housing boom, the company began carrying more wholesale products to cater to professional contractors. The housing boom brought such a demand for supplies that sales were often made out of the freight cars that ran by the store.

In 1952, Carl Buchan and Jim Lowe separated over differences in their views of the future of the business, with Buchan taking control of the hardware and building supply business. In 1960, Buchan died of a heart attack at the age of 44; his management team, which included Robert Strickland and Leonard Herring, assumed the leadership of the company. In 1961, the firm went public on the New York Stock Exchange, and in the next year was operating 21 stores with reported annual revenues of $32 million.

In the late 1970s, Lowe's experienced a slowdown as a result of a decline in housing construction. In response, the company began reaching out to retail consumers as well as to contractors. With fewer people building new homes, consumers were refurbishing their current homes, doing more of the work themselves. By 1983, Lowe's was making more money selling to consumers than it was selling to contractors.

At about the same time, Home Depot entered the market, setting a new trend of big warehouse-style stores that dwarfed the average Lowe's store. Nevertheless, Lowe's maintained its existing business model, thinking that smaller towns where it operated could not support the mega-stores. With time, however, Lowe's realized its mistake and began building its own mega-stores, creating the Lowe's we know today. While not as large as Home Depot, Lowe's is certainly a major competitor of Home Depot's, having 1,712 stores in the U.S. and 33 stores in Canada and Mexico, for a total of 1,745 stores. For the fiscal year ending February 2012, Lowe's had $50.2 billion in sales, with $1.9 billion in net income.

[2] *Our History* (n.d.), retrieved May 26, 2012 from: https://corporate.homedepot.com/OurCompany; History/Pages/default.aspx, retrieved June 1, 2012; The Home Depot (n.d.), retrieved May 15, 2012 from: http://www.thehistoryofcorporate.com; companies-by-industry/traderetail/the-home-depot, retrieved May 17, 2012; and Form 10-K, The Home Depot, Inc. for the year ended January 29, 2012, retrieved April 26, 2012.

[3] *Our Heritage* (n.d.), retrieved May 27, 2012 from: http://media.lowes.com/history; *Lowe's Companies, Inc. History* (n.d.), retrieved May 27, 2012 from: http://www.fundinguniverse.com; company-histories/lowe-s-companies-inc-history, retrieved May 27, 2012; and Form 10-K, Lowe's Companies, Inc. for the year ended February 3, 2012, retrieved May 25, 2012.

resources, information systems, and other groups within a firm can use financial ratios for a variety of other reasons.

## Concept Check

1. What is the basic purpose of *financial analysis*?
2. How does a firm use financial ratios? Who else might use financial ratios and why?
3. Where can we find financial ratios for different companies or for peer groups?

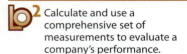

**2** Calculate and use a comprehensive set of measurements to evaluate a company's performance.

# Measuring Key Financial Relationships

Instructors usually take one of two approaches to teaching students about financial ratios. The first approach reviews the different types or categories of ratios, whereas the second approach uses ratios to answer important questions about a firm's operations. We prefer the latter approach and have chosen the following five questions to help you map out the process of using financial ratios:

1. How liquid is the firm?
2. Are the firm's managers generating adequate operating profits from the company's assets?
3. How is the firm financing its assets?
4. Are the firm's managers providing a good return on the capital provided by the shareholders?
5. Are the firm's managers creating shareholder value?

Let's look at each of these five questions in turn. In doing so, we will use Home Depot to illustrate the use of financial ratios. The company's financial statements for fiscal year ended January 30, 2011, which were originally presented in Chapter 3, are shown again in Table 4-1 and Table 4-2. As we remember from Chapter 3, the numbers in Home Depot's financial statements are expressed in millions, so that any number exceeding $1,000 million is actually over a billion dollars. We have color coded the numbers in the ratio computations so that you can readily determine whether a particular number is coming from the income statement (red numbers) or the balance sheet (blue numbers).

In addition to calculating Home Depot's financial ratios, we will provide the same ratios for Lowe's Companies, Inc., a home improvement stores company we learned about on the previous page in the Finance at Work box. By comparing Home Depot's results with Lowe's, we gain additional perspective about its performance relative to a major competitor.

| TABLE 4-1    The Home Depot, Inc. Income Statement for Year Ending January 30, 2011 ($ millions) | |
|---|---|
| Sales | $ 67,997 |
| Cost of goods sold | (44,693) |
| Gross profits | $ 23,304 |
| Operating expenses: | |
| Marketing expenses and general and administrative expenses | ($ 15,885) |
| Depreciation expenses | (1,616) |
| Total operating expenses | ($ 17,501) |
| Operating income | $ 5,803 |
| Interest expense | (530) |
| Earnings before taxes | $ 5,273 |
| Income taxes | (1,935) |
| Net income (earnings available to common stockholders) | $ 3,338 |
| Additional information: | |
| Numbers of common shares outstanding (millions) | 1,623 |
| Earnings per share (net income ÷ number of shares) | $ 2.06 |
| Dividends paid to stockholders | $ 1,569 |
| Dividends per share (total dividends ÷ number of shares) | $ 0.97 |

## TABLE 4-2  The Home Depot, Inc. Balance Sheets ($ millions) January 30, 2011

| Assets | |
|---|---|
| Cash | $ 545 |
| Account receivables | 1,085 |
| Inventories | 10,625 |
| Other current assets | 1,224 |
| Total current assets | $13,479 |
| Gross fixed assets | $38,471 |
| Accumulated depreciation | (13,411) |
| Net fixed assets | $25,060 |
| Other assets | 1,586 |
| Total assets | $40,125 |
| **Liabilities and Equity** | |
| Accounts payable | $ 9,080 |
| Short-term notes payable | 1,042 |
| Total current liabilities | $10,122 |
| Long-term debt | $11,114 |
| Total liabilities | $21,236 |
| Common equity: | |
| Common stock: | |
| Par value | $ 86 |
| Paid-in capital | 7,001 |
| Total common stock sold | $ 7,087 |
| Treasury stock | (3,193) |
| Total common stock | $ 3,894 |
| Retained earnings | 14,995 |
| Total common equity | $18,889 |
| Total liabilities and equity | $40,125 |

We will begin our analysis by addressing the first question shown above, "How liquid is the firm?" and then proceed through the remaining questions in the order listed.

## Question 1: How Liquid Is the Firm—Can It Pay Its Bills?

A liquid asset is one that can be converted quickly and routinely into cash at the current market price. So the **liquidity** of a business is a function of its ability to have cash available when needed to meet its financial obligations. Very simply, can we expect a company to be able to pay creditors on a timely basis?

We answer this question by comparing a firm's assets that can be converted quickly and easily into cash—namely its current assets—with the firm's current liabilities. In our analysis we are interested in both (1) the amount of current assets relative to current liabilities and (2) the *quality* of the individual current assets that will be used in meeting current debt payments.

When it comes to examining the relative size of current assets to current liabilities, the most commonly used measure of a firm's short-term solvency is the **current ratio**:

**liquidity** a firm's ability to pay its bills on time. Liquidity is related to the ease and speed with which a firm can convert its noncash assets into cash.

**current ratio** the firm's current assets divided by its current liabilities. This ratio indicates a company's degree of liquidity by comparing its current assets to its current liabilities.

$$\text{Current ratio} = \frac{\text{current assets}}{\text{current liabilities}} \tag{4-1}$$

For Home Depot:

$$\text{Current ratio} = \frac{\text{current assets}}{\text{current liabilities}} = \frac{\$13,479M}{\$10,122M} = 1.33$$

where M represents millions.

| Lowe's current ratio | 1.40 |
|---|---|

Based on the current ratio, Home Depot is less liquid than Lowe's. The company has $1.33 in current assets for every $1 in current liabilities, while Lowe's has $1.40.

When we use the current ratio, we assume that the firm's accounts receivable will be collected and turned into cash on a timely basis and that its inventories can be sold without any extended delay. Given that a company's inventory by its very nature is less liquid than its accounts receivable—it must first be sold before any cash can be collected—a more stringent measure of liquidity would exclude the inventories and include only the firm's cash and accounts receivable in the numerator. This revised ratio is called the **acid-test** (or **quick**) **ratio**. It is calculated as follows:

**acid-test (quick) ratio** the sum of a firm's cash and accounts receivable divided by its current liabilities. This ratio is a more stringent measure of liquidity than the current ratio because it excludes inventories and other current assets (those that are least liquid) from the numerator.

$$\text{Acid-test ratio} = \frac{\text{cash} + \text{accounts receivable}}{\text{current liabilities}} \tag{4-2}$$

For Home Depot:

$$\text{Acid-test ratio} = \frac{\text{cash} + \text{accounts receivable}}{\text{current liabilities}} = \frac{\$545M + \$1,085M}{\$10,122M} = 0.16$$

| Lowe's acid-test ratio | 0.12 |
|---|---|

Based on the acid-test ratio, Home Depot appears to be *more* liquid than Lowe's. It has $0.16 in cash and accounts receivable per $1 in current debt, compared to $0.12 for Lowe's.

So what should we conclude? The current ratio suggests that Lowe's is more liquid, while the acid-test ratio tells us that Home Depot is. The difference must come from the amount of inventories each firm has relative to their current liabilities; that is, the higher current ratio for Lowe's indicates that it has relatively more inventory then Home Depot. Thus, we will want to know more about the quality of Lowe's inventories compared to Home Depot's. That answer will come shortly.[4]

We now want to evaluate the quality of a firm's accounts receivable and inventories in terms of the firm's ability to convert these assets into cash on a timely basis. A firm might have a higher current ratio, as Lowe's does relative to Home Depot, but have more uncollectible receivables and/or be carrying a lot of obsolete inventory. So knowing the quality of these assets is necessary if we are to have a complete understanding of a firm's liquidity.

*Converting Accounts Receivable to Cash*  The conversion of accounts receivable into cash can be measured by computing how long it takes to collect the firm's receivables on average. We can answer this question by computing a firm's **days in receivables** (or **average collection period**) as follows:[5]

**days in receivables (average collection period)** a firm's accounts receivable divided by the company's average daily *credit* sales (annual credit sales ÷ 365). This ratio expresses how many days on average it takes to collect receivables.

$$\text{Days in receivables} = \frac{\text{accounts receivable}}{\text{daily credit sales}} = \frac{\text{accounts receivable}}{\text{annual credit sales} \div 365} \tag{4-3}$$

Note that in this equation, we are including only sales where the customer purchases on credit, omitting cash sales. As you would expect, businesses like Home Depot have mostly cash sales. Specifically, we estimate that only 30 percent of their sales are on credit, so credit sales

---

[4]Is it possible that a firm's current ratio or acid-test ratio could be too high? Absolutely. Liquid assets generally provide little in the way of profitability. For example, tying too much money up in inventories may prevent a company from investing in assets that will generate more profits. In other words, there is usually a tradeoff between having more liquidity and generating profits.

[5]When computing a given ratio that uses information from both the income statement and the balance sheet, we should remember that the income statement is for a given time period (for example, 2010), whereas balance sheet data are at a point in time (for example, January 30, 2011). If there has been a significant change in an asset balance from the beginning of the period to the end, it would be better to use the average balance for the year. For example, if the accounts receivable for a company have increased from $1,000 at the beginning of the year to $2,000 at the end of the year, it would be more appropriate to use the average accounts receivable of $1,500 in our computations. Nevertheless, in an effort to simplify, we will use year-end amounts from the balance sheet in our computations.

amounted to about $20.399 billion ($20.399 billion = $67.997 billion total sales × 30% credit sales). Thus, Home Depot's days in receivables is 19.41 days, computed as follows:

$$\text{Days in receivables} = \frac{\text{accounts receivable}}{\text{annual credit sales} \div 365}$$

$$= \frac{\$1,085M}{\$20,399M \div 365} = \frac{\$1,085M}{\$55.89M} = 19.41 \text{ days}$$

| Lowe's days in receivables | 16 days |
|---|---|

So on average Home Depot collected its accounts receivable in about 19.4 days compared to 16 days for Lowe's. Thus, Home Depot is slower at collecting its receivables than Lowe's, suggesting that its receivables are less liquid than Lowe's.

We could have reached the same conclusion by measuring how many times accounts receivable are "rolled over" during a year, using the **accounts receivable turnover ratio**. If Home Depot collects its accounts receivable every 19.41 days, then it is collecting 18.8 times per year (18.8 times = 365 days ÷ 19.41 days). The accounts receivable turnover can also be calculated as follows:

> **accounts receivable turnover ratio** a firm's credit sales divided by its accounts receivable. This ratio expresses how often accounts receivable are "rolled over" during a year.

$$\text{Accounts receivable turnover} = \frac{\text{annual credit sales}}{\text{accounts receivable}} \qquad (4\text{-}4)$$

For Home Depot:

$$\text{Accounts receivable turnover} = \frac{\text{annual credit sales}}{\text{accounts receivable}} = \frac{\$20,399M}{\$1,085M} = 18.80X$$

| Lowe's accounts receivable turnover | 22.81X |
|---|---|

Whether we use the days in receivables or the accounts receivable turnover ratio, the conclusion is the same. Home Depot collects its accounts receivable more slowly than Lowe's. In other words, Home Depot's accounts receivable are of lesser quality. (Think about this: If Home Depot's days in receivables were as low as Lowe's, it would have less accounts receivable and its current ratio would be lower.)

***Converting Inventories to Cash*** We now want to know the quality of Home Depot's inventory, as indicated by how long the inventory is held before being sold. This is called **days in inventory**, which is computed as follows:

> **days in inventory** inventory divided by daily cost of goods sold. This ratio measures the number of days a firm's inventories are held on average before being sold; it also indicates the quality of the inventory.

$$\text{Days in inventory} = \frac{\text{inventory}}{\text{daily cost of goods sold}} = \frac{\text{inventory}}{\text{annual cost of goods sold} \div 365} \qquad (4\text{-}5)$$

For Home Depot:

$$\text{Days in inventory} = \frac{\text{inventory}}{\text{annual cost of goods sold} \div 365}$$

$$= \frac{\$10,625M}{\$44,693M \div 365} = \frac{\$10,625M}{\$122.45M} = 86.77 \text{ days}$$

| Lowe's days in inventory | 95.80 days |
|---|---|

Note that when we calculated accounts receivable turnover or days in receivables, we use *sales* in our computation. But when calculating days in inventory or inventory turnover, we use cost of goods sold. We do this because inventory is measured at cost.

**inventory turnover** a firm's cost of goods sold divided by its inventory. This ratio measures the number of times a firm's inventories are sold and replaced during the year, that is, the relative liquidity of the inventories.

As we did with days in receivables and accounts receivable turnover, we can restate days in inventory as **inventory turnover**, which is calculated as follows:[6]

$$\text{Inventory turnover} = \frac{\text{cost of goods sold}}{\text{inventory}} \tag{4-6}$$

For Home Depot:

$$\text{Inventory turnover} = \frac{\$44,693M}{\$10,625M} = 4.21X$$

| Lowe's inventory turnover | 3.81X |
|---|---|

Hence, we see that Home Depot is moving (turning over) its inventory more quickly than Lowe's—4.21 times per year, compared with 3.81 times for Lowe's. This suggests that Home Depot's inventory is more liquid than Lowe's.

To conclude, the current ratio indicates that Home Depot is less liquid than Lowe's, but this result assumes that Home Depot's accounts receivable and inventory are of similar quality to Lowe's. However, this is not the case given Home Depot's lower accounts receivable turnover (more days in receivables) and higher inventory turnover (fewer days in inventory). The acid-test ratio, on the other hand, suggests that Home Depot is more liquid than Lowe's, but we know that Home Depot's accounts receivable are a bit less liquid than Lowe's. We therefore have a mixed outcome, and cannot say definitively whether Home Depot is more or less liquid. Thus, we have to conclude that Home Depot's liquidity and Lowe's liquidity are probably very similar.

We have completed our presentation of liquidity decision tools, which can be summarized as follows:

## FINANCIAL DECISION TOOLS

| Name of Tool | Formula | What It Tells You |
|---|---|---|
| Current ratio | $\dfrac{\text{current assets}}{\text{current liabilities}}$ | Measures a firm's liquidity. A higher ratio means greater liquidity. |
| Acid-test ratio | $\dfrac{\text{cash} + \text{accounts receivable}}{\text{current liabilities}}$ | Gives a more stringent measure of liquidity than the current ratio in that it excludes inventories and other current assets from the numerator. A higher ratio means greater liquidity. |
| Days in receivables | $\dfrac{\text{accounts receivable}}{\text{annual credit sales} \div 365}$ | Indicates how rapidly a firm is collecting its receivables. A longer (shorter) period means a slower (faster) collection of receivables and that the receivables are of lesser (greater) quality. |
| OR | | |
| Accounts receivable turnover | $\dfrac{\text{annual credit sales}}{\text{accounts receivable}}$ | Tells how many times a firm's accounts receivable are collected, or *turned over*, during a year. Provides the same information as the *days in receivables*, just expressed differently, where a high (low) number indicates fast (slow) collections. |
| Days in inventory | $\dfrac{\text{inventory}}{\text{annual cost of goods sold} \div 365}$ | Measures how many days a firm's inventories are held on average before being sold; the more (less) days required, the lower (higher) the quality of the inventory. |
| OR | | |
| Inventory turnover | $\dfrac{\text{cost of goods sold}}{\text{inventory}}$ | Gives the number of times a firm's inventory is sold and replaced during the year; as with days in inventory, serves as an indicator of the quality of the inventories; the higher the number, the better the inventory quality. |

[6]However, some of the industry norms provided by financial services are computed using sales in the numerator of inventory turnover. To make comparisons with ratios from these services, we will want to use sales in our computation of inventory turnover.

## EXAMPLE 4.1    Evaluating Disney's liquidity

The following information (expressed in $ millions) is taken from the Walt Disney Company's 2011 financial statements:

| | |
|---|---|
| Current assets | $ 13,757 |
| Cash | 2,722 |
| Accounts receivable | 6,182 |
| Inventories | 2,269 |
| Credit sales | 27,262 |
| Cash sales | 13,631 |
| Total sales | 40,893 |
| Cost of goods sold | 31,221 |
| Total current liabilities | 12,088 |

Source: Data from The Walt Disney Company's Fiscal Year 2011 Annual Financial Report.

Evaluate Disney's liquidity based on the following norms in the broadcasting and entertainment industry:

| | |
|---|---|
| Current ratio | 1.17 |
| Acid-test ratio | 0.92 |
| Accounts receivable turnover | 5.80X |
| Inventory turnover | 18.30X |

### STEP 1: FORMULATE A DECISION STRATEGY

We analyze a company's liquidity by looking at selected ratios. These include the current ratio, acid-test ratio, accounts receivable turnover (or days in receivables), and inventory turnover (or days in inventory). The formulas are:

$$\text{Current ratio} = \frac{\text{current assets}}{\text{current liabilities}}$$

$$\text{Acid-test ratio} = \frac{\text{cash} + \text{accounts receivable}}{\text{current liabilities}}$$

$$\text{Accounts receivable turnover} = \frac{\text{annual credit sales}}{\text{accounts receivable}}$$

$$\text{Inventory turnover} = \frac{\text{cost of goods sold}}{\text{inventory}}$$

### STEP 2: CRUNCH THE NUMBERS

| | DISNEY | INDUSTRY |
|---|---|---|
| Current ratio | 1.14 | 1.17 |
| Acid-test ratio | 0.74 | 0.92 |
| Accounts receivable turnover | 4.41X | 5.8X |
| Inventory turnover | 13.78X | 18.3X |

### STEP 3: ANALYZE YOUR RESULTS

Based on these results, Disney is not as liquid as the average firm in the industry! The company has smaller amounts of liquid assets relative to its current liabilities than does its average competitor. The firm does not convert its receivables to cash as quickly as do its competitors, and is slower at turning inventory.

## Concept Check _____

1. What information about the firm is provided by liquidity measures?

2. Describe the two perspectives available for measuring liquidity.

3. Why might a very high current ratio actually indicate there's a problem with a firm's inventory or accounts receivable management? What might be another reason for a high current ratio?

4. Why might a successful (liquid) firm have an acid-test ratio that is less than 1?

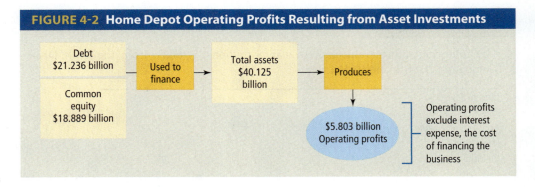

**FIGURE 4-2** Home Depot Operating Profits Resulting from Asset Investments

## Question 2: Are the Firm's Managers Generating Adequate Operating Profits from the Company's Assets?[7]

We now switch to a different dimension of performance—the firm's profitability. The question here is, "Do the firm's managers produce adequate profits from the company's assets?" From the perspective of the firm's shareholders, there is no more important question to be asked. One of the most important ways managers create shareholder value is to earn strong profits on the assets in which they have invested.

To answer this all-important question, think about the process of financing a company. In its simplest form, a firm's shareholders invest in a business. The company may also borrow additional money from other sources (banks and so forth). The purpose of making these investments is to create profits. Figure 4-2 graphically illustrates this process for Home Depot, where we see that the shareholders invested $18.889 billion in the company, and that the company borrowed another $21.236 billion, which together allowed the company to finance $40.125 billion of assets. These assets were then used to produce $5.803 billion in operating profits.

Notice that we are using *operating profits* rather than *net income*. Operating profits are the income generated from the firm's assets independent of how the firm is financed. The effect of financing will be explicitly considered in the two questions that follow, but for now we want to isolate only the operating aspects of the company's profits.

While knowing the dollar amount of a firm's operating profits is important, we also want to know the amount of operating profits relative to the total assets employed. In other words, we want to know how much operating profit is generated per dollar of assets used; that is, we are interested in a firm's return on its asset investment. We find this return by calculating the **operating return on assets (OROA)** as follows:

**operating return on assets (OROA)** the ratio of a firm's operating profits divided by its total assets. This ratio indicates the rate of return being earned on the firm's assets.

$$\text{Operating return on assets} = \frac{\text{operating profits}}{\text{total assets}} \tag{4-7}$$

For Home Depot:

$$\frac{\text{Operating return}}{\text{on assets}} = \frac{\text{operating profits}}{\text{total assets}} = \frac{\$5,803M}{\$40,125M} = 0.145 = 14.5\%$$

| Lowe's operating return on assets | 10.6% |
|---|---|

Thus, Home Depot earned a higher return on its assets relative to Lowe's—14.5 cents of operating profits for every $1 of assets for Home Depot, compared to 10.6 cents for Lowe's.

Clearly, Home Depot was doing something better than Lowe's when it came to earning a higher return on its assets. But what? The answer lies in two areas: (1) how effectively the company's income statement was being managed or what we will call **operations management**, which involves the day-to-day buying and selling of a firm's goods or services as reflected in the income statement; and (2) how efficiently assets are being

**operations management** how effectively management is performing in the day-to-day operations in terms of how well management is generating revenues and controlling costs and expenses; in other words, how well is the firm managing the activities that directly affect the income statement?

[7]We will use the term *operating profits* throughout this chapter. We could just as correctly use the term *operating income*. We also could use the term *earnings before interest and taxes*—frequently abbreviated as *EBIT*. After all, operating profits are usually the firm's earnings before subtracting interest and taxes. So you may see these terms used interchangeably in practice. Just understand that they are for the most part the same.

Chapter 4 • Evaluating a Firm's Financial Performance

managed to generate sales, or, **asset management**. That these two issues relate to the operating return on assets can be seen by using two other ratios—operating profit margin and total asset turnover. We can compute operating return on assets using the following revised equation and get the same answer as we did with equation (4-7):

**asset management** how efficiently management is using the firm's asset's to generate sales.

$$\begin{array}{c}\text{Operating return}\\ \text{on assets}\end{array} = \begin{array}{c}\text{operating profit}\\ \text{margin}\end{array} \times \begin{array}{c}\text{total asset}\\ \text{turnover}\end{array} \qquad (4\text{-}8a)$$

calculated as follows:

$$\begin{array}{c}\text{Operating return}\\ \text{on assets}\end{array} = \frac{\text{operating profit}}{\text{sales}} \times \frac{\text{sales}}{\text{total assets}} \qquad (4\text{-}8b)$$

The operating profit margin is the result of how a company manages its day-to-day operations (*operations management*), and the total asset turnover is the result of how efficiently the company's assets are being managed (*asset management*). Let's consider managing operations and asset management in turn.

**Managing Operations**   The first component of the operating return on assets (OROA), the operating profit margin, is an indicator of how well the company manages its operations—that is, how well revenues are being generated and costs and expenses controlled. The **operating profit margin** measures how well a firm is managing its cost of operations, in terms of both the cost of goods sold and operating expenses (marketing expenses, general and administrative expenses, and depreciation expenses) relative to the firm's revenues. All else being equal, the objective for managing operations is to keep costs and expenses low relative to sales. Thus, we use the operating profit margin to measure *how well the firm is managing its income statement*, where:

**operating profit margin** a firm's operating profits divided by sales. This ratio serves as an overall measure of operating effectiveness.

$$\text{Operating profit margin} = \frac{\text{operating profits}}{\text{sales}} \qquad (4\text{-}9)$$

For Home Depot:

$$\text{Operating profit margin} = \frac{\text{operating profits}}{\text{sales}} = \frac{\$5{,}803M}{\$67{,}997M} = 0.085 = 8.5\%$$

| Lowe's operating profit margin | 7.3% |
|---|---|

The foregoing result clearly indicates that Home Depot's managers were better at managing its cost of goods sold and operating expenses than Lowe's. Home Depot had lower costs per sales dollar, which resulted in a higher operating profit margin. Put another way, Home Depot was better than Lowe's at managing its income statement. Thus, one reason for Home Depot's higher operating return on assets was its higher operating profit margin.

Now let's look at the second driver of a company's operating return on assets—how efficiently assets are being managed.

**Managing Assets**   The second component in equation (4-8) is the **total asset turnover**. This ratio tells us how efficiently a firm is using its assets to generate sales. To clarify, assume that Company A generates $3 in sales for every $1 invested in assets, whereas Company B generates the same $3 in sales but has invested $2 in assets. In other words, Company A is using its assets more efficiently to generate sales, which leads to a higher return on the firm's investment in assets. This efficiency is captured by the total asset turnover ratio, shown again as follows:

**total asset turnover** a firm's sales divided by its total assets. This ratio is an overall measure of asset efficiency based on the relation between a firm's sales and the total assets.

$$\text{Total asset turnover} = \frac{\text{sales}}{\text{total assets}} \qquad (4\text{-}10)$$

For Home Depot:

$$\text{Total asset turnover} = \frac{\text{sales}}{\text{total assets}} = \frac{\$67{,}997M}{\$40{,}125M} = 1.69X$$

| Lowe's total asset turnover | 1.45X |
|---|---|

We now know that Home Depot is using its assets more efficiently than Lowe's, generating $1.69 in sales per dollar of assets, whereas Lowe's produces only $1.45. This is the second reason for Home Depot's higher operating return on assets—the first being the higher operating profit margin.

However, we should not stop here with our analysis of Home Depot's asset management. We have learned that, in general, Home Depot's managers are making efficient use of the firm's assets, but this may not be the case for each type of asset. We also want to know how well the firm is managing its main operating assets, accounts receivable, inventories, and fixed assets, respectively.

To answer this question, we can compute the turnover ratios for each of these asset categories. Of course, we have already calculated the turnover ratios for the company's accounts receivable and inventories and concluded that Home Depot's managers were not managing accounts receivable as efficiently as Lowe's, but were turning over inventories more quickly. We still need to compute the **fixed asset turnover**, which we do as follows:

**fixed asset turnover** a firm's sales divided by its net fixed assets. This ratio indicates how efficiently the firm is using its fixed assets.

$$\frac{\text{Fixed asset}}{\text{turnover}} = \frac{\text{sales}}{\text{net fixed assets}} \tag{4-11}$$

For Home Depot:

$$\frac{\text{Fixed asset}}{\text{turnover}} = \frac{\text{sales}}{\text{net fixed assets}} = \frac{\$67,997M}{\$25,060M} = 2.71X$$

| | |
|---|---|
| Lowe's fixed asset turnover | 2.21X |

Thus, Home Depot has a smaller investment in fixed assets relative to the firm's sales than does Lowe's.

We can now look at all the asset efficiency ratios together to summarize Home Depot's asset management:

| | HOME DEPOT | LOWE'S |
|---|---|---|
| Total asset turnover | 1.69X | 1.45X |
| Accounts receivable turnover | 18.80X | 22.81X |
| Inventory turnover | 4.21X | 3.81X |
| Fixed assets turnover | 2.71X | 2.21X |

Home Depot's situation with respect to asset management is now clear. Overall, Home Depot's managers are utilizing their firm's assets efficiently, based on the firm's total asset turnover. This overall asset efficiency results from better management of the firm's inventories and fixed assets (which have higher turnovers than Lowe's). However, the firm is not managing its accounts receivable as well: Home Depot's accounts receivable turnover is lower than Lowe's.

**FIGURE 4-3  Analysis of Home Depot's Operating Return on Assets**

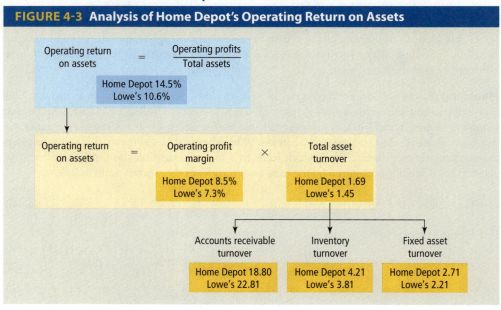

Figure 4-3 (on page 114) provides a summary of our evaluation of Home Depot's operating and asset management performance. We began by computing the operating return on assets to determine if managers were producing good returns on the assets. We then broke the operating return on assets into its two pieces, operations management (operating profit margin) and asset management (asset turnover ratios), to explain why Home Depot's operating return on assets was higher than Lowe's. We can also provide a summary of the financial ratios being used as tools to evaluate a firm's profitability as follows:

## FINANCIAL DECISION TOOLS

| Name of Tool | Formula | What It Tells You |
|---|---|---|
| Operating return on assets (OROA) | $$\frac{\text{operating profits}}{\text{total assets}}$$ or operating profit margin $\times$ total assets turnover | The rate of return being earned on a firm's assets. A higher (lower) return indicates more (less) operating profits per dollar of assets invested. |
| Operating profit margin | $$\frac{\text{operating profits}}{\text{sales}}$$ | Overall measure of day-to-day operating effectiveness—how well revenues are being generated and costs and expenses controlled. A higher (lower) margin means a firm is better (worse) at managing its day-to-day operations. |
| Total asset turnover | $$\frac{\text{sales}}{\text{total assets}}$$ | Measures how efficiently a firm is using its total assets. A higher turnover means the firm is using its assets more efficiently. |
| Days in receivables OR Accounts receivable turnover | $$\frac{\text{accounts receivable}}{\text{annual credit sales} \div 365}$$ $$\frac{\text{annual credit sales}}{\text{accounts receivable}}$$ | Measures how rapidly a firm is collecting its receivables. A longer (shorter) period means slower (faster) collections and a larger (smaller) investment in receivables. The number of times a firm's accounts receivable are collected, or *turned over*, during a year. Provides the same information as the *days in receivables*, just expressed differently. |
| Days in inventory OR Inventory turnover | $$\frac{\text{inventory}}{\text{annual cost of goods sold} \div 365}$$ $$\frac{\text{cost of goods sold}}{\text{inventory}}$$ | Measures how many days a firm's inventories are held on average before being sold; the more (less) days required, the larger (smaller) will be the investment in inventories. The number of times a firm's inventories are sold and replaced during the year; provides the same information as the *days in inventory*, just expressed differently. |
| Fixed asset turnover | $$\frac{\text{sales}}{\text{net fixed assets}}$$ | Measures how efficiently the firm is using its fixed assets. A higher (lower) turnover means the firm is using its fixed assets more (less) efficiently. |

## Concept Check

1. Which number in a company's income statement should be used to measure its profitability relative to its total assets? Why?

2. What two broad areas of the firm's management does the operating return on assets assess?

3. What factors influence the operating profit margin?

4. A low total asset turnover indicates that a firm's total assets are not being managed efficiently. What additional information would you want to know when this is the case?

> **EXAMPLE 4.2**    **Evaluating Disney's operating return on assets**
>
> Given the following financial information for the Walt Disney Company (expressed in $ millions), evaluate the firm's operating return on its assets (OROA).
>
> | | |
> |---|---|
> | Accounts receivable | $ 6,182 |
> | Inventories | 2,269 |
> | Sales | 40,893 |
> | Credit sales | 27,262 |
> | Cost of goods sold | 31,221 |
> | Operating profits | 7,781 |
> | Net fixed assets | 19,695 |
> | Total assets | 72,124 |
>
> Source: Data from The Walt Disney Company's Fiscal Year 2011 Annual Financial Report.
>
> The industry norms are as follows:
>
> | | |
> |---|---|
> | Operating return on assets | 7.25% |
> | Operating profit margin | 16.10% |
> | Total asset turnover | 0.45X |
> | Accounts receivable turnover | 7.10X |
> | Inventory turnover | 18.30X |
> | Fixed assets turnover | 1.05X |
>
> ### STEP 1: FORMULATE A DECISION STRATEGY
>
> The operating return on assets is determined by two factors: managing operations and managing assets. Recall equation (4-8a):
>
> $$\frac{\text{Operating}}{\text{return on assets}} = \frac{\text{operating profit}}{\text{margin}} \times \frac{\text{total asset}}{\text{turnover}}$$
>
> Substituting for the operating profit margin and total asset turnover (equation 4-8b):
>
> $$\frac{\text{Operating}}{\text{return on assets}} = \frac{\text{operating profits}}{\text{sales}} \times \frac{\text{sales}}{\text{total assets}}$$
>
> We can further analyze the total asset turnover ratio by looking at the efficiency of various components of total assets, including accounts receivable turnover, inventory turnover, and fixed assets turnover.
>
> ### STEP 2: CRUNCH THE NUMBERS
>
> | | DISNEY | INDUSTRY |
> |---|---|---|
> | Operating return on assets $\frac{\$7,781}{\$72,124}$ | 10.79% | 7.25% |
> | Operating profit margin $\frac{\$7,781}{\$40,893}$ | 19.03% | 16.10% |
> | Total asset turnover $\frac{\$40,893}{\$72,124}$ | 0.57X | 0.45X |
> | Accounts receivable turnover $\frac{\$27,262}{\$6,182}$ | 4.41X | 7.10X |
> | Inventory turnover $\frac{\$31,221}{\$2,269}$ | 13.76X | 18.30X |
> | Fixed assets turnover $\frac{\$40,893}{\$19,695}$ | 2.08X | 1.05X |

## STEP 3: ANALYZE YOUR RESULTS

Disney generated a higher return on its assets than the average firm in the industry, 10.79 percent compared to 7.25 percent for the industry. Disney provided a higher operating return on its assets by (1) managing its operations better, achieving a higher operating profit margin (19 percent compared to 16.10 percent), and (2) making better use of its assets, as indicated by a higher total asset turnover (0.57X versus 0.45X). However, the higher total asset turnover is caused entirely by a much higher fixed-asset turnover (2.08X compared to 1.05X), which more than offsets the lower accounts receivable turnover (4.41X as compared to 7.10X) and the less efficient management of inventories, as reflected by the lower inventory turnover (13.76X versus 18.30X).

## Question 3: How Is the Firm Financing Its Assets?

We now turn to the matter of how a firm is financed. (We will return to the issue of profitability shortly.) The key issue is management's choice between financing with debt or with equity. To begin, we want to know what percentage of the firm's assets is financed by debt, including both short-term and long-term debt, realizing that the remaining percentage must be financed by equity. To answer this question, we compute the **debt ratio** as follows:[8]

**debt ratio** a firm's total liabilities divided by its total assets. This ratio measures the extent to which a firm has been financed with debt.

$$\text{Debt ratio} = \frac{\text{total debt}}{\text{total assets}} \qquad (4\text{--}12)$$

For Home Depot:

$$\text{Debt ratio} = \frac{\text{total debt}}{\text{total assets}} = \frac{\$21,236M}{\$40,125M} = 0.53 = 53\%$$

| Lowe's debt ratio | 46% |
|---|---|

Home Depot finances 53 percent of its assets with debt (taken from Home Depot's balance sheet in Table 4-2), compared with Lowe's 46 percent. Stated differently, Home Depot finances with 47 percent equity, whereas Lowe's is 54 percent equity. Thus, Home Depot uses more debt than Lowe's. As we will see in later chapters, more debt financing results in more financial risk.

Our second perspective regarding the firm's financing decisions comes from looking at the income statement. When the firm borrows money, it must at least pay the interest on what it has borrowed. Thus, it is informative to compare (1) the amount of operating profits that are available to pay the interest with (2) the amount of interest that has to be paid. Stated as a ratio, we compute the number of times the firms is earning its interest. The **times interest earned** ratio is commonly used when examining a firm's debt position and is computed in the following manner:

**times interest earned** a firm's operating profits divided by interest expense. This ratio measures a firm's ability to meet its interest payments from its annual operating earnings.

$$\text{Times interest earned} = \frac{\text{operating profits}}{\text{interest expense}} \qquad (4\text{--}13)$$

For Home Depot:

$$\text{Times interest earned} = \frac{\text{operating profits}}{\text{interest expense}} = \frac{\$5,803M}{\$530M} = 10.9X$$

| Lowe's times interest earned | 9.0X |
|---|---|

Home Depot's interest expense is $530 million, which when compared to its operating profits of $5.803 billion ($5,803 million) indicates that its interest expense is consuming less of the operating profits than is the case for Lowe's. Home Depot's higher *times interest earned* can be attributed to the firm's relatively higher operating profits, as reflected in a

---

[8]Instead of using the debt ratio, we could use the debt–equity ratio. The debt–equity ratio is simply a transformation of the debt ratio:

$$\text{Debt–equity ratio} = \frac{\text{total debt}}{\text{total equity}} = \frac{\text{debt ratio}}{1 - \text{debt ratio}}; \text{Debt ratio} = \frac{\text{debt/equity}}{1 + \text{debt/equity}}$$

higher operating return on assets. The higher the profits, the higher will be the time interested earned. Home Depot's higher debt ratio would most likely lower the times interest earned, relative to Lowe's, since the more debt you have, the more interest you will pay. However, Home Depot's higher income apparently more than covers any additional interest expense on its greater amount of debt.

Before concluding our discussion regarding times interest earned, we should understand that interest is not paid with income but with cash. Moreover, in addition to the interest that must be paid, the firm will also be required to repay the debt principal. Thus, the times interest earned ratio is only a crude measure of the firm's capacity to service its debt. Nevertheless, it does give us a general indication of a company's financial risk and its capacity to borrow.

So the two ratios that can be used as financial decision tools are as follows:

### FINANCIAL DECISION TOOLS

| Name of Tool | Formula | What It Tells You |
|---|---|---|
| Debt Ratio | $\dfrac{\text{total debt}}{\text{total assets}}$ | The percentage of assets that is financed with debt. The higher (lower) the debt ratio, the more (less) financial risk the firm is assuming. |
| Times interest earned | $\dfrac{\text{operating profits}}{\text{interest expense}}$ | The number of times a firm is earning its interest expense. Indicates a company's ability to service its fixed interest payments. A higher (lower) value means the firm is more (less) able to service its debt. |

### EXAMPLE 4.3    Evaluate Disney's financing decisions

Given the information below (expressed in $ millions) for the Disney Corporation, calculate the firm's debt ratio and its times interest earned. How do Disney's ratios compare to those of the industry in which it operates? What are the implications of your findings?

| | |
|---|---|
| Total debt | $32,671 |
| Total assets | 72,124 |
| Operating profits | 7,781 |
| Interest expense | 526 |
| Industry norms: | |
|   Debt ratio | 34.21% |
|   Times interest earned | 8.5X |

### STEP 1: FORMULATE A DECISION STRATEGY

A company's financing decisions can be evaluated by considering two questions: (1) How much debt is used to finance the firm's assets, and (2) Does the company have the ability to service its interest payments? These two issues can be assessed by using the debt ratio and the times interest earned ratio, respectively, calculated as follows:

$$\text{Debt ratio} = \frac{\text{total debt}}{\text{total assets}}$$

$$\text{Times interest earned} = \frac{\text{operating profits}}{\text{interest expense}}$$

### STEP 2: CRUNCH THE NUMBERS

A comparison of Disney's debt ratio and times interest earned with the industry is as follows:

| | DISNEY | INDUSTRY |
|---|---|---|
| Debt ratio | 45.30% | 34.21% |
| Times interest earned | 14.79X | 8.50X |

### STEP 3: ANALYZE YOUR RESULTS

Disney uses significantly more debt financing than the average firm in the industry. The higher debt ratio implies that the firm has greater financial risk. Even so, Disney appears to have no difficulty servicing its debt, covering its interest almost 15 times compared to only 8.5 times for the average firm in the industry. Disney's higher times interest earned is attributable to significantly higher operating profits on its assets, which more than offsets the firm's use of more debt.

## Concept Check

1. What information is provided by the debt ratio?
2. Why is it important to calculate the times interest earned ratio, even for firms that have low debt ratios?
3. Why do operating profits not give a complete picture of a firm's ability to service its debt?

## Question 4: Are the Firm's Managers Providing a Good Return on the Capital Provided by the Shareholders?

We now want to determine if the firm's owners (shareholders) are receiving an attractive return on their equity investment when compared to the return on equity at competing firms. For this, we use the **return on equity** (frequently shortened to ROE), which is computed as follows:

$$\text{Return on equity} = \frac{\text{net income}}{\text{total common equity}} \tag{4–14}$$

**return on equity** a firm's net income divided by its common book equity. This ratio is the accounting rate of return earned on the common stockholders' investment.

For Home Depot:

$$\text{Return on equity} = \frac{\text{net income}}{\text{total common equity}} = \frac{\$3,338M}{\$18,889M} = 0.177 = 17.7\%$$

| Lowe's return on equity | 11.1% |
|---|---|

In the computation above, remember that the *total* common equity includes all common equity in the balance sheet, including par value, paid-in capital, and retained earnings, less any treasury stock. (After all, profits retained within the business are as much of an investment for the common stockholders as are their purchases of a company's stock.)

The returns on equity for Home Depot and Lowe's are 17.7 percent and 11.1 percent, respectively. Hence, the owners of Home Depot are receiving a higher return on their equity investment than are the shareholders of Lowe's. How are they doing it? To answer, we need to draw on what we have already learned, namely, that:

1. We know from our analysis of Question 2 that Home Depot is receiving a higher operating return on its assets—14.5 percent for Home Depot, compared to 10.6 percent for Lowe's. A higher (lower) return on the firm's assets will always result in a higher (lower) return on equity.
2. Home Depot uses more debt (less equity) financing than Lowe's—53 percent debt for Home Depot and 46 percent debt for Lowe's. As we will see shortly, the more debt a firm uses, the higher its return on equity will be, provided that the firm is earning a return on assets greater than the interest rate on its debt. Conversely, the less debt a firm uses, the lower its return on equity will be (again, provided that the firm is earning a return on assets greater than the interest rate on its debt). Thus, Home Depot has increased its return for the shareholders by using more debt. That's the good news. The bad news for Home Depot's shareholders is that the more debt a firm uses, the greater is the company's financial risk, which translates into more risk for the shareholders.

To help us understand the foregoing explanation for Home Depot's higher return on equity and its implications, consider the following hypothetical example.

Assume that two companies, Firms A and B, are identical in size. Both have $1,000 in total assets and an operating return on assets of 14 percent. However, they are different in one respect: Firm A uses all equity and no debt financing; Firm B finances 60 percent of its investments with debt and 40 percent with equity. We will also assume the interest rate on any debt is 6 percent, and for simplicity we will assume that there are no income taxes. The financial statements for the two companies would be as follows:

| | FIRM A | FIRM B | |
|---|---|---|---|
| **BALANCE SHEET** | | | |
| Total assets | $1,000 | $1,000 | |
| Debt (6% interest rate) | $0 | $ 600 | |
| Equity | 1,000 | 400 | |
| Total debt and equity | $1,000 | $1,000 | |
| **INCOME STATEMENT** | | | |
| Operating profits (OROA = 14%) | $ 140 | $ 140 | $140 = 0.14 OROA × $1,000 total assets |
| Interest expense (6%) | (0) | (36) | $36 = 0.06 interest rate × $600 debt principal |
| Net income | $ 140 | $ 104 | |

Computing the return on equity for both companies, we see that Firm B has a more attractive return of 26 percent compared with Firm A's 14 percent. The calculations are as follows:

| | | FIRM A | FIRM B |
|---|---|---|---|
| $\dfrac{\text{Return on}}{\text{common equity}} = \dfrac{\text{net income}}{\text{common equity}} =$ | | $\dfrac{\$140}{\$1,000} = 14\%$ | $\dfrac{\$104}{\$400} = 26\%$ |

Why the difference? The answer is straightforward. Firm B is earning 14 percent on all of its $1,000 in assets but only having to pay 6 percent to the lenders on the $600 debt principal. The difference between the 14 percent return on the firm's assets (operating return on assets) and the 6 percent interest rate goes to the owners, thus boosting Firm B's return on equity above that of Firm A.

This is an illustration of favorable financial leverage. What's favorable, you might ask. Well, the company is earning 14 percent on its assets while only paying 6 percent to the bankers, thus allowing the shareholders to receive the 8 percent spread (14 percent return on assets – 6 percent interest paid to the bankers) on each dollar of debt financing. The result is an increase in the return on equity for Firm B's owners when compared to Firm A's. What a great deal for Firm B's shareholders! So if debt enhances owners' returns, why doesn't Firm A borrow money or Firm B borrow even more money?

The good outcome for Firm B shareholders is based on the assumption that the firm does in fact earn a 14 percent operating return on its assets. But what if the economy falls into a deep recession, business declines sharply, and Firms A and B only earn a 2 percent operating return on their assets? Let's recompute the return on equity given the new conditions:

| | FIRM A | | FIRM B | |
|---|---|---|---|---|
| Operating profits (OROA = 2%) | $ 20 | | $ 20 | |
| Less interest expense | 0 | | (36) | |
| Net income | $ 20 | | ($ 16) | |
| Return on equity: | | | | |
| $\dfrac{\text{net income}}{\text{common equity}}$ | $\dfrac{\$ 20}{\$1,000}$ | = 2% | $\dfrac{(\$ 16)}{\$400}$ | = (4%) |

Now the use of financial leverage has a negative influence on the return on equity, with Firm B earning less than Firm A for its owners. This results from Firm B's earning less than the interest rate of 6 percent; consequently, the shareholders have to make up the difference. Thus, financial leverage is a two-edged sword: When times are good, financial leverage can make them very, very good, but when times are bad, financial leverage makes them very, very bad. Financial leverage can enhance the returns of the shareholders, but it also increases the possibility of losses, thereby increasing the uncertainty, or risk, for the owners. Chapter 12 will address financial leverage in greater detail.

Returning to Home Depot, Figure 4-4 provides a summary of our discussion of the return on equity and helps us visualize the two fundamental factors affecting a firm's return on equity:

1. There is a direct relationship between a firm's operating return on assets (OROA) and the resulting return on equity (ROE). As we have explained, the higher the operating return on assets (OROA), the higher will be the return on equity (ROE). Even more precisely, the greater the difference between the firm's operating return on assets (OROA) and the interest rate ($i$) being paid on the firm's debt, the higher the return on equity will be. So increasing the operating return on assets relative to the interest rate (OROA-$i$) increases the return on equity (ROE). But if OROA-$i$ decreases, then ROE will decrease as well.

2. Increasing the amount of debt financing relative to the amount of equity (increasing the debt ratio) increases the return on equity if the operating return on assets is higher than the interest rate being paid. If the operating return on assets falls below the interest rate, more debt financing will decrease the return on equity.

In short, the return on equity is driven by (1) the difference between the operating return on assets and the interest rate (OROA-$i$) and (2) how much debt is used, as measured by the debt ratio.

To recap, remember that the return on equity is the financial analysis tool that we use to measure the return on the owners' equity, which is shown as follows:

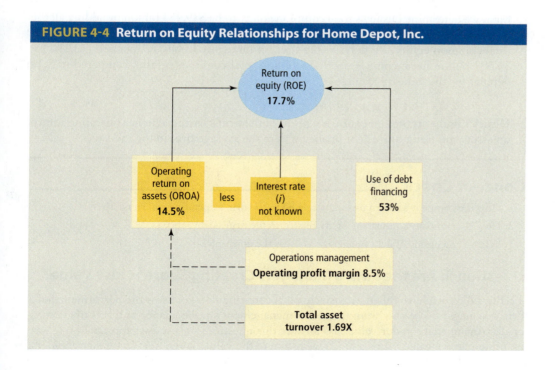

**FIGURE 4-4  Return on Equity Relationships for Home Depot, Inc.**

Return on equity (ROE)
17.7%

Operating return on assets (OROA)
14.5%

less

Interest rate ($i$)
not known

Use of debt financing
53%

Operations management
Operating profit margin 8.5%

Total asset turnover 1.69X

| FINANCIAL DECISION TOOLS | | |
| --- | --- | --- |
| **Name of Tool** | **Formula** | **What It Tells You** |
| Return on equity | $\dfrac{\text{net income}}{\text{total common equity}}$ | The shareholders' accounting return on their investment, which is the result of how well management does at generating a good operating return on assets and how the firm is financed. |

### EXAMPLE 4.4    Evaluating Disney's Return on equity

The net income and also the common equity invested by Disney's shareholders (expressed in $ millions) are provided here, along with the average return on equity for the industry. Evaluate the rate of return being earned on the common stockholders' equity investment. In addition to comparing the Disney Corporation's return on equity to the industry, consider the implications Disney's operating return on assets and its debt financing practices have on the firm's return on equity.

| | |
| --- | --- |
| Net income | $4,807 |
| Total common equity | |
|     Common stock (par value) | 27 |
|     Paid-in capital | 30,269 |
|     Retained earnings | 35,745 |
|     Treasury stock | (26,588) |
| Industry average return on equity | 8.31% |

#### STEP 1: FORMULATE A DECISION STRATEGY
To evaluate return on equity, recall equation 4-14:

$$\text{Return on equity} = \frac{\text{net income}}{\text{total common equity}}$$

#### STEP 2: CRUNCH THE NUMBERS
First, we determine Disney's total common equity to be $39.453 billion by adding all the individual equity items shown above. Then, dividing net income of $4.807 billion by the total common equity, we find Disney's return on equity to be 12.2 percent (12.2% = $4.807 billion net income ÷ $39.453 billion total common equity), compared to 8.31 percent for the industry average.

#### STEP 3: ANALYZE YOUR RESULTS
Disney's higher return on equity is a result of the firm's having a higher operating return on assets and using more debt financing than the average firm in the industry.

## Concept Check

1. How is a company's return on equity related to the firm's operating return on assets?
2. How is a company's return on equity related to the firm's debt ratio?
3. What is the upside of debt financing? What is the downside?

## Question 5: Are the Firm's Managers Creating Shareholder Value?

To this point, we have relied exclusively on accounting data to assess the performance of a firm's managers. We now want to look at management's performance in terms of creating or destroying shareholder value. To answer this question, we use two approaches: (1) we examine market-value ratios and (2) we estimate the value being created for shareholders, as measured by a popular technique called Economic Value Added (EVA™).

**Market-Value Ratios**    There are two ratios commonly used to compare a firm's stock price to its earnings and to accounting book value of its equity. These two ratios indicate what investors think of management's past performance and future prospects.

*Price/Earnings Ratio*    The **price/earnings** (P/E) **ratio** indicates how much investors are willing to pay for $1 of reported earnings. Returning to Home Depot, the firm had net income in the fiscal year of 2010 of $3.338 billion and 1.623 billion shares of common stock outstanding. (See Table 4-1.) Accordingly, its earnings per share were $2.06 ($2.06 = $3,338 million net income ÷ 1,623 million shares). At the time, the firm's stock was selling for $36.77 per share. Thus, the price/earnings ratio was 17.85 times, calculated as follows:

$$\text{Price/earnings ratio } = \frac{\text{market price per share}}{\text{earnings per share}} \qquad (4\text{-}15)$$

For Home Depot:

$$\text{Price/earnings ratio} = \frac{\text{market price per share}}{\text{earnings per share}} = \frac{\$36.77}{\$2.06} = 17.85\text{X}$$

| Lowe's price/earnings ratio | 16.90X |
|---|---|

Home Depot's price/earnings ratio tells us that the investors were willing to pay $17.85 for every dollar of earnings per share that Home Depot produced, compared to only $16.90 for $1 of earnings from Lowe's. Thus, investors were willing to pay somewhat more for Home Depot's earnings than they were for Lowe's. Why might that be? The price/earnings ratio will be higher for companies that investors think have strong earnings growth prospects and/or less risk. Thus, investors must perceive Home Depot to have more growth potential and/or smaller risk than Lowe's.

*Price/Book Ratio*    A second frequently used indicator of investors' assessment of the firm is its **price/book ratio**. This ratio compares the market value of a share of stock to its book value per share. Book value per share comes from of the firm's total common equity in its balance sheet. We already know that the market price of Home Depot's common stock was $36.77. To determine the equity book value per share, we divide the firm's equity book value (total common equity) by the number of shares of stock outstanding. From Home Depot's balance sheet (Table 4-2), we see that the equity book value was $18.889 billion. Given that Home Depot had 1.623 billion shares outstanding, the equity book value per share is $11.64 ($11.64 = $18.889 billion book equity value ÷ 1.623 billion shares. With this information, we determine the price/book ratio to be:

$$\text{Price/book ratio} = \frac{\text{market price per share}}{\text{equity book value per share}} \qquad (4\text{-}16)$$

For Home Depot:

$$\text{Price/book ratio } = \frac{\text{market price per share}}{\text{equity book value per share}} = \frac{\$36.77}{\$11.64} = 3.16\text{X}$$

| Lowe's price/book ratio | 1.95X |
|---|---|

Given that the book value per share is an accounting number that reflects historical costs, we can think of it roughly as the amount shareholders have invested in the business over its lifetime. Thus, a ratio greater than 1 indicates that investors believe the firm is more valuable than the amount shareholders have invested in it. Conversely, a ratio less than 1 suggests that investors do not believe the stock is worth the amount shareholders have invested in it. Clearly, investors believed that Home Depot's stock was worth more than was originally invested in the company, since they were willing to pay $3.16 per share for each dollar of equity book value (total common equity). In comparison, Lowe's stock was selling for only $1.95 for every $1 in book equity. Again, the investors were signaling that they believed that Home Depot had more growth prospects relative to its risk.

---

**price/earnings ratio** the price the market places on $1 of a firm's earnings. For example, if a firm has an earnings per share of $2, and a stock price of $30 per share, its price/earnings ratio is 15. ($30 ÷ $2).

**price/book ratio** the market value of a share of the firm's stock divided by the book value per share of the firm's reported equity in the balance sheet. Indicates the market price placed on $1 of capital that was invested by shareholders.

**Economic Value Added (EVA™)**    The price/book ratio, as just described, indicates whether the shareholders think the firm's equity is worth more or less than the amount of capital they originally invested. If the firm's market value is above the accounting book value (price/book > 1), then management has created value for shareholders, but if the firm's market value is below book value (price/book < 1), then management has destroyed shareholder value.

How is shareholder value created or destroyed? Quite simply, shareholder value is created when a firm earns a rate of return on the capital invested that is greater than the investors' required rate of return. If we invest in a firm and have a 12 percent required rate of return, and the firm earns 15 percent on our capital, then the firm's managers have created value for investors. If instead the firm earns only 10 percent, then value has been destroyed. This concept is regularly applied by firms when they decide whether or not to make large capital investments in plant and equipment; however, it has not been generally applied to the analysis of a firm's day-to-day operations. Instead, managers have traditionally focused on accounting results, such as earnings growth, profit margins, and the return on equity.

In recent years, however, investors have been demanding that managers show evidence that they are creating shareholder value. Although several techniques have been developed for making this assessment, the one that has received the most attention is Economic Value Added (EVA™).

---

### EXAMPLE 4.5    Computing Disney's price/earnings ratio and price/book ratio

Consider the following about Disney:

1.  At the time of our analysis, Disney's stock was selling for $33.
2.  The firm's net income was $3.963 billion, and its total common equity in the balance sheet (book equity) was $37.519 billion.
3.  There were 1.915 billion shares outstanding.

Given the information above, calculate the firm's earnings per share and its book value per share. Calculate the price/earnings ratio and the price/book ratio. The average firm in the industry sold for 11 times earnings and 1.6 times book value. What do the shareholders think about Disney's performance and future growth prospects relative to its competitors?

#### STEP 1: FORMULATE A DECISION STRATEGY

Calculating the price/earnings ratio and the price-to-book ratio for Disney shows how much investors are willing to pay for 1 dollar of Disney's earnings and how much value has been created on a dollar of equity capital invested (book value of equity). The equations to be used are as follows:

$$\text{Price/earnings ratio} = \frac{\text{market price per share}}{\text{earnings per share}}$$

$$\text{Price/book ratio} = \frac{\text{market price per share}}{\text{equity book value per share}}$$

#### STEP 2: CRUNCH THE NUMBERS

We compute Disney's price/earnings ratio and price/book ratio as follows:

$$\text{Earnings per share} = \frac{\text{net income}}{\text{number of shares}}$$

$$= \frac{\$3,963M}{1,915M \text{ shares}} = \$2.07$$

$$\text{Equity book value per share} = \frac{\text{total common equity}}{\text{number of shares}}$$

$$= \frac{\$37,519 \text{ million}}{1,915 \text{ million shares}} = \$19.59$$

$$\text{Price/earnings ratio} = \frac{\text{market price per share}}{\text{earning per share}} = \frac{\$33}{\$2.07} = 15.94X$$

$$\text{Price/book ratio} = \frac{\text{market price per share}}{\text{equity book value per share}}$$

$$= \frac{\$33.00}{\$19.59} = 1.68$$

### STEP 3: ANALYZE YOUR RESULTS

Disney's stock is selling for 15.94 times its earnings and 1.68 times its book value. At the same time, the average firm in the industry was selling for 11 times its earnings and 1.6 times its book value. Thus, investors see Disney as having greater growth prospects and/or less risk.

**Economic Value Added** is a financial performance measure developed by the investment consulting firm Stern Stewart & Co. EVA attempts to measure a firm's economic profit, rather than accounting profit, in a given year. Economic profits assign a cost to the equity capital (the opportunity cost of the funds provided by the shareholders) in addition to the interest cost on the firm's debt—even though accountants recognize only the interest expense as a financing cost when calculating a firm's net income.

For example, assume a firm has total assets of $1,000; 40 percent ($400) is financed with debt, and 60 percent ($600) is financed with equity. If the interest rate on the debt is 5 percent, the firm's interest expense is $20 ($20 = $400 × 0.05), which would be reported on the firm's income statement. However, there would be no cost shown on the income statement for the equity financing. To estimate economic profits, we include not only the $20 in interest expense but also the opportunity cost of the $600 equity capital invested in the firm. For example, if the shareholders could earn 15 percent on another investment of similar risk (their opportunity cost is 15 percent), then we should count that cost just as we do the interest expense. This would involve subtracting not only the $20 in interest but also $90 ($90 = $600 equity × 0.15) as the cost of equity. Thus, the firm has earned an economic profit only if its operating profit exceeds $110 ($20 interest cost + $90 opportunity cost of equity). Stated as a percentage, the firm must earn at least an 11 percent operating return on its assets (11% = $110 ÷ $1,000) in order to meet the investors' required rate of return.

We can calculate Economic Value Added (EVA)—the value created for the shareholders for a given year—as follows:

$$\text{EVA} = \left( \begin{array}{c} \text{operating return} \\ \text{on assets} \end{array} - \begin{array}{c} \text{cost of} \\ \text{capital} \end{array} \right) \times \text{total assets} \qquad (4\text{-}17)$$

where the cost of capital is the cost of the entire firm's capital, both debt and equity. That is, the value created by management is determined by (1) the amount a firm earns on its invested capital relative to the investors' required rate of return and (2) the total amount of capital invested in the firm (total assets).[9]

Continuing with our previous example, assume that our company is earning a 16 percent operating return on its assets (total invested capital). Then the firm's Economic Value Added is $50, calculated as follows:

$$\text{EVA} = \left( \begin{array}{c} \text{operating return} \\ \text{on assets} \end{array} - \begin{array}{c} \text{cost of} \\ \text{capital} \end{array} \right) \times \text{total assets}$$

$$= (0.16 - 0.11) \times \$1000 = \$50$$

Let's see what we find when we estimate Home Depot's Economic Value Added. We know from our previous calculations that in fiscal year ending January 30, 2011, Home Depot had an operating return on assets of 14.5 percent. In other words, the firm was earning operating profits of 14.5 percent on every dollar invested in assets, and it had invested a total of $40.125 billion in assets. If we assume that the firm's cost of capital (the required

**economic value added** measures a company's economic profits, as compared to its accounting profits, by including not only interest expense as a cost but also the shareholders' required rate of return on their investment.

[9]In Chapter 9, we will explain how the firm's cost of capital is calculated.

rate of all the investors) was 10 percent, then we can calculate the Economic Value Added for Home Depot as follows:

$$\text{EVA} = \left( \begin{array}{c} \text{operating return} \\ \text{on assets} \end{array} - \begin{array}{c} \text{cost of} \\ \text{capital} \end{array} \right) \times \text{total assets}$$

$$= (0.145 - 0.10) \times \$40.125 \text{ billion} = \$1.806 \text{ billion}$$

The foregoing explains the EVA concept in its simplest form. However, computing EVA requires converting a firm's financial statements from an accountant's perspective (GAAP) to an economic book value. This process is much more involved than we will go into here, but the basic premise involved in its computation is the same.

A summary of the ratios to be used to determine whether managers are creating shareholder value is as follows:

| FINANCIAL DECISION TOOLS | | |
| --- | --- | --- |
| Name of Tool | Formula | What It Tells You |
| Price/earnings ratio | $\dfrac{\text{market price per share}}{\text{earnings per share}}$ | The price that the market places on $1 of a firm's earnings. The higher (lower) the ratio, the more (less) value investors assign to the firm's earnings. |
| Price/book ratio | $\dfrac{\text{market price per share}}{\text{equity book value per share}}$ | The price that the market places on $1 of the shareholders' investment in the business, measured by the equity book value per share. The higher (lower) the number, the greater (lesser) the market value investors assign to each dollar invested in the company. |
| Economic value added | $\left( \begin{array}{c} \text{operating return} \\ \text{on assets} \end{array} - \begin{array}{c} \text{cost of} \\ \text{capital} \end{array} \right) \times \text{total assets}$ | A measure of a company's economic profits (as compared to its accounting profits), which includes not only interest expense as a cost but also the shareholders' required rate of return on their investment. A positive number says managers created shareholder value, while a negative number indicates that shareholder value was destroyed. |

To conclude, a summary of all the ratios we used to analyze the financial performance of Home Depot is provided in Table 4-3.

---

**EXAMPLE 4.6**   **Calculating Disney's Economic Value Added**

Earlier in the chapter, we determined that Disney's operating return on assets (OROA) was 10.79 percent. If Disney's cost of capital (the cost of both its debt and equity capital) was 9 percent at that time, what was the Economic Value Added (EVA) for the firm when its total assets were approximately $72.124 billion?

**STEP 1: FORMULATE A DECISION STRATEGY**
Economic Value Added includes the opportunity cost of the equity in the total cost of capital, to measure a firm's economic profit.

**STEP 2: CRUNCH THE NUMBERS**
Disney's Economic Value Added is calculated as follows:

$$\text{EVA} = \left( \begin{array}{c} \text{operating return} \\ \text{on assets} \end{array} - \begin{array}{c} \text{cost of} \\ \text{capital} \end{array} \right) \times \text{total assets}$$

$$= (0.1079 - 0.09) \times \$72.124 \text{ billion} = \$1.29 \text{ billion}$$

## STEP 3: ANALYZE YOUR RESULTS

Disney created approximately $1.29 billion in shareholder value by earning a rate of return on the firm's assets, 10.79 percent, that was higher than the investors' required rate of return of 9 percent.

| TABLE 4.3   Home Depot, Inc. Financial Ratio Analysis | | |
|---|---|---|
| **FINANCIAL RATIOS** | **HOME DEPOT** | **LOWE'S** |
| **1. FIRM LIQUIDITY** | | |
| Current ratio $= \dfrac{\text{current assets}}{\text{current liabilities}}$ | $\dfrac{\$13,479M}{\$10,122M} = 1.33$ | 1.40 |
| Acid-test ratio $= \dfrac{\text{cash + accounts receivable}}{\text{current liabilities}}$ | $\dfrac{\$545M + \$1,085M}{\$10,122M} = 0.16$ | 0.12 |
| Days in receivables $= \dfrac{\text{accounts receivable}}{\text{daily credit sales}}$ | $\dfrac{\$1,085M}{\$20,399M \div 365} = 19.41 \text{ days}$ | 16 days |
| Accounts receivable turnover $= \dfrac{\text{annual credit sales}}{\text{accounts receivable}}$ | $\dfrac{\$20,399M}{\$1,085M} = 18.80X$ | 22.81X |
| Days in inventory $= \dfrac{\text{inventory}}{\text{daily cost of goods sold}}$ | $\dfrac{\$10,625M}{\$44,693M \div 365} = 86.77 \text{ days}$ | 95.8 days |
| Inventory turnover $= \dfrac{\text{cost of goods sold}}{\text{inventory}}$ | $\dfrac{\$44,693M}{\$10,625M} = 4.21X$ | 3.81X |
| **2. OPERATING PROFITABILITY** | | |
| Operating return on assets $= \dfrac{\text{operating profits}}{\text{total assets}}$ | $\dfrac{\$5,803M}{\$40,125M} = 14.5\%$ | 10.6% |
| Operating profit margin $= \dfrac{\text{operating profits}}{\text{sales}}$ | $\dfrac{\$5,803M}{\$67,997M} = 8.50\%$ | 7.3% |
| Total asset turnover $= \dfrac{\text{sales}}{\text{total assets}}$ | $\dfrac{\$67,997M}{\$40,125M} = 1.69X$ | 1.45X |
| Accounts receivable turnover $= \dfrac{\text{annual credit sales}}{\text{accounts receivable}}$ | $\dfrac{\$20,399M}{\$1,085M} = 18.80X$ | 22.81X |
| Inventory turnover $= \dfrac{\text{cost of goods sold}}{\text{inventory}}$ | $\dfrac{\$44,693M}{\$10,625M} = 4.21X$ | 3.81X |
| Fixed asset turnover $= \dfrac{\text{sales}}{\text{net fixed assets}}$ | $\dfrac{\$67,997M}{\$25,060M} = 2.71X$ | 2.21X |
| **3. FINANCING DECISIONS** | | |
| Debt ratio $= \dfrac{\text{total debt}}{\text{total assets}}$ | $\dfrac{\$21,236M}{\$40,125M} = 53\%$ | 46% |
| Times interest earned $= \dfrac{\text{operating profits}}{\text{interest}}$ | $\dfrac{\$5,803M}{\$530M} = 10.9X$ | 9.0X |
| **4. RETURN ON EQUITY** | | |
| Return on equity $= \dfrac{\text{net income}}{\text{total common equity}}$ | $\dfrac{\$3,338M}{\$18,889M} = 17.7\%$ | 11.10% |

*(Continued)*

| TABLE 4.3    Home Depot, Inc. Financial Ratio Analysis (*Continued*) | | |
|---|---|---|
| **FINANCIAL RATIOS** | **HOME DEPOT** | **LOWE'S** |
| **5. CREATING SHAREHOLDER VALUE** | | |
| $\dfrac{\text{Price earrnings}}{\text{ratio}} = \dfrac{\text{market price per share}}{\text{earnings per share}}$ | $\dfrac{\$36.77}{\$2.06} = 17.85\text{X}$ | 16.90X |
| $\dfrac{\text{Price}}{\text{book ratio}} = \dfrac{\text{market price per share}}{\text{equity book value per share}}$ | $\dfrac{\$36.77}{\$11.64} = 3.16\text{X}$ | 1.95X |
| $\text{EVA} = \left(\dfrac{\text{operating return}}{\text{on assets}} - \dfrac{\text{cost of}}{\text{capital}}\right) \times \dfrac{\text{total}}{\text{assets}}$ | $(0.145 - 0.10) \times \$40.125 \text{ billion}$ $= \$1.806 \text{ billion}$ | Not computed |

## Concept Check

1. What determines whether a firm is creating or destroying shareholder value?
2. What measures can we use to determine whether a firm is creating shareholder value?
3. What is indicated by a price/book ratio that is greater than 1? Less than 1?
4. How does the information provided by a firm's price/book ratio differ from that provided by its price/earnings ratio?
5. How do the profits shown in an income statement differ from economic profits?
6. What is Economic Value Added? What does it tell you?

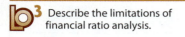

3 Describe the limitations of financial ratio analysis.

## The Limitations of Financial Ratio Analysis

We conclude this chapter by offering several caveats about using financial ratios. We have described how financial ratios can be used to understand a company's financial position. That said, anyone who works with these ratios needs to be aware of the limitations related to their use. The following list includes some of the more important pitfalls you will encounter as you compute and interpret financial ratios:

1. It is sometimes difficult to determine the industry to which a firm belongs when the firm engages in multiple lines of business. In this case, you must select your own set of peer firms and construct your own norms.
2. Published peer group or industry averages are only approximations. They provide the user with general guidelines, rather than scientifically determined averages of the ratios for all—or even a representative sample—of the firms within an industry.
3. An industry average is not necessarily a desirable target ratio or norm. There is nothing magical about an industry norm. At best, an industry average indicates the financial position of the average firm within the industry. It does not mean that value is the ideal or best value for the ratio. For various reasons, a well-managed company might be above the average, whereas another equally good firm might choose to be below the average.
4. Accounting practices differ widely among firms. For example, different firms choose different methods to depreciate their fixed assets. Differences such as these can make the computed ratios of different firms difficult to compare.
5. Financial ratios can be too high or too low. For example, a current ratio that exceeds the industry norm might signal the presence of excess liquidity, resulting in lower profits relative to the firm's investment in assets. On the other hand, a current ratio that falls below the norm might indicate that (1) the firm has inadequate liquidity and may at some future date be unable to pay its bills on time, or (2) the firm is managing its accounts receivable and inventories more efficiently than other, similar firms.
6. Many firms experience seasonal changes in their operations. As a result, their balance sheet entries and their corresponding ratios will vary with the time of year the statements are prepared. To avoid this problem, an average account balance should be used (one calculated

on the basis of several months or quarters during the year) rather than the year-end account balance. For example, an average of the firm's month-end inventory balance might be used to compute its inventory turnover ratio versus a year-end inventory balance.

In spite of their limitations, financial ratios are very useful tools for assessing a firm's financial condition. We should, however, be aware of their potential weaknesses. In many cases, the "real" value derived from the ratios is that they tell us what additional questions we need to ask about the firm.

## Concept Check

1. When comparing a firm to its peers, why is it difficult to determine the industry to which the firm belongs?
2. Why do differences in the accounting practices of firms limit the usefulness of financial ratios?
3. Why should you be careful when comparing a firm with industry norms?

# Chapter Summaries

### Explain the purpose and importance of financial analysis.  (pgs. 102–106)

**SUMMARY:** A variety of groups find financial ratios useful. For instance, both managers and shareholders use them to measure and track a company's performance over time. Financial analysts outside of the firm who have an interest in its economic well-being also use financial ratios. An example of this group would be a loan officer of a commercial bank who wishes to determine the creditworthiness of a loan applicant and its ability to pay the interest and principal associated with the loan request.

#### KEY TERMS

**Financial ratios, page 103** accounting data restated in relative terms in order to help people identify some of the financial strengths and weaknesses of a company.

### Calculate and use a comprehensive set of measurements to evaluate a company's performance.  (pgs 106–128)

**SUMMARY:** Financial ratios are the principal tool of financial analysis. Sometimes referred to simply as benchmarks, ratios standardize the financial information of firms so that comparisons can be made between firms of varying sizes.

Financial ratios can be used to answer at least five questions: (1) How liquid is the company? (2) Are the company's managers effectively generating profits on the firm's assets? (3) How is the firm financed? (4) Are the firm's managers providing a good return on the capital provided by the shareholders? (5) Are the firm's managers creating or destroying shareholder value?

Two methods can be used to analyze a firm's financial ratios. (1) We can examine the firm's ratios across time (say, for the past 5 years) to compare its current and past performance, and (2) we can compare the firm's ratios with those of other firms. In our example, Lowe's was chosen as a comparison firm for analyzing the financial position of Home Depot.

Financial ratios provide a popular way to evaluate a firm's financial performance. However, when evaluating a company's use of its assets (capital) to create firm value, a financial ratio analysis based entirely on the firm's financial statements may not be enough. If we want to understand how the market assesses the performance of a company's managers, we can use the market price of the firm's stock relative to its accounting earnings and equity book value.

Economic Value Added (EVA™) provides another approach for evaluating a firm's performance in terms of shareholder value creation. EVA is equal to the difference between the return on a company's invested capital and the investors' opportunity cost of the funds times the total amount of the capital invested.

## KEY TERMS

**Liquidity, page 107** a firm's ability to pay its bills on time. Liquidity is related to the ease and speed with which a firm can convert its noncash assets into cash, as well as to the size of the firm's investment in noncash assets relative to its short-term liabilities.

**Current ratio, page 107** a firm's current assets divided by its current liabilities. This ratio indicates the firm's degree of liquidity by comparing its current assets to its current liabilities.

**Acid-test (quick) ratio, page 108** the sum of a firm's cash and accounts receivable divided by its current liabilities. This ratio is a more stringent measure of liquidity than the current ratio because it excludes inventories and other current assets (those that are least liquid) from the numerator.

**Days in receivables (average collection period), page 108** a firm's accounts receivable divided by the company's average daily credit sales (annual credit sales ÷ 365). This ratio expresses how many days on average it takes to collect receivables.

**Accounts receivable turnover ratio, page 109** a firm's credit sales divided by its accounts receivable. This ratio expresses how often accounts receivable are "rolled over" during a year.

**Days in inventory, page 109** inventory divided by daily cost of goods sold. This ratio measures the number of days a firm's inventories are held on average before being sold; it also indicates the quality of the inventory.

**Inventory turnover, page 110** a firm's cost of goods sold divided by its inventory. This ratio measures the number of times a firm's inventories are sold and replaced during the year (that is, the relative liquidity of the inventories).

**Operating return on assets (OROA), page 112** the ratio of a firm's operating profits divided by its total assets. This ratio indicates the rate of return being earned on the firm's assets.

**Operations management, page 112** how effectively management is performing in the day-to-day operations in terms of how well management is generating revenues and controlling costs and expenses; in other words, how well is the firm managing the activities that directly affect the income statement?

**Asset management, page 113** how efficiently management is using the firm's asset's to generate sales.

**Operating profit margin, page 113** a firm's operating profits divided by sales. This ratio serves as an overall measure of operating effectiveness.

**Total asset turnover, page 113** a firm's sales divided by its total assets. This ratio is an overall measure of asset efficiency based on the relation between a firm's sales and the total assets.

**Fixed asset turnover, page 114** a firm's sales divided by its net fixed assets. This ratio indicates how efficiently the firm is using its fixed assets.

**Debt ratio, page 117** a firm's total liabilities divided by its total assets. This ratio measures the extent to which a firm has been financed with debt.

**Times interest earned, page 117** a firm's operating profits divided by interest expense. This ratio measures a firm's ability to meet its interest payments from its annual operating earnings.

**Return on equity, page 119** a firm's net income divided by its total common book equity. This ratio is the accounting rate of return earned on the common stockholders' investment.

**Price/earnings ratio, page 123** the price the market places on $1 of a firm's earnings. For example, if a firm has an earnings per share of $2, and a stock price of $30 per share, its price/earnings ratio is 15. ($30 ÷ $2).

**Price/book ratio, page 123** the market value of a share of the firm's stock divided by the book value per share of the firm's reported equity in the balance sheet. Indicates the market price placed on $1 of capital that was invested by shareholders.

**Economic value added, page 125** measures a company's economic profits, as compared to its accounting profits, by including not only interest expense as a cost but also the shareholders' required rate of return on their investment.

## KEY EQUATIONS

$$\text{Current ratio} = \frac{\text{current assets}}{\text{current liabilities}}$$

$$\text{Acid-test ratio} = \frac{\text{cash} + \text{accounts receivable}}{\text{current liabilities}}$$

$$\text{Days in receivable} = \frac{\text{accounts receivable}}{\text{daily credit sales}} = \frac{\text{accounts receivable}}{\text{annual credit sales} \div 365}$$

$$\text{Accounts receivable turnover} = \frac{\text{annual credit sales}}{\text{accounts receivable}}$$

$$\text{Days in inventory} = \frac{\text{inventory}}{\text{daily cost of goods sold}} = \frac{\text{inventory}}{\text{annual cost of goods sold} \div 365}$$

$$\text{Inventory turnover} = \frac{\text{cost of goods sold}}{\text{inventory}}$$

$$\text{Operating return on assets} = \frac{\text{operating profits}}{\text{total assets}}$$

$$\text{Operation return on assets} = \text{operating profit margin} \times \text{total asset turnover}$$

$$\text{Operation return on assets} = \frac{\text{operating profits}}{\text{sales}} \times \frac{\text{sales}}{\text{total assets}}$$

$$\text{Operating profit margin} = \frac{\text{operating profits}}{\text{sales}}$$

$$\text{Total asset turnover} = \frac{\text{sales}}{\text{total assets}}$$

$$\text{Fixed asset turnover} = \frac{\text{sales}}{\text{net fixed assets}}$$

$$\text{Debt ratio} = \frac{\text{total debt}}{\text{total assets}}$$

$$\text{Times interest earned} = \frac{\text{operating profits}}{\text{interest expense}}$$

$$\text{Return on equity} = \frac{\text{net income}}{\text{total common equity}}$$

$$\text{Price/earnings ratio} = \frac{\text{market price per share}}{\text{earnings per share}}$$

$$\text{Price/book ratio} = \frac{\text{market price per share}}{\text{equity book value per share}}$$

$$\text{EVA} = \left( \begin{array}{c} \text{operating return} \\ \text{on assets} \end{array} - \begin{array}{c} \text{cost of} \\ \text{capital} \end{array} \right) \times \text{total assets}$$

---

### Describe the limitations of financial ratio analysis.   (pgs. 128–129)

**SUMMARY:** The following are some of the limitations that you will encounter as you compute and interpret financial ratios:

1. It is sometimes difficult to determine an appropriate industry within which to place the firm.
2. Published industry averages are only approximations, not scientifically determined averages.
3. Accounting practices differ widely among firms and can lead to differences in computed ratios.
4. An industry average may not be a desirable target ratio or norm.
5. Many firms experience seasonal business conditions. As a result, the ratios calculated for them will vary with the time of year the statements are prepared.

In spite of their limitations, financial ratios provide us with a very useful tool for assessing a firm's financial condition.

# Review Questions

*All Review Questions are available in* MyFinanceLab.

**4-1.** Describe the "five-question approach" to using financial ratios.

**4-2.** Discuss briefly the two perspectives that can be taken when performing a ratio analysis.

**4-3.** Where can we obtain industry norms?

**4-4.** What are the limitations of industry average ratios? Discuss briefly.

**4-5.** What is liquidity, and what is the rationale for its measurement?

**4-6.** Distinguish between a firm's operating return on assets and operating profit margin.

**4-7.** Why is a firm's operating return on assets a function of its operating profit margin and total asset turnover?

**4-8.** What is the difference between a firm's gross profit margin, operating profit margin, and net profit margin?

**4-9.** What information do the price/earnings ratio and the price/book ratio give us about the firm and its investors?

**4-10.** Explain what determines a company's return on equity.

**4-11.** What is Economic Value Added? Why is it used?

**4-12.** Go to the Web site for IBM at www.ibm.com/investor. Click "Investor tools" and then "Investment guides" for a guide to reading financial statements. How does the guide differ from the presentation in Chapter 3 and this chapter?

# Study Problems

*All Study Problems are available in* MyFinanceLab.

**4-1.** (*Evaluating liquidity*) Brashear Inc. currently has $2,145,000 in current assets and $858,000 in current liabilities. The company's managers want to increase the firm's inventory, which will be financed by a short-term note with the bank. What level of inventories can the firm carry without its current ratio falling below 2.0?

**4-2.** (*Evaluating profitability*) The Allen Corporation had sales in 2013 of $65 million, total assets of $42 million, and total liabilities of $20 million. The interest rate on the company's debt is 6 percent and its tax rate is 30 percent. The operating profit margin was 12 percent. What were the company's operating profits and net income? What was the operating return on assets and return on equity? Assume that interest must be paid on all of the debt.

**4-3.** (*Evaluating profitability*) Last year, Davies Inc. had sales of $400,000 with a cost of goods sold of $112,000. The firm's operating expenses were $130,000, and its increase in retained earnings was $58,000. There are currently 22,000 common stock shares outstanding and the firm pays a $1.60 dividend per share.

    a.  Assuming the firm's earnings are taxed at 34 percent, construct the firm's income statement.
    b.  Compute the firm's operating profit margin.
    c.  What was the times interest earned?

**4-4.** (*Price book*) Greene Inc.'s balance sheet shows a stockholders' equity book value (total common equity) of $750,500. The firm's earnings per share were $3, resulting in a price/earnings ratio of 12.25X. There are 50,000 shares of common stock outstanding. What is the price/book ratio? What does this indicate about how shareholders view Greene Inc.?

**4-5.** (*Evaluating liquidity*) The Mitchem Marble Company has a target current ratio of 2.0 but has experienced some difficulties financing its expanding sales in the past few months. At present, the firm has current assets of $2.5 million and a current ratio of 2.5. If Mitchem expands its receivables and inventories using its short-term line of credit, how much additional short-term funding can it borrow before its current ratio standard is reached?

**4-6.** (*Ratio analysis*) The balance sheet and income statement for the J. P. Robard Mfg. Company are as follows:

**BALANCE SHEET ($000)**

| | |
|---|---|
| Cash | $   500 |
| Accounts receivable | 2,000 |
| Inventories | 1,000 |
| Current assets | $3,500 |
| Net fixed assets | 4,500 |
| Total assets | $8,000 |
| Accounts payable | $1,100 |
| Accrued expenses | 600 |
| Short-term notes payable | 300 |
| Current liabilities | $2,000 |
| Long-term debt | 2,000 |
| Owners' equity | 4,000 |
| Total liabilities and owners' equity | $8,000 |

**INCOME STATEMENT ($000)**

| | |
|---|---|
| Sales (all credit) | $8,000 |
| Cost of goods sold | (3,300) |
| Gross profit | 4,700 |
| Operating expenses (includes $500 depreciation) | (3,000) |
| Operating profits | $1,700 |
| Interest expense | (367) |
| Earnings before taxes | $1,333 |
| Income taxes (40%) | (533) |
| Net income | $   800 |

Calculate the following ratios:

| | |
|---|---|
| Current ratio | Operating return on assets |
| Times interest earned | Debt ratio |
| Inventory turnover | Average collection period |
| Total asset turnover | Fixed-asset turnover |
| Operating profit margin | Return on equity |

**4-7.** (*Analyzing operating return on assets*) The R. M. Smithers Corporation earned an operating profit margin of 10 percent based on sales of $10 million and total assets of $5 million last year.

a. What was Smithers' total asset turnover ratio?
b. During the coming year the company president has set a goal of attaining a total asset turnover of 3.5. How much must firm sales rise, other things being the same, for the goal to be achieved? (State your answer in both dollars and percentage increase in sales.)
c. What was Smithers' operating return on assets last year? Assuming the firm's operating profit margin remains the same, what will the operating return on assets be next year if the total asset turnover goal is achieved?

**4-8.** (*Evaluating liquidity*) The Brenmar Sales Company had a gross profit margin (gross profits ÷ sales) of 30 percent and sales of $9 million last year. Seventy-five percent of the firm's sales are on credit and the remainder are cash sales. Brenmar's current assets equal $1.5 million, its current liabilities equal $300,000, and it has $100,000 in cash plus marketable securities.

a. If Brenmar's accounts receivable are $562,500, what is its average collection period?
b. If Brenmar reduces its days in receivable (average collection period) to 20 days, what will be its new level of accounts receivable?
c. Brenmar's inventory turnover ratio is 9 times. What is the level of Brenmar's inventories?

**4-9.** (*Ratio analysis*) The financial statements and industry norms are shown below for Pamplin, Inc.:

a. Compute the financial ratios for Pamplin to compare both for 2012 and 2013 against the industry norms.
b. How liquid is the firm?
c. Are its managers generating an adequate operating profit on the firm's assets?
d. How is the firm financing its assets?
e. Are its managers generating a good return on equity?

| | INDUSTRY NORM |
|---|---|
| Current ratio | 5.00 |
| Acid-test (quick) ratio | 3.00 |
| Inventory turnover | 2.20 |
| Average collection period | 90.00 |
| Debt ratio | 0.33 |
| Times interest earned | 7.00 |
| Total asset turnover | 0.75 |
| Fixed-asset turnover | 1.00 |
| Operating profit margin | 20% |
| Return on common equity | 9% |

**Pamplin Inc. Balance Sheet at 12/31/2012 and 12/31/2013**

| ASSETS | | 2012 | | 2013 |
|---|---|---|---|---|
| Cash | | $ 200 | | $ 150 |
| Accounts receivable | | 450 | | 425 |
| Inventory | | 550 | | 625 |
| Current assets | | $1,200 | | $1,200 |
| Plant and equipment | $2,200 | | $ 2,600 | |
| Less accumulated depreciation | (1,000) | | (1,200) | |
| Net plant and equipment | | $1,200 | | $1,400 |
| Total assets | | $2,400 | | $2,600 |
| | | | | |
| **LIABILITIES AND OWNERS' EQUITY** | | | | |
| Accounts payable | | $ 200 | | $ 150 |
| Notes payable—current (9%) | | 0 | | 150 |
| Current liabilities | | $ 200 | | $ 300 |
| Bonds (8.33% interest) | | 600 | | 600 |
| Total debt | | $ 800 | | $ 900 |
| Owners' equity Common stock | $ 300 | | $ 300 | |
| Paid-in capital | 600 | | 600 | |
| Retained earnings | 700 | | 800 | |
| Total owners' equity | | $1,600 | | $1,700 |
| Total liabilities and owners' equity | | $2,400 | | $2,600 |

**Pamplin Inc. Income Statement for Years Ending 12/31/2012 and 12/31/2013**

|  | 2012 | | 2013 | |
|---|---|---|---|---|
| Sales* | | $1,200 | | $1,450 |
| Cost of goods sold | | 700 | | 850 |
| Gross profit | | $ 500 | | $ 600 |
| Operating expenses | 30 | | 40 | |
| Depreciation | 220 | 250 | 200 | 240 |
| Operating profits | | $ 250 | | $ 360 |
| Interest expense | | 50 | | 64 |
| Net income before taxes | | $ 200 | | $ 296 |
| Taxes (40%) | | 80 | | 118 |
| Net income | | $ 120 | | $ 178 |

\* 15% of sales are cash sales, with the remaining 85% being credit sales.

**4-10.** (*Evaluating current and proforma profitability*) (Financial ratios—investment analysis) The annual sales for Salco Inc. were $4.5 million last year. All sales are on credit. The firm's end-of-year balance sheet was as follows:

| Current assets | $  500,000 | Liabilities | $1,000,000 |
|---|---|---|---|
| Net fixed assets | 1,500,000 | Owners' equity | 1,000,000 |
| | $2,000,000 | | $2,000,000 |

The firm's income statement for the year was as follows:

| Sales | $4,500,000 |
|---|---|
| Less cost of goods sold | (3,500,000) |
| Gross profit | $1,000,000 |
| Less operating expenses | (500,000) |
| Operating profits | $ 500,000 |
| Less interest expense | (100,000) |
| Earnings before taxes | $ 400,000 |
| Less taxes (50%) | (200,000) |
| Net income | $ 200,000 |

a. Calculate Salco's total asset turnover, operating profit margin, and operating return on assets.
b. Salco plans to renovate one of its plants, which will require an added investment in plant and equipment of $1 million. The firm will maintain its present debt ratio of 0.5 when financing the new investment and expects sales to remain constant. The operating profit margin will rise to 13 percent. What will be the new operating return on assets for Salco after the plant's renovation?
c. Given that the plant renovation in part (b) occurs and Salco's interest expense rises by $50,000 per year, what will be the return earned on the common stockholders' investment? Compare this rate of return with that earned before the renovation.

**4-11.** (*Financial analysis*) The T. P. Jarmon Company manufactures and sells a line of exclusive sportswear. The firm's sales were $600,000 for the year just ended, and its total assets exceeded $400,000. The company was started by Mr. Jarmon just 10 years ago and has been profitable every year since its inception. The chief financial officer for the firm, Brent Vehlim, has decided to seek a line of credit totaling $80,000 from the firm's bank. In the past, the company has relied on its suppliers to finance a large part of its needs for inventory. However, in recent months tight money conditions have led the firm's suppliers to offer sizable cash discounts to speed up payments for purchases. Mr. Vehlim wants to use the line of credit to replace a large portion of the firm's payables during the summer, which is the firm's peak seasonal sales period.

The firm's two most recent balance sheets were presented to the bank in support of its loan request. In addition, the firm's income statement for the year just ended was provided. These statements are found in the following tables:

**T. P. Jarmon Company, Balance Sheet for 12/31/2012 and 12/31/2013**

|  | 2012 | 2013 |
|---|---|---|
| Cash | $ 15,000 | $ 14,000 |
| Marketable securities | 6,000 | 6,200 |
| Accounts receivable | 42,000 | 33,000 |
| Inventory | 51,000 | 84,000 |
| Prepaid rent | 1,200 | 1,100 |
| Total current assets | $115,200 | $138,300 |
| Net plant and equipment | 286,000 | 270,000 |
| Total assets | $401,200 | $408,300 |
| Accounts payable | $ 48,000 | $ 57,000 |
| Notes payable | 15,000 | 13,000 |
| Accruals | 6,000 | 5,000 |
| Total current liabilities | $ 69,000 | $ 75,000 |
| Long-term debt | 160,000 | 150,000 |
| Common stockholders' equity | 172,200 | 183,300 |
| Total liabilities and equity | $401,200 | $408,300 |

**T. P. Jarmon Company, Income Statement for the Year Ended 12/31/2013**

| | | |
|---|---|---|
| Sales (all credit) | | $600,000 |
| Less cost of goods sold | | 460,000 |
| Gross profit | | $140,000 |
| Less operating and interest expenses | | |
| General and administrative | $30,000 | |
| Interest | 10,000 | |
| Depreciation | 30,000 | |
| Total | | 70,000 |
| Earnings before taxes | | $ 70,000 |
| Less taxes | | 27,100 |
| Net income available to common stockholders | | $ 42,900 |
| Less cash dividends | | 31,800 |
| Change in retained earnings | | $ 11,100 |

Jan Fama, associate credit analyst for the Merchants National Bank of Midland, Michigan, was assigned the task of analyzing Jarmon's loan request.

    a. Calculate the financial ratios for 2013 corresponding to the industry norms provided as follows:

| RATIO | NORM |
|---|---|
| Current ratio | 1.8 |
| Acid-test ratio | 0.9 |
| Debt ratio | 0.5 |
| Times interest earned | 10.0 |
| Average collection period | 20.0 |
| Inventory turnover (based on cost of goods sold) | 7.0 |
| Return on common equity | 12.0% |
| Operating return on assets | 16.8% |
| Operating profit margin | 14.0% |
| Total asset turnover | 1.20 |
| Fixed asset turnover | 1.80 |

b. Which of the ratios reported in the industry norms do you feel should be most crucial in determining whether the bank should extend the line of credit?

c. Prepare Jarmon's statement of cash flows for the year ended December 31, 2013. Interpret your findings.

d. Use the information provided by the financial ratios and the cash flow statement to decide if you would support making the loan.

**4-12.** (*Economic Value Added*) Stegemoller Inc.'s managers want to evaluate the firm's prior-year performance in terms of its contribution to shareholder value. This past year, the firm earned an operating return on investment of 12 percent, compared to an industry norm of 11 percent. It has been estimated that the firm's investors have an opportunity cost on their funds of 14 percent, which is the same as its overall cost of capital. The firm's total assets for the year were $100 million. Compute the amount of economic value created or destroyed by the firm. How does your finding support or fail to support what you would conclude using ratio analysis to evaluate the firm's performance?

**4-13.** Being able to identify an industry to use for benchmarking your firm's results with similar companies is frequently not easy. Choose a type of business and go to www.naics.com. This Web site allows you to do a free search for the NAICS (North American Industry Classification System, pronounced "Nakes") number for different types of businesses. Choose keywords such as "athletic shoes" or "auto dealers" and others to see to which industry they have been assigned.

**4-14.** (*Market-value ratios*) Bremmer Industries has a price/earnings ratio of 16.29X.

a. If Bremmer's earnings per share are $1.35, what is the price per share of Bremmer's stock?

b. Using the price per share you found in part (a), determine the price/book ratio if Bremmer's equity book value per share is $9.58.

**4-15.** (*Financing decisions*) Ellie's Electronics Incorporated has total assets of $63 million and total debt of $42 million. The company also has operating profits of $21 million with interest expenses of $6 million.

a. What is Ellie's debt ratio?

b. What is Ellie's times interest earned?

c. Based on the information above, would you recommend to Ellie's management that the firm is in a strong enough position to assume more debt and increase interest expense to $9 million?

**4-16.** (*Economic Value Added*) Callaway Concrete uses Economic Value Added as a financial performance measure. Callaway has $240 million in assets, and the firm has financed its assets with 37 percent equity and 63 percent debt with an interest rate of 6 percent. The firm's opportunity cost on its funds is 12 percent, while the operating return on the firm's assets is 14 percent.

a. What is the Economic Value Added created or destroyed by Callaway Concrete?

b. What does Economic Value Added measure?

**4-17.** (*Ratio analysis*) Seward, Inc.'s financial statements for 2013 are shown below:

| | |
|---|---|
| Sales | $ 4,500 |
| Cost of goods sold | (2,800) |
| Gross profits | $ 1,700 |
| Operating expenses: | |
| Marketing and general and administrative expenses | $(1,000) |
| Depreciation expenses | (200) |
| Total operating expenses | $(1,200) |
| Operating profits | $ 500 |
| Interest expense | (60) |
| Earnings before taxes (taxable income) | $ 440 |
| Income taxes | (125) |
| Net Income | $ 315 |
| Cash | $ 500 |
| Account receivables | 600 |

*(Continued)*

| | |
|---|---:|
| Inventories | 900 |
| Total current assets | $ 2,000 |
| Gross fixed assets | $ 2,100 |
| Accumulated depreciation | (800) |
| Net fixed assets | $ 1,300 |
| Total assets | $ 3,300 |
| **LIABILITIES (DEBT) AND EQUITY** | |
| Accounts payable | $   500 |
| Short-term notes payable | 300 |
| Total current liabilities | $   800 |
| Long-term debt | 400 |
| Total liabilities | $1,200 |
| Common equity: | |
| Common stock (par and paid in capital) | $   500 |
| Retained earnings | 1,600 |
| Total common equity | $2,100 |
| Total liabilities and equity | $3,300 |

The chief financial officer for Seward has acquired industry averages for the following ratios:

| | |
|---|---|
| Current ratio | 3.0 |
| Acid-test ratio | 1.50 |
| Days in receivables | 40.0 |
| Days in inventories | 70.2 |
| Operating return on assets | 12.5% |
| Operating profit margin | 8.0% |
| Total asset turnover | 1.6 |
| Fixed-asset turnover | 3.1 |
| Debt ratio | 33% |
| Times interest earned | 6.0 |
| Return on equity | 11.0% |

a.  Compute the ratios listed above for Seward.
b.  Compared to the industry:
   1.  How liquid is the firm?
   2.  Are its managers generating attractive operating profit on the firm's assets?
   3.  How is the firm financing its assets?
   4.  Are its managers generating a good return on equity?

**4-18.** (*Computing ratios*) Use the information from the balance sheet and income statement below to calculate the following ratios:

| | |
|---|---|
| Current ratio | Days in receivables |
| Acid-test ratio | Operating return on assets |
| Times interest earned | Debt ratio |
| Inventory turnover | Return on equity |
| Total asset turnover | Fixed asset turnover |
| Operating profit margin | |

| | |
|---|---:|
| Cash | $100,000 |
| Accounts receivable | 30,000 |
| Inventory | 50,000 |
| Prepaid expenses | 10,000 |
| Total current assets | $190,000 |
| Gross plant and equipment | 401,000 |
| Accumulated depreciation | (66,000) |
| Total assets | $525,000 |
| Accounts payable | $ 90,000 |
| Accrued liabilities | 63,000 |
| Total current debt | $153,000 |
| Long-term debt | 120,000 |
| Common stock | 205,000 |
| Retained earnings | 47,000 |
| Total debt and equity | $525,000 |
| Sales* | $210,000 |
| Cost of goods sold | (90,000) |
| Gross profit | $120,000 |
| | |
| Selling, general, and administrative expenses | (29,000) |
| Depreciation expense | (26,000) |
| Operating profits | $65,000 |
| Interest expense | (8,000) |
| Earnings before taxes | $57,000 |
| Taxes | (16,000) |
| Net income | $41,000 |

*12% of sales are cash sales.

# Mini Case

*This Mini Case is available in MyFinanceLab.*

After graduating from college in December 2011, Alyssa Randall started her career at the G&S Corporation, a small- to medium-sized warehouse distributor in Nashville, Tennessee. The company was founded by Jack Griggs and Johnny Stites in 1998, after they had worked together in management at Wal-Mart. Although Randall had an offer from Sam's Club, she became excited about the opportunity with G&S. Griggs and Stites, as CEO and VP-marketing, respectively, assured her that she would be given every opportunity to take a leadership role in the business as quickly as she was ready.

In addition to receiving a competitive salary, Randall will immediately be entitled to a bonus based on how well the company does financially. The bonus is determined by the amount of Economic Value Added (EVA) that is generated in a year. To begin, she would receive 1 percent of the firm's EVA each year, to be paid half in stock and half in cash. In any year that the EVA is negative, she will not receive a bonus. Also, the firm's stock is traded publicly on the American Stock Exchange.

The year of 2012 turned out to be a good year financially for the business. But in the ensuing year, 2013, the company experienced a 5.3 percent sales reduction, where sales declined from $5.7 million to $5.4 million. The downturn then led to other financial problems, including a 50 percent reduction in the company's stock price. The share price went from $36 per share at the end of 2012 to $18 per share at the conclusion of 2013!

Financial information for G&S for both years is shown below, where all the numbers, except for per-share data, are shown in $ thousands.

    a. Using what you have learned in this chapter and Chapter 3, prepare a financial analysis of G&S, comparing the firm's financial performance between the two years. In addition to the financial information provided below, the company's chief financial officer, Mike Stegemoller, has estimated the company's average cost of capital for all its financing to be 10.5 percent.

    b. What conclusions can you make from your analysis?

    c. How much will Randall's bonus be in 2012 and 2013, both in the form of cash and stock? How many shares of the stock will Randall receive?

    d. What recommendations would you make to management?

**G&S Corporation Income Statements**

|  | 2012 | 2013 |
|---|---|---|
| Sales | $ 5,700 | $ 5,400 |
| Cost of goods sold | (3,700) | (3,600) |
| Gross profits | $ 2,000 | $ 1,800 |
| Operating expenses: |  |  |
| Selling and G&A expenses | $ (820) | $ (780) |
| Depreciation expenses | (340) | (500) |
| Total operating expenses | $(1,160) | $(1,280) |
| Operating profits | $ 840 | $ 520 |
| Interest expense | (200) | (275) |
| Earnings before taxes (taxable income) | $ 640 | $ 245 |
| Income taxes | (230) | (65) |
| Net Income | $ 410 | $ 180 |
| Additional information: |  |  |
| Number of common shares outstanding | 150 | 150 |
| Dividends paid to stockholders | $ 120 | $ 120 |
| Market price per share | $ 36 | $ 18 |

**G&S Corporation Balance Sheets**

|  | 2012 | 2013 |
|---|---|---|
| **ASSETS** | | |
| Cash | $ 300 | $ 495 |
| Accounts receivable | 700 | 915 |
| Inventories | 600 | 780 |
| Other current assets | 125 | 160 |
| Total current assets | $1,725 | $2,350 |
| Gross fixed assets | $4,650 | $4,950 |
| Accumulated depreciation | (1,700) | (2,200) |
| Net fixed assets | $2,950 | $2,750 |
| Total assets | $4,675 | $5,100 |
| **LIABILITIES (DEBT) AND EQUITY** | | |
| Accounts payable | $ 400 | $ 640 |
| Short-term notes payable | 250 | 300 |
| Total current liabilities | $ 650 | $ 940 |
| Long-term debt | 1,250 | 1,325 |
| Total liabilities | $1,900 | $2,265 |
| Common equity: | | |
| Common stock | $1,100 | $1,100 |
| Retained earnings | 1,675 | 1,735 |
| Total common equity | $2,775 | $2,835 |
| Total liabilities and equity | $4,675 | $5,100 |

# The Time Value of Money

## Learning Objectives

| | | |
|---|---|---|
| **1** | **Explain** the mechanics of compounding and bringing the value of money back to the present. | **Compound Interest, Future, and Present Value** |
| **2** | **Understand** annuities. | **Annuities** |
| **3** | **Determine** the future or present value of a sum when there are nonannual compounding periods. | **Making Interest Rates Comparable** |
| **4** | **Determine** the present value of an uneven stream of payments and understand perpetuities. | **The Present Value of an Uneven Stream and Perpetuities** |

In business, there is probably no other single concept with more power or applications than that of the time value of money. In his landmark book, *A History of Interest Rates*, Sidney Homer noted that if $1,000 was invested for 400 years at 8 percent interest, it would grow to $23 quadrillion—that would work out to approximately $5 million per person on earth. He was not giving a plan to make the world rich but effectively pointing out the power of the time value of money.

The time value of money is certainly not a new concept. Benjamin Franklin had a good understanding of how it worked when he left £1,000 each to Boston and Philadelphia. With the gift, he left instructions that the cities were to lend the money, charging the going interest rate, to worthy apprentices. Then, after the money had been invested in this way for 100 years, they were to use a portion of the investment to build something of benefit to the city and hold some back for the future. Two hundred years later, Franklin's Boston gift resulted in the construction of the Franklin Union, has helped countless medical students with loans, and still has over $3 million left in the account. Philadelphia, likewise, has reaped a significant reward from his gift with its portion of the gift growing to over $2 million. Bear in mind that all this has come from a gift of £2,000 with some serious help from the time value of money.

The power of the time value of money can also be illustrated through a story Andrew Tobias tells in his book *Money Angles*. There he tells of a peasant who wins a chess tournament put on by the king. The king asks the peasant what he would like as the prize. The peasant answers that he would like for his village one piece of grain to be placed on the first square of his chessboard, two pieces of grain on the second square, four pieces on the third, eight on the fourth, and so forth. The king, thinking he was getting off easy, pledged on his word of honor that it would be done. Unfortunately for the king, by the time all 64 squares on the chessboard were filled, there were 18.5 million trillion grains of wheat on the board—the kernels were compounding at a rate of 100 percent over the 64 squares of the chessboard. Needless to say, no one in the village ever went hungry; in fact, that is so much wheat that if each kernel were one-quarter inch long (quite frankly, I have no idea how long a kernel of

wheat is, but Andrew Tobias's guess is one-quarter inch), if laid end to end, they could stretch to the sun and back 391,320 times.

Understanding the techniques of compounding and moving money through time is critical to almost every business decision. It will help you to understand such varied things as how stocks and bonds are valued, how to determine the value of a new project, how much you should save for your children's education, and how much your mortgage payments will be.

In the next six chapters, we focus on determining the value of the firm and the desirability of the investments it considers making. A key concept that underlies this material is the time value of money; that is, a dollar today is worth more than a dollar received a year from now. Intuitively this idea is easy to understand. We are all familiar with the concept of interest. This concept illustrates what economists call an opportunity cost of passing up the earning potential of a dollar today. This opportunity cost is the time value of money.

To evaluate and compare investment proposals, we need to examine how dollar values might accrue from accepting these proposals. To do this, all the dollar values must first be comparable. In other words, we must move all dollar flows back to the present or out to a common future date. An understanding of the time value of money is essential, therefore, to an understanding of financial management, whether basic or advanced.

# Compound Interest, Future, and Present Value

 Explain the mechanics of compounding and bringing the value of money back to the present.

We begin our study of the time value of money with some basic tools for visualizing the time pattern of cash flows. While timelines seem simple at first glance, they can be a tremendous help for more complicated problems.

## Using Timelines to Visualize Cash Flows

As a first step in visualizing cash flows, we can construct a timeline, a linear representation of the timing of cash flows. A timeline identifies the timing and amount of a stream of cash flows—both cash received and cash spent—along with the interest rate it earns. Timelines are a critical first step used by financial analysts to solve financial problems. We will refer to them often throughout this text.

To illustrate how to construct a timeline, consider the following example, where we receive annual cash flows over the course of 4 years. The following timeline shows our cash inflows and outflows from time period 0 (the present) until the end of year 4:

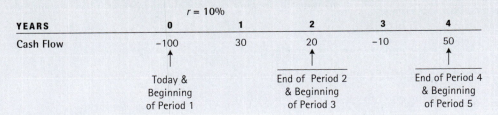

For our purposes, time periods are identified on the top of the timeline, and in this example, the time periods are measured in years, which are indicated on the far left of the timeline. Thus, time period 0 is both today and the beginning of the first year. The dollar amount of the cash flow received or spent at each time period is shown below the timeline. Positive values represent *cash inflows*. Negative values represent *cash outflows*. For example, in the timeline shown, a $100 cash outflow occurs today, or at time 0, followed by cash inflows of $30 and $20 at the end of years 1 and 2, a negative cash flow (a cash outflow) of $10 at the end of year 3, and finally a cash inflow of $50 at the end of year 4.

The units of measurement on the timeline are time periods and are typically expressed in years but could be expressed as months, days, or any unit of time. However, for now, let's assume we're looking at cash flows that occur annually. Thus, the distance between 0 and 1 represents the period between today and the end of the first year. Consequently, time period 0 indicates today, while time period 1 represents the end of the first year, which is also the beginning of the second year. (You can think of it as being both the last second of the first year and the first second of the second year.) The interest rate, which is 10 percent in this example, is listed above the timeline.

In this chapter and throughout the text, we will often refer to the idea of moving money through time. Because this concept is probably not familiar to everyone, we should take a moment to explain it. Most business investments involve investing money today. Then, in subsequent years, the investment produces cash that comes back to the business. To evaluate an investment, you need to compare the amount of money the investment requires today with the amount of money the investment will return to you in the future and adjust these numbers for the fact that a dollar today is worth more than a dollar in the future. Timelines simplify solving time value of money problems, and they are not just for beginners; experienced financial analysts use them as well. In fact, the more complex the problem you're trying to solve, the more valuable a timeline will be in terms of helping you visualize exactly what needs to be done.

Most of us encounter the concept of compound interest at an early age. Anyone who has ever had a savings account or purchased a government savings bond has received compound interest. **Compound interest** occurs when *interest paid on the investment during the first period is added to the principal; then, during the second period, interest is earned on this new sum.*

**compound interest** the situation in which interest paid on an investment during the first period is added to the principal. During the second period, interest is earned on the original principal plus the interest earned during the first period.

For example, suppose we place $100 in a savings account that pays 6 percent interest, compounded annually. How will our savings grow? At the end of the first year we have earned 6 percent, or $6 on our initial deposit of $100, giving us a total of $106 in our savings account, thus,

$$\text{Value at the end of year 1} = \text{present value} \times (1 + \text{interest rate})$$
$$= \$100(1 + 0.06)$$
$$= \$100(1.06)$$
$$= \$106$$

Carrying these calculations one period further, we find that we now earn the 6 percent interest on a principal of $106, which means we earn $6.36 in interest during the second year. Why do we earn more interest during the second year than we did during the first? Simply because we now earn interest on the sum of the original principal and the interest we earned in the first year. In effect we are now earning interest on interest; this is the concept of compound interest. Examining the mathematical formula illustrating the earning of interest in the second year, we find

**REMEMBER YOUR PRINCIPLES**

**Principle** In this chapter we develop the tools to incorporate **Principle 2: Money Has a Time Value** into our calculations. In coming chapters we use this concept to measure value by bringing the benefits and costs from a project back to the present.

$$\text{Value at the end of year 2} = \text{value at the end of year 1} \times (1 + r)$$

where $r =$ the annual interest (or discount) rate, which for our example gives

$$\text{Value at the end of year 2} = \$106 \times (1.06)$$
$$= \$112.36$$

Looking back, we can see that the **future value** at the end of year 1, or $106, is actually equal to the present value times $(1 + r)$, or $100(1 + 0.06)$. Moving forward to year 2 we find,

$$\text{Value at the end of year 2} = \text{present value} \times (1 + r) \times (1 + r)$$
$$= \text{present value} \times (1 + r)^2$$

Carrying this forward into the third year, we find that we enter the year with $112.36 and we earn 6 percent, or $6.74 in interest, giving us a total of $119.10 in our savings account. This can be expressed as

$$\text{Value at the end of year 3} = \text{present value} \times (1 + r) \times (1 + r) \times (1 + r)$$
$$= \text{present value} \times (1 + r)^3$$

By now a pattern is becoming apparent. We can generalize this formula to illustrate the future value of our investment if it is compounded annually at a rate of $r$ for $n$ years to be

$$\text{Future value} = \text{present value} \times (1 + r)^n$$

Letting $FV_n$ stand for the future value at the end of $n$ periods and $PV$ stand for the present value, we can rewrite this equation as

$$FV_n = PV(1 + r)^n \tag{5-1}$$

We also refer to $(1 + r)^n$ as the **future value factor**. Thus, to find the future value of a dollar amount, all you need to do is multiply that dollar amount times the appropriate future value factor,

$$\text{Future value} = \text{present value} \times (\text{future value factor})$$

where future value factor $= (1 + r)^n$.

Figure 5-1 illustrates how this investment of $100 would continue to grow for the first 20 years at a compound interest rate of 6 percent. Notice how the amount of interest earned annually increases each year. Again, the reason is that each year interest is

**future value** the amount to which your investment will grow, or a future dollar amount.

**future value factor** the value of $(1 + r)^n$ used as a multiple to calculate an amount's future value.

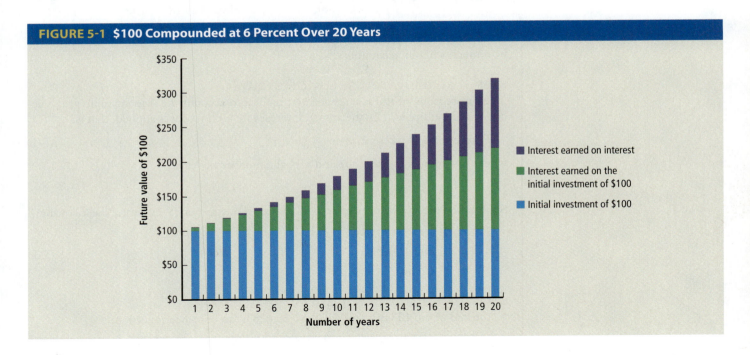

**FIGURE 5-1  $100 Compounded at 6 Percent Over 20 Years**

Future value of $100 (y-axis)

Number of years (x-axis)

■ Interest earned on interest
■ Interest earned on the initial investment of $100
■ Initial investment of $100

**FIGURE 5-2   The Future Value of $100 Initially Deposited and Compounded at 0, 5, 10, and 15 Percent**

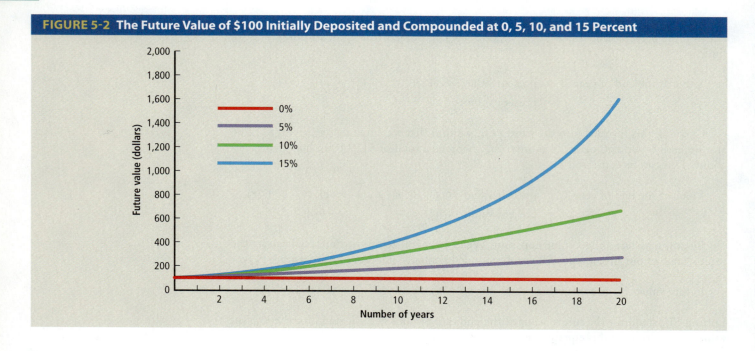

received on the sum of the original investment plus any interest earned in the past. The situation in which interest is earned on interest that was earned in the past is referred to as compound interest. *If you only earned interest on your initial investment*, it would be referred to as **simple interest**.

When we examine the relationship between the number of years an initial investment is compounded for and its future value, as shown graphically in Figure 5-2, we see that we can increase the future value of an investment by either increasing the number of years for which we let it compound or by compounding it at a higher interest rate. We can also see this from equation (5-1) because an increase in either $r$ or $n$ while the present value is held constant results in an increase in the future value.

**simple interest** if you only earned interest on your initial investment, it would be referred to as simple interest.

---

**EXAMPLE 5.1**   **Calculating the future value of an investment**

If we place $1,000 in a savings account paying 5 percent interest compounded annually, how much will our account accrue to in 10 years?

**STEP 1: FORMULATE A SOLUTION STRATEGY**
The future value of the savings account takes into account the present value of the account and multiplies it by the annual interest rate each year it is applied, that is,

$$\text{Future value} = \text{present value} \times (1 + r)^n \tag{5-1}$$

where $r$ = annual interest rate and $n$ = the number of years.

**STEP 2: CRUNCH THE NUMBERS**
Substituting present value, percent, and 10 years into equation (5-1), we get the following:

$$\begin{aligned} FV_n &= \$1,000(1 + 0.05)^{10} \\ &= \$1,000(1.62889) \\ &= \$1,628.89 \end{aligned} \tag{5-1}$$

**STEP 3: ANALYZE YOUR RESULTS**
At the end of the 10 years, we will have $1,628.89 in our savings account.

## Techniques for Moving Money Through Time

There are three different approaches that you can use to solve a time value of money problem. The first is to simply do the math. Financial calculators are a second alternative, and there are a number of them that do a good job of solving time value of money problems. Based on many years of experience, the Texas Instruments BA II Plus or the Hewlett-Packard 10BII calculators would be excellent choices. Finally, spreadsheets can move money through time, and in the real world, they are without question the tool of choice. Now let's take a look at all three alternatives.

**Mathematical Calculations**   If we want to calculate the future value of an amount of money, the mathematical calculations are relatively straightforward. However, as we will see, time value of money calculations are easier using a financial calculator or spreadsheet. Those are the chosen methods in the real world.

---

**EXAMPLE 5.2**   **Calculating future value of an investment**

If we invest $500 in a bank where it will earn 8 percent interest compounded annually, how much will it be worth at the end of 7 years?

**STEP 1: FORMULATE A SOLUTION STRATEGY**
The future value of the savings account is found using the same method as in Example 5.1 using equation (5-1) as follows:

$$\text{Future value} = \text{present value} \times (1 + r)^n \tag{5-1}$$

**STEP 2: CRUNCH THE NUMBERS**
Substituting into equation (5-1) we compute the future value of our account as follows:

$$FV = \$500(1 + 0.08)^7 = \$856.91$$

**STEP 3: ANALYZE YOUR RESULTS**
At the end of 7 years, we will have $856.91 in our savings account. In the future we will find several uses for equation (5-1); not only can we find the future value of an investment but we can also solve for the present value, $r$, or $n$.

---

**Using a Financial Calculator**   Before we review the use of the financial calculator, let's review the five "time value of money" keys on a financial calculator. Although the specific keystrokes used to perform time value of money calculations differ slightly when using financial calculators made by different companies, the symbols used are basically the same. Below are the keystrokes as they appear on a Texas Instruments BA II Plus calculator.

| MENU KEY | DESCRIPTION |
| --- | --- |
| Menu Keys we will use in this chapter include: | |
| N | Stores (or calculates) the total number of payments or compounding periods. |
| I/Y | Stores (or calculates) the interest (or discount or growth) rate per period. |
| PV | Stores (or calculates) the present value of a cash flow (or series of cash flows). |
| FV | Stores (or calculates) the future value, that is, the dollar amount of a final cash flow (or the compound value of a single flow or series of cash flows). |
| PMT | Stores (or calculates) the dollar amount of each annuity (or equal) payment deposited or received. |

The keys shown here correspond to the TI BA II Plus calculator. Other financial calculators have essentially the same keys. They are simply labeled a little differently. We should stop and point out that the labels on the keys of financial calculators are slightly different than what we have been using in our mathematical formulas. For example, we have used a lowercase $n$ to refer to the number of compounding periods, whereas an uppercase N appears on the Texas Instruments BA II Plus calculator. Likewise, the I/Y key refers to the rate of interest per period, whereas we have used $r$. Some financial calculators also have a CPT key, which stands for "compute." It is simply the key you press when you want the calculator to begin solving your problem. Finally, the PMT key refers to a fixed payment received or paid each period.

At this point you might be wondering exactly why we are using different symbols in this book than are used on calculators. The answer is that, unfortunately, the symbols used by the different companies that design and make financial calculators are not consistent. The symbols in Microsoft Excel are somewhat different as well.

An important thing to remember when using a financial calculator is that cash outflows (investments you make rather than receive) generally have to be entered as negative numbers. In effect, a financial calculator sees money as "leaving your hands" and therefore taking on a *negative* sign when you invest it. The calculator then sees the money "returning to your hands" and therefore taking on a *positive* sign after you've earned interest on it. Also, every calculator operates a bit differently with respect to entering variables. Needless to say, it is a good idea to familiarize yourself with exactly how your calculator functions.[1]

Once you've entered all the variables you know, including entering a zero for any variable with a value of zero, you can let the calculator do the math for you. If you own a Texas Instruments BA II Plus calculator, press the compute key (CPT), followed by the key corresponding to the unknown variable you're trying to determine. With a Hewlett-Packard calculator, once the known variables are entered, you need only press the key corresponding to the final variable to calculate its value.

A good starting place when working a problem is to write down all the variables you know. Then assign a value of zero to any variables that are not included in the problem. Once again, make sure that the sign you give to the different variables reflects the direction of the cash flow.

*Calculator Tips—Getting It Right*  Calculators are pretty easy to use. But there are some common mistakes that are often made. So, before you take a crack at solving a problem using a financial calculator ensure that you take the following steps:

1. **Set your calculator to one payment per year.** Some financial calculators use monthly payments as the default. Change it to annual payments. Then consider $n$ to be the number of periods and $r$ the interest rate per period.
2. **Set your calculator to display at least four decimal places or to floating decimal place (nine decimal places).** Most calculators are preset to display only two decimal places. Because interest rates are so small, change your decimal setting to at least four.
3. **Set your calculator to the "end" mode.** Your calculator will assume cash flows occur at the end of each time period.

*When you're ready to work a problem, remember:*

1. **Every problem must have at least one positive and one negative number.** The pre-programming within the calculator assumes that you are analyzing problems in which money goes out (outflows) and comes in (inflows), so you have to be sure to enter the sign appropriately. If you are using a BA II Plus calculator and get an "Error 5" message, that means you are solving for either $r$ or $n$ and you input both the present and future values as positive numbers—correct that and re-solve the problem.
2. **You must enter a zero for any variable that isn't used in a problem, or you have to clear the calculator before beginning a new problem.** If you don't clear your calculator or enter a value for one of the variables, your calculator won't assume that that variable is zero. Instead, your calculator will assume it carries the same number as

[1]Appendix A at www.pearsonhighered.com/keown provides a tutorial that covers both the Texas Instruments BA II Plus and the Hewlett-Packard 10BII calculators.

it did during the previous problem. So be sure to clear out the memory (CLR, TVM) or enter zeros for variables not included in the problem.

3. **Enter the interest rate as a percent, not a decimal.** That means 10 percent must be entered as 10 rather than 0.10.

Two popular financial calculators are the Texas Instruments BA II Plus (TI BA II Plus) and the Hewlett-Packard 10BII (HP 10BII). If you're using one of these calculators and encounter any problems, take a look at Appendix A at www.pearsonhighered.com/keown. It provides a tutorial for both of these calculators.

**Spreadsheets**   Practically speaking, most time value of money calculations are now done on computers with the help of spreadsheet software. Although there are competing spreadsheet programs, the most popular is Microsoft Corporation's Excel®. Just like financial calculators, Excel has "built-in" functions that make it really easy to do future value calculations.

*Excel Tips—Getting It Right*

1. **Take advantage of the formula help that Excel offers.** All Excel functions are set up the same way: First, with the "=" sign; second, with the function's name (for example, FV or PV); and third, with the inputs into that function enclosed in parentheses. The following, for example, is how the future value function looks:

   = FV(rate,nper,pmt,pv)

   When you begin typing in your Excel function in a spreadsheet cell (that is, a box where you enter a single piece of data), all the input variables will appear at the top of the spreadsheet in their proper order, so you will know what variable must be entered next. For example, = FV(**rate**,nper,pmt,pv,type) will come into view, with **rate** appearing in bold because rate is the next variable to enter. This means you don't really need to memorize the functions because they will appear when you begin entering them.

2. **If you're lost, click on "Help."** On the top row of your Excel spreadsheet you'll notice the word *Help* listed—another way to get to the help link is to hit the F1 button. When you're lost, the help link is your friend. Click on it and enter "PV" or "FV" in the search bar, and the program will explain how to calculate each. All of the other financial calculations you might want to find can be found the same way.

3. **Be careful about rounding the *r* variable.** For example, suppose you're dealing with the interest rate 6.99 percent compounded monthly. This means you will need to enter the interest rate per month, which is = 6.99%/12, and since you are performing division in the cell, you need to put an "=" sign before the division is performed. Don't round the result of 0.0699/12 to 0.58 and enter 0.58 as *r*. Instead, enter = 6.99/12 or as a decimal = 0.0699/12 for *r*.

   Also, you'll notice that while the inputs using an Excel spreadsheet are almost identical to those on a financial calculator, the interest rate in Excel is entered as *either* a decimal (0.06) *or* a whole number followed by a % sign (6%) rather than a 6 (as you would enter if you were using a financial calculator).

4. **Don't let the Excel notation fool you.** Excel doesn't use *r* or I/Y to note the interest rate. Instead, it uses the term *rate*. Don't let this bother you. All of these notations refer to the same thing—the interest rate. Similarly, Excel doesn't use *n* to denote the number of periods. Instead, it uses *nper*. Once again, don't let this bother you. Both *n* and *nper* refer to the number of periods.

5. **Don't be thrown off by the "Type" input variable.** You'll notice that Excel asks for a new variable that we haven't talked about yet, "type." Again, if you type "= FV" in a cell, "= FV(rate,nper,pmt,pv,type)" will immediately appear just below that cell. Don't let this new variable, "type," throw you off. The variable "type" refers to whether the payments, pmt, occur at the end of each period (which is considered type = 0) or the beginning of each period (which is considered type = 1). But you don't have to worry about it at all because the default on "type" is 0. *Thus, if you don't enter a value for "type," it will assume that the payments occur at the end of each period.* We're going to assume they

occur at the end of each period, and if they don't, we'll deal with them another way that will be introduced later in this chapter. You'll also notice that since we assume that all payments occur at the end of each period unless otherwise stated, we ignore the "type" variable.

Some of the more important Excel functions that we will be using throughout the book include the following (again, we are ignoring the "type" variable because we are assuming cash flows occur at the end of the period):

| CALCULATION (WHAT IS BEING SOLVED FOR) | FORMULA |
| --- | --- |
| Present value | $= PV$(rate, nper, pmt, fv) |
| Future value | $= FV$(rate, nper, pmt, pv) |
| Payment | $= PMT$(rate, nper, pv, fv) |
| Number of periods | $= NPER$(rate, pmt, pv, fv) |
| Interest rate | $= RATE$(nper, pmt, pv, fv) |

Reminders: First, just as in using a financial calculator, the outflows have to be entered as negative numbers. In general, each problem will have two cash flows—one positive and one negative. Second, a small, but important, difference between a spreadsheet and a financial calculator: When using a financial calculator, you enter the interest rate as a percent. For example, 6.5 percent is entered as 6.5. However, with the spreadsheet, the interest rate is entered as a decimal, thus 6.5 percent would be entered as 0.065 or, alternatively, as 6.5 followed by a % sign.

---

**EXAMPLE 5.3** **Calculating the future value of an investment**

If you put $1,000 into an investment paying 20 percent interest compounded annually, how much will your account grow to in 10 years?

### STEP 1: FORMULATE A SOLUTION STRATEGY

Let's start with a timeline to help you visualize the problem:

| | $r = 20\%$ | | | | | | | | | | |
| --- | --- | --- | --- | --- | --- | --- | --- | --- | --- | --- | --- |
| **YEARS** | **0** | **1** | **2** | **3** | **4** | **5** | **6** | **7** | **8** | **9** | **10** |
| Cash Flows | $-1,000$ | | | | | | | | | | Future Value = ? |

The future value of our savings account can be computed using equation (5-1) as follows:

$$\text{Future value} = \text{present value} \times (1 + r)^n \tag{5-1}$$

### STEP 2: CRUNCH THE NUMBERS

**Using the Mathematical Formulas**

Substituting present value $= \$1,000$, $r = 20$ percent, and $n = 10$ years into equation (5-1), we get

$$\text{Future value} = \text{present value} \times (1 + r)^n \tag{5-1}$$

$$= \$1,000(1 + 0.20)^{10}$$

$$= \$1,000(6.19174)$$

$$= \$6,191.74$$

Thus, at the end of 10 years, you will have $6,191.74 in your investment. In this problem we've invested $1,000 at 20 percent and found that it will grow to $6,191.74 after 10 years. These are actually equivalent values expressed in terms of dollars from different time periods where we've assumed a 20 percent compound rate.

### Using a Financial Calculator

A financial calculator makes this even simpler. If you are not familiar with the use of a financial calculator, or if you have any problems with these calculations, check out the tutorial on financial calculators in Appendix A at www.pearsonhighered.com/keown. There you'll find an introduction to financial calculators and the time value of money along with calculator tips to make sure that you come up with the right answers.

| Enter | 10 | 20 | − 1,000 | 0 | |
|---|---|---|---|---|---|
| | N | I/N | PV | PMT | FV |
| Solve for | | | | | 6,192 |

Notice that you input the present value with a negative sign. In effect, a financial calculator sees money as "leaving your hands" and therefore taking on a negative sign when you invest it. In this case you are investing $1,000 right now, so it takes on a negative sign—as a result, the answer takes on a positive sign.

### Using an Excel Spreadsheet

You'll notice the inputs using an Excel spreadsheet are almost identical to those on a financial calculator. The only difference is that the interest rate in Excel is entered as *either* a decimal (0.20) *or* a whole number followed by a % sign (20%) rather than as 20 (as you would enter if you were using a financial calculator). Again, the present value should be entered with a negative value so that the answer takes on a positive sign.

| | A | B |
|---|---|---|
| 1 | interest rate (rate) = | 20.00% |
| 2 | number of periods (nper) = | 10 |
| 3 | payment (pmt) = | $0 |
| 4 | present value (pv) = | ($1,000) |
| 5 | | |
| 6 | future value (fv) = | $6,192 |
| 7 | | |
| 8 | Excel formula =FV(rate,nper,pmt,pv) | |
| 9 | Entered in cell b6: =FV(b1,b2,b3,b4) | |

### STEP 3: ANALYZE YOUR RESULTS

Thus, at the end of 10 years, you will have $6,192 in your investment. In this problem we've invested $1,000 at 20 percent and found that it will grow to $6,192 after 10 years. These are actually equivalent values expressed in terms of dollars from different time periods where we've assumed a 20 percent compound rate.

## Two Additional Types of Time Value of Money Problems

Sometimes the time value of money does not involve determining either the present value or future value of a sum, but instead deals with either the number of periods in the future, $n$, or the rate of interest, $r$. For example, to answer the following question you will need to calculate the value for $n$.

◆ How many years will it be before the money I have saved will be enough to buy a second home?

Similarly, questions such as the following must be answered by solving for the interest rate, $r$.

◆ What rate do I need to earn on my investment to have enough money for my newborn child's college education ($n = 18$ years)?
◆ What interest rate has my investment earned?

Fortunately, with the help of a financial calculator or an Excel spreadsheet, you can easily solve for $r$ or $n$ in any of the above situations. It can also be done using the mathematical formulas, but it's much easier with a calculator or spreadsheet, so we'll stick to them.

**Solving for the Number of Periods**    Suppose you want to know how many years it will take for an investment of $9,330 to grow to $20,000 if it's invested at 10 percent annually. Let's take a look at solving this using a financial calculator and an Excel spreadsheet.

*Using a Financial Calculator*  With a financial calculator, all you do is substitute in the values for I/Y, PV, and FV and solve for N:

| Enter | | 10 | – 9,330 | 0 | 20,000 |
|---|---|---|---|---|---|
| | N | I/Y | PV | PMT | FV |
| Solve for | 8 | | | | |

You'll notice that PV is input with a negative sign. In effect, the financial calculator is programmed to assume that the $9,330 is a cash outflow, whereas the $20,000 is money that you receive. If you don't give one of these values a negative sign, you can't solve the problem.

*Using an Excel Spreadsheet*  With Excel, solving for $n$ is straightforward. You simply use the = NPER function and input values for rate, pmt, pv, and fv.

| | A | B |
|---|---|---|
| 1 | interest rate (rate) = | 10.00% |
| 2 | payment (pmt) = | 0 |
| 3 | present value (pv) = | ($9,330) |
| 4 | future value (fv) = | $20,000 |
| 5 | | |
| 6 | number of periods (nper) = | 8 |
| 7 | | |
| 8 | Excel formula =nper(rate,pmt,pv,fv) | |
| 9 | Entered in cell b6: =nper(b1,b2,b3,b4) | |

**Solving for the Rate of Interest**    You have just inherited $34,946 and want to use it to fund your retirement in 30 years. If you have estimated that you will need $800,000 to fund your retirement, what rate of interest would you have to earn on your $34,946 investment? Let's take a look at solving this using a financial calculator and an Excel spreadsheet to calculate the interest rate.

*Using a Financial Calculator*  With a financial calculator, all you do is substitute in the values for N, PV, and FV, and solve for I/Y:

| Enter | | 30 | | – 34,946 | 0 | 800,000 |
|---|---|---|---|---|---|---|
| | N | I/Y | PV | PMT | FV |
| Solve for | | 11 | | | | |

*Using an Excel Spreadsheet*  With Excel, the problem is also very easy. You simply use the = RATE function and input values for nper, pmt, pv, and fv.

| | A | B |
|---|---|---|
| 1 | number of periods (nper) = | 30 |
| 2 | payment (pmt) = | 0 |
| 3 | present value (pv) = | ($34,946) |
| 4 | future value (fv) = | $800,000 |
| 5 | | |
| 6 | interest rate (rate) = | 11.00% |
| 7 | | |
| 8 | Excel formula =rate(nper,pmt,pv,fv) | |
| 9 | Entered in cell b6: =rate(b1,b2,b3,b4) | |

## Applying Compounding to Things Other Than Money

While this chapter focuses on moving money through time at a given interest rate, the concept of compounding applies to almost anything that grows. For example, let's assume you're interested in knowing how big the market for wireless printers will be in 5 years and assume the demand for them is expected to grow at a rate of 25 percent per year over the next 5 years. We can calculate the future value of the market for printers using the same formula we used to calculate future value for a sum of money. If the market is currently 25,000 printers per year, then 25,000 would be the present value, $n$ would be 5, $r$ would be 25%, and substituting into equation (5-1) you would be solving $FV$,

$$\text{Future value} = \text{present value} \times (1 + r)^n \tag{5-1}$$
$$= 25{,}000(1 + 0.20)^5 = 76{,}293$$

In effect, you can view the interest rate, $r$, as a compound growth rate and solve for the number of periods it would take for something to grow to a certain level—what something will grow to in the future. Or you could solve for $r$, that is, solve for the rate that something would have to grow at in order to reach a target level.

## Present Value

Up to this point we have been moving money forward in time; that is, we know how much we have to begin with and are trying to determine how much that sum will grow in a certain number of years when compounded at a specific rate. We are now going to look at the reverse question: What is the value in today's dollars of a sum of money to be received in the future? The answer to this question will help us determine the desirability of investment projects in Chapters 10 and 11. In this case we are moving future money back to the present. We will determine the **present value** of a lump sum, which in simple terms is the *current value of a future payment*. In fact, we will be doing nothing other than inverse compounding. The differences in these techniques come about merely from the investor's point of view. In compounding, we talked about the compound interest rate and the initial investment; in determining the present value, we will talk about the discount rate and present value of future cash flows. Determining the discount rate is the subject of Chapter 9 and can be defined as the rate of return available on an investment of equal risk to what is being discounted. Other than that, the technique and the terminology remain the same, and the mathematics are simply reversed. In equation (5-1) we were attempting to determine the future value of an initial investment. We now want to determine the initial investment or present value. By dividing both sides of equation (5-1) by $(1 + r)^n$, we get

> **present value** the value in today's dollars of a future payment discounted back to present at the required rate of return.

$$\text{Present value} = \text{future value at the end of year } n \times \left[\frac{1}{(1 + r)^n}\right]$$

or

$$PV = FV_n\left[\frac{1}{(1 + r)^n}\right] \tag{5-2}$$

The term in the brackets in equation (5-2) is referred to as the **present value factor**. Thus, to find the present value of a future dollar amount, all you need to do is multiply that future dollar amount times the appropriate present value factor:

> **present value factor** the value of $\frac{1}{(1 + r)^n}$ used as a multiplier to calculate an amount's present value.

$$\text{Present value} = \text{future value (present value factor)}$$

where

$$\text{Present value factor} = \left[\frac{1}{(1 + r)^n}\right]$$

Because the mathematical procedure for determining the present value is exactly the inverse of determining the future value, we also find that the relationships among $n$, $r$, and present value are just the opposite of those we observed in future value. The present value of a future sum of money is inversely related to both the number of years until the payment will be received and the discount rate. This relationship is shown in Figure 5-3. Although the present value equation

**FIGURE 5-3** The Present Value of $100 to Be Received at a Future Date and Discounted Back to the Present at 0, 5, 10, and 15 Percent

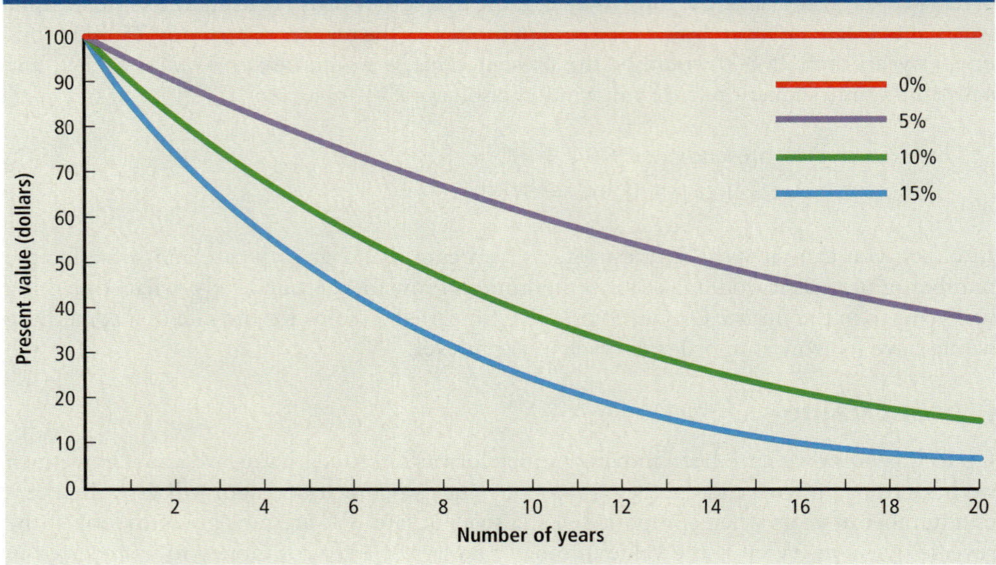

[equation (5-2)] is used extensively to evaluate new investment proposals, it should be stressed that the equation is actually the same as the future value, or compounding equation [equation (5-1)], only it solves for present value instead of future value.

---

**EXAMPLE 5.4**    **Calculating the discounted value to be received in 10 years**

What is the present value of $500 to be received 10 years from today if our discount rate is 6 percent?

**STEP 1: FORMULATE A SOLUTION STRATEGY**
The present value to be received can be calculated using equation (5-2) as follows:

$$\text{Present value} = FV_n\left[\frac{1}{(1 + r)^n}\right] \tag{5-2}$$

**STEP 2: CRUNCH THE NUMBERS**
Substituting $FV = \$500$, $n = 10$, and $r = 6$ percent into equation (5-2), we find:

$$
\begin{aligned}
\text{Present value} &= \$500\left[\frac{1}{(1 + 0.06)^{10}}\right] \\
&= \$500(0.5584) \\
&= \$279.20
\end{aligned}
$$

**STEP 3: ANALYZE YOUR RESULTS**
Thus, the present value of the $500 to be received in 10 years is $279.20.

**CALCULATOR SOLUTION**

| Data Input | Function Key |
|---|---|
| 10 | N |
| 6 | I/Y |
| −500 | FV |
| 0 | PMT |

| Function Key | Answer |
|---|---|
| CPT | |
| PV | 279.20 |

---

**EXAMPLE 5.5**    **Calculating the present value of a savings bond**

You're on vacation in a rather remote part of Florida and see an advertisement stating that if you take a sales tour of some condominiums "you will be given $100 just for taking the tour." However, the $100 that you get is in the form of a savings bond that will not pay you the $100 for 10 years. What is the present value of $100 to be received 10 years from today if your discount rate is 6 percent?

### STEP 1: FORMULATE A SOLUTION STRATEGY

The present value of our savings bond can be computed using equation (5-2) as follows:

$$\text{Present value} = FV_n\left[\frac{1}{(1 + r)^n}\right] \tag{5-2}$$

### STEP 2: CRUNCH THE NUMBERS

Substituting $FV = \$100$, $n = 10$, and $r = 6$ percent into equation (5-2), we compute the present value as follows:

$$\begin{aligned}
\text{Present value} &= \$100\left[\frac{1}{(1 + 0.06)^{10}}\right] \\
&= \$100(0.5584) \\
&= \$55.84
\end{aligned}$$

### STEP 3: ANALYZE YOUR RESULTS

Thus, the value in today's dollars of that $100 savings bond is only $55.84.

**CALCULATOR SOLUTION**

| Data Input | Function Key |
|---|---|
| 10 | N |
| 6 | I/Y |
| −100 | FV |
| 0 | PMT |

| Function Key | Answer |
|---|---|
| CPT | |
| PV | 55.84 |

## CAUTIONARY TALE

### FORGETTING PRINCIPLE 4: MARKET PRICES ARE GENERALLY RIGHT

In the Cautionary Tale for Chapter 2, we looked at the role the mortgage crisis played in the recent financial collapse from the viewpoint of conflicts of interest and failed corporate governance. But there are many lenses through which we can look to analyze the crisis. One such lens is the principle of efficient markets.

In 2007, several U.S. real estate markets entered a housing bubble. To look more closely at the underlying factors that led to the recent housing bubble (and burst), let's take a step back for a moment.

Beginning in the mid-1990s, the federal government made moves to relax conventional lending standards. In one such move, the government required the Federal National Mortgage Association, commonly known as Fannie Mae, and the Federal Home Loan Mortgage Corporation, known as Freddie Mac, to increase their holdings of loans to low- and moderate-income borrowers. Then in 1999, the U.S. Department of Housing and Urban Development (HUD) regulations required Fannie Mae and Freddie Mac to accept more loans with little or no down payment. As a result, the government had opened the door to very risky loans that would not have been made without this government action.

After the 2001 terrorist attack on the World Trade Center, the government made another move that acted against what we know about competitive markets. The Fed lowered short-term interest rates to ensure that the economy did not seize up. These low, short-term interest rates made adjustable rate loans with low down payments highly attractive to homebuyers. As a result of the low interest rate, when individuals took out variable rate mortgages, they often qualified for bigger mortgages than they could have afforded during a normal interest rate period. But in 2005 and 2006, to control inflation, the Fed returned these short-term interest rates to higher levels and the adjustable rates reset, causing the monthly payments on these loans to increase. Housing prices began to fall and defaults soared.

These actions prevented supply and demand from acting naturally. As a result, housing prices were unnaturally inflated and the listed value of the mortgages, when packaged as securities, was a poor indicator of their actual worth. When homeowners defaulted on their loans in spades, investors were left holding the bad mortgages. These defaulted mortgages also led to a lot more houses on the market that the banks couldn't sell, which led to the market drying up, as it then became very difficult for anyone to get a *new* loan.

We now know that these events put into motion the housing bubble that contributed to our recent economic downturn. Competitive markets operate with natural forces of supply and demand, and while they tend to eliminate huge returns, competitive markets can also help to prevent the occurrence of short-lived false values—such as the temporarily low monthly interest payments for new homebuyers—that lead to an eventual crash. If we take one lesson away from this, it should be this: Don't mess with efficient markets. if the markets move interest rates to higher levels, it's for a reason.

Again, we have only one present-value–future-value equation; that is, equations (5-1) and (5-2) are different formats of the same equation. We have introduced them as separate equations to simplify our calculations; in one case we are determining the value in future dollars, and in the other case the value in today's dollars. In either case, the reason is the same: to compare values on alternative investments and to recognize that the value of a dollar received today is not the same as that of a dollar received at some future date. In other words, we must measure the dollar values in dollars of the same time period. For example, if we looked at these projects—one that promised $1,000 in 1 year, one that promised $1,500 in 5 years, and one that promised $2,500 in 10 years—the concept of present value allows us to bring their flows back to the present and make those projects comparable. Moreover, because all present values are comparable (they are all measured in dollars of the same time period), we can add and subtract the present value of inflows and outflows to determine the present value of an investment. Let's now look at an example of an investment that has two cash flows in different time periods and determine the present value of this investment.

## STEP 1
CALCULATOR SOLUTION

| Data Input | Function Key |
|---|---|
| 7 | N |
| 6 | I/Y |
| −1,000 | FV |
| 0 | PMT |

| Function Key | Answer |
|---|---|
| CPT | |
| PV | 665.06 |

## STEP 2
CALCULATOR SOLUTION

| Data Input | Function Key |
|---|---|
| 10 | N |
| 6 | I/Y |
| −1,000 | FV |
| 0 | PMT |

| Function Key | Answer |
|---|---|
| CPT | |
| PV | 558.39 |

## STEP 3
Add the two present values that you just calculated together:

$ 665.06
558.39
$1,223.45

---

**EXAMPLE 5.6**  **Calculating the present value of an investment**

What is the present value of an investment that yields $1,000 to be received in 7 years and $1,000 to be received in 10 years if the discount rate is 6 percent?

### STEP 1: FORMULATE A SOLUTION STRATEGY
The present value of our investment can be computed using equation (5-2) for each yield, then adding these values together as follows:

$$\text{Present value} = FV_n\left[\frac{1}{(1 + r)^n}\right] + FV_n\left[\frac{1}{(1 + r)^n}\right] \tag{5-2}$$

### STEP 2: CRUNCH THE NUMBERS
Substituting into equation (5-2), we compute the future value as follows:

$$\text{Present value} = \$1,000\left[\frac{1}{(1 + 0.06)^7}\right] + \$1,000\left[\frac{1}{(1 + 0.06)^{10}}\right]$$
$$= \$665.06 + \$558.39 = \$1,223.45$$

### STEP 3: ANALYZE YOUR RESULTS
Again, present values are comparable because they are measured in the same time period's dollars.

With a financial calculator, this becomes a three-step solution, as shown in the margin. First, you'll solve for the present value of the $1,000 received at the end of 7 years, then you'll solve for the present value of the $1,000 received at the end of 10 years, and finally, you'll add the two present values together. Remember, once you've found the present value of those future cash flows you can add them together because they're measured in the same period's dollars.

---

## CAN YOU DO IT?

### SOLVING FOR THE PRESENT VALUE WITH TWO FLOWS IN DIFFERENT YEARS

What is the present value of an investment that yields $500 to be received in 5 years and $1,000 to be received in 10 years if the discount rate is 4 percent?
(The solution can be found on page 158.)

## Concept Check

1. Principle 2 states that "money has a time value." Explain this statement.
2. How does compound interest differ from simple interest?
3. Explain the formula $FV_n = PV(1 + r)^n$.
4. Why is the present value of a future sum always less than that sum's future value?

# Annuities

 **2** Understand annuities.

An **annuity** is a *series of equal dollar payments for a specified number of years*. When we talk about annuities, we are referring to **ordinary annuities** unless otherwise noted. With an ordinary annuity *the payments occur at the end of each period*. Because annuities occur frequently in finance—for example, as bond interest payments—we treat them specially. Although compounding and determining the present value of an annuity can be dealt with using the methods we have just described, these processes can be time-consuming, especially for larger annuities. Thus, we have modified the single cash flow formulas to deal directly with annuities.

**annuity** a series of equal dollar payments made for a specified number of years.

**ordinary annuity** an annuity where the cash flows occur at the end of each period.

## Compound Annuities

A **compound annuity** involves *depositing or investing an equal sum of money at the end of each year for a certain number of years and allowing it to grow*. Perhaps we are saving money for education, a new car, or a vacation home. In any case, we want to know how much our savings will have grown at some point in the future.

Actually, we can find the answer by using equation (5-1), our compounding equation, and compounding each of the individual deposits to its future value. For example, if to provide for a college education we are going to deposit $500 at the end of each year for the next 5 years in a bank where it will earn 6 percent interest, how much will we have at the end of 5 years? Compounding each of these values using equation (5-1), we find that we will have $2,818.50 at the end of 5 years.

**compound annuity** depositing an equal sum of money at the end of each year for a certain number of years and allowing it to grow.

$$
\begin{aligned}
FV_5 &= \$500(1 + 0.6)^4 + \$500(1 + 0.6)^3 + \$500(1 + 0.6)^2 + \$500(1 + 0.6) + \$500 \\
&= \$500(1.262) + \$500(1.191) + \$500(1.124) + \$500(1.060) + \$500 \\
&= \$631.00 + \$595.50 + \$562.00 + \$530.00 + \$500.00 \\
&= \$2,818.50
\end{aligned}
$$

By examining the mathematics involved and the graph of the movement of money through time in Table 5-1, we can see that all we are really doing is adding up the future values of different cash flows that initially occurred in different time periods. Fortunately, there is also an equation that helps us calculate the future value of an annuity:

$$
\begin{aligned}
\text{Future value of an annuity} &= PMT\left[\frac{\text{future value factor} - 1}{r}\right] \\
&= PMT\left[\frac{(1 + r)^n - 1}{r}\right]
\end{aligned}
\tag{5-3}
$$

**TABLE 5-1  Growth of a 5-Year, $500 Annuity Compounded at 6 Percent**

| YEAR | 0 | 1 | 2 | 3 | 4 | 5 |
|---|---|---|---|---|---|---|
| | | $r = 6\%$ | | | | |
| Dollar deposits at end of year | | 500 | 500 | 500 | 500 | 500 |
| | | | | | | $ 500.00 |
| | | | | | | 530.00 |
| | | | | | | 562.00 |
| | | | | | | 595.50 |
| | | | | | | 631.00 |
| Future value of the annuity | | | | | | $2,818.50 |

# DID YOU GET IT?

## SOLVING FOR THE PRESENT VALUE WITH TWO FLOWS IN DIFFERENT YEARS

There are several different ways you can solve this problem—using the mathematical formulas, a financial calculator, or a spreadsheet—each one giving you the same answer.

1. **Using the Mathematical Formula.** Substituting the values of $n = 5$, $r = 4$ percent, and $FV_5 = \$500$; and $n = 10$, $r = 4$ percent, and $FV_{10} = \$1,000$ into equation (5-2) and adding these values together, we find

$$\text{Present value} = \$500\left[\frac{1}{(1 + 0.04)^5}\right] + \$1,000\left[\frac{1}{(1 + 0.04)^{10}}\right]$$

$$= \$500(0.822) + \$1,000(0.676)$$

$$= \$411 + \$676 = \$1,087$$

2. **Using a Financial Calculator.** Again, it is a three-step process. First calculate the present value of each cash flow individually, and then add the present values together.

| STEP 1 | | STEP 2 | | STEP 3 |
|---|---|---|---|---|
| **CALCULATOR SOLUTION** | | **CALCULATOR SOLUTION** | | Add the two present values that you just calculated together: |

| Data Input | Function Key | | Data Input | Function Key | | |
|---|---|---|---|---|---|---|
| 5 | N | | 10 | N | | $ 410.96 |
| 4 | I/Y | | 4 | I/Y | | 675.56 |
| −500 | FV | | −1,000 | PV | | $1,086.52 |
| 0 | PMT | | 0 | PMT | | |

| Function Key | Answer | | Function Key | Answer |
|---|---|---|---|---|
| CPT | | | CPT | |
| PV | 410.96 | | PV | 675.56 |

3. **Using an Excel Spreadsheet.** Using Excel, the cash flows are brought back to the present using the =PV function. If the future values were entered as positive values, our answer will come out as a negative number.

**annuity future value factor** the value of $\left[\frac{(1 + r)^n - 1}{r}\right]$ used as a multiplier to calculate the future value of an annuity.

**CALCULATOR SOLUTION**

| Data Input | Function Key |
|---|---|
| 8 | N |
| 6 | I/Y |
| −10,000 | FV |
| 0 | PV |

| Function Key | Answer |
|---|---|
| CPT | |
| PMT | 1,010.36 |

To simplify our discussion, we will refer to the value in brackets in equation (5-3) as the **annuity future value factor**. It is defined as $\left[\frac{(1 + r)^n - 1}{r}\right]$.

Using this new notation, we can rewrite equation (5-3) as follows:

$$FV_n = PMT\left[\frac{(1 + r)^n - 1}{r}\right] = PMT(\text{annuity future value factor})$$

Rather than asking how much we will accumulate if we deposit an equal sum in a savings account each year, a more common question to ask is how much we must deposit each year to accumulate a certain amount of savings. This problem frequently occurs with respect to saving for large expenditures.

For example, if we know that we need $10,000 for college in 8 years, how much must we deposit in the bank at the end of each year at 6 percent interest to have the college money ready? In this case we know the values of $n$, $r$, and $FV_n$ in equation (5-3); what we do not know is the value of $PMT$. Substituting these example values in equation (5-3), we find

$$\$10,000 = PMT\left[\frac{(1 + 0.06)^8 - 1}{0.06}\right]$$

$$\$10,000 = PMT(9.8975)$$

$$\frac{\$10,000}{9.8975} = PMT$$

$$\$1,010.36 = PMT$$

Thus, we must deposit $1,010.36 in the bank at the end of each year for 8 years at 6 percent interest to accumulate $10,000 at the end of 8 years.

---

**EXAMPLE 5.7**    **Calculating deposit amount to accumulate $5,000**

How much must we deposit in an 8 percent savings account at the end of each year to accumulate $5,000 at the end of 10 years?

**STEP 1: FORMULATE A SOLUTION STRATEGY**
In order to determine the amount we must deposit, we have to use equation (5-3) as follows:

$$FV = PMT\left[\frac{(1 + r)^n - 1}{r}\right] \tag{5-3}$$

**STEP 2: CRUNCH THE NUMBERS**
Substituting into equation (5-3), we compute the future value as follows:

$$\$5,000 = PMT\left[\frac{(1 + 0.06)^8 - 1}{0.06}\right]$$

$$\$5,000 = PMT(14.4866)$$

$$\frac{5,000}{14.4866} = PMT = \$345.15$$

| CALCULATOR SOLUTION | |
|---|---|
| Data Input | Function Key |
| 10 | N |
| 8 | I/Y |
| −5,000 | FV |
| 0 | PV |
| Function Key | Answer |
| CPT | |
| PMT | 345.15 |

**STEP 3: ANALYZE YOUR RESULTS**
Thus, we must deposit $345.15 per year for 10 years at 8 percent to accumulate $5,000.

---

## The Present Value of an Annuity

Pension payments, insurance obligations, and the interest owed on bonds all involve annuities. To compare these three types of investments we need to know the present value of each. For example, if we wish to know what $500 received at the end of each of the next 5 years is worth today given a discount rate of 6 percent, we can simply substitute the appropriate values into equation (5-2), such that

$$PV = \$500\left[\frac{1}{(1 + 0.06)^1}\right] + \$500\left[\frac{1}{(1 + 0.06)^2}\right] + \$500\left[\frac{1}{(1 + 0.06)^3}\right]$$

$$+ \$500\left[\frac{1}{(1 + 0.06)^4}\right] + \$500\left[\frac{1}{(1 + 0.06)^5}\right]$$

$$= \$500(0.943) + \$500(0.890) + \$500(0.840) + \$500(0.792) + \$500(0.747)$$

$$= \$2,106$$

Thus, the present value of this annuity is $2,106.00. By examining the mathematics involved and the graph of the movement of money through time in Table 5-2, we can see that all we are really doing is adding up the present values of different cash flows that initially occurred in different time periods. Fortunately, there is also an equation that helps us calculate the present value of an annuity:

$$\text{Present value of an annuity} = PMT\left[\frac{1 - \text{present value factor}}{r}\right]$$

$$= PMT\left[\frac{1 - (1 + r)^{-n}}{r}\right] \tag{5-4}$$

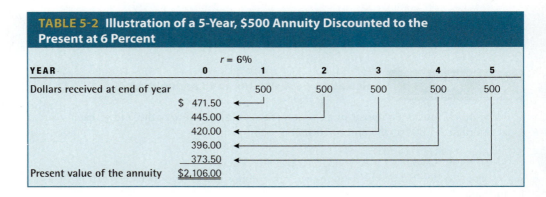

**TABLE 5-2** Illustration of a 5-Year, $500 Annuity Discounted to the Present at 6 Percent

| | | $r = 6\%$ | | | | |
|---|---|---|---|---|---|---|
| **YEAR** | **0** | **1** | **2** | **3** | **4** | **5** |
| Dollars received at end of year | | 500 | 500 | 500 | 500 | 500 |
| | $ 471.50 | | | | | |
| | 445.00 | | | | | |
| | 420.00 | | | | | |
| | 396.00 | | | | | |
| | 373.50 | | | | | |
| Present value of the annuity | $2,106.00 | | | | | |

To simplify our discussion, we will refer to the value in the brackets in equation (5-4) as the **annuity present value factor**. It is defined as $\left[\dfrac{1 - (1 + r)^{-n}}{r}\right]$.

**annuity present value factor** the value of $\left[\dfrac{1 - (1 + r)^{-n}}{r}\right]$ used as a multiplier to calculate the present value of an annuity

---

**EXAMPLE 5.8**  **Calculating the present value of an annuity**

What is the present value of a 10-year $1,000 annuity discounted back to the present at 5 percent?

**STEP 1: FORMULATE A SOLUTION STRATEGY**
The present value of the annuity can be computed using equation (5-4) as follows:

$$PV = PMT\left[\frac{1 - (1 + r)^{-n}}{r}\right] \tag{5-4}$$

**STEP 2: CRUNCH THE NUMBERS**
Substituting into equation (5-4), we compute the present value as follows:

$$PV = \$1,000\left[\frac{1 - (1 + 0.05)^{-10}}{0.05}\right]$$
$$= \$1,000(7.722)$$
$$= \$7,722$$

**STEP 3: ANALYZE YOUR RESULTS**
Thus, the present value of this annuity is $7,722.

---

**CALCULATOR SOLUTION**

| Data Input | Function Key |
|---|---|
| 10 | N |
| 5 | I/Y |
| −1,000 | PMT |
| 0 | PV |

| Function Key | Answer |
|---|---|
| CPT | |
| PV | 7,722 |

---

**CALCULATOR SOLUTION**

| Data Input | Function Key |
|---|---|
| 5 | N |
| 8 | I/Y |
| −5,000 | PV |
| 0 | FV |

| Function Key | Answer |
|---|---|
| CPT | |
| PMT | 1,252 |

---

When we solve for *PMT*, the financial interpretation of this action would be: How much can be withdrawn, perhaps as a pension or to make loan payments, from an account that earns *r* percent compounded annually for each of the next *n* years if we wish to have nothing left at the end of *n* years? For example, if we have $5,000 in an account earning 8 percent interest, how large of an annuity can we draw out each year if we want nothing left at the end of 5 years? In this case the present value, *PV*, of the annuity is $5,000, $n = 5$ years, $r = 8$ percent, and *PMT* is unknown. Substituting this into equation (5-4), we find

$$\$5,000 = PMT\left[\frac{1 - (1 + 0.08)^{-5}}{0.08}\right] = PMT(3.993)$$

$$\$1,252 = PMT$$

Thus, this account will fall to zero at the end of 5 years if we withdraw $1,252 at the end of each year.

## Annuities Due

**Annuities due** are really just *ordinary annuities in which all the annuity payments have been shifted forward by 1 year*. Compounding them and determining their future and present value is actually quite simple. With an annuity due, each annuity payment occurs at the beginning of each period rather than at the end of the period. Let's first look at how this affects our compounding calculations.

Because an annuity due merely shifts the payments from the end of the year to the beginning of the year, we now compound the cash flows for one additional year. Therefore, the compound sum of an annuity due is simply

$$\text{Future value of an annuity due} = \text{future value of an annuity} \times (1 + r)$$

$$FV_n(\text{annuity due}) = PMT\left[\frac{(1 + r)^n - 1}{r}\right](1 + r) \qquad (5\text{-}5)$$

In an earlier example on saving for college, we calculated the value of a 5-year ordinary annuity of $500 invested in the bank at 6 percent to be $2,818.50. If we now assume this to be a 5-year annuity due, its future value increases from $2,818.50 to $2,987.66.

$$FV_5 = \$500\left[\frac{(1 + 0.06)^5 - 1}{0.06}\right](1 + 0.06)$$

$$= \$500(5.637093)(1.06)$$

$$= \$2,987.66$$

Likewise, with the present value of an annuity due, we simply receive each cash flow 1 year earlier—that is, we receive it at the beginning of each year rather than at the end of each year. Thus, because each cash flow is received 1 year earlier, it is discounted back for one less period. To determine the present value of an annuity due, we merely need to find the present value of an ordinary annuity and multiply that by $(1 + r)$, which in effect cancels out 1 year's discounting.

$$\text{Present value of an annuity due} = \text{present value of an annuity} \times (1 + r)$$

$$PV(\text{annuity due}) = PMT\left[\frac{1 - (1 + r)^{-n}}{r}\right](1 + r) \qquad (5\text{-}6)$$

Reexamining the earlier college saving example in which we calculated the present value of a 5-year ordinary annuity of $500 given a discount rate of 6 percent, we now find that if it is an annuity due rather than an ordinary annuity, the present value increases from $2,106 to $2,232.55.

$$PV = \$500\left[\frac{1 - (1 + 0.06)^{-5}}{0.06}\right](1 + 0.06)$$

$$= \$500(4.21236)(1.06)$$

$$= \$2,232.55$$

With a financial calculator, first treat it as if it were an ordinary annuity and find the future or present value. Then multiply the present value times $(1 + r)$, in this case times 1.06; this is shown in the margin.

The result of all this is that both the future and present values of an annuity due are larger than those of an ordinary annuity because in each case all payments are received earlier. Thus, when *compounding*, an annuity due compounds for 1 additional year, whereas when *discounting*, an annuity due discounts for 1 less year. Although annuities due are used with some frequency in accounting, their usage is quite limited in finance. Therefore, in the remainder of this text, whenever the term *annuity* is used, you should assume that we are referring to an ordinary annuity.

**annuity due** an annuity in which the payments occur at the beginning of each period.

Future value of an annuity due:

**STEP 1**
CALCULATOR SOLUTION

| Data Input | Function Key |
|---|---|
| 5 | N |
| 6 | I/Y |
| 0 | PV |
| −500 | PMT |

| Function Key | Answer |
|---|---|
| CPT | |
| FV | 2,818.55 |

**STEP 2**

$2,818.55
× 1.06
$2,987.66

Present value of an annuity due:

**STEP 1**
CALCULATOR SOLUTION

| Data Input | Function Key |
|---|---|
| 5 | N |
| 6 | I/Y |
| −500 | PMT |
| 0 | FV |

| Function Key | Answer |
|---|---|
| CPT | |
| PV | 2,106.18 |

**STEP 2**

$2,106.18
× 1.06
$2,232.55

| **EXAMPLE 5.9** | **Calculating the Lotto payments on $2 million** |

Forty-three states run lotteries and most of those lotteries are similar: You must select 6 out of 44 numbers correctly in order to win the jackpot. If you come close, there are some significantly lesser prizes, which we ignore for now. For each million dollars in the lottery jackpot, you receive $50,000 per year for 20 years, and your chance of winning is 1 in 7.1 million. A recent advertisement for a particular state lottery went as follows: "Okay, you got two kinds of people. You've got the kind who play Lotto all the time, and the kind who play Lotto some of the time. You know, like only on a Saturday when they stop in at the store on the corner for some peanut butter cups and diet soda and the jackpot happens to be really big. I mean, my friend Ned? He's like 'Hey, it's only $2 million this week.' Well, hellloooo, anybody home? I mean, I don't know about you, but I wouldn't mind having a measly 2 mill coming *my* way. . . ."

What is the present value of these payments?

**STEP 1: FORMULATE A SOLUTION STRATEGY**

The answer to this question depends on what assumption you make about the time value of money. In this case, let's assume that your required rate of return on an investment with this level of risk is 10 percent. Keeping in mind that the Lotto is an annuity due—that is, on a $2 million lottery you would get $100,000 immediately and $100,000 at the end of each of the next 19 years. Thus, the present value of this 20-year annuity due discounted back to present at 10 percent becomes:

$$PV(\text{annuity due}) = PMT\left[\frac{1 - (1 + r)^{-n}}{r}\right]$$

**STEP 2: CRUNCH THE NUMBERS**

Solving this is a two-step process. In step 1, you treat the jackpot as if it were an ordinary annuity and find the present value. Then multiply the present value times $(1 + r)$, in this case times 1.10.

Substituting into equation (5-6), we compute the present value as follows:

$$PV = \$100,000\left[\frac{1 - (1 + 0.10)^{-20}}{0.10}\right](1 + 0.10)$$

$$= \$100,000(8.51356)(1.10)$$

$$= \$936,492$$

**STEP 3: ANALYZE YOUR RESULTS**

Thus, the present value of the $2 million Lotto jackpot is less than $1 million if 10 percent is the discount rate. Moreover, because the chance of winning is only 1 in 7.1 million, the expected value of each dollar "invested" in the lottery is only $(1/7.1 \text{ million}) \times (\$936,492) = 13.19¢$. That is, for every dollar you spend on the lottery you should expect to get, on average, about 13 cents back—not a particularly good deal. Although this ignores the minor payments for coming close, it also ignores taxes. In this case, it looks like "my friend Ned" is doing the right thing by staying clear of the lottery. Obviously, the main value of the lottery is entertainment. Unfortunately, without an understanding of the time value of money, it can sound like a good investment.

Present value of an annuity due:

**STEP 1**
**CALCULATOR SOLUTION**

| Data Input | Function Key |
|---|---|
| 20 | N |
| 10 | I/Y |
| −100,000 | PMT |
| 0 | FV |

| Function Key | Answer |
|---|---|
| CPT | |
| PV | 851,356 |

**STEP 2**

$851,356
× 1.10
$936,492

## Amortized Loans

The procedure of solving for *PMT*, the annuity payment value when *r*, *n*, and *PV* are known, is also used to determine what payments are associated with paying off a loan in equal installments over time. *Loans that are paid off this way, in equal periodic payments,* are called **amortized loans**. Actually, the word *amortization* comes from the Latin word meaning "about to die." When you pay off a loan using regular, fixed payments, that loan is amortized. Although the payments are fixed, different amounts of each payment are applied

**amortized loan** a loan that is paid off in equal periodic payments.

## FIGURE 5-4  The Amortization Process

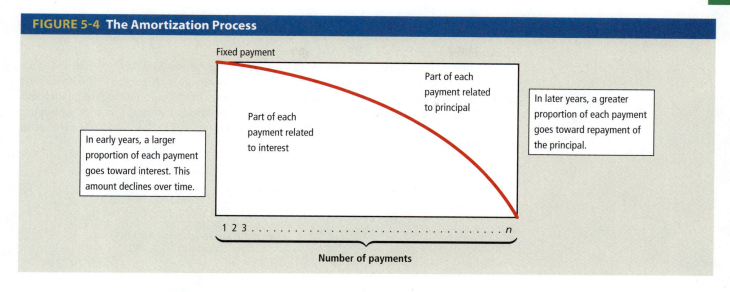

toward the principal and the interest. With each payment, you owe a bit less toward the principal. As a result, the amount that has to go toward the interest payment declines with each payment, whereas the portion of each payment that goes toward the principal increases. Figure 5-4 illustrates the process of amortization.

For example, suppose a firm wants to purchase a piece of machinery. To do this, it borrows $6,000 to be repaid in four equal payments at the end of each of the next 4 years, and the interest rate that is paid to the lender is 15 percent on the outstanding portion of the loan. To determine what the annual payments associated with the repayment of this debt will be, we simply use equation (5-4) and solve for the value of *PMT*, the annual annuity. In this case, we know *PV*, *r*, and *n*. *PV*, the present value of the annuity, is $6,000; *r*, the annual interest rate, is 15 percent; and *n*, the number of years for which the annuity will last, is 4 years. *PMT*, the annuity payment received (by the lender and paid by the firm) at the end of each year, is unknown. Substituting these values into equation (5-4), we find

$$\$6{,}000 = PMT\left[\frac{1 - (1 + 0.15)^{-4}}{0.15}\right]$$

$$\$6{,}000 = PMT(2.85498)$$

$$\$2{,}101.59 = PMT$$

To repay the principal and interest on the outstanding loan in 4 years, the annual payments would be $2,101.59. The breakdown of interest and principal payments is given in the *loan amortization schedule* in Table 5-3, with very minor rounding error. As you can see, the interest portion of the payment declines each year as the loan outstanding balance declines.

**CALCULATOR SOLUTION**

| Data Input | Function Key |
|---|---|
| 4 | N |
| 15 | I/Y |
| −6,000 | PV |
| 0 | FV |

| Function Key | Answer |
|---|---|
| CPT | |
| PMT | 2,101.59 |

## TABLE 5-3  Loan Amortization Schedule Involving a $6,000 Loan at 15 Percent to Be Repaid in 4 Years

| Year | Annuity | Interest Portion of the Annuity[a] | Repayment of the principal Portion of the Annuity[b] | Outstanding Loan Balance After the Annuity Payment |
|---|---|---|---|---|
| 0 | 0 | 0 | 0 | $6,000.00 |
| 1 | $2,101.59 | $900.00 | $1,201.59 | 4,798.41 |
| 2 | 2,101.59 | 719.76 | 1,381.83 | 3,416.58 |
| 3 | 2,101.59 | 512.49 | 1,589.10 | 1,827.48 |
| 4 | 2,101.59 | 274.12 | 1,827.48 | |

[a]The interest portion of the annuity is calculated by multiplying the outstanding loan balance at the beginning of the year by the interest rate of 15 percent. Thus, for year 1 it was $6,000 × 0.15 = $900.00, for year 2 it was $4,798.41 × 0.15 = $719.76, and so on.

[b]Repayment of the principal portion of the annuity was calculated by subtracting the interest portion of the annuity (column 2) from the annuity (column 1).

Now let's use a spreadsheet to look at a loan amortization problem and calculate the monthly mortgage payment, and then determine how much of a specific payment goes toward interest and principal.

To buy a new house you take out a 25-year mortgage for $100,000. What will your monthly payments be if the interest rate on your mortgage is 8 percent? To solve this problem, you must first convert the annual rate of 8 percent into a monthly rate by dividing it by 12. Second, you have to convert the number of periods into months by multiplying 25 years times 12 months per year for a total of 300 months. We'll look at this process in more detail in the next section.

| | A | B |
|---|---|---|
| 1 | interest rate (rate) = | 0.6667% |
| 2 | number of periods (nper) = | 300 |
| 3 | present value (pv) = | $100,000 |
| 4 | future value (fv) = | $0 |
| 5 | | |
| 6 | payment (pmt) = | ($771.82) |
| 7 | | |
| 8 | Excel formula =pmt(rate,nper,pv,fv) | |
| 9 | Entered in cell b6: =pmt((8/12)%,b2,b3,b4) | |

You can also use Excel to calculate the interest and principal portion of any loan amortization payment. You can do this using the following Excel functions:

| CALCULATION | FUNCTION |
|---|---|
| Interest portion of payment | = IPMT(rate, per, nper, pv, fv) |
| Principal portion of payment where per refers to the number of an individual periodic payment | = PPMT(rate, per, nper, pv, fv) |

For this example, you can determine how much of the 48th monthly payment goes toward interest and principal as follows,

| | A | B |
|---|---|---|
| 1 | interest rate (rate) = | 0.6667% |
| 2 | payment number (per) = | 48 |
| 3 | number of periods (nper) = | 300 |
| 4 | present value (pv) = | $100,000 |
| 5 | future value (fv) = | $0 |
| 6 | | |
| 7 | Interest portion of the 48th payment = | ($628.12) |
| 8 | Principal portion of the 48th loan payment = | ($143.69) |
| 9 | | |
| 10 | Entered values in cell b7: =IPMT((8/12)%,b2,b3,b4,b5) | |
| 11 | Entered values in cell b8: =PPMT((8/12)%,b2,b3,b4,b5) | |

## Concept Check

1. What is an amortized loan?
2. What functions in Excel help determine the amount of interest and principal in a mortgage payment?

# Making Interest Rates Comparable

 Determine the future or present value of a sum when there are nonannual compounding periods.

In order to make intelligent decisions about where to invest or borrow money, it is important that we make the stated interest rates comparable. Unfortunately, some rates are quoted as compounded annually, whereas others are quoted as compounded quarterly or compounded daily. But it is not fair to compare interest rates with different compounding periods to each other. Thus, the only way interest rates can logically be compared is to convert them to a common compounding period.

In order to understand the process of making different interest rates comparable, it is first necessary to define the nominal, or quoted, interest rate. The nominal, or quoted, rate is the rate of interest stated on the contract. For example, if you shop around for loans and are quoted 8 percent compounded annually and 7.85 percent compounded quarterly, then 8 percent and 7.85 percent would both be nominal rates. Unfortunately, because on one rate the interest is compounded annually, but on the other interest is compounded quarterly, the two rates are not comparable. In fact, it is never appropriate to compare nominal rates *unless* they include the same number of compounding periods per year. To make them comparable, we must calculate their equivalent rate at some common compounding period. We do this by calculating the **effective annual rate (EAR)**. This is *the annual compound rate that produces the same return as the nominal or quoted rate.*

**effective annual rate (EAR)** the annual compound rate that produces the same return as the nominal, or quoted, rate when something is compounded on a nonannual basis. In effect, the EAR provides the true rate of return.

Let's assume that you are considering borrowing money from a bank at 12 percent compounded monthly. If you borrow $1 at 1 percent per month for 12 months you'd owe,

$$\$1.00(1.01)^{12} = \$1.126825$$

In effect, you are borrowing at 12.6825 percent rather than just by 12 percent. Thus, the EAR for 12 percent compounded monthly is 12.6825. It tells us the annual rate that would produce the same loan payments as the nominal rate. In other words, you'll end up with the same monthly payments if you borrow at 12.6825 percent compounded annually or 12 percent compounded monthly. Thus, 12.6825 is the effective annual rate (EAR) for 12 percent compounded monthly.

Generalizing on this process, we can calculate the EAR using the following equation:

$$EAR = \left(1 + \frac{\text{quoted rate}}{m}\right)^m - 1 \tag{5-7}$$

where *EAR* is the effective annual rate and *m* is the number of compounding periods within a year. Given the wide variety of compounding periods used by businesses and banks, it is important to know how to make these rates comparable so that logical decisions can be made.

---

**EXAMPLE 5.10**    **Calculating the EAR on a credit card**

You've just received your first credit card and the problem is the rate. It looks pretty high to you. The quoted rate is 21.7 percent, and when you look closer, you notice that the interest is compounded daily. What's the EAR, or effective annual rate, on your credit card?

**STEP 1: FORMULATE A SOLUTION STRATEGY**
To calculate the EAR we can use equation (5-7) as follows:

$$EAR = \left[1 + \frac{\text{quoted rate}}{m}\right]^m - 1$$

**STEP 2: CRUNCH THE NUMBERS**

Substituting into equation (5-7), we compute the EAR as follows:

$$EAR = \left[1 + \frac{0.217}{365}\right]^{365} - 1$$

$$EAR = 1.242264 - 1 = 0.242264, \text{ or } 24.2264 \text{ percent.}$$

**STEP 3: ANALYZE YOUR RESULTS**

Thus, in reality, the effective annual rate is actually 24.2264 percent.

## Finding Present and Future Values with Nonannual Periods

The same logic that applies to calculating the EAR also applies to calculating present and future values when the periods are semiannual, quarterly, or any other nonannual period. Previously when we moved money through time we assumed that the cash flows occurred annually and the compounding or discounting period was always annual. However, it need not be, as evidenced by the fact that bonds generally pay interest semiannually and most mortgages require monthly payments.

For example, if we invest our money for 5 years at 8 percent interest compounded semiannually, we are really investing our money for ten 6-month periods during which we receive 4 percent interest each period. If it is 8 percent compounded quarterly for 5 years, we receive 2 percent interest per period for twenty 3-month periods. This process can easily be generalized, giving us the following formula for finding the future value of an investment for which interest is compounded in nonannual periods:

$$FV_n = PV\left[1 + \frac{r}{m}\right]^{m \cdot n}$$

where $FV_n$ = the future value of the investment at the end of $n$ years

$n$ = the number of years during which the compounding occurs

$r$ = annual interest (or discount) rate

$PV$ = the present value or original amount invested at the beginning of the first year

$m$ = the number of times compounding occurs during the year

In fact, all the formulas for moving money through time can be easily modified to accommodate nonannual periods. In each case, we begin with the formulas we introduced in this chapter, and make two adjustments—the first where $n$, the number of years, appears, and the second where $r$, the annual interest rate, appears. Thus, the adjustment involves two steps:

- ◆ $n$ becomes the number of periods or $n$ (the number of years) times $m$ (the number of times compounding occurs per year). Thus, if it is monthly compounding for 10 years, $n$ becomes $10 \times 12 = 120$ months in 10 years, and if it is daily compounding over 10 years, it becomes $10 \times 365 = 3,650$ days in 10 years.

## CAN YOU DO IT?

### HOW MUCH CAN YOU AFFORD TO SPEND ON A HOUSE? AN AMORTIZED LOAN WITH MONTHLY PAYMENTS

You've been house shopping and aren't sure how big a house you can afford. You figure you can handle monthly mortgage payments of $1,250 and you can get a 30-year loan at 6.5 percent. How big of a mortgage can you afford? In this problem, you are solving for *PV*, which is the amount of money you can borrow today.
(The solution can be found on page 168.)

**TABLE 5-4  The Value of $100 Compounded at Various Intervals**

| FOR 1 YEAR AT *r* PERCENT | | | | |
| --- | --- | --- | --- | --- |
| r = | 2% | 5% | 10% | 15% |
| Compounded annually | $102.00 | $105.00 | $110.00 | $115.00 |
| Compounded semiannually | 102.01 | 105.06 | 110.25 | 115.56 |
| Compounded quarterly | 102.02 | 105.09 | 110.38 | 115.87 |
| Compounded monthly | 102.02 | 105.12 | 110.47 | 116.08 |
| Compounded weekly (52) | 102.02 | 105.12 | 110.51 | 116.16 |
| Compounded daily (365) | 102.02 | 105.13 | 110.52 | 116.18 |
| **FOR 10 YEARS AT *r* PERCENT** | | | | |
| r = | 2% | 5% | 10% | 15% |
| Compounded annually | $121.90 | $162.89 | $259.37 | $404.56 |
| Compounded semiannually | 122.02 | 163.86 | 265.33 | 424.79 |
| Compounded quarterly | 122.08 | 164.36 | 268.51 | 436.04 |
| Compounded monthly | 122.10 | 164.70 | 270.70 | 444.02 |
| Compounded weekly (52) | 122.14 | 164.83 | 271.57 | 447.20 |
| Compounded daily (365) | 122.14 | 164.87 | 271.79 | 448.03 |

♦ *r* becomes the interest rate per period or *r* (the annual interest rate) divided by *m* (the number of times compounding occurs per year). Thus, if it is a 6 percent annual rate with monthly compounding, *r* becomes 6% ÷ 12 = 0.5 percent per month, and if it is a 6 percent annual rate compounded daily, then *r* becomes (6% ÷ 365) per day.

We can see the value of intrayear compounding by examining Table 5-4. Because "interest is earned on interest" more frequently as the length of the compounding period declines, there is an inverse relationship between the length of the compounding period and the effective annual interest rate: The shorter the compounding period is, the higher the effective interest rate will be. Conversely, the longer the compounding period is, the lower the effective interest rate will be.

**EXAMPLE 5.11    Calculating the growth of an investment**

If we place $100 in a savings account that yields 12 percent compounded quarterly, what will our investment grow to at the end of 5 years?

**STEP 1: FORMULATE A SOLUTION STRATEGY**
The future value of our savings account can be computed using equation (5-8) as follows:

$$\text{Future value} = \text{present value} \times \left(1 + \frac{r}{m}\right)^{m \cdot n}$$

**STEP 2: CRUNCH THE NUMBERS**
Substituting into equation (5-8), we compute the future value as follows:

$$FV = \$100\left(1 + \frac{0.12}{4}\right)^{4 \cdot 5}$$
$$= \$100(1.8061) = \$180.61$$

**STEP 3: ANALYZE YOUR RESULTS**
Thus, we will have $180.61 at the end of 5 years. In this problem, *n* becomes the number of quarters in 5 years while *r/m* becomes the interest rate per period—in effect, 3 percent per quarter for 20 quarters.

**CALCULATOR SOLUTION**

| Data Input | Function Key |
| --- | --- |
| 20 | N |
| 12/4 | I/Y |
| 100 | PV |
| 0 | PMT |

| Function Key | Answer |
| --- | --- |
| CPT | |
| FV | −180.61 |

# DID YOU GET IT?

## HOW MUCH CAN YOU AFFORD TO SPEND ON A HOUSE? AN AMORTIZED LOAN WITH MONTHLY PAYMENTS

There are several different ways you can solve this problem—using the mathematical formulas, a financial calculator, or a spreadsheet—each one giving you the same answer.

1. **Using the Mathematical Formulas.** Again, you need to multiply *n* times *m* and divide *r* by *m*, where *m* is the number of compounding periods per year. Thus,

$$PV = \$1{,}250 \left[ \frac{1 - \dfrac{1}{\left(1 + \dfrac{0.065}{12}\right)^{30 \cdot 12}}}{\dfrac{0.065}{12}} \right]$$

$$PV = \$1{,}250 \left[ \frac{1 - \dfrac{1}{(1 + 0.00541667)^{360}}}{0.00541667} \right]$$

$$PV = \$1{,}250 \left[ \frac{1 - \dfrac{1}{6.99179797}}{0.00541667} \right]$$

$$PV = \$1{,}250(158.210816)$$

$$PV = \$197{,}763.52$$

2. **Using a Financial Calculator.** First, you must convert everything to months. To do this you would first convert *n* into months by multiplying *n* times *m* (30 times 12) and enter this into $\boxed{N}$. Next you would enter the interest rate as a monthly rate by dividing *r* by *m* and entering this number into $\boxed{I/Y}$. Finally, make sure that the value entered as $\boxed{PMT}$ is a monthly figure, that is, it is the monthly payment value.

CALCULATOR SOLUTION

| Data Input | Function Key |
|---|---|
| 360 | $\boxed{N}$ |
| 6.5/12 | $\boxed{I/Y}$ |
| −1,250 | $\boxed{PMT}$ |
| 0 | $\boxed{FV}$ |

| Function Key | Answer |
|---|---|
| $\boxed{CPT}$ | |
| $\boxed{PV}$ | 197,763.52 |

3. **Using an Excel Spreadsheet.**

| | A | B |
|---|---|---|
| 1 | interest rate (rate) = | 0.5417% |
| 2 | number of periods (nper) = | 360 |
| 3 | payment (pmt) = | 1,250 |
| 4 | future value (fv) = | 0 |
| 5 | | |
| 6 | present value (pv) = | ($197,763.52) |
| 7 | Entered values in cell b6: | |
| 8 | =PV((6.5/12)%,b2,b3,b4) | |

---

CALCULATOR SOLUTION

| Data Input | Function Key |
|---|---|
| 13.0/12 | $\boxed{I/Y}$ |
| 10,000 | $\boxed{PV}$ |
| −400 | $\boxed{PMT}$ |
| 0 | $\boxed{FV}$ |

| Function Key | Answer |
|---|---|
| $\boxed{CPT}$ | |
| $\boxed{N}$ | 29.3 |

**EXAMPLE 5.12**    **Calculating the future value of an investment**

In 2009 the average U.S. household owed about $10,000 in credit card debt, and the average interest rate on credit card debt was 13.0 percent. On many credit cards the minimum monthly payment is 4 percent of the debt balance. If the average household paid off 4 percent of the initial amount it owed each month, that is, made payments of $400 each month, how many months would it take to repay this credit card debt? Use a financial calculator to solve this problem.

### STEP 1: FORMULATE A SOLUTION STRATEGY

The easiest approach here is to either use your financial calculator or use Excel to solve for N, the number of periods. Using Excel, you would simply use the =NPER function and input values for rate, pmt, pv, and fv. Using your financial calculator, you would simply solve for N; however, you'll need to make sure that I/Y is expressed as a monthly rate because you are solving for the number of months necessary to repay the credit card.

### STEP 2: CRUNCH THE NUMBERS

The solution, using a financial calculator, appears in the margin. You'll notice in the solution that the value for PMT goes in as a negative.

**STEP 3: ANALYZE YOUR RESULTS**

The answer is over 29 months before you pay off your credit card if you pay off 4 percent of the initial amount owed each month—obviously, if you keep using the credit card, it will take longer.

## Concept Check

1. Why does the future value of a given amount increase when interest is compounded nonannually as opposed to annually?
2. How do you adjust the present- and future-value formulas when interest is compounded monthly?

# The Present Value of an Uneven Stream and Perpetuities

Although some projects will involve a single cash flow and some will involve annuities, many projects will involve uneven cash flows over several years. Chapter 10, which examines investments in fixed assets, presents this situation repeatedly. There we will be comparing not only the present value of cash flows generated by different projects but also the cash inflows and outflows generated by a particular project to determine that project's present value. However, this will not be difficult because the present value of any cash flow is measured in today's dollars and thus can be compared, through addition for inflows and subtraction for outflows, to the present value of any other cash flow also measured in today's dollars. For example, if we wished to find the present value of the following cash flows

| YEAR | CASH FLOW | YEAR | CASH FLOW |
|------|-----------|------|-----------|
| 1 | $ 0 | 6 | 500 |
| 2 | 200 | 7 | 500 |
| 3 | −400 | 8 | 500 |
| 4 | 500 | 9 | 500 |
| 5 | 500 | 10 | 500 |

given a 6 percent discount rate, we would merely discount the flows back to the present and total them by adding in the positive flows and subtracting the negative ones. However, this problem is complicated by the annuity of $500 that runs from years 4 through 10. To accommodate this, we can first discount the annuity back to the beginning of period 4 (or end of period 3) and get its present value at that point in time. We then bring this single cash flow (which is the present value of the 7-year annuity) back to the present. In effect, we discount twice, first back to the end of period 3, then back to the present. This is shown graphically in Table 5-5 and numerically in Table 5-6. Thus, the present value of this uneven stream of cash flows is $2,185.69.

 **4** Determine the present value of an uneven stream of payments and understand perpetuities.

**STEP 1**
Bring the $200 at the end of year 2 back to present:

CALCULATOR SOLUTION

| Data Input | Function Key |
|------------|--------------|
| 2 | N |
| 6 | I/Y |
| 200 | FV |
| 0 | PMT |

| Function Key | Answer |
|--------------|--------|
| CPT | |
| PV | −178.00 |

**STEP 2**
Bring the negative $400 at the end of year 3 back to present:

CALCULATOR SOLUTION

| Data Input | Function Key |
|------------|--------------|
| 3 | N |
| 6 | I/Y |
| 0 | PMT |
| −400 | FV |

| Function Key | Answer |
|--------------|--------|
| CPT | |
| PV | 335.85 |

**STEP 3**
Bring the 7-year, $500 annuity beginning at the end of year 4 back to the beginning of year 4, which is the same as the end of year 3:

CALCULATOR SOLUTION

| Data Input | Function Key |
|------------|--------------|
| 7 | N |
| 6 | I/Y |
| 500 | PMT |
| 0 | FV |

| Function Key | Answer |
|--------------|--------|
| CPT | |
| PV | −2,791.19 |

**TABLE 5-5  The Present Value of an Uneven Stream Involving One Annuity Discounted to the Present at 6 Percent: An Example**

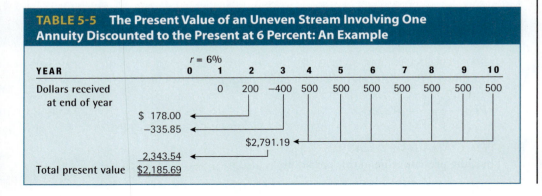

| YEAR | $r = 6\%$ 0 | 1 | 2 | 3 | 4 | 5 | 6 | 7 | 8 | 9 | 10 |
|------|-------------|---|---|---|---|---|---|---|---|---|----|
| Dollars received at end of year | | 0 | 200 | −400 | 500 | 500 | 500 | 500 | 500 | 500 | 500 |

$ 178.00
−335.85
$2,791.19
2,343.54
Total present value  $2,185.69

## STEP 4
Bring the value we just calculated, which is the value of the 7-year annuity of $500 at the end of year 3, back to present.

**CALCULATOR SOLUTION**

| Data Input | Function Key |
|---|---|
| 3 | N |
| 6 | I/Y |
| 2,791.19 | FV |
| 0 | PMT |

| Function Key | Answer |
|---|---|
| CPT | |
| PV | −2,343.54 |

## STEP 5
Add the present value of the cash inflows and subtract the present value of the cash outflow (the $400 from the end of year 3) calculated in steps 1, 2, and 4.

$$\begin{aligned} &\$\ \ 178.00 \\ &-335.85 \\ &\underline{+2,343.54} \\ &\$\,2,185.69 \end{aligned}$$

**perpetuity** an annuity with an infinite life.

---

**TABLE 5-6  Determining the Present Value of an Uneven Stream Involving One Annuity Discounted to the Present at 6 Percent: An Example**

| | |
|---|---|
| 1. Present value of $200 received at the end of 2 years at 6% = | $   178.00 |
| 2  Present value of a $400 outflow at the end of 3 years at 6% = | −335.85 |
| 3. (a)  Value at end of year 3 of a $500 annuity, years 4–10 at 6% = $2,791.19<br>   (b)  Present value of $2,791.19 received at the end of year 3 at 6% = | 2,343.54 |
| 4. Total present value = | $2,185.69 |

Remember, once the cash flows from an investment have been brought back to the present, they can be combined by adding and subtracting to determine the project's total present value.

## Concept Check

1. How would you calculate the present value of an investment that produced cash flows of $100 received at the end of year 1 and $700 at the end of year 2?

## Perpetuities

A **perpetuity** is *an annuity that continues forever*; that is, every year following its establishment this investment pays the same dollar amount. An example of a perpetuity is preferred stock that pays a constant dollar dividend infinitely. Determining the present value of a perpetuity is delightfully simple; we merely need to divide the constant flow by the discount rate. For example, the present value of a $100 perpetuity discounted back to the present at 5 percent is $100/0.05 = $2,000. Thus, the equation representing the present value of a perpetuity is

$$PV = \frac{PP}{r} \tag{5-9}$$

where: $PV$ = the present value of the perpetuity
$PP$ = the constant dollar amount provided by the perpetuity
$r$ = the annual interest (or discount) rate

---

**EXAMPLE 5.13**   **Calculating the future value of an investment**

What is the present value of a $500 perpetuity discounted back to the present at 8 percent?

**STEP 1: FORMULATE A SOLUTION STRATEGY**
The present value of the perpetuity can be calculated using equation (5-9) as follows:

$$PV = \frac{PP}{r}$$

**STEP 2: CRUNCH THE NUMBERS**
Substituting $PP$ = $500 and $r$ = 0.08 into equation (5-9), we find

$$PV = \frac{\$500}{0.08} = \$6,250$$

**STEP 3: ANALYZE YOUR RESULTS**
Thus, the present value of this perpetuity is $6,250.

## Concept Check

1. What is a perpetuity?

2. When $r$, the annual interest (or discount) rate, increases, what happens to the present value of a perpetuity? Why?

| TABLE 5-7 | Summary of Time Value of Money Equations |
|---|---|
| **Calculation** | **Equation** |
| Future value of a single payment | $FV_n = PV(1 + r)^n$ |
| Present value of a single payment | $PV = FV_n\left[\dfrac{1}{(1 + r)^n}\right]$ |
| Future value of an annuity | $FV \text{ of an annuity} = PMT\left[\dfrac{(1 + r)^n - 1}{r}\right]$ |
| Present value of an annuity | $PV \text{ of an annuity} = PMT\left[\dfrac{1 - (1 + r)^{-n}}{r}\right]$ |
| Future value of an annuity due | $FV_n(\text{annuity due}) = \text{future value of an annuity} \times (1 + r)$ |
| Present value of an annuity due | $PV(\text{annuity due}) = \text{present value of an annuity} \times (1 + r)$ |
| Effective annual return (EAR) $=$ | $\left[1 + \dfrac{\text{quoted rate}}{m}\right]^m - 1$ |
| Future value of a single payment with nonannual compounding | $FV_n = PV\left(1 + \dfrac{r}{m}\right)^{mn}$ |
| Present value of a perpetuity | $PV = \dfrac{PP}{r}$ |

Notations: $FV_n$ = the future value of the investment at the end of $n$ years
$n$ = the number of years until payment will be received or during which compounding occurs
$r$ = the annual interest or discount rate
$PV$ = the present value of the future sum of money
$m$ = the number of times compounding occurs during the year
$PMT$ = the annuity payment deposited or received at the end of each year
$PP$ = the constant dollar amount provided by the perpetuity

# Chapter Summaries

## Explain the mechanics of compounding and bringing the value of money back to the present. (pgs. 143–157)

**SUMMARY:** Compound interest occurs when interest paid on an investment during the first period is added to the principal; then, during the second period, interest is earned on this new sum. The formula for this appears in Table 5-7.

Although there are several ways to move money through time, they all give you the same result. In the business world, the primary method is through the use of a financial spreadsheet, with Excel being the most popular. If you can use a financial calculator, you can easily apply your skills to a spreadsheet.

Actually, we have only one formula with which to calculate both present value and future value—we simply solve for different variables—$FV$ and $PV$. This single compounding formula is $FV_n = PV(1 + r)^n$ and is presented in Table 5-7.

### KEY TERMS

**Compound interest, page 144**  The situation in which interest paid on an investment during the first period is added to the principal. During the second period, interest is earned on the original principal plus the interest earned during the first period.

**Future value, page 145**  The amount to which your investment will grow, or a future dollar amount.

**Future value factor, page 145**  The value of $(1 + r)^n$ used as a multiple to calculate an amount's future value.

**Simple interest, page 146**  If you only earned interest on your initial investment, it would be referred to as simple interest.

**Present value, page 153**  The value in today's dollars of a future payment discounted back to present at the required rate of return.

**Present value factor, page 153**  The value of $\dfrac{1}{(1 + r)^n}$ used as a multiplier to calculate an amount's present value.

### KEY EQUATIONS

Future value at the end of year $n$ = present value $\times (1 + r)^n$

Present value = future value at the end of year $n \times \dfrac{1}{(1 + r)^n}$

---

 **2**   **Understand annuities.**   (pgs. 157–164)

**SUMMARY:** An annuity is a series of equal payments made for a specified number of years. In effect, it is calculated as the sum of the present or future value of the individual cash flows over the life of the annuity. The formula for an annuity due is given in Table 5-7.

If the cash flows from an annuity occur at the end of each period, the annuity is referred to as an ordinary annuity. If the cash flows occur at the beginning of each period, the annuity is referred to as an annuity due. We will assume that cash flows occur at the end of each period unless otherwise stated.

The procedure for solving for PMT, the annuity payment value when $i$, $n$, and $PV$ are known, is also used to determine what payments are associated with paying off a loan in equal installments over time. Loans that are paid off this way, in equal periodic payments, are called amortized loans. Although the payments are fixed, different amounts of each payment are applied toward the principal and the interest. With each payment you make, you owe a bit less on the principal. As a result, the amount that goes toward the interest payment declines with each payment made, whereas the portion of each payment that goes toward the principal increases.

### KEY TERMS

**Annuity, page 157**  A series of equal dollar payments made for a specified number of years.

**Ordinary annuity, page 157**  An annuity where the cash flows occur at the end of each period.

**Compound annuity, page 157**  Depositing an equal sum of money at the end of each year for a certain number of years and allowing it to grow.

**Annuity future value factor, page 158**  The value of $\left[\dfrac{(1 + r)^n - 1}{r}\right]$ used as a multiplier to calculate the future value of an annuity.

**Annuity present value factor, page 160**  The value of $\left[\dfrac{1 - (1 + r)^{-n}}{r}\right]$ used as a multiplier to calculate the present value of an annuity.

**Annuity due, page 161**  An annuity in which the payments occur at the beginning of each period.

**Amortized loan, page 162**  A loan that is paid off in equal periodic payments.

**KEY EQUATIONS**

$$\text{Future value of an annuity} = PMT \left[ \frac{(1 + r)^n - 1}{r} \right]$$

$$\text{Present value of an annuity} = PMT \left[ \frac{1 - \dfrac{1}{(1 + r)^n}}{r} \right]$$

$$\text{Future value of an annuity due} = PMT \left[ \frac{(1 + r)^n - 1}{r} \right] \times (1 + r)$$

$$\text{Present value of an annuity} = PMT \left[ \frac{1 - \dfrac{1}{(1 + r)^n}}{r} \right] \times (1 + r)$$

## Determine the future or present value of a sum when there are nonannual compounding periods. (pgs. 165–169)

**SUMMARY:** With nonannual compounding, interest is earned on interest more frequently because the length of the compounding period is shorter. As a result, there is an inverse relationship between the length of the compounding period and the effective annual interest rate. The formula for solving for the future value of a single payment with nonannual compounding is given in Table 5-7.

**KEY TERM**

**Effective annual rate (EAR), page 165** The annual compound rate that produces the same return as the nominal, or quoted, rate when something is compounded on a nonannual basis. In effect, the EAR provides the true rate of return.

**KEY EQUATIONS**

$$\text{Effective annual rate } (EAR) = \left( 1 + \frac{\text{quoted rate}}{m} \right)^m - 1$$

$$FV_n = PV \left[ 1 + \frac{r}{m} \right]^{m \cdot n}$$

## Determine the present value of an uneven stream of payments and understand perpetuities. (pgs. 169–171)

**SUMMARY:** Although some projects will involve a single cash flow and some will involve annuities, many projects will involve uneven cash flows over several years. However, finding the present or future value of these flows is not difficult because the present value of any cash flow measured in today's dollars can be compared, by adding the inflows and subtracting the outflows, to the present value of any other cash flow also measured in today's dollars.

A perpetuity is an annuity that continues forever; that is, every year following its establishment the investment pays the same dollar amount. An example of a perpetuity is preferred stock, which pays a constant dollar dividend infinitely. Determining the present value of a perpetuity is delightfully simple. We merely need to divide the constant flow by the discount rate.

**KEY TERM**

**Perpetuity, page 170** An annuity with an infinite life.

**KEY EQUATION**

$$\text{Present value of a perpetuity} = \frac{\text{constant dollar amount provided by the perpetuity}}{r}$$

# Review Questions

*All Review Questions are available in* MyFinanceLab.

**5-1.** What is the time value of money? Why is it so important?

**5-2.** The process of discounting and compounding are related. Explain this relationship.

**5-3.** How would an increase in the interest rate ($r$) or a decrease in the holding period ($n$) affect the future value ($FV_n$) of a sum of money? Explain why.

**5-4.** Suppose you were considering depositing your savings in one of three banks, all of which pay 5 percent interest; bank A compounds annually, bank B compounds semiannually, and bank C compounds daily. Which bank would you choose? Why?

**5-5.** What is an annuity? Give some examples of annuities. Distinguish between an annuity and a perpetuity.

**5-6.** Compare some of the different financial calculators that are available on the Internet. Look at www.dinkytown.net, www.bankrate.com/calculators.aspx, and www.interest.com/calculators. Which financial calculators do you find to be the most useful? Why?

# Study Problems

*All Study Problems are available in* MyFinanceLab.

**5-1.** (*Compound interest*) To what amount will the following investments accumulate?
- a. $5,000 invested for 10 years at 10 percent compounded annually
- b. $8,000 invested for 7 years at 8 percent compounded annually
- c. $775 invested for 12 years at 12 percent compounded annually
- d. $21,000 invested for 5 years at 5 percent compounded annually

**5-2.** (*Compound value solving for* n) How many years will the following take?
- a. $500 to grow to $1,039.50 if invested at 5 percent compounded annually
- b. $35 to grow to $53.87 if invested at 9 percent compounded annually
- c. $100 to grow to $298.60 if invested at 20 percent compounded annually
- d. $53 to grow to $78.76 if invested at 2 percent compounded annually

**5-3.** (*Compound value solving for* r) At what annual rate would the following have to be invested?
- a. $500 to grow to $1,948.00 in 12 years
- b. $300 to grow to $422.10 in 7 years
- c. $50 to grow to $280.20 in 20 years
- d. $200 to grow to $497.60 in 5 years

**5-4.** (*Present value*) What is the present value of the following future amounts?
- a. $800 to be received 10 years from now discounted back to the present at 10 percent
- b. $300 to be received 5 years from now discounted back to the present at 5 percent
- c. $1,000 to be received 8 years from now discounted back to the present at 3 percent
- d. $1,000 to be received 8 years from now discounted back to the present at 20 percent

**5-5.** (*Compound value*) Stanford Simmons, who recently sold his Porsche, placed $10,000 in a savings account paying annual compound interest of 6 percent.
- a. Calculate the amount of money that will have accrued if he leaves the money in the bank for 1, 5, and 15 years.
- b. If he moves his money into an account that pays 8 percent or one that pays 10 percent, rework part (a) using these new interest rates.
- c. What conclusions can you draw about the relationship between interest rates, time, and future sums from the calculations you have completed in this problem?

**5-6.** (*Future value*) Sarah Wiggum would like to make a single investment and have $2 million at the time of her retirement in 35 years. She has found a mutual fund that will earn 4 percent annually. How much will Sarah have to invest today? What if Sarah were a finance major and learned how to earn a 14 percent annual return, how much would she have to invest today?

**5-7.** (*Future value*) Sales of a new finance book were 15,000 copies this year and were expected to increase by 20 percent per year. What are expected sales during each of the next 3 years? Graph this sales trend and explain.

**5-8.** (*Future value*) Albert Pujols hit 47 home runs in 2009. If his home-run output grew at a rate of 12 percent per year, what would it have been over the following 5 years?

**5-9.** (*Solving for* r *in compound interest*) If you were offered $1,079.50 10 years from now in return for an investment of $500 currently, what annual rate of interest would you earn if you took the offer?

**5-10.** (*Solving for* r *in compound interest*) You lend a friend $10,000, for which your friend will repay you $27,027 at the end of 5 years. What interest rate are you charging your "friend"?

**5-11.** (*Present-value comparison*) You are offered $1,000 today, $10,000 in 12 years, or $25,000 in 25 years. Assuming that you can earn 11 percent on your money, which should you choose?

**5-12.** (*Solving for* r *in compound interest—financial calculator needed*) In September 1963, the first issue of the comic book *X-MEN* was issued. The original price for that issue was $0.12. By September 2013, 50 years later, the value of the near-mint copy of this comic book had risen to $33,000. What annual rate of interest would you have earned if you had bought the comic in 1963 and sold it in 2013?

**5-13.** (*Compounding using a calculator*) Bart Simpson, age 10, wants to be able to buy a really cool new car when he turns 16. His really cool car costs $15,000 today, and its cost is expected to increase 3 percent annually. Bart wants to make one deposit today (he can sell his mint-condition original *Nuclear Boy* comic book) into an account paying 7.5 percent annually in order to buy his car in 6 years. How much will Bart's car cost, and how much does Bart have to save today in order to buy this car at age 16?

**5-14.** (*Compounding using a calculator*) Lisa Simpson wants to have $1 million in 45 years by making equal annual end-of-the-year deposits into a tax-deferred account paying 8.75 percent annually. What must Lisa's annual deposit be?

**5-15.** (*Future value*) Bob Terwilliger received $12,345 for his services as financial consultant to the mayor's office of his hometown of Springfield. Bob says that his consulting work was his civic duty and that he should not receive any compensation. So, he has invested his paycheck into an account paying 3.98 percent annual interest and left the account in his will to the city of Springfield on the condition that the city could not collect any money from the account for 200 years. How much money will the city receive from Bob's generosity in 200 years?

**5-16.** (*Solving for* r) Kirk Van Houten, who has been married for 23 years, would like to buy his wife an expensive diamond ring with a platinum setting on their 30-year wedding anniversary. Assume that the cost of the ring will be $12,000 in 7 years. Kirk currently has $4,510 to invest. What annual rate of return must Kirk earn on his investment to accumulate enough money to pay for the ring?

**5-17.** (*Solving for* n) Jack asked Jill to marry him, and she has accepted under one condition: Jack must buy her a new $330,000 Rolls-Royce Phantom. Jack currently has $45,530 that he may invest. He has found a mutual fund that pays 4.5% annual interest in which he will place the money. How long will it take Jack to win Jill's hand in marriage?

**5-18.** (*Present value*) Ronen Consulting has just realized an accounting error which has resulted in an unfunded liability of $398,930 due in 28 years. Toni Flanders, the company's CEO, is scrambling to discount the liability to the present to assist in valuing the firm's stock. If the appropriate discount rate is 7 percent, what is the present value of the liability?

**5-19.** (*Future value*) Selma and Patty Bouvier are twins and both work at the Springfield DMV. Selma and Patty Bouvier decide to save for retirement, which is 35 years away. They'll both receive an 8 percent annual return on their investment over the next 35 years. Selma invests $2,000 per year at the end of each year *only* for the first 10 years of the 35-year period—for a total of $20,000 saved. Patty doesn't start saving for 10 years and then saves $2,000 per year at the end of each year for the remaining 25 years—for a total of $50,000 saved. How much will each of them have when they retire?

---

**5-20.** (*Compound annuity*) What is the accumulated sum of each of the following streams of payments?

a. $500 a year for 10 years compounded annually at 5 percent
b. $100 a year for 5 years compounded annually at 10 percent
c. $35 a year for 7 years compounded annually at 7 percent
d. $25 a year for 3 years compounded annually at 2 percent

**5-21.** (*Present value of an annuity*) What is the present value of the following annuities?

a. $2,500 a year for 10 years discounted back to the present at 7 percent
b. $70 a year for 3 years discounted back to the present at 3 percent

c. $280 a year for 7 years discounted back to the present at 6 percent

d. $500 a year for 10 years discounted back to the present at 10 percent

**5-22.** (*Solving for* r *with annuities*) Nicki Johnson, a sophomore mechanical engineering student, receives a call from an insurance agent, who believes that Nicki is an older woman ready to retire from teaching. He talks to her about several annuities that she could buy that would guarantee her an annual fixed income. The annuities are as follows:

| ANNUITY | INITIAL PAYMENT INTO ANNUITY (AT $t = 0$) | AMOUNT OF MONEY RECEIVED PER YEAR | DURATION OF ANNUITY (YEARS) |
|---|---|---|---|
| A | $50,000 | $8,500 | 12 |
| B | $60,000 | $7,000 | 25 |
| C | $70,000 | $8,000 | 20 |

If Nicki could earn 11 percent on her money by placing it in a savings account, should she place it instead in any of the annuities? Which ones, if any? Why?

**5-23.** (*Loan amortization*) Mr. Bill S. Preston, Esq., purchased a new house for $80,000. He paid $20,000 down and agreed to pay the rest over the next 25 years in 25 equal end-of-year payments plus 9 percent compound interest on the unpaid balance. What will these equal payments be?

**5-24.** (*Solving for* PMT *of an annuity*) To pay for your child's education, you wish to have accumulated $15,000 at the end of 15 years. To do this you plan on depositing an equal amount into the bank at the end of each year. If the bank is willing to pay 6 percent compounded annually, how much must you deposit each year to reach your goal?

**5-25.** (*Future value of an annuity*) In 10 years you are planning on retiring and buying a house in Oviedo, Florida. The house you are looking at currently costs $100,000 and is expected to increase in value each year at a rate of 5 percent. Assuming you can earn 10 percent annually on your investments, how much must you invest at the end of each of the next 10 years to be able to buy your dream home when you retire?

**5-26.** (*Compound value*) The Aggarwal Corporation needs to save $10 million to retire a $10 million mortgage that matures in 10 years. To retire this mortgage, the company plans to put a fixed amount into an account at the end of each year for 10 years, with the first payment occurring at the end of 1 year. The Aggarwal Corporation expects to earn 9 percent annually on the money in this account. What equal annual contribution must it make to this account to accumulate the $10 million in 10 years?

**5-27.** (*Loan amortization*) On December 31, Beth Klemkosky bought a yacht for $50,000, paying $10,000 down and agreeing to pay the balance in 10 equal end-of-year installments and 10 percent interest on the declining balance. How big would the annual payments be?

**5-28.** (*Solving for* r *of an annuity*) You lend a friend $30,000, which your friend will repay in five equal annual end-of-year payments of $10,000, with the first payment to be received 1 year from now. What rate of return does your loan receive?

**5-29.** (*Loan amortization*) A firm borrows $25,000 from the bank at 12 percent compounded annually to purchase some new machinery. This loan is to be repaid in equal installments at the end of each year over the next 5 years. How much will each annual payment be?

**5-30.** (*Compound annuity*) You plan on buying some property in Florida 5 years from today. To do this you estimate that you will need $20,000 at that time for the purchase. You would like to accumulate these funds by making equal annual deposits in your savings account, which pays 12 percent annually. If you make your first deposit at the end of this year, and you would like your account to reach $20,000 when the final deposit is made, what will be the amount of your deposits?

**5-31.** (*Loan amortization*) On December 31, Son-Nan Chen borrowed $100,000, agreeing to repay this sum in 20 equal end-of-year installments and 15 percent interest on the declining balance. How large must the annual payments be?

**5-32.** (*Loan amortization*) To buy a new house you must borrow $150,000. To do this you take out a $150,000, 30-year, 10 percent mortgage. Your mortgage payments, which are made at the end of each year (one payment each year), include both principal and 10 percent interest on the declining balance. How large will your annual payments be?

**5-33.** (*Spreadsheet problem*) If you invest $900 in a bank in which it will earn 8 percent compounded annually, how much will it be worth at the end of 7 years? Use a spreadsheet to do your calculations.

**5-34.** (*Spreadsheet problem*) In 20 years you'd like to have $250,000 to buy a vacation home, but you have only $30,000. At what rate must your $30,000 be compounded annually for it to grow to $250,000 in 20 years? Use a spreadsheet to calculate your answer.

**5-35.** (*Compounding using a calculator and annuities due*) Springfield mogul Montgomery Burns, age 80, wants to retire at age 100 in order to steal candy from babies full time. Once Mr. Burns retires, he wants to withdraw $1 billion at the beginning of each year for 10 years from a special offshore account that will pay 20 percent annually. In order to fund his retirement, Mr. Burns will make 20 equal end-of-the-year deposits in this same special account that will pay 20 percent annually. How much money will Mr. Burns need at age 100, and how large of an annual deposit must he make to fund this retirement account?

**5-36.** (*Compounding using a calculator and annuities due*) Imagine Homer Simpson actually invested $100,000 5 years ago at a 7.5 percent annual interest rate. If he invests an additional $1,500 a year at the beginning of each year for 20 years at the same 7.5 percent annual rate, how much money will Homer have 20 years from now?

**5-37.** (*Solving for r in an annuity*) Your folks just called and would like some advice from you. An insurance agent just called them and offered them the opportunity to purchase an annuity for $21,074.25 that will pay them $3,000 per year for 20 years, but they don't have the slightest idea what return they would be making on their investment of $21,074.25. What rate of return will they be earning?

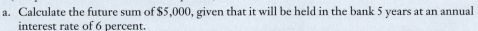

**5-38.** (*Compound interest with nonannual periods*)

   a. Calculate the future sum of $5,000, given that it will be held in the bank 5 years at an annual interest rate of 6 percent.

   b. Recalculate part (a) using compounding periods that are (1) semiannual and (2) bimonthly.

   c. Recalculate parts (a) and (b) for a 12 percent annual interest rate.

   d. Recalculate part (a) using a time horizon of 12 years (annual interest rate is still 6 percent).

   e. With respect to the effect of changes in the stated interest rate and holding periods on future sums in parts (c) and (d), what conclusions do you draw when you compare these figures with the answers found in parts (a) and (b)?

**5-39.** (*Compound interest with nonannual periods*) After examining the various personal loan rates available to you, you find that you can borrow funds from a finance company at 12 percent compounded monthly or from a bank at 13 percent compounded annually. Which alternative is more attractive?

**5-40.** (*Solving for n with nonannual periods*) About how many years would it take for your investment to grow fourfold if it were invested at 16 percent compounded semiannually?

**5-41.** (*Spreadsheet problem*) To buy a new house you take out a 25-year mortgage for $300,000. What will your monthly payments be if the interest rate on your mortgage is 8 percent? Use a spreadsheet to calculate your answer. Now, calculate the portion of the 48th monthly payment that goes toward interest and principal.

**5-42.** (*Nonannual compounding using a calculator*) Prof. Finance is thinking about trading cars. He estimates he will still have to borrow $25,000 to pay for his new car. How large will Prof. Finance's monthly car loan payment be if he can get a 5-year (60 equal monthly payments) car loan from the university's credit union at 6.2 percent?

**5-43.** (*Nonannual compounding using a calculator*) Bowflex's television ads say you can get a fitness machine that sells for $999 for $33 a month for 36 months. What rate of interest are you paying on this Bowflex loan?

**5-44.** (*Nonannual compounding using a calculator*) Ford's current incentives include 4.9 percent financing for 60 months or $1,000 cash back for a Mustang. Let's assume Suzie Student wants to buy the premium Mustang convertible, which costs $25,000, and she has no down payment other than the cash back from Ford. If she chooses the $1,000 cash back, Suzie can borrow from the VTech Credit Union at 6.9 percent for 60 months (Suzie's credit isn't as good as Prof. Finance's). What will Suzie Student's monthly payment be under each option? Which option should she choose?

**5-45.** (*Nonannual compounding using a calculator*) Ronnie Rental plans to invest $1,000 at the end of each quarter for 4 years into an account that pays 6.4 percent compounded quarterly. He will use this money as a down payment on a new home at the end of the 4 years. How large will his down payment be 4 years from today?

**5-46.** (*Nonannual compounding using a calculator*) Dennis Rodman has a $5,000 debt balance on his Visa card that charges 12.9 percent compounded monthly. Dennis's current minimum monthly payment is 3 percent of his debt balance, which is $150. How many months (round up) will it take Dennis to pay off his credit card if he pays the current minimum payment of $150 at the end of each month?

**5-47.** (*Nonannual compounding using a calculator*) Should we have bet the kids' college fund at the dog track? Let's look at one specific case of a college professor (let's call him Prof. ME) with two young children. Two years ago, Prof. ME invested $160,000 hoping to have $420,000 available 12 years later when the first child started college. However, the account's balance is now only $140,000. Let's figure out what is needed to get Prof. ME's college savings plan back on track.

   a. What was the original annual rate of return needed to reach Prof. ME's goal when he started the fund 2 years ago?
   b. Now with only $140,000 in the fund and 10 years remaining until his first child starts college, what annual rate of return would the fund have to earn to reach Prof. ME's $420,000 goal if he adds nothing to the account?
   c. Shocked by his experience of the past 2 years, Prof. ME feels the college mutual fund has invested too much in stocks. He wants a low-risk fund in order to ensure he has the necessary $420,000 in 10 years, and he is willing to make end-of-the-month deposits to the fund as well. He later finds a fund that promises to pay a guaranteed return of 6 percent compounded monthly. Prof. ME decides to transfer the $140,000 to this new fund and make the necessary monthly deposits. How large of a monthly deposit must Prof. ME make into this new fund to meet his $420,000 goal?
   d. Now Prof. ME gets sticker shock from the necessary monthly deposit he has to make into the guaranteed fund in the preceding question. He decides to invest the $140,000 today and $500 at the end of each month for the next 10 years into a fund consisting of 50 percent stock and 50 percent bonds and hope for the best. What annual rate of return would the fund have to earn in order to reach Prof. ME's $420,000 goal?

**5-48.** (*Present value of an uneven stream of payments*) You are given three investment alternatives to analyze. The cash flows from these three investments are as follows:

| END OF YEAR | INVESTMENT | | |
| --- | --- | --- | --- |
| | A | B | C |
| 1 | $10,000 | | $10,000 |
| 2 | 10,000 | | |
| 3 | 10,000 | | |
| 4 | 10,000 | | |
| 5 | 10,000 | $10,000 | |
| 6 | | 10,000 | 50,000 |
| 7 | | 10,000 | |
| 8 | | 10,000 | |
| 9 | | 10,000 | |
| 10 | | 10,000 | 10,000 |

Assuming a 20 percent discount rate, find the present value of each investment.

**5-49.** (*Present value*) The Kumar Corporation is planning on issuing bonds that pay no interest but can be converted into $1,000 at maturity, 7 years from their purchase. To price these bonds competitively with other bonds of equal risk, it is determined that they should yield 10 percent, compounded annually. At what price should the Kumar Corporation sell these bonds?

**5-50.** (*Perpetuities*) What is the present value of the following?

    a. A $300 perpetuity discounted back to the present at 8 percent

    b. A $1,000 perpetuity discounted back to the present at 12 percent

    c. A $100 perpetuity discounted back to the present at 9 percent

    d. A $95 perpetuity discounted back to the present at 5 percent

**5-51.** (*Complex present value*) How much do you have to deposit today so that beginning 11 years from now you can withdraw $10,000 a year for the next 5 years (periods 11 through 15) plus an *additional* amount of $20,000 in that last year (period 15)? Assume an interest rate of 6 percent.

**5-52.** (*Complex present value*) You would like to have $50,000 in 15 years. To accumulate this amount you plan to deposit each year an equal sum in the bank, which will earn 7 percent interest compounded annually. Your first payment will be made at the end of the year.

    a. How much must you deposit annually to accumulate this amount?

    b. If you decide to make a large lump-sum deposit today instead of the annual deposits, how large should this lump-sum deposit be? (Assume you can earn 7 percent on this deposit.)

    c. At the end of 5 years you will receive $10,000 and deposit this in the bank toward your goal of $50,000 at the end of 15 years. In addition to this deposit, how much must you deposit in equal annual deposits to reach your goal? (Again assume you can earn 7 percent on this deposit.)

**5-53.** (*Comprehensive present value*) You are trying to plan for retirement in 10 years, and currently you have $100,000 in a savings account and $300,000 in stocks. In addition you plan on adding to your savings by depositing $10,000 per year in your savings account at the end of each of the next 5 years and then $20,000 per year at the end of each year for the final 5 years until retirement.

    a. Assuming your savings account returns 7 percent compounded annually, and your investment in stocks will return 12 percent compounded annually, how much will you have at the end of 10 years? (Ignore taxes.)

    b. If you expect to live for 20 years after you retire, and at retirement you deposit all of your savings in a bank account paying 10 percent, how much can you withdraw each year after retirement (20 equal withdrawals beginning 1 year after you retire) to end up with a zero balance upon your death?

**5-54.** (*Present value*) The state lottery's million-dollar payout provides for $1 million to be paid over 19 years in 20 payments of $50,000. The first $50,000 payment is made immediately, and the 19 remaining $50,000 payments occur at the end of each of the next 19 years. If 10 percent is the appropriate discount rate, what is the present value of this stream of cash flows? If 20 percent is the appropriate discount rate, what is the present value of the cash flows?

**5-55.** (*Complex annuity*) Upon graduating from college 35 years ago, Dr. Nick Riviera was already thinking of retirement. Since then he has made deposits into his retirement fund on a quarterly basis in the amount of $300. Nick has just completed his final payment and is at last ready to retire. His retirement fund has earned 9% interest compounded quarterly.

    a. How much has Nick accumulated in his retirement account?

    b. In addition to all this, 15 years ago, Nick received an inheritance check for $20,000 from his beloved uncle. He decided to deposit the entire amount into his retirement fund. What is his current balance in the fund?

**5-56.** (*Complex annuity and future value*) Milhouse, 22, is about to begin his career as a rocket scientist for a NASA contractor. Being a rocket scientist, Milhouse knows that he should begin saving for retirement immediately. Part of his inspiration came from reading an article on Social Security in *Newsweek*, where he saw that the ratio of workers paying taxes to retirees collecting checks will drop dramatically in the future. In fact, the ratio was 8.6 workers for every retiree in 1955; today the ratio is 3.3, and it will drop to 2 workers for every retiree in 2040. Milhouse's retirement plan pays 9 percent interest annually and allows him to make equal yearly contributions. Upon retirement Milhouse plans to buy a new boat, which he estimates will cost him $300,000 in 43 years (he plans to retire at age 65). He also estimates that in order to live comfortably he will require a yearly income of $80,000 for each year after he retires. Based on family history, Milhouse expects to live until age 80 (that is, he would like to receive 15 payments of $80,000 at the end of each year). When he retires, Milhouse will purchase his boat in one lump sum and place the remaining balance into an account, which pays 6% interest, from which he will withdraw his $80,000 per year. If Milhouse's first contribution is made

1 year from today, and his last is made the day he retires, how much money must he contribute each year to his retirement fund?

**5-57.** (*Present value of a complex stream*) Don Draper has signed a contract that will pay him $80,000 at the end of each year for the next 6 years, plus an additional $100,000 at the end of year 6. If 8 percent is the appropriate discount rate, what is the present value of this contract?

**5-58.** (*Present value of a complex stream*) Don Draper has signed a contract that will pay him $80,000 at the *beginning* of each year for the next 6 years, plus an additional $100,000 at the end of year 6. If 8 percent is the appropriate discount rate, what is the present value of this contract?

**5-59.** (*Complex stream of cash flows*) Roger Sterling has decided to buy an ad agency and is going to finance the purchase with seller financing—that is, a loan from the current owners of the agency. The loan will be for $2,000,000 financed at a 7 percent nominal annual interest rate. This loan will be paid off over 5 years with end-of-month payments along with a $500,000 balloon payment at the end of year 5. That is, the $2 million loan will be paid off with monthly payments and there will also be a final payment of $500,000 at the end of the final month. How much will the monthly payments be?

**5-60.** (*Future and present value using a calculator*) In 2013 Bill Gates was worth about $28 billion after he reduced his stake in Microsoft from 21 percent to around 14 percent by moving billions into his charitable foundation. Let's see what Bill Gates can do with his money in the following problems.

    a. I'll take Manhattan? Manhattan's native tribe sold Manhattan Island to Peter Minuit for $24 in 1626. Now, 387 years later in 2013, Bill Gates wants to buy the island from the "current natives." How much would Bill have to pay for Manhattan if the "current natives" want a 6 percent annual return on the original $24 purchase price? Could he afford it?

    b. (*Nonannual compounding using a calculator*) How much would Bill have to pay for Manhattan if the "current natives" want a 6% return compounded monthly on the original $24 purchase price?

    c. Microsoft Seattle? Bill Gates decides to pass on Manhattan and instead plans to buy the city of Seattle, Washington, for $60 billion in 10 years. How much would Mr. Gates have to invest today at 10 percent compounded annually in order to purchase Seattle in 10 years?

    d. Now assume Bill Gates wants to invest only about half his net worth today, $14 billion, in order to buy Seattle for $60 billion in 10 years. What annual rate of return would he have to earn in order to complete his purchase in 10 years?

    e. Margaritaville? Instead of buying and running large cities, Bill Gates is considering quitting the rigors of the business world and retiring to work on his golf game. To fund his retirement, Bill Gates would invest his $28 billion fortune in safe investments with an expected annual rate of return of 7 percent. Also, Mr. Gates wants to make 40 equal annual withdrawals from this retirement fund beginning a year from today. How much can Mr. Gates's annual withdrawal be in this case?

# Mini Case

*This Mini Case is available in* MyFinanceLab.

For your job as the business reporter for a local newspaper, you are given the task of putting together a series of articles that explain the power of the time value of money to your readers. Your editor would like you to address several specific questions in addition to demonstrating for the readership the use of time value of money techniques by applying them to several problems. What would be your response to the following memorandum from your editor?

    To: Business Reporter
    From: Perry White, Editor, *Daily Planet*
    Re: Upcoming Series on the Importance and Power of the Time Value of Money

In your upcoming series on the time value of money, I would like to make sure you cover several specific points. In addition, before you begin this assignment, I want to make sure we are all reading from the same script, as accuracy has always been the cornerstone of the *Daily Planet*. In this regard, I'd like a response to the following questions before we proceed:

    a. What is the relationship between discounting and compounding?

    b. What is the relationship between the present-value factor and the annuity present-value factor?

c.  1. What will $5,000 invested for 10 years at 8 percent compounded annually grow to?
    2. How many years will it take $400 to grow to $1,671 if it is invested at 10 percent compounded annually?
    3. At what rate would $1,000 have to be invested to grow to $4,046 in 10 years?

d. Calculate the future sum of $1,000, given that it will be held in the bank for 5 years and earn 10 percent compounded semiannually.

e. What is an annuity due? How does this differ from an ordinary annuity?

f. What is the present value of an ordinary annuity of $1,000 per year for 7 years discounted back to the present at 10 percent? What would be the present value if it were an annuity due?

g. What is the future value of an ordinary annuity of $1,000 per year for 7 years compounded at 10 percent? What would be the future value if it were an annuity due?

h. You have just borrowed $100,000, and you agree to pay it back over the next 25 years in 25 equal end-of-year payments plus 10 percent compound interest on the unpaid balance. What will be the size of these payments?

i. What is the present value of a $1,000 perpetuity discounted back to the present at 8 percent?

j. What is the present value of a $1,000 annuity for 10 years, with the first payment occurring at the end of year 10 (that is, ten $1,000 payments occurring at the end of year 10 through year 19), given a discount rate of 10 percent?

k. Given a 10 percent discount rate, what is the present value of a perpetuity of $1,000 per year if the first payment does not begin until the end of year 10?

# The Meaning and Measurement of Risk and Return

## Learning Objectives

**LO1** **Define and measure** the expected rate of return of an individual investment.

Expected Return Defined and Measured

**LO2** **Define and measure** the riskiness of an individual investment.

Risk Defined and Measured

**LO3** **Compare** the historical relationship between risk and rates of return in the capital markets.

Rates of Return: The Investor's Experience

**LO4** **Explain** how diversifying investments affects the riskiness and expected rate of return of a portfolio or combination of assets.

Risk and Diversification

**LO5** **Explain** the relationship between an investor's required rate of return on an investment and the riskiness of the investment.

The Investor's Required Rate of Return

One of the most important concepts in finance is *risk and return*, which is the total focus of our third principle of finance—**Risk Requires a Reward.** You only have to look at what happened in the stock markets during the past 5 years from 2007 to 2012 to see an overwhelming presence of investment risk. To illustrate, if you had been so unfortunate to buy a portfolio consisting of stocks making up the Standard & Poor's 500 Index in July 2007 and sold in February 2009, you would have lost 54 percent of your investment value. But if you had instead purchased the stock in July 2009 and held until March 2012, you would have a gain of 105 percent. Then if you had held the portfolio of stock for the entire 5 years, 2007–2012, you would still have lost 10 percent of your investment.

Instead of investing in a portfolio of stocks, as represented by the Standard & Poor's 500 Index, you could have chosen to invest in a single stock, such as JP Morgan Chase. If you were so fortunate as to buy the stock in November 2010 and sell 5 months later in April 2011, you would have doubled your money! On the other hand, if you had bought in April 2011, by June 2012 you would have lost half of your investment. Of course, you could have bought Apple at the beginning of 2012 and by June 2012 have a gain of 50 percent. Finally, if you were one of the investors who were eager to buy Facebook stock when it was issued to the public in May 2012, within 3 weeks your investment would have lost 30 percent of its value.

Clearly, owning stocks in recent times has not been for the faint of heart, where in a single day you could have earned as much as 5 percent on your investment, or lost even more. The market crash and extreme volatility in stock prices in 2008 and 2009 are what Nassim Nicholas Taleb would call a black swan—a highly improbable event that has a massive impact.[1] As a consequence, our confidence in forecasting the future has been undermined. Furthermore, our lives have been impacted and future plans delayed. We are much more cognizant of the financial risks that we face, both individually and in business.

In this chapter, we will help you understand the nature of risk and how risk *should* relate to expected returns on investments. We will look back beyond the past few years to see what we can learn about long-term historical risk-and-return relationships. These are topics that should be of key interest to us all in this day and age.

The need to recognize risk in financial decisions has already been apparent in earlier chapters. In Chapter 2, we referred to the discount rate, or the interest rate, as the opportunity cost of funds, but we did not look at the reasons why that rate might be high or low. For example, we did not explain why in June 2012 you could buy bonds issued by Office Depot that promised to pay a 6.8 percent rate of return, or why you could buy Dole Foods bonds that would give you an 8.0 percent rate of return, provided that both firms make the payments to the investors as promised.

In this chapter, we learn that risk is an integral force underlying rates of return. To begin our study, we define expected return and risk and offer suggestions about how these important concepts of return and risk can be measured quantitatively. We also compare the historical relationship between risk and rates of return. We then explain how diversifying investments can affect the expected return and riskiness of those investments. We also consider how the riskiness of an investment should affect the required rate of return on an investment.

Let's begin our study by looking at what we mean by the expected rate of return and how it can be measured.

[1]In his book *The Black Swan: The Impact of the Highly Improbable* (New York: Random House, 2007), Nassim Nicholas Taleb uses the analogy of a black swan, which represents a highly unlikely event. Until black swans were discovered in Australia, everyone assumed that all swans were white. Thus, for Taleb, the black swan symbolizes an event that no one thinks possible.

**1** Define and measure the expected rate of return of an individual investment.

**holding-period return (historical or realized rate of return)** the rate of return earned on an investment, which equals the dollar gain divided by the amount invested.

# Expected Return Defined and Measured

The expected benefits, or returns, an investment generates come in the form of cash flows. Cash flow, not accounting profit, is the relevant variable the financial manager uses to measure returns. This principle holds true regardless of the type of security, whether it is a debt instrument, preferred stock, common stock, or any mixture of these (such as convertible bonds).

To begin our discussion about an asset's expected rate of return, let's first understand how to compute a **historical** or **realized rate of return** on an investment. It may also be called a **holding-period return.** For instance, consider the dollar return you would have earned had you purchased a share of Google on April 23, 2012, for $598.45 and sold it less than 1 month later on May 17 for $637.85. The dollar return on your investment would have been $39.40 ($39.40 = $637.85−$598.45), assuming that the company paid no dividend. In addition to the dollar gain, we can calculate the rate of return as a percentage. It is useful to summarize the return on an investment in terms of a percentage because that way we can see the return per dollar invested, which is independent of how much we actually invest.

The rate of return earned from the investment in Google can be calculated as the ratio of the dollar return of $39.40 divided by your $598.45 investment in the stock, or 6.58 percent (6.58% = 0.0658 = $39.40 ÷ $598.45).

We can formalize the return calculations using equations (6-1) and (6-2):

Holding-period dollar gain would be:

$$\text{Holding-period dollar gain, DG} = \text{price}_{\text{end of period}} + \underset{\text{(dividend)}}{\text{cash distribution}} - \text{price}_{\text{beginning of period}} \qquad (6\text{-}1)$$

and for the holding-period rate of return

$$\text{Holding-period rate of return, } r = \frac{\text{dollar gain}}{\text{price}_{\text{beginning of period}}} = \frac{\text{price}_{\text{end of period}} + \text{dividend} - \text{price}_{\text{beginning of period}}}{\text{price}_{\text{beginning of period}}}$$
$$(6\text{-}2)$$

The method we have just used to compute the holding-period return on our investment in Google tells us the return we actually earned during a historical time period. However, the risk–return trade-off that investors face on a day-to-day basis is based *not* on realized rates of return but on what the investor *expects* to earn on an investment in the future. We can think of the rate of return that will ultimately be realized from making a risky investment in terms of a range of possible return outcomes, much like the distribution of grades for this class at the end of the term. To describe this range of possible returns, it is customary to use the average of the different possible returns. We refer to the average of the possible rates of return as the investment's **expected rate of return**.

**expected rate of return** The arithmetic mean or average of all possible outcomes where those outcomes are weighted by the probability that each will occur.

Accurately measuring expected future cash flows is not easy in a world of uncertainty. To illustrate, assume you are considering an investment costing $10,000, for which the future cash flows from owning the security depend on the state of the economy, as estimated in Table 6-1.

| TABLE 6-1 Measuring the Expected Return of an Investment | | | |
|---|---|---|---|
| State of the Economy | Probability of the States[a] | Cash Flows from the Investment | Percentage Returns (Cash Flow ÷ Investment Cost) |
| Economic recession | 20% | $1,000 | 10% ($1,000 ÷ $10,000) |
| Moderate economic growth | 30% | 1,200 | 12% ($1,200 ÷ $10,000) |
| Strong economic growth | 50% | 1,400 | 14% ($1,400 ÷ $10,000) |

[a]The probabilities assigned to the three possible economic conditions have to be determined subjectively, which requires managers to have a thorough understanding of both the investment cash flows and the general economy.

In any given year, the investment could produce any one of three possible cash flows, depending on the particular state of the economy. With this information, how should we select the cash flow estimate that means the most for measuring the investment's expected rate of return? One approach is to calculate an *expected* cash flow. The expected cash flow is simply the weighted average of the *possible* cash flow outcomes such that the weights are the probabilities of the various states of the economy occurring. Stated as an equation:

$$\text{Expected cash flow, } \overline{CF} = \left( \begin{array}{c} \text{cash flow} \\ \text{in state 1} \\ (CF_1) \end{array} \times \begin{array}{c} \text{probability} \\ \text{of state 1} \\ (Pb_1) \end{array} \right) + \left( \begin{array}{c} \text{cash flow} \\ \text{in state 2} \\ (CF_2) \end{array} \times \begin{array}{c} \text{probability} \\ \text{of state 2} \\ (Pb_2) \end{array} \right)$$

$$+ \ldots + \left( \begin{array}{c} \text{cash flow} \\ \text{in state 3} \\ (CF_3) \end{array} \times \begin{array}{c} \text{probability} \\ \text{of state 3} \\ (Pb_3) \end{array} \right) \tag{6-3}$$

For the present illustration:

$$\text{Expected cash flow} = (0.2)(\$1,000) + (0.3)(\$1,200)$$
$$+ (0.5)(\$1,400)$$
$$= \$1,260$$

In addition to computing an expected dollar return from an investment, we can also calculate an expected rate of return earned on the $10,000 investment. Similar to the expected cash flow, the expected rate of return is *a weighted average of all the possible returns, weighted by the probability that each return will occur*. As the last column in Table 6-1 shows, the $1,400 cash inflow, assuming strong economic growth, represents a 14 percent return ($1,400 ÷ $10,000). Similarly, the $1,200 and $1,000 cash flows result in 12 percent and 10 percent returns, respectively. Using these percentage returns in place of the dollar amounts, the expected rate of return can be expressed as follows:

$$\text{Expected rate of return, } \overline{r} = \left( \begin{array}{c} \text{rate of return} \\ \text{for state 1} \\ (r_1) \end{array} \times \begin{array}{c} \text{probability} \\ \text{of state 1} \\ (Pb_1) \end{array} \right) + \left( \begin{array}{c} \text{rate of return} \\ \text{for state 2} \\ (r_2) \end{array} \times \begin{array}{c} \text{probability} \\ \text{of state 2} \\ (Pb_2) \end{array} \right)$$

$$+ \ldots + \left( \begin{array}{c} \text{rate of return} \\ \text{for state 3} \\ (r_3) \end{array} \times \begin{array}{c} \text{probability} \\ \text{of state 3} \\ (Pb_3) \end{array} \right) \tag{6-4}$$

In our example:

$$\overline{r} = (0.2)(10\%) + (0.3)(12\%) + (0.5)(14\%) = 12.6\%$$

## CAN YOU DO IT?

### COMPUTING EXPECTED CASH FLOW AND EXPECTED RETURN

You are contemplating making a $5,000 investment that would have the following possible outcomes in cash flow each year. What is the expected value of the future cash flows and the expected rate of return?

| PROBABILITY | CASH FLOW |
|---|---|
| 0.30 | $350 |
| 0.50 | 625 |
| 0.20 | 900 |

(The solution can be found on page 187.)

To this point, we have learned how to calculate a *historical* holding-period return, expressed both in dollars and percentages. Also, we have seen how to estimate dollar and percentage returns that we expect to earn in the future. These financial tools may be summarized as follows:

## FINANCIAL DECISION TOOLS

| Name of Tool | Formula | What It Tells You |
|---|---|---|
| Holding-period dollar gain | Holding-period dollar gain, DG $=$ price$_{\text{end of period}}$ $+$ cash distribution (dividend) $-$ price$_{\text{beginning of period}}$ | Measures the dollar gain on an investment for a period of time |
| Holding-period rate of return | Holding-period rate of return, $r$ $= \dfrac{\text{dollar gain}}{\text{price}_{\text{beginning of period}}}$ $= \dfrac{\text{price}_{\text{end of period}} + \text{dividend} - \text{price}_{\text{beginning of period}}}{\text{price}_{\text{beginning of period}}}$ | Calculates the percentage rate of return for a security held for a period of time |
| Expected cash flow | Expected cash flow, $\overline{CF}$ $= \left( \begin{array}{c} \text{cash flow} \\ \text{in state 1} \times \\ (CF_1) \end{array} \begin{array}{c} \text{probability} \\ \text{of state 1} \\ (Pb_1) \end{array} \right)$ $+ \left( \begin{array}{c} \text{cash flow} \\ \text{in state 2} \times \\ (CF_2) \end{array} \begin{array}{c} \text{probability} \\ \text{of state 2} \\ (Pb_2) \end{array} \right)$ $+ \ldots + \left( \begin{array}{c} \text{cash flow} \\ \text{in state 3} \times \\ (CF_3) \end{array} \begin{array}{c} \text{probability} \\ \text{of state 3} \\ (Pb_3) \end{array} \right)$ | Estimates the cash flows that can be expected from an investment, recognizing that there are multiple possible outcomes from the investment |
| Expected rate of return | Expected rate of return, $\bar{r}$ $= \left( \begin{array}{c} \text{rate of return} \\ \text{for state 1} \times \\ (r_1) \end{array} \begin{array}{c} \text{probability} \\ \text{of state 1} \\ (Pb_1) \end{array} \right)$ $+ \left( \begin{array}{c} \text{rate of return} \\ \text{for state 2} \times \\ (r_2) \end{array} \begin{array}{c} \text{probability} \\ \text{of state 2} \\ (Pb_2) \end{array} \right)$ $+ \ldots + \left( \begin{array}{c} \text{rate of return} \\ \text{for state 3} \times \\ (r_3) \end{array} \begin{array}{c} \text{probability} \\ \text{of state 3} \\ (Pb_3) \end{array} \right)$ | An estimate of the expected rate of return on an investment, recognizing that there are multiple possible outcomes from the investment |

With our concept and measurement of expected returns, let's consider the other side of the investment coin: risk.

## Concept Check

1. When we speak of "benefits" from investing in an asset, what do we mean?
2. Why is it difficult to measure future cash flows?
3. Define *expected rate of return*.

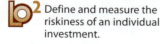
Define and measure the riskiness of an individual investment.

# Risk Defined and Measured

Because we live in a world where events are uncertain, the way we see risk is vitally important in almost all dimensions of our life. The Greek poet and statesman Solon, writing in the sixth century B.C., put it this way:

> There is risk in everything that one does, and no one knows where he will make his landfall when his enterprise is at its beginning. One man, trying to act effectively, fails to foresee something and falls into great and grim ruination, but to another man, one who is acting ineffectively, a god gives good fortune in everything and escape from his folly.[2]

[2] From *Iambi et Elegi Graeci ante Alexandrum Cantati*, vol. 2. Edited by M.L. West, translated by Arthur W.H. Adkins. (Oxford: Clarendon Press, 1972).

## DID YOU GET IT?
### COMPUTING EXPECTED CASH FLOW AND EXPECTED RETURN

| | POSSIBLE | | EXPECTED | |
| --- | --- | --- | --- | --- |
| **PROBABILITY** | **CASH FLOW** | **RETURN** | **CASH FLOW** | **RETURN** |
| 0.30 | $350 | 7.0% | $105.00 | 2.1% |
| 0.50 | 625 | 12.5% | 312.50 | 6.3% |
| 0.20 | 900 | 18.0% | 180.00 | 3.6% |
| Expected cash flow and rate of return | | | $597.50 | 12.0% |

The possible returns are equal to the possible cash flows divided by the $5,000 investment. The expected cash flow and return are equal to the possible cash flows and possible returns multiplied by the probabilities.

Solon would have given more of the credit to Zeus than we would for the outcomes of our ventures. However, his insight reminds us that little is new in this world, including the need to acknowledge and compensate as best we can for the risks we encounter. In fact, the significance of risk and the need for understanding what it means in our lives is noted by Peter Bernstein in the following excerpt:

> What is it that distinguishes the thousands of years of history from what we think of as modern times? The answer goes way beyond the progress of science, technology, capitalism, and democracy.
>
> The distant past was studded with brilliant scientists, mathematicians, inventors, technologists, and political philosophers. . . . [T]he skies had been mapped, the great library of Alexandria built, and Euclid's geometry taught. . . . Coal, oil, iron, and copper have been at the service of human beings for millennia. . . .
>
> The revolutionary idea that defines the boundary between modern times and the past is the mastery of risk. . . . Until human beings discovered a way across that boundary, the future was a mirror of the past or the murky domain of oracles and soothsayers. . . .[3]

In our study of risk, we want to consider these questions:

1. What is risk?
2. How do we know the amount of risk associated with a given investment; that is, how do we measure risk?
3. If we choose to diversify our investments by owning more than one asset, as most of us do, will such diversification reduce the riskiness of our combined portfolio of investments?

Without intending to be trite, risk means different things to different people, depending on the context and on how they feel about taking chances. For the student, risk is the possibility of failing an exam or the chance of not making his or her best grades. For the coal miner or the oil field worker, risk is the chance of an explosion in the mine or at the well site. For the retired person, risk means perhaps not being able to live comfortably on a fixed income. For the entrepreneur, risk is the chance that a new venture will fail.

While certainly acknowledging these different kinds of risk, we limit our attention to the risk inherent in an investment. In this context, **risk** is the *potential variability in future cash flows*. The wider the range of possible events that can occur, the greater the risk.[4] If we think about it, this is a relatively intuitive concept.

**risk** potential variability in future cash flows.

---

[3]From "Introduction" in *Against the Gods: The Remarkable Story of Risk* by Peter Bernstein, published by John Wiley & Sons, Inc., New York: 1996.

[4]When we speak of possible events, we must not forget that it is the highly unlikely event that we cannot anticipate that may have the greatest impact on the outcome of an investment. So, we evaluate investment opportunities based on the best information available, but there may be a *black swan* that we cannot anticipate.

To help us grasp the fundamental meaning of risk within this context, consider two possible investments:

1. The first investment is a U.S. Treasury bond, a government security that matures in 10 years and promises to pay an annual return of 2 percent. If we purchase and hold this security for 10 years, we are virtually assured of receiving no more and no less than 2 percent on an annualized basis. For all practical purposes, the risk of loss is nonexistent.

2. The second investment involves the purchase of the stock of a local publishing company. Looking at the past returns of the firm's stock, we have made the following estimate of the annual returns from the investment:

| CHANCE OF OCCURRENCE | RATE OF RETURN ON INVESTMENT |
| --- | --- |
| 1 chance in 10 (10% chance) | −10% |
| 2 chances in 10 (20% chance) | 5% |
| 4 chances in 10 (40% chance) | 15% |
| 2 chances in 10 (20% chance) | 25% |
| 1 chance in 10 (10% chance) | 30% |

Investing in the publishing company could conceivably provide a return as high as 30 percent if all goes well, or a loss of 10 percent if everything goes against the firm. However, in future years, both good and bad, we could expect a 14 percent return on average.[5]

$$\text{Expected return} = (0.10)(-10\%) + (0.20)(5\%) + (0.40)(15\%) + (0.20)(25\%)$$
$$+ (0.10)(30\%)$$
$$= 14\%$$

Comparing the Treasury bond investment with the publishing company investment, we see that the Treasury bond offers an expected 2 percent annualized rate of return, whereas the publishing company has a much higher expected rate of return of 14 percent. However, our investment in the publishing firm is clearly more "risky"—that is, there is greater uncertainty about the final outcome. Stated somewhat differently, there is a greater variation or dispersion of possible returns, which in turn implies greater risk.[6] Figure 6-1 shows these differences graphically in the form of discrete probability distributions.

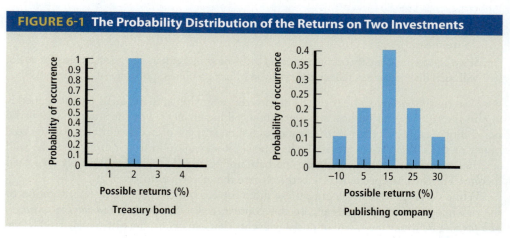

**FIGURE 6-1  The Probability Distribution of the Returns on Two Investments**

[5]We assume that the particular outcome or return earned in 1 year does *not* affect the return earned in the subsequent year. Technically speaking, the distribution of returns in any year is assumed to be independent of the outcome in any prior year.

[6]How can we possibly view variations above the expected return as risk? Should we even be concerned with the positive deviations above the expected return? Some would say "no," viewing risk as only the negative variability in returns from a predetermined minimum acceptable rate of return. However, as long as the distribution of returns is symmetrical, the same conclusions will be reached.

Although the return from investing in the publishing firm is clearly less certain than for Treasury bonds, quantitative measures of risk are useful when the difference between two investments is not so evident. We can quantify the risk of an investment by computing the variance in the possible investment returns and its square root, the **standard deviation** ($\sigma$). For the case where there are $n$ possible returns (that is, states of the economy), we calculate the variance as follows:

**standard deviation** a statistical measure of the spread of a probability distribution calculated by squaring the difference between each outcome and its expected value, weighting each value by its probability, summing over all possible outcomes, and taking the square root of this sum.

$$
\begin{aligned}
\text{Variance in rates of return } (\sigma^2) =\ & \left[\left(\begin{array}{c}\text{rate of return} \\ \text{for state 1} \\ (r_1)\end{array} - \begin{array}{c}\text{expected rate} \\ \text{of return} \\ \bar{r}\end{array}\right)^2 \times \begin{array}{c}\text{probability} \\ \text{of state 1} \\ (Pb_1)\end{array}\right] \\
+\ & \left[\left(\begin{array}{c}\text{rate of return} \\ \text{for state 2} \\ (r_2)\end{array} - \begin{array}{c}\text{expected rate} \\ \text{of return} \\ \bar{r}\end{array}\right)^2 \times \begin{array}{c}\text{probability} \\ \text{of state 2} \\ (Pb_2)\end{array}\right] \\
+ \cdots +\ & \left[\left(\begin{array}{c}\text{rate of return} \\ \text{for state } n \\ (r_n)\end{array} - \begin{array}{c}\text{expected rate} \\ \text{of return} \\ \bar{r}\end{array}\right)^2 \times \begin{array}{c}\text{probability} \\ \text{of state } n \\ (Pb_n)\end{array}\right]
\end{aligned}
$$

(6-5)

For the publishing company's common stock, we calculate the standard deviation using the following five-step procedure:

**STEP 1** Calculate the expected rate of return of the investment, which was calculated above to be 14 percent.

**STEP 2** Subtract the expected rate of return of 14 percent from each of the possible rates of return and square the difference.

**STEP 3** Multiply the squared differences calculated in step 2 by the probability that those outcomes will occur.

**STEP 4** Sum all the values calculated in step 3 together. The sum is the variance of the distribution of possible rates of return. Note that the variance is actually the *average squared difference between the possible rates of return and the expected rate of return*.

**STEP 5** Take the square root of the variance calculated in step 4 to calculate the standard deviation of the distribution of possible rates of return.

Table 6-2 illustrates the application of this process, which results in an estimated standard deviation for the common stock investment of 11.14 percent. This compares to the Treasury bond investment, which is risk-free, and has a standard deviation of zero percent. The more risky the investment, the higher is its standard deviation.

**TABLE 6-2  Measuring the Variance and Standard Deviation of the Publishing Company Investment**

| State of the World | Rate of Return | Chance or Probability | $D = B \times C$ | Step 2 $E = (B - \bar{r})^2$ | Step 3 $F = E \times C$ |
|---|---|---|---|---|---|
| A | B | C | | | |
| 1 | −10% | 0.10 | −1% | 576% | 57.6% |
| 3 | 5% | 0.20 | 1% | 81% | 16.2% |
| 4 | 15% | 0.40 | 6% | 1% | 0.40% |
| 4 | 25% | 0.20 | 5% | 121% | 24.2% |
| 5 | 30% | 0.10 | 3% | 256% | 25.6% |

**Step 1:** Expected Return ($\bar{r}$) = ⟶ 14%

**Step 4:** Variance = ⟶ 124%

**Step 5:** Standard Deviation = ⟶ 11.14%

# CAN YOU DO IT?

## COMPUTING THE STANDARD DEVIATION

In the preceding "Can You Do It?" on page 185, we computed the expected cash flow of $597.50 and the expected return of 12 percent on a $5,000 investment. Now let's calculate the standard deviation of the returns. The probabilities of possible returns are given as follows:

| PROBABILITY | RETURNS |
|---|---|
| 0.30 | 7.0% |
| 0.50 | 12.5% |
| 0.20 | 18.0% |

(The solution can be found on page 193.)

Alternatively, we could use equation (6-5) to calculate the standard deviation in investment returns as follows:

$$\sigma = \left[ \begin{array}{l} (-10\% - 14\%)^2(0.10) + (5\% - 14\%)^2(0.20) \\ + (15\% - 14\%)^2(0.40) + (25\% - 14\%)^2(0.20) \\ + (30\% - 14\%)^2(0.10) \end{array} \right]^{\frac{1}{2}}$$

$$= \sqrt{124\%} = 11.14\%$$

Although the standard deviation of returns provides us with a quantitative measure of an asset's riskiness, how should we interpret the result? What does it mean? Is the 11.14 percent standard deviation for the publishing company investment good or bad? First, we should remember that statisticians tell us that two-thirds of the time, an event will fall within 1 standard deviation of the expected value (assuming the distribution is normally distributed; that is, it is shaped like a bell). Thus, given a 14 percent expected return and a standard deviation of 11.14 percent for the publishing company investment, we can reasonably anticipate that the actual returns will fall between 2.86 percent and 25.14 percent (14% ± 11.14%) two-thirds of the time. In other words, there is not much certainty with this investment.

A second way of answering the question about the meaning of the standard deviation comes by comparing the investment in the publishing firm against other investments. Obviously the attractiveness of a security with respect to its return and risk cannot be determined in isolation. Only by examining other available alternatives can we reach a conclusion about a particular investment's risk. For example, if another investment, say, an investment in a firm that owns a local radio station, has the same expected return as the publishing company, 14 percent, but with a standard deviation of 7 percent, we would consider the risk associated with the publishing firm, 11.14 percent, to be excessive. In the technical jargon of modern portfolio theory, the radio station investment is said to "dominate" the publishing firm investment. In commonsense terms, this means that the radio station investment has the same expected return as the publishing company investment but is less risky.

# FINANCE AT WORK

## A DIFFERENT PERSPECTIVE OF RISK

The first Chinese symbol shown here represents danger; the second stands for opportunity. The Chinese define risk as the combination of danger and opportunity. Greater risk, according to the Chinese, means we have greater opportunity to do well but also greater danger of doing badly.

What if we compare the investment in the publishing company with one in a quick oil-change franchise, an investment in which the expected rate of return is an attractive 24 percent but the standard deviation is estimated at 13 percent? Now what should we do? Clearly, the oil-change franchise has a higher expected rate of return, but it also has a larger standard deviation. In this example, we see that the real challenge in selecting the better investment comes when one investment has a higher expected rate of return but also exhibits greater risk. *Here the final choice is determined by our attitude toward risk, and there is no single right answer.* You might select the publishing company, whereas I might choose the oil-change investment, and neither of us would be wrong. We would simply be expressing our tastes and preferences about risk and return.

To summarize, the riskiness of an investment is of primary concern to an investor, where the standard deviation is the conventional measure of an investment's riskiness. This decision tool is represented as follows:

## FINANCIAL DECISION TOOLS

| Name of Tool | Formula | What It Tells You |
|---|---|---|
| Variance in rates of return $(\sigma^2)$ <br><br> Standard deviation in rates of return $= \sqrt{\text{variance}}$ | $= \left[\left(\begin{array}{c}\text{rate of return}\\\text{for state 1}\\(r_1)\end{array} - \begin{array}{c}\text{expected rate}\\\text{of return}\\\bar{r}\end{array}\right)^2 \times \begin{array}{c}\text{probability}\\\text{of state 1}\\(Pb_1)\end{array}\right]$ <br> $+ \left[\left(\begin{array}{c}\text{rate of return}\\\text{for state 2}\\(r_2)\end{array} - \begin{array}{c}\text{expected rate}\\\text{of return}\\\bar{r}\end{array}\right)^2 \times \begin{array}{c}\text{probability}\\\text{of state 2}\\(Pb_2)\end{array}\right]$ <br> $+ \dots + \left[\left(\begin{array}{c}\text{rate of return}\\\text{for state } n\\(r_n)\end{array} - \begin{array}{c}\text{expected rate}\\\text{of return}\\\bar{r}\end{array}\right)^2 \times \begin{array}{c}\text{probability}\\\text{of state } n\\(Pb_n)\end{array}\right]$ | A measure of risk, as determined by the square root of the variance of cash flows or rates of returns, which measures the volatility of cash flows or returns |

### EXAMPLE 6.1    Computing the expected return and standard deviation

You are considering two investments, X and Y. The distributions of possible returns are shown below:

| | POSSIBLE RETURNS | |
|---|---|---|
| PROBABILITY | INVESTMENT X | INVESTMENT Y |
| 0.05 | −10% | 0% |
| 0.25 | 5% | 5% |
| 0.40 | 20% | 16% |
| 0.25 | 30% | 24% |
| 0.05 | 40% | 32% |

Compute the expected return and standard deviation for each investment. Do you have a preference for one investment over the other if you were making the decision?

### STEP 1: FORMULATE A SOLUTION STRATEGY

To compute the expected return for each investment, equation (6-4) is used, where there are five possible outcomes or states:

$$\begin{array}{l}\text{Expected rate}\\\text{of return, } \bar{r}\end{array} = \left(\begin{array}{cc}\text{rate of return} & \text{probability of}\\\text{for state 1} \times & \text{state 1}\\(r_1) & (Pb_1)\end{array}\right)$$

$$+ \left(\begin{array}{cc}\text{rate of return} & \text{probability of}\\\text{for state 2} \times & \text{state 2}\\(r_2) & (Pb_2)\end{array}\right) + \dots + \left(\begin{array}{cc}\text{rate of return} & \text{probability of}\\\text{for state 5} \times & \text{state 5}\\(r_5) & (Pb_5)\end{array}\right)$$

To calculate the riskiness of each investment, as measured by the standard deviation of returns, we rely on equation (6-5) for five possible outcomes:

$$
\begin{aligned}
\text{Variance in} \\
\text{rates of return} \\
(\sigma^2)
\end{aligned}
=
\left[ \left( \begin{array}{c} \text{rate of return} \\ \text{for state 1} \\ (r_1) \end{array} - \begin{array}{c} \text{expected rate} \\ \text{of return} \\ \overline{r} \end{array} \right)^2 \times \begin{array}{c} \text{probability} \\ \text{of state 1} \\ (Pb_1) \end{array} \right]
$$

$$
+ \left[ \left( \begin{array}{c} \text{rate of return} \\ \text{for state 2} \\ (r_2) \end{array} - \begin{array}{c} \text{expected rate} \\ \text{of return} \\ \overline{r} \end{array} \right)^2 \times \begin{array}{c} \text{probability} \\ \text{of state 2} \\ (Pb_2) \end{array} \right]
$$

$$
+ \cdots + \left[ \left( \begin{array}{c} \text{rate of return} \\ \text{for state } n \\ (r_n) \end{array} - \begin{array}{c} \text{expected rate} \\ \text{of return} \\ \overline{r} \end{array} \right)^2 \times \begin{array}{c} \text{probability} \\ \text{of state } n \\ (Pb_n) \end{array} \right]
$$

Standard deviation $(\sigma) = \sqrt{\text{variance}}$

## STEP 2: CRUNCH THE NUMBERS

*For investment X:*

$$
\begin{aligned}
\text{Expected rate} \\
\text{of return, } \overline{r}
\end{aligned}
= (0.05)(-10\%) + (0.25)(5\%) + (0.40)(20\%)
$$
$$
+ (0.25)(30\%) + (0.05)(40\%)
$$
$$
= 18.25\%
$$

$$
\begin{aligned}
\text{Variance in} \\
\text{rates of returns} \\
(\sigma^2)
\end{aligned}
= (0.05)(-10\% - 18.25\%)^2 + (0.25)(5\% - 18.25\%)^2
$$
$$
+ (0.40)(20\% - 18.25\%)^2 + (0.25)(30\% - 18.25\%)^2
$$
$$
+ (0.05)(40\% - 18.25\%)^2
$$
$$
= 143.19\%
$$

$$
\begin{aligned}
\text{Standard deviation of} \\
\text{rates of returns} \\
(\sigma)
\end{aligned}
= \sqrt{\text{variance}} = \sqrt{143.19\%} = 11.97\%
$$

*For investment Y:*

$$
\begin{aligned}
\text{Expected rate} \\
\text{of return, } \overline{r}
\end{aligned}
= (0.05)(0\%) + (0.25)(5\%) + (0.40)(16\%) + (0.25)(24\%)
$$
$$
+ (0.05)(32\%)
$$
$$
= 15.25\%
$$

$$
\begin{aligned}
\text{Variance in} \\
\text{rates of returns} \\
(\sigma^2)
\end{aligned}
= (0.05)(0\% - 15.25\%)^2 + (0.25)(5\% - 15.25\%)^2
$$
$$
+ (0.40)(16\% - 15.25\%)^2 + (0.25)(24\% - 15.25\%)^2
$$
$$
+ (0.05)(32\% - 15.25\%)^2
$$
$$
= 71.29\%
$$

$$
\begin{aligned}
\text{Standard deviation of} \\
\text{rates of returns} \\
(\sigma)
\end{aligned}
= \sqrt{\text{variance}} = \sqrt{71.29\%} = 8.44\%
$$

## STEP 3: ANALYZE YOUR RESULTS

The results are as follows:

| INVESTMENT | EXPECTED RETURN | STANDARD DEVIATION |
| --- | --- | --- |
| Investment X | 18.25% | 11.97% |
| Investment Y | 15.25% | 8.44% |

In this case, you will have to take on more risk if you want additional expected return. (There is no money tree.) Thus, the choice depends on the investor's preference for risk and return. There is no single right answer.

## DID YOU GET IT?
### COMPUTING THE STANDARD DEVIATION

| DEVIATION (POSSIBLE RETURN − 12% EXPECTED RETURN) | DEVIATION SQUARED | PROBABILITY | PROBABILITY × DEVIATION SQUARED |
|---|---|---|---|
| −5.0% | 25.00% | 0.30 | 7.500% |
| 0.5% | 0.25% | 0.50 | 0.125% |
| 6.0% | 36.00% | 0.20 | 7.200% |
| Sum of squared deviations × probability (variance) | | | 14.825% |
| Standard deviation | | | 3.85% |

## Concept Check

1. How is risk defined?
2. How does the standard deviation help us measure the riskiness of an investment?
3. Does greater risk imply a bad investment?

# Rates of Return: The Investor's Experience

 **3** Compare the historical relationship between risk and rates of return in the capital markets.

So far, we have mostly used hypothetical examples of expected rates of return and risk; however, it is also interesting to look at returns that investors have actually received on different types of securities. For example, Ibbotson Associates publishes the long-term historical annual rates of return for the following types of investments beginning in 1926 and continuing to the present:

1. Common stocks of large companies
2. Common stocks of small firms
3. Long-term corporate bonds
4. Long-term U.S. government bonds
5. Intermediate-term U.S. government bonds
6. U.S. Treasury bills (short-term government securities)

Before comparing these returns, we should think about what to expect. First, we would intuitively expect a Treasury bill (short-term government securities) to be the least risky of the six portfolios. Because a Treasury bill has a short-term maturity date, the price is less volatile (less risky) than the price of an intermediate- or long-term government security. In turn, because there is a chance of default on a corporate bond, which is essentially nonexistent for government securities, a long-term government bond is less risky than a long-term corporate bond. Finally, the common stocks of large companies are more risky than corporate bonds, with small-company stocks being more risky than large-firm stocks.

With this in mind, we could reasonably expect different rates of return to the holders of these varied securities. If the market rewards an investor for assuming risk, the average annual rates of return should increase as risk increases.

A comparison of the annual rates of return for five portfolios and the inflation rate for the years 1926 to 2011 is provided in Figure 6-2. Four aspects of these returns are included: (1) the nominal average annual rate of return; (2) the standard deviation of the returns, which measures the volatility, or riskiness, of the returns; (3) the real average annual rate of return, which is the nominal return less the inflation rate; and (4) the risk premium, which represents the additional return received beyond the risk-free rate (Treasury bill rate) for assuming risk. Looking at the

## FIGURE 6-2  Historical Rates of Return

| Securities | Nominal Average Annual Returns | Standard Deviation of Returns | Real Average Annual Returns[a] | Risk Premium[b] |
|---|---|---|---|---|
| Large-company stocks | 11.8% | 20.3% | 8.7% | 8.0% |
| Small-company stocks | 16.5% | 32.5% | 13.4% | 12.7% |
| Corporate bonds | 6.4% | 8.4% | 3.3% | 2.6% |
| Intermediate-term government bonds | 5.5% | 5.7% | 3.0% | 2.3% |
| U.S. Treasury bills | 3.8% | 3.1% | 0.7% | 0.0% |
| Inflation | 3.1% | 4.2% | | |

[a]The real return equals the nominal returns less the inflation rate of 3.1 percent.
[b]The risk premium equals the nominal security return less the average risk-free rate (Treasury bills) of 3.8 percent.

Source: Data from Summary Statistics of Annual Total Returns: 1926 to 2011 Yearbook. Copyright® 2012 Ibbotson Associates Inc.

first two columns of nominal average annual returns and standard deviations, we get a good overview of the risk–return relationships that have existed over the 86 years ending in 2011. In every case, there has been a positive relationship between risk and return, with Treasury bills being least risky and small-company stocks being most risky.

The return information in Figure 6-2 clearly demonstrates that only common stock has in the long run served as an inflation hedge and provided any substantial risk premium. However, it is equally apparent that the common stockholder is exposed to a sizable amount of risk, as is demonstrated by the 20.3 percent standard deviation for large-company stocks and the 32.5 percent standard deviation for small-company stocks. In fact, in the 1926 to 2011 time frame, common shareholders of large firms received negative returns in 22 of the 86 years, compared with only 1 (1938) in 86 years for Treasury bills.

### Concept Check

1. What is the additional compensation for assuming greater risk called?
2. In Figure 6-2, which rate of return is the risk-free rate? Why?

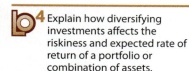

4 Explain how diversifying investments affects the riskiness and expected rate of return of a portfolio or combination of assets.

# Risk and Diversification

More can be said about risk, especially about its nature, when we own more than one asset in our investment portfolio. Let's consider for the moment how risk is affected if we diversify our investment by holding a variety of securities.

Let's assume that you graduated from college in December 2011. Not only did you get the good job you had hoped for but you also finished the year with a little nest egg—not enough to take that summer fling to Europe like some of your college friends but a nice surplus. Besides, you suspected that they used credit cards to go anyway. So right after graduation, you used some of your nest egg to buy Harley-Davidson stock. Then a couple of months later, you purchased Starbucks stock. (As the owner of a Harley Softail motorcycle, you've had a passion for riding since your high school days. And you give Starbucks credit for helping you get through many long study sessions.) But since making these investments, you have focused on your career and seldom thought about your investments. Your first extended break from work came in June 2012. After a lazy Saturday morning, you decided to get on the Internet to see how your investments had done over the previous several months. You bought Harley-Davidson for $37, and the stock was now trading at almost $50. "Not bad," you thought. But then the bad news—Starbucks was selling for $54, compared to the $62 that you paid for the stock.

Clearly, what we have described about Harley-Davidson and Starbucks were events unique to these two companies, and as we would expect, investors reacted accordingly; that is, the value of the stock changed in light of the new information. Although we might have wished we had owned only Starbucks stock at the time, most of us would prefer to avoid such uncertainties; that is, we are risk averse. Instead, we would like to reduce the risk associated with our investment portfolio, without having to accept a lower expected return. Good news: It is possible by diversifying your portfolio!

## Diversifying Away the Risk

If we diversify our investments across different securities rather than invest in only one stock, the variability in the returns of our portfolio should decline. The reduction in risk will occur if the stock returns within our portfolio do not move precisely together over time—that is, if they are not perfectly correlated. Figure 6-3 shows graphically what we could expect to happen to the variability of returns as we add additional stocks to the portfolio. The reduction occurs because some of the volatility in returns of a stock are unique to that security. The unique variability of a single stock tends to be countered by the uniqueness of another security. However, we should not expect to eliminate all risk from our portfolio. In practice, it would be rather difficult to cancel all the variations in returns of a portfolio, because stock prices have some tendency to move together. Thus, we can divide the total risk (total variability) of our portfolio into two types of risk: (1) **company-unique risk**, or **unsystematic risk**, and (2) **market risk**, or **systematic risk**. Company-unique risk might also be called **diversifiable risk**, in that it *can be diversified away*. Market risk is **nondiversifiable risk**; it *cannot be eliminated through random diversification*. These two types of risk are shown graphically in Figure 6-3. Total risk declines until we have approximately 20 securities, and then the decline becomes very slight.

The remaining risk, which would typically be about 40 percent of the total risk, is the portfolio's systematic, or market, risk. At this point, our portfolio is highly correlated with all securities in the marketplace. Events that affect our portfolio now are not so much unique events as changes in the general economy, major political events, and sociological changes. Examples include changes in interest rates in the economy, changes in tax legislation that affect all companies, or increasing public concern about the effect of business practices on the environment. Our measure of risk should, therefore, measure how responsive a stock or portfolio is to changes in a market portfolio, such as the New York Stock Exchange or the S&P 500 Index.[7]

**company-unique risk** see unsystematic risk.

**unsystematic risk** the risk related to an investment return that can be eliminated through diversification. Unsystematic risk is the result of factors that are unique to the particular firm. Also called company-unique risk or diversifiable risk.

**market risk** see systematic risk.

**systematic risk** (1) the risk related to an investment return that cannot be eliminated through diversification. Systematic risk results from factors that affect all stocks. Also called market risk or nondiversifiable risk. (2) The risk of a project from the viewpoint of a well-diversified shareholder. This measure takes into account that some of the project's risk will be diversified away as the project is combined with the firm's other projects, and, in addition, some of the remaining risk will be diversified away by shareholders as they combine this stock with other stocks in their portfolios.

**diversifiable risk** see unsystematic risk.

**nondiversifiable risk** see systematic risk.

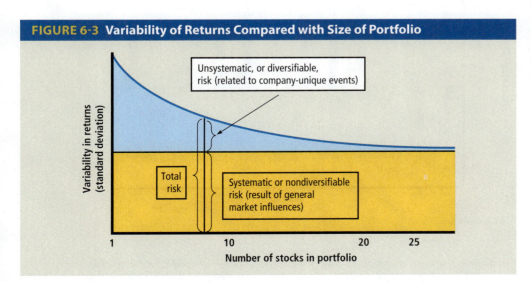

**FIGURE 6-3  Variability of Returns Compared with Size of Portfolio**

- Variability in returns (standard deviation) — vertical axis
- Number of stocks in portfolio — horizontal axis (1, 10, 20, 25)
- Unsystematic, or diversifiable, risk (related to company-unique events)
- Total risk
- Systematic or nondiversifiable risk (result of general market influences)

[7]The New York Stock Exchange Index is an index that reflects the performance of all stocks listed on the New York Stock Exchange. The Standard & Poor's (S&P) 500 Index is similarly an index that measures the combined stock-price performance of the companies that constitute the 500 largest companies in the United States, as designated by Standard & Poor's.

## Measuring Market Risk

To help clarify the idea of systematic risk, let's examine the relationship between the common stock returns of Home Depot and the returns of the S&P 500 Index.

The monthly returns for Home Depot and the S&P 500 Index for the 12 months ending June 2012 are presented in Table 6-3 and Figure 6-4. These *monthly returns*, or *holding-period returns*, as they are often called, are calculated as follows.[8]

$$\text{Monthly holding return} = \frac{\text{price}_{\text{end of month}} - \text{price}_{\text{beginning of month}}}{\text{price}_{\text{beginning of month}}}$$

$$= \frac{\text{price}_{\text{end of month}}}{\text{price}_{\text{beginning of month}}} - 1 \tag{6-6}$$

For instance, the holding-period return for Home Depot and the S&P 500 Index for January 2012 is computed as follows:

$$\text{The Home Depot return} = \frac{\text{stock price at end of January 2012}}{\text{stock price at end of December 2011}} - 1$$

$$= \frac{\$44.39}{\$42.04} - 1 = 0.0559 = 5.59\%$$

$$\text{The S\&P 500 Index return} = \frac{\text{index value at end of January 2012}}{\text{index value at end of December 2011}} - 1$$

$$= \frac{\$1,312.41}{\$1,257.60} - 1 = 0.0436 = 4.36\%$$

At the bottom of Table 6-3, we have also computed the averages of the returns for the 12 months, for both Home Depot and the S&P 500 Index, and the standard deviation for these returns. Because we are using historical return data, we assume each observation has

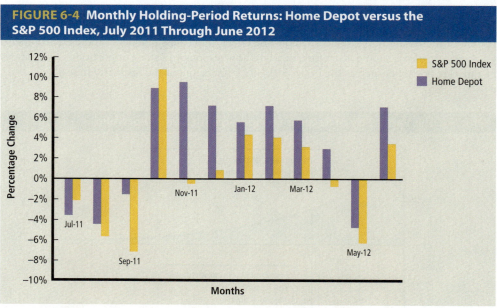

**FIGURE 6-4  Monthly Holding-Period Returns: Home Depot versus the S&P 500 Index, July 2011 Through June 2012**

Source: Data from Yahoo Finance

---

[8]For simplicity's sake, we are ignoring the dividend that the investor receives from the stock as part of the total return. In other words, letting $D_t$ equal the dividend received by the investor in month $t$, the holding-period return would more accurately be measured as

$$r_1 = \frac{P_t + D_t}{P_{t-1}} - 1 \tag{6-7}$$

**TABLE 6-3** Monthly Holding-Period Returns, Home Depot versus the S&P 500 Index, June 2011 Through June 2012

| Month and Year | Home Depot | | S&P 500 Index | |
|---|---|---|---|---|
| | Price | Returns | Price | Returns |
| **2011** | | | | |
| June | $36.22 | | $1,320.64 | |
| July | 34.93 | −3.56% | 1,292.28 | −2.15% |
| August | 33.38 | −4.44% | 1,218.89 | −5.68% |
| September | 32.87 | −1.53% | 1,131.42 | −7.18% |
| October | 35.80 | 8.91% | 1,253.30 | 10.77% |
| November | 39.22 | 9.55% | 1,246.96 | −0.51% |
| December | 42.04 | 7.19% | 1,257.60 | 0.85% |
| **2012** | | | | |
| January | 44.39 | 5.59% | 1,312.41 | 4.36% |
| February | 47.57 | 7.16% | 1,365.68 | 4.06% |
| March | 50.31 | 5.76% | 1,408.47 | 3.13% |
| April | 51.79 | 2.94% | 1,397.91 | −0.75% |
| May | 49.34 | −4.73% | 1,310.33 | −6.27% |
| June | 52.83 | 7.07% | 1,355.69 | 3.46% |
| Average return | | 3.33% | | 0.34% |
| Standard deviation | | 5.40% | | 5.23% |

Source: Data from Yahoo Finance

an equal probability of occurrence. Thus, the average holding-period return is found by summing the returns and dividing by the number of months; that is,

$$\text{Average holding-period return} = \frac{\text{return in month 1} + \text{return in month 2} + \cdots + \text{return in last month}}{\text{number of monthly returns}}$$

(6-8)

and the standard deviation is computed as follows:

Standard deviation

$$= \sqrt{\frac{(\text{return in month 1} - \text{average return})^2 + (\text{return in month 2} - \text{average return})^2 + \cdots + (\text{return in last month} - \text{average return})^2}{\text{number of monthly returns} - 1}}$$

(6-9)

In looking at Table 6-3 and Figure 6-4, we notice the following things about Home Depot's holding-period returns over the 12 months ending in June 2012.

1. Home Depot's shareholders realized significantly higher monthly holding-period returns on average than the general market, as represented by the Standard & Poor's 500 Index (S&P 500). Over the 12 months, Home Depot's stock had an average 3.33 percent monthly return compared only to 0.34 percent for the S&P 500 Index.

2. While Home Depot had higher average monthly holding-period returns than the general market (S&P 500 Index), at least for the 12-month period ending June 2012, the volatility (standard deviation) of the returns was only slightly higher for Home Depot than for the market—5.40 percent for Home Depot versus 5.23 percent for the S&P 500 Index.

3. We should also notice the tendency, although not perfect, of Home Depot's stock price to increase when the value of the S&P 500 Index increases and vice versa. This was the case in 10 of the 12 months. That is, there is a moderate positive relationship between Home Depot's stock returns and the S&P 500 Index returns.

With respect to our third observation, that there is a relationship between the stock returns of Home Depot and the S&P 500 Index, it is helpful to see this relationship by graphing Home Depot's returns against the S&P 500 Index returns. We provide such a graph in

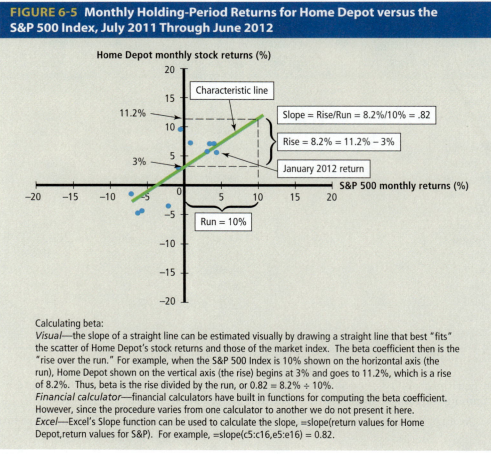

**FIGURE 6-5** Monthly Holding-Period Returns for Home Depot versus the S&P 500 Index, July 2011 Through June 2012

Calculating beta:

*Visual*—the slope of a straight line can be estimated visually by drawing a straight line that best "fits" the scatter of Home Depot's stock returns and those of the market index. The beta coefficient then is the "rise over the run." For example, when the S&P 500 Index is 10% shown on the horizontal axis (the run), Home Depot shown on the vertical axis (the rise) begins at 3% and goes to 11.2%, which is a rise of 8.2%. Thus, beta is the rise divided by the run, or 0.82 = 8.2% ÷ 10%.

*Financial calculator*—financial calculators have built in functions for computing the beta coefficient. However, since the procedure varies from one calculator to another we do not present it here.

*Excel*—Excel's Slope function can be used to calculate the slope, =slope(return values for Home Depot,return values for S&P). For example, =slope(c5:c16,e5:e16) = 0.82.

Source: Data from Yahoo Finance

Figure 6-5. In the figure, we have plotted Home Depot's returns on the vertical axis and the returns for the S&P 500 Index on the horizontal axis. Each of the 12 dots in the figure represents the returns of Home Depot and the S&P 500 Index for a particular month. For instance, the returns for January 2012 for Home Depot and the S&P 500 Index were 5.59 percent and 4.36 percent, respectively, which are noted in the figure.

In addition to the dots in the graph, we have drawn a line of "best fit," which we call the **characteristic line**. *The slope of the characteristic line measures the average relationship between a stock's returns and those of the S&P 500 Index*; or stated differently, *the slope of the line indicates the average movement in a stock's price in response to a movement in the S&P 500 Index price*. We can estimate the slope of the line visually by fitting a line that appears to cut through the middle of the dots. We then compare the rise (increase of the line on the vertical axis) to the run (increase on the horizontal axis). Alternatively, we can enter the return data into a financial calculator or in an Excel spreadsheet, which will calculate the slope based on statistical analysis. For Home Depot, the slope of the line is 0.82, which means that on average that as the market returns (S&P 500 Index returns) increase or decrease 1 percent, the return for Home Depot on average increases or decreases 0.82 percentage points.

We can also think of the 0.82 slope of the characteristic line as indicating that Home Depot's returns are 0.82 times as volatile on average as those of the overall market (S&P 500 Index). This slope has come to be called **beta** ($\beta$) in investor jargon, and it *measures the average relationship between a stock's returns and the market's returns*. It is a term you will see almost any time you read an article written by a financial analyst about the riskiness of a stock.

Looking once again at Figure 6-5, we see that the dots (returns) are scattered all about the characteristic line—most of the returns do not fit neatly on the characteristic line. That is, the average relationship may be 0.82, but the variation in Home Depot's returns is only partly explained by the stock's average relationship with the S&P 500 Index. There are other driving forces unique to Home Depot that also affect the firm's stock returns. (Earlier, we called this company-unique risk.) If we were, however, to diversify our

**characteristic line** the line of "best fit" through a series of returns for a firm's stock relative to the market's returns. The slope of the line, frequently called beta, represents the average movement of the firm's stock returns in response to a movement in the market's returns.

**beta** the relationship between an investment's returns and the market's returns. This is a measure of the investment's nondiversifiable risk.

**FIGURE 6-6**  Holding-Period Returns for a Hypothetical Portfolio and the S&P 500 Index

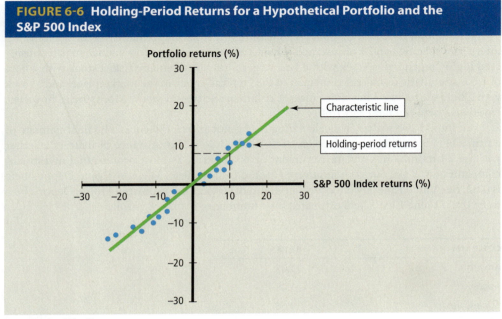

Source: Data from Yahoo Finance

holdings and own, say, 20 stocks with betas of 0.82, we could essentially eliminate the variation about the characteristic line. That is, we would remove almost all the volatility in returns, except for that caused by the general market, which is represented by the slope of the line in Figure 6-5. If we plotted the returns of our 20-stock portfolio against the S&P 500 Index, the points in our new graph would fit nicely along a straight line with a slope of 0.82, which means that the beta ($\beta$) of the portfolio is also 0.82. The new graph would look something like the one shown in Figure 6-6. In other words, by diversifying our portfolio, we can essentially eliminate the variations about the characteristic line, leaving only the variation in returns for a company that comes from variations in the general market returns.

So beta ($\beta$)—the slope of the characteristic line—is a measure of a firm's market risk or systematic risk, which is the risk that remains for a company even after we have diversified

## CAN YOU DO IT?

### ESTIMATING BETA

Below, we provide the end-of-month prices for Toyota stock and the Standard & Poor's 500 Index for December 2011 through June 2012. Given the information, compute the following both for Toyota and the S&P 500: (1) the monthly holding-period returns, (2) the average monthly returns, and (3) the standard deviation of the returns. Next, graph the holding-period returns of Toyota on the vertical axis against the holding-period returns of the S&P 500 on the horizontal axis. Draw a line on your graph similar to what we did in Figure 6-5 to estimate the average relationship between the stock returns of Toyota and the returns of the overall market as represented by the S&P 500. What is the approximate slope of your line? What does this tell you?

(In working this problem, it would be easier if you used an Excel spreadsheet including the slope function.)

| DATE | TOYOTA | S&P 500 INDEX |
| --- | --- | --- |
| Dec-11 | $66.13 | $1,257.60 |
| Jan-12 | 73.48 | 1,312.41 |
| Feb-12 | 82.71 | 1,365.68 |
| Mar-12 | 86.82 | 1,408.47 |
| Apr-12 | 81.78 | 1,397.91 |
| May-12 | 76.89 | 1,310.33 |
| June-12 | 76.30 | 1,355.69 |

(The solution can be found on page 204.)

our portfolio. It is this risk—and only this risk—that matters for investors who have broadly diversified portfolios.

Although we have said that beta is a measure of a stock's systematic risk, how should we interpret a specific beta? For instance, when is a beta considered low and when is it considered high? In general, a stock with a beta of zero has no systematic risk; a stock with a beta of 1 has systematic or market risk equal to the "typical" stock in the marketplace; and a stock with a beta exceeding 1 has more market risk than the typical stock. Most stocks, however, have betas between 0.60 and 1.60.

We should also realize that calculating beta is not an exact science. The final estimate of a firm's beta is heavily dependent on one's methodology. For instance, it matters whether you use 24 months in your measurement or 60 months, as most professional investment companies do. Take our computation of Home Depot's beta. We said Home Depot's beta is 0.82, but Value Line, a well-known investment service, has estimated Home Depot's beta to be 0.95. Value Line's beta estimates for a number of firms are as follows:

| COMPANY NAME | BETAS |
|---|---|
| Amazon | 1.05 |
| Apple | 1.05 |
| Coca-Cola | 0.60 |
| eBay | 1.10 |
| ExxonMobil | 0.80 |
| General Electric | 1.20 |
| IBM | 0.85 |
| Lowe's | 0.95 |
| Merck | 0.80 |
| Nike | 0.85 |
| PepsiCo | 0.60 |
| WalMart | 0.60 |

**EXAMPLE 6.2** | **Calculating monthly returns, average returns, standard deviation, and estimating beta**

Given the following price data for Harley-Davidson and the S&P 500 Index, compare the returns and the volatility of the returns, and estimate the relationship of the returns for Harley-Davidson and the S&P 500 Index. What do you conclude?

| DATE | HARLEY-DAVIDSON | S&P 500 INDEX |
|---|---|---|
| June-11 | $ 40.97 | $1,320.64 |
| July-11 | 43.39 | 1,292.28 |
| Aug-11 | 38.66 | 1,218.89 |
| Sept-11 | 34.33 | 1,131.42 |
| Oct-11 | 38.90 | 1,253.30 |
| Nov-11 | 36.77 | 1,246.96 |
| Dec-11 | 38.87 | 1,257.60 |
| Jan-12 | 44.19 | 1,312.41 |
| Feb-12 | 46.58 | 1,365.68 |
| Mar-12 | 49.08 | 1,408.47 |
| Apr-12 | 52.33 | 1,397.91 |
| May-12 | 48.18 | 1,310.33 |
| June-12 | 46.18 | 1,355.69 |

## STEP 1: FORMULATE A DECISION STRATEGY

The following equations are needed to solve the problem:

Monthly holding-period returns:

$$\text{Monthly holding return} = \frac{\text{price}_{\text{end of month}} - \text{price}_{\text{beginning of month}}}{\text{price}_{\text{beginning of month}}}$$

$$= \frac{\text{price}_{\text{end of month}}}{\text{price}_{\text{beginning of month}}} - 1$$

Average monthly returns:

$$\text{Average holding-period return} = \frac{\text{return in month 1} + \text{return in month 2} + \cdots + \text{return in last month}}{\text{number of monthly returns}}$$

Standard deviation of the returns:

$$\text{Standard deviation} = \sqrt{\frac{(\text{return in month 1} - \text{average return})^2 + (\text{return in month 2} - \text{average return})^2 + \cdots + (\text{return in last month} - \text{average return})^2}{\text{number of monthly returns} - 1}}$$

Determining the historical relationship between Harley-Davidson's stock returns and those of the S&P 500 Index requires our eye balling the line that best fits the average relationship, or using a financial calculator, or using a spreadsheet.

## STEP 2: CRUNCH THE NUMBERS

Given the price data, we have calculated the monthly returns, the average returns, and the standard deviation of returns as follows, as well as the slope of the characteristic line (using a spreadsheet):

| MONTH | HARLEY-DAVIDSON | | S&P 500 INDEX | |
|---|---|---|---|---|
| | PRICE | RETURN | PRICE | RETURN |
| Jun-11 | $40.97 | | $1,320.64 | |
| Jul-11 | 43.39 | 5.9% | 1,292.28 | −2.1% |
| Aug-11 | 38.66 | −10.9% | 1,218.89 | −5.7% |
| Sep-11 | 34.33 | −11.2% | 1,131.42 | −7.2% |
| Oct-11 | 38.9 | 13.3% | 1,253.30 | 10.8% |
| Nov-11 | 36.77 | −5.5% | 1,246.96 | −0.5% |
| Dec-11 | 38.87 | 5.7% | 1,257.60 | 0.9% |
| Jan-12 | 44.19 | 13.7% | 1,312.41 | 4.4% |
| Feb-12 | 46.58 | 5.4% | 1,365.68 | 4.1% |
| Mar-12 | 49.08 | 5.4% | 1,408.47 | 3.1% |
| Apr-12 | 52.33 | 6.6% | 1,397.91 | −0.7% |
| May-12 | 48.18 | −7.9% | 1,310.33 | −6.3% |
| Jun-12 | 46.18 | −4.2% | 1,355.69 | 3.5% |
| Average return | | 1.36% | | 0.34% |
| Standard deviation | | 8.87% | | 5.23% |
| Slope of the characteristic line | | | | 1.34 |

The relationship between the Harley-Davidson returns and the S&P 500 Index are shown in the graph below:

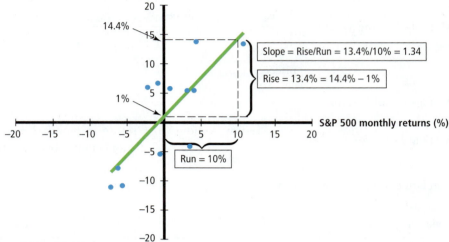

Source: Data from Yahoo Finance.

### STEP 3: ANALYZE YOUR RESULTS

We can see that the average return for Harley-Davidson was significantly higher than the returns for the S&P 500. (Remember these are only monthly returns.) But the volatility of the returns for Harley-Davidson is also higher than for the S&P 500. Then when we regress the Harley-Davidson returns on the market (S&P 500) returns, we see that the average relationship is 1.34, which is a measure of systematic risk. That is, for every 1 percent that the market returns move up or down, Harley-Davidson's returns will on average move 1.34 percent.

To this point, we have talked about measuring an individual stock's beta. We will now consider how to measure the beta for a portfolio of stocks.

## Measuring a Portfolio's Beta

**portfolio beta** the relationship between a portfolio's returns and the market returns. It is a measure of the portfolio's nondiversifiable risk.

What if we were to diversify our portfolio, as we have just suggested, but instead of acquiring stocks with the same beta as Home Depot (0.82), we buy 8 stocks with betas of 1.0 and 12 stocks with betas of 1.5. What would the beta of our portfolio become? As it works out, the **portfolio beta** is merely the average of the individual stock betas. It is a *weighted average of the individual securities' betas, with the weights being equal to the proportion of the portfolio invested in each security.* Thus, the beta ($\beta$) of a portfolio consisting of $n$ stocks is equal to

$$
\begin{aligned}
\text{Portfolio} \atop \text{beta} = &\left( \begin{array}{c} \text{percentage of} \\ \text{portfolio invested} \\ \text{in asset 1} \end{array} \times \begin{array}{c} \text{beta for} \\ \text{asset 1} \\ (\beta_1) \end{array} \right) \\
+ &\left( \begin{array}{c} \text{percentage of} \\ \text{portfolio invested} \\ \text{in asset 2} \end{array} \times \begin{array}{c} \text{beta for} \\ \text{asset 2} \\ (\beta_2) \end{array} \right) \\
+ \ldots + &\left( \begin{array}{c} \text{percentage of} \\ \text{portfolio invested} \\ \text{in asset } n \end{array} \times \begin{array}{c} \text{beta for} \\ \text{asset } n \\ (\beta_n) \end{array} \right)
\end{aligned}
\tag{6-10}
$$

So, assuming we bought equal amounts of each stock in our new 20-stock portfolio, the beta would simply be 1.3, calculated as follows:

$$
\text{Portfolio beta} = \left( \frac{8}{20} \times 1.0 \right) + \left( \frac{12}{20} \times 1.50 \right) = 1.3
$$

Thus, whenever the general market increases or decreases 1 percent, our new portfolio's returns would change 1.3 percent on average, which means that our new portfolio has more systematic, or market, risk than the market has as a whole.

We can conclude that the beta of a portfolio is determined by the betas of the individual stocks. If we have a portfolio consisting of stocks with low betas, then our portfolio will have a low beta. The reverse is true as well. Figure 6-7 presents these situations graphically.

Before leaving the subject of risk and diversification, we want to share a study that demonstrates the effects of diversifying our investments, not just across different stocks but also across different types of securities.

## Risk and Diversification Demonstrated

To this point, we have described the effect of diversification on risk and return in a general way. Also, when we spoke of diversification, we were diversifying by holding more stocks in our portfolio. Now let's look briefly on how risk and return change as we (1) diversify between two different types of assets—stocks and bonds, and (2) increase the length of time that we hold a portfolio of assets.

Notice that when we previously spoke about diversification, we were diversifying by holding more stock, but the portfolio still consisted of all stocks. Now we examine diversifying between a portfolio of stocks and a portfolio of bonds. Diversifying among different kinds of assets is called **asset allocation**, compared with diversification within the different asset classes, such as stocks, bonds, real estate, and commodities. We know from experience that the benefit we receive from diversifying is far greater through effective asset allocation than from astutely selecting individual stocks to include with an asset category.

Figure 6-8 presents the range of rolling returns for several mixtures of stocks and bonds depending on whether we held the investments 12 months, 60 months, or 120 months between 1926 and 2011. For the 12-month holding period, we would have purchased the investment at the beginning of each year and sold at the end of each year, repeating this process every year from 1926 to 2011. Then for the 60 months, we would have invested at the beginning of the year and held the investment for 60 months. In other words, we invested at the beginning of 1926 and sold at the end of 1930, then did the same for 1927–1931, repeating the process for all 60-month periods all the way through 2011. Finally, we would have invested at the beginning of each year, holding each investment for 120 months.

**asset allocation** identifying and selecting the asset classes appropriate for a specific investment portfolio and determining the proportions of those assets within the portfolio.

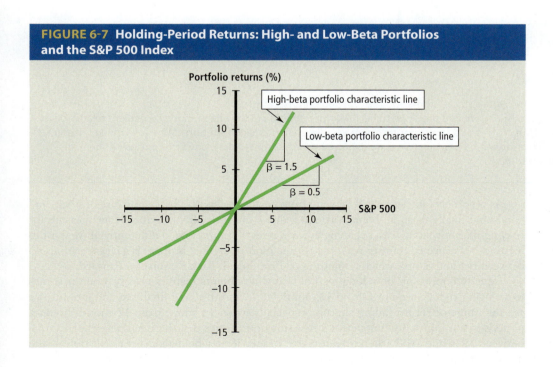

**FIGURE 6-7  Holding-Period Returns: High- and Low-Beta Portfolios and the S&P 500 Index**

# DID YOU GET IT?

## ESTIMATING BETA

The holding-period returns, average monthly returns, and the standard deviations for Toyota and the S&P 500 data are as follows:

| | TOYOTA | | S&P 500 | |
|---|---|---|---|---|
| | **PRICES** | **RETURNS** | **PRICES** | **RETURNS** |
| Dec-11 | $66.13 | | $1,257.60 | |
| Jan-12 | 73.48 | 11.11% | 1,312.41 | 4.36% |
| Feb-12 | 82.71 | 12.56% | 1,365.68 | 4.06% |
| Mar-12 | 86.82 | 4.97% | 1,408.47 | 3.13% |
| Apr-12 | 81.78 | −5.81% | 1,397.91 | −0.75% |
| May-12 | 76.89 | −5.98% | 1,310.33 | −6.27% |
| Jun-12 | 76.30 | −0.77% | 1,355.69 | 3.46% |
| Average return | | 2.68% | | 1.33% |
| Standard deviation | | 8.16% | | 4.16% |
| Slope | | 1.54 | | |

The graph would appear as follows:

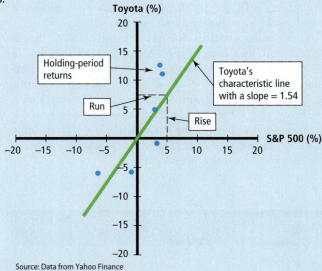

Source: Data from Yahoo Finance

The average relationship between Toyota's stock returns and the S&P 500's returns is estimated by the slope of the characteristic line in the graph above. Using a spreadsheet, we find the slope to be 1.54, where the rise of the line is about 7.5 percent relative to a run (horizontal axis) of 5 percent. Thus, Toyota's stock returns are more volatile than the market's returns. When the market rises (or falls) 1 percent, Toyota's stock will rise (or fall) 1.5 percent. (We should, however, be hesitant to draw any firm conclusions here, given the limited number of return observations.)

As we observe in Figure 6-8, moving from an all-stock portfolio to a mixture of stocks and bonds and finally to an all-bond portfolio reduces the variability of returns (our measure for risk) significantly along with declining average rates of return. Stated differently, if we want to increase our expected returns, we must assume more risk. That is, there is a clear relationship between risk and return, which reminds us of **Principle 3: Risk Requires a Reward.**

Equally important, how long we hold our investments matters greatly when it comes to reducing risk. As we move from 12 months to 60 months, and finally to 120 months, we see the range of return falling sharply, especially when we move from 12-month holding periods to 60-month holding periods. As a side note, notice that there has never been a time between 1926 and 2011 when investors lost money if they held an all-stock portfolio—the most risky portfolio—for 10 years. In other words, *the market rewards the patient investor*.

**FIGURE 6-8  The Effect of Diversifying and Investing for Longer Periods of Time on Risk and Returns**

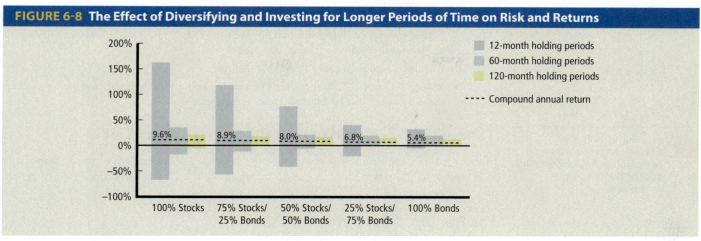

Source: Data from Summary Statistics of Annual Total Returns: 1926 to 2011 Yearbook. Copyright® 2012 Ibbotson Associates, Inc.

In the next section, we complete our study of risk and returns by connecting risk—market or systematic risk—to the investor's *required* rate of return. After all, although risk is an important issue, it is primarily important in its effect on the investor's required rate of return.

We now can recap the financial decision tools used to measure market risk for a single investment and for a portfolio of investments. They can be shown as follows:

## FINANCIAL DECISION TOOLS

| Name of Tool | Formula | What It Tells You |
|---|---|---|
| Monthly holding-period return | $\text{Monthly holding-period return} = \dfrac{\text{Price}_{end\ of\ month} - \text{Price}_{beginning\ of\ month}}{\text{Price}_{beginning\ of\ month}}$<br><br>$= \dfrac{\text{Price}_{end\ of\ month}}{\text{Price}_{beginning\ of\ month}} - 1$ | Calculates the percentage rate of return for a security held for a single month. |
| Average monthly holding-period rate of return | $\text{Average monthly holding-period return} = \dfrac{\text{return in month 1} + \text{return in month 2} + \cdots + \text{return in last month}}{\text{number of monthly returns}}$ | Finds the average monthly holding-period return for a number of monthly returns. |
| Standard deviation of monthly holding-period returns | $\text{Standard Deviation}$ $= \sqrt{\dfrac{(\text{return in month 1} - \text{average return})^2 + (\text{return in month 2} - \text{average return})^2 + \cdots + (\text{return in last month} - \text{average return})^2}{\text{number of monthly returns} - 1}}$ | Measure of the volatility of monthly holding-period returns over a series of months. |
| Portfolio beta | $\begin{aligned}\text{Portfolio beta} &= \left(\begin{array}{c}\text{percentage of} \\ \text{portfolio invested} \\ \text{in asset 1}\end{array} \times \begin{array}{c}\text{beta for} \\ \text{asset 1} \\ (\beta_1)\end{array}\right) \\ &+ \left(\begin{array}{c}\text{percentage of} \\ \text{portfolio invested} \\ \text{in asset 2}\end{array} \times \begin{array}{c}\text{beta for} \\ \text{asset 2} \\ (\beta_2)\end{array}\right) \\ &+ \cdots + \left(\begin{array}{c}\text{percentage of} \\ \text{portfolio invested} \\ \text{in asset } n\end{array} \times \begin{array}{c}\text{beta for} \\ \text{asset } n \\ (\beta_n)\end{array}\right)\end{aligned}$ | Finds the beta for an entire portfolio of stocks. |

## Concept Check

1. Give specific examples of systematic and unsystematic risk. How many different securities must be owned to essentially diversify away unsystematic risk?
2. What method is used to measure a firm's market risk?
3. After reviewing Figure 6-5, explain the difference between the plotted dots and the firm's characteristic line. What must be done to eliminate the variations?

 **5** Explain the relationship between an investor's required rate of return on an investment and the riskiness of the investment.

# The Investor's Required Rate of Return

In this section, we examine the concept of the investor's required rate of return, especially as it relates to the riskiness of an asset, and then we see how the required rate of return might be measured.

## The Required Rate of Return Concept

**required rate of return** minimum rate of return necessary to attract an investor to purchase or hold a security.

An investor's **required rate of return** can be defined as the *minimum rate of return necessary to attract an investor to purchase or hold a security*. This definition considers the investor's opportunity cost of funds of making an investment in *the next-best investment*. This forgone return is an opportunity cost of undertaking the investment and, consequently, is the investor's required rate of return. In other words, we invest with the intention of achieving a rate of return sufficient to warrant making the investment. The investment will be made only if the purchase price is low enough relative to expected future cash flows to provide a rate of return greater than or equal to our required rate of return.

To help us better understand the nature of an investor's required rate of return, we can separate the return into its basic components: the risk-free rate of return plus a risk premium. Expressed as an equation:

$$\begin{matrix} \text{Investor's required} \\ \text{rate of return} \end{matrix} = \begin{matrix} \text{risk-free rate of} \\ \text{return} \end{matrix} + \begin{matrix} \text{risk} \\ \text{premium} \end{matrix} \qquad (6\text{-}11)$$

**risk-free rate of return** the rate of return on risk-free investments. The interest rates on short-term U.S. government securities are commonly used to measure this rate.

**risk premium** the additional return expected for assuming risk.

The **risk-free rate of return** is the *required rate of return, or discount rate, for riskless investments*. Typically, our measure for the risk-free rate of return is the U.S. Treasury bill rate. The **risk premium** is the *additional return we must expect to receive for assuming risk*. As the level of risk increases, we will demand additional expected returns. Even though we may or may not actually receive this incremental return, we must have reason to expect it; otherwise, why expose ourselves to the chance of losing all or part of our money?

To illustrate, assume you are considering the purchase of a stock that you believe will provide a 10 percent return over the next year. If the expected risk-free rate of return, such as the rate of return for 90-day Treasury bills, is 2 percent, then the risk premium you are demanding to assume the additional risk is 8 percent (10% – 2%).

## Measuring the Required Rate of Return

We have seen that (1) systematic risk is the only relevant risk—the rest can be diversified away, and (2) the required rate of return, *k*, equals the risk-free rate plus a risk premium. We will now examine how we can estimate investors' required rates of return.

The finance profession has had difficulty in developing a practical approach to measure an investor's required rate of return; however, financial managers often use a method called

**capital asset pricing model (CAPM)** an equation stating that the expected rate of return on an investment (in this case a stock) is a function of (1) the risk-free rate, (2) the investment's systematic risk, and (3) the expected risk premium for the market portfolio of all risky securities.

the **capital asset pricing model (CAPM)**. The capital asset pricing model is *an equation that equates the expected rate of return on a stock to the risk-free rate plus a risk premium for the stock's systematic risk*. Although certainly not without its critics, the CAPM provides an intuitive approach for thinking about the return that an investor should require on an investment, given the asset's systematic or market risk.

Equation (6-11) above provides the natural starting point for measuring the investor's required rate of return and sets us up for using the CAPM. Rearranging this equation to solve for the risk premium we have

$$\begin{matrix} \text{Risk} \\ \text{premium} \end{matrix} = \begin{matrix} \text{investor's required} \\ \text{rate of return, } r \end{matrix} - \begin{matrix} \text{risk-free rate of} \\ \text{return, } r_f \end{matrix} \qquad (6\text{-}12)$$

## FINANCE AT WORK

### DOES BETA ALWAYS WORK?

At the start of 1998, Apple Computer was in deep trouble. As a result, its stock price fluctuated wildly—far more than other computer firms, such as IBM. However, based on the capital asset pricing model (CAPM) and its measure of beta, the required return of Apple's investors would have been only 8 percent, compared with 12 percent for IBM's stockholders. Equally interesting, when Apple's situation improved in the spring of that year, and its share price became less volatile, Apple's investors, at least according to the CAPM, would have required a rate of return of 11 percent—a 3 percentage point increase from the earlier required rate of return. That is not what intuition would suggest should have happened.

So what should we think? Just when Apple's future was most in doubt and its shares most volatile, its beta was only 0.47, suggesting that Apple's stock was only half as volatile as the overall stock market. In reality, beta is meaningless here. The truth is that Apple was in such a dire condition that its stock price simply "decoupled" itself from the stock market. So, as IBM and its peer stock prices moved up and down with the rest of the market, Apple shares reacted solely to news about the company, without regard for the market's movements. The stock's beta thus created the false impression that Apple shares were more stable than the stock market.

The lesson here is that beta may at times be misleading when used with individual companies. Instead, its use is far more reliable when applied to a portfolio of companies. If a firm that was interested in acquiring Apple Computer in 1998, for instance, had used the beta in computing the required rate of return for the acquisition, it would without a doubt have overvalued Apple.

So does that mean that CAPM is worthless? No, not as long as company-unique risk is not the main driving force in a company's stock price movements or if investors are able to diversify away specific company risk. Then they would bid up the price of such shares until they reflected only market risk. For example, a mutual fund that specializes in "distressed stocks" might purchase a number of "Apple Computer-type companies," each with its own problems, but for different reasons. For such investors, betas work pretty well. Thus, the moral of the story is to exercise common sense and judgment when using a beta.

which simply says that the risk premium for a security equals the investor's required return less the risk-free rate existing in the market. For example, if the required return is 12 percent and the risk-free rate is 3 percent, the risk premium is 9 percent. Also, if the required return for the market portfolio is 10 percent, and the risk-free rate is 3 percent, the risk premium for the market would be 7 percent. This 7 percent risk premium would apply to any security having systematic (nondiversifiable) risk equivalent to the general market, or a beta ($\beta$) of 1.

In this same market, a security with a beta ($\beta$) of 2 should provide a risk premium of 14 percent, or twice the 7 percent risk premium existing for the market as a whole. Hence, in general, the appropriate required rate of return for a given security should be determined by

$$\begin{array}{l} \text{Required return on} \\ \text{security, } r \end{array} = \begin{array}{l} \text{risk free} \\ \text{rate of return, } r_f \end{array}$$

$$+ \begin{array}{l} \text{beta for} \\ \text{security, } \beta \end{array} \times \left( \begin{array}{l} \text{required return} \\ \text{on the market portfolio, } r_m \end{array} - \begin{array}{l} \text{risk-free} \\ \text{rate of return, } r_f \end{array} \right)$$

(6-13)

Equation (6-13) is the CAPM. This equation designates the risk–return trade-off existing in the market, where risk is measured in terms of beta. Figure 6-9 graphs the CAPM as the **security market line**.[9] The security market line is *the graphic representation of the CAPM. It is the line that shows the appropriate required rate of return given a stock's systematic risk*

**security market line** the return line that reflects the attitudes of investors regarding the minimum acceptable return for a given level of systematic risk associated with a security.

---

[9]Two key assumptions are made in using the security market line. First, we assume that the marketplace where securities are bought and sold is highly efficient. Market efficiency indicates that the price of an asset responds quickly to new information, thereby suggesting that the price of a security reflects all available information. As a result, the current price of a security is considered to represent the best estimate of its future price. Second, the model assumes that a perfect market exists. A perfect market is one in which information is readily available to all investors at a nominal cost. Also, securities are assumed to be infinitely divisible, with any transaction costs incurred in purchasing or selling a security being negligible. Furthermore, investors are assumed to be single-period wealth maximizers who agree on the meaning and significance of the available information. Finally, within the perfect market, all investors are *price takers*, which simply means that a single investor's actions cannot affect the price of a security. These assumptions are obviously not descriptive of reality. However, from the perspective of positive economics, the mark of a good theory is the accuracy of its predictions, not the validity of the simplifying assumptions that underlie its development.

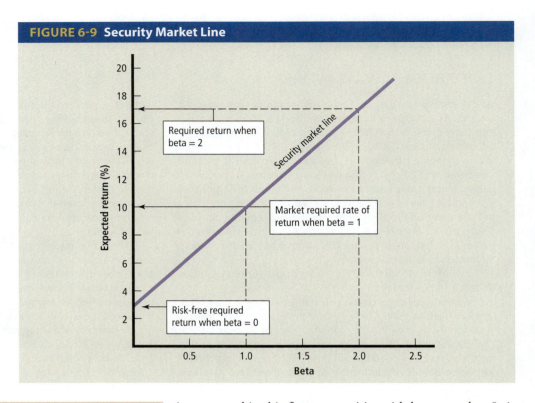

**FIGURE 6-9  Security Market Line**

As presented in this figure, securities with betas equal to 0, 1, and 2, should have required rates of return as follows:

If $\beta = 0$: required rate of return $= 3\% + 0(10\% - 3\%) = 3\%$
If $\beta = 1$: required rate of return $= 3\% + 1(10\% - 3\%) = 10\%$
If $\beta = 2$: required rate of return $= 3\% + 2(10\% - 3\%) = 17\%$

where the risk-free rate is 3 percent, and the required return for the market portfolio is 10 percent.

A large part of this chapter has been spent in explaining and measuring an investment's expected rate of return and the corresponding amount of risk. However, one step remains—providing the financial tool or criterion to determine if the investment should be made. Only by knowing the investor's required rate of return for a particular investment can we answer this question. The formulas used to answer this question were presented in this section and can be summarized as follows:

## FINANCIAL DECISION TOOLS

| Name of Tool | Formula | What It Tells You |
|---|---|---|
| Investor's required rate of return | Investor's required rate of return = risk-free rate of return + risk premium | Measures an investor's required rate of return based on a risk-free rate plus a return premium for assuming risk |
| Risk premium | Risk premium = investor's required rate of return, $r$ − risk-free rate of return, $r_f$ | Indicates the additional return an investor should require to assume additional risk |
| Investor's required rate of return | $\text{Required return on security, } r = \text{risk free rate of return, } r_f + \text{beta for security, } \beta \times \left( \text{required return on the market portfolio, } r_m - \text{risk-free rate of return, } r_f \right)$ | Calculates the rate of return an investor should require based on the capital asset pricing model, which only considers systematic risk to determine the appropriate risk premium |

## CAN YOU DO IT?

### COMPUTING A REQUIRED RATE OF RETURN

Determine a fair expected (or required) rate of return for a stock that has a beta of 1.25 when the risk-free rate is 3 percent and the expected market return is 9 percent.

(The solution can be found below.)

## Concept Check

1. How does opportunity cost affect an investor's required rate of return?
2. What are the two components of the investor's required rate of return?
3. How does beta fit into factoring the risk premium in the CAPM equation?
4. Assuming the market is efficient, what is the relationship between a stock's price and the security market line?

## DID YOU GET IT?

### COMPUTING A REQUIRED RATE OF RETURN

The appropriate rate of return would be:

Required return = risk-free rate + [beta × (market return − risk-free rate)]
             = 3% + [1.25 × (9% − 3%)]
             = 10.5%

# Chapter Summaries

In Chapter 2, we referred to the discount rate as the interest rate, or the opportunity cost of funds. At that point, we considered a number of important factors that influence interest rates, including the price of time, expected or anticipated inflation, the risk premium related to maturity (liquidity), and the variability of future returns. In this chapter, we have returned to our study of rates of return and looked ever so carefully at the relationship between risk and rates of return.

### Define and measure the expected rate of return of an individual investment. (pgs 184–186)

**SUMMARY:** When we speak of "returns" on an investment, either we are talking about *historical* return, what we earned on an investment in the past, or *expected* returns, where we are attempting to determine the return we can "expect" to receive in the future. In a world of uncertainty, we cannot make forecasts with certitude. Thus, we must speak in terms of expected events. The expected return on an investment may therefore be stated as a weighted average of all possible returns, weighted by the probability that each will occur.

#### KEY TERMS

**Holding-period return (historical or realized rate of return), page 184**  The rate of return earned on an investment, which equals the dollar gain divided by the amount invested.

**Expected rate of return, page 184**  The arithmetic mean or average of all possible outcomes where those outcomes are weighted by the probability that each will occur.

## KEY EQUATIONS

Holding-period dollar gain, DG

$$= \text{price}_{\text{end of period}} + \text{cash distribution (dividend)} - \text{price}_{\text{beginning of period}}$$

Holding-period rate of return, $r$

$$= \frac{\text{dollar gain}}{\text{price}_{\text{beginning of period}}} = \frac{\text{price}_{\text{end of period}} + \text{dividend} - \text{price}_{\text{beginning of period}}}{\text{price}_{\text{beginning of period}}}$$

$$
\begin{aligned}
\text{Expected cash flow, } \overline{CF} = &\left( \begin{array}{c} \text{cash flow} \\ \text{in state 1} \\ (CF_1) \end{array} \times \begin{array}{c} \text{probability} \\ \text{of state 1} \\ (Pb_1) \end{array} \right) + \left( \begin{array}{c} \text{cash flow} \\ \text{in state 2} \\ (CF_2) \end{array} \times \begin{array}{c} \text{probability} \\ \text{of state 2} \\ (Pb_2) \end{array} \right) \\
&+ \dots + \left( \begin{array}{c} \text{cash flow} \\ \text{in state } n \\ (CF_n) \end{array} \times \begin{array}{c} \text{probability} \\ \text{of state } n \\ (Pb_n) \end{array} \right)
\end{aligned}
$$

$$
\begin{aligned}
\text{Expected rate of return, } \overline{r} = &\left( \begin{array}{c} \text{rate of return} \\ \text{for state 1} \\ (r_1) \end{array} \times \begin{array}{c} \text{probability} \\ \text{of state 1} \\ (Pb_1) \end{array} \right) + \left( \begin{array}{c} \text{rate of return} \\ \text{for state 2} \\ (r_2) \end{array} \times \begin{array}{c} \text{probability} \\ \text{of state 2} \\ (Pb_2) \end{array} \right) \\
&+ \dots + \left( \begin{array}{c} \text{rate of return} \\ \text{for state } n \\ (r_n) \end{array} \times \begin{array}{c} \text{probability} \\ \text{of state } n \\ (Pb_n) \end{array} \right)
\end{aligned}
$$

---

 **Define and measure the riskiness of an individual investment.** (pgs 186–193)

**SUMMARY:** Risk associated with a single investment is the variability of cash flows or returns and can be measured by the standard deviation.

### KEY TERMS

**Risk, page 187** Potential variability in future cash flows.

**Standard deviation, page 189** A statistical measure of the spread of a probability distribution calculated by squaring the difference between each outcome and its expected value, weighting each value by its probability, summing over all possible outcomes, and taking the square root of this sum.

### KEY EQUATION

$$
\begin{aligned}
\begin{array}{c} \text{Variance in} \\ \text{rates of return} \\ (\sigma^2) \end{array} = &\left[ \left( \begin{array}{c} \text{rate of return} \\ \text{for state 1} \\ (r_1) \end{array} - \begin{array}{c} \text{expected rate} \\ \text{of return} \\ \overline{r} \end{array} \right)^2 \times \begin{array}{c} \text{probability} \\ \text{of state 1} \\ (Pb_1) \end{array} \right] \\
&+ \left[ \left( \begin{array}{c} \text{rate of return} \\ \text{for state 2} \\ (r_2) \end{array} - \begin{array}{c} \text{expected rate} \\ \text{of return} \\ \overline{r} \end{array} \right)^2 \times \begin{array}{c} \text{probability} \\ \text{of state 2} \\ (Pb_2) \end{array} \right] \\
&+ \dots + \left[ \left( \begin{array}{c} \text{rate of return} \\ \text{for state } n \\ (r_n) \end{array} - \begin{array}{c} \text{expected rate} \\ \text{of return} \\ \overline{r} \end{array} \right)^2 \times \begin{array}{c} \text{probability} \\ \text{of state } n \\ (Pb_n) \end{array} \right]
\end{aligned}
$$

---

 **Compare the historical relationship between risk and rates of return in the capital markets.** (pgs 193–194)

**SUMMARY:** Ibbotson Associates have provided us with annual rates of return earned on different types of security investments as far back as 1926. They summarize among other things, the annual returns for six portfolios of securities made up of

1. Common stocks of large companies
2. Common stocks of small firms
3. Long-term corporate bonds

**4.** Long-term U.S. government bonds

**5.** Intermediate-term U.S. government bonds

**6.** U.S. Treasury bills

A comparison of the annual rates of return for these respective portfolios for the years 1926 to 2011 shows a positive relationship between risk and return, with Treasury bills being least risky and common stocks of small firms being most risky. From the data, we are able to see the benefit of diversification in terms of improving the return–risk relationship. Also, the data clearly demonstrate that only common stock has in the long run served as an inflation hedge, and that the risk associated with common stock can be reduced if investors are patient in receiving their returns.

## Explain how diversifying investments affects the riskiness and expected rate of return of a portfolio or combination of assets. (pgs 194–206)

**SUMMARY:** We made an important distinction between nondiversifiable risk and diversifiable risk. We concluded that the only relevant risk, given the opportunity to diversify our portfolio, is a security's nondiversifiable risk, which we called by two other names: systematic risk and market-related risk.

### KEY TERMS

**Systematic risk (market risk or nondiversifiable risk), page 195** (1) The risk related to an investment return that cannot be eliminated through diversification. Systematic risk results from factors that affect all stocks. Also called market risk or nondiversifiable risk. (2) The risk of a project from the viewpoint of a well-diversified shareholder. This measure takes into account that some of the project's risk will be diversified away as the project is combined with the firm's other projects, and, in addition, some of the remaining risk will be diversified away by shareholders as they combine this stock with other stocks in their portfolios.

**Unsystematic risk (company unique risk or diversifiable risk), page 195** The risk related to an investment return that can be eliminated through diversification. Unsystematic risk is the result of factors that are unique to the particular firm. Also called company-unique risk or diversifiable risk.

**Characteristic line, page 198** The line of "best fit" through a series of returns for a firm's stock relative to the market's returns. The slope of the line, frequently called beta, represents the average movement of the firm's stock returns in response to a movement in the market's returns.

**Beta, page 198** The relationship between an investment's returns and the market's returns. This is a measure of the investment's nondiversifiable risk.

**Portfolio beta, page 202** The relationship between a portfolio's returns and the market returns. It is a measure of the portfolio's nondiversifiable risk.

**Asset allocation, page 203** Identifying and selecting the asset classes appropriate for a specific investment portfolio and determining the proportions of those assets within the portfolio.

### KEY EQUATIONS

$$\text{Monthly holding return} = \frac{\text{Price}_{\text{end of month}} - \text{Price}_{\text{beginning of month}}}{\text{Price}_{\text{beginning of month}}}$$

$$= \frac{\text{Price}_{\text{end of month}}}{\text{Price}_{\text{beginning of month}}} - 1$$

$$\text{Average holding-period return} = \frac{\text{return in month 1} + \text{return in month 2} + \cdots + \text{return in last month}}{\text{number of monthly returns}}$$

Standard deviation

$$= \sqrt{\frac{(\text{return in month 1} - \text{average return})^2 + (\text{return in month 2} - \text{average return})^2 + \cdots (\text{return in last month} - \text{average return})^2}{\text{number of monthly returns} - 1}}$$

$$\begin{aligned}
\text{Portfolio} \atop \text{beta} = & \left( \begin{array}{ccc} \text{percentage of} & & \text{beta for} \\ \text{portfolio invested} & \times & \text{asset 1} \\ \text{in asset 1} & & (\beta_1) \end{array} \right) \\
+ & \left( \begin{array}{ccc} \text{percentage of} & & \text{beta for} \\ \text{portfolio invested} & \times & \text{asset 2} \\ \text{in asset 2} & & (\beta_2) \end{array} \right) \\
+ \ldots + & \left( \begin{array}{ccc} \text{percentage of} & & \text{beta for} \\ \text{portfolio invested} & \times & \text{asset } n \\ \text{in asset } n & & (\beta_n) \end{array} \right)
\end{aligned}$$

  **Explain the relationship between an investor's required rate of return on an investment and the riskiness of the investment.** (pgs. 206–209)

**SUMMARY:** The capital asset pricing model provides an intuitive framework for understanding the risk–return relationship. The CAPM suggests that investors determine an appropriate required rate of return, depending upon the amount of systematic risk inherent in a security. This minimum acceptable rate of return is equal to the risk-free rate plus a risk premium for assuming risk.

### KEY TERMS

**Required rate of return, page 206** Minimum rate of return necessary to attract an investor to purchase or hold a security.

**Risk-free rate of return, page 206** The rate of return on risk-free investments. The interest rates on short-term U.S. government securities are commonly used to measure this rate.

**Risk premium, page 206** The additional return expected for assuming risk.

**Capital asset pricing model (CAPM), page 206** An equation stating that the

expected rate of return on an investment (in this case a stock) is a function of (1) the risk-free rate, (2) the investment's systematic risk, and (3) the expected risk premium for the market portfolio of all risky securities.

**Security market line, page 207** The return line that reflects the attitudes of investors regarding the minimum acceptable return for a given level of systematic risk associated with security.

### KEY EQUATIONS

Investor's required rate of return = risk-free rate of return + risk premium

Risk premium = investor's required rate of return, $r$ − risk-free rate of return, $r_f$

$$\begin{aligned}
\text{Required return on} \atop \text{security, } r = & \ \text{risk free} \atop \text{rate of return, } r_f \\
+ & \ {\text{beta for} \atop \text{security, } \beta} \times \left( {\text{required return} \atop \text{on the market portfolio, } r_m} - {\text{risk-free} \atop \text{rate of return, } r_f} \right)
\end{aligned}$$

# Review Questions

*All Review Questions are available in* MyFinanceLab.

**6-1.** a. What is meant by the investor's required rate of return?

   b. How do we measure the riskiness of an asset?

   c. How should the proposed measurement of risk be interpreted?

**6-2.** What is (a) unsystematic risk (company-unique or diversifiable risk) and (b) systematic risk (market or nondiversifiable risk)?

**6-3.** What is a beta? How is it used to calculate $r$, the investor's required rate of return?

**6-4.** What is the security market line? What does it represent?

**6-5.** How do we measure the beta of a portfolio?

**6-6.** If we were to graph the returns of a stock against the returns of the S&P 500 Index, and the points did not follow a very ordered pattern, what could we say about that stock? If the stock's returns tracked the S&P 500 returns very closely, then what could we say?

**6-7.** Over the past eight decades, we have had the opportunity to observe the rates of return and the variability of these returns for different types of securities. Summarize these observations.

**6-8.** What effect will diversifying your portfolio have on your returns?

# Study Problems

*All Study Problems are available in MyFinanceLab.*

**6-1.** (*Expected return and risk*) Universal Corporation is planning to invest in a security that has several possible rates of return. Given the following probability distribution of returns, what is the expected rate of return on the investment? Also compute the standard deviations of the returns. What do the resulting numbers represent?

| PROBABILITY | RETURN |
| --- | --- |
| 0.10 | −10% |
| 0.20 | 5% |
| 0.30 | 10% |
| 0.40 | 25% |

**6-2.** (*Average expected return and risk*) Given the holding-period returns shown here, calculate the average returns and the standard deviations for the Kaifu Corporation and for the market.

| MONTH | KAIFU CORP. | MARKET |
| --- | --- | --- |
| 1 | 4% | 2% |
| 2 | 6 | 3 |
| 3 | 0 | 1 |
| 4 | 2 | −1 |

**6-3.** (*Expected rate of return and risk*) Carter Inc. is evaluating a security. Calculate the investment's expected return and its standard deviation.

| PROBABILITY | RETURN |
| --- | --- |
| 0.15 | 6% |
| 0.30 | 9% |
| 0.40 | 10% |
| 0.15 | 15% |

**6-4.** (*Expected rate of return and risk*) Summerville Inc. is considering an investment in one of two common stocks. Given the information that follows, which investment is better, based on the risk (as measured by the standard deviation) and return of each?

| COMMON STOCK A | | COMMON STOCK B | |
| --- | --- | --- | --- |
| PROBABILITY | RETURN | PROBABILITY | RETURN |
| 0.30 | 11% | 0.20 | −5% |
| 0.40 | 15% | 0.30 | 6% |
| 0.30 | 19% | 0.30 | 14% |
| | | 0.20 | 22% |

**6-5.** (*Standard deviation*) Given the following probabilities and returns for Mik's Corporation, find the standard deviation.

| PROBABILITY | RETURNS |
|---|---|
| 0.40 | 7% |
| 0.25 | 4% |
| 0.15 | 18% |
| 0.20 | 10% |

**6-6.** (*Expected return*) Go to http://finance.yahoo.com. Select the link Investing, and then choose Education. Go to Financial Glossary. Find the terms Expected Return and Expected Value in the glossary. What did you learn from these definitions?

**6-7.** Go to www.investopedia.com/university/beginner, where there is an article on "Investing 101: Introduction." Read the article and explain what it says about risk tolerance.

**6-8.** Go to www.moneychimp.com. Select the link Volatility. Complete the retirement planning calculator, making the assumptions that you believe are appropriate for you. Then go to the Monte Carlo simulation calculator. Assume that you invest in large-company common stocks during your working years and then invest in long-term corporate bonds during retirement. Use the nominal average returns and standard deviations shown in Figure 6-2. What did you learn?

**6-9.** (*Holding-period returns*) From the price data that follow, compute the holding-period returns for periods 2 through 4.

| PERIOD | STOCK PRICE |
|---|---|
| 1 | $10 |
| 2 | 13 |
| 3 | 11 |
| 4 | 15 |

**6-10.** (*Computing holding-period returns*)

a.  From the price data here, compute the holding-period returns for Jazman and Solomon for periods 2 through 4.

| PERIOD | JAZMAN | SOLOMON |
|---|---|---|
| 1 | $ 9 | $27 |
| 2 | 11 | 28 |
| 3 | 10 | 32 |
| 4 | 13 | 29 |

b.  How would you interpret the meaning of a holding-period return?

**6-11.** (*Measuring risk and rates of return*)

a.  Given the holding-period returns shown here, compute the average returns and the standard deviations for the Zemin Corporation and for the market.

| MONTH | ZEMIN CORP. | MARKET |
|---|---|---|
| 1 | 6% | 4% |
| 2 | 3 | 2 |
| 3 | −1 | 1 |
| 4 | −3 | −2 |
| 5 | 5 | 2 |
| 6 | 0 | 2 |

b. If Zemin's beta is 1.54 and the risk-free rate is 4 percent, what would be an appropriate required return for an investor owning Zemin? (*Note:* Because the returns of Zemin Corporation are based on monthly data, you will need to annualize the returns to make them compatible with the risk-free rate. For simplicity, you can convert from monthly to yearly returns by multiplying the average monthly returns by 12.)

c. How does Zemin's historical average return compare with the return you believe to be a fair return, given the firm's systematic risk?

**6-12.** (*Holding period dollar gain and return*) Suppose you purchased 16 shares of Disney stock for $24.22 per share on May 1, 2012. On September 1 of the same year, you sold 12 shares of the stock for $25.68. Calculate the holding-period dollar gain for the shares you sold, assuming no dividend was distributed, and the holding-period rate of return.

**6-13.** (*Asset allocation*) Go to http://cgi.money.cnn.com/tools and then go to the heading, investing and click the link Fix Your Asset Allocation. Answer the questions and click, Calculate. Try different options and see how the calculator suggests you allocate your investments.

---

**6-14.** (*Expected return, standard deviation, and capital asset pricing model*) The following are the end-of-month prices for both the Standard & Poor's 500 Index and Nike's common stock.

a. Using the data here, calculate the holding-period returns for each of the months.

| | NIKE | S&P 500 INDEX |
|---|---|---|
| **2011** | | |
| June | $89.98 | $1,320.64 |
| July | 90.15 | 1,292.28 |
| August | 86.65 | 1,218.89 |
| September | 85.51 | 1,131.42 |
| October | 96.35 | 1,253.30 |
| November | 96.18 | 1,246.96 |
| December | 96.37 | 1,257.60 |
| **2012** | | |
| January | 103.99 | 1,312.41 |
| February | 107.92 | 1,365.68 |
| March | 108.44 | 1,408.47 |
| April | 111.87 | 1,397.91 |
| May | 108.18 | 1,310.33 |
| June | 98.45 | 1,355.69 |

b. Calculate the average monthly return and the standard deviation for both the S&P 500 and Nike.

c. Develop a graph that shows the relationship between the Nike stock returns and the S&P 500 Index. (Show the Nike returns on the vertical axis and the S&P 500 Index returns on the horizontal axis as done in Figure 6-5.)

d. From your graph, describe the nature of the relationship between Nike stock returns and the returns for the S&P 500 Index.

**6-15.** (*Capital asset pricing model*) Using the CAPM, estimate the appropriate required rate of return for the three stocks listed here, given that the risk-free rate is 5 percent and the expected return for the market is 12 percent.

$$\bar{r}_a = r_f + \beta_a (\bar{r}_m - r_f) \qquad CAPM$$

$$5 + 0.75(12 - 5)$$

| STOCK | BETA |
|---|---|
| A | 0.75 |
| B | 0.90 |
| C | 1.40 |

**6-16.** (*Expected return, standard deviation, and the Capital Asset Pricing Model*) Below you have been provided the prices for Merck and the S&P 500 Index.

|  | MERCK | S&P 500 INDEX |
|---|---|---|
| **2011** | | |
| June | $32.27 | $1,320.64 |
| July | 32.75 | 1,292.28 |
| August | 30.87 | 1,218.89 |
| September | 29.49 | 1,131.42 |
| October | 31.83 | 1,253.30 |
| November | 29.59 | 1,246.96 |
| December | 30.33 | 1,257.60 |
| **2012** | | |
| January | 31.60 | 1,312.41 |
| February | 35.74 | 1,365.68 |
| March | 36.90 | 1,408.47 |
| April | 41.02 | 1,397.91 |
| May | 39.19 | 1,310.33 |
| June | 42.50 | 1,355.69 |

a. Calculate the monthly holding-period returns for Merck and the S&P 500 Index.
b. What are the average monthly returns and standard deviations for each?
c. Graph the Merck returns against the S&P 500 Index returns.
d. Use a spreadsheet to compute the slope of the characteristic line.
e. Interpret your findings.

**6-17.** (*Security market line*)

a. Determine the expected return and beta for the following portfolio:

| STOCK | PERCENTAGE OF PORTFOLIO | BETA | EXPECTED RETURN |
|---|---|---|---|
| 1 | 40% | 1.00 | 12% |
| 2 | 25 | 0.75 | 11 |
| 3 | 35 | 1.30 | 15 |

b. Given the foregoing information, draw the security market line and show where the securities and portfolio fit on the graph. Assume that the risk-free rate is 2 percent and that the expected return on the market portfolio is 8 percent. How would you interpret these findings?

**6-18.** (*Required rate of return using CAPM*)

a. Compute a fair rate of return for Intel common stock, which has a 1.2 beta. The risk-free rate is 2 percent, and the market portfolio (New York Stock Exchange stocks) has an expected return of 11 percent.
b. Why is the rate you computed a fair rate?

**6-19.** (*Estimating beta*) From the graph in the margin relating the holding-period returns for Aram Inc. to the S&P 500 Index, estimate the firm's beta.

**6-20.** (*Capital asset pricing model*) Levine Manufacturing Inc. is considering several investments. The rate on Treasury bills is currently 2.75 percent, and the expected return for the market is 12 percent. What should be the required rates of return for each investment (using the CAPM)?

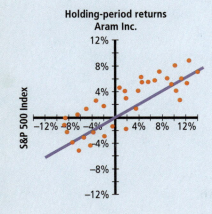

**Holding-period returns Aram Inc.**

| SECURITY | BETA |
|---|---|
| A | 1.50 |
| B | 0.90 |
| C | 0.70 |
| D | 1.15 |

**6-21.** (*Capital asset pricing model*) MFI Inc. has a beta of 0.86. If the expected market return is 11.5 percent and the risk-free rate is 3 percent, what is the appropriate required return of MFI (using the CAPM)?

**6-22.** (*Capital asset pricing model*) The expected return for the general market is 12.8 percent, and the risk premium in the market is 9.3 percent. Tasaco, LBM, and Exxos have betas of 0.864, 0.693, and 0.575, respectively. What are the corresponding required rates of return for the three securities?

**6-23.** (*Portfolio beta and security market line*) You own a portfolio consisting of the stocks below:

| STOCK | PERCENTAGE OF PORTFOLIO | BETA | EXPECTED RETURN |
|---|---|---|---|
| 1 | 20% | 1.00 | 12% |
| 2 | 30 | 0.85 | 8 |
| 3 | 15 | 1.20 | 12 |
| 4 | 25 | 0.60 | 7 |
| 5 | 10 | 1.60 | 16 |

The risk-free rate is 3 percent. Also, the expected return on the market portfolio is 11 percent.

a. Calculate the expected return of your portfolio. (*Hint:* The expected return of a portfolio equals the weighted average of the individual stocks' expected returns, where the weights are the percentage invested in each stock.)
b. Calculate the portfolio beta.
c. Given the foregoing information, plot the security market line on paper. Plot the stocks from your portfolio on your graph.
d. From your plot in part (c), which stocks appear to be your winners and which ones appear to be losers?
e. Why should you consider your conclusion in part (d) to be less than certain?

**6-24.** (*Portfolio beta*) Assume you have the following portfolio.

| | STOCK WEIGHT | BETA |
|---|---|---|
| Apple | 38% | 1.50 |
| Green Mountain Coffee | 15% | 1.44 |
| Disney | 27% | 1.15 |
| Target | 20% | 1.20 |

What is the portfolio's beta?

# Mini Case

*This Mini Case is available in* MyFinanceLab.
*Note:* Although not absolutely necessary, you are advised to use a computer spreadsheet to work the following problem.

a. Use the price data from the table that follows for the Standard & Poor's 500 Index, Wal-mart, and Target to calculate the holding-period returns for the 24 months from July 2010 through June 2012.

| MONTH | S&P 500 | WAL-MART | TARGET |
|---|---|---|---|
| June-10 | $1,030.71 | $48.07 | $49.17 |
| Jul-10 | 1,101.60 | 51.19 | 51.32 |
| Aug-10 | 1,049.33 | 50.14 | 51.16 |
| Sep-10 | 1,141.20 | 53.52 | 53.44 |
| Oct-10 | 1,183.26 | 54.17 | 51.94 |
| Nov-10 | 1,180.55 | 54.09 | 56.94 |
| Dec-10 | 1,257.64 | 53.93 | 60.13 |
| Jan-11 | 1,286.12 | 56.07 | 54.83 |
| Feb-11 | 1,327.22 | 51.98 | 52.55 |
| Mar-11 | 1,325.83 | 52.05 | 50.01 |
| Apr-11 | 1,363.61 | 54.98 | 49.10 |
| May-11 | 1,345.20 | 55.22 | 49.53 |
| Jun-11 | 1,320.64 | 53.14 | 46.91 |
| Jul-11 | 1,292.28 | 52.71 | 51.49 |
| Aug-11 | 1,218.89 | 53.19 | 51.67 |
| Sep-11 | 1,131.42 | 51.90 | 49.04 |
| Oct-11 | 1,253.30 | 56.72 | 54.75 |
| Nov-11 | 1,246.96 | 58.90 | 52.70 |
| Dec-11 | 1,257.60 | 59.76 | 51.22 |
| Jan-12 | 1,312.41 | 61.36 | 50.81 |
| Feb-12 | 1,365.68 | 59.08 | 56.69 |
| Mar-12 | 1,408.47 | 61.20 | 58.27 |
| Apr-12 | 1,397.91 | 58.91 | 57.94 |
| May-12 | 1,310.33 | 65.82 | 57.91 |
| Jun-12 | 1,355.69 | 67.70 | 57.40 |

b. Calculate the average monthly holding-period returns and the standard deviation of these returns for the S&P 500 Index, Wal-mart, and Target.

c. Plot (1) the holding-period returns for Wal-mart against the Standard & Poor's 500 Index, and (2) the Target holding-period returns against the Standard & Poor's 500 Index. (Use Figure 6-5 as the format for your graph.)

d. From your graphs in part (c), describe the nature of the relationship between the stock returns for Wal-mart and the returns for the S&P 500 Index. Make the same comparison for Target.

e. Assume that you have decided to invest one-half of your money in Wal-mart and the remainder in Target. Calculate the monthly holding-period returns for your two-stock portfolio. (*Hint:* The monthly return for the portfolio is the average of the two stocks' monthly returns.)

f. Plot the returns of your two-stock portfolio against the Standard & Poor's 500 Index as you did for the individual stocks in part (c). How does this graph compare to the graphs for the individual stocks? Explain the difference.

g. The following table shows the returns on an *annualized* basis that were realized from holding long-term government bonds for the same period. Calculate the average *monthly* holding-period returns and the standard deviations of these returns. (*Hint:* You will need to convert the annual returns to monthly returns by dividing each return by 12 months.)

| MONTH AND YEAR | ANNUALIZED RATE OF RETURN |
|---|---|
| Jun-10 | 4.03% |
| Jul-10 | 3.71% |
| Aug-10 | 3.82% |
| Sep-10 | 3.35% |
| Oct-10 | 3.40% |
| Nov-10 | 3.66% |
| Dec-10 | 3.95% |
| Jan-11 | 4.18% |
| Feb-11 | 4.37% |
| Mar-11 | 4.24% |
| Apr-11 | 4.27% |
| May-11 | 4.14% |
| Jun-11 | 3.83% |
| Jul-11 | 4.12% |
| Aug-11 | 3.72% |
| Sep-11 | 3.10% |
| Oct-11 | 2.51% |
| Nov-11 | 2.73% |
| Dec-11 | 2.82% |
| Jan-12 | 2.67% |
| Feb-12 | 2.65% |
| Mar-12 | 2.80% |
| Apr-12 | 3.00% |
| May-12 | 2.76% |
| Jun-12 | 2.13% |

h. Now assuming that you have decided to invest equal amounts of money in Wal-mart, Target, and long-term government securities, calculate the monthly returns for your three-asset portfolio. What is the average return and the standard deviation?

i. Make a comparison of the average returns and the standard deviations for all the individual assets and the two portfolios that we designed. What conclusions can be reached by your comparison?

j. According to Standard & Poor's, the betas for Wal-mart and Target are 0.45 and 0.60, respectively. Compare the meaning of these betas relative to the standard deviations calculated above.

k. Assume that the current Treasury bill rate is 3 percent and that the expected market return is 10 percent. Given the betas for Wal-mart and Target in part (j), estimate an appropriate rate of return for the two firms.

# The Valuation and Characteristics of Bonds

## Learning Objectives

**1** **Distinguish** between different kinds of bonds.

Types of Bonds

**2** **Explain** the more popular features of bonds.

Terminology and Characteristics of Bonds

**3** **Define** the term *value* as used for several different purposes.

Defining Value

**4** **Explain** the factors that determine value.

What Determines Value?

**5** **Describe** the basic process for valuing assets.

Valuation: The Basic Process

**6** **Estimate** the value of a bond.

Valuing Bonds

**7** **Compute** a bond's expected rate of return and its current yield.

Bond Yields

**8** **Explain** three important relationships that exist in bond valuation.

Bond Valuation: Three Important Relationships

On August 16, 2011, the headlines read, "AT&T Sells $5 Billion of Bonds to Help Refinance Maturing Debt." Bonds are a form of long-term debt issued by companies needing financing for a variety of reasons, including the need to repay debt that is coming due, as was the case for AT&T when it issued the $5 billion in new bonds. Some of the bonds matured in 5 years, some in 10 years, and others not until 30 years. Just 3 months earlier the company had issued $3 billion in bonds. Then in June 2012 the company decided to issue more bonds in the amount of $2 billion. Although few companies could begin to issue billions of dollars in bonds as AT&T does, this form of debt is an important source of financing for many publicly traded companies. Companies were particularly tempted to issue bonds in 2011 and

2012 when interest rates were at all-time lows. AT&T, for example, only had to pay about 3 percent in interest on bonds that were being issued in 2011 and 2012.

When AT&T's management was deciding to issue bonds, there were a number of decisions that had to be made, such as the type of bond—not all bonds are the same—and the terms to be offered to the investors. Then there is always the issue of valuing the bond.

Understanding how to value financial securities is essential if managers are to meet the objective of maximizing the value of the firm. If they are to maximize the investors' value, they must know what drives the value of an asset. Specifically, they need to understand how bonds and stocks are valued in the marketplace; otherwise, they cannot act in the best interest of the firm's investors.

In this chapter, we begin by identifying the different kinds of bonds. We next look at the features or characteristics of most bonds. We then examine the concepts of and procedures for valuing an asset and apply these ideas to valuing bonds.

We now begin our study by considering the different kinds of bonds.

## Types of Bonds

A **bond** is a *type of debt or long-term promissory note, issued by the borrower, promising to pay its holder a predetermined and fixed amount of interest per year and the face value of the bond at maturity*. However, there is a wide variety of such creatures. Just to mention a few, we have

| | |
|---|---|
| Debentures | Eurobonds |
| Subordinated debentures | Convertible bonds |
| Mortgage bonds | |

The following sections briefly explain each of these types of bonds.

### Debentures

The term **debenture** applies to *any unsecured long-term debt*. Because these bonds are unsecured, the earning ability of the issuing corporation is of great concern to the bondholder. They are also viewed as being more risky than secured bonds and, as a result, must provide investors with a higher yield than secured bonds provide. Often the firm issuing debentures attempts to provide some protection to the holder of the debenture by agreeing not to issue more secured long-term debt that would further tie up the firm's assets. To the issuing firm, the major advantage of debentures is that no property has to be secured by them. This allows the firm to issue debt and still preserve some future borrowing power.

 Distinguish between different kinds of bonds.

**bond** a long-term (10-year or more) promissory note issued by the borrower, promising to pay the owner of the security a predetermined, fixed amount of interest each year.

**debenture** any unsecured long-term debt.

221

## Subordinated Debentures

**subordinated debenture** a debenture that is subordinated to other debentures in terms of its payments in case of insolvency.

Many firms have more than one issue of debentures outstanding. In this case a hierarchy may be specified, in which some debentures are given *subordinated standing in case of insolvency*. The claims of the **subordinated debentures** are honored only after the claims of secured debt and unsubordinated debentures have been satisfied.

## Mortgage Bonds

**mortgage bond** a bond secured by a lien on real property.

A **mortgage bond** is a *bond secured by a lien on real property*. Typically, the value of the real property is greater than that of the mortgage bonds issued. This provides the mortgage bondholders with a margin of safety in the event the market value of the secured property declines. In the case of foreclosure, *trustees*, who represent the bondholders and act on their behalf, have the power to sell the secured property and use the proceeds to pay the bondholders. The bond trustee, usually a banking institution or trust company, oversees the relationship between the bondholder and the issuing firm, protecting the bondholder and seeing that the terms of the indenture are carried out. In the event that the proceeds from this sale do not cover the bonds, the bondholders become general creditors, similar to debenture bondholders, for the unpaid portion of the debt.

## Eurobonds

**Eurobond** a bond issued in a country different from the one in which the currency of the bond is denominated; for example, a bond issued in Europe or Asia by an American company that pays interest and principal to the lender in U.S. dollars.

**Eurobonds** are not so much a different type of security. They are simply securities, in this case *bonds, issued in a country different from the one in which the currency of the bond is denominated*. For example, a bond that is issued in Europe or in Asia by an American company and that pays interest and principal to the lender in U.S. dollars would be considered a Eurobond. Thus, even if the bond is not issued in Europe, it merely needs to be sold in a country different from the one in which the bond's currency is denominated to be considered a Eurobond.

The primary attractions of Eurobonds to borrowers, aside from favorable rates, are the relative lack of regulation (Eurobonds are not registered with the Securities and Exchange Commission [SEC]), less-rigorous disclosure requirements than those of the SEC, and the speed with which they can be issued. Interestingly, not only are Eurobonds not registered with the SEC, but they may not be offered to U.S. citizens and residents.

## Convertible Bonds

**convertible bond** a debt security that can be converted into a firm's stock at a prespecified price.

**Convertible bonds** are debt securities that can be converted into a firm's stock at a prespecified price. For instance, you might have a convertible bond with a face, or par, value of $1,000 that pays 6 percent interest, or $60, each year. The bond matures in 5 years, at which time the company must pay the $1,000 par value to the bondholder. However, at the time the bond was issued, the firm gave the bondholder the option of either collecting the $1,000 or receiving shares of the firm's stock at a conversion price of $50. In other words, the bondholder would receive 20 shares (20 = $1,000 par value ÷ $50 conversion price). What would you do if you were the bondholder? If the stock were selling for more than $50, then you would want to give up the $1,000 par value and take the stock. Thus, it's the investor's choice either to take the $1,000 promised when the bond was issued or to convert the bond into the firm's stock.

Consider Ingersoll Rand Company, a diversified equipment manufacturer. In 2009, the firm issued $300 million of 5 percent convertible debt. The bonds can be converted at any time into Ingersoll Rand common stock at a conversion price of $17.94 per share. Because the par value for each bond is $1,000, a bondholder can convert one bond into 55.74 shares (55.74 shares = $1,000 ÷ $17.94 price per share). This option allows the investor to be repaid the $1,000 par value or to convert into stock if the total value of the stock exceeds $1,000. Thus, with convertible bonds, the investor gets to participate in the upside if the company does well. For instance, 3 months after the bonds were issued, the firm's stock was selling for $27. If you had been an investor, you could have converted the bonds into 55.74 shares of stock, which would be worth about $1,500. Not bad for 3 months.

Now that you have an understanding of the kinds of bonds firms might issue, let's look at some of the characteristics and terminology of bonds.

## Concept Check

1. How do debentures, subordinated debentures, and mortgage bonds differ with regard to their risk? How would investors respond to the varying types of risk?
2. How is a Eurobond different from a bond issued in Asia that is denominated in dollars?
3. Why would a convertible bond increase much more in value than a bond that is not convertible?

# Terminology and Characteristics of Bonds

**2** Explain the more popular features of bonds.

Before valuing bonds, we first need to understand the terminology related to bonds. Then we will be better prepared to determine the value of a bond.

When a firm or nonprofit institution needs financing, one source is bonds. As already noted, this type of financing instrument is simply a long-term promissory note, issued by the borrower, promising to pay its holder a predetermined and fixed amount of interest each year. Some of the more important terms and characteristics that you might hear about bonds are as follows:

Claims on assets and income    Call provision
Par value                      Indenture
Coupon interest rate           Bond ratings
Maturity

Let's consider each in turn.

## Claims on Assets and Income

In the case of insolvency, claims of debt, including bonds, are generally honored before those of both common stock and preferred stock. In general, if the interest on bonds is not paid, the bond trustees can classify the firm as insolvent and force it into bankruptcy. Thus, the bondholders' claim on income is more likely to be honored than that of the common stockholders, whose dividends are paid at the discretion of the firm's management. However, different types of debt can have a hierarchy among themselves as to the order of their claims on assets.

## Par Value

The **par value** of a bond is its *face value, which is returned to the bondholder at maturity*. In general, corporate bonds are issued in denominations of $1,000, although there are some exceptions to this rule. Also, when bond prices are quoted, either by financial managers or in the financial press, prices are generally expressed as a percentage of the bond's par value. For example, a Morgan Stanley bond was recently quoted as selling for $103.83. That does not mean you can buy the bond for $103.83. It means that this bond is selling for 103.83 percent of its par value of $1,000. Hence, the market price of this bond is actually $1,038.30. At maturity in 2017, the bondholder will receive $1,000.

**par value** on the face of a bond, the stated amount that the firm is to repay upon the maturity date.

## Coupon Interest Rate

The **coupon interest rate** on a bond indicates the *percentage of the par value of the bond that will be paid out annually in the form of interest*. Thus, regardless of what happens to the price of a bond with a 5 percent coupon interest rate and a $1,000 par value, it will pay out $50 annually in interest until maturity (0.05 × $1,000 = $50). For the Morgan Stanley bonds, the coupon rate is 5.95 percent; thus an investor owning the bonds would receive 5.95 percent of its par value of $1,000, or $59.50 ($59.50 = 0.0595 × $1,000) per year. The investor receives a fixed dollar income each year from the interest; thus, these bonds are called **fixed-rate bonds**.

**coupon interest rate** the interest rate contractually owed on a bond as a percent of its par value.

**fixed-rate bond** a bond that pays a fixed amount of interest to the investor each year.

**zero coupon bond** a bond issued at a substantial discount from its $1,000 face value and that pays little or no interest.

Occasionally, a firm will issue bonds that have zero or very low coupon rates, thus the name **zero coupon bonds.** Instead of paying interest, the company sells the bonds at a substantial discount below the $1,000 par or face value. Thus, the investor receives a large part (or all with zero coupon bonds) of the return from the appreciation of the bond value as it moves in time to maturity. For example, Amgen, the biotech company, issued $3.95 billion face value bonds with a coupon rate of only 1/8th of 1 percent. Thus, the investors would hardly receive any interest income. But the bonds were issued to the investors at $500 for each $1,000 face value bond. Investors who purchased these bonds for $500 could hold them until they mature and would then receive the $1,000 par value.

## Maturity

**maturity** the length of time until the bond issuer returns the par value to the bondholder and terminates the bond.

The **maturity** of a bond indicates *the length of time until the bond issuer returns the par value to the bondholder and terminates or redeems the bond.*

## Call Provision

**callable bond (redeemable bond)** an option available to a company issuing a bond whereby the issuer can call (redeem) the bond before it matures. This is usually done if interest rates decline below what the firm is paying on the bond.

**call protection period** a prespecified time period during which a company cannot recall a bond.

If a company issues bonds and then later the prevailing interest rate declines, the firm may want to pay off the bonds early and then issue new bonds with a lower interest rate. To do so, the bond must be **callable**, or **redeemable**; otherwise, the firm cannot force the bondholder to accept early payment. The issuer, however, usually must pay the bondholders a premium, such as 1 year's interest. Also, there frequently is a **call protection period** where the firm cannot call the bond for a prespecified time period.

## Indenture

**indenture** the legal agreement between the firm issuing bonds and the bond trustee who represents the bondholders, providing the specific terms of the loan agreement.

An **indenture** is the *legal agreement between the firm issuing the bonds and the trustee who represents the bondholders.* The indenture provides the specific terms of the loan agreement, including a description of the bonds, the rights of the bondholders, the rights of the issuing firm, and the responsibilities of the trustee. This legal document may run 100 pages or more in length, with the majority of it devoted to defining protective provisions for the bondholder.

Typically, the restrictive provisions included in the indenture attempt to protect the bondholders' financial position relative to that of other outstanding securities. Common provisions involve (1) prohibiting the sale of the firm's accounts receivable, (2) limiting common stock dividends, (3) restricting the purchase or sale of the firm's fixed assets, and (4) setting limits on additional borrowing by the firm. Not allowing the sale of accounts receivable is specified because such sales would benefit the firm's short-run liquidity position at the expense of its future liquidity position. Common stock dividends may not be allowed if the firm's liquidity falls below a specified level, or the maximum dividend payout might be limited to some fraction, say, 50 or 60 percent of earnings. Fixed-asset restrictions generally require permission before they can be liquidated or used as collateral on new loans. Constraints on additional borrowing usually involve limiting the amount and type of additional long-term debt that can be issued. All these restrictions have one thing in common: They attempt to prohibit actions that would improve the status of other securities at the expense of bonds and to protect the status of bonds from being weakened by any managerial action.

## Bond Ratings

John Moody first began to rate bonds in 1909. Since that time three rating agencies—Moody's, Standard & Poor's, and Fitch Investor Services—have provided ratings on corporate bonds. These ratings involve a judgment about the future risk potential of the bonds. Although they deal with expectations, several historical factors seem to play a significant role in their determination. Bond ratings are favorably affected by (1) a greater reliance on equity as opposed to debt in financing the firm, (2) profitable operations, (3) a low variability in past earnings, (4) large firm

> **REMEMBER YOUR PRINCIPLES**
>
> **P**rinciple  When we say that a lower bond rating means a higher interest rate charged by the investors (bondholders), we are observing an application of **Principle 3: Risk Requires a Reward.**

**TABLE 7-1  Standard & Poor's Corporate Bond Ratings**

| | |
|---|---|
| AAA | This is the highest rating assigned by Standard & Poor's for debt obligation and indicates an extremely strong capacity to pay principal and interest. |
| AA | Bonds rated AA also qualify as high-quality debt obligations. Their capacity to pay principal and interest is very strong; in the majority of instances, they differ from AAA issues only by a small degree. |
| A | Bonds rated A have a strong capacity to pay principal and interest, although they are somewhat more susceptible to the adverse effects of changes in circumstances and economic conditions. |
| BBB | Bonds rated BBB are regarded as having an adequate capacity to pay principal and interest. Whereas they normally exhibit adequate protection parameters, adverse economic conditions or changing circumstances are more likely to lead to a weakened capacity to pay principal and interest for bonds in this category than for bonds in the A category. |
| BB<br>B<br>CCC<br>CC | Bonds rated BB, B, CCC, and CC are regarded, on balance, as predominantly speculative with respect to the issuer's capacity to pay interest and repay principal in accordance with the terms of the obligation. BB indicates the lowest degree of speculation and CC the highest. Although such bonds will likely have some quality and protective characteristics, these are outweighed by large uncertainties or major risk exposures to adverse conditions. |
| C | The rating C is reserved for income bonds on which no interest is being paid. |
| D | Bonds rated D are in default, and payment of principal and/or interest is in arrears. |

Plus (+) or Minus (−): To provide more detailed indications of credit quality, the ratings from AA to BB may be modified by the addition of a plus or minus sign to show relative standing within the major rating categories.

Source: Adapted from www.standardandpoors.com, December 2005.

size, and (5) little use of subordinated debt. In turn, the rating a bond receives affects the interest rate demanded on the bond by the investors. The poorer the bond rating, the higher the interest rate demanded by investors. (Table 7-1 describes these ratings.) Thus, bond ratings are extremely important for the financial manager. They provide an indicator of default risk that in turn affects the interest rate that must be paid on borrowed funds.

Toward the bottom end of the rating spectrum, we have **junk bonds**, which are high-risk debt with *ratings of BB or below* by Moody's and Standard & Poor's. The lower the rating, the higher the chance of default. The lowest rating is CC for Standard & Poor's

**junk bond** any bond rated BB or below.

# FINANCE AT WORK

## J.C. PENNEY CREDIT RATING REDUCED TO JUNK

In March 2012, J.C. Penney reported that it had a net loss of $163 million in the first quarter of the year, mainly due to the firm's new pricing strategy for its products. The plan eliminated Penney's practice of frequent sales in favor of everyday prices that were 40 percent below the sales prices the year before. Penney's customers, accustomed to big markdowns and coupons, resisted the new approach. The outcome was a 20-percent reduction in revenues.

As a consequence, in May Standard & Poor's announced it was cutting Penney's credit rating from BB+ to BB, which is a rating category for junk bonds. Fitch, another rating agency, also lowered the firm's credit ratings to junk.

The two rating agencies attributed the cut to poor performance in the first quarter of the year. In addition, S&P placed all of Penney's bonds on CreditWatch "with negative implications." The CreditWatch indicates that the rating was vulnerable to a further downgrade after Standard & Poor's reassessed the company's business and financial strategies.

Then in June, Mike Francis, the new president and a former Target executive, left the company unexpectedly. Francis was in charge of marketing the new pricing strategy.

One month later in July, Standard & Poor's further lowered Penney's credit rating from BB to B+, which means that the rating agency believes that the firm may have difficulty not only in paying interest, but also repaying the debt principal as it comes due. An even bigger issue was the growing concern that management may not be able to turn the business around.

In the meantime, Penney's stock fell by half in a mere five months. Only time will tell if the business can be saved.

Sources: Lance Murray, "J.C. Penney's Credit Rating Cut Again by S&P," *Dallas Business Journal*, http://cxa.gtm.idmanagedsolutions.com/finra/BondCenter/BondDetail.aspx?ID=NTk0OTE4QU02, accessed June 26, 2012; "S&P Cuts J.C. Penney Rating to 'BB'/, Reuters, http://www.reuters.com/article/2012/05/17/idUSWNA755420120517, accessed June 26, 2012; and Melodie Warner, "S&P Cuts J.C. Penney Rating to Junk," Market Watch, *Wall Street Journal*, http://www.marketwatch.com/story/sp-cuts-jc-penney-rating-to-junk-2012-03-07, assessed June 26, 2012, and http://www.kansascity.com/2012/07/11/3701158/sp-cuts-jc-penney-credit-rating.html#storylink=cpy, accessed August 15, 2012.

**high-yield bond** see junk bond.

and Ca for Moody's. Originally, the term *junk bonds* was used to describe firms with sound financial histories that were facing severe financial problems and suffering from poor credit ratings. Junk bonds are also called **high-yield bonds** because of the high interest rates they pay the investor. Typically, they have an interest rate between 3 and 5 percent more than AAA-grade long-term debt.

Until the early 1970s, credit-rating agencies were paid by the investors who wanted impartial information about a firm's creditworthiness. But beginning in the 1970s, the firms issuing bonds began paying the agencies for their services. This arrangement has frequently raised a concern that the agencies have a conflict of interest, where the company being evaluated is also their client. This criticism became particularly loud during the financial crisis beginning in 2007. The agencies gave some types of debt securities high ratings, only for them to default when the borrower could no longer pay on the loan.

We are now ready to think about bond valuation. To begin, we must first clarify precisely what we mean by *value*. Next, we need to understand the basic concepts of valuation and the process for valuing an asset. Then we may apply these concepts to valuing a bond, and in Chapter 8, to valuing stocks.

> **REMEMBER YOUR PRINCIPLES**
>
> **P**rinciple  Some have thought junk bonds were fundamentally different from other securities, but they are not. They are bonds with a great amount of risk and, therefore, promise high expected returns. Thus, **Principle 3: Risk Requires a Reward**.

## Concept Check

1. What are some important features of a bond? Which features determine the cash flows associated with a bond?
2. What restrictions are typically included in an indenture in order to protect the bondholder?
3. How does the bond rating affect an investor's required rate of return? What actions could a firm take to receive a more favorable rating?

**LO3** Define the term *value* as used for several different purposes.

**book value** (1) the value of an asset as shown on the firm's balance sheet. It represents the historical cost of the asset rather than its current market value or replacement cost. (2) The depreciated value of a company's assets (original cost less accumulated depreciation) less outstanding liabilities.

**liquidation value** the dollar sum that could be realized if an asset were sold.

**market value** the value observed in the marketplace.

**intrinsic, or economic, value** the present value of an asset's expected future cash flows. This value is the amount the investor considers to be fair value, given the amount, timing, and riskiness of future cash flows.

**fair value** the present value of an asset's expected future cash flows.

# Defining Value

The term *value* is often used in different contexts, depending on its application. **Book value** is the *value of an asset as shown on a firm's balance sheet*. It represents the historical cost of the asset rather than its current worth. For instance, the book value of a company's common stock is the amount the investors originally paid for the stock and, therefore, the amount the firm received when the stock was issued.

**Liquidation value** is the *dollar sum that could be realized if an asset were sold individually and not as part of a going concern*. For example, if a firm's operations were discontinued and its assets were divided up and sold, the sales price would represent the asset's liquidation value.

The **market value** of an asset is the *observed value for the asset in the marketplace*. This value is determined by supply and demand forces working together in the marketplace, whereby buyers and sellers negotiate a mutually acceptable price for the asset. For instance, the market price for Harley-Davidson's common stock on June 20, 2012, was $50 per share. This price was reached by a large number of buyers and sellers working through the New York Stock Exchange. In theory, a market price exists for all assets. However, many assets have no readily observable market price because trading seldom occurs. For instance, the market price for the common stock of Liberty Capital Bank, a new bank in Dallas, Texas, would be more difficult to establish than the market value of Harley-Davidson's common stock.

The **intrinsic, or economic, value** of an asset—also called the **fair value**—is the *present value of the asset's expected future cash flows*. This value is the amount an investor should be willing to pay for the asset given the amount, timing, and riskiness of its future cash flows. Once the investor has estimated the intrinsic value of a security, this value could be compared with its market value when available. If the intrinsic value is greater than the market value, then the security is undervalued in the eyes of the investor. Should the market value exceed the investor's intrinsic value, then the security is overvalued.

We hasten to add that if the securities market is working efficiently, the market value and the intrinsic value of a security will be equal. Whenever a security's intrinsic value differs from its current market price, the competition among investors seeking opportunities to make a profit will quickly drive the market price back to its intrinsic value. Thus, we may define an **efficient market** as one in which *the values of all securities at any instant fully reflect all available public information*, which results in the market value and the intrinsic value being the same. If the markets are efficient, it is extremely difficult for an investor to make extra profits from an ability to predict prices.

**efficient market** market where the values of all securities fully recognize all available public information.

Should we expect markets to be efficient or inefficient? For a market to be inefficient, there would need to be a trading strategy that allows investors to make money without assuming a proportionate amount of risk. But for that to happen, there must be traders who are willing to sell underpriced stocks to you and buy overpriced stocks from you. Instead, if you buy a stock because you believe it to be underpriced, the investor selling the stock must believe it is overpriced. Furthermore, if there were a strategy that allowed you to make profits without assuming risk, then other investors would adopt the strategy until the opportunity to make excess profits would disappear.

The market could be inefficient because investors act irrationally. For this reason, financial economists have been interested in studying to see if investors are rational in their investment behavior. Competitive markets assume that investors act rationally in their decisions. Thus, the field of **behavioral finance** studies the rationality of investors when making decisions. For example, they suggest that some investors may be overconfident in their own opinions when making investments and ignore information that becomes available if it does not support their own opinion.

**behavioral finance** the field of study examining when investors act rationally or irrationally when making investment decisions.

What does the evidence suggest about market efficiency? There have been thousands of studies testing for market efficiency over the past several decades. Some of the studies found evidence that the markets have at times been somewhat inefficient. However, with time these anomalies have been largely eliminated by professional investors who seek out such opportunities. Thus, we would agree that the markets are certainly not perfectly efficient, but any such inefficiencies probably only provide enough return to cover the cost of implementing a given strategy. But no doubt this issue will continue to cause debate in the years ahead.

> **REMEMBER YOUR PRINCIPLES**
>
> **Principle** The fact that investors have difficulty identifying stocks that are undervalued relates to **Principle 4: Market Prices Are Generally Right**. In an efficient market, the price reflects all available public information about the security and, therefore, it is priced fairly.

## Concept Check

1. Explain the different types of value.
2. Why should the market value equal the intrinsic value?

# What Determines Value?

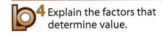

4 Explain the factors that determine value.

For our purposes, *the value of an asset is its intrinsic value or the present value of its expected future cash flows*, when these cash flows are discounted back to the present using the investor's required rate of return. This statement is true for valuing all assets, and it serves as the basis of almost all that we do in finance. Thus, value is affected by three elements:

1. The amount and timing of the asset's expected cash flows
2. The riskiness of these cash flows
3. The investor's required rate of return for undertaking the investment

The first two factors are characteristics of the asset. The third one, the required rate of return, is the minimum rate of return necessary to attract an investor to purchase or hold a security. This rate of return is determined by *the rates of return available on similar investments*, or what we learned in Chapter 2 is called the opportunity cost of funds. This rate must be high enough to compensate the investor for risk perceived in the asset's future cash flows. (The required rate of return was explained in Chapter 6.)

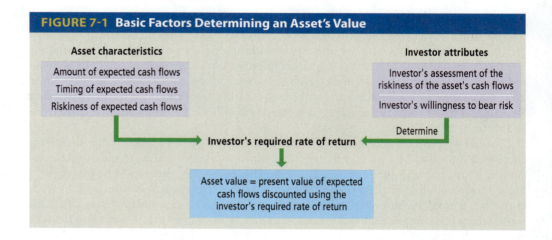

**FIGURE 7-1  Basic Factors Determining an Asset's Value**

Asset characteristics

Amount of expected cash flows
Timing of expected cash flows
Riskiness of expected cash flows

Investor attributes

Investor's assessment of the riskiness of the asset's cash flows
Investor's willingness to bear risk

Determine

Investor's required rate of return

Asset value = present value of expected cash flows discounted using the investor's required rate of return

## REMEMBER YOUR PRINCIPLES

**Principle**  Our discussions should remind us of three of our principles that help us understand finance:

**Principle 1: Cash Flow Is What Matters.**
**Principle 2: Money Has a Time Value.**
**Principle 3: Risk Requires a Reward.**

Determining the economic worth or value of an asset always relies on these three principles. Without them, we would have no basis for explaining value. With them, we can know that the amount and timing of cash, not earnings, drive value. Also, we must be rewarded for taking risk; otherwise, we will not invest.

Figure 7-1 depicts the basic factors involved in valuation. As the figure shows, finding the value of an asset involves the following steps:

1. Assessing the asset's characteristics, which include the amount and timing of the expected cash flows and the riskiness of these cash flows

2. Determining the investor's required rate of return, which embodies the investor's attitude about assuming risk and the investor's perception of the riskiness of the asset

3. Discounting the expected cash flows back to the present, using the investor's required rate of return as the discount rate

Thus, intrinsic value is a function of the cash flows yet to be received, the riskiness of these cash flows, and the investor's required rate of return.

## Concept Check

1. What are the three important elements of asset valuation?

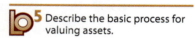
5 Describe the basic process for valuing assets.

# Valuation: The Basic Process

The valuation process can be described as follows: It is assigning value to an asset by calculating the present value of its expected future cash flows using the investor's required rate of return as the discount rate. The investor's required rate of return, $r$, is determined by the level of the risk-free rate of interest and risk premium that the investor feels is necessary compensation. Therefore, a basic asset valuation model can be defined mathematically as follows:

$$\frac{\text{Asset}}{\text{value}} = \frac{\text{cash flow in year 1}}{\left(1 + \frac{\text{required}}{\text{rate of return}}\right)^1} + \frac{\text{cash flow in year 2}}{\left(1 + \frac{\text{required}}{\text{rate of return}}\right)^2} + \cdots + \frac{\text{cash flow in year } n}{\left(1 + \frac{\text{required}}{\text{rate of return}}\right)^n} \quad (7\text{-}1a)$$

Or stated in symbols, we have:

$$V = \frac{C_1}{(1 + r)^1} + \frac{C_2}{(1 + r)^2} + \cdots + \frac{C_n}{(1 + r)^n} \quad (7\text{-}1b)$$

where $V$ = the intrinsic value, or present value, of an asset producing expected future cash flows, $C_t$, in years 1 through $n$

$C_t$ = cash flow to be received at time $t$

$r$ = the investor's required rate of return

Using equation (7-1), there are three basic steps in the valuation process:

**STEP 1**   Estimate the $C_t$ in equation (7-1), which is the amount and timing of the future cash flows the security is expected to provide.

**STEP 2**   Determine $r$, the investor's required rate of return.

**STEP 3**   Calculate the intrinsic value, $V$, as the present value of expected future cash flows discounted at the investor's required rate of return.

Equation (7-1), which measures the present value of future cash flows, is the basis of the valuation process. It is the most important equation in this chapter because all the remaining equations in this chapter and in Chapter 8 are merely reformulations of this one equation. If we understand equation (7-1), all the valuation work we do, and a host of other topics as well, will be much clearer in our minds.

With the foregoing principles of valuation as our foundation, let's now look at how bonds are valued.

## Valuing Bonds

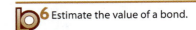 6 Estimate the value of a bond.

The value of a bond is the present value of both the future interest to be received and the par or maturity value of the bond. It's that simple.

The process for valuing a bond, as depicted in Figure 7-2, requires knowing three essential elements: (1) the amount and timing of the cash flows to be received by the investor, (2) the time to maturity of the bond, and (3) the investor's required rate of return. The amount of cash flows is dictated by the periodic interest to be received and by the par value to be paid at maturity. Given these elements, we can compute the value of the bond, or the present value.

To illustrate the process for valuing a bond, consider a bond issued by Pioneer Natural Resources with a maturity date of 2016 and a stated annual coupon rate of 5.875 percent.[1]

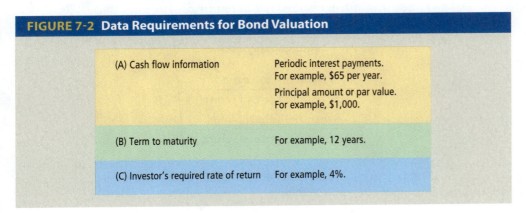

**FIGURE 7-2**  **Data Requirements for Bond Valuation**

| | |
|---|---|
| (A) Cash flow information | Periodic interest payments. For example, $65 per year. |
| | Principal amount or par value. For example, $1,000. |
| (B) Term to maturity | For example, 12 years. |
| (C) Investor's required rate of return | For example, 4%. |

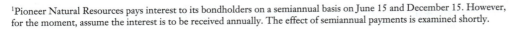

[1]Pioneer Natural Resources pays interest to its bondholders on a semiannual basis on June 15 and December 15. However, for the moment, assume the interest is to be received annually. The effect of semiannual payments is examined shortly.

In 2012, with 4 years left to maturity, investors owning the bonds were requiring a 4.16 percent rate of return. We can calculate the value of the bonds to these investors using the following three-step valuation procedure:

**STEP 1**   Estimate the amount and timing of the expected future cash flows. Two types of cash flows are received by the bondholder:

   a. Annual interest payments equal to the coupon rate of interest times the face value of the bond. In this example, the bond's coupon interest rate is 5.875 percent; thus, the annual interest payment is $58.75 ($58.75 = .05875 × $1,000). Assuming that 2012 interest payments have already been made, these cash flows will be received by the bondholder in each of the 4 years before the bond matures (2013 through 2016 = 4 years).

   b. The face value of $1,000 to be received in 2016.

To summarize, the cash flows received by the bondholder are as follows:

| 2013 | 2014 | 2015 | 2016 |
|------|------|------|------|
| $58.75 | $58.75 | $58.75 | $    58.75 |
| | | | $1,000.00 |
| | | | $1,058.75 |

**STEP 2**   Determine the investor's required rate of return by evaluating the riskiness of the bond's future cash flows. A 4.16 percent required rate of return for the bondholders is given. However, we should recall from Chapter 6 that an investor's required rate of return is equal to a rate earned on a risk-free security plus a risk premium for assuming risk.

   In this case, the Pioneer Natural Resources bonds are rated BBB by Standard & Poor's, which indicates that the bonds are not considered high-risk bonds (junk bonds), but neither are they AAA investment grade. Thus, S&P believes the company has the capacity to make interest and principal payments, provided that circumstances do not change adversely.

**STEP 3**   Calculate the intrinsic value of the bond as the present value of the expected future interest and principal payments discounted at the investor's required rate of return.

In general, the present value of a bond is found as follows:

$$\text{Bond value} = V_b = \frac{\$ \text{ interest in year 1}}{(1 + \text{required rate of return})^1} \tag{7-2a}$$

$$+ \frac{\$ \text{ interest in year 2}}{(1 + \text{required rate of return})^2}$$

$$+ \frac{\$ \text{ interest in year 3}}{(1 + \text{required rate of return})^3}$$

$$+ \cdots$$

$$+ \frac{\$ \text{ interest in year } n}{(1 + \text{required rate of return})^n}$$

$$+ \frac{\$ \text{ maturity value of bond}}{(1 + \text{required rate of return})^n}$$

Using $I_t$ to represent the interest payment in year $t$, $M$ to represent the bond's maturity (or par) value, and $r_b$ to equal the bondholder's required rate of return, we can express the value of a bond maturing in year $n$ as follows:

$$V_b = \frac{\$I_1}{(1 + r_b)^1} + \frac{\$I_2}{(1 + r_b)^2} + \frac{\$I_3}{(1 + r_b)^3} + \cdots + \frac{\$I_n}{(1 + r_b)^n} + \frac{\$M}{(1 + r_b)^n} \tag{7-2b}$$

## DID YOU GET IT?

### COMPUTING AN ASSET'S VALUE

The value of an asset generating $5,000 per year for 4 years, given a 6 percent required rate of return, would be $17,325.53. Using a TI BA II Plus calculator, we find the answer as follows:

**CALCULATOR SOLUTION**

| Data Input | Function Key |
|---|---|
| 6 | I/Y |
| 4 | N |
| −5,000 | +/− PMT |
| 0 | FV |

| Function Key | Answer |
|---|---|
| CPT | |
| PV | $17,325.53 |

If an investor owns an asset that pays $1,062.02 in cash flows each year for 4 years, he would earn exactly his required rate of return of 6 percent if he paid $17,325.53 today.

Notice that equation (7-2b) is a restatement of equation (7-1), where now the cash flows are represented by the interest received each period and the par value of the bond when it matures. In either equation, the value of an asset is the present value of its future cash flows.

The equation for finding the value of the Pioneer bonds would be as follows:

$$V_b = \frac{\$58.75}{(1 + 0.0416)^1} + \frac{\$58.75}{(1 + 0.0416)^2} + \frac{\$58.75}{(1 + 0.0416)^3} + \frac{\$58.75}{(1 + 0.0416)^4} + \frac{\$1,000}{(1 + 0.0416)^4}$$

Finding the value of the Pioneer bonds can be represented graphically as follows:

| YEAR | 0 | 2013 | 2014 | 2015 | 2016 |
|---|---|---|---|---|---|
| Dollars received at end of year | | $58.75 | $58.75 | $58.75 | $   58.75 +$1,000.00 $1,058.75 |
| Present value | $1,062.02 ◄ | | | | |

Using a TI BA II Plus financial calculator, we find the value of the bond to be $1,062.02, as calculated in the margin.[2] Thus, if investors consider 4.16 percent to be an appropriate required rate of return in view of the risk level associated with Pioneer bonds, paying a price of $1,062.02 would satisfy their return requirement.

We can also solve for the value of Pioneer's bonds using a spreadsheet. The solution using Excel appears as follows:

**CALCULATOR SOLUTION**

| Data Input | Function Key |
|---|---|
| 4 | N |
| 4.16 | I/Y |
| 58.75 | +/− PMT |
| 1,000 | +/− FV |

| Function Key | Answer |
|---|---|
| CPT | |
| PV | 1,062.02 |

| | A | B | C | D |
|---|---|---|---|---|
| 1 | Required rate of return | Rate | 4.16% | |
| 2 | Years left to maturity | Nper | 4 | |
| 3 | Annual interest payment | Pmt | −58.75 | |
| 4 | Future value | FV | −1,000 | |
| 5 | Present value | PV | 1,062.02 | |
| 6 | | | | |
| 7 | | Equation: =PV(Rate,Nper,Pmt,FV) = PV(C1,C2,C3,C4) | | |
| 8 | | | | |
| 9 | | | | |
| 10 | | | | |
| 11 | | | | |

[2]As noted in Chapter 5, we are using the TI BA II Plus. You may want to return to the Chapter 5 section "Moving Money Through Time with the Aid of a Financial Calculator" or Appendix A at www.pearsonhighered.com/keown, to see a more complete explanation of using the TI BA II Plus.

| EXAMPLE 7.1 | Valuing a bond |
|---|---|

Verso Paper Holdings, a producer of coated papers, has a bond outstanding with a coupon interest rate of 8.75 percent that will mature in 7 years. The investors who have purchased the bonds are requiring a really high rate of return of 25.34 percent! Compute the value of the bonds for the current investors. Earning a 25 percent rate of return is fantastic—sure beats government Treasury bond rates. So why would many investors choose not to invest in these bonds, in spite of the high rate of return?

### STEP 1: FORMULATE A SOLUTION STRATEGY

The formula for valuing a bond is shown below:

$$\text{Bond value} = V_b = \frac{\$\text{ interest in year 1}}{(1 + \text{ required rate of return})^1}$$
$$+ \frac{\$\text{ interest in year 2}}{(1 + \text{ required rate of return})^2}$$
$$+ \frac{\$\text{ interest in year 3}}{(1 + \text{ required rate of return})^3}$$
$$+ \cdots$$
$$+ \frac{\$\text{ interest in year } n}{(1 + \text{ required rate of return})^n}$$
$$+ \frac{\$\text{ maturity value of bond}}{(1 + \text{ required rate of return})^n}$$

### STEP 2: CRUNCH THE NUMBERS

The value of the Verso bonds can be computed by using either a financial calculator or a spreadsheet. But first we must determine the annual interest payment, which is $87.50 ($87.50 = 0.0875 coupon interest rate × $1,000 par value). As shown below, the value of the bond is $480.02.

Using a financial calculator:

*Interest ↑*
*Price ↓*

**CALCULATOR SOLUTION**

| Data Input | Function Key |
|---|---|
| 7 | N |
| 25.34 | I/Y |
| 87.50 | +/− PMT |
| 1,000 | +/− FV |
| **Function Key** | **Answer** |
| CPT | |
| PV | 480.02 |

Then, using a spreadsheet:

| | A | B | C | D | |
|---|---|---|---|---|---|
| 1 | Required rate of return | Rate | 25.34% | | |
| 2 | Years left to maturity | Nper | 7 | | |
| 3 | Annual interest payment | Pmt | − 87.50 | | |
| 4 | Future value (par value) | FV | −1,000 | | |
| 5 | | | | | |
| 6 | Solve for present value (bond value) | PV | $480.02 | | |
| 7 | | | | | |
| 8 | | Equation: | | | |
| 9 | | =PV(Rate,Nper,Pmt,FV) = PV(C1,C2,C3,C4) | | | |
| 10 | | | | | |

## STEP 3: ANALYZE YOUR RESULTS

Only by buying the bond at a low price compared to the bond's par value, $480.02, relative to $1,000 (par value) can the investors earn such a high rate of return of 25.34 percent. Furthermore, for a bond to sell at such a large discount and thereby provide a high rate of return indicates that investors perceive there to be a high likelihood of default. In other words, the 25.34 percent is not the true *expected* rate of return, but rather the rate that will be earned if Verso does not default on interest or principal payments. There is certainly the possibility that the investors will receive the high return, but there is apparently considerable risk that the company will default. So only investors who are prepared to accept a large dose of risk will be interested in buying the bond.

To this point we have provided the basic present-value equation to determine the value of an asset based on its expected future cash flows. This same equation was then applied to valuing a bond. These two equations served as the financial tools for valuing an asset and are represented as follows:

### FINANCIAL DECISION TOOLS

| Name of Tool | Formula | What It Tells You |
|---|---|---|
| Asset value | $\text{Asset value} = \dfrac{\text{cash flow in year 1}}{\left(1 + \text{required rate of return}\right)^1} + \dfrac{\text{cash flow in year 2}}{\left(1 + \text{required rate of return}\right)^2} + \cdots + \dfrac{\text{cash flow in year } n}{\left(1 + \text{required rate of return}\right)^n}$ | Indicates that the value of an asset, be it a security or an investment in plant and equipment, is equal to the present value of future cash flows expected to be received from the investment. |
| Bond value | $\text{Bond value} = V_b = \dfrac{\$ \text{ interest in year 1}}{(1 + \text{required rate of return})^1}$ $+ \dfrac{\$ \text{ interest in year 2}}{(1 + \text{required rate of return})^2}$ $+ \dfrac{\$ \text{ interest in year 3}}{(1 + \text{required rate of return})^3}$ $+ \cdots$ $+ \dfrac{\$ \text{ interest in year } n}{(1 + \text{required rate of return})^n}$ $+ \dfrac{\$ \text{ maturity value of bond}}{(1 + \text{required rate of return})^n}$ and $V_b = \dfrac{\$I_1}{(1 + r_b)^1} + \dfrac{\$I_2}{(1 + r_b)^2} + \dfrac{\$I_3}{(1 + r_b)^3} + \cdots + \dfrac{\$I_n}{(1 + r_b)^n} + \dfrac{\$M}{(1 + r_b)^n}$ | Calculates the value of a bond as the present value both of future interest payments and the par value of the bond to be received at maturity. |

## Concept Check

1. What two factors determine an investor's required rate of return?
2. How does the required rate of return affect a bond's value?

## CAN YOU DO IT?

### COMPUTING A BOND'S VALUE

La Fiesta Restaurants issued bonds that have a 6 percent coupon interest rate. Interest is paid annually. The bonds mature in 12 years. If your required rate of return is 8 percent, what is the value of a bond to you?
(The solution can be found on page 235.)

In the preceding illustration using Pioneer Natural Resources, the interest payments were assumed to be paid annually. However, companies typically pay interest to bondholders semiannually. For example, Pioneer actually pays a total of $58.75 for each bond per year, but disburses the interest semiannually ($29.375 each June 15 and December 15).

Several steps are involved in adapting equation (7-2b) for semiannual interest payments.[3] First, thinking in terms of *periods* instead of years, a bond with a life of $n$ years paying interest semiannually has a life of $2n$ periods. In other words, a 4-year bond ($n = 4$) that remits its interest on a semiannual basis actually makes 8 payments. Although the number of periods has doubled, the *dollar* amount of interest being sent to the investors for each period and the bondholders' required rate of return are half of the equivalent annual figures. $I_t$ becomes $I_t/2$ and $r_b$ is changed to $r_b/2$; thus, for semiannual compounding, equation (7-2b) becomes

$$V_b = \frac{\$I_1/2}{\left(1 + \frac{r_b}{2}\right)^1} + \frac{\$I_2/2}{\left(1 + \frac{r_b}{2}\right)^2} + \frac{\$I_3/2}{\left(1 + \frac{r_b}{2}\right)^3} + \cdots + \frac{\$I_{2n}/2}{\left(1 + \frac{r_b}{2}\right)^{2n}} + \frac{\$M}{\left(1 + \frac{r_b}{2}\right)^{2n}} \quad (7\text{-}3)$$

We can now compute the value of the Pioneer bonds, recognizing that interest is being paid semiannually. We simply change the number of periods from 4 years to 8 semiannual periods and the required rate of return from 4.16 percent annually to 2.08 percent per semiannual period and divide interest payment by 2 to get $29.375. The value of the bond would now be $1,062.60. Not a big change, but just more accurate when interest is paid semiannually.

This solution can be found using a calculator as shown in the margin or a spreadsheet that would look as follows:

**CALCULATOR SOLUTION**

| Data Input | Function Key |
|---|---|
| $2n \rightarrow 2 \times 4 \rightarrow 8$ | N |
| $4.16 \div 2 \rightarrow 2.08$ | I/Y |
| 29.375 | +/− PMT |
| 1,000 | +/− FV |

| Function Key | Answer |
|---|---|
| CPT | |
| PV | 1,062.60 |

|  | A | B | C | D | E |
|---|---|---|---|---|---|
| 1 | Required rate of return | Rate | 2.08% | | |
| 2 | Years left to maturity | Nper | 8 | | |
| 3 | Annual interest payment | Pmt | −29.375 | | |
| 4 | Future value | FV | −1,000 | | |
| 5 | Present value | PV | 1,062.60 | | |
| 6 | | | | | |
| 7 | | | | | |
| 8 | | | | | |
| 9 | | | | | |
| 10 | | | | | |
| 11 | | | | | |

Equation:
=PV(Rate,Nper,Pmt,FV) = PV(C1,C2,C3,C4)

To conclude, we previously valued bonds assuming that interest was paid to the investors on an annual basis. However, since bonds typically pay interest semiannually, we need a slightly revised financial tools shown as follows:

## FINANCIAL DECISION TOOLS

| Name of Tool | Formula | What It Tells You |
|---|---|---|
| Bond value when interest is paid semiannually | $V_b = \dfrac{\$I_1/2}{\left(1 + \frac{r_b}{2}\right)^1} + \dfrac{\$I_2/2}{\left(1 + \frac{r_b}{2}\right)^2} + \dfrac{\$I_3/2}{\left(1 + \frac{r_b}{2}\right)^3} + \cdots + \dfrac{\$I_{2n}/2}{\left(1 + \frac{r_b}{2}\right)^{2n}} + \dfrac{\$M}{\left(1 + \frac{r_b}{2}\right)^{2n}}$ | Calculates the value of a bond as the present value both of future interest payments received semi-annually and the par value of the bond to be received at maturity. |

[3]The logic for calculating the value of a bond that pays interest semiannually is similar to the material presented in Chapter 5, where compound interest with nonannual periods was discussed.

## DID YOU GET IT?
### COMPUTING A BOND'S VALUE

The La Fiesta bond with a 6 percent coupon rate pays $60 in interest per year ($60 = 0.06 coupon rate × $1,000 par value). Thus, you would receive $60 per year for 12 years plus the $1,000 in par value in year 12. Assuming an 8 percent required rate of return, the value of the bond would be $849.28.

**CALCULATOR SOLUTION**

| Data Input | Function Key |
|---|---|
| 8 | I/Y |
| 12 | N |
| 60 | +/– PMT |
| 1,000 | +/– FV |

| Function | Key Answer |
|---|---|
| CPT | |
| PV | 849.28 |

If an investor owns a bond that pays $60 in interest each year for 12 years, she would earn exactly her required rate of return of 8 percent if she paid $849.28 today.

## Concept Check

1. How do semiannual interest payments affect the asset valuation equation?

Now that we know how to value a bond, we will next examine a bondholder's rate of return from investing in a bond, or what is called bond yields.

# Bond Yields

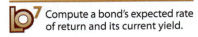
7 Compute a bond's expected rate of return and its current yield.

There are two calculations used to measure the rate of return a bondholder receives from owning a bond: the yield to maturity and the current yield.

## Yield to Maturity

Theoretically, each bondholder could have a different required rate of return for a particular bond. However, the financial manager is interested only in the expected rate of return that is implied by the market prices of the firm's bonds, or what we call the yield to maturity.

To measure the bondholder's **expected rate of return**, $\bar{r}_b$, we would find the *discount rate that equates the present value of the future cash flows (interest and maturity value) with the current market price of the bond.*[4] It is also the *rate of return the investor will earn if the bond is held to maturity*, thus the name **yield to maturity**. So, when referring to bonds, the terms *expected rate of return* and *yield to maturity* are often used interchangeably.

To solve for the expected rate of return for a bond, we would use the following equation:

**expected rate of return** (1) the discount rate that equates the present value of the future cash flows (interest and maturity value) of a bond with its current market price. It is the rate of return an investor will earn if the bond is held to maturity. (2) The rate of return the investor expects to receive on an investment by paying the existing market price of the security.

**yield to maturity** The rate of return a bondholder will receive if the bond is held to maturity. (It is equivalent to the expected rate of return.)

$$\text{Market price} = P_0 = \frac{\$ \text{ interest in year 1}}{(1 + \text{expected rate of return})^1} \tag{7-4}$$

$$+ \frac{\$ \text{ interest in year 2}}{(1 + \text{expected rate of return})^2}$$

$$+ \frac{\$ \text{ interest in year 3}}{(1 + \text{expected rate of return})^3}$$

$$+ \cdots$$

$$+ \frac{\$ \text{ interest in year } n}{(1 + \text{expected rate of return})^n}$$

$$+ \frac{\$ \text{ maturity value of bond}}{(1 + \text{expected rate of return})^n}$$

[4]When we speak of computing an expected rate of return, we are not describing the situation very accurately. Expected rates of return are ex ante (before the fact) and are based on "expected and unobservable future cash flows" and, therefore, can only be "estimated."

To illustrate this concept, consider the Brister Corporation's bonds, which are selling for $1,100. The bonds carry a coupon interest rate of 6 percent and mature in 10 years. (Remember, the coupon rate determines the interest payment—coupon rate × par value.)

To determine the expected rate of return ($\bar{r}_b$) implicit in the current market price, we need to find the rate that discounts the anticipated cash flows back to a present value of $1,100, the current market price ($P_0$) for the bond.

The expected return for the Brister Corporation bondholders is 4.72 percent, which can be found as presented in the margin by using the TI BA II Plus calculator, or by using a computer spreadsheet, as follows:

| | A | B | C | D | |
|---|---|---|---|---|---|
| 1 | Years left to maturity | Nper | 10 | | |
| 2 | Annual interest payment | Pmt | 60 | | |
| 3 | Present value | PV | −1,100 | | |
| 4 | Future value | FV | 1,000 | | |
| 5 | Required rate of return | Rate | 4.72% | | |
| 6 | | | | | |
| 7 | | Equation: | | | |
| 8 | | =RATE(Nper,Pmt,PV,FV) = RATE(C1,C2,C3,C4) | | | |
| 9 | | | | | |
| 10 | | | | | |

---

**EXAMPLE 7.2**     **Solving for the yield to maturity (expected rate of return)**

In Example 7.1 you were asked to calculate the value of bonds issued by Verso Paper Holdings, where the coupon interest rate was 8.75 percent, which indicated an interest payment of $87.50, and the maturity date was 7 years. The investors who had purchased the bonds were requiring a rate of return of 25.34 percent. Given this information, we found the bond value to be $480.02; if you had gone to www.finance.yahoo.com, on June 28, 2012, you would have found that the market price for the bonds was indeed $480. But what if investors changed their required rates of return to the point that the bonds were selling for $700? In that case, what would be the expected rate of return, or yield to maturity, if you purchased the bonds at the higher value? Explain what happened.

**STEP 1: FORMULATE A SOLUTION STRATEGY**
The formula for computing the expected rate of return (yield to maturity) for the Verso bonds at a market price of $700 is shown below:

$$\text{Market price} = P_0 = \frac{\$ \text{ interest in year 1}}{(1 + \text{expected rate of return})^1}$$
$$+ \frac{\$ \text{ interest in year 2}}{(1 + \text{expected rate of return})^2}$$
$$+ \frac{\$ \text{ interest in year 3}}{(1 + \text{expected rate of returns})^3}$$
$$+ \cdots$$
$$+ \frac{\$ \text{ interest in year } n}{(1 + \text{expected rate of return})^n}$$
$$+ \frac{\$ \text{ maturity value of bond}}{(1 + \text{expected rate of return})^n}$$

where we are solving for the expected rate of return in the equation.

**STEP 2: CRUNCH THE NUMBERS**
The expected rate of return (yield to maturity) for the Verso bonds can be computed by using either a financial calculator a spreadsheet.

Using a TI BA II Plus financial calculator, the expected rate of return is found to be 16.23 percent:

CALCULATOR SOLUTION

| Data Input | Function Key |
|---|---|
| 7 | N |
| 700 | +/− PV |
| 87.50 | PMT |
| 1,000 | FV |

| Function Key | Answer |
|---|---|
| CPT | |
| I/Y | 16.23 |

Then using a spreadsheet:

| | A | B | C | D | |
|---|---|---|---|---|---|
| 1 | Years left to maturity | Nper | 7 | | |
| 2 | Annual interest payment | Pmt | 87.50 | | |
| 3 | Present value | PV | −700 | | |
| 4 | Future value | FV | 1,000 | | |
| 5 | Expected rate of return | Rate | 16.23% | | |
| 6 | | | | | |
| 7 | | | | | |
| 8 | | | | | |
| 9 | | | | | |
| 10 | | | | | |
| 11 | | | | | |

Equation:
=RATE(Nper,Pmt,PV,FV) = RATE(C1,C2,C3,C4)

### STEP 3: ANALYZE YOUR RESULTS

If you are willing to pay the higher price of $700 for the Verso bonds, it means that you are prepared to accept a lower yield to maturity (expected rate of return) on your investment. In other words, you are willing to accept the riskiness of the investment and receive a smaller expected return. Thus, as rates of return decrease, the value of a security of a security will always increase.

## Current Yield

The **current yield** on a bond refers to the *ratio of the annual interest payment to the bond's current market price*. If, for example, we have a bond with a 4 percent coupon interest rate, a par value of $1,000, and a market price of $920, it would have a current yield of 4.35 percent:

**current yield** the ratio of a bond's annual interest payment to its market price.

$$\text{Current yield} = \frac{\text{annual interest payment}}{\text{current market price of the bond}} \tag{7-5}$$

In our example

$$\text{Current yield} = \frac{0.04 \times \$1,000}{\$920} = \frac{\$40}{\$920} = 0.0435 = 4.35\%$$

We should understand that the current yield, although frequently quoted in the popular press, is an incomplete picture of the expected rate of return from holding a bond. The current yield indicates the cash income that results from holding a bond in a given year, but it fails to recognize the capital gain or loss that will occur if the bond is held to maturity. As such, it is not an accurate measure of the bondholder's expected rate of return.

We now have financial tools to determine the rate of return a bondholder can expect to earn: (1) if the bond is held until it matures when the bondholder receives the par value of the bond, and (2) if we only consider the interest payment being received relative to the current market price of the bond. These two financial tools are stated as follows:

## FINANCIAL DECISION TOOLS

| Name of Tool | Formula | What It Tells You |
|---|---|---|
| Yield to maturity or expected rate of return | $\text{Market price} = P_0 = \dfrac{\$ \text{ interest in year 1}}{(1 + \text{expected rate of return})^1}$ $+ \dfrac{\$ \text{ interest in year 2}}{(1 + \text{expected rate of return})^2}$ $+ \dfrac{\$ \text{ interest in year 3}}{(1 + \text{expected rate of return})^3}$ $+ \cdots$ $+ \dfrac{\$ \text{ interest in year } n}{(1 + \text{expected rate of return})^n}$ $+ \dfrac{\$ \text{ maturity value of bond}}{(1 + \text{expected rate of return})^n}$ | The expected rate of return (yield to maturity) of a bond if held until maturity, given its current market price. |
| Current yield | $\text{Current yield} = \dfrac{\text{annual interest payment}}{\text{current market price of the bond}}$ | The yield today determined by dividing the interest payment by the current market price. |

## Concept Check

1. What assumption is being made about the length of time a bond is held when computing the yield to maturity?
2. What does the current yield tell us?
3. How are the yield to maturity and the current yield different?

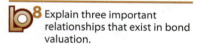
8 Explain three important relationships that exist in bond valuation.

# Bond Valuation: Three Important Relationships

We have now learned to find the value of a bond ($V_b$), given (1) the amount of interest payments ($I_t$), (2) the maturity value ($M$), (3) the length of time to maturity ($n$ periods), and (4) the investor's required rate of return, $r_b$. We also know how to compute the expected rate of return ($\bar{r}_b$), which also happens to be the current interest rate on the bond, given (1) the current market value ($P_0$), (2) the amount of interest payments ($I_t$), (3) the maturity value ($M$), and (4) the length of time to maturity ($n$ periods). We now have the basics. But let's go further in our understanding of bond valuation by studying several important relationships:

♦ **Relationship 1.** The value of a bond is inversely related to changes in the investor's present required rate of return. In other words, as interest rates increase (decrease), the value of the bond decreases (increases).

   To illustrate, assume that an investor's required rate of return for a given bond is 5 percent. The bond has a par value of $1,000 and annual interest payments of $50, indicating a 5 percent coupon interest rate ($50 ÷ $1,000 = 5%). Assuming a 5-year maturity date, the bond would be worth $1,000, computed as follows:

$$V_b = \frac{\$I_1}{(1 + r_b)^1} + \cdots + \frac{\$I_n}{(1 + r_b)^n} + \frac{\$M}{(1 + r_b)^n}$$

## CAN YOU DO IT?

### COMPUTING THE YIELD TO MATURITY AND CURRENT YIELD

The Argon Corporation bonds are selling for $1,100. They have a 5 percent coupon interest rate paid annually and mature in 8 years. What is the yield to maturity for the bonds if an investor buys them at the $1,100 market price? What is the current yield? (The solution can be found on page 240.)

In our example,

$$V_b = \frac{\$50}{(1 + 0.05)^1} + \frac{\$50}{(1 + 0.05)^2} + \frac{\$50}{(1 + 0.05)^3} + \frac{\$50}{(1 + 0.05)^4} + \frac{\$50}{(1 + 0.05)^5} + \frac{\$1,000}{(1 + 0.05)^5}$$

Using a calculator, we find the value of the bond to be $1,000.

CALCULATOR SOLUTION

| Data Input | Function Key |
|---|---|
| 5 | I/Y |
| 5 | N |
| 50 | +/– PMT |
| 1,000 | +/– FV |

| Function Key | Answer |
|---|---|
| CPT | |
| PV | 1,000 |

If, however, the investors' required rate of return increases from 5 percent to 8 percent, the value of the bond would decrease to $880.22, computed as follows:

CALCULATOR SOLUTION

| Data Input | Function Key |
|---|---|
| 8 | I/Y |
| 5 | N |
| 50 | +/– PMT |
| 1,000 | +/– FV |

| Function Key | Answer |
|---|---|
| CPT | |
| PV | 880.22 |

On the other hand, if the investor's required rate of return decreases to 2 percent, the bond would increase in value to $1,141.40.

CALCULATOR SOLUTION

| Data Input | Function Key |
|---|---|
| 2 | I/Y |
| 5 | N |
| 50 | +/– PMT |
| 1,000 | +/– FV |

| Function Key | Answer |
|---|---|
| CPT | |
| PV | $1,141.40 |

This inverse relationship between the investor's required rate of return and the value of a bond is presented in Figure 7-3. Clearly, as investors demand a higher rate of return, the value of a bond decreases: The higher rate of return can be achieved only by paying less for the bond. Conversely, a lower required rate of return yields a higher market value for the bond.

# DID YOU GET IT?

## COMPUTING THE YIELD TO MATURITY AND CURRENT YIELD

The Argon bonds pay $50 in interest per year ($50 = 0.05 coupon rate × $1,000 par value) for the duration of the bond, or for 8 years. The investor will then receive $1,000 at the bond's maturity. Given a market price of $1,100 the yield to maturity would be 3.54 percent.

CALCULATOR SOLUTION

| Data Input | Function Key |
|---|---|
| 8 | N |
| 1,100 | PV |
| 50 | +/– PMT |
| 1,000 | +/– FV |

| Function Key | Answer |
|---|---|
| CPT | |
| I/Y | 3.54 |

$$\text{Current yield} = \frac{\text{annual interest payment}}{\text{current market price of the bond}}$$

$$= \frac{\$50}{\$1,100} = 0.0455 = 4.55\%$$

If an investor paid $1,100 for a bond that pays $50 in interest each year for 8 years, along with the $1,000 par value in the eighth year, he would earn exactly 3.54 percent on the investment.

Changes in bond prices represent an element of uncertainty for the bond investor. If the current interest rate (required rate of return) changes, the price of a bond also fluctuates. An increase in interest rates causes the bondholder to incur a loss in market value. Because future interest rates and the resulting bond value cannot be predicted with certainty, a bond investor is exposed to the *risk of changing values as interest rates vary*. This risk has come to be known as **interest rate risk**.

**interest rate risk** the variability in a bond's value caused by changing interest rates.

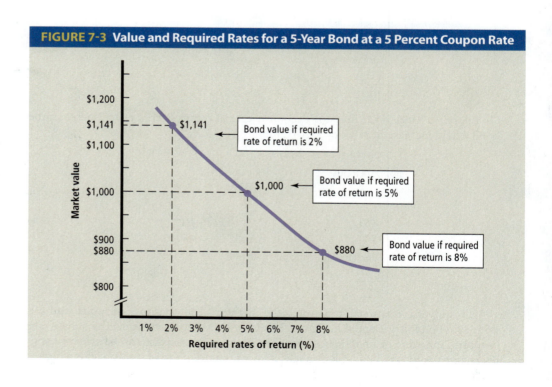

**FIGURE 7-3** Value and Required Rates for a 5-Year Bond at a 5 Percent Coupon Rate

◆ **Relationship 2.** The market value of a bond will be less than the par value if the required rate of return of investors is above the coupon interest rate; but it will be valued above par value if the required rate of return of investors is below the coupon interest rate.

Using the previous example, we observed that

- The bond has a *market value* of $1,000, equal to the par, or maturity, value, when the required rate of return demanded by investors equals the 5 percent coupon interest rate. In other words, if

  *required rate* = *coupon rate*, then *market value* = *par value*

    5%   =   5%,   then   $1,000  = $1,000

- When the required rate is 8 percent, which exceeds the 5 percent coupon rate, the market value of the bond falls below par value to $880.22; that is, if

  *required rate* > *coupon rate*, then *market value* < *par value*

    8%   >   5%,   then   $880.22  < $1,000

  In this case the *bond sells at a discount below par value*; thus, it is called a **discount bond**.

  > **discount bond** a bond that sells at a discount, or below par value.

- When the required rate is only 2 percent, or less than the 5 percent coupon rate, the market value, $1,141.40, exceeds the bond's par value. In this instance, if

  *required rate* < *coupon rate*, then *market value* > *par value*

    2%   <   5%,   then   $1,141.40  > $1,000

The *bond is now selling at a premium above par value*; thus, it is a **premium bond**.

◆ **Relationship 3.** Long-term bonds have greater interest rate risk than do short-term bonds.

> **premium bond** a bond that is selling above its par value.

As already noted, a change in current interest rates (the required rate of return) causes an inverse change in the market value of a bond. However, the impact on value is greater for long-term bonds than it is for short-term bonds.

In Figure 7-3 we observed the effect of interest rate changes on a 5-year bond paying a 5 percent coupon interest rate. What if the bond did not mature until 10 years from today instead of 5 years? Would the changes in market value be the same? Absolutely not. The changes in value would be more significant for the 10-year bond. For example, what if the current interest rates increase from 2 percent to 5 percent and then to 8 percent? In this case, a 10-year bond's value would drop more sharply than a 5-year bond's value would. The values for both the 5-year and the 10-year bonds are shown here.

| | MARKET VALUE FOR A 5% COUPON-RATE BOND MATURING IN | |
|---|---|---|
| **REQUIRED RATE** | **5 YEARS** | **10 YEARS** |
| 2% | $1,141.40 | $1,269.48 |
| 5% | 1,000.00 | 1,000.00 |
| 8% | 880.22 | 798.70 |

The reason long-term bond prices fluctuate more than short-term bond prices in response to interest rate changes is simple. Assume an investor bought a 10-year bond yielding a 5 percent interest rate. If the current interest rate for bonds of similar risk increased to 8 percent, the investor would be locked into the lower rate for 10 years. If, on the other hand, a shorter-term bond had been purchased—say, one maturing in 2 years—the investor would have to accept the lower return for only 2 years and not the full 10 years. At the end of year 2, the investor would receive the maturity value of $1,000 and could buy a bond offering the higher 8 percent rate for the remaining 8 years. Thus, interest rate risk is determined, at least in part, by the length of time an investor is required to commit to an investment.

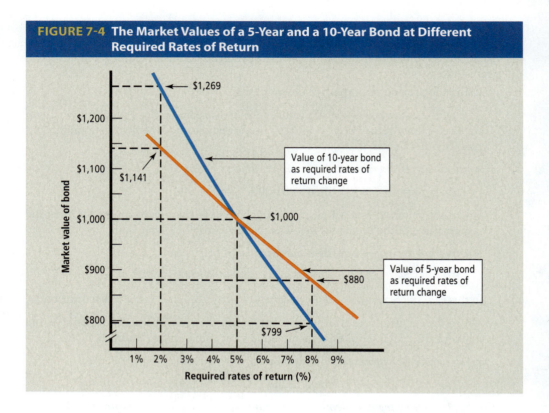

**FIGURE 7-4  The Market Values of a 5-Year and a 10-Year Bond at Different Required Rates of Return**

Using these values and the required rates, we can graph the changes in values for the two bonds relative to different interest rates. These comparisons are provided in Figure 7-4. The figure clearly illustrates that the price of a long-term bond (say, 10 years) is more responsive or sensitive to interest rate changes than the price of a short-term bond (say, 5 years). However, the holder of a long-term bond can take some comfort from the fact that long-term interest rates are usually not as volatile as short-term rates.

## Concept Check

1. Why does a bond sell at a discount when the coupon rate is lower than the required rate of return and vice versa?

2. As interest rates increase, why does the price of a long-term bond decrease more than that of a short-term bond?

# Chapter Summaries

### Distinguish between different kinds of bonds.  (pgs 221–223)

**SUMMARY:** There is a variety of types of bonds, including:

Debentures                     Eurobonds
Subordinated debentures        Convertible bonds
Mortgage bonds

## KEY TERMS

**Bond, page 221**  A long-term (10-year or more) promissory note issued by the borrower, promising to pay the owner of the security a predetermined, fixed amount of interest each year.

**Debenture, page 221**  Any unsecured long-term debt.

**Subordinated debenture, page 222**  A debenture that is subordinated to other debentures in terms of its payments in case of insolvency.

**Mortgage bond, page 222**  A bond secured by a lien on real property.

**Eurobond, page 222**  A bond issued in a country different from the one in which the currency of the bond is denominated; for example, a bond issued in Europe or Asia by an American company that pays interest and principal to the lender in U.S. dollars.

**Convertible bond, page 222**  A debt security that can be converted into a firm's stock at a prespecified price.

---

## Explain the more popular features of bonds. (pgs 223–226)

**SUMMARY:** Some of the more popular terms and characteristics used to describe bonds include the following:

Claims on assets and income
Par value
Coupon interest rate
Maturity

Call provision
Indenture
Bond ratings

## KEY TERMS

**Par value, page 223**  On the face of a bond, the stated amount that the firm is to repay upon the maturity date.

**Coupon interest rate, page 223**  The interest rate contractually owed on a bond as a percent of its par value.

**Fixed-rate bond, page 223**  A bond that pays a fixed amount of interest to the investor each year.

**Zero coupon bond, page 224**  A bond issued at a substantial discount from its $1,000 face value and that pays little or no interest.

**Maturity, page 224**  The length of time until the bond issuer returns the par value to the bondholder and terminates the bond.

**Callable bond (redeemable bond), page 224**  An option available to a company issuing a bond whereby the issuer can call (redeem) the bond before it matures. This is usually done if interest rates decline below what the firm is paying on the bond.

**Call protection period, page 224**  A prespecified time period during which a company cannot recall a bond.

**Indenture, page 224**  The legal agreement between the firm issuing bonds and the bond trustee who represents the bondholders, providing the specific terms of the loan agreement.

**Junk bond, page 225**  Any bond rated BB or below.

**High-yield bond, page 226**  See junk bond.

---

## Define the term *value* as used for several different purposes. (pgs 226–227)

**SUMMARY:** Value is defined differently depending on the context. But for us, value is the present value of future cash flows expected to be received from an investment, discounted at the investor's required rate of return.

## KEY TERMS

**Book value, page 226**  (1) The value of an asset as shown on the firm's balance sheet. It represents the historical cost of the asset rather than its current market value or replacement cost. (2) The depreciated value of a company's assets (original cost less accumulated depreciation) less outstanding liabilities.

**Liquidation value, page 226**  The dollar sum that could be realized if an asset were sold.

**Market value, page 226**  The value observed in the marketplace.

**Intrinsic, or economic, value, page 226**  The present value of an asset's expected future cash flows. This value is the amount the investor considers to be fair value, given the amount, timing, and riskiness of future cash flows.

**Fair value, page 226** The present value of an asset's expected future cash flows.

**Efficient market, page 227** Market where the values of all securities fully recognize all available public information.

**Behavioral finance, page 227** The field of study examining when investors act rationally or irrationally when making investment decisions.

 **4    Explain the factors that determine value.** (pgs 227–228)

**SUMMARY:** Three basic factors determine an asset's value: (1) the amount and timing of future cash flows, (2) the riskiness of the cash flows, and (3) the investor's attitude about the risk.

 **5    Describe the basic process for valuing assets.** (pgs 228–229)

**SUMMARY:** The valuation process can be described as follows: It is assigning value to an asset by calculating the present value of its expected future cash flows using the investor's required rate of return as the discount rate. The investor's required rate of return, $r$, equals the risk-free rate of interest plus a risk premium to compensate the investor for assuming risk.

**KEY EQUATIONS**

$$\frac{\text{Asset}}{\text{value}} = \frac{\text{cash flow in year 1}}{\left(1 + \frac{\text{required}}{\text{rate of return}}\right)^1} + \frac{\text{cash flow in year 2}}{\left(1 + \frac{\text{required}}{\text{rate of return}}\right)^2} + \cdots + \frac{\text{cash flow in year } n}{\left(1 + \frac{\text{required}}{\text{rate of return}}\right)^n}$$

$$V = \frac{C_1}{(1 + r)^1} + \frac{C_2}{(1 + r)^2} + \cdots + \frac{C_n}{(1 + r)^n}$$

 **6    Estimate the value of a bond.** (pgs 229–235)

**SUMMARY:** The value of a bond is the present value of both future interest to be received and the par or maturity value of the bond.

**KEY EQUATIONS**

$$\text{Bond value} = V_b = \frac{\$ \text{ interest in year 1}}{(1 + \text{required rate of return})^1}$$

$$+ \frac{\$ \text{ interest in year 2}}{(1 + \text{required rate of return})^2}$$

$$+ \frac{\$ \text{ interest in year 3}}{(1 + \text{required rate of return})^3}$$

$$+ \cdots$$

$$+ \frac{\$ \text{ interest in year } n}{(1 + \text{required rate of return})^n}$$

$$+ \frac{\$ \text{ maturity value of bond}}{(1 + \text{required rate of return})^n}$$

$$V_b = \frac{\$I_1}{(1 + r_b)^1} + \frac{\$I_2}{(1 + r_b)^2} + \frac{\$I_3}{(1 + r_b)^3} + \cdots + \frac{\$I_n}{(1 + r_b)^n} + \frac{\$M}{(1 + r_b)^n}$$

$$V_b = \frac{\$I_1/2}{\left(1 + \frac{r_b}{2}\right)^1} + \frac{\$I_2/2}{\left(1 + \frac{r_b}{2}\right)^2} + \frac{\$I_3/2}{\left(1 + \frac{r_b}{2}\right)^3} + \cdots + \frac{\$I_n/2}{\left(1 + \frac{r_b}{2}\right)^{2n}} + \frac{\$M}{\left(1 + \frac{r_b}{2}\right)^{2n}}$$

## Compute a bond's expected rate of return and its current yield. (pgs 235–238)

**SUMMARY:** To measure bondholder's expected rate of return, we find the discount rate that equates the present value of the future cash flows (interest and maturity value) with the current market price of the bond. The expected rate of return for a bond is also the rate of return the investor will earn if the bond is held to maturity, or the yield to maturity. We may also compute the current yield as the annual interest payment divided by the bond's current market price, but this is not an accurate measure of a bondholder's expected rate of return.

### KEY TERMS

**Expected rate of return, page 235** (1) The discount rate that equates the present value of the future cash flows (interest and maturity value) of a bond with its current market price. It is the rate of return an investor will earn if the bond is held to maturity. (2) The rate of return the investor expects to receive on an investment by paying the existing market price of the security.

**Yield to maturity, page 235** The rate of return a bondholder will receive if the bond is held to maturity. (It is equivalent to the expected rate of return.)

**Current yield, page 237** The ratio of a bond's annual interest payment to its market price.

### KEY EQUATIONS

$$
\text{Market price} = P_0 = \frac{\$ \text{ interest in year } 1}{(1 + \text{ expected rate of return })^1}
$$

$$
+ \frac{\$ \text{ interest in year } 2}{(1 + \text{ expected rate of return})^2}
$$

$$
+ \frac{\$ \text{ interest in year } 3}{(1 + \text{ expected rate of return })^3}
$$

$$
+ \cdots
$$

$$
+ \frac{\$ \text{ interest in year } n}{(1 + \text{ expected rate of return })^n}
$$

$$
+ \frac{\$ \text{ maturity value of bond}}{(1 + \text{ expected rate of return })^n}
$$

$$
\text{Current yield} = \frac{\text{annual interest payment}}{\text{current market price of the bond}}
$$

## Explain three important relationships that exist in bond valuation. (pgs 238–242)

**SUMMARY:** Certain key relationships exist in bond valuation, these being:

1. A decrease in interest rates (the required rates of return) will cause the value of a bond to increase; by contrast, an interest rate increase will cause a decrease in value. The change in value caused by changing interest rates is called interest rate risk.

2. If the required rate of return (current interest rate):
   a. Equals the coupon interest rate, the bond will sell at par, or maturity value.
   b. Exceeds the bond's coupon rate, the bond will sell below par value, or at a discount.
   c. Is less than the bond's coupon rate, the bond will sell above par value, or at a premium.

3. A bondholder owning a long-term bond is exposed to greater interest rate risk than one owning a short-term bond.

### KEY TERMS

**Interest rate risk, page 240** The variability in a bond's value caused by changing interest rates.

**Discount bond, page 241** A bond that sells at a discount, or below par value.

**Premium bond, page 241** A bond that is selling above its par value.

# Review Questions

*All Review Questions are available in* MyFinanceLab.

**7-1.** Distinguish between debentures and mortgage bonds.

**7-2.** Define (a) Eurobonds, (b) zero coupon bonds, and (c) junk bonds.

**7-3.** Describe the bondholder's claim on the firm's assets and income.

**7-4.** a.  How does a bond's par value differ from its market value?

   b.  Explain the difference between a bond's coupon interest rate, current yield, and required rate of return.

**7-5.** What factors determine a bond's rating? Why is the rating important to the firm's manager?

**7-6.** What are the basic differences between book value, liquidation value, market value, and intrinsic value?

**7-7.** What is a general definition of the intrinsic value of an asset?

**7-8.** Explain the three factors that determine the intrinsic, or economic, value of an asset.

**7-9.** Explain the relationship between the required rate of return and the value of a security.

**7-10.** Define the expected rate of return to bondholders.

# Study Problems

*All Study Problems are available in* MyFinanceLab.

**7-1.** (*Bond valuation*) Trico bonds have an annual coupon rate of 8 percent and a par value of $1,000 and will mature in 20 years. If you require a return of 7 percent, what price would you be willing to pay for the bond? What happens if you pay *more* for the bond? What happens if you pay *less* for the bond?

**7-2.** (*Bond valuation*) Sunn Co.'s bonds, maturing in 7 years, pay 4 percent interest on a $1,000 face value. However, interest is paid semiannually. If your required rate of return is 5 percent, what is the value of the bond? How would your answer change if the interest were paid annually?

**7-3.** (*Bond valuation*) You own a 20-year, $1,000 par value bond paying 7 percent interest annually. The market price of the bond is $875, and your required rate of return is 10 percent.

   a.  Compute the bond's expected rate of return.
   b.  Determine the value of the bond to you, given your required rate of return.
   c.  Should you sell the bond or continue to own it?

**7-4.** (*Bond valuation*) Calculate the value of a bond that will mature in 14 years and has a $1,000 face value. The annual coupon interest rate is 5 percent, and the investor's required rate of return is 7 percent.

**7-5.** (*Bond valuation*) At the beginning of the year, you bought a $1,000 par value corporate bond with a 6 percent annual coupon rate and a 10-year maturity date. When you bought the bond, it had an expected yield to maturity of 8 percent. Today the bond sells for $1,060.

   a.  What did you pay for the bond?
   b.  If you sold the bond at the end of the year, what would be your one-period return on the investment?

**7-6.** (*Bond valuation*) Shelly Inc. bonds have a 6 percent coupon rate. The interest is paid semiannually, and the bonds mature in 8 years. Their par value is $1,000. If your required rate of return is 4 percent, what is the value of the bond? What is the value if the interest is paid annually?

**7-7.** (*Bond relationship*) Crawford Inc. has two bond issues outstanding, both paying the same annual interest of $55, called Series A and Series B. Series A has a maturity of 12 years, whereas Series B has a maturity of 1 year.

   a.  What would be the value of each of these bonds when the going interest rate is (1) 4 percent, (2) 7 percent, and (3) 10  percent? Assume that there is only one more interest payment to be made on the Series B bonds.
   b.  Why does the longer-term (12-year) bond fluctuate more when interest rates change than does the shorter-term (1-year) bond?

**7-8.** (*Bond valuation*) ExxonMobil 20-year bonds pay 6 percent interest annually on a $1,000 par value. If bonds sell at $945, what is the bonds' expected rate of return?

**7-9.** (*Bond valuation*) National Steel 15-year, $1,000 par value bonds pay 5.5 percent interest annually. The market price of the bonds is $1,085, and your required rate of return is 7 percent.

    a. Compute the bond's expected rate of return.
    b. Determine the value of the bond to you, given your required rate of return.
    c. Should you purchase the bond?

**7-10.** (*Bond valuation*) You own a bond that pays $70 in annual interest, with a $1,000 par value. It matures in 15 years. Your required rate of return is 7 percent.

    a. Calculate the value of the bond.
    b. How does the value change if your required rate of return (1) increases to 9 percent or (2) decreases to 5 percent?
    c. Explain the implications of your answers in part (b) as they relate to interest rate risk, premium bonds, and discount bonds.
    d. Assume that the bond matures in 5 years instead of 15 years. Recompute your answers in part (b).
    e. Explain the implications of your answers in part (d) as they relate to interest rate risk, premium bonds, and discount bonds.

**7-11.** (*Bond valuation*) New Generation Public Utilities issued a bond with a $1,000 par value that pays $30 in annual interest. It matures in 20 years. Your required rate of return is 4 percent.

    a. Calculate the value of the bond.
    b. How does the value change if your required rate of return (1) increases to 7 percent or (2) decreases to 2 percent?
    c. Explain the implications of your answers in part (b) as they relate to interest rate risk, premium bonds, and discount bonds.
    d. Assume that the bond matures in 10 years instead of 20 years. Recompute your answers in part (b).
    e. Explain the implications of your answers in part (d) as they relate to interest rate risk, premium bonds, and discount bonds.

**7-12.** (*Bond valuation—zero coupon*) The Logos Corporation is planning on issuing bonds that pay no interest but can be converted into $1,000 at maturity, 7 years from their purchase. To price these bonds competitively with other bonds of equal risk, it is determined that they should yield 6 percent, compounded annually. At what price should the Logos Corporation sell these bonds?

**7-13.** (*Bond valuation*) You are examining three bonds with a par value of $1,000 (you receive $1,000 at maturity) and are concerned with what would happen to their market value if interest rates (or the market discount rate) changed. The three bonds are

    Bond A—a bond with 3 years left to maturity that has a 6 percent annual coupon interest rate, but the interest is paid semiannually.
    Bond B—a bond with 7 years left to maturity that has a 6 percent annual coupon interest rate, but the interest is paid semiannually.
    Bond C—a bond with 20 years left to maturity that has a 6 percent annual coupon interest rate, but the interest is paid semiannually.

What would be the value of these bonds if the market discount rate were
    a. 6 percent per year compounded semiannually?
    b. 3 percent per year compounded semiannually?
    c. 9 percent per year compounded semiannually?
    d. What observations can you make about these results?

**7-14.** (*Bond valuation*) Bank of America has bonds that pay a 6.5 percent coupon interest rate and mature in 5 years. If an investor has a 4.3 percent required rate of return, what should she be willing to pay for the bond? What happens if she pays more or less?

**7-15.** (*Bond valuation*) Xerox issued bonds that pay $67.50 in interest each year and will mature in 5 years. You are thinking about purchasing the bonds. You have decided that you would need to receive a 5 percent return on your investment. What is the value of the bond to you, first assuming that the interest is paid annually and then semiannually?

**7-16.** (*Bondholders' expected rate of return*) Sharp Co. bonds are selling in the market for $1,045. These 15-year bonds pay 7 percent interest annually on a $1,000 par value. If they are purchased at the market price, what is the expected rate of return?

**7-17.** (*Bondholders' expected rate of return*) The market price is $900 for a 10-year bond ($1,000 par value) that pays 6 percent interest (6 percent semiannually). What is the bond's expected rate of return?

**7-18.** (*Bondholders' expected rate of return*) You own a bond that has a par value of $1,000 and matures in 5 years. It pays a 5 percent annual coupon rate. The bond currently sells for $1,100. What is the bond's expected rate of return?

**7-19.** (*Expected rate of return and current yield*) Time Warner has bonds that are selling for $1,371. The coupon interest rate on the bonds is 9.15 percent and they mature in 21 years. What is the yield to maturity on the bonds? What is the current yield?

**7-20.** (*Expected rate of return and current yield*) Citigroup issued bonds that pay a 5.5 percent coupon interest rate. The bonds mature in 5 years. They are selling for $1,076. What would be your expected rate of return (yield to maturity) if you bought the bonds? What would the current yield be?

**7-21.** (*Bondholders' expected rate of return*) Zenith Co.'s bonds mature in 12 years and pay 7 percent interest annually. If you purchase the bonds for $1,150, what is your expected rate of return?

**7-22.** (*Yield to maturity*) Assume the market price of a 5-year bond for Margaret Inc. is $900, and it has a par value of $1,000. The bond has an annual interest rate of 6 percent that is paid semiannually. What is the yield to maturity of the bond?

**7-23.** (*Current yield*) Assume you have a bond with a semiannual interest payment of $35, a par value of $1,000, and a current market of $780. What is the current yield of the bond?

**7-24.** (*Yield to maturity*) An 8-year bond for Katy Corporation has a market price of $700 and a par value of $1,000. If the bond has an annual interest rate of 6 percent, but pays interest semiannually, what is the bond's yield to maturity?

**7-25.** (*Expected rate of return*) Assume you own a bond with a market value of $820 that matures in 7 years. The par value of the bond is $1,000. Interest payments of $30 are paid semiannually. What is your expected rate of return on the bond?

**7-26.** (*Yield to maturity*) You own a 10-year bond that pays 6 percent interest annually. The par value of the bond is $1,000 and the market price of the bond is $900. What is the yield to maturity of the bond?

**7-27.** (*Bondholders' expected rate of return*) You purchased a bond for $1,100. The bond has a coupon rate of 8 percent, which is paid semiannually. It matures in 7 years and has a par value of $1,000. What is your expected rate of return?

# Mini Case

This Mini Case is available in MyFinanceLab.

Here are data on $1,000 par value bonds issued by Microsoft, GE Capital, and Morgan Stanley at the end of 2012. Assume you are thinking about buying these bonds as of January 2013. Answer the following questions:

    a. Assuming interest is paid annually, calculate the values of the bonds if your required rates of return are as follows: Microsoft, 6 percent; GE Capital, 8 percent; and Morgan Stanley, 10 percent; where

| | MICROSOFT | GE CAPITAL | MORGAN STANLEY |
|---|---|---|---|
| Coupon interest rate | 5.25% | 4.25% | 4.75% |
| Years to maturity | 30 | 10 | 5 |

b. At the end of 2008, the bonds were selling for the following amounts:

| Microsoft | $1,100 |
| GE Capital | $1,030 |
| Morgan Stanley | $1,015 |

What were the expected rates of return for each bond?

c. How would the value of the bonds change if (1) your required rate of return ($r_b$) increased 2 percentage points or (2) decreased 2 percentage points?

d. Explain the implications of your answers in part (b) in terms of interest rate risk, premium bonds, and discount bonds.

e. Should you buy the bonds? Explain.

# 8

# The Valuation and Characteristics of Stock

## Learning Objectives

| | | |
|---|---|---|
| **1** | **Identify** the basic characteristics of preferred stock. | **Preferred Stock** |
| **2** | **Value** preferred stock. | **Valuing Preferred Stock** |
| **3** | **Identify** the basic characteristics of common stock. | **Common Stock** |
| **4** | **Value** common stock. | **Valuing Common Stock** |
| **5** | **Calculate** a stock's expected rate of return. | **The Expected Rate of Return of Stockholders** |

In the entertainment industry, Netflix was a well-recognized success story. That is, it was a success until 2011 when it changed how it charged its customers who subscribed to its services. Previously, you could stream videos to your television or computer or order videos through the mail, all for about $10. The firm's management changed the subscription plan so that you had to purchase the two plans separately, paying about $8 for each. Thus, if you wanted to continue with what you had previously, the cost became almost $16—a 60-percent increase in your cost. The price increase sparked 80,000 comments on the company's Facebook page. Netflix lost subscribers as well as stock market value in the wake of the controversial price increase.

To compound the problem, pay channel Starz, which controls the rights to movies from Sony Pictures and Walt Disney Pictures, announced it would not renew a deal allowing Netflix to stream those films. Some analysts considered the partnership with Starz to be worth as much as $300 million.

Netflix's CEO responded with a letter, saying, "We hate making our subscribers upset with us, but we feel like we provide a fantastic service and we're working hard to further improve the quality and range of our streaming content."

Not only did Netflix lose customers, but the stockholders saw the value of their stock plummet. In one day, the price was down 17 percent. By year end, the stock price had declined from almost $300 to slightly more than $70, with the price still in the $80 range in June 2012. Lazard Capital Markets analyst Barton Crockett called the news "a rare, large and surprising misstep" for the company.

How much value was destroyed for the firm's owners? The total value of Netflix's stock declined by some $12 billion to slightly over $4 billion! It could be that the large loss in stock value, which is tied to the loss in customers, has kept the Netflix management up late at night. After all, creating shareholder value, not destroying it, is a basic goal for management. In this chapter, we will look closely at how stock is valued, which is vital for a manager to understand.

In Chapter 7, we developed a general concept about valuation, and economic value was defined as the present value of the expected future cash flows generated by an asset. We then applied that concept to valuing bonds.

We continue our study of valuation in this chapter, but we now give our attention to valuing stocks, both preferred stock and common stock. As already noted at the outset of our study of finance and on several occasions since, the financial manager's objective should be to maximize the value of the firm's common stock. Thus, we need to understand what determines stock value. Also, only with an understanding of valuation can we compute a firm's cost of capital, a concept essential to making effective capital investment decisions—an issue to be discussed in Chapter 9.

# Preferred Stock

 **Identify the basic characteristics of preferred stock.**

**Preferred stock** is often referred to as a *hybrid security* because it has *many characteristics of both common stock and bonds*. Preferred stock is similar to common stock in that (1) it has no fixed maturity date, (2) if the firm fails to pay dividends, it does not bring on bankruptcy, and (3) dividends are not deductible for tax purposes. On the other hand, preferred stock is similar to bonds in that dividends are fixed in amount.

The amount of the preferred stock dividend is generally fixed either as a dollar amount or as a percentage of the par value. For example, Georgia Pacific has preferred stock outstanding that pays an annual dividend of $53, whereas AT&T has some 6⅜ percent preferred stock outstanding. The AT&T preferred stock has a par value of $25; hence, each share pays 6.375 percent × $25, or $1.59 in dividends annually.

To begin, we first discuss several features associated with almost all preferred stock. Then we take a brief look at methods of retiring preferred stock. We close by learning how to value preferred stock.

**preferred stock** a hybrid security with characteristics of both common stock and bonds. Preferred stock is similar to common stock in that it has no fixed maturity date, the nonpayment of dividends does not bring on bankruptcy, and dividends are not deductible for tax purposes. Preferred stock is similar to bonds in that dividends are limited in amount.

## The Characteristics of Preferred Stock

Although each issue of preferred stock is unique, a number of characteristics are common to almost all issues. Some of these more frequent traits include

♦ Multiple series of preferred stock
♦ Preferred stock's claim on assets and income

Source: Ben Fritz, "Netflix Shares Tumble as Subscribers Leave After Price Increase," *Los Angeles Times*, September 11, 2011, http://latimesblogs.latimes.com/entertainmentnewsbuzz/2011/09/netflix-shares-tumble-as-subscribers-leave-following-price-increase.html, accessed May 26, 2012; "Netflix to Lose Starz, Its Most Valuable Source of New Movies," *Los Angeles Times*, September 1, 2011, http://latimesblogs.latimes.com/entertainmentnewsbuzz/2011/09/netflix-to-lose-starz-its-most-valuable-source-of-new-movies.html, accessed May 27, 2012; "Netflix Revenue and Guidance Disappoints Wall Street," *Los Angeles Times*, July 25, 2011, http://latimesblogs.latimes.com/entertainmentnewsbuzz/2011/07/netflix-stock-drops-as-wall-street-disappointed-with-revenue-and-guidance.html, accessed May 27, 2012: and "Netflix Misses on Revenve, Stock Plunges" by Matt Rosoff, from BUSINESS INSIDER, July 25, 2011."

♦ Cumulative dividends
♦ Protective provisions
♦ Convertibility
♦ Retirement provisions

All these features are presented in the discussion that follows.

**Multiple Series**   If a company desires, it can issue more than one series of preferred stock, and each series can have different characteristics. In fact, it is quite common for firms that issue preferred stock to issue more than one series. These issues can be differentiated in that some are convertible into common stock and others are not, and they have varying protective provisions in the event of bankruptcy. For instance, the Xerox Corporation has a Series B and Series C preferred stock.

**Claim on Assets and Income**   Preferred stock has priority over common stock with regard to claims on assets in the case of bankruptcy. The preferred stock claim is honored after that of bonds and before that of common stock. Multiple issues of preferred stock may be given an order of priority. Preferred stock also has a claim on income before common stock. That is, the firm must pay its preferred stock dividends before it pays common stock dividends. Thus, in terms of risk, preferred stock is safer than common stock because it has a prior claim on assets and income. However, it is riskier than long-term debt because its claims on assets and income come after those of debt, such as bonds.

**cumulative feature** a requirement that all past, unpaid preferred stock dividends be paid before any common stock dividends are declared.

**Cumulative Dividends**   Most preferred stocks carry a **cumulative feature** that *requires all past, unpaid preferred stock dividends be paid before any common stock dividends are declared.* The purpose is to provide some degree of protection for the preferred shareholder.

**protective provisions** provisions for preferred stock that protect the investor's interest. The provisions generally allow for voting in the event of nonpayment of dividends, or they restrict the payment of common stock dividends if sinking-fund payments are not met or if the firm is in financial difficulty.

**convertible preferred stock** preferred shares that can be converted into a predetermined number of shares of common stock, if investors so choose.

**call provision** a provision that entitles the corporation to repurchase its preferred stock from investors at stated prices over specified periods.

**Protective Provisions**   In addition to the cumulative feature, protective provisions are common to preferred stock. These **protective provisions** generally *allow for voting rights in the event of nonpayment of dividends, or they restrict the payment of common stock dividends if the preferred stock payments are not met or if the firm is in financial difficulty.* For example, consider the stocks of Tenneco Corporation and Reynolds Metals. Tenneco preferred stock has a protective provision that provides preferred stockholders with voting rights whenever six quarterly dividends are in arrears. At that point, the preferred shareholders are given the power to elect a majority of the board of director's. Reynolds Metals preferred stock includes a protective provision that precludes the payment of common stock dividends during any period in which the preferred stock payments are in default. Both provisions offer preferred stockholders protection beyond that provided by the cumulative provision and further reduce their risk. Because of these protective provisions, preferred stockholders do not require as high a rate of return. That is, they will accept a lower dividend payment.

**Convertibility**   Much of the preferred stock that is issued today is **convertible preferred stock**; that is, *at the discretion of the holder, the stock can be converted into a predetermined number of shares of common stock.* In fact, today about one-third of all preferred stock issued has a convertibility feature. The convertibility feature is, of course, desirable to the investor and, thus, reduces the cost of the preferred stock to the issuer.

**Retirement Provisions**   Although preferred stock does not have a set maturity date associated with it, issuing firms generally provide for some method of retiring the stock, usually in the form of a call provision or a sinking fund. A **call provision** *entitles a company to repurchase its preferred stock from holders at stated prices over a given time period.* In fact, the Securities and Exchange Commission discourages firms from issuing preferred stock without some call provision. For example,

---

**REMEMBER YOUR PRINCIPLES**

**P**rinciple   Valuing preferred stock relies on three of our principles presented in Chapter 1, namely:

**Principle 1: Cash Flow Is What Matters.**
**Principle 2: Money Has a Time Value.**
**Principle 3: Risk Requires a Reward.**

Determining the economic worth, or value, of an asset always relies on these three principles. Without them, we would have no basis for explaining value. With them, we can know that the amount and timing of cash, not earnings, drives value. Also, we must be rewarded for taking risk; otherwise, we will not invest.

Apartment Investment and Management Company, a real estate investment trust that engages in acquiring and managing apartment properties, published the following news release:

> **Denver, January 26, 2012 (BUSINESS WIRE)**—Apartment Investment and Management Company ("Aimco") announced it will redeem all outstanding shares of its Cumulative Preferred Stock.… Redemptions will occur on July 26, 2012, at $25.00 per share plus an amount equal to accumulated and unpaid dividends of $0.0646 per share. The total redemption payments of $25.0646 per share is payable only in cash. After the redemption date, the Preferred Stock no longer will be outstanding and holders of Preferred Stock will have only the right to receive payment of the redemption price in exchange for their Preferred Stock certificates.

The call feature on preferred stock usually requires buyers to pay an initial premium of approximately 10 percent above the par value or issuing price of the preferred stock. Then, over time, the call premium generally decreases. By setting the initial call price above the initial issue price and allowing it to decline slowly over time, the firm protects the investor from an early call that carries no premium. A call provision also allows the issuing firm to plan the retirement of its preferred stock at predetermined prices.

A **sinking-fund provision** *requires the firm to periodically set aside an amount of money for the retirement of its preferred stock.* This money is then used to purchase the preferred stock in the open market or to call the stock, whichever method is cheaper. For instance, the Xerox Corporation has two preferred stock issues, one that has a 7-year sinking-fund provision and another with a 17-year sinking-fund provision.

> **sinking-fund provision** a protective provision that requires the firm periodically to set aside an amount of money for the retirement of its preferred stock. This money is then used to purchase the preferred stock in the open market or through the use of the call provision, whichever method is cheaper.

# Valuing Preferred Stock

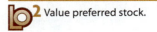 Value preferred stock.

As already explained, the owner of preferred stock generally receives a constant dividend from the investment in each period. In addition, most preferred stocks are perpetuities (nonmaturing). In this instance, finding the value (present value) of preferred stock, ($V_{ps}$), with a level cash-flow stream continuing indefinitely, may best be explained by an example.

Consider Pacific & Gas Electric's preferred stock issue. In similar fashion to valuing bonds in Chapter 7, we use a three-step valuation procedure.

**STEP 1**   Estimate the amount and timing of the receipt of the future cash flows the preferred stock is expected to provide. PG&E's preferred stock pays an annual dividend of $1.25. The shares do not have a maturity date; that is, they are a perpetuity.

**STEP 2**   Evaluate the riskiness of the preferred stock's future dividends and determine the investor's required rate of return. The investor's required rate of return is assumed to equal 5 percent for the preferred stock.[1]

**STEP 3**   Calculate the economic, or intrinsic, value of the PG&E share of preferred stock, which is the present value of the expected dividends discounted at the investor's required rate of return. The valuation model for a share of preferred stock, $V_{ps}$, is therefore defined as follows:

$$\text{Preferred Stock Value} = \frac{\text{dividend in year 1}}{(1 + \text{required rate of return})^1} \tag{8-1}$$
$$+ \frac{\text{dividend in year 2}}{(1 + \text{required rate of return})^2}$$
$$+ \cdots + \frac{\text{dividend in infinity}}{(1 + \text{required rate of return})^\infty}$$
$$= \frac{D_1}{(1 + r_{ps})^1} + \frac{D_2}{(1 + r_{ps})^2} + \cdots + \frac{D_\infty}{(1 + r_{ps})^\infty}$$

---

[1]In Chapter 6, we learned about measuring an investor's required rate of return.

# FINANCE AT WORK

## READING A STOCK QUOTE IN THE *WALL STREET JOURNAL*

If you want to check on a stock, you can look in the hard copy of the *Wall Street Journal* to find the ticker symbol, the closing prices of the stock on the previous day, and the percentage change in the price from the day before. However, the list only includes the 1,000 largest companies. If you would like to have more information for all publicly traded stock, you will need to go to the online version of the *Wall Street Journal* (http://online.wsj.com), choose *markets*, and select *stocks*. You can then select from a number of options for finding stock quotes. For instance, if you want to look at all the stocks traded on the New York Stock Exchange, you would choose the link for *markets*, then the *market data* link, and then the link for *U.S. stocks*. At that point, you will see a list of different exchanges. Choose the *NYSE stocks* link. You will then see all the stocks listed on the New York Exchange.

At this link, you will find more complete information about a stock, including:

- The stock's ticker symbol
- The opening, high, low, and closing price for the day, as well as the high and low prices for the past 52 weeks
- The dollar and percentage change in the price of the stock from the prior day
- The percentage change in the stock price from a year ago
- The number of shares that were traded during the day
- The stock's dividend per share, dividend yield (dividend per share ÷ stock price), and the price/earnings ratio (stock price ÷ earnings per share)

To illustrate, on July 5, 2012, the following information was provided for General Electric:

| | PRICES FOR JULY 5, 2012 | | | | | |
|---|---|---|---|---|---|---|
| **SYMBOL** | **OPEN** | **HIGH** | **LOW** | **CLOSE** | **NET CHG** | **% CHG** |
| GE | 20.34 | 20.48 | 20.29 | 20.33 | −0.1 | −0.049 |

| **VOLUME OF SHARES TRADED** | **52 WEEK HIGH** | **52 WEEK LOW** | **DIVIDEND PER SHARE** | **DIVIDEND YIELD** | **PRICE TO EARNINGS** | **YTD % CHG** |
|---|---|---|---|---|---|---|
| 28,622,062 | 21.00 | 14.02 | 0.68 | 3.34 | 16.51 | 13.51 |

Notice that equation (8-1) is a restatement in a slightly different form of equation (7-1) in Chapter 7. Recall that equation (7-1) states that the value of an asset is the present value of future cash flows to be received by the investor.

Because the dividends in each period are equal for preferred stock, equation (8-1) can be reduced to the following relationship:[2]

$$\text{Preferred stock value} = \frac{\text{annual dividend}}{\text{required rate of return}} = \frac{D}{r_{ps}} \qquad (8\text{-}2)$$

[2]To verify this result, we begin with equation (8-1):

$$V_{ps} = \frac{D_1}{(1 + r_{ps})^1} + \frac{D_2}{(1 + r_{ps})^2} + \cdots + \frac{D_n}{(1 + r_{ps})^n}$$

If we multiply both sides of this equation by $(1 + r_{ps})$, we have

$$V_{ps}(1 + r_{ps}) = D_1 + \frac{D_2}{(1 + r_{ps})} + \cdots + \frac{D_n}{(1 + r_{ps})^{n-1}} \qquad (8\text{-}1\text{i})$$

Subtracting (8-1) from (8-1i) yields

$$V_{ps}(1 + r_{ps} - 1) = D_1 - \frac{D_n}{(1 + r_{ps})^n} \qquad (8\text{-}1\text{ii})$$

As $n$ approaches infinity, $D_n/(1 + r_{ps})^n$ approaches zero. Consequently,

$$V_{ps} r_{ps} = D_1 \text{ and } V_{ps} = \frac{D_1}{r_{ps}} \qquad (8\text{-}1\text{iii})$$

Because $D_1 = D_2 = \cdots = D_n$, we need not designate the year. Therefore,

$$V_{ps} = \frac{D}{r_{ps}} \qquad (8\text{-}2)$$

Equation (8-2) represents the present value of an infinite stream of cash flows, when the cash flows are the same each year.

We can now determine the value of the PG&E preferred stock, as described on page 253, as follows:

$$V_{PS} = \frac{D}{r_p} = \frac{\$1.25}{0.05} = \$25$$

In summary, the value of a preferred stock is the present value of all future dividends. But because most preferred stocks are nonmaturing—the dividends continue to infinity—we rely on a shortcut for finding value as represented by equation (8-2).

---

**EXAMPLE 8.1**    **Solving for the value of a preferred stock**

Deutsche Bank has several preferred stock issues outstanding. One issue, a 7.35 percent preferred stock, was sold at its par value of $25. The stock pays an annual dividend of $1.84. The firm has the right to redeem the stock at 10 percent above par.

1. If investors have a 6 percent required rate of return today, in order to be interested in buying the stock, what value would they assign to the stock?
2. How would your answer change if their required return was only 4 percent? What if it increased to 9 percent?
3. How do you feel about the stock being redeemable?

**STEP 1: FORMULATE A SOLUTION STRATEGY**

The basic framework for valuing preferred stock is provided by equation (8-1), which is shown as follows:

$$
\begin{aligned}
\text{Preferred stock value} &= \frac{\text{dividend in year 1}}{(1 + \text{required rate of return})^1} \\
&+ \frac{\text{dividend in year 2}}{(1 + \text{required rate of return})^2} \\
&+ \cdots + \frac{\text{dividend in infinity}}{(1 + \text{required rate of return})^\infty} \\
&= \frac{D_1}{(1 + r_{ps})^1} + \frac{D_2}{(1 + r_{ps})^2} + \cdots + \frac{D_\infty}{(1 + r_{ps})^\infty}
\end{aligned}
$$

While equation (8-1) conveys the fundamental concept that the value of a preferred stock is equal to the present value of all dividends continuing in perpetuity, it does not allow us to solve the problem. Instead, equation (8-2) reduces equation (8-1) to a workable solution, as long as the dividends are constant each year and the security does not mature.

$$\text{Preferred stock value} = \frac{\text{annual dividend}}{\text{required rate of return}} = \frac{D}{r_{ps}} \qquad (8\text{-}2)$$

**STEP 2: CRUNCH THE NUMBERS**

Values of the Deutsche Bank preferred stock for the different required rates of return are as follows:

| REQUIRED RATE OF RETURN | SOLUTION | ANSWER |
|---|---|---|
| 6% | $\dfrac{\$1.84}{0.06}$ | = $30.67 |
| 4% | $\dfrac{\$1.84}{0.04}$ | = $46.00 |
| 9% | $\dfrac{\$1.84}{0.09}$ | = $20.44 |

**STEP 3: ANALYZE YOUR RESULTS**

When the Deutsche Bank preferred stock was sold at the $25 par value, the investors' required rate of return was equal to the coupon dividend rate of 7.35 percent. However, there is an inverse relationship between value and rates of return. As an investor's required rate of return increases (decreases) the security value decreases (increases).

You would prefer that the stock not be redeemable. The firm will recall the stock only if it is in its best interest, not yours. For instance if with time the firm could issue preferred stock with a lower dividend rate, it would be inclined to do so, and at the same time you might not be able to find a comparable stock with the same return. Thus, an investor should require a slightly higher required rate of return if a stock is redeemable.

In conclusion, we can understand the process for valuing preferred stock as well as the method for valuing preferred stock by using the following two financial tools:

## FINANCIAL DECISION TOOLS

| Name of Tool | Formula | What It Tells You |
|---|---|---|
| Preferred stock valuation equation | $\text{Preferred stock value} = \dfrac{\text{dividend in year 1}}{(1 + \text{required rate of return})^1}$ $+ \dfrac{\text{dividend in year 2}}{(1 + \text{required rate of return})^2}$ $+ \cdots + \dfrac{\text{dividend in infinity}}{(1 + \text{required rate of return})^\infty}$ $= \dfrac{D_1}{(1 + r_{ps})^1} + \dfrac{D_2}{(1 + r_{ps})^2} + \cdots + \dfrac{D_\infty}{(1 + r_{ps})^\infty}$ | The value of a preferred stock is equal to the present value of all future dividends in perpetuity. |
| Preferred stock valuation with constant dividend | $V_{ps} = \dfrac{\text{annual dividend}}{\text{required rate of return}} = \dfrac{D}{r_{ps}}$ | The value of a preferred stock where all dividends are equal in perpetuity. |

## Concept Check

1. What features of preferred stock are different from bonds?
2. What provisions are available to protect a preferred stockholder?
3. What cash flows associated with preferred stock are included in the valuation model equation (8-1)? Why is the valuation model simplified in equation (8-2)?

## CAN YOU DO IT?

### VALUING PREFERRED STOCK

If a preferred stock pays 4 percent on its par, or stated, value of $100, and your required rate of return is 7 percent, what is the stock worth to you?
(The solution can be found on page 257.)

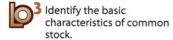 **3** Identify the basic characteristics of common stock.

**common stock** shares that represent the ownership in a corporation.

# Common Stock

**Common stock** is *a certificate that indicates ownership in a corporation*. (An example of a stock certificate is shown in Figure 8-1.) In effect, bondholders and preferred stockholders can be viewed as creditors, whereas the common stockholders are the true owners of the firm. Common stock does not have a maturity date but exists as long as the firm does. Common stock also does not have an upper limit on its dividend payments. Dividend payments must be declared each period (usually quarterly) by the firm's board of directors. In the event of bankruptcy, the common stockholders, as owners of the corporation, will not receive any payment until the firm's creditors, including the bondholders and preferred shareholders, have been paid. Next we look at several characteristics of common stock. Then we focus on valuing common stock.

## FIGURE 8-1  Sample Stock

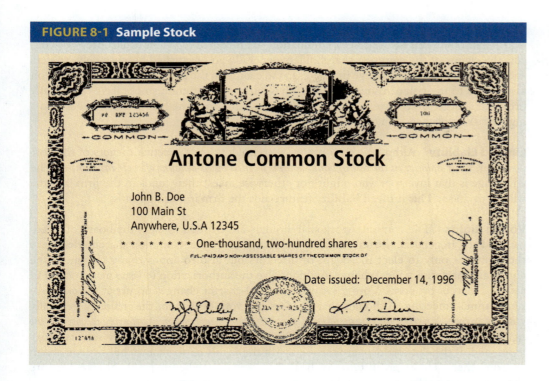

## The Characteristics of Common Stock

We now examine common stock's claim on income and assets, its limited liability feature, and holders' voting and preemptive rights.

**Claim on Income**   As the owners, the common shareholders have the right to the residual income after creditors and preferred stockholders have been paid. This income may be paid directly to the shareholders in the form of dividends or retained within the firm and reinvested in the business. Although it is obvious the shareholder benefits immediately from the distribution of income in the form of dividends, the reinvestment of earnings also benefits the shareholder. Plowing back earnings into the firm should result in an increase in the value of the firm, its earning power, future dividends, and, ultimately, an increase in the value of the stock. In effect, residual income is distributed directly to shareholders in the form of dividends or indirectly in the form of capital gains (value increases) on their common stock.

The right to residual income has advantages and disadvantages for the common stockholder. The advantage is that the potential return is limitless. Once the claims of the senior securities, such as bonds and preferred stock, have been satisfied, the remaining income flows to the common stockholders in the form of dividends or capital gains. The disadvantage is that if the bond and preferred stock claims on income totally absorb earnings, common shareholders receive nothing. In years when earnings fall, it is the common shareholders who suffer first.

## DID YOU GET IT?
### VALUING PREFERRED STOCK

The value of the preferred stock would be $57.14:

$$\text{Value} = \frac{\text{dividend}}{\text{required rate return}} = \frac{0.04 \times \$100}{0.07} = \frac{\$4}{0.07} = \$57.14$$

In other words, a preferred stock, or any security for that matter, that pays a constant $4 annually in perpetuity because it has no maturity date is valued by dividing the annual payment by the investor's required rate of return. With this simple computation, you are finding the present value of the future cash-flow stream.

**Claim on Assets**    Just as common stock has a residual claim on income, it also has a residual claim on assets in the case of liquidation. Unfortunately, when bankruptcy does occur, the claims of the common shareholders generally go unsatisfied because debt holders and preferred stockholders have first and second claims on the assets. This residual claim on assets adds to the risk of common stock. Thus, although common stocks have historically provided a large return, averaging 10 percent annually since the late 1920s, there is also a higher risk associated with common stock.

**Limited Liability**    Although the common shareholders are the actual owners of the corporation, their *liability in the case of bankruptcy is limited to the amount of their investment*. The advantage is that investors who might not otherwise invest their funds in the firm become willing to do so. This **limited liability** feature aids the firm in raising funds.

> **limited liability** a protective provision whereby the investor is not liable for more than the amount he or she has invested in the firm.

**Voting Rights**    The common stock shareholders are entitled to elect the board of directors and are, in general, the only security holders given a vote. Common shareholders have the right not only to elect the board of directors but also to approve any change in the corporate charter. A typical change might involve the authorization to issue new stock or to accept a merger proposal. Voting for directors and charter changes occurs at the corporation's annual meeting. Although shareholders can vote in person, the majority generally vote by proxy. A **proxy** *gives a designated party the temporary power of attorney to vote for the signee at the corporation's annual meeting*. The firm's management generally solicits proxy votes, and, if the shareholders are satisfied with the firm's performance, has little problem securing them. However, in times of financial distress or when managerial takeovers are threatened, **proxy fights**—*battles between rival groups for proxy votes*—occur.

> **proxy** a means of voting in which a designated party is provided with the temporary power of attorney to vote for the signee at the corporation's annual meeting.

> **proxy fight** a battle between rival groups for proxy votes in order to control the decisions made in a stockholders' meeting.

Although each share of common stock carries the same number of votes, the voting procedure is not always the same from company to company. The two procedures commonly used are majority and cumulative voting. Under **majority voting**, *each share of stock allows the shareholder one vote and each position on the board of directors is voted on separately*. Because each member of the board of directors is elected by a simple majority, a majority of shares has the power to elect the entire board of directors.

> **majority voting** voting in which each share of stock allows the shareholder one vote and each position on the board of directors is voted on separately. As a result, a majority of shares has the power to elect the entire board of directors.

With **cumulative voting**, *each share of stock allows the stockholder a number of votes equal to the number of directors being elected*. The shareholder can then cast all of his or her votes for a single candidate or split them among the various candidates. The advantage of a cumulative voting procedure is that it gives minority shareholders the power to elect a director.

> **cumulative voting** voting in which each share of stock allows the shareholder a number of votes equal to the number of directors being elected. The shareholder can then cast all of his or her votes for a single candidate or split them among the various candidates.

In theory, the shareholders pick the corporate board of directors, generally through proxy voting, and the board of directors, in turn, picks the management. In reality, shareholders are offered a slate of nominees selected by management from which to choose. The end result is that management effectively selects the directors, who then may have more allegiance to the managers than to the shareholders. This sets up the potential for agency problems in which a divergence of interests between managers and shareholders is allowed to exist, with the board of directors not monitoring the managers on behalf of the shareholders as they should.

**Preemptive Rights**    The **preemptive right** *entitles the common shareholder to maintain a proportionate share of ownership in the firm*. When new shares are issued, common shareholders have the first right of refusal. If a shareholder owns 25 percent of the corporation's stock, then he or she is entitled to purchase 25 percent of the new shares. *Certificates issued to the shareholders giving them an option to purchase a stated number of new shares of stock at a specified price during a 2- to 10-week period* are called **rights**. These rights can be exercised (generally at a price set by management below the common stock's current market price), allowed to expire, or sold in the open market.

> **preemptive right** the right entitling the common shareholder to maintain his or her proportionate share of ownership in the firm.

> **right** a certificate issued to common stockholders giving them an option to purchase a stated number of new shares at a specified price during a 2- to 10-week period.

> **LO4** Value common stock.

# Valuing Common Stock

Like bonds and preferred stock, a common stock's value is equal to the present value of all future cash flows—dividends in this case—expected to be received by the stockholder. However, in contrast to preferred stock dividends, common stock does not provide the investor with a predetermined, constant dividend. For common stock, the dividend is based on the profitability of the firm and its decision to pay dividends or to retain the profits for reinvestment. As a consequence, dividend streams tend to increase with the growth in corporate earnings. Thus, the growth of future dividends is a prime distinguishing feature of common stock.

***The Growth Factor in Valuing Common Stock***   What is meant by the term *growth* when used in the context of valuing common stock? A company can grow in a variety of ways. It can become larger by borrowing money to invest in new projects. Likewise, it can issue new stock for expansion. Managers can also acquire another company to merge with the existing firm, which would increase the firm's assets. Although it can accurately be said that the firm has grown, the original stockholders may or may not participate in this growth. Growth is realized through the infusion of new capital. The firm size clearly increases, but unless the original investors increase their investment in the firm, they will own a smaller portion of the expanded business.

Another means of growing is **internal growth**, which requires that *managers retain some or all of the firm's profits for reinvestment in the firm*, resulting in the growth of future earnings and, hopefully, the value of the common stock. This process underlies the essence of potential growth for the firm's current stockholders and is the only relevant growth for our purposes of valuing a firm's common shares.[3]

**internal growth** a firm's growth rate resulting from reinvesting the company's profits rather than distributing them as dividends. The growth rate is a function of the amount retained and the return earned on the retained funds.

To illustrate the nature of internal growth, assume that the return on equity for PepsiCo is 16 percent.[4] If PepsiCo decides to pay all the profits out in dividends to its stockholders, the firm will experience no growth internally. It might become larger by borrowing more money or issuing new stock, but internal growth will come only through the retention of profits. If, on the other hand, PepsiCo retains all of the profits, the stockholders' investment in the firm would grow by the amount of profits retained, or by 16 percent. If, however, PepsiCo keeps only 50 percent of the profits for reinvestment, the common shareholders' investment would increase only by half of the 16 percent return on equity, or by 8 percent. We can express this relationship by the following equation:

$$g = ROE \times pr \tag{8-3}$$

where $g$ = the growth rate of future earnings and the growth in the common stockholders' investment in the firm

$ROE$ = the return on equity (net income/common book value)

$pr$ = *the company's percentage of profits retained*, called the **profit-retention rate**[5]

**profit-retention rate** the company's percentage of profits retained.

Therefore, if only 25 percent of the profits were retained by PepsiCo, we would expect the common stockholders' investment in the firm and the value of the stock price to increase, or grow, by 4 percent; that is,

$$g = 16\% \times 0.25 = 4\%$$

In summary, common stockholders frequently rely on an increase in the stock price as a source of return. If the company is retaining a portion of its earnings for reinvestment, future profits and dividends should grow. This growth should be reflected by an increase in the market price of the common stock in future periods. Therefore, both types of return (dividends and price appreciation) must be recognized in valuing common stock.

---

[3]We are not arguing that the existing common stockholders never benefit from the use of external financing; however, such benefit is nominal if capital markets are efficient.

[4]The return on equity is the accounting rate of return on the common shareholders' investment in the company and is computed as follows:

$$\text{Return on equity} = \frac{\text{net income}}{(\text{common stock} + \text{retained earnings})}$$

[5]The retention rate is also equal to (1 − the percentage of profits paid out in dividends). *The percentage of profits paid out in dividends* is often called the **dividend-payout ratio**.

**dividend-payout ratio** dividends as a percentage of earnings.

***Dividend Valuation Model***  The value of a common stock when defining value as the present value of future dividends relies on the same basic equation that we used with preferred stock [equation (8-1)], with the exception that we are using the required rate of return of common stockholders, $r_{cs}$. That is,

$$V_{cs} = \frac{D_1}{(1 + r_{cs})^1} + \frac{D_2}{(1 + r_{cs})^2} + \cdots + \frac{D_n}{(1 + r_{cs})^n} + \cdots + \frac{D_\infty}{(1 + r_{cs})^\infty} \qquad (8\text{-}4)$$

If you turn back to Chapter 7 and compare equation (7-1) with equation (8-4), you will notice that equation (8-4) is merely a restatement of equation (7-1). Recall that equation (7-1), which is the basis for our work in valuing securities, states that the value of an asset is the present value of future cash flows to be received by the investor. Equation (8-4) simply applies equation (7-1) to valuing common stock.

Equation (8-4) indicates that we are discounting the dividend at the end of the first year, $D_1$, back 1 year; the dividend in the second year, $D_2$, back 2 years; the dividend in the $n$th year back $n$ years; and the dividend in infinity back an infinite number of years. The required rate of return is $r_{cs}$. In using equation (8-4), note that the value of the stock is established at the beginning of the year, say January 1, 2013. The most recent past dividend, $D_0$, would have been paid the previous day, December 31, 2012. Thus, if we purchased the stock on January 1, the first dividend would be received in 12 months, on December 31, 2013, which is represented by $D_1$.

Fortunately, equation (8-4) can be reduced to a much more manageable form if dividends grow each year at a constant rate, $g$. The constant-growth, common-stock valuation equation can be presented as follows:[6]

$$\text{Common stock value} = \frac{\text{dividend in year 1}}{\text{required rate of return} - \text{growth rate}}$$

$$V_{cs} = \frac{D_1}{r_{cs} - g} \qquad (8\text{-}5)$$

In other words, the intrinsic value (present value) of a share of common stock whose dividends grow at a constant annual rate can be calculated using equation (8-5). Although the interpretation of this equation might not be intuitively obvious, simply remember that it solves for the present value of the future dividend stream growing at a rate, $g$, to infinity, assuming that $r_{cs}$ is greater than $g$.

To illustrate the process of valuing a common stock, consider the valuation of a share of common stock that paid a $2 dividend at the end of last year and is expected to pay a cash

---

[6]When common stock dividends grow at a constant rate of $g$ every year, we can express the dividend in any year in terms of the dividend paid at the end of the previous year, $D_0$. For example, the expected dividend year 1 hence is simply $D_0(1 + g)$. Likewise, the dividend at the end of $t$ years is $D_0(1 + g)^t$. Using this notation, the common stock valuation equation in (8-4) can be rewritten as follows:

$$V_{cs} = \frac{D_0 (1 + r_{cs})^1}{(1 + g)^1} + \frac{D_0 (1 + g)^2}{(1 + r_{cs})^2} + \cdots + \frac{D_0 (1 + g)^n}{(1 + r_{cs})^n} + \cdots + \frac{D_0 (1 + g)^\infty}{(1 + r_{cs})^\infty} \qquad (8\text{-}4\text{i})$$

If both sides of equation (8-4i) are multiplied by $(1 + r_{cs})/(1 + g)$ and then equation (8-5) is subtracted from the product, the result is

$$\frac{V_{cs} (1 + r_{cs})}{1 + g} - V_{cs} = D_0 - \frac{D_0 (1 + g)^\infty}{(1 + r_{cs})^\infty} \qquad (8\text{-}4\text{ii})$$

If $r_{cs} > g$, which normally should hold, $[D_0(1 + g)/(1 + r_{cs})^\infty]$ approaches zero. As a result,

$$\frac{V_{cs} (1 + r_{cs})}{1 + g} - V_{cs} = D_0$$

$$V_{cs}\left(\frac{1 + r_{cs}}{1 + g}\right) - V_{cs}\left(\frac{1 + g}{1 + g}\right) = D_0$$

$$V_{cs}\left[\frac{(1 + r_{cs}) - (1 + g)}{1 + g}\right] = D_0 \qquad (8\text{-}4\text{iii})$$

$$V_{cs} (r_{cs} - g) = D_0 (1 + g)$$

$$V_{cs} = \frac{D_1}{r_{cs} - g}$$

## CAN YOU DO IT?

### MEASURING JOHNSON & JOHNSON'S GROWTH RATE

In 2012, Johnson & Johnson had a return on equity of 19.47 percent, as computed to the right. The firm's earnings per share was $4.63 and it paid $1.87 in dividends per share. If these relationships hold in the future, what will be the firm's internal growth rate?

(The solution can be found on page 262.)

$$\text{Return on equity (ROE)} = \frac{\text{net income}}{\text{common stock} + \text{retained earnings}}$$

$$= \frac{\$12,849}{\$66,499}$$

$$= 0.1932 = 19.32\%$$

dividend every year from now to infinity. Each year the dividends are expected to grow at a rate of 4 percent. Based on an assessment of the riskiness of the common stock, the investor's required rate of return is 14 percent. Using this information, we would compute the value of the common stock as follows:

1. Because the $2 dividend was paid last year, we must compute the next dividend to be received, that is, $D_1$, where

$$D_1 = D_0 (1 + g)$$
$$= \$2(1 + 0.04)$$
$$= \$2.08$$

2. Now, using equation (8-5),

$$V_{cs} = \frac{D_1}{r_{cs} - g}$$
$$= \frac{\$2.08}{0.14 - 0.04}$$
$$= \$20.80$$

We have argued that the value of a common stock is equal to the present value of all future dividends, which is without question a fundamental premise of finance. In practice, however, managers, along with many security analysts, often talk about the relationship between stock value and earnings, rather than dividends. We would encourage you to be very cautious in using earnings to value a stock. Even though it may be a popular practice, significant available evidence suggests that investors look to the cash flows generated by the firm, not the earnings, for value. A firm's value truly is the present value of the cash flows it produces.

### EXAMPLE 8.2    Solving for the value of a common stock

During 2012, Starbucks Coffee's common stock had been selling for between $30 and $60. Its most recent earnings per share was $1.73, and the firm was expected to pay a dividend of $0.68. The company's return on equity (net income ÷ total common equity) has been 25 percent. You are planning on investing in 100 shares of the stock, but you want a 17 percent return on your investment. Given the limited information, what growth rate would you estimate for Starbucks? What price would be required for you to earn your required return?

#### STEP 1: FORMULATE A SOLUTION STRATEGY

Solving for the value of the Starbucks stock requires you to estimate a future growth rate, which we have suggested you do by multiplying the firm's return on equity times the percentage of its earnings being retained to be reinvested in the company. The equation (8-3) is as follows:

$$g = ROE \times pr$$

We then solve for the stock value, using equation (8-5):

$$\text{Common stock value} = \frac{\text{dividend in year 1}}{\text{required rate of return} - \text{growth rate}}$$

$$V_{cs} = \frac{D_1}{r_{cs} - g}$$

### STEP 2: CRUNCH THE NUMBERS

Starbucks pays out 39 percent of its earning to the shareholders (39% = $0.68 dividends per share ÷ $1.73 earnings per share). Thus, it is retaining 61 percent (61% = 100% − 39%).

Given the firm's return on equity of 25 percent, we could expect the company to grow at 15.25 percent:

Growth rate = 25% return on equity × 61% earnings retention = 15.25%

Then solving for the stock value that would satisfy a 17 percent required rate of return:

$$\text{Value} = \frac{\text{dividend}}{\text{required rate of return} - \text{growth rate}}$$

$$= \frac{\$0.68}{0.17 - 0.1525}$$

$$= \$38.86$$

### STEP 3: ANALYZE YOUR RESULTS

While Starbucks was selling for about $50 when this problem was written, you should not be willing to pay the $50 market price; otherwise, if our assumptions are reasonable you would not earn your required rate of return. Besides, Starbucks was experiencing growth problems in 2012, actually closing some stores.

## DID YOU GET IT?
### MEASURING JOHNSON & JOHNSON'S GROWTH RATE

To compute Johnson & Johnson's internal growth rate, we must know (1) the firm's return on equity, and (2) what percentage of the earnings are being retained and reinvested in the business—that is, used to grow the business.

The return on equity was computed to be 19.47 percent. We then calculate the percentage of the profits that is being retained as follows:

$$\frac{\text{Percentage of}}{\text{profits retained}} = 1 - \frac{\text{dividends per share}}{\text{earnings per share}}$$

$$= 1 - \frac{\$1.87}{\$4.63}$$

$$= 1 - 0.404$$

$$= 0.596 = 59.6\%$$

Thus, Johnson & Johnson is paying out 40.4 percent of its earnings, which means it is retaining 59.6 percent.

Then we compute the internal growth rate as follows:

$$\frac{\text{Internal growth}}{\text{rate}} = \frac{\text{return on}}{\text{equity}} \times \frac{\text{percentage of}}{\text{earnings retained}}$$

$$= 19.47\% \times 59.6\%$$

$$= 11.6\%$$

The ability of a firm to grow is critical to its future, but only if the firm has attractive opportunities in which to invest. Also, there must be a way to finance the growth, which can occur by borrowing more, issuing stock, or not distributing the profits to the owners (not paying dividends). The last option is called internal growth. Johnson & Johnson was able to grow internally by almost 12 percent by earning 19.47 percent on the equity's investment and retaining about 60 percent of the profits in the business.

## CAN YOU DO IT?
### CALCULATING COMMON STOCK VALUE

The Abraham Corporation paid $1.32 in dividends per share *last year*. The firm's projected growth rate is 6 percent for the foreseeable future. If the investor's required rate of return for a firm with Abraham's level of risk is 10 percent, what is the value of the stock? (The solution can be found on page 264.)

We now have the financial decision tools to value common stock assuming that dividends grow at a constant rate in perpetuity, which are shown as follows:

| FINANCIAL DECISION TOOLS | | |
|---|---|---|
| **Name of Tool** | **Formula** | **What It Tells You** |
| Dividend growth rate | Growth = return on equity × percentage of profits retained | Estimation of a company's growth rate to be used in valuing the stock. |
| Common stock valuation | $V_{cs} = \dfrac{D_1}{(1 + r_{cs})^1} + \dfrac{D_2}{(1 + r_{cs})^2} + \cdots + \dfrac{D_n}{(1 + r_{cs})^n} + \cdots + \dfrac{D_\infty}{(1 + r_{cs})^\infty}$ | The value of a common stock is the present value of all future dividends in perpetuity. |
| Common stock valuation assuming constant dividend growth | Common stock value = $\dfrac{\text{dividend in year 1}}{\text{required rate of return} - \text{growth rate}}$ $$V_{cs} = \dfrac{D_1}{r_{cs} - g}$$ | The value of common stock assuming that dividends are growing at a constant growth rate in perpetuity. |

## Concept Check

1. What features of common stock indicate ownership in the corporation versus preferred stock or bonds?
2. In what two ways does a shareholder benefit from ownership?
3. How does internal growth versus the infusion of new capital affect the original shareholders?
4. Describe the process for common stock valuation.

### REMEMBER YOUR PRINCIPLES

**Principle** Valuing common stock is no different from valuing preferred stock; only the pattern of the cash flows changes. Thus, the valuation of common stock relies on the same three principles developed in Chapter 1 that were used in valuing preferred stock:

**Principle 1: Cash Flow Is What Matters.**

**Principle 2: Money Has a Time Value.**

**Principle 3: Risk Requires a Reward.**

Determining the economic worth, or value, of an asset always relies on these three principles. Without them, we would have no basis for explaining value. With them, we can know that the amount and timing of cash, not earnings, drives value. Also, we must be rewarded for taking risk; otherwise, we will not invest.

# The Expected Rate of Return of Stockholders

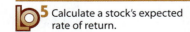

5 Calculate a stock's expected rate of return.

As stated in Chapter 7, the expected rate of return, or yield to maturity, on a bond is the return the bondholder expects to receive on the investment by paying the existing market price for the security. This rate of return is of interest to the financial manager because it tells the manager about investors' expectations. The same can be said for the financial manager needing to know the expected rate of return of the firm's stockholders, which is the topic of this section.

## DID YOU GET IT?

### CALCULATING COMMON STOCK VALUE

Abraham's stock value would be $35:

$$\text{Value} = \frac{\text{dividend year 1}}{\text{required rate of return} - \text{growth rate}}$$

$$= \frac{\$1.32 \times (1 + .06)}{0.10 - 0.06} = \frac{\$1.40}{0.04} = \$35$$

So the value of a common stock, much like preferred stock, is the present value of all future dividends. However, unlike preferred stock, common stock dividends are assumed to increase as the firm's profits increase. So the dividend is growing over time. And with a bit of calculus—keep the faith, baby—we can find the stock value by taking the dividend that is expected to be received at the end of the coming year and dividing it by the investor's required rate of return less the assumed constant growth rate. When we do, we have the present value of the dividends, which is the value of the stock.

### The Expected Rate of Return of Preferred Stockholders

To compute the expected rate of return of preferred stockholders, we use the valuation equation for preferred stock. Earlier, equation (8-2) specified the value of a preferred stock, $V_{ps}$, as

$$\text{Preferred stock value } (V_{ps}) = \frac{\text{annual dividend}}{\text{required rate of return}} = \frac{D}{r_{ps}}$$

Solving equation (8-2) for $r_{ps}$, we have

$$\text{Required rate of return } (r_{ps}) = \frac{\text{annual dividend}}{\text{preferred stock value}} = \frac{D}{V_{ps}} \tag{8-6}$$

Thus, the *required* rate of return of preferred stockholders simply equals the stock's annual dividend divided by the stock's intrinsic value. We can also use this equation to solve for a preferred stock's *expected* rate of return, $\bar{r}_{ps}$, as follows:[7]

$$\text{Expected rate of return } (\bar{r}_{ps}) = \frac{\text{annual dividend}}{\text{preferred stock market price}} = \frac{D}{P_{ps}} \tag{8-7}$$

Note that we have merely substituted the current market price, $P_{ps}$, for the intrinsic value, $V_{ps}$. The expected rate of return, $\bar{r}_{ps}$, therefore, equals the annual dividend relative to the price the stock is currently selling for, $P_{ps}$. Thus, the **expected rate of return**, $\bar{r}_{ps}$, is *the rate of return the investor can expect to earn from the investment if it is bought at the current market price.*

For example, if the present market price of the preferred stock is $50, and it pays a $3.64 annual dividend, the expected rate of return implicit in the present market price is

$$\bar{r}_{ps} = \frac{D}{P_{ps}} = \frac{\$3.64}{\$50} = 7.28\%$$

Therefore, investors (who pay $50 per share for a preferred security that is paying $3.64 in annual dividends) are expecting a 7.28 percent rate of return.

So we now have the decision tools for calculating a stockholder's required rate of return and the stock's expected rate of return shown as follows:

**expected rate of return** The rate of return investors expect to receive on an investment by paying the current market price of the security.

[7]We will use $\bar{r}$ to represent a security's *expected* rate of return versus $r$ for investors' *required* rate of return.

| **FINANCIAL DECISION TOOLS** | | |
|---|---|---|
| **Name of Tool** | **Formula** | **What It Tells You** |
| Preferred stockholder's *required* rate of return | $r_{ps} = \dfrac{\text{annual dividend}}{\text{preferred stock value}} = \dfrac{D}{V_{ps}}$ | The required rate of return for a preferred stockholder, given the value the investor assigns to the stock. |
| Preferred stock *expected* rate of return | $\bar{r}_{ps} = \dfrac{\text{annual dividend}}{\text{preferred stock market price}} = \dfrac{D}{P_{ps}}$ | Calculates the expected rate of return for a preferred stock, given the current market price of the stock. |

---

**EXAMPLE 8.3**    **Solving for the expected rate of return for a preferred stock**

In Example 8-1, we calculated the value of Deutsche Bank's preferred stock, where the stock had a par value of $25 and a coupon dividend rate of 7.35 percent, which resulted in a $1.84 dividend. In the earlier example, we computed the value of the stock given different required rates of returns. At the time, the stock was actually selling for $26 in the market. What is the expected rate of return if you purchased the stock at the current market price?

**STEP 1: FORMULATE A SOLUTION STRATEGY**
To determine the expected rate of return for preferred stock. We need only compute the stock's dividend yield, as measured in equations (8-7), as follows:

$$\bar{r}_{ps} = \frac{\text{annual dividend}}{\text{preferred stock market price}} = \frac{D}{P_{ps}}$$

**STEP 2: CRUNCH THE NUMBERS**

$$\text{Expected rate of return} = \frac{\$1.84}{\$26} = 0.0708 = 7.08\%$$

**STEP 3: ANALYZE YOUR RESULTS**
The investors owning the Deutsche Bank stock are expecting to earn less than the coupon dividend rate of 7.35 percent. This outcome is the result of the investors being willing to pay above the par value of the stock.

## The Expected Rate of Return of Common Stockholders

The valuation equation for common stock was defined earlier in equation (8-4) as

$$\text{Common stock value} = \frac{\text{dividend in year 1}}{(1 + \text{required rate of return})^1}$$
$$+ \frac{\text{dividend in year 2}}{(1 + \text{required rate of return})^2}$$
$$+ \cdots + \frac{\text{dividend in year infinity}}{(1 + \text{required rate of return})^\infty}$$

$$V_{cs} = \frac{D_1}{(1 + r_{cs})^1} + \frac{D_2}{(1 + r_{cs})^2} + \cdots + \frac{D_\infty}{(1 + r_{cs})^\infty}$$

Owing to the difficulty of discounting to infinity, we made the key assumption that the dividends, $D_t$, increase at a constant annual compound growth rate of $g$. If this assumption is valid, equation (8-5) was shown to be equivalent to

$$\text{Common stock value} = \frac{\text{dividend in year 1}}{\text{required rate of return} - \text{growth rate}}$$

$$V_{cs} = \frac{D_1}{r_{cs} - g}$$

Thus, $V_{cs}$ represents the maximum value that investors having a required rate of return of $r_{cs}$ would pay for a security having an anticipated dividend in year 1 of $D_1$ that is expected to grow in future years at rate $g$. Solving equation (8-5) for $r_{cs}$, we can compute the common stockholders' required rate of return as follows:[8]

$$r_{cs} = \frac{D_1}{V_{cs}} + g \qquad (8\text{-}8)$$

According to this equation, the required rate of return is equal to the dividend yield plus a growth factor. Although the growth rate, $g$, applies to the growth in the company's dividends, given our assumptions, the stock's value can also be expected to increase at the same rate. For this reason, $g$ represents the annual percentage growth in the stock value. In other words, the required rate of return of investors is satisfied by their receiving dividends *and* capital gains, as reflected by the expected percentage growth rate in the stock price.

As was done for preferred stock earlier, we may revise equation (8-8) to measure a common stock's *expected* rate of return, $\bar{r}_{cs}$. Replacing the intrinsic value, $V_{cs}$, in equation (8-8) with the stock's current market price, $P_{cs}$, we may express the stock's expected rate of return as follows:

> ### REMEMBER YOUR PRINCIPLES
>
> **Principle** We have just learned that, on average, the expected return will be equal to the investor's required rate of return. This equilibrium condition is achieved by investors paying for an asset only the amount that will exactly satisfy their required rate of return. Thus, finding the expected rate of return based on the current market price for the security relies on two of the principles given in Chapter 1:
>
> **Principle 2: Money Has Time Value.**
>
> **Principle 3: Risk Requires a Reward.**

$$\bar{r}_{cs} = \frac{\text{dividend in year 1}}{\text{market price}} + \text{growth rate} = \frac{D_1}{P_{cs}} + g \qquad (8\text{-}9)$$

To illustrate, Pearson, Inc. will pay a dividend of $2 this year. Management anticipates that the firm will grow at about 6 percent per year. You are interested in buying 100 shares of the stock, which is currently priced at $45. Your required rate of return is 12 percent. Should you buy the stock?

$$\bar{r}_{cs} = \frac{\$2}{\$45} + 0.06 = 4.44\% + 6\% = 10.44\%$$

You would not want to buy the stock. The expected return is less than your required return.

Historically, most of the returns on stocks come from price appreciation, or capital gains, with a smaller part of the return coming from dividends, with 2008–2009 being the

---

> **EXAMPLE 8.4**   **Solving for the expected rate of return of a common stock**
>
> In Example 8-2, we valued Starbucks Coffee at $38.86, given your required rate of return of 17 percent. This answer was based on an anticipated growth rate of 15.25 percent.
>
> Also, the stock was expected to pay a $0.68 dividend. The stock was actually selling for $50 at the time. What would be the expected rate of return for investors purchasing the stock at the current price of $50?
>
> **STEP 1: FORMULATE A SOLUTION STRATEGY**
>
> To estimate the expected rate of return on a common stock, we use the following equation:

---

[8]At times the expected dividend at year-end ($D_1$) is not given. Instead, we might only know the most recent dividend (paid yesterday), that is, $D_0$. If so, equation (8-5) must be restated as follows:

$$V_{cs} = \frac{D_1}{(r_{cs} - g)} = \frac{D_0(1 + g)}{(r_{cs} - g)}$$

$$\bar{r}_{cs} = \frac{\text{dividend in year 1}}{\text{market price}} + \text{growth rate} = \frac{D_1}{P_{cs}} + g$$

### STEP 2: CRUNCH THE NUMBERS

The expected rate of return for the Starbucks stock would be 16.61 percent.

$$\begin{aligned}
\text{Expected rate of return} &= \frac{\text{dividend}}{\text{market price}} + \text{growth rate} \\
&= \frac{\$0.68}{\$50} + 0.1525 \\
&= 0.0136 + 0.1525 = 0.1661 = 16.61\%
\end{aligned}$$

### STEP 3: ANALYZE YOUR RESULTS

Of the expected rate of return at the $50 market price, only a small portion is attributable to the dividend received by the investors. The investors are essentially relying on the firm to achieve a growth rate of about 15 percent per year into the future. Not an easy thing to do for many firms.

exception. The Standard & Poor's 500 Index, for example, returned a 10 percent annual return on average since 1926. But the dividend yield (dividend ÷ stock price) accounted for only about 2–3 percent of the return. The remaining 7–8 percent resulted from price appreciation.

---

## CAN YOU DO IT?

### COMPUTING THE EXPECTED RATE OF RETURN

Calculate the expected rate of return for the two following stocks:

Preferred stock: The stock is selling for $80 and pays a 5 percent dividend on its $100 par or stated value.

Common stock: The stock paid a dividend of $4 last year and is expected to increase each year at a 5 percent growth rate. The stock sells for $75.

(The solution can be found below.)

---

## DID YOU GET IT?

### COMPUTING THE EXPECTED RATE OF RETURN

Preferred stock:

$$\text{Expected return} = \frac{\text{dividend}}{\text{stock price}} = \frac{\$5}{\$80} = 0.0625, \text{ or } 6.25\%$$

Common stock:

$$\begin{aligned}
\text{Expected return} &= \frac{\text{dividend in year 1}}{\text{stock price}} + \text{growth rate} \\
&= \frac{\$4 \times (1 + 0.05)}{\$75} + 5\% = \frac{\$4.20}{\$75} + 5\% \\
&= 5.6\% + 5\% = 10.6\%
\end{aligned}$$

At this point, we are not concerned what the value of the stock is to us. Instead, we want to know what rate of return we could expect if we buy a common stock at the current market price. So the price is given, and we are finding the corresponding expected return based on the current market price. We can then ask ourselves if the expected rate of return is acceptable, given the amount of risk we would be assuming.

As a final note, we should understand that the *expected* rate of return implied by a given market price equals the *required* rate of return for investors at the margin. For these investors, the expected rate of return is just equal to their required rate of return and, therefore, they are willing to pay the current market price for the security. These investors' required rate of return is of particular significance to the financial manager because it represents the cost of new financing to the firm.

In summary, we can use the following decision tools to estimate a common stockholder's required rate of return and the stocks expected return:

## FINANCIAL DECISION TOOLS

| Name of Tool | Formula | What It Tells You |
|---|---|---|
| Common stockholder's *required* rate of return | $$r_{cs} = \frac{D_1}{V_{cs}} + g$$  dividend yield    annual growth rate | Calculates the required rate of return for a common stockholder, given the value the investor assigns to the stock. |
| Common stock *expected* rate of return | $$\bar{r}_{cs} = \frac{\text{dividend in year 1}}{\text{market price}} + \text{growth rate} = \frac{D_1}{P_{cs}} + g$$ | Calculates the expected rate of return for a common stock, given the current market price of the stock and the projected growth rate in future dividends. |

## Concept Check

1. In computing the required rate of return for common stock, why should the growth factor be added to the dividend yield?

2. Explain the difference between a stockholder's required and expected rates of return.

3. How does an efficient market affect the required and expected rates of return?

# Chapter Summaries

Valuation is an important process in financial management. An understanding of valuation, both the concepts and procedures, supports the financial objective of creating shareholder value.

 **Identify the basic characteristics of preferred stock.** (pgs. 251–253)

**SUMMARY:** Preferred stock has no fixed maturity date, and the dividends are fixed in amount. Some of the more common characteristics of preferred stock include the following:

- There are multiple classes of preferred stock.
- Preferred stock has a priority claim on assets and income over common stock.
- Any dividends, if not paid as promised, must be paid before any common stock dividends may be paid; that is, they are cumulative.
- Protective provisions are included in the contract with the shareholder to reduce the investor's risk.
- Some preferred stocks are convertible into common stock shares.
- In addition, there are provisions frequently used to retire an issue of preferred stock, such as the ability of the firm to call its preferred stock or to use a sinking-fund provision.

## KEY TERMS

**Preferred stock, page 251** A hybrid security with characteristics of both common stock and bonds. Preferred stock is similar to common stock in that it has no fixed maturity date, the nonpayment of dividends does not bring on bankruptcy, and dividends are not deductible for tax purposes. Preferred stock is similar to bonds in that dividends are limited in amount.

**Cumulative feature, page 252** A requirement that all past, unpaid preferred stock dividends be paid before any common stock dividends are declared.

**Protective provisions, page 252** Provisions for preferred stock that protect the investor's interest. The provisions generally allow for voting in the event of nonpayment of dividends, or they restrict the payment of common stock dividends if sinking-fund

payments are not met or if the firm is in financial difficulty.

**Convertible preferred stock, page 252** Preferred shares that can be converted into a predetermined number of shares of common stock, if investors so choose.

**Call provision, page 252** A provision that entitles the corporation to repurchase its preferred stock from investors at stated prices over specified periods.

**Sinking-fund provision, page 253** A protective provision that requires the firm periodically to set aside an amount of money for the retirement of its preferred stock. This money is then used to purchase the preferred stock in the open market or through the use of the call provision, whichever method is cheaper.

---

## Value preferred stock. (pgs. 253–256)

**SUMMARY:** Value is the present value of future cash flows discounted at the investor's required rate of return. Although the valuation of any security entails the same basic principles, the procedures used in each situation vary. For example, we learned in Chapter 7 that valuing a bond involves calculating the present value of the future interest to be received plus the present value of the principal returned to the investor at the maturity of the bond. For securities with cash flows that are constant in each year but with no specified maturity, such as preferred stock, the present value equals the dollar amount of the annual dividend divided by the investor's required rate of return.

### KEY EQUATION

$$\text{Preferred Stock Value } (V_{ps}) = \frac{\text{dividend in year 1}}{(1 + \text{required rate of return})^1}$$
$$+ \frac{\text{dividend in year 2}}{(1 + \text{required rate of return})^2}$$
$$+ \cdots + \frac{\text{dividend in infinity}}{(1 + \text{required rate of return})^\infty}$$
$$= \frac{D_1}{(1 + r_{ps})^1} + \frac{D_2}{(1 + r_{ps})^2} + \cdots + \frac{D_\infty}{(1 + r_{ps})^\infty}$$

$$\text{Preferred stock value } (V_{ps}) = \frac{\text{annual dividend}}{\text{required rate of return}} = \frac{D}{r_{ps}}$$

---

## Identify the basic characteristics of common stock. (pgs. 256–258)

**SUMMARY:** Common stock involves ownership in the corporation. In effect, bondholders and preferred stockholders can be viewed as creditors, whereas common stockholders are the owners of the firm. Common stock does not have a maturity date but exists as long as the firm does. Nor does common stock have an upper limit on its dividend payments. Dividend payments must be declared by the firm's board of directors before they are issued. In the event of bankruptcy, the common stockholders, as owners of the corporation, cannot exercise claims on assets until the firm's creditors, including its bondholders and preferred shareholders, have been satisfied. However, common stockholders' liability is limited to the amount of their investment.

The common stockholders are entitled to elect the firm's board of directors and are, in general, the only security holders given a vote. Common shareholders also have the right to approve any change in the company's corporate charter. Although each share of stock carries the same number of votes, the voting procedure is not always the same from company to company.

The preemptive right entitles the common shareholder to maintain a proportionate share of ownership in the firm.

### KEY TERMS

**Common stock, page 256** Shares that represent the ownership in a corporation.

**Limited liability, page 258** A protective provision whereby the investor is not liable for more than the amount he or she has invested in the firm.

**Proxy, page 258** A means of voting in which a designated party is provided with the temporary power of attorney to vote for the signee at the corporation's annual meeting.

**Proxy fight, page 258** A battle between rival groups for proxy votes in order to control the decisions made in a stockholders' meeting.

**Majority voting, page 258** Voting in which each share of stock allows the shareholder one vote and each position on the board of directors is voted on separately. As a result, a

majority of shares has the power to elect the entire board of directors.

**Cumulative voting, page 258** Voting in which each share of stock allows the shareholder a number of votes equal to the number of directors being elected. The shareholder can then cast all of his or her votes for a single candidate or split them among the various candidates.

**Preemptive right, page 258** The right entitling the common shareholder to maintain his or her proportionate share of ownership in the firm.

**Right, page 258** A certificate issued to common stockholders giving them an option to purchase a stated number of new shares at a specified price during a 2- to 10-week period.

---

 **4   Value common stock.** (pgs 258–263)

**SUMMARY:** As with bonds and preferred stock, the value of a common stock is equal to the present value of future cash flows.

When using the dividend-growth model to value a stock, growth relates to internal growth only—growth achieved by retaining part of the firm's profits and reinvesting them in the firm—as opposed to growth achieved by issuing new stock or acquiring another firm.

Growth in and of itself does not mean that a firm is creating value for its stockholders. Only if profits are reinvested at a rate of return greater than the investor's required rate of return will growth result in increased stockholder value.

### KEY TERMS

**Internal growth, page 259** A firm's growth rate resulting from reinvesting the company's profits rather than distributing them as dividends. The growth rate is a function of the amount retained and the return earned on the retained funds.

**Profit-retention rate, page 259** The company's percentage of profits retained.

**Dividend-payout ratio, page 259** Dividends as a percentage of earnings.

### KEY EQUATIONS

Growth = return on equity × percentage of profits retained in the firm

$$\text{Common stock value } (V_{cs}) = \frac{D_1}{(1 + r_{cs})^1} + \frac{D_2}{(1 + r_{cs})^2} + \cdots + \frac{D_n}{(1 + r_{cs})^n} + \cdots + \frac{D_\infty}{(1 + r_{cs})^\infty}$$

$$\text{Common stock value} = \frac{\text{dividend in year 1}}{\text{required rate of return} - \text{growth rate}}$$

$$V_{cs} = \frac{D_1}{r_{cs} - g}$$

---

 **5   Calculate a stock's expected rate of return.** (pgs. 263–268)

**SUMMARY:** The expected rate of return on a security is the required rate of return of investors who are willing to pay the present market price for the security, but no more. This rate of return is important to the financial manager because it equals the required rate of return of the firm's investors.

### KEY TERM

**Expected rate of return, page 264** The rate of return investors expect to receive on an

investment by paying the current market price of the security.

## KEY EQUATIONS

$$\text{Required rate of return } (r_{ps}) = \frac{\text{annual dividend}}{\text{preferred stock value}} = \frac{D}{V_{ps}}$$

$$\text{Expected rate of return } (\bar{r}_{ps}) = \frac{\text{annual dividend}}{\text{preferred stock market price}} = \frac{D}{P_{ps}}$$

$$r_{cs} = \frac{D_1}{V_{cs}} + g$$

$$\underbrace{\phantom{\frac{D_1}{V_{cs}}}}_{\text{dividend yield}} \quad \underbrace{\phantom{g}}_{\text{annual growth rate}}$$

$$\bar{r}_{cs} = \frac{\text{dividend in year 1}}{\text{market price}} + \text{growth rate} = \frac{D_1}{P_{cs}} + g$$

# Review Questions

*All Review Questions are available in* MyFinanceLab.

**8-1.** Why is preferred stock referred to as a hybrid security? It is often said to combine the worst features of common stock and bonds. What is meant by this statement?

**8-2.** Because preferred stock dividends in arrears must be paid before common stock dividends, should they be considered a liability and appear on the right-hand side of the balance sheet?

**8-3.** Why would a preferred stockholder want the stock to have a cumulative dividend feature and protective provisions?

**8-4.** Why is preferred stock frequently convertible? Why is it callable?

**8-5.** Compare valuing preferred stock and common stock.

**8-6.** Define investors' expected rate of return.

**8-7.** State how investors' expected rate of return is computed.

**8-8.** The common stockholders receive two types of return from their investment. What are they?

# Study Problems

*All Study Problems are available in* MyFinanceLab.

**8-1.** (*Preferred stock valuation*) What is the value of a preferred stock when the dividend rate is 16 percent on a $100 par value? The appropriate discount rate for a stock of this risk level is 12 percent.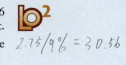

**8-2.** (*Preferred stock valuation*) The preferred stock of Armlo pays a $2.75 dividend. What is the value of the stock if your required return is 9 percent?

$2.75/9\% = 30.56$

**8-3.** (*Preferred stock valuation*) What is the value of a preferred stock when the dividend rate is 14 percent on a $100 par value? The appropriate discount rate for a stock of this risk level is 12 percent.

$\dfrac{14\% \times 100}{12\%}$

**8-4.** (*Preferred stock valuation*) Pioneer preferred stock is selling for $33 per share in the market and pays a $3.60 annual dividend.

   a. What is the expected rate of return on the stock?
   b. If an investor's required rate of return is 10 percent, what is the value of the stock for that investor?
   c. Should the investor acquire the stock?

**8-5.** (*Preferred stock valuation*) Calculate the value of a preferred stock that pays a dividend of $6 per share if your required rate of return is 12 percent.

**8-6.** (*Preferred stock valuation*) You are considering an investment in one of two preferred stocks, TCF Capital or TAYC Capital Trust. TCF Capital pays an annual dividend of $2.69, while TAYC Capital pays an annual dividend of $2.44. If your required return is 12 percent, what value would you assign to the stocks?

**8-7.** (*Preferred stock valuation*) You are considering an investment in Double Eagle Petroleum's preferred stock. The preferred stock pays a dividend of $2.31. Your required return is 12 percent. Value the stock.

**8-8.** (*Common stock valuation*) Crosby Corporation common stock paid $1.32 in dividends last year and is expected to grow indefinitely at an annual 7 percent rate. What is the value of the stock if you require an 11 percent return?

**8-9.** (*Measuring growth*) The Fisayo Corporation wants to achieve a steady 7 percent growth rate. If it can achieve a 12 percent return on equity, what percentage of earnings must Fisayo retain for investment purposes?

**8-10.** (*Common stock valuation*) Dalton Inc. has an 11.5 percent return on equity and retains 55 percent of its earnings for reinvestment purposes. It recently paid a dividend of $3.25 and the stock is currently selling for $40.

    a. What is the growth rate for Dalton Inc.?
    b. What is the expected return for Dalton's stock?
    c. If you require a 13 percent return, should you invest in the firm?

**8-11.** (*Common stock valuation*) Bates Inc. pays a dividend of $1 and is currently selling for $32.50. If investors require a 12 percent return on their investment from buying Bates stock, what growth rate would Bates Inc. have to provide the investors?

**8-12.** (*Common stock valuation*) You intend to purchase Marigo common stock at $50 per share, hold it 1 year, and then sell it after a dividend of $6 is paid. How much will the stock price have to appreciate for you to satisfy your required rate of return of 15 percent?

**8-13.** (*Common stock valuation*) Header Motor Inc. paid a $3.50 dividend last year. At a constant growth rate of 5 percent, what is the value of the common stock if the investors require a 20 percent rate of return?

**8-14.** (*Measuring growth*) Given that a firm's return on equity is 18 percent and management plans to retain 40 percent of earnings for investment purposes, what will be the firm's growth rate?

**8-15.** (*Common stock valuation*) Honeywag common stock is expected to pay $1.85 in dividends next year, and the market price is projected to be $42.50 per share by year-end. If investors require a rate of return of 11 percent, what is the current value of the stock?

**8-16.** (*Common stock valuation*) The common stock of NCP paid $1.32 in dividends last year. Dividends are expected to grow at an 8 percent annual rate for an indefinite number of years.

    a. If NCP's current market price is $23.50 per share, what is the stock's expected rate of return?
    b. If your required rate of return is 10.5 percent, what is the value of the stock for you?
    c. Should you make the investment?

**8-17.** (*Measuring growth*) Pepperdine Inc.'s return on equity is 16 percent, and the management plans to retain 60 percent of earnings for investment purposes. What will be the firm's growth rate?

**8-18.** (*Common stock valuation*) Abercrombie & Fitch's common stock pays a dividend of $0.70. It is currently selling for $34.14. If the firm's investors require a 10 percent return on their investment from buying Abercrombie & Fitch stock, what growth rate would Abercrombie & Fitch have to provide the investors?

**8-19.** (*Common stock valuation*) Schlumberger is selling for $64.91 per share and paid a dividend of $1.10 last year. The dividend is expected to grow at 4 percent indefinitely. What is the stock's expected rate of return?

**8-20.** (*Preferred stockholder expected return*) You own 250 shares of Dalton Resources preferred stock, which currently sells for $38.50 per share and pays annual dividends of $3.25 per share.

    a. What is your expected return?
    b. If you require an 8 percent return, given the current price, should you sell or buy more stock?

**8-21.** (*Preferred stock expected return*) You are planning to purchase 100 shares of preferred stock and must choose between Stock A and Stock B. Stock A pays an annual dividend of $4.50 and is currently selling for $35. Stock B pays an annual dividend of $4.25 and is selling for $36. If your required return is 12 percent, which stock should you choose?

**8-22.** (*Preferred stockholder expected return*) Solitron preferred stock is selling for $42.16 per share and pays $1.95 in dividends. What is your expected rate of return if you purchase the security at the market price?

**8-23.** (*Preferred stockholder expected return*) You own 200 shares of Somner Resources preferred stock, which currently sells for $40 per share and pays annual dividends of $3.40 per share.

    a. What is your expected return?
    b. If you require an 8 percent return, given the current price, should you sell or buy more stock?

**8-24.** (*Preferred stock expected return*) You are planning to purchase 100 shares of preferred stock and must choose between stock in Kristen Corporation and Titus Corporation. Your required rate of return is 9 percent. If the stock in Kristen pays a dividend of $2 and is selling for $23 and the stock in Titus pays a dividend of $3.25 and is selling for $31, which stock should you choose?

**8-25.** (*Preferred stockholder expected return*) You own 150 shares of James Corporation preferred stock at a market price of $22 per share. James pays dividends of $1.55. What is your expected rate of return? If you have a required rate of return of 9 percent, should you buy more stock?

**8-26.** (*Preferred stock expected return*) You are considering the purchase of 150 shares of preferred stock. Your required return is 11 percent. If the stock is currently selling for $40 and pays a dividend of $5.25, should you purchase the stock?

**8-27.** (*Preferred stockholder expected return*) You are considering the purchase of Davis stock at a market price of $36.72 per share. Assume the stock pays an annual dividend of $2.33. What would be your expected return? Should you purchase the stock if your required return is 8 percent?

**8-28.** (*Common stockholder expected return*) Blackburn & Smith common stock currently sells for $23 per share. The company's executives anticipate a constant growth rate of 10.5 percent and an end-of-year dividend of $2.50.
   a.  What is your expected rate of return?
   b.  If you require a 17 percent return, should you purchase the stock?

**8-29.** (*Common stockholder expected return*) Made-It common stock currently sells for $22.50 per share. The company's executives anticipate a constant growth rate of 10 percent and an end-of-year dividend of $2.
   a.  What is your expected rate of return if you buy the stock for $22.50?
   b.  If you require a 17 percent return, should you purchase the stock?

**8-30.** (*Common stockholder expected return*) The common stock of Zaldi Co. is selling for $32.84 per share. The stock recently paid dividends of $2.94 per share and has a projected constant growth rate of 9.5 percent. If you purchase the stock at the market price, what is your expected rate of return?

**8-31.** (*Common stockholder expected return*) The market price for Hobart common stock is $43 per share. The price at the end of 1 year is expected to be $48, and dividends for next year should be $2.84. What is the expected rate of return?

**8-32.** (*Common stockholder expected return*) If you purchased 125 shares of common stock that pays an end-of-year dividend of $3, what is your expected rate of return if you purchased the stock for $30 per share? Assume the stock is expected to have a constant growth rate of 7 percent.

**8-33.** (*Common stockholder expected return*) Daisy executives anticipate a growth rate of 12 percent for the company's common stock. The stock is currently selling for $42.65 per share and pays an end-of-year dividend of $1.45. What is your expected rate of return if you purchase the stock for its current market price of $42.65?

# Mini Case

*This Mini Case is available in* MyFinanceLab.

You have finally saved $10,000 and are ready to make your first investment. You have the three following alternatives for investing that money:

- Bank of America bonds with a par value of $1,000, that pays a 6.35 percent on its par value in interest, sells for $1,020, and matures in 5 years.
- Southwest Bancorp preferred stock paying a dividend of $2.63 and selling for $26.25.
- Emerson Electric common stock selling for $52, with a par value of $5. The stock recently paid a $1.60 dividend and the firm's earnings per share has increased from $2.23 to $3.30 in the past 5 years. The firm expects to grow at the same rate for the foreseeable future.

Your required rates of return for these investments are 5 percent for the bond, 8 percent for the preferred stock, and 12 percent for the common stock. Using this information, answer the following questions.

   a.  Calculate the value of each investment based on your required rate of return.
   b.  Which investment would you select? Why?
   c.  Assume Emerson Electric's managers expect an earnings to grew at 1 percent above the historical growth rate. How does this affect your answers to parts (a) and (b)?
   d.  What required rates of return would make you indifferent to all three options?

# 9

# The Cost of Capital

## Learning Objectives

**1 Understand** the concepts underlying the firm's cost of capital

The Cost of Capital: Key Definitions and Concepts

**2 Evaluate** the costs of the individual sources of capital

Determining the Costs of the Individual Sources of Capital

**3 Calculate** a firm's weighted average cost of capital

The Weighted Average Cost of Capital

**4 Estimate** divisional costs of capital

Calculating Divisional Costs of Capital

In the third quarter of 2011 ExxonMobil (XON) earned a record $9.4 billion, which was almost double what it earned in the same quarter of 2008! But is ExxonMobil creating value for its shareholders? The key to answering this question rests not just on the level of the firm's earnings but also on (i) how large an investment has been made in the company in order to produce these earnings and (ii) how risky the firm's investors perceive the company's investments to be. In other words, we need to know two things: What *rate* of return did the company earn on its invested capital, and what is the *market's required rate of return* on that invested capital (the company's cost of capital)?

The firm's cost of capital provides an estimate of the rate of return the firm's combined investors expect from the company. Estimating a firm's cost of capital is very intuitive in theory but can be somewhat tedious in practice. In theory, what is required is the following: (i) identify all of the firm's sources of capital and their relative importance (that is, what fraction of the firm's invested capital comes from each source); (ii) estimate the market's required rate of return for each source of capital the firm has used; (iii) calculate an average of the required rates of return for each source of capital where the required rate of return for each source has been weighted by its contribution to the total capital invested in the firm.

The cost of capital is not only important when evaluating the company's overall performance but is also used when evaluating individual investment decisions made by the firm. For example, when ExxonMobil is considering the development of a new oil production property in Nigeria, the company needs to estimate just how much return is needed to justify the investment. Similarly, when it is considering a chemical plant in Southeast Asia the company's analysts need a benchmark return to compare to the investment's expected return. The cost of capital provides this benchmark.

Not to hold you in suspense any longer, in 2011 ExxonMobil Corporation earned a whopping 26.93 percent rate of return on the book value of the firm's equity and a 10 percent rate of return on the market value of the firm's total assets. Given that the firm had to earn less than 10 percent to satisfy all of its investors (both equity and debt), it created a lot of value for its investors even in the midst of a worsening financial crisis. In this chapter, we investigate how to estimate the cost of funds to the firm. We will refer to the combined cost of borrowed money and money invested in the company by the firm's stockholders as the weighted average cost of capital or simply the firm's cost of capital.

Having studied the connection between risk and investor required rates of return (Chapter 6) and, specifically, investor required rates of return for bondholders and stockholders in Chapters 7 and 8, we are now ready to consider required rates of return for the firm as a whole. That is, just as the individuals that lend the firm money (bondholders) and those that invest in its stock have their individual required rates of return, we can also think about a combined required rate of return for the firm as a whole. This required rate of return for the firm is a blend of the required rates of return of all investors that we will estimate using a weighted average of the individual rates of return called the firm's **weighted average cost of capital** or simply the firm's cost of capital. Just like any cost of doing business, the firm must earn at least this cost if it is to create value for its owners.

In this chapter, we discuss the fundamental determinants of a firm's cost of capital and the rationale for its calculation and use. This entails developing the logic for estimating the cost of debt capital, preferred stock, and common stock. Chapter 12 takes up consideration of the impact of the firm's financing mix on the cost of capital.

**weighted average cost of capital** an average of the individual costs of financing used by the firm. A firm's weighted cost of capital is a function of (1) the individual costs of capital, and (2) the capital structure mix.

**1** Understand the concepts underlying the firm's cost of capital.

# The Cost of Capital: Key Definitions and Concepts

## Opportunity Costs, Required Rates of Return, and the Cost of Capital

The firm's cost of capital is sometimes referred to as the firm's **opportunity cost** of capital. The term *opportunity cost* comes from the study of economics and is defined as the cost of making a choice in terms of the next best opportunity that is foregone. For example, the opportunity cost of taking a part-time job at Starbucks (SBUX) is the lost wages from the on-campus job you would have taken otherwise. Similarly, when a firm chooses to invest money it has raised from investors, it is in essence deciding not to return the money to the investors. Thus, the opportunity cost of investing the money is the cost the firm incurs by keeping the money and not returning it to the investors, which is the firm's cost of capital.

Is the investor's required rate of return the same thing as the cost of capital? Not exactly. Consequently, in this chapter we will use the symbol $k$ to refer to the cost of financing, whereas in Chapters 7 and 8 we used $r$ to refer to the investor's required rate of return. Two

**opportunity cost** the cost of making a choice defined in terms of the next best alternative that is foregone.

factors drive a wedge between the investor's required rate of return and the cost of capital to the firm.

1. **Taxes.** When a firm borrows money to finance the purchase of an asset, the interest expense is deductible for federal income tax calculations. Consider a firm that borrows at 9 percent and then deducts its interest expense from its revenues before paying taxes at a rate of 34 percent. For each dollar of interest it pays, the firm reduces its taxes by $0.34. Consequently, the actual cost of borrowing to the firm is only 5.94% $[0.09 - (0.34 \times 0.09) = 0.09(1 - 0.34) = 0.0594$, or 5.94%].

2. **Flotation costs.** Here we are referring to the costs the firm incurs *when it raises funds by issuing a particular type of security.* As you learned in Chapter 2, these are sometimes called transaction costs. For example, if a firm sells new shares for $25 per share but incurs transaction costs of $5 per share, then the cost of capital for the new common equity is increased. Assume that the investor's required rate of return is 15 percent for each $25 share; then $0.15 \times \$25 = \$3.75$ must be earned each year to satisfy the investor's required return. However, the firm has only $20 to invest, so the cost of capital ($k$) is calculated as the rate of return that must be earned on the $20 net proceeds that will produce a return of $3.75; that is,

$$\$20k = \$25 \times 0.15 = \$3.75$$

$$k = \frac{\$3.75}{\$20.00} = 0.1875, \text{ or } 18.75\%$$

We will have more to say about both these considerations shortly when we discuss the costs of the individual sources of capital to the firm.

### The Firm's Financial Policy and the Cost of Capital

**financial policy** the firm's policies regarding the sources of financing it plans to use and the particular mix (proportions) in which they will be used.

A firm's **financial policy**—that is, *the policies regarding the sources of finances it plans to use and the particular mix (proportions) in which they will be used*—governs its use of debt and equity financing. The particular mixture of debt and equity that the firm uses can impact the firm's cost of capital. However, in this chapter, we assume that the firm maintains a fixed financial policy that is reflected in a fixed debt-equity ratio. Determining the target mix of debt and equity financing is the subject of Chapter 12.

### Concept Check

1. How is an investor's required rate of return related to an opportunity cost?
2. How do flotation costs impact the firm's cost of capital?

**LO2** Evaluate the costs of the individual sources of capital.

# Determining the Costs of the Individual Sources of Capital

In order to attract new investors, companies have created a wide variety of financing instruments or securities. In this chapter, we stick to three basic types: debt, preferred stock, and common stock. In calculating the respective cost of financing using each of these types of securities, we estimate the investor's required rate of return after properly adjusting for any transaction or flotation costs. In addition, because we will be discounting after-tax cash flows, we adjust our cost of capital for the effects of corporate taxes. In summary, the cost of a particular source of capital is equal to the investor's required rate of return after adjusting for the effects of both flotation costs and corporate taxes.

## The Cost of Debt

**cost of debt** the rate that has to be received from an investment in order to achieve the required rate of return for the creditors.

In Chapter 7 we learned that the value of a bond can be described in terms of the present value of the bond's future interest and principal payments. For example, if the bond has 3 years until maturity and pays interest annually, its value can be expressed as follows:

$$\begin{aligned}
\text{Bond} \\
\text{market} \\
\text{price}
\end{aligned} = \frac{\begin{array}{c}\text{interest paid}\\\text{in year 1}\end{array}}{\left(1 + \begin{array}{c}\text{bondholder's required}\\\text{rate of return }(r_d)\end{array}\right)^1} + \frac{\begin{array}{c}\text{interest paid}\\\text{in year 2}\end{array}}{\left(1 + \begin{array}{c}\text{bondholder's required}\\\text{rate of return }(r_d)\end{array}\right)^2}$$

$$+ \frac{\begin{array}{c}\text{interest paid}\\\text{in year 3}\end{array}}{\left(1 + \begin{array}{c}\text{bondholder's required}\\\text{rate of return }(r_d)\end{array}\right)^3} + \frac{\text{principal}}{\left(1 + \begin{array}{c}\text{bondholder's required}\\\text{rate of return }(r_d)\end{array}\right)^3} \quad (9\text{-}1)$$

In Chapter 7, we use the above bond price equation to estimate the bondholder's required rate of return. This required rate of return is commonly referred to as the bond's yield to maturity.

Since firms must pay **flotation costs** when they sell bonds, the net proceeds per bond received by the firm is less than the market price of the bond. Consequently, the cost of debt capital ($k_d$) is higher than the bondholder's required rate of return and is calculated using equation (9-2) as follows:

**flotation costs** the costs incurred by the firm when it issues securities to raise funds.

$$\begin{aligned}\text{Net proceeds}\\\text{per bond}\end{aligned} = \frac{\begin{array}{c}\text{interest paid}\\\text{in year 1}\end{array}}{\left(1 + \begin{array}{c}\text{cost of debt}\\\text{capital or }k_d\end{array}\right)^1} + \frac{\begin{array}{c}\text{interest paid}\\\text{in year 2}\end{array}}{\left(1 + \begin{array}{c}\text{cost of debt}\\\text{capital or }k_d\end{array}\right)^2}$$

$$+ \frac{\begin{array}{c}\text{interest paid}\\\text{in year 3}\end{array}}{\left(1 + \begin{array}{c}\text{cost of debt}\\\text{capital or }k_d\end{array}\right)^3} + \frac{\text{principal}}{\left(1 + \begin{array}{c}\text{cost of debt}\\\text{capital or }k_d\end{array}\right)^3} \quad (9\text{-}2)$$

Note that the adjustment for flotation costs simply involves replacing the market price of the bond with the net proceeds per bond received by the firm after paying these costs. The result of this adjustment is that the discount rate that solves equation (9-2) is now the firm's cost of debt financing before adjusting for the effect of corporate taxes—that is, the before-tax cost of debt ($k_d$). The final adjustment we make is to account for the fact that interest is tax deductible. Thus, the after-tax cost of debt capital is simply the before-tax cost of debt ($k_d$) times 1 minus the corporate tax rate.

## DID YOU GET IT?

### DETERMINING HOW FLOTATION COSTS AFFECT THE COST OF CAPITAL

If the required rate of return on the shares was 18 percent, and the shares sold for $22.00 with $2.00 in transaction costs incurred per share, then the cost of equity capital for Chipotle Mexican Grill is found by grossing up the investor's required rate of return as follows:

$$\text{Cost of equity capital} = \frac{\text{investor's required rate of return}}{(1 - \text{\% flotation costs})} = \frac{18\%}{1 - \left(\dfrac{\$2.00}{\$22.00}\right)} = 19.80\%$$

Incidentally, although the shares were sold to the public for $22.00 per share, they doubled to $44.00 by the end of the day after being traded in the secondary market.

# CAN YOU DO IT?

## CALCULATING THE COST OF DEBT FINANCING

General Auto Parts Corporation recently issued a 2-year bond with a face value of $20 million and a coupon rate of 5.5 percent per year (assume interest is paid annually). The subsequent cash flows to General Auto Parts were as follows:

|  | TODAY | YEAR 1 | YEAR 2 |
|---|---|---|---|
| Principal | $18 million | ($0.00 million) | ($20 million) |
| Interest |  | ($0.99 million) | ($0.99 million) |
| Total | $18 million | ($0.99 million) | ($20.99 million) |

What was the cost of capital to General Auto Parts for the debt issue?
(The solution can be found on page 280.)

---

**EXAMPLE 9.1** **Calculating the after-tax cost of debt financing**

Synopticom Inc. plans a bond issue for the near future and wants to estimate its current cost of debt capital. After talking with the firm's investment banker, the firm's chief financial officer has determined that a 20-year maturity bond with a $1,000 face value and 8 percent coupon (paying 8% × $1,000 = $80 per year in interest) can be sold to investors for net proceeds of $908.32. If the Synopticom tax rate is 34 percent, what is the after-tax cost of debt financing to the firm?

### STEP 1: FORMULATE A SOLUTION STRATEGY

The cost of debt financing is estimated as the bondholder's required rate of return, which we learned in Chapter 7 is the discount rate used to calculate the value of a bond, that is, using equation (9-1):

$$\text{Net proceeds per bond} = \frac{\text{interest paid in year 1}}{\left(1 + \frac{\text{bondholder's required}}{\text{rate of return } (k_d)}\right)^1} + \frac{\text{interest paid in year 2}}{\left(1 + \frac{\text{bondholder's required}}{\text{rate of return } (k_d)}\right)^2} + \cdots$$

$$+ \frac{\text{interest paid in year } N}{\left(1 + \frac{\text{bondholder's required}}{\text{rate of return } (k_d)}\right)^N} + \frac{\text{principle paid in year } N}{\left(1 + \frac{\text{bondholder's required}}{\text{rate of return } (k_d)}\right)^N}$$

Note that we allow for $N$ years of interest payments but omitted writing in the payments for years 3 through $N - 1$ for space considerations. Substituting what we know about the Synopticom bond into equation (9-1) above, we can then solve for the bondholder's required rate of return, $k_d$. Finally, we calculate the after-tax required rate of return by multiplying $k_d$ by 1 minus the tax rate, $T$, or

$$\frac{\text{After-tax}}{\text{cost of debt}} = \frac{\text{bondholder's required}}{\text{rate of return } (k_d)} \times \left(1 - \frac{\text{tax}}{\text{rate}}\right)$$

### STEP 2: CRUNCH THE NUMBERS

Substituting the characteristics of Synopticom's bond issue into equation (9-1), we get the following:

$$\$908.32 = \frac{0.08 \times \$1,000}{(1 + k_d)^1} + \frac{0.08 \times \$1,000}{(1 + k_d)^2} + \cdots + \frac{0.08 \times \$1,000}{(1 + k_d)^{20}} + \frac{\$1,000}{(1 + k_d)^{20}}$$

We can solve for $r_d$ using the calculator, which equals 9 percent, as demonstrated in the margin. The after-tax cost of debt can now be calculated as follows:

$$\begin{array}{l}\frac{\text{After-tax}}{\text{cost of debt}} = \frac{\text{bondholder's required}}{\text{rate of return }(k_d)} \times \left(1 - \frac{\text{tax}}{\text{rate}}\right) \\ = 0.09 \times (1 - 0.34) = 0.0594, \text{ or } 5.94\%\end{array}$$

### STEP 3: ANALYZE YOUR RESULTS

It appears that Synopticom's bondholders require a 9 percent rate of return when they purchase the firm's bonds at their current market price of $908.32. However, since Synopticom can deduct the interest it pays on its debt from its taxable income, the firm saves $0.34 for each dollar of interest it pays. As a consequence, the 9 percent required return of the firm's bondholders only costs the firm 5.94 percent.

If Synopticom is issuing new bonds, then it will incur the costs of selling the new bonds (that is, flotation costs). If the firm estimates that it will net $850 per new bond like the one described above since it must pay $58.32 per bond in flotation costs, then we substitute $850 for the bond price and compute the required rate of return (after flotation costs) to be 9.73 percent, and the corresponding after-tax cost of newly issued bonds is 6.422 percent.

**CALCULATOR SOLUTION**

| Data Input | Function Key |
|---|---|
| 20 | N |
| −850 | PV |
| 80 | PMT |
| 1,000 | FV |

| Function Key | Answer |
|---|---|
| CPT | |
| I/Y | 9.73 |

## The Cost of Preferred Stock

You may recall from Chapter 8 that the price of a share of preferred stock (**cost of preferred equity**) is equal to the present value of the constant stream of preferred stock dividends, that is,

$$\frac{\text{Price of a share of}}{\text{preferred stock}} = \frac{\text{preferred stock dividend}}{\begin{array}{c}\text{required rate of}\\ \text{return of the preferred stockholder }(r_{ps})\end{array}} \qquad (9\text{-}3)$$

**cost of preferred equity** the rate of return that must be earned on the preferred stockholders' investment in order to satisfy their required rate of return.

If we can observe the price of the share of preferred stock and we know the preferred stock dividend, we can calculate the preferred stockholder's required rate of return as follows:

$$\frac{\text{Required rate of return}}{\text{of the preferred stockholder }(r_{ps})} = \frac{\text{preferred stock dividend}}{\begin{array}{c}\text{price of a share of}\\ \text{preferred stock}\end{array}} \qquad (9\text{-}4)$$

Once again, because flotation costs are usually incurred when new preferred shares are sold, the investor's required rate of return is less than the cost of preferred capital to the firm. To calculate the cost of preferred stock, we must adjust the required rate of return to reflect these flotation costs. We replace the price of a preferred share in equation (9-4) with the net proceeds per share from the sale of new preferred shares. The resulting formula can be used to calculate the cost of preferred stock to the firm.

$$\text{Cost of preferred stock }(k_{ps}) = \frac{\text{preferred stock dividend}}{\text{net proceeds per preferred share}} \qquad (9\text{-}5)$$

Note that the net proceeds per share are equal to the price per share of preferred stock minus flotation cost per share of newly issued preferred stock.

What about corporate taxes? In the case of preferred stock, no tax adjustment must be made because, unlike interest payments, preferred dividends are not tax deductible.

---

## CAN YOU DO IT?

### CALCULATING THE COST OF PREFERRED STOCK FINANCING

Carson Enterprises recently issued $25 million in preferred stock at a price of $2.50 per share. The preferred shares carry a 10 percent dividend, or $0.25 per share (assume that it is paid annually). After paying all the fees and costs associated with the preferred issue the firm realized $2.25 per share issued.

What was the cost of capital to Carson Enterprises from the preferred stock issue?

(The solution can be found on page 281.)

> **EXAMPLE 9.2**    **Calculating the cost of preferred stock financing**
>
> San Antonio Edison has a preferred stock issue outstanding on which it pays an annual dividend of $4.25 per share. On August 24, 2011, the stock price was $58.50 per share. If the firm were to sell a new issue of preferred stock today with the same characteristics as its outstanding issue, it would incur flotation costs of $1.375 per share. Based on the most recent closing price for the preferred stock, what would you estimate the cost of preferred stock financing to be for the firm?
>
> **STEP 1: FORMULATE A SOLUTION STRATEGY**
>
> The cost of preferred stock financing can be computed from the basic valuation equation for a share of preferred stock just like we estimate the cost of debt financing from the valuation equation for a bond. Specifically, solving for the cost of preferred stock we can be computed using equation (9-5) as follows:
>
> $$\text{Cost of preferred stock } (k_{ps}) = \frac{\text{preferred stock dividend}}{\text{net proceeds per preferred share}}$$
>
> Note that net proceeds per preferred share reflects the difference in the price for which each preferred share is sold and the flotation costs per share incurred to sell new shares.
>
> **STEP 2: CRUNCH THE NUMBERS**
>
> Substituting into equation (9-5), we compute the cost of a new preferred stock issue as follows:
>
> $$\text{Cost of preferred stock } (k_{ps}) = \frac{\$4.25}{(\$58.50 - \$1.375)} \doteq 0.0744, \text{ or } 7.44\%$$
>
> **STEP 3: ANALYZE YOUR RESULTS**
>
> If San Antonio Edison were to issue preferred stock today, it could sell the shares for $58.50 per share (assuming the preferred stock paid the same dividend as the outstanding shares). However, in order to sell the shares it would have to pay an investment banker a fee to market the issue, and the cost of doing this is $1.375 per share. Thus, after considering the costs of selling the issue, the firm would incur a cost of 7.44 percent in order to raise preferred stock financing.

# DID YOU GET IT?

## CALCULATING THE COST OF DEBT FINANCING

General Auto Parts Corporation receives $18 million from the sale of the bonds (after paying flotation costs) and is required to make principal plus interest payments at the end of the next 2 years. The total cash flows (both the inflow and the outflows) are summarized below:

|           | TODAY        | YEAR 1            | YEAR 2            |
|-----------|--------------|-------------------|-------------------|
| Principal | $18 million  | ($0.00 million)   | ($20 million)     |
| Interest  |              | ($0.99 million)   | ($0.99 million)   |
| Total     | $18 million  | ($0.99 million)   | ($20.99 million)  |

We can estimate the before-tax cost of capital from the bond issue by solving for $k_d$ in the following bond valuation equation:

$$\text{Net bond proceeds}_{today} = \frac{\text{interest paid in year 1}}{(1 + k_d)^1} + \frac{\text{interest paid in year 2}}{(1 + k_d)^2} + \frac{\text{principal paid in year 2}}{(1 + k_d)^2}$$

$$\$18,000,000 = \frac{\$990,000}{(1 + k_d)^1} + \frac{\$990,000}{(1 + k_d)^2} + \frac{\$20,000,000}{(1 + k_d)^2}$$

$$k_d = 10.77\%$$

## The Cost of Common Equity

Common equity is unique in two respects. First, the **cost of common equity** is more difficult to estimate than the cost of debt or cost of preferred stock because the common stockholders' required rate of return is not observable. For example, there is no stated coupon rate or set dividend payment they receive. This results from the fact that common stockholders are the residual owners of the firm, which means that their return is equal to what is left of the firm's earnings after paying the firm's bondholders their contractually set interest and principal payments and the preferred stockholders their promised dividends. Second, common equity can be obtained either from the retention and reinvestment of firm earnings or through the sale of new shares. The costs associated with each of these sources are different from one another because the firm does not incur any flotation costs when it retains earnings, but it does incur costs when it sells new common shares.

> **cost of common equity** the rate of return that must be earned on the common stockholders' investment in order to satisfy their required rate of return.

We discuss two methods for estimating the common stockholders' required rate of return, which is the foundation for our estimate of the firm's cost of equity capital. These methods are based on the dividend growth model and the capital asset pricing model, which were both discussed in Chapter 8 when we discussed stock valuation.

## The Dividend Growth Model

Recall from Chapter 8 that the value of a firm's common stock is equal to the present value of all future dividends. When dividends are expected to grow at a rate $g$ forever, and $g$ is less than the investor's required rate of return, $k_{cs}$, then the value of a share of common stock, $P_{cs}$, can be written as

$$P_{cs} = \frac{D_1}{k_{cs} - g} \tag{9-6}$$

where $D_1$ is the dividend expected to be received by the firm's common shareholders 1 year hence. The expected dividend is simply the current dividend ($D_0$) multiplied by 1 plus the annual rate of growth in dividends (that is, $D_1 = D_0 (1 + g)$). The investor's required rate of return then is found by solving equation (9-6) for $k_{cs}$.

$$k_{cs} = \frac{D_1}{P_{cs}} + g \tag{9-7}$$

Note that $k_{cs}$ is the investor's required rate of return for investing in the firm's stock. It also serves as our estimate of the cost of equity capital, where new equity capital is obtained by retaining a part of the firm's current-period earnings. Recall that common equity financing can come from one of two sources: the retention of earnings or the sale of new common shares. When the firm retains earnings, it doesn't incur any flotation costs; thus, the investor's required rate of return is the same as the firm's cost of new equity capital in this instance.

If the firm issues new shares to raise equity capital, then it incurs flotation costs. Once again we adjust the investor's required rate of return for flotation costs by substituting the net proceeds per share, $NP_{cs}$, for the stock price, $P_{cs}$, in equation (9-7) to estimate the cost of new common stock, $k_{ncs}$.

$$k_{ncs} = \frac{D_1}{NP_{cs}} + g \tag{9-8}$$

## DID YOU GET IT?
### CALCULATING THE COST OF PREFERRED STOCK FINANCING

Carson Enterprises sold its shares of preferred stock for net proceeds of $2.25 a share, and each share entitles the holder to a $0.25 cash dividend every year. Because the dividend payment is constant for all future years, we can calculate the cost of capital raised by the sale of preferred stock ($k_{ps}$) as follows:

$$\text{Cost of preferred stock } (k_{ps}) = \frac{\text{preferred stock dividend}}{\text{net proceeds per preferred share}} = \frac{\$0.25}{\$2.25} = 11.11\%$$

| EXAMPLE 9.3 | Calculating the cost of common stock financing |
|---|---|

The Talbot Corporation's common shareholders anticipate receiving a $2.20 per share dividend next year, based on the fact that they received $2 last year and expect dividends to grow 10 percent next year. Furthermore, analysts predict that dividends will continue to grow at a rate of 10 percent into the foreseeable future. If Talbot were to issue new common stock, the firm would incur a $7.50 per share cost to sell the new shares. Based on the most recent closing price for the firm's common stock, what would you estimate the cost of a common stock to be for the firm? What is the cost of a new common stock issue?

### STEP 1: FORMULATE A SOLUTION STRATEGY

The cost of common stock financing can be computed from the basic valuation equation for a share of common stock just like we estimate the cost of debt financing from the valuation equation for a bond. Specifically, solving for the cost of common stock, it can be computed using equation (9-7) as follows:

$$\text{Cost of common stock } (k_{cs}) = \frac{\text{common stock dividend}}{\text{price per common share}} + \text{growth rate } (g)$$

If Talbot were to issue new common stock, then the $7.50 per share flotation costs would be incurred, such that the cost of a new common stock issue would be computed using equation (9-8) as follows:

$$\text{Cost of common stock } (k_{ncs}) = \frac{\text{common stock dividend}}{\text{net proceeds per common share}} + \text{growth rate } (g)$$

Note that net proceeds per common share reflects the difference in the price for which each common share is sold and the flotation costs per share incurred to sell new shares.

### STEP 2: CRUNCH THE NUMBERS

Inputting the numbers into equation (9-7), we compute the cost of common stock as follows:

$$\text{Cost of common stock } (k_{cs}) = \frac{\$2.20}{\$50.00} + 0.10 = 0.144, \text{ or } 14.4\%$$

The cost of a new common stock issue is computed by substituting net proceeds per new common share issued for the firm's stock price, that is,

$$\text{Cost of common stock } (k_{ncs}) = \frac{\$2.20}{\$50.00 - \$7.50} + 0.10 = 0.1518, \text{ or } 15.18\%$$

### STEP 3: ANALYZE YOUR RESULTS

The cost of common stock or common equity to Talbot is 14.4 percent; however, if the firm makes a new stock issue, it will incur an issue or flotation cost of $7.50 such that the cost of a new common stock issue is 15.18 percent.

## Issues in Implementing the Dividend Growth Model

The principal advantage of the dividend growth model as a basis for calculating the firm's cost of capital as it relates to common stock is the model's simplicity. To estimate an investor's required rate of return, the analyst needs only to observe the current dividend and stock price and to estimate the rate of growth in future dividends. The primary drawback relates to the applicability or appropriateness of the valuation model. That is, the dividend growth model is based on the fundamental assumption that dividends are expected to grow at a constant rate $g$ forever. To avoid this assumption, analysts frequently utilize more complex valuation models in which dividends are expected to grow for, say, 5 years at one rate and then grow at a lower rate from year 6 forward. We do not consider these more complex models here.

Even if the constant growth rate assumption is acceptable, we must arrive at an estimate of that growth rate. We could estimate the rate of growth in historical dividends ourselves or go to published sources of growth rate expectations. Investment advisory services such as Value Line provide their own analysts' estimates of earnings growth rates (generally spanning up to 5 years), and the Institutional Brokers' Estimate System (I/B/E/S) collects and publishes earnings per share forecasts made by more than 1,000 analysts for a broad list of stocks. These estimates are helpful but still require the careful judgment of an analyst in their use because they relate to earnings (not dividends) and extend only 5 years into the future (not forever, as required by the dividend growth model). Nonetheless, these estimates provide a useful guide to making your initial dividend growth rate estimate.

## The Capital Asset Pricing Model

Recall from Chapter 6 that the capital asset pricing model (CAPM) provides a basis for determining the investor's expected or required rate of return from investing in a firm's common stock. The model depends on three things:

1. The risk-free rate, $r_f$
2. The systematic risk of the common stock's returns relative to the market as a whole, or the stock's beta coefficient, $\beta$
3. The market-risk premium, which is equal to the difference in the expected rate of return for the market as a whole, that is, the expected rate of return for the "average security" minus the risk-free rate, or in symbols, $r_m - r_f$

Using the CAPM, the investor's required rate of return can be written as follows:

$$k_{cs} = r_f + \beta(r_m - r_f) \tag{9-9}$$

**EXAMPLE 9.4**

**Calculating the cost of common stock financing using the CAPM**

The Talbot Corporation's beta coefficient is estimated to be 1.40. Furthermore, the risk-free rate of interest is currently 3.75%, and the expected rate of return on a diversified portfolio of all common stocks is 12 percent. Use the capital asset pricing model (CAPM) to estimate the cost of equity capital for Talbot.

### STEP 1: FORMULATE A SOLUTION STRATEGY

In Example 9.3 we estimated the cost of common stock using a constant rate of growth and the discounted cash-flow model. In this example, we estimate that same cost of common stock using the capital asset pricing model, or CAPM. Specifically, the cost of common stock can be estimated using equation (9-9) as follows:

$$\text{Cost of common stock } (k_{cs}) = r_f + \beta(r_m - r_f)$$

### STEP 2: CRUNCH THE NUMBERS

Inserting the values into equation (9-9), we compute the cost of a common stock as follows:

$$\text{Cost of common stock } (k_{cs}) = r_f + \beta(r_m - r_f) = 0.0375 + 1.4(0.12 - 0.0375) = 0.153, \text{ or } 15.3\%$$

### STEP 3: ANALYZE YOUR RESULTS

Our estimate of the cost of common stock or common equity to Talbot using the CAPM is 15.3 percent. Note that since no transaction costs are considered when using the CAPM, this estimate is for the cost of internal common equity or the retention of earnings.

## CAN YOU DO IT?

### CALCULATING THE COST OF NEW COMMON STOCK USING THE DIVIDEND GROWTH MODEL

In March of 2012 the Mayze Corporation sold an issue of common stock in a public offering. The shares sold for $100 per share. Mayze's dividend in 2011 was $8 per share, and analysts expect that the firm's earnings and dividends will grow at a rate of 6 percent per year for the foreseeable future. What is the common stock investor's required rate of return (and the cost of retained earnings)?

Although the shares sold for $100 per share, Mayze received net proceeds from the issue of only $95 per share. The difference represents the flotation cost paid to the investment banker.

What is your estimate of the cost of new equity for Mayze using the dividend growth model?
(The solution can be found on page 285.)

## CAN YOU DO IT?

### CALCULATING THE COST OF COMMON STOCK USING THE CAPM

The Mayze Corporation issued common stock in March 2012 for $100 per share. However, before the issue was made, the firm's chief financial officer (CFO) asked one of his financial analysts to estimate the cost of the common stock financing using the CAPM. The analyst looked on Yahoo! Finance and got an estimate of 0.90 for the firm's beta coefficient. She also consulted online sources to get the current yield on a 10-year U.S. Treasury bond, which was 5.5 percent. The final estimate she needed to complete her calculation of the cost of equity using the CAPM was the market-risk premium, or the difference in the expected rate of return on all equity securities and the rate of return on the 10-year U.S. Treasury bond. After a bit of research she decided that the risk premium should be based on a 12 percent expected rate of return for the market portfolio and the 5.5 percent rate on the Treasury bond.

What is your estimate of the cost of common stock for Mayze using the CAPM?
(The solution can be found on page 286.)

## Issues in Implementing the CAPM

The CAPM approach has two primary advantages when it comes to calculating a firm's cost of capital as it relates to common stock. First, the model is simple and easy to understand and implement. The model variables are readily available from public sources, with the possible exception of beta coefficients for small firms and/or privately held firms. Second, because the model does not rely on dividends or any assumption about the growth rate in dividends, it can be applied to companies that do not currently pay dividends or are not expected to experience a constant rate of growth in dividends.

Of course, using the CAPM requires that we obtain estimates of each of the three model variables—$r_f$, $\beta$, and $(r_m - r_f)$. Let's consider each in turn. First, the analyst has a wide range of U.S. government securities on which to base an estimate of the risk-free rate $(r_f)$. Treasury securities with maturities from 30 days to 20 years are readily available. Unfortunately, the CAPM offers no guidance about the appropriate choice. In fact, the model itself assumes that there is but one risk-free rate, and it corresponds to a one-period return (the length of the period is not specified, however). Consequently, we are left to our own judgment about which maturity we should use to represent the risk-free rate. For applications of the cost of capital involving long-term capital expenditure decisions, it seems reasonable to select a risk-free rate of comparable maturity. So, if we are calculating the cost of capital to be used as the basis for evaluating investments that will provide returns over the next 20 years, it seems appropriate to use a risk-free rate corresponding to a U.S. Treasury bond of comparable maturity.

Second, estimates of security beta $(\beta)$ coefficients are available from a wide variety of investment advisory services, including Merrill Lynch and Value Line, among others. Alternatively, we could collect historical stock market returns for the company of interest as well as a general market index (such as the Standard and Poor's 500 Index) and estimate the stock's beta as the slope of the relationship between the two return series—as we did in Chapter 6. However, because beta estimates are widely available for a large majority of publicly traded firms, analysts frequently rely on published sources for betas.

Finally, estimating the market-risk premium can be accomplished by looking at the history of stock returns and the premium earned over (under) the risk-free rate of interest. In Chapter 6, we reported a summary of the historical returns earned on risk-free securities and common stocks in Figure 6-2. We saw that on average over the past 70 years, common stocks have earned a premium of roughly 5.5 percent over long-term government bonds. Thus, for our purposes, we will utilize this estimate of the market-risk premium ($r_m - r_f$) when estimating the investor's required rate of return on equity using the CAPM.

## FINANCE AT WORK

### IPOs: SHOULD A FIRM GO PUBLIC?

When a privately owned company decides to distribute its shares to the general public, it goes through a process known as an initial public offering (IPO). There are a number of advantages to having a firm's shares traded in the public equity market, including the following:

- **New capital is raised.** When the firm sells its shares to the public, it acquires new capital that can be invested in the firm.
- **The firm's owners gain liquidity of their share holdings.** Publicly traded shares are more easily bought and sold, so the owners can more easily liquidate all or part of their investment in the firm.
- **The firm gains future access to the public capital market.** Once a firm has raised capital in the public markets, it is easier to go back a second and third time.
- **Being a publicly traded firm can benefit the firm's business.** Public firms tend to enjoy a higher profile than their privately held counterparts. This may make it easier to make sales and attract vendors to supply goods and services to the firm.

However, all is not rosy as a publicly held firm. There are a number of potential disadvantages, including the following:

- **Reporting requirements can be onerous.** Publicly held firms are required to file periodic reports with the Securities and Exchange Commission (SEC). This is not only onerous in terms of the time and effort required but also some business owners feel they must reveal information to their competitors that could be potentially damaging.

- **The private equity investors now must share any new wealth with the new public investors.** Once the firm is a publicly held company, the new shareholders share on an equal footing with the company founders the good (and bad) fortune of the firm.
- **The private equity investors lose a degree of control over the organization.** Outsiders gain voting control over the firm to the extent that they own its shares.
- **An IPO is expensive.** A typical firm may spend 15 to 25 percent of the money raised on expenses directly connected to the IPO. This cost is increased further if we consider the cost of lost management time and disruption of business associated with the IPO process.
- **Exit of the company's owners is usually limited.** The company's founders may want to sell their shares through the IPO, but this is not allowed for an extended period of time following the IPO. Therefore, this is not usually a good mechanism for cashing out the company founders.
- **Everyone involved faces legal liability.** The IPO participants are jointly and severally liable for each others' actions. This means that they can be sued for any omissions from the IPO's prospectus should the market valuation fall below the IPO offering price.

Carefully weighing the financial consequences of each of these advantages and disadvantages can provide a company's owners (and managers) with some basis for answering the question of whether they want to become a public corporation.

Other Sources: Professor Ivo Welch's Web site, welch.som.yale.edu, provides a wealth of information concerning IPOs.

## DID YOU GET IT?
### CALCULATING THE COST OF NEW COMMON STOCK USING THE DIVIDEND GROWTH MODEL

We can estimate the cost of equity capital using the dividend growth model by substituting into the following equation:

$$\text{Cost of new common stock } (k_{ncs}) = \frac{\text{expected dividend next year } (D_1)}{\text{net proceeds per share } (NP_{cs})} + \text{dividend growth rate } (g) = \frac{\$8.00\,(1.06)}{\$95.00} + 0.06 = 14.92\%$$

## DID YOU GET IT?
### CALCULATING THE COST OF COMMON STOCK USING THE CAPM

The CAPM can be used to estimate the investor's required rate of return as follows:

$$\begin{matrix} \text{Cost of} \\ \text{common equity } (k_{cs}) \end{matrix} = \begin{pmatrix} \text{risk-free} \\ \text{rate of interest } (r_f) \end{pmatrix} + \begin{pmatrix} \text{Mayze's beta} \\ \text{coefficient } (\beta) \end{pmatrix} \times \begin{bmatrix} \text{expected market} \\ \text{rate of return } (r_m) \end{bmatrix} - \begin{matrix} \text{risk-free} \\ \text{rate of interest } (r_f) \end{matrix} \end{bmatrix}$$

Making the appropriate substitutions, we get the following estimate of the investor's required rate of return using the CAPM model:

$$\text{Cost of common equity } (k_{cs}) = 0.055 + 0.90 \times (0.12 - 0.055) = 0.1135, \text{ or } 11.35\%$$

In addition to the historical average market-risk premium, we can also utilize surveys of professional economists' opinions regarding future premiums.[1] For example, in a survey conducted in 1998 by Yale economist Ivo Welch, the median 30-year market-risk premium for all survey participants was 7 percent. When the survey was repeated in 2000, the corresponding market-risk premium had fallen to 5 percent. These results suggest two things. First, the market-risk premium is not fixed. It varies through time with the general business cycle. In addition, it appears that using a market-risk premium somewhere between 5 percent and 7 percent is reasonable when estimating the cost of capital using the capital asset pricing model.

### Concept Check

1. Define the cost of debt, preferred equity, and common equity financing.
2. The cost of common equity financing is more difficult to estimate than the costs of debt and preferred equity. Explain why.
3. What is the dividend growth model, and how is it used to estimate the cost of common equity financing?
4. Describe the capital asset pricing model and how it can be used to estimate the cost of common equity financing.
5. What practical problems are encountered in using the CAPM to estimate common equity capital cost?

## The Weighted Average Cost of Capital

 3 Calculate a firm's weighted average cost of capital.

Now that we have calculated the individual costs of capital for each of the sources of financing the firm might use, we turn to the combination of these capital costs into a single weighted average cost of capital. To estimate the weighted average cost of capital, we need to know the cost of each of the sources of capital used and the capital structure mix. We use the term **capital structure** to refer to *the proportions of each source of financing used by the firm.* Although a firm's capital structure can be quite complex, we focus our examples on the three basic sources of capital: bonds, preferred stock, and common equity.

In words, we calculate the weighted average cost of capital for a firm that uses only debt and common equity using the following equation:

**capital structure** the mix of long-term sources of funds used by the firm. This is also called the firm's capitalization. The relative total (percentage) of each type of fund is emphasized.

$$\begin{matrix} \text{Weighted} \\ \text{average cost} \\ \text{of capital} \end{matrix} = \begin{pmatrix} \text{after-tax} \\ \text{cost of} \times \\ \text{debt} \end{pmatrix} \begin{matrix} \text{proportion} \\ \text{of debt} \\ \text{financing} \end{matrix} + \begin{pmatrix} \text{cost of} \\ \text{equity} \times \end{pmatrix} \begin{matrix} \text{proportion} \\ \text{of equity} \\ \text{financing} \end{matrix} \qquad (9\text{-}10)$$

[1]The results reported here come from Ivo Welch, "Views of Financial Economists on the Equity Premium and on Professional Controversies," *Journal of Business* 73–74 (October 2000), pp. 501–537; and Ivo Welch, "The Equity Premium Consensus Forecast Revisited," Cowles Foundation Discussion Paper No. 1325 (September 2001).

For example, if a firm borrows money at 6 percent after taxes, pays 10 percent for equity, and raises its capital in equal proportions from debt and equity, its weighted average cost of capital is 8 percent, that is,

Weighted average cost of capital $= [0.06 \times 0.5] + [0.10 \times 0.5] = 0.08$, or 8%

In practice, the calculation of the cost of capital is more complex than this example. For one thing, firms often have multiple debt issues with different required rates of return, and they also use preferred equity as well as common equity financing. Furthermore, when common equity capital is raised, it is sometimes the result of retaining and reinvesting the firm's earnings, and at other times it involves a new stock offering. Of course, in the case of retained earnings, the firm does not incur the costs associated with selling new common stock. This means that equity from retained earnings is less costly than a new stock offering. In the examples that follow, we address each of these complications.

## Capital Structure Weights

The reason we calculate a cost of capital is that it enables us to evaluate one or more of the firm's investment opportunities. Remember that the cost of capital should reflect the riskiness of the project being evaluated, so a firm should calculate multiple costs of capital when it makes investments in multiple divisions or business units having different risk characteristics. Thus, for the calculated cost of capital to be meaningful, it must correspond directly to the riskiness of the particular project being analyzed. That is, in theory the cost of capital should reflect the particular way in which the funds are raised (the capital structure used) and the systemic risk characteristics of the project. Consequently, the correct way to calculate capital structure weights is to use the actual dollar amounts of the various sources of capital actually used by the firm.[2]

In practice, *the mixture of financing sources used by a firm will vary from year to year*. For this reason, many firms find it expedient to use target capital structure proportions when calculating the firm's weighted average cost of capital. For example, a firm might use its target mix of 40 percent debt and 60 percent equity to calculate its weighted average cost of capital even though, in that particular year, it raised the majority of its financing requirements by borrowing. Similarly, it would continue to use the target proportions in the subsequent year, when it might raise the majority of its financing needs by reinvesting earnings or issuing new stock.

## Calculating the Weighted Average Cost of Capital

The weighted average cost of capital, $k_{wacc}$, is simply a weighted average of all the capital costs incurred by the firm. Table 9-1 illustrates the procedure used to estimate $k_{wacc}$ for a firm that has debt, preferred stock, and common equity in its target capital structure mix. Two possible scenarios are described in the two panels. First, in Panel A the firm is able to finance all of its target capital structure requirements for common equity using retained earnings. Second, in Panel B the firm must use a new equity offering to raise the equity capital it requires. For example, if the firm has set a 75 percent target for equity financing and has current earnings of $750,000, then it can raise up to $750,000/0.75 = $1,000,000 in new financing before it has to sell new equity. For $1,000,000 or less in capital spending, the firm's weighted average cost of capital would be calculated using the cost of equity from retained earnings (following Panel A of Table 9-1). For more than $1,000,000 in new capital, the cost of capital would rise to reflect the impact of the higher cost of using new common stock (following Panel B of Table 9-1).

---

[2]There are instances when we will want to calculate the cost of capital for the firm as a whole. In this case, the appropriate weights to use are based on the market value of the various capital sources used by the firm. Market values rather than book values properly reflect the sources of financing used by a firm at any particular point in time. However, when a firm is privately owned, it is not possible to get market values of its securities, and book values are often used.

**TABLE 9-1  Calculating the Weighted Average Cost of Capital**

**PANEL A: COMMON EQUITY RAISED BY RETAINED EARNINGS**
Capital Structure

| Source of Capital | Weights | × Cost of Capital | = Product |
|---|---|---|---|
| Bonds | $w_d$ | $k_d(1-T_c)$ | $w_d \times k_d(1-T_c)$ |
| Preferred stock | $w_{ps}$ | $k_{ps}$ | $w_{ps} \times k_{ps}$ |
| Common equity | | | |
|   Retained earnings | $w_{cs}$ | $k_{cs}$ | $w_{cs} \times k_{cs}$ |
| Sum = | 100% | Sum = | $k_{wacc}$ |

**PANEL B: COMMON EQUITY RAISED BY SELLING NEW COMMON STOCK**
Capital Structure

| Source of Capital | Weights | × Cost of Capital | = Product |
|---|---|---|---|
| Bonds | $w_d$ | $k_d(1-T_c)$ | $w_d \times k_d(1-T_c)$ |
| Preferred stock | $w_{ps}$ | $k_{ps}$ | $w_{ps} \times k_{ps}$ |
| Common equity | | | |
|   Common stock | $w_{ncs}$ | $k_{ncs}$ | $w_{ncs} \times k_{ncs}$ |
| Sum = | 100% | Sum = | $k_{wacc}$ |

---

**EXAMPLE 9.5    Calculating a firm's weighted average cost of capital**

Ash Inc.'s capital structure and estimated capital costs are found in Table 9-2. Note that the sum of the capital structure weights must equal 100 percent if we have properly accounted for all sources of financing and in the correct amounts. For example, Ash plans to invest a total of $3 million in common equity to fund a $5 million investment. Because Ash has earnings equal to the $3,000,000 it needs in new equity financing, the entire amount of new equity will be raised by retaining earnings.

**STEP 1: FORMULATE A SOLUTION STRATEGY**
We calculate the weighted average cost of capital following the procedure described in Panel A of Table 9-1 and using the information found in Table 9-2. Note that the cost of capital for Ash Inc. varies with the amount of financing being considered. For example, for up to $5 million in new capital the firm can use retained earnings to supply the needed common equity to make up 60 percent of the total. However, for each dollar over $5 million Ash Inc. will have to issue new common shares, which carry a higher cost of financing than retained earnings since transaction costs are incurred to sell more common stock.

The formula used to calculate the weighted average cost of capital, $k_{wacc}$, is summarized in Table 9-1; however, we can write the equation down as follows:

$$k_{wacc} = w_d \times k_d \times (1 - T_c) + (w_{ps} \times k_{cs}) + (w_{cs} \times k_{cs})$$

Note that $k_{wacc}$ is simply an average of the after-tax costs of debt, preferred stock, and common stock where these costs are weighted by their relative importance in the firm's capital structure. To compute the cost of raising more than $5 million in total financing we simply substitute the cost of new common stock, $k_{ncs}$, for the cost of equity.

**STEP 2: CRUNCH THE NUMBERS**
Panel A of Table 9-3 computes an estimate of Ash Inc.'s weighted average cost of up to $5 million in new capital, which is 12.7 percent. Should the firm need to raise more than $5 million, then new shares of common stock will have to be issued and the cost of this equity capital is 18 percent (compared to 16 percent for internally generated common equity or retained earnings). The net result is that the firm's cost of capital for each dollar over $5 million rises to 13.9 percent.

**TABLE 9-2  Capital Structure and Capital Costs for Ash Inc.**

| Source of Capital | Amount of Funds Raised ($) | Percentage of Total | After-Tax Cost of Capital |
|---|---|---|---|
| Bonds | 1,750,000 | 35% | 7% |
| Preferred stock | 250,000 | 5% | 13% |
| Retained earnings | 3,000,000 | 60% | 16% |
| Total | 5,000,000 | 100% | |

**TABLE 9-3  The Weighted Average Cost of Capital for Ash Inc.**

**PANEL A: COST OF CAPITAL FOR $0 TO $5,000,000 IN NEW CAPITAL**

Capital Structure

| Source of Capital | Weights | Cost of Capital | Product |
|---|---|---|---|
| Bonds | 35% | 7% | 2.45% |
| Preferred stock | 5% | 13% | 0.65% |
| Retained earnings | 60% | 16% | 9.60% |
| Total | 100% | $k_{wacc} =$ | 12.70% |

**PANEL B: COST OF CAPITAL FOR MORE THAN $5,000,000**

Capital Structure

| Source of Capital | Weights | Cost of Capital | Product |
|---|---|---|---|
| Bonds | 35% | 7% | 2.45% |
| Preferred stock | 5% | 13% | 0.65% |
| New common stock | 60% | 18% | 10.80% |
| Total | 100% | $k_{wacc} =$ | 13.90% |

### STEP 3: ANALYZE YOUR RESULTS

The firm's weighted average cost of capital is an estimate of the blend of sources of capital the firm has used. For Ash Inc., the cost of raising up to $5 million is 12.70 percent, whereas raising more than $5 million requires the firm to issue new shares of common stock and incur flotation costs such that the overall weighted average cost of capital rises to 13.9 percent.

## CAUTIONARY TALE

### FORGETTING PRINCIPLE 3: RISK REQUIRES A REWARD

What happens to a firm's cost of capital when the capital market that the firm depends on for financing simply stops working? Investment banking firm Goldman Sachs discovered the answer to this question the hard way. In 2008, as potential lenders became very nervous about the future of the economy, the credit markets from which Goldman Sachs borrowed money on a regular basis simply stopped functioning. The effect of this shutdown was that Goldman Sachs no longer had access to cheap short-term debt financing. And this meant the firm was at greater risk of financial distress. This high risk of firm failure caused its equity holders to demand a much higher rate of return and thus, Goldman Sachs's cost of equity financing skyrocketed.

Ultimately, faced with a crisis, Goldman arranged for a $10 billion loan from the U.S. Government's Troubled Asset Relief Fund (TARP) and obtained a $5 billion equity investment from famed investor Warren Buffett. The combined effects of these actions stabilized the firm's financial situation and lowered the firm's cost of capital dramatically. Goldman Sachs and Morgan Stanley are the only two large investment banking firms to survive the financial crisis.

So what can Goldman Sachs learn from this experience? Debt financing, and in particular short-term debt financing, may offer higher returns in the short run, but this use of financial leverage comes with a significant increase in risk to the equity holders, and this translates to higher costs of equity financing for the firm.

## Concept Check

1. A firm's capital structure and its target capital structure proportions are important determinants of a firm's weighted average cost of capital. Explain.

2. Explain in words the calculation of a firm's weighted average cost of capital. What exactly are we averaging and what do the weights represent?

 **4** Estimate divisional costs of capital

# Calculating Divisional Costs of Capital

## Estimating Divisional Costs of Capital

Firms that have multiple operating divisions where each division's risk is unique and different from that of the firm as a whole often use different costs of capital for each division in an effort to properly account for risk. The idea here is that the divisions take on investment projects with unique levels of risk and, consequently, the WACC used in each division is potentially unique to that division. Generally, divisions are defined either by geographical regions (for example, the Latin American division) or industry (for example, exploration and production, pipelines, and refining for a large integrated oil company).

**divisional WACC** the cost of capital for a specific business unit or division.

The advantages of using a **divisional WACC** include the following:

◆ It provides different discount rates that reflect differences in the systematic risk of the projects evaluated by the different divisions.
◆ It entails only one cost of capital estimate per division (as opposed to unique discount rates for each project), thereby minimizing the time and effort of estimating the cost of capital.
◆ The use of a common discount rate throughout the division limits managerial latitude and the attendant influence costs as managers would otherwise be tempted to lobby for a lower cost of capital for pet projects.

## Using Pure Play Firms to Estimate Divisional WACCs

One approach that can be taken to deal with differences in the costs of capital for each of the firm's business units involves identifying what we will call "pure play" comparison firms (or "comps") that operate in only one of the individual business areas (where possible). For example, Valero Energy Corporation (VLO) is a Fortune 500 manufacturer and marketer of transportation fuels headquartered in San Antonio, Texas. The firm owns 14 refineries and is one of the largest U.S. retail operators with over 5,800 retail stores. Specifically, the firm's operations are concentrated in the "downstream" segment of the petroleum industry, which involves refining crude oil into gasoline and other transportation fuels and the sale of those products to the public.

To estimate the cost of capital for each of these different types of activities, we use the WACCs for comparison firms that are not fully integrated and operate in only one of Valero's business segments. For example, to estimate the WACC for its business unit engaged in refining crude oil, Valero might use a WACC estimate for firms that operate in the refinery industry (SIC industry 2911) to estimate the relevant WACC for this division.[3] To estimate the WACC for the retail component of Valero's operations, we could use firms that operate primarily in the retail convenience store industry, which is SIC 5411.

**Divisional WACC Example**   Table 9-4 contains hypothetical estimates of the divisional WACC for the refining and retail (convenience store) industries.

Panel A contains estimates of the after-tax cost of debt financing to the refining and retailing industries where the firm's marginal income tax rate is assumed to be 38 percent. Note that the borrowing costs are slightly different, which reflects both the amount of money borrowed (see Panel C) and the risk differences perceived by lenders to the two industries. Panel B contains the after-tax cost of equity capital based on the capital asset

[3]SIC is the four-digit Standard Industrial Classification code that is widely used to identify different industries.

**TABLE 9-4  Divisional WACC Computations**

### PANEL A. AFTER-TAX COST OF DEBT

| | Pre-Tax Cost of Debt | × | (1 − Tax Rate) | After-Tax Cost of Debt |
|---|---|---|---|---|
| Refining | 9.00% | × | 0.62 | 0.0558 |
| Retailing—Convenience Stores | 7.50% | × | 0.62 | 0.0465 |

### PANEL B. AFTER-TAX COST OF EQUITY

| | Risk-Free Rate | + | Beta | × | Market-Risk Premium | = | Cost of Equity |
|---|---|---|---|---|---|---|---|
| Refining | 0.02 | + | 1.1 | × | 0.07 | = | 0.097 |
| Retailing—Convenience Stores | 0.02 | + | 0.8 | × | 0.07 | = | 0.076 |

### PANEL C. TARGET DEBT RATIOS

| | Target Debt Ratio |
|---|---|
| Refining | 10% |
| Retailing—Convenience Stores | 50% |

### PANEL D. DIVISIONAL WACC FOR REFINING

| | Capital Structure Weight | × | After-Tax Cost of Capital | = | Product |
|---|---|---|---|---|---|
| Debt | 0.10 | × | 0.0558 | = | 0.0056 |
| Equity | 0.90 | × | 0.0970 | = | 0.0873 |
| | | | WACC | = | 0.0929 or 9.29% |

### PANEL E. DIVISIONAL WACC FOR RETAIL (CONVENIENCE STORES)

| | Capital Structure Weight | × | After-Tax Cost of Capital | = | Product |
|---|---|---|---|---|---|
| Debt | 0.50 | × | 0.0465 | = | 0.0233 |
| Equity | 0.50 | × | 0.0760 | = | 0.03580 |
| | | | WACC | = | 0.0613 or 6.13% |

pricing model. The only difference in the cost of equity for the two industries corresponds to the beta estimates. Finally, in Panels D and E we estimate the WACCs for the two industry segments. The refining industry has a 9.29 percent WACC estimate, while the retail industry has a 6.13 percent WACC. If the firm were to use a composite of the two WACC estimates to evaluate new projects, the WACC would be somewhere between these two industry estimates. This would mean that the firm would take on too many refining projects and too few retail investments.

**Divisional WACC—Estimation Issues and Limitations**  Although the divisional WACC is generally a significant improvement over the single, company-wide WACC, the way that it is often implemented using industry-based comparison firms has a number of potential limitations:

◆ The sample of those in a given industry may firms include those that are not good matches for the firm or one of its divisions. For example, the Valero company analyst may select two or three firms whose risk profiles more nearly match their refining division as opposed to using a composite made of all firms found in the petroleum refining industry (SIC 2911). The firm's management can easily address this problem by selecting appropriate comparison firms with similar risk profiles from among the many firms included in these industries.

◆ The division being analyzed may not have a capital structure that is similar to the sample of firms in the industry data. The division may be more or less leveraged than the firms whose costs of capital are used to proxy for the divisional cost of capital. For example, ExxonMobil raised only 4 percent of its capital using debt financing, whereas Valero Energy (VLO) has raised 35 percent of its capital with debt at the end of 2011[4].

◆ The firms in the chosen industry that are used to proxy for divisional risk may not be good reflections of project risk. Firms, by definition, are engaged in a variety of activities, and it can be very difficult to identify a group of firms that are predominantly engaged in activities that are truly comparable to a given project. Even within divisions, individual projects can have very different risk profiles. This means that even if we are able to match divisional risks very closely, there may still be significant differences in risk across projects undertaken within a division. For example, some projects may entail extensions of existing production capabilities, while others involve new-product development. Both types of investments take place within a given division, but they have very different risk profiles.

◆ Good comparison firms for a particular division may be difficult to find. Most publicly traded firms report multiple lines of business, yet each company is classified into a single industry group. In the case of Valero we found two operating divisions (refining and retail) and identified an industry proxy for each.

The preceding discussion suggests that although the use of divisional WACCs to determine project discount rates may represent an improvement over the use of a company-wide WACC, this methodology is far from perfect. However, if the firm has investment opportunities with risks that vary principally with industry-risk characteristics, the use of a divisional WACC has clear advantages over the use of the firm's WACC. It provides a methodology that allows for different discount rates, and it avoids some of the influence costs associated with giving managers complete leeway to select project-specific discount rates. Table 9-5 summarizes the cases for using a single-firm WACC and divisional WACCs to evaluate investment opportunities.

**TABLE 9-5    Choosing the Right WACC—Discount Rates and Project Risk**

There are good reasons for using a single, company-wide WACC to evaluate the firm's investments even where there are differences in the risks of the projects the firm undertakes. The most common practice among firms that use a variety of discount rates to evaluate new investments in an effort to accommodate risk differences is the divisional WACC. The latter represents something of a compromise that minimizes some of the problems encountered when attempting to estimate both the project-specific costs of capital and the costs that arise where a single discount rate is used that is equal to the firm's WACC.

| Method | Description | Advantages | Disadvantages | When to Use |
|---|---|---|---|---|
| WACC | Estimated WACC for the firm as an entity; used as the discount rate on *all* projects. | • Familiar concept to most business executives.<br>• Minimizes estimation costs, as there is only one cost of capital calculation for the firm.<br>• Reduces the problem of influence cost issues. | • Does not adjust discount rates for differences in project risk.<br>• Does not provide for flexibility in adjusting for differences in project debt in the capital structure. | • Projects are similar in risk to the firm as a whole.<br>• Using multiple discount rates creates significant problems with influence costs. |
| Divisional WACC | Estimated WACC for individual business units or divisions within the firm; used as the only discount rates within each division. | • Uses division-level risk to adjust discount rates for individual projects.<br>• Reduces influence costs to the competition among division managers to lower their division's cost of capital. | • Does not capture intra-division risk differences in projects.<br>• Does not account for differences in project debt capacities within divisions.<br>• Potential influence costs associated with the choice of discount rates across divisions.<br>• Difficult to find single-division firms to proxy for divisions. | • Individual projects within each division have similar risks and debt capacities.<br>• Discount rate discretion creates significant influence costs within divisions but not between divisions. |

[4]This estimate is based on year-end 2011 financial statements, using book values of interest-bearing short- and long-term debt and the market value of the firm's equity on March 30, 2012.

## FINANCE AT WORK

### THE PILLSBURY COMPANY ADOPTS EVA WITH A GRASSROOTS EDUCATION PROGRAM

A key determinant of the success of any incentive-based program is employee buy-in. If employees simply view a new performance measurement and reward system as "just another" reporting requirement, the program will have little impact on their behavior and, consequently, little effect on the firm's operating performance. In addition, if a firm's employees do not understand the measurement system, it is very likely that it will be distrusted and may even have counterproductive effects on the firm's performance.

So how do you instill in your employees the notion that your performance measurement and reward system does indeed lead to the desired result? Pillsbury took a unique approach to the problem by using a simulation exercise in which the value of applying the principles of Economic Value Added (EVA®) could be learned by simulating the operations of a hypothetical factory. Employees used the simulation to follow the value-creation process from the factory's revenue, to net operating profit after taxes, to the weighted average cost of capital. The results were gratifying. One Pillsbury manager noted, "you saw the lights go on in people's eyes" as employees realized, "Oh, this really does impact my work environment."

Briggs and Stratton used a similar training program to instill the basic principles of EVA in its employees. Its business-simulation example was even more basic than the Pillsbury factory. Briggs and Stratton used a convenience store's operations to teach line workers the importance of controlling waste, utilizing assets fully, and managing profit margins. Stern Stewart and Company, which coined the term *EVA*, has also developed a training tool, the EVA Training Tutor.™ The EVA Training Tutor addresses four basic issues using CD-ROM technology:

- Why is creating shareholder wealth an important corporate and investor goal?
- What is the best way to measure wealth and business success?
- Which business strategies have created wealth, and which have failed?
- What can you do to create wealth and increase the stock price of your company?

The educational programs described briefly here are examples of how major corporations are seeing the need to improve the financial literacy of their employees to make the most of their human and capital resources.

Sources: Adapted from George Donnelly, "Grassroots EVA," CFO.com (May 1, 2000), www.cfo.com and The EVA Training Tutor™ (Stern Stewart and Company).

## CAN YOU DO IT?

### CALCULATING THE WEIGHTED AVERAGE COST OF CAPITAL

In the fall of 2009, Grey Manufacturing was considering a major expansion of its manufacturing operations. The firm has sufficient land to accommodate the doubling of its operations, which will cost $200 million. To raise the needed funds Grey's management has decided to simply mimic the firm's present capital structure as follows:

| SOURCE OF CAPITAL | AMOUNT OF FUNDS RAISED ($) | PERCENTAGE OF TOTAL | AFTER-TAX COST OF CAPITAL* |
|---|---|---|---|
| Debt | $ 80,000,000 | 40% | 5.20% |
| Common stock | 120,000,000 | 60% | 14.50% |
| Total | $200,000,000 | 100% | |

What is your estimate of Grey's weighted average cost of capital?

*You may assume that these after-tax costs of capital have been appropriately adjusted for any transaction costs incurred when raising the funds.

(The solution appears below.)

## DID YOU GET IT?

### CALCULATING THE WEIGHTED AVERAGE COST OF CAPITAL

The weighted average cost of capital (WACC) for Grey Manufacturing can be calculated using the following table:

| SOURCE OF CAPITAL | PERCENTAGE OF TOTAL CAPITAL | AFTER-TAX COST OF CAPITAL | PRODUCT |
|---|---|---|---|
| Debt | 40% | 5.20% | 2.0800% |
| Common stock | 60% | 14.50% | 8.7000% |
| | | WACC = | 10.7800% |

Consequently, we estimate Grey's WACC to be 10.78 percent.

Calculating a firm's cost of capital involves using a number of financial decision tools. Specifically, the analyst must estimate the after-tax cost of debt, the cost of preferred stock financing, the cost of common equity financing, and the weighted average cost of capital itself.

## FINANCIAL DECISION TOOLS

| Name of Tool | Formula | What It Tells You |
|---|---|---|
| After-tax cost of debt | Step 1: The cost of debt (before taxes) is calculated as follows:<br><br>$$\frac{\text{Net Proceeds}}{(NP_d)} = \frac{\text{interest (year 1)}}{(1 + k_d)^1} + \frac{\text{interest (year 2)}}{(1 + k_d)^2} + \cdots$$<br>$$+ \frac{\text{principal}}{(1 + k_d)^2}$$<br><br>Step 2: The after-tax cost of debt is calculated as follows:<br>$$k_d(1 - T_c)$$<br>Where $T_c$ is the corporate tax rate. | The cost of borrowed funds to the firm after considering the tax deductibility of interest expense |
| Cost of preferred stock | The ratio of the present value of the future free cash flows to the initial outlay:<br><br>$$k_{ps} = \frac{\text{preferred stock dividend}}{\text{net proceeds per share of preferred stock } (NP_{ps})}$$ | The cost of raising funds by selling new shares of preferred stock |
| Cost of common equity (dividend growth model) | Cost of raising common equity by retaining and reinvesting firm earnings:<br><br>$$k_{cs} = \frac{\text{common stock dividend in year 1}}{\text{current price of common stock } (P_{cs})} + \frac{\text{dividend growth}}{\text{rate } (g)}$$<br><br>Cost of raising external equity funding by selling new shares of common stock:<br><br>$$k_{cs} = \frac{\text{common stock dividend in year 1}}{\text{net proceeds per share of preferred stock } (NP_{cs})} + \frac{\text{dividend growth}}{\text{rate } (g)}$$ | The cost of raising common equity funds |
| Cost of common equity (capital asset pricing model) | $$k_{cs} = \frac{\text{risk-free}}{\text{rate } (r_f)} + \frac{\text{equity}}{\text{beta } (\beta)}\left(\frac{\text{market}}{\text{return } (r_m)} - \frac{\text{risk-free}}{\text{rate } (r_f)}\right)$$ | The cost of raising common equity funds |
| Weighted average cost of capital (WACC) | $$WACC = \left(\begin{matrix}\text{after-tax} \\ \text{cost of} \\ \text{debt}\end{matrix} \times \begin{matrix}\text{proportion} \\ \text{of debt} \\ \text{financing}\end{matrix}\right) + \left(\begin{matrix}\text{cost of} \\ \text{equity}\end{matrix} \times \begin{matrix}\text{proportion} \\ \text{of equity} \\ \text{financing}\end{matrix}\right)$$ | • The opportunity cost of money invested in the firm<br>• Projects that earn higher rates of return than the WACC create shareholder wealth |

## Using a Firm's Cost of Capital to Evaluate New Capital Investments

If a firm has traditionally used a single cost of capital for all projects undertaken within each of several operating divisions (or companies) with very different risk characteristics, then the company will likely encounter resistance from the high-risk divisions if it changes to a divisional cost of capital structure. Consider the case of the hypothetical firm Global Energy, whose divisional costs of capital are illustrated in Figure 9-1. Global Energy is an integrated oil company that engages in a wide range of hydrocarbon-related businesses, including exploration and development, pipelines, and refining. Each of these businesses has its unique set of risks. In Figure 9-1 we see that the overall, or enterprise-wide, cost of capital for Global Energy is 11 percent, reflecting an average of the firm's divisional costs of capital, ranging from a low of 8 percent for pipelines up to 18 percent for exploration and development.

At present, Global Energy is using a cost of capital of 11 percent to evaluate its new investment proposals from all three operating divisions. This means that exploration and development projects earning as little as 11 percent are being accepted even though the capital market dictates that projects of this risk should earn 18 percent. Thus, Global Energy overinvests in high-risk projects. Similarly, the company will underinvest in its two lower-risk divisions, where the company-wide cost of capital is used.

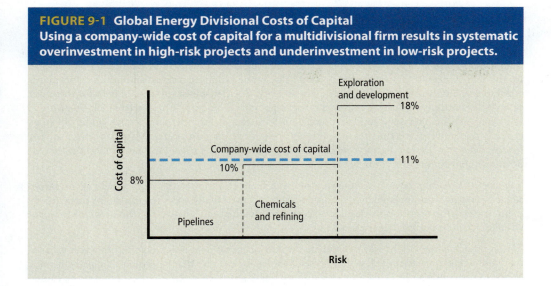

**FIGURE 9-1  Global Energy Divisional Costs of Capital**
**Using a company-wide cost of capital for a multidivisional firm results in systematic overinvestment in high-risk projects and underinvestment in low-risk projects.**

Now consider the prospect of moving to division costs of capital and the implications this might have for the three divisions. Specifically, the managers of the exploration and development division are likely to see this as an adverse move for them because it will surely cut the level of new investment capital flowing into their operations. In contrast, the managers of the remaining two divisions will see the change as good news because, under the company-wide cost of capital system, they have been rejecting projects earning more than their market-based costs of capital (8 percent and 10 percent for pipelines and refining, respectively) but less than the company's 11 percent cost of capital.

## Concept Check

1. What are the implications for a firm's capital investment decisions of using a company-wide cost of capital when the firm has multiple operating divisions that each have unique risk attributes and capital costs?

2. If a firm has decided to move from a situation in which it uses a company-wide cost of capital to divisional costs of capital, what problems is it likely to encounter?

# Chapter Summaries

## Understand the concepts underlying the firm's cost of capital. (pgs. 275–276)

**SUMMARY:** A firm's cost of capital is equal to a weighted average of the opportunity costs of each source of capital used by the firm, including debt, preferred stock, and common equity. To properly capture the cost of all these sources of capital, the individual costs are based on current market conditions and not historical costs.

### KEY TERMS

**Weighted average cost of capital, page 275** an average of the individual costs of financing used by the firm.

**Opportunity cost, page 275** The cost of making a choice defined in terms of the next best alternative that is foregone.

**Financial policy, page 276** the firm's policies regarding the sources of financing it plans to use and the particular mix (proportions) in which they will be used.

**2**    **Evaluate the costs of the individual sources of capital.** (pgs. 276–286)

**SUMMARY:** The after-tax cost of debt is typically estimated as the yield-to-maturity of the promised principal and interest payments for an outstanding debt agreement. This means that we solve for the rate of interest that makes the present value of the promised interest and principal payments equal to the current market value of the debt security. We then adjust this cost of debt for the effect of taxes by multiplying it by 1 minus the firm's tax rate. The cost of preferred stock financing is estimated in a manner very similar to debt but with two differences. First, since preferred stock typically does not mature, the present-value equation for valuing the preferred stock involves solving for the value of a level perpetuity. Second, since preferred dividends are not tax deductible, there is no adjustment to the cost of preferred stock for taxes.

The cost of common equity is somewhat more difficult to estimate than either debt or preferred stock since the common stockholders do not have a contractually specified return on their investment. Instead, the common stockholders receive the residual earnings of the firm or what's left over after all other claims have been paid.

Two approaches are widely used to estimate the cost of common equity financing. The first is based on the dividend growth model, which is used to solve for the rate that will equate the present value of future dividends with the current price of the firm's shares of stock. The second uses the capital asset pricing model.

### KEY TERMS

**Cost of debt, page 277** The rate that has to be received from an investment in order to achieve the required rate of return for the creditors. This rate must be adjusted for the fact that an increase in interest payments will result in lower taxes. The cost is based on the debt holders' opportunity cost of debt in the capital markets.

**Flotation costs, page 277** The costs incurred by the firm when it issues securities to raise funds.

**Cost of preferred equity, page 279** The rate of return that must be earned on the

preferred stockholders' investment in order to satisfy their required rate of return. The cost is based on the preferred stockholders' opportunity cost of preferred stock in the capital markets.

**Cost of common equity, page 281** The rate of return that must be earned on the common stockholders' investment in order to satisfy their required rate of return. The cost is based on the common stockholders' opportunity cost of common stock in the capital markets.

### KEY EQUATIONS

The cost of debt financing can be calculated as follows:

$$\begin{aligned} \text{Net proceeds} \atop \text{per bond} &= \frac{\text{interest paid in year 1}}{\left(1 + {\text{cost of debt} \atop \text{financing } (k_d)}\right)^1} + \frac{\text{interest paid in year 2}}{\left(1 + {\text{cost of debt} \atop \text{financing } (k_d)}\right)^2} \\ &+ \frac{\text{interest paid in year 3}}{\left(1 + {\text{cost of debt} \atop \text{financing } (k_d)}\right)^3} + \frac{\text{principal paid in year 3}}{\left(1 + {\text{cost of debt} \atop \text{financing } (k_d)}\right)^3} \end{aligned}$$

This equation works for a 3-year bond. Longer-term bonds include more interest payments. The result is an estimate of the before-tax cost of debt financing to the firm. To adjust for taxes, we multiply this rate of return by 1 minus the corporate tax rate.

The cost of preferred stock is calculated by solving for $k_{ps}$:

$$\begin{aligned} \text{Net proceeds} \atop \text{per preferred} \atop \text{share} = \frac{\text{preferred dividend}}{\text{cost of preferred stock } (k_{ps})} \end{aligned}$$

The cost of common stock—discounted cash-flow method is calculated using the following equation:

$$\begin{aligned} \text{Cost of common} \atop \text{stock } (k_{cs}) = \frac{\text{common stock dividend for year 1}}{\text{market price of common stock}} + \left(\text{growth rate in} \atop \text{dividends}\right) \end{aligned}$$

The cost of common stock—capital asset pricing method is calculated as follows:

$$\underset{\text{stock } (k_{cs})}{\text{Cost of common}} = \underset{\text{rate}}{\text{risk-free}} + \underset{\text{coefficient}}{\text{equity beta}} \left( \underset{\text{the market portfolio}}{\text{expected return on}} - \underset{\text{rate}}{\text{risk-free}} \right)$$

## Calculate a firm's weighted average cost of capital. (pgs. 286–290)

**SUMMARY:** The firm's WACC is defined as follows:

$$\underset{\text{of capital (WACC)}}{\underset{\text{average cost}}{\text{Weighted}}} = \left[ \left( \underset{\text{of debt } (k_d)}{\text{after-tax cost}} \right) \times \left( \underset{(w_d)}{\underset{\text{debt financing}}{\text{proportion of}}} \right) \right]$$
$$+ \left[ \left( \underset{(k_{cs})}{\text{cost of equity}} \right) \times \left( \underset{(w_{cs})}{\underset{\text{equity financing}}{\text{proportion of}}} \right) \right]$$

where $k_d$, $k_{ps}$, and $k_{cs}$ are the cost of capital for the firm's debt, preferred stock, and common equity, respectively. Note that the costs of these sources of capital must be properly adjusted for the effect of issuance or flotation costs. $T$ is the marginal corporate tax rate and $w_d$, $w_{ps}$, and $w_{cs}$ are the fractions of the firm's total financing (weights) that are comprised of debt, preferred stock, and common equity, respectively. The weights used to calculate WACC should theoretically reflect the market values of each capital source as a fraction of the total market value of all capital sources (that is, the market value of the firm). In some cases, market values are not observed and analysts use book values instead.

### KEY TERM

**capital structure, 286** The mix of long-term sources of funds used by the firm. This is also called the firm's capitalization. The rela- tive total (percentage) of each type of fund is emphasized.

## Estimate divisional costs of capital. (pgs. 290–295)

**SUMMARY:** Finance theory is very clear about the appropriate rate at which the cash flows of investment projects should be discounted. The appropriate discount rate should reflect the opportunity cost of capital, which in turn reflects the risk of the investment being evaluated.

However, an investment evaluation policy that allows managers to use different discount rates for different investment opportunities may be difficult to implement. First, coming up with discount rates for individual projects can be time-consuming and difficult and may simply not be worth the effort. In addition, when firms allow the cost of capital to vary for each project, overzealous managers may waste corporate resources lobbying for a lower discount rate to help ensure the approval of their pet projects.

To reduce these estimation and lobbying costs, most firms have either just one corporate cost of capital or a single cost of capital for each division of the company. Divisional WACCs are generally determined by using information from publicly traded single-segment firms.

### KEY TERM

**Divisional WACC, page 290** The cost of capital for a specific business unit or division.

# Review Questions

*All Review Questions are available in* MyFinanceLab.

**9-1.** Define the term *cost of capital*.

**9-2.** In 2009, ExxonMobil (XOM) acquired XTO Energy for $41 billion. The acquisition pro- vided ExxonMobil an opportunity to engage in the development of shale and unconventional nat- ural gas resources within the continental United States. This acquisition added to ExxonMobil's existing upstream (exploration and development) activities. In addition to this business segment, ExxonMobil was also engaged in chemicals and downstream operations related to the refining of crude oil into a variety of consumer and industrial products. How do you think the company should approach the determination of its cost of capital for making new capital investment decisions?

**9-3.** Why do firms calculate their weighted average cost of capital?

**9-4.** In computing the cost of capital, which sources of capital should be considered?

**9-5.** How does a firm's tax rate affect its cost of capital? What is the effect of the flotation costs associated with a new security issue on a firm's weighted average cost of capital?

**9-6.** a. Distinguish between internal common equity and new common stock.
   b. Why is there a cost associated with internal common equity?
   c. Describe two approaches that could be used in computing the cost of common equity.

**9-7.** What might we expect to see in practice in the relative costs of different sources of capital?

# Study Problems

*All Study Problems are available in* MyFinanceLab.

**9-1.** (*Terminology*) Match the following terms with their definitions:

| TERMS | DEFINITIONS |
|---|---|
| Opportunity cost | The target mix of sources of funds that the firm uses when raising new money to invest in the firm. |
| Financial policy | A weighted average of the required rates of return of the firm's sources of capital (after adjusting for flotation costs and tax considerations). |
| Cost of capital | The cost of making a choice in terms of the next best alternative that must be foregone. |
| Transaction costs | The expenses that a firm incurs when raising funds by issuing a particular type of security. |

**9-2.** (*Individual or component costs of capital*) Compute the cost of the following:
   a. A bond that has $1,000 par value (face value) and a contract or coupon interest rate of 11 percent. A new issue would have a flotation cost of 5 percent of the $1,125 market value. The bonds mature in 10 years. The firm's average tax rate is 30 percent and its marginal tax rate is 34 percent.
   b. A new common stock issue that paid a $1.80 dividend last year. The par value of the stock is $15, and earnings per share have grown at a rate of 7 percent per year. This growth rate is expected to continue into the foreseeable future. The company maintains a constant dividend–earnings ratio of 30 percent. The price of this stock is now $27.50, but 5 percent flotation costs are anticipated.
   c. Internal common equity when the current market price of the common stock is $43. The expected dividend this coming year should be $3.50, increasing thereafter at a 7 percent annual growth rate. The corporation's tax rate is 34 percent.
   d. A preferred stock paying a 9 percent dividend on a $150 par value. If a new issue is offered, flotation costs will be 12 percent of the current price of $175.
   e. A bond selling to yield 12 percent after flotation costs, but before adjusting for the marginal corporate tax rate of 34 percent. In other words, 12 percent is the rate that equates the net proceeds from the bond with the present value of the future cash flows (principal and interest).

**9-3.** (*Cost of equity*) Salte Corporation is issuing new common stock at a market price of $27. Dividends last year were $1.45 and are expected to grow at an annual rate of 6 percent forever. Flotation costs will be 6 percent of market price. What is Salte's cost of equity?

**9-4.** (*Cost of debt*) Belton is issuing a $1,000 par value bond that pays 7 percent annual interest and matures in 15 years. Investors are willing to pay $958 for the bond. Flotation costs will be 11 percent of market value. The company is in an 18 percent tax bracket. What will be the firm's after-tax cost of debt on the bond?

**9-5.** (*Cost of preferred stock*) The preferred stock of Julian Industries sells for $36 and pays $3.00 in dividends. The net price of the security after issuance costs is $32.50. What is the cost of capital for the preferred stock?

**9-6.** (*Cost of debt*) The Zephyr Corporation is contemplating a new investment to be financed 33 percent from debt. The firm could sell new $1,000 par value bonds at a net price of $945. The coupon interest rate is 12 percent, and the bonds would mature in 15 years. If the company is in a 34 percent tax bracket, what is the after-tax cost of capital to Zephyr for bonds?

**9-7.** (*Cost of preferred stock*) Your firm is planning to issue preferred stock. The stock sells for $115; however, if new stock is issued, the company would receive only $98. The par value of the stock is $100, and the dividend rate is 14 percent. What is the cost of capital for the stock to your firm?

**9-8.** (*Cost of internal equity*) Pathos Co.'s common stock is currently selling for $23.80. Dividends paid last year were $0.70. Flotation costs on issuing stock will be 10 percent of market price. The dividends and earnings per share are projected to have an annual growth rate of 15 percent. What is the cost of internal common equity for Pathos?

**9-9.** (*Cost of equity*) The common stock for the Bestsold Corporation sells for $58. If a new issue is sold, the flotation costs are estimated to be 8 percent. The company pays 50 percent of its earnings in dividends, and a $4 dividend was recently paid. Earnings per share 5 years ago were $5. Earnings are expected to continue to grow at the same annual rate in the future as during the past 5 years. The firm's marginal tax rate is 34 percent. Calculate the cost of (a) internal common equity and (b) external common equity.

**9-10.** (*Growth rate in stock dividends and the cost of equity*) Clearview Productions is a publicly held company whose common stock has recently been selling for $50.00 a share. The firm is expected to pay an annual cash dividend of $5.00 a share next year, and the firm's investors anticipate an annual rate of return of 15%.

   a. If the firm is expected to provide a constant annual rate of growth in dividends, what is that growth rate?
   b. If the risk-free rate of interest is 3% and the market risk premium is 6%, what must the firm's beta be to warrant a 15% expected rate of return on the firm's stock?

**9-11.** (*Individual or component costs of capital*) Compute the cost for the following sources of financing:

   a. A $1,000 par value bond with a market price of $970 and a coupon interest rate of 10 percent. Flotation costs for a new issue would be approximately 5 percent. The bonds mature in 10 years and the corporate tax rate is 34 percent.
   b. A preferred stock selling for $100 with an annual dividend payment of $8. The flotation cost will be $9 per share. The company's marginal tax rate is 30 percent.
   c. Retained earnings totaling $4.8 million. The price of the common stock is $75 per share, and dividend per share was $9.80 last year. The dividend is not expected to change in the future.
   d. New common stock when the most recent dividend was $2.80. The company's dividends per share should continue to increase at an 8 percent growth rate into the indefinite future. The market price of the stock is currently $53; however, flotation costs of $6 per share are expected if the new stock is issued.

**9-12.** (*Cost of debt*) Sincere Stationery Corporation needs to raise $500,000 to improve its manufacturing plant. It has decided to issue a $1,000 par value bond with a 14 percent annual coupon rate and a 10-year maturity. The investors require a 9 percent rate of return.

   a. Compute the market value of the bonds.
   b. What will the net price be if flotation costs are 10.5 percent of the market price?
   c. How many bonds will the firm have to issue to receive the needed funds?
   d. What is the firm's after-tax cost of debt if its average tax rate is 25 percent and its marginal tax rate is 34 percent?

**9-13.** (*Cost of debt*)

   a. Rework Problem 9-12 as follows: Assume an 8 percent coupon rate. What effect does changing the coupon rate have on the firm's after-tax cost of capital?
   b. Why is there a change?

**9-14.** (*Capital structure weights*) Caraway Seeds estimated its weighted average cost of capital to be 9.2% based on the fact that its after-tax cost of debt financing was 6 percent and its cost of equity was 10 percent. What are the firm's capital structure weights (that is, the proportion of financing that came from debt and equity)?

**9-15.** (*Weighted average cost of capital*) Crawford Enterprises is a publicly held company located in Arnold, Kansas. The firm began as a small tool and die shop but grew over its 35-year life to become a leading supplier of metal fabrication equipment used in the farm tractor industry. At the close of 2009 the firm's balance sheet appeared as follows:

| | | | |
|---|---|---|---|
| Cash | $ 540,000 | | |
| Accounts receivable | 4,580,000 | | |
| Inventories | 7,400,000 | Long-term debt | $12,590,000 |
| Net property, plant, and equipment | 18,955,000 | Common equity | 18,885,000 |
| Total assets | $31,475,000 | Total debt and equity | $31,475,000 |

At present the firm's common stock is selling for a price equal to its book value, and the firm's bonds are selling at par. Crawford's managers estimate that the market requires a 15 percent return on its common stock, the firm's bonds command a yield to maturity of 8 percent, and the firm faces a tax rate of 34 percent.

    a. What is Crawford's weighted average cost of capital?

    b. If Crawford's stock price were to rise such that it sold at 1.5 times book value, causing the cost of equity to fall to 13 percent, what would the firm's cost of capital be (assuming the cost of debt and tax rate do not change)?

**9-16.** (*Weighted average cost of capital*) The capital structure for the Carion Corporation is provided here. The company plans to maintain its debt structure in the future. If the firm has a 5.5 percent after-tax cost of debt, a 13.5 percent cost of preferred stock, and an 18 percent cost of common stock, what is the firm's weighted average cost of capital?

| CAPITAL STRUCTURE ($000) | |
|---|---|
| Bonds | $1,083 |
| Preferred stock | 268 |
| Common stock | 3,681 |
| | $5,032 |

**9-17.** (*Weighted average cost of capital*) ABBC Inc. operates a very successful chain of yogurt and coffee shops spread across the southwestern part of the United States and needs to raise funds for its planned expansion into the Northwest. The firm's balance sheet at the close of 2009 appeared as follows:

| | | | |
|---|---|---|---|
| Cash | $ 2,010,000 | | |
| Accounts receivable | 4,580,000 | | |
| Inventories | 1,540,000 | Long-term debt | $ 8,141,000 |
| Net property, plant, and equipment | 32,575,000 | Common equity | 32,564,000 |
| Total assets | $40,705,000 | Total debt and equity | $40,705,000 |

At present the firm's common stock is selling for a price equal to 2.5 times its book value, the firm's investors require an 18 percent return, the firm's bonds command a yield to maturity of 8 percent, and the firm faces a tax rate of 35 percent. At the end of the previous year ABBC's common stock was selling for a price of 2.5 times its book value, and its bonds were trading near their par value.

    a. What does ABBC's capital structure look like?

    b. What is ABBC's weighted average cost of capital?

    c. If ABBC's stock price were to rise such that it sold at 3.5 times its book value and the cost of equity fell to 15 percent, what would the firm's weighted average cost of capital be (assuming the cost of debt and tax rate do not change)?

**9-18.** (*Determining a firm's capital budget*) Newcomb Vending Company manages soft drink dispensing machines in western Tennessee for several of the major bottling companies in the area. When a machine malfunctions the company sends out a repair technician, and if he cannot repair it on the spot he puts in a replacement machine so that the broken one can be taken to the firm's repair facility in Murfreesboro, Tennessee. Betsy Newcomb recently completed her BBA from a nearby university and has been trying to incorporate as much of what she learned as possible into the operations of her family business. Specifically, Betsy recently reviewed the firm's capital structure and estimated that the firm's weighted average cost of capital is approximately 12%. She hopes to help her father determine which of several major capital expenditures he should make in the current year based on a comparison of the rates of return she estimated for each project (that is, the internal rate of return) and the firm's cost of capital. Specifically, the firm is considering the following projects (ranked by their internal rate of return):

| PROJECT | INVESTED CAPITAL | INTERNAL RATE OF RETURN |
|---------|------------------|-------------------------|
| A | $ 450,000 | 18% |
| B | 1,200,000 | 16% |
| C | 800,000 | 13% |
| D | 600,000 | 10% |
| E | 1,450,000 | 8% |

If all five of the investments being considered by Newcomb are of similar risk and that risk is very similar to that of the company as a whole, which project(s) should Betsy recommend the firm undertake? You may assume that the firm can raise all the capital it needs to fund its investments at the cost of capital of 12%. Explain your answer.

**9-19.** (Divisional costs of capital) LPT Inc. is an integrated oil company headquartered in Dallas, Texas. The company has three operating divisions: oil exploration and production (commonly referred to as E&P), pipelines, and refining. Historically, LPT did not spend a great deal of time thinking about the opportunity costs of capital for each of its divisions and used a company-wide weighted average cost of capital of 14 percent for all new capital investment projects. Recent changes in its businesses have made it abundantly clear to LPT's management that this is not a reasonable approach. For example, investors demand a much higher expected rate of return for exploration and production ventures than for pipeline investments. Although LPT's management agrees, in principle at least, that different operating divisions should face an opportunity cost of capital that reflects their individual risk characteristics, they are not in agreement about whether a move toward divisional costs of capital is a good idea based on practical considerations.

a. Pete Jennings is the chief operating officer for the E&P division, and he is concerned that going to a system of divisional costs of capital may restrain his ability to undertake very promising exploration opportunities. He argues that the firm really should be concerned about finding those opportunities that offer the highest possible rate of return on invested capital. Pete contends that using the firm's scarce capital to take on the most promising projects would lead to the greatest increase in shareholder value. Do you agree with Pete? Why or why not?

b. The pipeline division manager, Donna Selma, has long argued that charging her division the company-wide cost of capital of 14 percent severely penalizes her opportunities to increase shareholder value. Do you agree with Donna? Explain.

**9-20.** (*Divisional costs of capital and investment decisions*) In May of this year Newcastle Mfg. Company's capital investment review committee received two major investment proposals. One of the proposals was put forth by the firm's domestic manufacturing division, and the other came from the firm's distribution company. Both proposals promise internal rates of return equal to approximately 12 percent. In the past Newcastle has used a single firm-wide cost of capital to evaluate new investments.

However, managers have long recognized that the manufacturing division is significantly more risky than the distribution division. In fact, comparable firms in the manufacturing division have equity betas of about 1.6, whereas distribution companies typically have equity betas of only 1.1. Given the size of the two proposals, Newcastle's management feels it can undertake only one, so it wants to be sure that it is taking on the more promising investment. Given the importance of getting the cost of capital estimate as close to correct as possible, the firm's chief financial officer has asked you to prepare cost of capital estimates for each of the two divisions. The requisite information needed to accomplish your task is contained here:

♦ The cost of debt financing is 8 percent before taxes of 35 percent. You may assume this cost of debt is after any flotation costs the firm might incur.

♦ The risk-free rate of interest on long-term U.S. Treasury bonds is currently 4.8 percent, and the market-risk premium has averaged 7.3 percent over the past several years.

♦ Both divisions adhere to target debt ratios of 40 percent.

♦ The firm has sufficient internally generated funds such that no new stock will have to be sold to raise equity financing.

    a. Estimate the divisional costs of capital for the manufacturing and distribution divisions.

    b. Which of the two projects should the firm undertake (assuming it cannot do both due to labor and other nonfinancial restraints)? Discuss.

**9-21.** (*Divisional costs of capital and investment decisions*) Belton Oil and Gas Inc. is a Houston-based independent oil and gas firm. In the past Belton's managers have used a single firmwide cost of capital of 13 percent to evaluate new investments. However, the firm has long recognized that its exploration and production division is significantly more risky than the pipeline and transportation division. In fact, comparable firms to Belton's E&P division have equity betas of about 1.7, whereas distribution companies typically have equity betas of only 0.8. Given the importance of getting the cost of capital estimate as close to correct as possible, the firm's chief financial officer has asked you to prepare cost of capital estimates for each of the two divisions. The requisite information needed to accomplish your task is contained here:

♦ The cost of debt financing is 7 percent before taxes of 35 percent. However, if the E&P division were to borrow based on its projects alone, the cost of debt would probably be 9 percent, and the pipeline division could borrow at 5.5 percent. You may assume these costs of debt are after any flotation costs the firm might incur.

♦ The risk-free rate of interest on long-term U.S. Treasury bonds is currently 4.8 percent, and the market-risk premium has averaged 7.3 percent over the past several years.

♦ The E&P division adheres to a target debt ratio of 10 percent, whereas the pipeline division utilizes 40 percent borrowed funds.

♦ The firm has sufficient internally generated funds such that no new stock will have to be sold to raise equity financing.

    a. Estimate the divisional costs of capital for the E&P and pipeline divisions.

    b. What are the implications of using a company-wide cost of capital to evaluate new investment proposals in light of the differences in the costs of capital you estimated previously?

# Mini Cases

*These Mini Cases are available in* MyFinanceLab.

**9-1.** Nealon Energy Corporation engages in the acquisition, exploration, development, and production of natural gas and oil in the continental United States. The company has grown rapidly over the last 5 years as it has expanded into horizontal drilling techniques for the development of the massive deposits of both gas and oil in shale formations. The company's operations in the Haynesville shale (located in northwest Louisiana) have been so significant that it needs to construct a natural gas gathering and processing center near Bossier City, Louisiana, at an estimated cost of $70 million.

To finance the new facility Nealon has $20 million in profits that it will use to finance a portion of the expansion and plans to sell a bond issue to raise the remaining $50 million. The decision to use so much debt financing for the project was largely due to the argument by company CEO (Douglas Nealon Sr.) that debt financing is relatively cheap relative to common stock (which the firm has used in the past). Company CFO Doug Nealon Jr. (son of the company founder) did not object to the decision to use all debt but pondered the issue of what cost of capital to use for the expansion project. There is no doubt but that the out-of-pocket cost of financing was equal to the new interest that must be paid on the debt. However, the CFO also knew that by using debt for this project the firm would eventually have to use equity in the future if it wanted to maintain the balance of debt and equity it had in its capital structure and not become overly dependent on borrowed funds.

The following balance sheet reflects the mix of capital sources that Nealon has used in the past. Although the percentages would vary over time, the firm tended to manage its capital structure back toward these proportions:

| SOURCE OF FINANCING | TARGET CAPITAL STRUCTURE WEIGHTS |
|---|---|
| Bonds | 40% |
| Common Stock | 60% |

The firm currently has one issue of bonds outstanding. The bonds have a par value of $1,000 per bond, carry an 8 percent coupon rate of interest, have 16 years to maturity, and are selling for $1,035. Nealon's common stock has a current market price of $35 and the firm paid a $2.50 dividend last year that is expected to increase at an annual rate of 6 percent for the foreseeable future.

a. What is the yield to maturity for Nealon's bonds under current market conditions?

b. What is the cost of new debt financing to Nealon based on current market prices after both taxes (you may use a 34 percent marginal tax rate for your estimate) and flotation costs of $30 per bond have been considered?

c. What is the investor's required rate of return for Nealon's common stock? If Nealon were to sell new shares of common stock, it would incur a cost of $2.00 per share. What is your estimate of the cost of new equity financing raised from the sale of common stock?

d. Compute the weighted average cost of capital for Nealon's investment using the weights reflected in the actual financing mix (that is, $20 million in retained earnings and $50 million in bonds).

e. Compute the weighted average cost of capital for Nealon where the firm maintains its target capital structure by reducing its debt offering to 40 percent of the $70 million in new capital, or $28 million, using $20 million in retained earnings and raising $22 million through a new equity offering.

f. If you were the CFO for the company, would you prefer to use the calculation of the cost of capital in part (d) or (e) to evaluate the new project? Why?

**9-2.** ExxonMobil (XOM) is one of the half-dozen major oil companies in the world. The firm has four primary operating divisions (upstream, downstream, chemical, and global services) as well as a number of operating companies that it has acquired over the years. A recent major acquisition was XTO Energy, which was acquired in 2009 for $41 billion. The XTO acquisition gave ExxonMobil a significant presence in the development of domestic unconventional natural gas resources, including the development of shale gas formations, which was booming at the time.

Assume that you have just been hired to be an analyst working for ExxonMobil's chief financial officer. Your first assignment was to look into the proper cost of capital for use in making corporate investments across the company's many business units.

a. Would you recommend that ExxonMobil use a single company-wide cost of capital for analyzing capital expenditures in all its business units? Why or why not?

b. If you were to evaluate divisional costs of capital, how would you go about estimating these costs of capital for ExxonMobil? Discuss how you would approach the problem in terms of how you would evaluate the weights to use for various sources of capital as well as how you would estimate the costs of individual sources of capital for each division.

# 10

# Capital-Budgeting Techniques and Practice

## Learning Objectives

 **Discuss** the difficulty encountered in finding profitable projects in competitive markets and the importance of the search.

**Finding Profitable Projects**

 **Determine** whether a new project should be accepted or rejected using the payback period, the net present value, the profitability index, and the internal rate of return.

**Capital-Budgeting Decision Criteria**

 **Explain** how the capital-budgeting decision process changes when a dollar limit is placed on the capital budget.

**Capital Rationing**

**Discuss** the problems encountered when deciding among mutually exclusive projects.

**Ranking Mutually Exclusive Projects**

Back in 1955, the Walt Disney Company changed the face of entertainment when it opened Disneyland, its first theme park, in Anaheim, California, at a cost of $17.5 million. Since then Disney has opened theme parks in Orlando, Florida; Tokyo, Japan; Paris, France; and in September 2005, 香港迪士尼樂園, or Hong Kong Disneyland, was opened. This $3.5 billion project, with much of that money provided by the Hong Kong government, was opened in hopes of reaching what has largely been an untapped Chinese market. For Disney, a market this size was simply too large to pass up.

Unfortunately, while Hong Kong Disneyland's opening was spectacular, it has yet to earn a profit. One of the unexpected problems it has faced has been knockoff rides by rival Asian theme parks, which used the Hong Kong Disneyland's advance publicity to design their rides and put them in use before Hong Kong Disneyland's opening.

For Disney, keeping its theme parks and resorts division healthy is extremely important because this division accounts for over one-quarter of the company's revenues. Certainly, there are opportunities for Disney in China; with a population of 1.26 billion people, it accounts for 20 percent of the entire world's total population and Hong Kong Disneyland was supposed to provide Disney with a foothold in the potentially lucrative China market. While Hong Kong Disneyland has not lived up to Disney's expectations, Disney has not given up

on the Chinese market and with 330 million people living within a 3-hour drive or train ride from Shanghai, it picked its next location. Work has already begun on the Shanghai Disney Resort, which will be the home to Shanghai Disneyland, targeted to open at the end of 2015. Learning from its mistakes in Hong Kong, Disney's new proposed park will be much larger and easier for Chinese families to visit, but Disney has been a bit vague on the specifics of the park in an attempt to avoid a repeat of competition from knockoff rides that it experienced in Hong Kong.

To say the least, with a total investment of over $8 billion shared by Disney and its Chinese partner, the outcome of this decision will have a major effect on Disney's future. Whether this was a good or a bad decision, only time will tell. The question we will ask in this chapter is: How did Disney go about making this decision to enter the Chinese market and build Hong Kong Disneyland, and, after losing money on its Hong Kong venture, how did it go about making the decision to build Shanghai Disney Resort? The answer is that the company did it using the decision criteria we will examine in this chapter.

This chapter is actually the first of two chapters dealing with the process of decision making with respect to making investments in fixed assets—that is, should a proposed project be accepted or rejected? We will refer to this process as capital budgeting. In this chapter, we will look at the methods used to evaluate new projects. In deciding whether to accept a new project, we will focus on free cash flows. Free cash flows represent the benefits generated from accepting a capital-budgeting proposal. We will assume we know what level of free cash flows is generated by a project and will work on determining whether that project should be accepted. In the following chapter, we will examine what a free cash flow is and how we measure it. We will also look at how risk enters into this process.

# Finding Profitable Projects

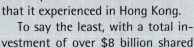 Discuss the difficulty encountered in finding profitable projects in competitive markets and the importance of the search.

**capital budgeting** the process of decision making with respect to investments made in fixed assets—that is, should a proposed project be accepted or rejected.

Without question it is easier to *evaluate profitable projects or investments in fixed assets, a process referred to as* **capital budgeting**, than it is to find them. In competitive markets, generating ideas for profitable projects is extremely difficult. The competition is brisk for new profitable projects, and once they have been uncovered, competitors generally rush in, pushing down prices and profits. For this reason a firm must have a systematic strategy for generating capital-budgeting projects based on these ideas. Without this flow of new projects and ideas, the firm cannot grow or even survive for long. Instead, it will be forced to live off the profits from existing projects with limited lives. So where do these ideas come from for new products, or for ways to improve existing products or make them more profitable? The answer is from inside the firm—from everywhere inside the firm, in fact.

Typically, a firm has a research and development (R&D) department that searches for ways of improving existing products or finding new products. These ideas may come

305

from within the R&D department or may be based on referral ideas from executives, sales personnel, anyone in the firm, or even customers. For example, at Ford Motor Company before the 1990s, ideas for product improvements had typically been generated in Ford's R&D department. Unfortunately, this strategy was not enough to keep Ford from losing much of its market share to Japanese competitors. In an attempt to cut costs and improve product quality, Ford moved from strict reliance on an R&D department to seeking the input of employees at all levels for new ideas. Bonuses are now provided to workers for their cost-cutting suggestions, and assembly-line personnel who can see the production process from a hands-on point of view are now brought into the hunt for new projects. The effect on Ford has been positive and it helped Ford avoid the bankruptcy problems that befell GM and Chrysler. Although not all suggested projects prove to be profitable, many new ideas generated from within the firm turn out to be good ones.

Another way an existing product can be applied to a new market is illustrated by Kimberly-Clark, the manufacturer of Huggies disposable diapers. The company took its existing diaper product line, made the diapers more waterproof, and began marketing them as disposable swim pants called Little Swimmers. Sara Lee Hosiery boosted its market by expanding its offerings to appeal to more customers and more customer needs. For example, Sara Lee Hosiery introduced Sheer Energy pantyhose for support, Just My Size pantyhose aimed at larger-women sizes, and Silken Mist pantyhose in shades better suited for African American women.

Big investments such as these go a long way toward determining the future of the company, but they don't always work as planned. Just look at Burger King's development of its new french fries. It looked like a slam-dunk great idea. Burger King took an uncooked french fry and coated it with a layer of starch that made it crunchier and kept it hot longer. The company spent over $70 million on the new fries and even gave away 15 million orders on a "Free Fryday." Unfortunately, the product didn't go down with consumers, and Burger King was left to eat the loss. Given the size of the investment we're talking about, you can see why such a decision is so important.

## Concept Check

1. Why is it so difficult to find an exceptionally profitable project?

2. Why is the search for new profitable projects so important?

## CAUTIONARY TALE

### FORGETTING PRINCIPLE 3: RISK REQUIRES A REWARD AND PRINCIPLE 4: MARKET PRICES ARE GENERALLY RIGHT

In the world of investing, you win some, you lose some. A common misconception is that high-risk investments always provide high returns. In fact, there are no guarantees. That's why consistently high returns paid year in and year out from a fund known for its exclusivity and its double-digit rates of return should have given investors pause.

In December of 2008 an investor in the fund, quoted in *Time* magazine, wrote, "All we knew was that my wife's entire family had been in the fund for decades and lived well on the returns, which ranged from 15 percent to 22 percent. It was all very secretive and tough to get into, which, looking back, was a brilliant strategy to lure suckers."

The fund in question is the one we now know as the Ponzi scheme orchestrated by Bernard "Bernie" Madoff. A Ponzi scheme is an investment that pays returns to investors from the money they originally invested along with money provided by new investors, rather than any profits earned. A Ponzi scheme is destined to collapse because the payments made exceed any earnings from the investment. Madoff's scam is considered to be the biggest Wall Street fraud ever attempted. Prosecutors estimate the size of the scam as somewhere between $50 billion to $54.8 billion.

In efficient markets, high returns are extremely difficult to achieve in good and bad years. Harry Markopolos, who once worked for one of Madoff's competitors, long suspected that Madoff's returns were simply too good to be true and wrote letters for at least a decade to the Securities and Exchange Commission trying to persuade them to investigate Madoff. As Markopolos observed, one thing that we know from efficient markets is that if an investment promises a return that looks too good to be true, it probably is.

Source: Robert Chew, "How I Got Screwed by Bernie Madoff," *Time*, December 15, 2008, http://www.time.com/time/business/article/0,8599,1866398,00.html.

# Capital-Budgeting Decision Criteria

As we explained, when deciding whether to accept a new project, we focus on cash flows because cash flows represent the benefits generated from accepting a capital-budgeting proposal. In this chapter we assume a given cash flow is generated by a project and work on determining whether that project should be accepted.

We consider four commonly used criteria for determining the acceptability of investment proposals. The first one is the least sophisticated in that it does not incorporate the time value of money into its calculations; the other three do take it into account. For the time being, the problem of incorporating risk into the capital-budgeting decision is ignored. This issue is examined in Chapter 11. In addition, we assume that the appropriate discount rate, required rate of return, or cost of capital is given.

## The Payback Period

The **payback period** is the *number of years needed to recover the initial cash outlay related to an investment*. Thus, the payback period becomes the number of years prior to the year of complete recovery of the initial outlay plus the unrecovered dollar amount at the beginning of the year recovery is completed divided by the cash flow in the year in which recovery is completed:

$$\text{Payback period} = \begin{array}{c}\text{number of years just}\\ \text{prior to complete}\\ \text{payback}\end{array} + \dfrac{\begin{array}{c}\text{unpaid-back amount}\\ \text{at beginning of year}\end{array}}{\begin{array}{c}\text{free cash flow in year}\\ \text{payback is completed}\end{array}} \quad (10\text{-}1)$$

The accept/reject criteria for the payback period is if the payback period is less than the required payback period, then the project is accepted. Shorter payback periods are preferred over longer payback periods because the shorter the payback period, the quicker you get your money back. Because this criterion measures how quickly the project will return its original investment, it deals with free cash flows, which measure the true timing of the benefits, rather than accounting profits. Unfortunately, it also ignores the time value of money and does not discount these free cash flows back to the present. Rather, the accept/reject criterion centers on whether the project's payback period is less than or equal to the firm's maximum desired payback period. For example, if a firm's maximum desired payback period is 3 years, and an investment proposal requires an initial cash outlay of $10,000 and yields the following set of annual cash flows, what is its payback period? Should the project be accepted?

| YEAR | FREE CASH FLOW |
|------|----------------|
| 1 | $2,000 |
| 2 | 4,000 |
| 3 | 3,000 |
| 4 | 3,000 |
| 5 | 9,000 |

In this case, after 3 years the firm will have recaptured $9,000 on an initial investment of $10,000, leaving $1,000 of the initial investment to be recouped. During the fourth year $3,000 will be returned from this investment, and, assuming it will flow into the firm at a constant rate over the year, it will take one-third of the year ($1,000/$3,000) to recapture the remaining $1,000. Thus, the payback period on this project is 3½ years, which is more than the desired payback period. Using the payback period criterion, the firm would reject this project without even considering the $9,000 cash flow in year 5.

Although the payback period is used frequently, it does have some rather obvious drawbacks that are best demonstrated through the use of an example. Consider two investment projects, A and B, which involve an initial cash outlay of $10,000 each and produce the annual cash flows shown in Table 10-1. Both projects have a payback period of 2 years; therefore, in terms of the payback criterion both are equally acceptable. However, if we had our choice, it is clear we would select A over B, for at least two reasons. First, regardless of what happens after the payback period, project A returns more of our initial investment to us faster within the payback period ($6,000 in year 1 versus $5,000). Thus, because there is a time value of money, the cash flows occurring within the payback period should not be

**2** Determine whether a new project should be accepted or rejected using the payback period, the net present value, the profitability index, and the internal rate of return.

**payback period** the number of years it takes to recapture a project's initial outlay.

| TABLE 10-1  Payback Period Example | | |
|---|---|---|
| | **PROJECTS** | |
| | **A** | **B** |
| Initial cash outlay | −$10,000 | −$10,000 |
| Annual free cash inflows | | |
| Year 1 | $ 6,000 | $ 5,000 |
| 2 | 4,000 | 5,000 |
| 3 | 3,000 | 0 |
| 4 | 2,000 | 0 |
| 5 | 1,000 | 0 |

weighted equally, as they are. In addition, all cash flows that occur after the payback period are ignored. This violates the principle that investors desire more in the way of benefits rather than less—a principle that is difficult to deny, especially when we are talking about money. Finally, the choice of the maximum desired payback period is arbitrary. That is, there is no good reason why the firm should accept projects that have payback periods less than or equal to 3 years rather than 4 years.

Although these deficiencies limit the value of the payback period as a tool for investment evaluation, the payback period has several positive features. First, it deals with cash flows, as opposed to accounting profits, and therefore focuses on the true timing of the project's benefits and costs, even though it does not adjust the cash flows for the time value of money. Second, it is easy to visualize, quickly understood, and easy to calculate. Third, the payback period may make sense for the capital-constrained firm, that is, the firm that needs funds and is having problems raising additional money. These firms need cash flows early on to allow them to continue in business and to take advantage of future investments. Finally, although the payback period has serious deficiencies, it is often used as a rough screening device to eliminate projects whose returns do not materialize until later years. This method emphasizes the earliest returns, which in all likelihood are less uncertain, and provides for the liquidity needs of the firm. Although its advantages are certainly significant, its disadvantages severely limit its value as a discriminating capital-budgeting criterion.

**Discounted Payback Period**    To deal with the criticism that the payback period ignores the time value of money, some firms use the discounted payback period approach. The **discounted payback period** method is similar to the traditional payback period except that it uses discounted free cash flows rather than actual undiscounted free cash flows in calculating the payback period. The discounted payback period is defined as *the number of years it takes to recapture a project's initial outlay from the discounted free cash flows*. This equation can be written as

**discounted payback period** the number of years it takes to recapture a project's initial outlay from the discounted free cash flows.

$$\begin{array}{c} \text{Discounted} \\ \text{payback} \\ \text{period} \end{array} = \begin{array}{c} \text{number of years just prior} \\ \text{to complete payback} \\ \text{from discounted free} \\ \text{cash flows} \end{array} + \dfrac{\begin{array}{c}\text{unpaid-back amount at} \\ \text{the beginning} \\ \text{of year}\end{array}}{\begin{array}{c}\text{discounted free cash} \\ \text{flow in year} \\ \text{payback is completed}\end{array}} \qquad (10\text{-}2)$$

The accept/reject criterion then becomes whether the project's discounted payback period is less than or equal to the firm's maximum desired discounted payback period. Using the assumption that the required rate of return on projects A and B illustrated in Table 10-1 is 17 percent, the discounted cash flows from these projects are given in Table 10-2. On project A, after 3 years, only $74 of the initial outlay remains to be recaptured, whereas year 4 brings in a discounted free cash flow of $1,068. Thus, if the $1,068 comes in at a constant rate over the year, it will take about 7/100 of the year ($74/$1,068) to recapture the remaining $74. The discounted payback period for project A is 3.07 years, calculated as follows:

$$\text{Discounted payback period}_A = 3.0 + \$74/\$1,068 = 3.07 \text{ years}$$

## TABLE 10-2  Discounted Payback, Period Example Using a 17 Percent Required Rate of Return

### PROJECT A

| Year | Undiscounted Free Cash Flows | Discounted Free Cash Flows at 17% | Cumulative Discounted Free Cash Flows |
|------|------|------|------|
| 0 | −$10,000 | −$10,000 | −$10,000 |
| 1 | 6,000 | 5,130 | −4,870 |
| 2 | 4,000 | 2,924 | −1,946 |
| 3 | 3,000 | 1,872 | −74 |
| 4 | 2,000 | 1,068 | 994 |
| 5 | 1,000 | 456 | 1,450 |

### PROJECT B

| Year | Undiscounted Free Cash Flows | Discounted Free Cash Flows at 17% | Cumulative Discounted Free Cash Flows |
|------|------|------|------|
| 0 | −$10,000 | −$10,000 | −$10,000 |
| 1 | 5,000 | 4,275 | −5,725 |
| 2 | 5,000 | 3,655 | −2,070 |
| 3 | 0 | 0 | −2,070 |
| 4 | 0 | 0 | −2,070 |
| 5 | 0 | 0 | −2,070 |

If project A's discounted payback period was less than the firm's maximum desired discounted payback period, then project A would be accepted. Project B, however, does not have a discounted payback period because it never fully recovers the project's initial cash outlay and thus should be rejected. The major problem with the discounted payback period comes in setting the firm's maximum desired discounted payback period. This is an arbitrary decision that affects which projects are accepted and which ones are rejected. In addition, cash flows that occur after the discounted payback period are not included in the analysis. Thus, although the discounted payback period is superior to the traditional payback period, in that it accounts for the time value of money in its calculations, its use is limited by the arbitrariness of the process used to select the maximum desired payback period. Moreover, as we will soon see, the net present value criterion is theoretically superior and no more difficult to calculate. These two payback period rules can be summarized as follows:

## FINANCIAL DECISION TOOLS

| Name of Tool | Formula | What It Tells You |
|------|------|------|
| Payback period | Number of years required to recapture the initial investment from the free cash flows:<br><br>$$\text{Payback period} = \begin{array}{c}\text{number of years} \\ \text{just prior to} \\ \text{complete} \\ \text{payback}\end{array} + \dfrac{\text{unpaid-back amount at beginning of year}}{\text{free cash flow in year payback is completed}}$$ | • How long it will take to recapture the initial investment<br>• The shorter the payback period, the better<br>• If it is less than the maximum acceptable payback period, it is accepted |
| Discounted payback period | Number of years required to recapture the initial investment from the discounted free cash flows:<br><br>$$\text{Discounted payback period} = \begin{array}{c}\text{number of years} \\ \text{just prior to} \\ \text{complete} \\ \text{payback from} \\ \text{discounted free} \\ \text{cash flows}\end{array} + \dfrac{\text{unpaid-back amount at beginning of year}}{\text{discounted free cash flow in year payback is completed}}$$ | • How long it will take to recapture the initial investment from the discounted cash flows<br>• The shorter the discounted payback period, the better<br>• If it is less than the maximum acceptable discounted payback period, it is accepted. |

## The Net Present Value

**net present value (NPV)** the present value of an investment's annual free cash flows less the investment's initial outlay.

The **net present value (NPV)** of an investment proposal is equal to the *present value of its annual free cash flows less the investment's initial outlay*. The net present value can be expressed as follows:

$$NPV = \text{(present value of all the future annual free cash flows)} - \text{(the initial cash outlay)}$$

$$= \frac{FCF_1}{(1+k)^1} + \frac{FCF_2}{(1+k)^2} + \cdots + \frac{FCF_n}{(1+k)^n} - IO \qquad (10\text{-}1)$$

where $FCF_t$ = the annual free cash flow in time period $t$ (this can take on either positive or negative values)

$k$ = the firm's required rate of return or cost of capital[1]

$IO$ = the initial cash outlay

$n$ = the project's expected life

If any of the future free cash flows (*FCFs*) are cash outflows rather than inflows, say for example that there is another large investment in year 2 that results in the $FCF_2$ being negative, then the $FCF_2$ would take on a negative sign when calculating the project's net present value. In effect, the *NPV* can be thought of as the present value of the benefits minus the present value of the costs,

$$NPV = PV_{\text{benefits}} - PV_{\text{costs}}$$

### REMEMBER YOUR PRINCIPLES

**Principle** The final three capital-budgeting criteria all incorporate Principle 2: Money Has a Time Value in their calculations. If we are to make rational business decisions, we must recognize that money has a time value. In examining the following three capital-budgeting techniques, you will notice that this principle is the driving force behind each of them.

A project's *NPV* measures the net value of the investment proposal in terms of today's dollars. Because all cash flows are discounted back to the present, comparing the difference between the present value of the annual cash flows and the investment outlay recognizes the time value of money. The difference between the present value of the annual cash flows and the initial outlay determines the net value of the investment proposal. Whenever the project's *NPV* is greater than or equal to zero, we will accept the project; whenever the *NPV* is negative, we will reject the project. If the project's *NPV* is zero, then it returns the required rate of return and should be accepted. This accept/reject criterion is represented as follows:

$NPV \geq 0.0$: accept

$NPV < 0.0$: reject

Realize, however, that the worth of the *NPV* calculation is a function of the accuracy of the cash-flow predictions.

The following example illustrates the use of *NPV* as a capital-budgeting criterion.

### EXAMPLE 10.1    Calculating net present value

Ski-Doo is considering new machinery that would reduce manufacturing costs associated with its Mach Z snowmobile for which the free cash flows are shown in Table 10-3. If the firm has a 12 percent required rate of return, what is the NPV of the project? Should the company accept the project?

#### STEP 1: FORMULATE A SOLUTION STRATEGY

The net present value (*NPV*) of an investment proposal is equal to the present value of its annual free cash flows less the investment's initial outlay. Given the company's free cash flows information, the *NPV* can be calculated as:

---

[1]The required rate of return or cost of capital is the rate of return necessary to justify raising funds to finance the project or, alternatively, the rate of return necessary to maintain the firm's current market price per share. These terms were defined in detail in Chapter 9.

**TABLE 10-3  Ski-Doo's Investment in New Machinery and Its Associated Free Cash Flows**

|  | Free Cash Flow |
| --- | --- |
| Initial outlay | −$40,000 |
| Inflow year 1 | 15,000 |
| Inflow year 2 | 14,000 |
| Inflow year 3 | 13,000 |
| Inflow year 4 | 12,000 |
| Inflow year 5 | 11,000 |

$$NPV = \text{(present value of all the future annual free cash flows)} - \text{(the initial cash outlay)}$$

$$= \frac{FCF_1}{(1+k)^1} + \frac{FCF_2}{(1+k)^2} + \cdots + \frac{FCF_n}{(1+k)^n} - IO \qquad (10\text{-}1)$$

where $FCF_t$ = the annual free cash flow in time period $t$ (this can take on either positive or negative values)

$k$ = the firm's required rate of return or cost of capital

$IO$ = the initial cash outlay

$n$ = the project's expected life

### STEP 2: CRUNCH THE NUMBERS

If the firm has a 12 percent required rate of return, the present value of the free cash flow is $47,675, as calculated in Table 10-4. Subtracting the $40,000 initial outlay leaves an *NPV* of $7,675.

**TABLE 10-4  Calculating the *NPV* of Ski-Doo's Investment in New Machinery**

| | | PRESENT VALUE | | |
| --- | --- | --- | --- | --- |
| | Free Cash Flow | × | Factor at 12 Percent | = Present Value |
| Inflow year 1 | $15,000 | × | $\dfrac{1}{(1+0.12)^1}$ | = $13,393 |
| Inflow year 2 | 14,000 | × | $\dfrac{1}{(1+0.12)^2}$ | = 11,161 |
| Inflow year 3 | 13,000 | × | $\dfrac{1}{(1+0.12)^3}$ | = 9,253 |
| Inflow year 4 | 12,000 | × | $\dfrac{1}{(1+0.12)^4}$ | = 7,626 |
| Inflow year 5 | 11,000 | × | $\dfrac{1}{(1+0.12)^5}$ | = 6,242 |
| Present value of free cash flows | | | | $47,675 |
| Initial outlay | | | | −40,000 |
| Net present value | | | | $ 7,675 |

**CALCULATOR SOLUTION (USING A TEXAS INSTRUMENTS BA II PLUS):**

| Data and Key Input | Display |
| --- | --- |
| CF ; −40,000; ENTER | CFo = −40,000. |
| ↓ ; 15,000; ENTER | C01 = 15,000. |
| ↓ ; 1; ENTER | F01 = 1.00 |
| ↓ ; 14,000; ENTER | C02 = 14,000. |
| ↓ ; 1; ENTER | F02 = 1.00 |
| ↓ ; 13,000; ENTER | C03 = 13,000. |
| ↓ ; 1; ENTER | F03 = 1.00 |
| ↓ ; 12,000; ENTER | C04 = 12,000. |
| ↓ ; 1; ENTER | F04 = 1.00 |
| ↓ ; 11,000; ENTER | C05 = 11,000 |
| ↓ ; 1; ENTER | F05 = 1.00 |
| NPV | I = 0.00 |
| 12; ENTER | I = 1200 |
| ↓ ; CPT | NPV = 7,675. |

### STEP 3: ANALYZE YOUR RESULTS

The *NPV* tells us how much value is created if the project is accepted, and if the *NPV* is positive, value is created; if the *NPV* is negative, the project destroys value. In this case because this value is greater than zero, this project creates value and should be accepted.

The *NPV* criterion is the capital-budgeting decision tool we find most favorable for several reasons. First of all, it deals with free cash flows rather than accounting profits. In this regard it is sensitive to the true timing of the benefits resulting from the project. Moreover, recognizing the time value of money allows the benefits and costs to be compared in a logical manner. Finally, because projects are accepted only if a positive *NPV* is associated with them, the acceptance of a project using this criterion will increase the value of the firm, which is consistent with the goal of maximizing the shareholders' wealth.

The disadvantage of the *NPV* method stems from the need for detailed, long-term forecasts of the free cash flows accruing from the project's acceptance. Despite this drawback, the *NPV* is the most theoretically correct criterion that we will examine. The following example provides an additional illustration of its application.

---

**EXAMPLE 10.2**   **Calculating net present value**

A firm is considering the purchase of a new computer system, which will cost $30,000 initially, to aid in credit billing and inventory management. The free cash flows resulting from this project are provided below:

|  | FREE CASH FLOW |
| --- | --- |
| Initial outlay | −$30,000 |
| Inflow year 1 | 15,000 |
| Inflow year 2 | 15,000 |
| Inflow year 3 | 15,000 |

The required rate of return demanded by the firm is 10 percent. Determine the system's *NPV*. Should the firm accept the project?

**STEP 1: FORMULATE A SOLUTION STRATEGY**

To determine the system's *NPV*, the 3-year $15,000 cash flow annuity is first discounted back to the present at 10 percent. The present value of the $15,000 annuity can be found using a calculator (as is done in the margin), or by using the relationship from equation (5-4),

$$PV = PMT \left[ \frac{1 - \frac{1}{(1 + k)^n}}{k} \right].$$

**STEP 2: CRUNCH THE NUMBERS**

Using the mathematical relationship we get:

$$PV = \$15,000 \left[ \frac{1 - \frac{1}{(1 + 0.10)^3}}{0.10} \right] = \$15,000 \, (2.4869) = \$37,303$$

**STEP 3: ANALYZE YOUR RESULTS**

Seeing that the cash inflows have been discounted back to the present, they can now be compared with the initial outlay because both of the flows are now stated in terms of today's dollars. Subtracting the initial outlay ($30,000) from the present value of the cash inflows ($37,303), we find that the system's *NPV* is $7,303. Because the *NPV* on this project is positive, the project should be accepted.

---

**CALCULATOR SOLUTION**

**STEP 1**
Calculate payment value of inflows

| Data Input | Function Key |
| --- | --- |
| 3 | N |
| 10 | I/Y |
| −15,000 | PMT |
| 0 | FV |

| Function Key | Answer |
| --- | --- |
| CPT | |
| PV | 37,303 |

**STEP 2**
Subtract initial outlay from present value of inflows

$37,303
−30,000
$ 7,303

---

## Using Spreadsheets to Calculate the Net Present Value

Although we can calculate the *NPV* by hand or with a financial calculator, it is more commonly done with the help of a spreadsheet. Just as with the keystroke calculations on a

## CAN YOU DO IT?

### DETERMINING THE *NPV* OF A PROJECT

Determine the *NPV* for a new project that costs $7,000, is expected to produce 10 years' worth of annual free cash flows of $1,000 per year, and has a required rate of return of 5 percent.
(The solution can be found on page 314.)

financial calculator, a spreadsheet can make easy work of *NPV* calculations. The only real glitch here is that in Excel, along with most other spreadsheets, the =*NPV* function calculates the present value of only the future cash flows and ignores the initial outlay in its *NPV* calculations. Sounds strange? Well, it is. It is essentially just a carryforward of an error in one of the first spreadsheets. That means that the actual *NPV* is the Excel-calculated *NPV* minus the initial outlay:

Actual *NPV* = Excel-calculated *NPV* − initial outlay

This can be input into a spreadsheet cell as:

=*NPV* (rate,inflow 1,inflow 2, . . . inflow 29)-initial outlay

Looking back at the Ski-Doo example in Table 10-3, we can use a spreadsheet to calculate the net present value of the investment in machinery as long as we remember to subtract the initial outlay in order to get the correct number.

| | A | B | C | D | E |
|---|---|---|---|---|---|
| 2 | | Spreadsheets and NPV – the Ski-Doo Example | | | |
| 3 | | | | | |
| 4 | | Looking at the example in Table 10-3, given a 12 percent | | | |
| 5 | | discount rate and the following after-tax cash flows, the | | | |
| 6 | | Net Present Value could be calculated as follows: | | | |
| 7 | | | | | |
| 8 | | | rate (*k*) = | 12% | |
| 9 | | | | | |
| 10 | | | Year | Cash Flow | |
| 11 | | | Initial Outlay | ($40.000) | |
| 12 | | | 1 | $15.000 | |
| 13 | | | 2 | $14.000 | |
| 14 | | | 3 | $13.000 | |
| 15 | | | 4 | $12.000 | Entered value in cell c18: |
| 16 | | | 5 | $11.000 | =NPV(D8,D12:D16)−40000 |
| 17 | | | | | |
| 18 | | NPV = | $7,674.63 | | |
| 19 | | | | | |
| 20 | Excel formula: =NPV(rate,inflow1,inflow2, ...,inflow29) | | | | |
| 21 | | | | | |
| 22 | Again, from the Excel NPV calculation we must then | | | | |
| 23 | subtract out the initial outlay in order to calculate the | | | | |
| 24 | actual NPV. | | | | |
| 25 | | | | | |
| 26 | | | | | |
| 27 | | | | | |

## The Profitability Index (Benefit–Cost Ratio)

The **profitability index (*PI*), or benefit–cost ratio**, is the *ratio of the present value of the future free cash flows to the initial outlay*. Although the *NPV* investment criterion gives a measure of the absolute dollar desirability of a project, the profitability index provides a relative

**profitability index (*PI*) or benefit–cost ratio** the ratio of the present value of an investment's future free cash flows to the investment's initial outlay.

measure of an investment proposal's desirability—that is, the ratio of the present value of its future net benefits to its initial cost. The profitability index can be expressed as follows:

$$PI = \frac{\text{present value of all the future annual free cash flows}}{\text{initial cash outlay}}$$

$$= \frac{\dfrac{FCF_1}{(1+k)^1} + \dfrac{FCF_2}{(1+k)^2} + \cdots + \dfrac{FCF_n}{(1+k)^n}}{IO} \tag{10-2}$$

where $FCF_t$ = the annual free cash flow in time period $t$ (this can take on either positive or negative values)

$k$ = the firm's required rate of return or cost of capital

$IO$ = the initial cash outlay

$n$ = the project's expected life

The decision criterion is to accept the project if the $PI$ is greater than or equal to 1.00 and to reject the project if the $PI$ is less than 1.00.

$PI \geq 1.0$: accept
$PI < 1.0$: reject

Looking closely at this criterion, we see that it yields the same accept/reject decision as the $NPV$ criterion. Whenever the present value of the project's free cash flows is greater than the initial cash outlay, the project's $NPV$ will be positive, signaling a decision to accept. When this is true, then the project's $PI$ will also be greater than 1 because the present value of the free cash flows (the $PI$'s numerator) is greater than the initial outlay (the $PI$'s denominator). Thus, these two decision criteria will always yield the same decision, although they

---

# DID YOU GET IT?
## DETERMINING THE *NPV* OF A PROJECT

You were asked to determine the *NPV* for a project with an initial outlay of $7,000 and free cash flows in years 1 through 10 of $1,000, given a 5 percent required rate of return.

$NPV$ = (present value of all future free cash flows) − (initial outlay)

1. **Using the Mathematical Formulas.**

    **STEP 1**  Determine the present value of the future cash flows.

    Substituting these example values in equation (5-4), we find

$$PV = \$1,000 \left[ \frac{1 - \dfrac{1}{(1+0.05)^{10}}}{0.05} \right]$$

$$= \$1,000\,[(1 - 1/1.62889463)/0.05]$$
$$= \$1,000\,[(1 - 0.61391325)/0.05]$$
$$= \$1,000\,(7.72173493) = \$7,721.73$$

    **STEP 2**  Subtract the initial outlay from the present value of the free cash flows.

    $7,721.73
    −$7,000.00
    $  721.73

2. **Using a Financial Calculator.**

    **STEP 1**  Determine the present value of the future cash flows.

| Data Input | Function Key |
|---|---|
| 10 | N |
| 5 | I/Y |
| −1,000 | PMT |
| 0 | FV |

| Function Key | Answer |
|---|---|
| CPT | |
| PV | 7,721.73 |

**STEP 2**  Subtract the initial outlay from present value of the free cash flows.

$7,721.73
−$7,000.00
$  721.73

Alternatively, you could use the CF button on your calculator (using a TI BA II Plus).

| Data and Key Input | Display |
|---|---|
| CF ; 2nd ; CE/C | CFo = 0. (this clears out any past cash flows) |
| −7,000; ENTER | CFo = −7,000. |
| ↓ ; 1,000; ENTER | C01 = 1,000. |
| ↓ ; 10; ENTER | F01 = 10.00 |
| NPV | I = 0. |
| 5; ENTER | I = 5.00 |
| ↓ | NPV = 0. |
| CPT | NPV = 721.73 |

will not necessarily rank acceptable projects in the same order. This problem of conflicting ranking is dealt with at a later point.

Because the *NPV* and *PI* criteria are essentially the same, they have the same advantages over the other criteria examined. Both employ free cash flows, recognize the timing of the cash flows, and are consistent with the goal of maximizing shareholders' wealth. The major disadvantage of the *PI* criterion, similar to the *NPV* criterion, is that it requires long, detailed free cash flow forecasts.

---

**EXAMPLE 10.3** | **Calculating the profitability index**

A firm with a 10 percent required rate of return is considering investing in a new machine with an expected life of 6 years. The free cash flows resulting from this investment are given in Table 10-5. Determine the firm's profitability index. According to the profitability index, should the firm accept the investment?

**TABLE 10-5  The Free Cash Flows Associated with an Investment in New Machinery**

|  | Free Cash Flow |
| --- | --- |
| Initial outlay | −$50.000 |
| Inflow year 1 | 15,000 |
| Inflow year 2 | 8,000 |
| Inflow year 3 | 10,000 |
| Inflow year 4 | 12,000 |
| Inflow year 5 | 14,000 |
| Inflow year 6 | 16,000 |

### STEP 1: FORMULATE A SOLUTION STRATEGY

The profitability index can be calculated using equation (10-2) as follows:

$$PI = \frac{\text{present value of all the furure annual free cash flows}}{\text{initial cash outlay}}$$

$$= \frac{\frac{FCF_1}{(1+k)^1} + \frac{FCF_2}{(1+k)^2} + \cdots + \frac{FCF_n}{(1+k)^n}}{IO}$$

where $FCF_t$ = the annual free cash flow in time period $t$ (this can take on either positive or negative values)

$k$ = the firm's required rate of return or cost of capital

$IO$ = the initial cash outlay

$n$ = the project's expected life

### STEP 2: CRUNCH THE NUMBERS

Discounting the project's future net free cash flows back to the present yields a present value of $53,682; dividing this value by the initial outlay of $50,000 yields a profitability index of 1.0736, as shown in Table 10-6.

### STEP 3: ANALYZE YOUR RESULTS

This tells us that the present value of the future benefits accruing from this project is 1.0736 times the level of the initial outlay. Because the profitability index is greater than 1.0, the project should be accepted. In addition, because the profitability index is greater than 1.0 we also know that the *NPV* is positive—that's because the present value of the future benefits is greater than the initial outlay. These two measures always give consistent accept/reject decisions on investment projects.

**TABLE 10-6 Calculating the *PI* of an Investment in New Machinery**

| | Free Cash Flow | × | Present Value Factor at 10 Percent | = | Present Value |
|---|---|---|---|---|---|
| Inflow year 1 | 15,000 | × | $\dfrac{1}{(1 + 0.10)^1}$ | = | 13,636 |
| Inflow year 2 | 8,000 | × | $\dfrac{1}{(1 + 0.10)^2}$ | = | 6,612 |
| Inflow year 3 | 10,000 | × | $\dfrac{1}{(1 + 0.10)^3}$ | = | 7,513 |
| Inflow year 4 | 12,000 | × | $\dfrac{1}{(1 + 0.10)^4}$ | = | 8,196 |
| Inflow year 5 | 14,000 | × | $\dfrac{1}{(1 + 0.10)^5}$ | = | 8,693 |
| Inflow year 6 | 16,000 | × | $\dfrac{1}{(1 + 0.10)^6}$ | = | 9,032 |

$$PI = \dfrac{\dfrac{FCF_1}{(1 + k)^1} + \dfrac{FCF_2}{(1 + k)^2} + \cdots + \dfrac{FCF_n}{(1 + k)^n}}{IO}$$

$$= \dfrac{\$13,636 + \$6,612 + \$7,513 + \$8,196 + \$8,693 + \$9,032}{\$50,000}$$

$$= \dfrac{\$53,682}{\$50,000} = 1.0736$$

## The Internal Rate of Return

**internal rate of return (*IRR*)** the rate of return that the project earns. For computational purposes, the internal rate of return is defined as the discount rate that equates the present value of the project's free cash flows with the project's initial cash outlay.

The **internal rate of return (*IRR*)** attempts to answer the question, what rate of return does this project earn? For computational purposes, the internal rate of return is defined as *the discount rate that equates the present value of the project's free cash flows with the project's initial cash outlay.* Mathematically, the internal rate of return is defined as the value *IRR* in the following equation:

*IRR* = the rate of return that equates the present value of the project's free cash flows with the initial outlay

$$IO = \frac{FCF_1}{(1 + IRR)^1} + \frac{FCF_2}{(1 + IRR)^2} + \cdots + \frac{FCF_n}{(1 + IRR)^n} \tag{10-3}$$

where $FCF_t$ = the annual free cash flow in time period *t* (this can take on either positive or negative values)

  *IO* = the initial cash outlay

  *n* = the project's expected life

  *IRR* = the project's internal rate of return

In effect, the *IRR* is analogous to the concept of the yield to maturity for bonds, which was examined in Chapter 7. In other words, a project's *IRR* is simply the rate of return that the project earns.

The decision criterion is to accept the project if the *IRR* is greater than or equal to the firm's required rate of return. We reject the project if its *IRR* is less than the required rate of return. This accept/reject criterion can be stated as

*IRR* ≥ firm's required rate of return or cost of capital: accept
*IRR* < firm's required rate of return or cost of capital: reject

If the *IRR* on a project is equal to the firm's required rate of return, then the project should be accepted because the firm is earning the rate that its shareholders are demanding. By contrast, accepting a project with an *IRR* below the investors' required rate of return will decrease the firm's stock price.

If the *NPV* is positive, then the *IRR* must be greater than the required rate of return, *k*. Thus, all the discounted cash-flow criteria are consistent and will result in similar accept/reject decisions. One disadvantage of the *IRR* relative to the *NPV* deals with the implied reinvestment rate assumptions made by these two methods. The *NPV* assumes that cash flows over the life of the project are reinvested back in projects that earn the required rate of return. That is, if we have a mining project with a 10-year expected life that produces a $100,000 cash flow at the end of the second year, the *NPV* technique assumes that this $100,000 is reinvested over years 3 though 10 at the required rate of return. The use of the *IRR*, however, implies that cash flows over the life of the project can be reinvested at the *IRR*. Thus, if the mining project we just looked at has a 40 percent *IRR*, the use of the *IRR* implies that the $100,000 cash flow that is received at the end of year 2 could be reinvested at 40 percent over the remaining life of the project. In effect, *the NPV method implicitly assumes that cash flows over the life of the project can be reinvested at the project's required rate of return, whereas the use of the IRR method implies that these cash flows could be reinvested at the IRR.* The better assumption is the one made by the *NPV*—that the cash flows can be reinvested at the required rate of return because they can either be (1) returned in the form of dividends to shareholders, who demand the required rate of return on their investments, or (2) reinvested in a new investment project. If these cash flows are invested in a new project, then they are simply substituting for external funding on which the required rate of return is again demanded. Thus, the opportunity cost of these funds is the required rate of return.

The bottom line of all this is that the *NPV* method makes the best reinvestment rate assumption, and, as such, is superior to the *IRR* method. Why should we care which method is used if both methods result in similar accept/reject decisions? The answer, as we will see, is that although they may result in the same accept/reject decision, they may rank projects differently in terms of desirability.

**Computing the *IRR* with a Financial Calculator** With today's calculators, determining an *IRR* is merely a matter of a few keystrokes. In Chapter 5, whenever we were solving time value of money problems for *i*, we were really solving for the *IRR*. For instance, in Chapter 5 when we solve for the rate at which $100 must be compounded annually for it to grow to $179.10 in 10 years, we are actually solving for that problem's *IRR*. Thus, with financial calculators we need only input the initial outlay, the cash flows, and their timing and then input the function key "I/Y" or the "IRR" button to calculate the *IRR*. On some calculators it is necessary to press the compute key, CPT, before pressing the function key to be calculated.

**Computing the *IRR* with a Spreadsheet** Calculating the *IRR* using a spreadsheet is extremely simple. Once the cash flows have been entered on the spreadsheet, all you need to do is input the Excel *IRR* function into a spreadsheet cell and let the spreadsheet do the calculations for you. Of course, at least one of the cash flows must be positive and at least one must be negative. The *IRR* function to be input into a spreadsheet cell is: = **IRR(values)**, where "values" is simply the range of cells in which the cash flows including the initial outlay are stored.

Entered value in cell B14:=IRR(B8:B12)
Entered value in cell C14:=IRR(C8:C12)
Entered value in cell D14:=IRR(D8:D12)

|  | A | B | C | D | E |
|---|---|---|---|---|---|
| 1 | | | | | |
| 2 | | **Spreadsheets and the IRR** | | | |
| 3 | | | | | |
| 4 | Three investment proposals being examined have the following | | | | |
| 5 | cash flows: | | | | |
| 6 | | | | | |
| 7 | Year | Project A | Project B | Project C | |
| 8 | Initial Outlay | ($10.000) | ($10.000) | ($10.000) | |
| 9 | 1 | 3.362 | 0 | 1.000 | |
| 10 | 2 | 3.362 | 0 | 3.000 | |
| 11 | 3 | 3.362 | 0 | 6.000 | |
| 12 | 4 | 3.362 | 13.605 | 7.000 | |
| 13 | | | | | |
| 14 | IRR= | 13.001% | 8.000% | 19.040% | |
| 15 | | | | | |
| 16 | Excel Formula: =IRR(values) | | | | |
| 17 | | | | | |
| 18 | where: | | | | |
| 19 | values = | the range of cells where the cash flows are stored. | | | |
| 20 | | Note: There must be at least one positive and one | | | |
| 21 | | negative cash flow. | | | |

**Computing the *IRR* for Uneven Cash Flows with a Financial Calculator**  Solving for the *IRR* when the cash flows are uneven is quite simple with a calculator: One need only key in the initial cash outlay, the cash flows, and their timing and press the "IRR" button. Let's take a look at how you might solve a problem with uneven cash flows using a financial calculator. Every calculator works a bit differently, so you'll want to be familiar with how to input data into yours, but that being said, they all work essentially the same way. As you'd expect, you will enter all the cash flows, then solve for the project's *IRR*. With a Texas Instruments BA II Plus calculator, you begin by hitting the CF button. Then, CFo indicates the initial outlay, which you'll want to give a negative value; C01 is the first free cash flow; and F01 is the number of years in which the first free cash flow appears. Thus, if the free cash flows in years 1, 2, and 3 are all $1,000, then F01 = 3. C02 then becomes the second free cash flow, and F02 is the number of years in which the second free cash flow appears. You'll notice that you move between the different cash flows using the down arrow (↓) located on the top row of your calculator. Once you have inputted the initial outlay and all the free cash flows, you then calculate the project's *IRR* by hitting the "IRR" button followed by "CPT," the compute button. Let's look at a quick example. Consider the following investment proposal:

| | |
|---|---|
| Initial outlay | −$5,000 |
| *FCF* in year 1 | 2,000 |
| *FCF* in year 2 | 2,000 |
| *FCF* in year 3 | 3,000 |

**CALCULATOR SOLUTION (USING A TI BA II PLUS):**

| Data and Key Input | Display |
|---|---|
| CF ; −5,000; ENTER | CFo = −5,000.00 |
| ↓ 2,000; ENTER | C01 = 2,000.00 |
| ↓ 2; ENTER | F01 = 2.00 |
| ↓ 3,000; ENTER | C02 = 3,000.00 |
| ↓ 1; ENTER | F02 = 1.00 |
| IRR ; CPT | IRR = 17.50% |

**EXAMPLE 10.4  Calculating internal rate of return**

Consider the following investment proposal:

| | |
|---|---|
| Initial outlay | −$10,010 |
| FCF in year 1 | 1,000 |
| FCF in year 2 | 3,000 |
| FCF in year 3 | 6,000 |
| FCF in year 4 | 7,000 |

If the required rate of return is 15 percent, should this project be accepted?

**STEP 1: FORMULATE A SOLUTION STRATEGY**
Because the cash flows are uneven, you'll want to either use Excel or use a financial calculator. Let's use a financial calculator; specifically, let's use a Texas Instruments BA II Plus calculator.

# CAN YOU DO IT?
## DETERMINING THE *IRR* OF A PROJECT

Determine the *IRR* for a new project that costs $5,019 and is expected to produce 10 years' worth of annual free cash flows of $1,000 per year.
(The solution can be found on page 319.)

## STEP 2: CRUNCH THE NUMBERS

Calculate the internal rate of return using the calculator.

CALCULATOR SOLUTION
(USING A TI BA II PLUS)

| Data and Key Input | Display |
|---|---|
| CF ; −10,010; ENTER | CFo = −10,010.00 |
| ↓ 1,000; ENTER | C01 = 1,000.00 |
| ↓ 1; ENTER | F01 = 1.00 |
| ↓ 3,000; ENTER | C02 = 3,000.00 |
| ↓ 1; ENTER | F02 = 1.00 |
| ↓ 6,000; ENTER | C03 = 6,000.00 |
| ↓ 1; ENTER | F03 = 1.00 |
| ↓ 7,000; ENTER | C04 = 7,000.00 |
| ↓ 1; ENTER | F04 = 1.00 |
| IRR ; CPT | IRR = 19.00% |

## STEP 3: ANALYZE YOUR RESULTS

In this case, the project's *IRR* is 19 percent, which is above the required rate of return of 15 percent. That means that this project would add value to the firm and should be accepted. In addition, we also know that since the *IRR* is greater than the required rate of return, the *NPV* must also be positive.

## Viewing the *NPV–IRR* Relationship: The Net Present Value Profile

Perhaps the easiest way to understand the relationship between the *IRR* and the *NPV* value is to view it graphically through the use of a **net present value profile**. A net present value profile is simply *a graph showing how a project's NPV changes as the discount rate changes*. To graph a project's net present value profile, you simply need to determine the project's *NPV*, first using a 0 percent discount rate, then slowly increasing the discount rate until a representative curve has been plotted. How does the *IRR* enter into the net present value profile? The *IRR* is the discount rate at which the *NPV* is zero.

**net present value profile** a graph showing how a project's *NPV* changes as the discount rate changes.

Let's look at an example of a project that involves an after-tax initial outlay of $105,517 with free cash flows expected to be $30,000 per year over the project's 5-year life. Calculating the *NPV* of this project at several different discount rates results in the following:

| Discount Rate | Project's *NPV* |
|---|---|
| 0% | $44,483 |
| 5% | $24,367 |
| 10% | $ 8,207 |
| 13% | $ 0 |
| 15% | −$ 4,952 |
| 20% | −$15,798 |
| 25% | −$24,839 |

## DID YOU GET IT?

### DETERMINING THE *IRR* OF A PROJECT

You were asked to determine the *IRR* for a project with an initial outlay of $5,019 and free cash flows in years 1 through 10 of $1,000.

1. **Using a Financial Calculator.** Substituting in a financial calculator, we are solving for *i*.

| Data Input | Function Key |
|---|---|
| 10 | N |
| −5,019 | PV |
| 1,000 | PMT |
| 0 | FV |

| Function Key | Answer |
|---|---|
| CPT | |
| I/Y | 15 |

Alternatively, you could use the CF button on your calculator (using a TI BA II Plus):

| Data and Key Input | Display |
|---|---|
| CF ; −5,019; ENTER | CFo = −5,019. |
| ↓ ; 1,000; ENTER | C01 = 1,000. |
| ↓ ; 10; ENTER | F01 = 10.00 |
| IRR ; CPT | IRR = 15 |

2. **Using Excel.** Using Excel, the *IRR* could be calculated using the = **IRR** function.

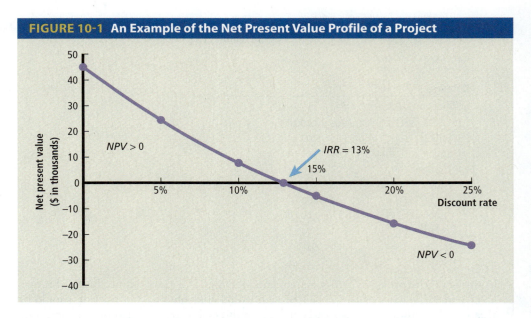

**FIGURE 10-1** An Example of the Net Present Value Profile of a Project

Plotting these values yields the net present value profile in Figure 10-1.

Where is the *IRR* in this figure? Recall that the *IRR* is the discount rate that equates the present value of the inflows with the present value of the outflows; thus, the *IRR* is the point at which the *NPV* is equal to zero—in this case, 13 percent. This is exactly the process that we use in computing the *IRR* for a series of uneven cash flows—we simply calculate the project's *NPV* using different discount rates and the discount rate that makes the *NPV* equal to zero is the project's *IRR*.

From the net present value profile you can easily see how a project's *NPV* varies inversely with the discount rate—as the discount rate is raised, the *NPV* drops. By analyzing a project's net present value profile, you can also see how sensitive the project is to your selection of the discount rate. The more sensitive the *NPV* is to the discount rate, the more important it is that you use the correct one in your calculations.

## Complications with the *IRR*: Multiple Rates of Return

Although any project can have only one *NPV* and one *PI*, a single project under certain circumstances can have more than one *IRR*. The reason for this can be traced to the calculations involved in determining the *IRR*. Equation (10-3) states that the *IRR* is the discount rate that equates the present value of the project's future net cash flows with the project's initial outlay:

$$IO = \frac{FCF_1}{(1 + IRR)^1} + \frac{FCF_2}{(1 + IRR)^2} + \cdots + \frac{FCF_n}{(1 + IRR)^n} \tag{10-3}$$

However, because equation (10-3) is a polynomial of a degree $n$, it has $n$ solutions. Now if the initial outlay (*IO*) is the only negative cash flow and all the annual free cash flows (*FCF*) are positive, then all but one of these $n$ solutions is either a negative or an imaginary number and there is no problem. But problems occur when there are sign reversals in the cash-flow stream; in fact, there can be as many solutions as there are sign reversals. A normal, or "conventional," pattern with a negative initial outlay and positive annual free cash flows after that (−, +, +, +, . . . , +) has only one sign reversal, hence, only one positive *IRR*. However, an "unconventional" pattern with more than one sign reversal can have more than one *IRR*.

| | FREE CASH FLOW |
|---|---|
| Initial outlay | −$ 1,600 |
| Year 1 free cash flow | +$10,000 |
| Year 2 free cash flow | −$10,000 |

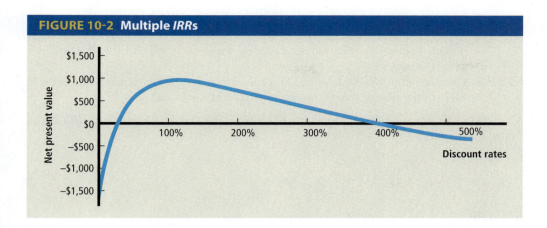

**FIGURE 10-2  Multiple *IRRs***

In this pattern of cash flows, there are two sign reversals: one from −$1,600 to +$10,000 and one from +$10,000 to −$10,000, so there can be as many as two positive *IRR*s that will make the present value of the free cash flows equal to the initial outlay. In fact, two internal rates of return solve this problem: 25 percent and 400 percent. Graphically, what we are solving for is the discount rate that makes the project's *NPV* equal to zero. As Figure 10-2 illustrates, this occurs twice.

Which solution is correct? The answer is that neither solution is valid. Although each fits the definition of *IRR*, neither provides any insight into the true project returns. In summary, when there is more than one sign reversal in the cash-flow stream, the possibility of multiple *IRR*s exists, and the normal interpretation of the *IRR* loses its meaning. In this case, try the *NPV* criterion instead.

## The Modified Internal Rate of Return (*MIRR*)[2]

Problems with multiple rates of return and the reinvestment rate assumption make the *NPV* superior to the *IRR* as a capital-budgeting technique. However, because of the ease of interpretation, the *IRR* is preferred by many practitioners. Recently, a new technique, the **modified internal rate of return (MIRR)**, has gained popularity as an alternative to the *IRR* method because it avoids multiple *IRR*s and allows the decision maker to directly specify the appropriate reinvestment rate. As a result, the *MIRR* provides the decision maker with the intuitive appeal of the *IRR* coupled with an improved reinvestment rate assumption.

Is this really a problem? The answer is yes. One of the problems of the *IRR* is that it creates unrealistic expectations both for the corporation and for its shareholders. For example, the consulting firm McKinsey & Company examined one firm that approved 23 major projects over 5 years based on average *IRR*s of 77 percent.[3] However, when McKinsey adjusted the reinvestment rate on these projects to the firm's required rate of return, this return rate fell to 16 percent. The ranking of the projects also changed with the top-ranked project falling to the 10th most attractive project. Moreover, the returns on the highest-ranked projects with *IRR*s of 800, 150, and 130 percent dropped to 15, 23, and 22 percent, respectively, once the reinvestment rate was adjusted downward.

The driving force behind the *MIRR* is the assumption that all free cash flows over the life of the project are reinvested at the required rate of return until the termination of the project. Thus, to calculate the *MIRR*, we:

**STEP 1**   Determine the present value of the project's free cash *out*flows. We do this by discounting all the free cash *out*flows back to the present at the required rate of return. If the initial outlay is the only free cash *out*flow, then the initial outlay is the present value of the free cash *out*flows.

**modified internal rate of return (*MIRR*)**
the discount rate that equates the present value of the project's future free cash flows with the terminal value of the cash inflows.

[2]This section is relatively complex and can be omitted without loss of continuity.
[3]John C. Kellecher and Justin J. MacCormack, "Internal Rate of Return: A Cautionary Tale," *McKinsey Quarterly*, September 24, 2004, pp. 1–4.

**STEP 2**   Determine the future value of the project's free cash *in*flows. Take all the annual free cash *in*flows and find their future value at the end of the project's life, compounded forward at the required rate of return. We will call this the project's *terminal value*, or *TV*.

**STEP 3**   Calculate the *MIRR*. The *MIRR* is the discount rate that equates the present value of the free cash outflows with the project's terminal value.[4]

Mathematically, the modified internal rate of return is defined as the value of *MIRR* in the following equation:

$$PV_{\text{outflows}} = \frac{TV_{\text{inflows}}}{(1 + MIRR)^n} \qquad (10\text{-}4)$$

where $PV_{\text{outflows}}$ = the present value of the project's free cash *out*flows

$TV_{\text{inflows}}$ = the project's terminal value, calculated by taking all the annual free cash *in*flows and finding their future value at the end of the project's life, compounded forward at the required rate of return

$n$ = the project's expected life

$MIRR$ = the project's modified internal rate of return

In terms of decision rules, if the project's *MIRR* is greater than or equal to the project's required rate of return, it should be accepted. While we have now introduced a number of different capital-budgeting decision rules, interestingly the *NPV*, *PI*, *IRR*, and *MIRR* will always give the same accept/reject decision for independent projects. These financial decision rules can be summarized as follows:

## FINANCIAL DECISION TOOLS

| Name of Tool | Formula | What It Tells You |
|---|---|---|
| Net present value (*NPV*) | The present value of all the future annual free cash flows minus the initial cash outlay: $$= \frac{FCF_1}{(1+k)^1} + \frac{FCF_2}{(1+k)^2} + \cdots + \frac{FCF_n}{(1+k)^n} - IO$$ | • The amount of wealth that is created if the project is accepted<br>• If the *NPV* is positive, then wealth is created and the project should be accepted. |
| Profitability index (*PI*)<br><br>(Also referred to as the benefit–cost ratio) | The ratio of the present value of the future free cash flows to the initial outlay: $$= \frac{\dfrac{FCF_1}{(1+k)^1} + \dfrac{FCF_2}{(1+k)^2} + \cdots + \dfrac{FCF_n}{(1+k)^n}}{IO}$$ | • The ratio of the present value of future benefits to the initial cost<br>• If it is greater than 1.0, the *NPV* must be positive; the project creates value and should be accepted. |
| Internal rate of return (*IRR*) | The discount rate that equates the present value of the project's future free cash flows with the project's initial outlay: $$IO = \frac{FCF_1}{(1+IRR)^1} + \frac{FCF_2}{(1+IRR)^2} + \cdots + \frac{FCF_n}{(1+IRR)^n}$$ Where *IRR* = the project's internal rate of return | • The rate of return that the project earns<br>• If the project earns more than the required rate of return, then the *NPV* must be positive; the project creates value and should be accepted. |
| Modified internal rate of return (*MIRR*) | The discount rate that equates the present value of the project's future free cash flows with the terminal value of the cash inflows $$PV_{\text{outflows}} = \frac{TV_{\text{inflows}}}{(1 + MIRR)^n}$$ | • What the *IRR* would be if it was based upon the assumption that cash flows are reinvested at the required rate of return |

---

[4]You will notice that we differentiate between annual cash inflows and annual cash outflows, compounding all the inflows to the end of the project and bringing all the outflows back to the present as part of the present value of the cost. Although there are alternative definitions of the *MIRR*, this is the most widely accepted definition.

| EXAMPLE 10.5 | Calculating the *MIRR* |
|---|---|

Let's look at an example of a project with a 3-year life and a required rate of return of 10 percent assuming the following cash flows are associated with it:

|  | FREE CASH FLOWS |
|---|---|
| Initial outlay | −$6,000 |
| Year 1 | 2,000 |
| Year 2 | $3,000 |
| Year 3 | 4,000 |

Determine the *MIRR* of the project.

### STEP 1: FORMULATE A SOLUTION STRATEGY

The calculation of the *MIRR* can be viewed as a three-step process:

**STEP 1**  Determine the present value of the project's free cash outflows.
**STEP 2**  Determine the terminal value of the project's free cash inflows.
**STEP 3**  Determine the discount rate that equates the present value of the terminal value and the present value of the project's cash outflows.

Mathematically, the modified internal rate of return is defined as the value of *MIRR* in the following equation:

$$PV_{outflows} = \frac{TV_{inflows}}{(1 + MIRR)^n} \tag{10-4}$$

where $PV_{outflows}$ = the present value of project's free cash *out*flows
 $TV_{inflows}$ = the project's terminal value, calculated by taking all the annual free cash *in*flows and finding their future value at the end of the project's life, compounded forward at the required rate of return
 $n$ = the project's expected life
 $MIRR$ = the project's modified internal rate of return

### STEP 2: CRUNCH THE NUMBERS

Using the three-step process:

**STEP 1**  Determine the present value of the project's free cash outflows. In this case, the only outflow is the initial outlay of $6,000, which is already at the present; thus, it becomes the present value of the cash outflows.
**STEP 2**  Determine the terminal value of the project's free cash inflows. To do this, we merely use the project's required rate of return to calculate the future value of the project's three cash inflows at the termination of the project. In this case, the terminal value becomes $9,720.
**STEP 3**  Determine the discount rate that equates the present value of the terminal value and the present value of the project's cash outflows. Thus, the MIRR is calculated to be 17.446 percent.

The calculations are as follows:

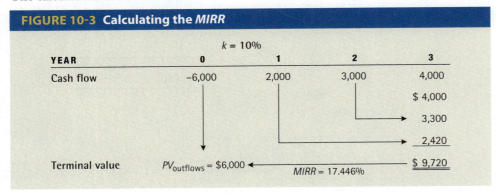

**FIGURE 10-3  Calculating the *MIRR***

$$\$6{,}000 = \frac{TV_{\text{inflows}}}{(1 + MIRR)^n}$$

$$\$6{,}000 = \frac{\$2{,}000(1 + 0.10)^2 + \$3{,}000(1 + 0.10)^1 + \$4{,}000(1 + 0.10)^0}{(1 + MIRR)^3}$$

$$\$6{,}000 = \frac{\$2{,}420 + \$3{,}300 + \$4{,}000}{(1 + MIRR)^3}$$

$$\$6{,}000 = \frac{\$9{,}720}{(1 + MIRR)^3}$$

$$MIRR = 17.45\%$$

### STEP 3: ANALYZE YOUR RESULTS

Thus, the *MIRR* for this project (17.45 percent) is less than its *IRR*, which comes out to 20.614 percent. In this case, it only makes sense that the *IRR* should be greater than the *MIRR*, because the *IRR* implicitly assumes intermediate cash inflows to grow at the *IRR* rather than the required rate of return.

In terms of decision rules, if the project's *MIRR* is greater than or equal to the project's required rate of return, then the project should be accepted; if not, it should be rejected:

*MIRR* ≥ required rate of return: accept
*MIRR* < required rate of return: reject

Because of the frequent use of the *IRR* in the real world as a decision-making tool and its limiting reinvestment rate assumption, the *MIRR* has become increasingly popular as an alternative decision-making tool.

## Using Spreadsheets to Calculate the *MIRR*

As with other financial calculations using a spreadsheet, calculating the *MIRR* is extremely simple. The only difference between this calculation and that of the traditional *IRR* is that with a spreadsheet you also have the option of specifying both a *financing rate* and a *reinvestment rate*. The financing rate refers to the rate at which you borrow the money needed for the investment, whereas the reinvestment rate is the rate at which you reinvest the cash flows. Generally, it is assumed that these two values are one and the same. Thus, we enter the value of $k$, the appropriate discount rate, for both of these values. Once the cash flows have been entered on the spreadsheet, all you need to do is input the Excel *MIRR* function into a spreadsheet cell and let the spreadsheet do the calculations for you. Of course, as with the *IRR* calculation, at least one of the cash flows must be positive and at least one must be negative. The *MIRR* function to be input into a spreadsheet cell is **=MIRR(values,finance rate,reinvestment rate)**, where values is simply the range of cells where the cash flows are stored, and $k$ is entered for both the finance rate and the reinvestment rate.

| | A | B | C | D | E |
|---|---|---|---|---|---|
| 1 | | | | | |
| 2 | **Using a Spreadsheet to Calculate the MIRR** | | | | |
| 3 | | | | | |
| 4 | Looking back on the previous example, we can also calculate the | | | | |
| 5 | MIRR using a spreadsheet. However, with a spreadsheet you also | | | | |
| 6 | have the option of specifying both a financing rate and a reinvestment | | | | |
| 7 | rate. The *financing rate* would be the rate at which you borrow the money | | | | |
| 8 | you need for the investment, while the *reinvestment rate* is the rate | | | | |
| 9 | at which you reinvest the cash flows. In our calculations we assume | | | | |
| 10 | these values to be identical. Thus we will put $k$, the appropriate | | | | |
| 11 | discount rate, in for both of these values. Going back to the | | | | |
| 12 | previous example: | | | | |
| 13 | | | | | |
| 14 | | Year | Cash Flow | | |
| 15 | | Initial Outlay | ($6,000) | | |
| 16 | | 1 | 2000 | | |
| 17 | | 2 | 3000 | | |
| 18 | | 3 | 4000 | | |
| 19 | | | | | |
| 20 | | MIRR = | 17.446% | | |
| 21 | | | | | |
| 22 | Excel formula: =MIRR(values,finance rate,reinvestment rate) | | | | |
| 23 | | | | | |
| 24 | | where: | | | |
| 25 | | values = | the range of cells where the cash flows are stored. | | |
| 26 | | | Note: There must be at least one positive and one | | |
| 27 | | | negative cash flow. | | |
| 28 | | finance rate = | the rate at which you borrow the money needed | | |
| 29 | | | for the investment. Generally assumed to be $k$. | | |
| 30 | | reinvestment rate = | the reinvestment rate. Generally assumed to be $k$. | | |
| 31 | | | | | |

Entered value in cell C20:
=MIRR(C15:C18,10%,10%)

## Concept Check

1. Provide an intuitive definition of an internal rate of return for a project.
2. What does a net present value profile tell you, and how is it constructed?
3. What is the difference between the *IRR* and the *MIRR*?
4. Why do the net present value and profitability index always yield the same accept/reject decision for any project?

# Capital Rationing

 Explain how the capital-budgeting decision process changes when a dollar limit is placed on the capital budget.

**capital rationing** placing a limit on the dollar size of the capital budget.

The use of our capital-budgeting decision rules developed in this chapter implies that the size of the capital budget is determined by the availability of acceptable investment proposals. However, a firm may *place a limit on the dollar size of the capital budget*. This situation is called **capital rationing**. As we will see, examining capital rationing not only better enables us to deal with complexities of the real world but also serves to demonstrate the superiority of the *NPV* method over the *IRR* method for capital budgeting. It is always somewhat uncomfortable to deal with problems associated with capital rationing because, under rationing, projects with positive net present values are rejected. This is a situation that violates the firm's goal of shareholder wealth maximization. However, in the real world, capital rationing does exist, and managers must deal with it. Often when firms impose capital constraints, they are recognizing that they do not have the ability to profitably handle more than a certain number of new and/or large projects.

Using the *IRR* as the firm's decision rule, a firm accepts all projects with an *IRR* greater than the firm's required rate of return. This rule is illustrated in Figure 10-4, where projects A through E would be chosen. However, when capital rationing is imposed, the dollar size of the total investment is limited by the budget constraint. In Figure 10-4, the budget constraint of $X precludes the acceptance of an attractive investment, project E. This situation obviously contradicts prior decision rules. Moreover, choosing the projects with the highest *IRR* is complicated by the fact that some projects are indivisible. For example, it may be illogical to recommend that half of project D be undertaken.

## The Rationale for Capital Rationing

In general, three principal reasons are given for imposing a capital-rationing constraint. First, managers may think market conditions are temporarily adverse. In the period surrounding the downturn in the economy in the late 2000s, this reason was frequently given. At that time stock prices were depressed, which made the cost of funding projects high. Second, there may be a shortage of qualified managers to direct new projects; this can happen when projects are of a highly technical nature. Third, there may be intangible considerations. For example, managers may simply fear debt, wishing to avoid interest payments at any cost. Or perhaps the firm wants to limit the issuance of common stock to maintain a stable dividend policy.

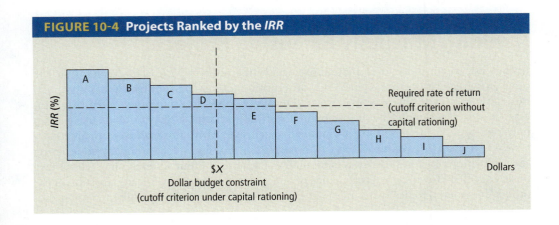

**FIGURE 10-4  Projects Ranked by the *IRR***

| TABLE 10-7 | Capital Rationing: Choosing Among Five Indivisible Projects | | |
|---|---|---|---|
| Project | Initial Outlay | Profitability Index | Net Present Value |
| A | $200,000 | 2.4 | $280,000 |
| B | 200,000 | 2.3 | 260,000 |
| C | 800,000 | 1.7 | 560,000 |
| D | 300,000 | 1.3 | 90,000 |
| E | 300,000 | 1.2 | 60,000 |

So what is capital rationing's effect on the firm? In brief, the effect is negative. To what degree it is negative depends on the severity of the rationing. If the rationing is minor and short-lived, the firm's share price will not suffer to any great extent. In this case, capital rationing can probably be excused, although it should be noted that any capital-rationing action that rejects projects with positive *NPV*s is contrary to the firm's goal of maximization of shareholders' wealth. If the capital rationing is a result of the firm's decision to limit dramatically the number of new projects or to use only internally generated funds for projects, then this policy will eventually have a significantly negative effect on the firm's share price. For example, a lower share price will eventually result from lost competitive advantage if, because of a decision to arbitrarily limit its capital budget, a firm fails to upgrade its products and manufacturing processes.

## Capital Rationing and Project Selection

If a firm decides to impose a capital constraint on its investment projects, the appropriate decision criterion is to select the set of projects with the highest *NPV* subject to the capital constraint. In effect, it should select the projects that increase shareholders' wealth the most. This guideline may preclude merely taking the highest-ranked projects in terms of the *PI* or the *IRR*. If the projects shown in Figure 10-4 are divisible, the last project accepted will be only partially accepted. Although partial acceptance may be possible, as we have said, in some cases, the indivisibility of most capital investments prevents it. For example, purchasing half a sales outlet or half a truck is impossible.

Consider a firm with a budget constraint of $1 million and five indivisible projects available to it, as given in Table 10-7. If the highest-ranked projects were taken, projects A and B would be taken first. At that point there would not be enough funds available to take on project C; hence, projects D and E would be taken on. However, a higher total *NPV* is provided by the combination of projects A and C. Thus, projects A and C should be selected from the set of projects available. This illustrates our guideline: to select the set of projects that maximizes the firm's *NPV*.

## Concept Check

1. What is capital rationing?
2. How might capital rationing conflict with the goal of maximizing shareholders' wealth?
3. What are mutually exclusive projects? How might they complicate the capital-budgeting process?

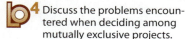 **4** Discuss the problems encountered when deciding among mutually exclusive projects.

# Ranking Mutually Exclusive Projects

In the past, we have proposed that all projects with a positive *NPV*, a *PI* greater than 1.0, or an *IRR* greater than the required rate of return be accepted, assuming there is no capital rationing. However, this acceptance is not always possible. In some cases, when two projects are judged acceptable by the discounted cash-flow criteria, it may be necessary to select only one of them because they are mutually exclusive. **Mutually exclusive projects** *are projects that, if undertaken, would serve the same purpose.* For example, a company considering the installation of a computer system might evaluate three or four systems, all of which have positive *NPV*s. However, the acceptance of one system automatically means rejection of the others. In general, to deal with mutually exclusive projects, we simply rank them by means

**mutually exclusive projects** projects that, if undertaken, would serve the same purpose. Thus, accepting one will necessarily mean rejecting the others.

of the discounted cash-flow criteria and select the project with the highest ranking. On occasion, however, problems of conflicting ranking may arise. As we will see, in general, the *NPV* method is the preferred decision-making tool because it leads to the selection of the project that increases shareholder wealth the most.

When dealing with mutually exclusive projects, there are three general types of ranking problems: the size-disparity problem, the time-disparity problem, and the unequal-lives problem. Each involves the possibility of conflict in the ranks yielded by the various discounted cash-flow, capital-budgeting criteria. As noted previously, when one discounted cash-flow criterion gives an accept signal, they will all give an accept signal, but they will not necessarily rank all projects in the same order. In most cases this disparity is not critical; however, for mutually exclusive projects the ranking order is important.

## The Size-Disparity Problem

The size-disparity problem occurs when mutually exclusive projects of unequal size are examined. This problem is most easily clarified with an example.

---

**EXAMPLE 10.6**    **The size-disparity problem**

Suppose a firm is considering two mutually exclusive projects, A and B; both have required rates of return of 10 percent. Project A involves a $200 initial outlay and a cash inflow of $300 at the end of year 1, whereas project B involves an initial outlay of $1,500 and a cash inflow of $1,900 at the end of year 1. The net present values, profitability indexes, and internal rates of return for these projects are given in Table 10-8.

**TABLE 10-8**   **The Size-Disparity Ranking Problem**

| PROJECT A | | |
|---|---|---|
| | | $k = 10\%$ |
| **YEARS** | **0** | **1** |
| Cash Flow | −200 | 300 |
|   $NPV = \$72.73$ | | |
|   $PI = 1.36$ | | |
|   $IRR = 50\%$ | | |

| PROJECT B | | |
|---|---|---|
| | | $k = 10\%$ |
| **YEARS** | **0** | **1** |
| Cash Flow | −1,500 | 1,900 |
|   $NPV = \$227.28$ | | |
|   $PI = 1.15$ | | |
|   $IRR = 27\%$ | | |

In this case, if the *NPV* criterion is used, project B should be accepted; whereas if the *PI* or *IRR* criterion is used, project A should be chosen. The question now becomes, which project is better?

### STEP 1: FORMULATE A SOLUTION STRATEGY
The answer depends on whether capital rationing exists.

### STEP 2: CRUNCH THE NUMBERS
Without capital rationing, project B is better because it provides the largest increase in shareholders' wealth; that is, it has a larger *NPV*. If there is a capital constraint, the problem then focuses on what can be done with the additional $1,300 that is freed up if project A is chosen (costing $200, as opposed to $1,500). If the firm can earn more on project A plus the project financed with the additional $1,300 than it can on project B, then project A and the marginal project should be accepted. In effect, we are attempting to select the set of projects that maximize the firm's *NPV*. Thus, if the marginal project has an *NPV* greater than $154.55 ($227.28 − $72.73), selecting it plus project A with an *NPV* of $72.73 will provide an *NPV* greater than $227.28, the *NPV* for project B.

### STEP 3: ANALYZE YOUR RESULTS

In summary, whenever the size-disparity problem results in conflicting rankings between mutually exclusive projects, the project with the largest *NPV* will be selected, provided there is no capital rationing. When capital rationing exists, the firm should select the set of projects with the largest *NPV*.

## The Time-Disparity Problem

The time-disparity problem and the conflicting rankings that accompany it result from the differing reinvestment assumptions made by the net present value and internal rate of return decision criteria. The *NPV* criterion assumes that cash flows over the life of the project can be reinvested at the required rate of return or cost of capital, whereas the *IRR* criterion implicitly assumes that the cash flows over the life of the project can be reinvested at the *IRR*. One possible solution to this problem is to use the *MIRR* method introduced earlier. As you recall, this method allows you to explicitly state the rate at which cash flows over the life of the project will be reinvested. Again, this problem may be illustrated through the use of an example.

---

**EXAMPLE 10.7**    **The time-disparity problem**

Suppose a firm with a required rate of return or cost of capital of 10 percent and with no capital constraint is considering the two mutually exclusive projects illustrated in Table 10-9. How to solve this time-disparity problem?

**TABLE 10-9  The Time-Disparity Ranking Problem**

**PROJECT A**

| | $k = 10\%$ | | | |
|---|---|---|---|---|
| **YEARS** | **0** | **1** | **2** | **3** |
| Cash Flow | −1,000 | 100 | 200 | 2,000 |
| $NPV = \$758.83$ | | | | |
| $PI = 1.759$ | | | | |
| $IRR = 35\%$ | | | | |

**PROJECT B**

| | $k = 10\%$ | | | |
|---|---|---|---|---|
| **YEARS** | **0** | **1** | **2** | **3** |
| Cash Flow | −1,000 | 650 | 650 | 650 |
| $NPV = \$616.45$ | | | | |
| $PI = 1.616$ | | | | |
| $IRR = 43\%$ | | | | |

### STEP 1: FORMULATE A SOLUTION STRATEGY

Which criterion would be followed depends on which reinvestment assumption is used. The *NPV* and *PI* indicate that project A is the better of the two, whereas the *IRR* indicates that project B is the better. Project B receives its cash flows earlier than project A, and the different assumptions made about how these flows can be reinvested result in the difference in rankings.

### STEP 2: CRUNCH THE NUMBERS

The *NPV* criterion assumes that cash flows over the life of the project can be reinvested at the required rate of return or cost of capital, whereas the *IRR* criterion implicitly assumes that the cash flows over the life of the project can be reinvested at the *IRR*.

### STEP 3: ANALYZE YOUR RESULTS

The *NPV* criterion is preferred in this case because it makes the most acceptable assumption for the wealth-maximizing firm. It is certainly the most conservative assumption that can be made, because the required rate of return is the lowest possible reinvestment rate. Moreover, as we have already noted, the *NPV* method maximizes the value of the firm and the shareholders' wealth.

## The Unequal-Lives Problem

The final ranking problem to be examined asks whether it is appropriate to compare mutually exclusive projects with different life spans. The incomparability of projects with different lives arises because future, profitable investment proposals will be precluded without ever having been considered. For example, let's say you own an older hotel on some prime beachfront property on Hilton Head Island, and you're considering either remodeling the hotel, which will extend its life by 5 years, or tearing it down and building a new hotel that has an expected life of 10 years. Either way you're going to make money because beachfront property is exactly where everyone would like to stay. But clearly, you can't do both.

Is it fair to compare the *NPV*s on these two projects? No. Why not? Because if you accept the 10-year project, you will not only be rejecting the 5-year project but also the chance to do something else profitable with the property in years 5 through 10. In effect, if the project with the shorter life were taken, at its termination you could either remodel again or rebuild and receive additional benefits, whereas accepting the project with the longer life would exclude this possibility, which is not included in the analysis. The key question thus becomes: Does today's investment decision include all future profitable investment proposals in its analysis? If not, the projects are not comparable.

| EXAMPLE 10.8 | **The unequal-lives problem** |

Suppose a firm with a 10 percent required rate of return must replace an aging machine and is considering two replacement machines, one with a 3-year life and one with a 6-year life. The relevant cash-flow information for these projects is given in Figure 10-5.

### FIGURE 10-5  Unequal Lives Ranking Problem

PROJECT A:

$k = 10\%$

| YEARS | 0 | 1 | 2 | 3 |
|---|---|---|---|---|
| Cash Flows | −1,000 | 500 | 500 | 500 |

NPV = $243.43
PI = 1.243
IRR = 23.4%

PROJECT B:

$k = 10\%$

| YEARS | 0 | 1 | 2 | 3 | 4 | 5 | 6 |
|---|---|---|---|---|---|---|---|
| Cash Flows | −1,000 | 300 | 300 | 300 | 300 | 300 | 300 |

NPV = $306.58
PI = 1.307
IRR = 19.9%

Examining the discounted cash-flow criteria, we find that the net present value and profitability index criteria indicate that project B is the better project, whereas the internal rate of return favors project A. This ranking inconsistency is caused by the different life spans of the projects being compared. In this case, the decision is a difficult one because the projects are not comparable. How to solve this unequal-lives problem?

## STEP 1: FORMULATE A SOLUTION STRATEGY

There are several methods to deal with this situation. The first option is to assume that the cash inflows from the shorter-lived investment will be reinvested at the required rate of return until the termination of the longer-lived asset. Although this approach is the simplest because it merely involves calculating the net present value, It actually ignores the problem at hand—the possibility of undertaking another replacement opportunity with a positive net present value. Thus, the proper solution involves projecting reinvestment opportunities into the future—that is, making assumptions about possible future investment opportunities. Unfortunately, whereas the first method is too simplistic to be of any value, the second is extremely difficult, requiring extensive cash-flow forecasts. The final technique for confronting the problem is to assume that the firm's reinvestment opportunities in the future will be similar to its current ones. The two most common ways of doing this are by creating a replacement chain to equalize the life spans of projects or by calculating the equivalent annual annuity (*EAA*) of the projects.

Using a replacement chain, the present example would call for the creation of a two-chain cycle for project A; that is, we assume that project A can be replaced with a similar investment at the end of 3 years. Thus, project A would be viewed as two A projects occurring back to back, as illustrated in Figure 10-6. The first project begins with a $1,000 outflow in year 0, or the beginning of year 1. The second project would have an initial outlay of $1,000 at the beginning of year 4, or end of year 3, followed by $500 cash flows in years 4 through 6. As a result, in year 3 there would be a $500 inflow associated with the first project along with a $1,000 outflow associated with repeating the project, resulting in a net cash flow in year 3 of −$500. The net present value on this replacement chain is $426.32, which can be compared with project B's net present value.

### FIGURE 10-6 Replacement Chain Illustration: Two Project A's Back to Back

|  | $k = 10\%$ | | | | | | |
| --- | --- | --- | --- | --- | --- | --- | --- |
| **YEARS** | **0** | **1** | **2** | **3** | **4** | **5** | **6** |
| Cash Flows | −1,000 | 500 | 500 | −500 | 500 | 500 | 500 |
| *NPV* = $426.32 | | | | | | | |

Therefore, project A should be accepted because the net present value of its replacement chain is greater than the net present value of project B. One problem with replacement chains is that, depending on the life of each project, it can be quite difficult to come up with equivalent lives. For example, if the two projects had 7- and 13-year lives, because the lowest common denominator is $7 \times 13 = 91$, a 91-year replacement chain would be needed to establish equivalent lives. In this case, it is easier to determine the project's **equivalent annual annuity (*EAA*)**. A project's *EAA* is simply an annuity cash flow that yields the same present value as the project's *NPV*.

To calculate an *EAA*, we need only calculate a project's *NPV* and then determine what annual annuity (PMT on your financial calculator) it is equal to. This can be done in two steps as follows:

**STEP 1**   Calculate the project's *NPV*.
**STEP 2**   Calculate the *EAA*.

## STEP 2: CRUNCH THE NUMBERS

**STEP 1**   Calculate the project's *NPV*. In Figure 10-5 we determined that project A had an *NPV* of $243.43, whereas project B had an *NPV* of $306.58.
**STEP 2**   Calculate the *EAA*. The *EAA* is determined by using the *NPV* as the project's present value (PV), the number of years in the project as N, the required rate

**equivalent annual annuity (*EAA*)** an annuity cash flow that yields the same present value as the project's *NPV*.

of return as I/Y, entering a 0 for the future value (FV), and solving for the annual annuity (PMT). This determines the level of an annuity cash flow that would produce the same *NPV* as the project. For project A the calculations are:

**CALCULATOR SOLUTION**

| Data Input | Function Key |
|---|---|
| 3 | N |
| 10 | I/Y |
| −243.43 | PV |
| 0 | FV |
| **Function Key** | **Answer** |
| CPT | |
| PMT | 97.89 |

For project B, the calculations are:

**CALCULATOR SOLUTION**

| Data Input | Function Key |
|---|---|
| 6 | N |
| 10 | I/Y |
| −306.58 | PV |
| 0 | FV |
| **Function Key** | **Answer** |
| CPT | |
| PMT | 70.39 |

### STEP 3: ANALYZE YOUR RESULTS

How do we interpret the *EAA*? For a project with an *n*-year life, it tells us what the dollar value is of an *n*-year annual annuity that would provide the same *NPV* as the project. Thus, for project A, it means that a 3-year annuity of $97.89 with a discount rate of 10 percent would produce a net present value the same as project A's net present value, which is $243.43. We can now compare the equivalent annual annuities directly to determine which project is better. We can do this because we now have found the level of annual annuity that produces an *NPV* equivalent to the project's *NPV*. Thus, because they are both annual annuities, they are comparable.

## FINANCIAL DECISION TOOLS

| Name of Tool | Formula | What It Tells You |
|---|---|---|
| Equivalent annual annuity (*EAA*) | The annuity cash flow that yields the same present value as the project's *NPV* | • It makes mutually exclusive projects with unequal lives comparable by determining the level of an annual annuity that produces an *NPV* equivalent to the project's *NPV*.<br>• The *EAAs* for projects with unequal lives can be compared because they represent annual annuities. |

## Concept Check

1. What are the three general types of ranking problems?

# ETHICS IN FINANCIAL MANAGEMENT

## THE FINANCIAL DOWNSIDE OF POOR ETHICAL BEHAVIOR

As we discussed in Chapter 1, ethics and trust are essential elements of the business world. Knowing the inevitable outcome— for truth does percolate—why do bright and experienced people ignore it? For even if the truth is known only within the confines of the company, it will get out. Circumstances beyond even the best manager's control take over once the chance has passed to act on the moment of truth. Consider the following cases:

Dow Corning didn't deserve its bankruptcy or the multibillion-dollar settlements for its silicone implants because the science didn't support the alleged damages. However, there was a moment of truth when those implants, placed on a blotter, left a stain. The company could have disclosed the possible leakage, researched the risk, and warned doctors and patients. Given the congressional testimony on the implants, many women would have chosen them despite the risk. Instead, they sued because they were not warned.

Beech-Nut's crisis was a chemical concoction instead of apple juice in its baby food products. Executives there ignored an in-house chemist who tried to tell them they were selling adulterated products.

Kidder-Peabody fell despite warnings from employees about a glitch in its accounting system that was reporting bond swaps as sales and income.

In 2004, Merck removed one of the world's best-selling painkillers from the market after a study showed Vioxx caused an increased risk of serious cardiovascular events, such as stroke and heart attack. Producing Vioxx wasn't Merck's problem; its problem was that, according to an editorial in the *New England Journal of Medicine,* Merck was alleged to have withheld data and information that would affect conclusions drawn in an earlier study that appeared in the *New England Journal of Medicine* in

2000. Now, Merck faces thousands of lawsuits, and studies continue to deliver bad news about the drug. In fact, in one case, a jury awarded $51 million to a retired FBI agent who suffered a heart attack after taking the drug.

As a now-infamous memo reveals, Ford and Firestone did not feel obligated to reveal to the U.S. Transportation Department that certain tires were being recalled in overseas markets. The companies should have realized that it was not a question of whether the recall would be reported but by whom.

These cases all have several things in common. First, their moments of truth came and went while the companies took no action. Second, employees who raised the issue were ignored or, in some cases, fired. Third, there were lawyers along for the ride, as they were with Ford and Firestone.

Never rely on a lawyer in these moments of truth. Lawyers are legal experts but are not particularly good at controlling damage. They shouldn't make business decisions; managers should. More importantly, moments of truth require managers with strong ethics who will do more than the law requires.

Do businesses ever face a moment of truth wisely? One example is Foxy brand lettuce, which in 2006, shortly after E. coli–contaminated spinach was linked to three deaths, recalled all its lettuce after it discovered irrigation water on its farms tested positive for the bacterium. Although the lettuce was not found to be carrying any bacterium, it did everything possible to protect the public and, as a result, has very loyal customers.

Source: Kevin Kingsbury, "Corporate News: Merck Settles Claims Over Vioxx Ads," *Wall Street Journal*, May 21, 2008, p. B3; "Manager's Journal: Ford-Firestone Lesson: Heed the Moment of Truth," *Wall Street Journal*, September 11, 2000, p. A44; "Foxy's lettuce recalled after E. coli scare," *USA Today*, October 9, 2006, p. A10; and Joe Queenan, "Juice Men—Ethics and the Beech-Nut Sentences," *Barron's*, June 20, 1988, p. 14.

# Chapter Summaries

 **Discuss the difficulty encountered in finding profitable projects in competitive markets and the importance of the search.** (pgs. 305–306)

**SUMMARY:** The process of capital budgeting involves decision making with respect to investments in fixed assets. Before a profitable project can be adopted, it must be identified or found. Unfortunately, coming up with ideas for new products, for ways to improve existing products, or for ways to make existing products more profitable is extremely difficult. In general, the best source of ideas for new, potentially profitable products is within the firm.

**KEY TERM**

**Capital budgeting, page 305**   The process of decision making with respect to investments made in fixed assets—that is, should a proposed project be accepted or rejected.

**Determine whether a new project should be accepted or rejected using the payback period, the net present value, the profitability index, and the internal rate of return.** (pgs. 307–325)

**SUMMARY:** We examine four commonly used criteria for determining the acceptance or rejection of capital-budgeting proposals. The first method, the payback period, does not incorporate the time value of money into its calculations. However, the net present value, profitability index, and internal rate of return methods do account for the time value of money. These methods are summarized in Table 10-10.

---

### TABLE 10-10  Capital-Budgeting Methods: A Summary

1A. Payback period = number of years required to recapture the initial investment from the free cash flows

    Accept if payback period ≤ maximum acceptable payback period
    Reject if payback period > maximum acceptable payback period

| **Advantages:** | **Disadvantages:** |
|---|---|
| • Uses free cash flows. | • Ignores the time value of money. |
| • Is easy to calculate and understand. | • Ignores cash flows occurring after the payback period. |
| • Benefits the capital-constrained firm. | • Selection of the maximum acceptable payback period is |
| • May be used as rough screening device. |   arbitrary. |

1B. Discounted payback period = the number of years needed to recover the initial cash outlay from the *discounted free cash flows*

    Accept if discounted payback ≤ maximum acceptable discounted payback period
    Reject if discounted payback > maximum acceptable discounted payback period

| **Advantages:** | **Disadvantages:** |
|---|---|
| • Uses cash flows. | • Ignores cash flows occurring after the payback period. |
| • Is easy to calculate and understand. | • Selection of the maximum acceptable discounted payback |
| • Considers time value of money. |   period is arbitrary. |

2. Net present value = present value of the future free cash flows less the investment's initial outlay
    *NPV* = present value of all the future annual free cash flows − the initial cash outlay

    Accept if *NPV* ≥ 0.0
    Reject if *NPV* < 0.0

| **Advantages:** | **Disadvantage:** |
|---|---|
| • Uses free cash flows. | • Requires detailed long-term forecasts of a project's cash flows. |
| • Recognizes the time value of money. | |
| • Is consistent with the firm's goal of shareholder wealth maximization. | |

3. Profitability index = the ratio of the present value of the future free cash flows to the initial outlay.

    Accept if *PI* ≥ 1.0
    Reject if *PI* < 1.0

| **Advantages:** | **Disadvantage:** |
|---|---|
| • Uses free cash flows. | • Requires detailed long-term forecasts of a project's cash flows. |
| • Recognizes the time value of money. | |
| • Is consistent with the firm's goal of shareholder wealth maximization. | |

4A. Internal rate of return = the discount rate that equates the present value of the project's future free cash flows with the project's initial outlay
    *IRR* = the rate of return that equates the present value of the project's free cash flows with the initial outlay

    Accept if *IRR* ≥ required rate of return
    Reject if *IRR* < required rate of return

| **Advantages:** | **Disadvantages:** |
|---|---|
| • Uses free cash flows. | • Requires detailed long-term forecasts of a project's cash flows. |
| • Recognizes the time value of money. | • Possibility of multiple *IRR*s. |
| • Is, in general, consistent with the firm's goal of shareholder wealth maximization. | • Assumes cash flows over the life of the project can be reinvested at the *IRR*. |

*(Continued)*

**TABLE 10-10** (*Continued*)

4B. Modified internal rate of return = the discount rate that equates the present value of the cash outflows with the terminal value of the cash inflows

Accept if *MIRR* ≥ required rate of return

Reject if *MIRR* < required rate of return

**Advantages:**

- Uses free cash flows.
- Recognizes the time value of money.
- Is consistent with the firm's goal of shareholder wealth maximization.
- Allows reinvestment rate to be directly specified.

**Disadvantage:**

- Requires detailed long-term cash-flow forecasts.

## KEY TERMS

**Payback period, page 307** The number of years it takes to recapture a project's initial outlay.

**Discounted payback period, page 308** The number of years it takes to recapture a project's initial outlay from the discounted free cash flows.

**Net present value (*NPV*), page 310** The present value of an investment's annual free cash flows less the investment's initial outlay.

**Profitability Index (*PI*) or benefit–cost ratio, page 313** The ratio of the present value of an investment's future free cash flows to the investment's initial outlay.

**Internal rate of return (*IRR*), page 316** The rate of return that the project earns. For computational purposes, the internal rate of return is defined as the discount rate that equates the present value of the project's free cash flows with the project's initial cash outlay.

**Net present value profile, page 319** A graph showing how a project's *NPV* changes as the discount rate changes.

**Modified internal rate of return (*MIRR*), page 321** The discount rate that equates the present value of the project's future free cash flows with the terminal value of the cash inflows.

## KEY EQUATIONS

$$\text{Payback period} = \begin{pmatrix} \text{number of years just} \\ \text{prior to complete} \\ \text{payback} \end{pmatrix} + \frac{\text{unpaid-back amount}}{\text{free cash flow in year}} \\ \text{at beginning of year}}{\text{free cash flow in year}} \\ \text{payback is completed}}$$

$$\text{Discounted payback period} = \begin{pmatrix} \text{number of years just prior} \\ \text{to complete payback} \\ \text{from discounted free} \\ \text{cash flows} \end{pmatrix} + \frac{\text{unpaid-back amount at}}{\text{the beginning}} \\ \text{of year}}{\text{discounted free cash}} \\ \text{flow in year}}{\text{payback is completed}}$$

$$\text{Net present value} = \frac{FCF_1}{(1 + k)^1} + \frac{FCF_2}{(1 + k)^2} + \cdots + \frac{FCF_n}{(1 + k)^n} - IO$$

$$\text{Profitability index } (PI) \text{ or benefit–cost ratio} = \frac{\dfrac{FCF_1}{(1 + k)^1} + \dfrac{FCF_2}{(1 + k)^2} + \cdots + \dfrac{FCF_n}{(1 + k)^n}}{IO}$$

$$\text{Internal rate of return } (IRR): IO = \frac{FCF_1}{(1 + IRR)^1} + \frac{FCF_2}{(1 + IRR)^2} + \cdots + \frac{FCF_n}{(1 + IRR)^n}$$

$$\text{Modified internal rate of return } (MIRR): PV_{\text{outflows}} = \frac{TV_{\text{inflows}}}{(1 + MIRR)^n}$$

**Explain how the capital-budgeting decision process changes when a dollar limit is placed on the capital budget.** (pgs. 325–326)

**SUMMARY:** There are several complications related to the capital-budgeting process. First, we examined capital rationing and the problems it can create by imposing a limit on the dollar size of the capital budget. Although capital rationing does not, in general, maximize shareholders' wealth, it does exist. The goal of maximizing shareholders' wealth remains, but it is now subject to a budget constraint.

**KEY TERM**

**Capital rationing, page 325** Placing a limit on the dollar size of the capital budget.

**Discuss the problems encountered when deciding among mutually exclusive projects.** (pgs. 326–331)

**SUMMARY:** There are a number of problems associated with evaluating mutually exclusive projects. Mutually exclusive projects occur when different investments, if undertaken, would serve the same purpose. In general, to deal with mutually exclusive projects, we rank them by means of the discounted cash-flow criteria and select the project with the highest ranking. Conflicting rankings can arise because of the projects' size disparities, time disparities, and unequal lives. The incomparability of projects with different life spans is not simply a result of the different life spans; rather, it arises because future profitable investment proposals will be rejected without being included in the initial analysis. Replacement chains and equivalent annual annuities can solve this problem.

A perpetuity is an annuity that continues forever; that is, every year following its establishment the investment pays the same dollar amount. An example of a perpetuity is preferred stock, which pays a constant dollar dividend infinitely. Determining the present value of a perpetuity is delightfully simple. We merely need to divide the constant flow by the discount rate.

**KEY TERMS**

**Mutually exclusive projects, page 326** Projects that, if undertaken, would serve the same purpose. Thus, accepting one will necessarily mean rejecting the others.

**Equivalent annual annuity (*EAA*), page 330** An annuity cash flow that yields the same present value as the project's *NPV*.

# Review Questions

*All Review Questions are available in* MyFinanceLab.

**10-1.** Why is capital budgeting such an important process? Why are capital-budgeting errors so costly?

**10-2.** What are the disadvantages of using the payback period as a capital-budgeting technique? What are its advantages? Why is it so frequently used?

**10-3.** In some countries, the expropriation (seizure) of foreign investments is a common practice. If you were considering an investment in one of those countries, would the use of the payback period criterion seem more reasonable than it otherwise might? Why or why not?

**10-4.** Briefly compare and contrast the *NPV*, *PI*, and *IRR* criteria. What are the advantages and disadvantages of using each of these methods?

**10-5.** What are mutually exclusive projects? Why might the existence of mutually exclusive projects cause problems in the implementation of the discounted cash-flow capital-budgeting criteria?

**10-6.** What are common reasons for capital rationing? Is capital rationing rational?

**10-7.** How should managers compare two mutually exclusive projects of unequal size? Should the approach change if capital rationing is a factor?

**10-8.** What causes the time-disparity ranking problem? What reinvestment rate assumptions are associated with the *NPV* and *IRR* capital-budgeting criteria?

**10-9.** When might two mutually exclusive projects having unequal lives be incomparable? How should managers deal with this problem?

# Study Problems

*All Study Problems are available in MyFinanceLab.*

**10-1.** (*IRR calculation*) Determine the *IRR* on the following projects:

    a. An initial outlay of $10,000 resulting in a single free cash flow of $17,182 after 8 years

    b. An initial outlay of $10,000 resulting in a single free cash flow of $48,077 after 10 years

    c. An initial outlay of $10,000 resulting in a single free cash flow of $114,943 after 20 years

    d. An initial outlay of $10,000 resulting in a single free cash flow of $13,680 after 3 years

**10-2.** (*IRR calculation*) Determine the *IRR* on the following projects:

    a. An initial outlay of $10,000 resulting in a free cash flow of $1,993 at the end of each year for the next 10 years

    b. An initial outlay of $10,000 resulting in a free cash flow of $2,054 at the end of each year for the next 20 years

    c. An initial outlay of $10,000 resulting in a free cash flow of $1,193 at the end of each year for the next 12 years

    d. An initial outlay of $10,000 resulting in a free cash flow of $2,843 at the end of each year for the next 5 years

**10-3.** (*IRR calculation*) Determine to the nearest percent the *IRR* on the following projects:

    a. An initial outlay of $10,000 resulting in a free cash flow of $2,000 at the end of year 1, $5,000 at the end of year 2, and $8,000 at the end of year 3

    b. An initial outlay of $10,000 resulting in a free cash flow of $8,000 at the end of year 1, $5,000 at the end of year 2, and $2,000 at the end of year 3

    c. An initial outlay of $10,000 resulting in a free cash flow of $2,000 at the end of years 1 through 5 and $5,000 at the end of year 6

**10-4.** (*NPV, PI, and IRR calculations*) Fijisawa Inc. is considering a major expansion of its product line and has estimated the following cash flows associated with such an expansion. The initial outlay would be $1,950,000, and the project would generate incremental free cash flows of $450,000 per year for 6 years. The appropriate required rate of return is 9 percent.

    a. Calculate the *NPV*.

    b. Calculate the *PI*.

    c. Calculate the *IRR*.

    d. Should this project be accepted?

**10-5.** (*Payback period, NPV, PI, and IRR calculations*) You are considering a project with an initial cash outlay of $80,000 and expected free cash flows of $20,000 at the end of each year for 6 years. The required rate of return for this project is 10 percent.

    a. What is the project's payback period?

    b. What is the project's *NPV*?

    c. What is the project's *PI*?

    d. What is the project's *IRR*?

**10-6.** (*NPV, PI, and IRR calculations*) You are considering two independent projects, project A and project B. The initial cash outlay associated with project A is $50,000, and the initial cash outlay associated with project B is $70,000. The required rate of return on both projects is 12 percent. The expected annual free cash inflows from each project are as follows:

|  | PROJECT A | PROJECT B |
| --- | --- | --- |
| Initial outlay | −$50,000 | −$70,000 |
| Inflow year 1 | 12,000 | 13,000 |
| Inflow year 2 | 12,000 | 13,000 |
| Inflow year 3 | 12,000 | 13,000 |
| Inflow year 4 | 12,000 | 13,000 |
| Inflow year 5 | 12,000 | 13,000 |
| Inflow year 6 | 12,000 | 13,000 |

Calculate the *NPV*, *PI*, and *IRR* for each project and indicate if the project should be accepted.

**10-7.** (*Payback period calculations*) You are considering three independent projects, project A, project B, and project C. Given the following cash-flow information, calculate the payback period for each.

|  | PROJECT A | PROJECT B | PROJECT C |
|---|---|---|---|
| Initial outlay | −$1,000 | −$10,000 | −$5,000 |
| Inflow year 1 | 600 | 5,000 | 1,000 |
| Inflow year 2 | 300 | 3,000 | 1,000 |
| Inflow year 3 | 200 | 3,000 | 2,000 |
| Inflow year 4 | 100 | 3,000 | 2,000 |
| Inflow year 5 | 500 | 3,000 | 2,000 |

If you require a 3-year payback before an investment can be accepted, which project(s) would be accepted?

**10-8.** (*NPV with varying required rates of return*) Gubanich Sportswear is considering building a new factory to produce aluminum baseball bats. This project would require an initial cash outlay of $5,000,000 and will generate annual free cash inflows of $1,000,000 per year for 8 years. Calculate the project's *NPV* given:

    a. A required rate of return of 9 percent
    b. A required rate of return of 11 percent
    c. A required rate of return of 13 percent
    d. A required rate of return of 15 percent

**10-9.** (*IRR calculations*) Given the following free cash flows, determine the *IRR* for the three independent projects A, B, and C.

|  | PROJECT A | PROJECT B | PROJECT C |
|---|---|---|---|
| Initial outlay | −$50,000 | −$100,000 | −$450,000 |
| Cash inflows: |  |  |  |
| Year 1 | $10,000 | $125,000 | $200,000 |
| Year 2 | 15,000 | 25,000 | 200,000 |
| Year 3 | 20,000 | 25,000 | 200,000 |
| Year 4 | 25,000 | 25,000 | — |
| Year 5 | 30,000 | 25,000 | — |

**10-10.** (*NPV with varying required rates of return*) Big Steve's, a maker of swizzle sticks, is considering the purchase of a new plastic stamping machine. This investment requires an initial outlay of $100,000 and will generate free cash inflows of $18,000 per year for 10 years.

    a. If the required rate of return is 10 percent, what is the project's *NPV*?
    b. If the required rate of return is 15 percent, what is the project's *NPV*?
    c. Would the project be accepted under part (a) or (b)?
    d. What is the project's *IRR*?

**10-11.** (*NPV with different required rates of return*) Mooby's is considering building a new theme park. After estimating the future cash flows, but before the project could be evaluated, the economy picked up and with that surge in the economy interest rates rose. That rise in interest rates was reflected in the required rate of return Mooby's used to evaluate new products. As a result, the required rate of return for the new theme park jumped from 9.5 percent to 11.00 percent. If the initial outlay for the park is expected to be $250 million and the project is expected to return free cash flows of $50 million in years 1 through 5 and $75 million in years 6 and 7, what is the project's *NPV* using the new required rate of return? How much did the project's *NPV* change as a result of the rise in interest rates?

**10-12.** (*IRR with uneven cash flows*) The Tiffin Barker Corporation is considering introducing a new currency verifier that has the ability to identify counterfeit dollar bills. The required rate of return on this project is 12 percent. What is the *IRR* on this project if it is expected to produce the following cash flows?

| | |
|---|---|
| Initial outlay | −$927,917 |
| *FCF* in year 1 | 200,000 |
| *FCF* in year 2 | 300,000 |
| *FCF* in year 3 | 300,000 |
| *FCF* in year 4 | 200,000 |
| *FCF* in year 5 | 200,000 |
| *FCF* in year 6 | 160,000 |

**10-13.** (*NPV calculation*) Calculate the *NPV* given the following cash flows if the appropriate required rate of return is 10%.

| YEAR | CASH FLOWS |
|---|---|
| 0 | −$60,000 |
| 1 | 20,000 |
| 2 | 20,000 |
| 3 | 10,000 |
| 4 | 10,000 |
| 5 | 30,000 |
| 6 | 30,000 |

Should the project be accepted?

**10-14.** (*NPV calculation*) Calculate the *NPV* given the following cash flows if the appropriate required rate of return is 10%.

| YEAR | CASH FLOWS |
|---|---|
| 0 | −$70,000 |
| 1 | 30,000 |
| 2 | 30,000 |
| 3 | 30,000 |
| 4 | −30,000 |
| 5 | 30,000 |
| 6 | 30,000 |

Should the project be accepted?

**10-15.** (*MIRR calculation*) Calculate the *MIRR* given the following cash flows if the appropriate required rate of return is 10% (use this as the reinvestment rate).

| YEAR | CASH FLOWS |
|---|---|
| 0 | −$50,000 |
| 1 | 25,000 |
| 2 | 25,000 |
| 3 | 25,000 |
| 4 | −25,000 |
| 5 | 25,000 |
| 6 | 25,000 |

Should the project be accepted?

**10-16.** (*PI calculation*) Calculate the *PI* given the following cash flows if the appropriate required rate of return is 10%.

| YEAR | CASH FLOWS |
|------|------------|
| 0 | −$55,000 |
| 1 | 10,000 |
| 2 | 10,000 |
| 3 | 10,000 |
| 4 | 10,000 |
| 5 | 10,000 |
| 6 | 10,000 |

Should the project be accepted? Without calculating the *NPV*, do you think it would be positive or negative? Why?

**10-17.** (*Discounted payback period*) Gio's Restaurants is considering a project with the following expected cash flows:

| YEAR | PROJECT CASH FLOW |
|------|-------------------|
| 0 | −$150 million |
| 1 | 90 million |
| 2 | 70 million |
| 3 | 90 million |
| 4 | 100 million |

If the project's appropriate discount is 12 percent, what is the project's discounted payback?

**10-18.** (*Discounted payback period*) You are considering a project with the following cash flows:

| YEAR | PROJECT CASH FLOW |
|------|-------------------|
| 0 | −$50,000 |
| 1 | 20,000 |
| 2 | 20,000 |
| 3 | 20,000 |
| 4 | 20,000 |

If the appropriate discount rate is 10 percent, what is the project's discounted payback period?

**10-19.** (*Discounted payback period*) Assuming an appropriate discount rate of 11 percent, what is the discounted payback period on a project with an initial outlay of $100,000 and the following cash flows?

Year 1 = $30,000

Year 2 = $35,000

Year 3 = $25,000

Year 4 = $25,000

Year 5 = $30,000

Year 5 = $20,000

**10-20.** (*IRR*) Jella Cosmetics is considering a project that costs $800,000, and is expected to last for 10 years and produce future cash flows of $175,000 per year. If the appropriate discount rate for this project is 12 percent, what is the project's *IRR*?

**10-21.** (*IRR*) Your investment advisor has offered you an investment that will provide you with one cash flow of $10,000 at the end of 20 years if you pay premiums of $200 per year at the end of each year for 20 years. Find the internal rate of return on this investment.

**10-22.** (*IRR, payback, and calculating a missing cash flow*) Mode Publishing is considering a new printing facility that will involve a large initial outlay and then result in a series of positive cash flows for 4 years. The estimated cash flows associated with this project are:

| YEAR | PROJECT CASH FLOW |
|---|---|
| 0 (initial outlay) | ? |
| 1 | $800 million |
| 2 | 400 million |
| 3 | 300 million |
| 4 | 500 million |

If you know that the project has a regular payback of 2.5 years, what is the project's internal rate of return?

**10-23.** (*Discounted payback period*) Sheinhardt Wig Company is considering a project that has the following cash flows:

| YEAR | PROJECT CASH FLOW |
|---|---|
| 0 | −$100,000 |
| 1 | 20,000 |
| 2 | 60,000 |
| 3 | 70,000 |
| 4 | 50,000 |
| 5 | 40,000 |

If the appropriate discount rate is 10 percent, what is the project's discounted payback?

**10-24.** (*IRR of uneven cash-flow stream*) Microwave Oven Programming, Inc. is considering the construction of a new plant. The plant will have an initial cash outlay of $7 million, and will produce cash flows of $3 million at the end of year 1, $4 million at the end of year 2, and $2 million at the end of years 3 through 5. What is the internal rate of return on this new plant?

**10-25.** (*MIRR*) Dunder Mifflin Paper Company is considering purchasing a new stamping machine that costs $400,000. This new machine will produce cash inflows of $150,000 each year at the end of years 1 through 5, then at the end of year 7 there will be a cash *out*flow of $200,000. The company has a weighted average cost of capital of 12 percent (use this as the reinvestment rate). What is the *MIRR* of the investment?

**10-26.** (*MIRR calculation*) Artie's Wrestling Stuff is considering building a new plant. This plant would require an initial cash outlay of $8 million and will generate annual free cash inflows of $2 million per year for 8 years. Calculate the project's *MIRR* given:

    a. A required rate of return of 10 percent
    b. A required rate of return of 12 percent
    c. A required rate of return of 14 percent

**10-27.** (*Capital rationing*) The Cowboy Hat Company of Stillwater, Oklahoma, is considering seven capital investment proposals for which the total funds available are limited to a maximum of $12 million. The projects are independent and have the following costs and profitability indexes associated with them:

| PROJECT | COST | PROFITABILITY INDEX |
|---|---|---|
| A | $4,000,000 | 1.18 |
| B | 3,000,000 | 1.08 |
| C | 5,000,000 | 1.33 |
| D | 6,000,000 | 1.31 |
| E | 4,000,000 | 1.19 |
| F | 6,000,000 | 1.20 |
| G | 4,000,000 | 1.18 |

a.  Under strict capital rationing, which projects should be selected?
b.  What problems are there with capital rationing?

**10-28.** (*Mutually exclusive projects*) Nanotech, Inc. currently has a production electronics facility and it is cost-prohibitive to expand this production facility. Nanotech is deciding between the following four contracts:

|   | CONTRACT'S *NPV* | USE OF PRODUCTION FACILITY |
|---|---|---|
| A | $100 million | 100% |
| B | $ 90 million | 80% |
| C | $ 60 million | 60% |
| D | $ 50 million | 40% |

Which project or projects should they accept?

**10-29.** (*Mutually exclusive projects and NPV*) You have been assigned the task of evaluating two mutually exclusive projects with the following projected cash flows:

| YEAR | PROJECT A CASH FLOW | PROJECT B CASH FLOW |
|---|---|---|
| 0 | −$100,000 | −$100,000 |
| 1 | 33,000 | 0 |
| 2 | 33,000 | 0 |
| 3 | 33,000 | 0 |
| 4 | 33,000 | 0 |
| 5 | 33,000 | 220,000 |

If the appropriate discount rate on these projects is 10 percent, which would be chosen and why?

**10-30.** (*Size-disparity problem*) The D. Dorner Farms Corporation is considering purchasing one of two fertilizer-herbicides for the upcoming year. The more expensive of the two is better and will produce a higher yield. Assume these projects are mutually exclusive and that the required rate of return is 10 percent. Given the following free cash flows:

|   | PROJECT A | PROJECT B |
|---|---|---|
| Initial outlay | −$500 | −$5,000 |
| Inflow year 1 | 700 | 6,000 |

a.  Calculate the *NPV* of each project.
b.  Calculate the *PI* of each project.
c.  Calculate the *IRR* of each project.
d.  If there is no capital-rationing constraint, which project should be selected? If there is a capital-rationing constraint, how should the decision be made?

**10-31.** (*Time-disparity problem*) The State Spartan Corporation is considering two mutually exclusive projects. The free cash flows associated with those projects are as follows:

|   | PROJECT A | PROJECT B |
|---|---|---|
| Initial outlay | −$50,000 | −$ 50,000 |
| Inflow year 1 | 15,625 | 0 |
| Inflow year 2 | 15,625 | 0 |
| Inflow year 3 | 15,625 | 0 |
| Inflow year 4 | 15,625 | 0 |
| Inflow year 5 | 15,625 | 100,000 |

The required rate of return on these projects is 10 percent.

    a. What is each project's payback period?
    b. What is each project's *NPV*?
    c. What is each project's *IRR*?
    d. What has caused the ranking conflict?
    e. Which project should be accepted? Why?

**10-32.** (*Replacement chains*) Destination Hotels currently owns an older hotel on the best beach-front property on Hilton Head Island, and it is considering either remodeling the hotel or tearing it down and building a new convention hotel, but because they both would occupy the same physical location, the company can only do one—that is, these are mutually exclusive projects. Both these projects have the same initial outlay of $1,000,000. The first project, since it is a remodel of an existing hotel, has an expected life of 8 years and will provide free cash flows of $250,000 at the end of each year for all 8 years. In addition, this project can be repeated at the end of 8 years at the same cost and with the same set of future cash flows. The proposed new convention hotel has an expected life of 16 years and will produce cash flows of $175,000 per year. The required rate of return on both of these projects is 10 percent. Calculate the *NPV* using replacement chains to compare these two projects.

**10-33.** (*Equivalent annual annuity*) Rib & Wings-R-Us is considering the purchase of a new smoker oven for cooking barbecue, ribs, and wings. It is looking at two different ovens. The first is a relatively standard smoker and would cost $50,000, last for 8 years, and produce annual cash flows of $16,000 per year. The alternative is the deluxe, award-winning Smoke-alator, which costs $78,000 and, because of its patented humidity control, produces the "moistest, tastiest barbecue in the world." The Smoke-alator would last for 11 years and produce cash flows of $23,000 per year. Assuming a 10 percent required rate of return on both projects, compute their equivalent annual annuity (*EAA*).

# Mini Case

*This Mini Case is available in* MyFinanceLab.

Your first assignment in your new position as assistant financial analyst at Caledonia Products is to evaluate two new capital-budgeting proposals. Because this is your first assignment, you have been asked not only to provide a recommendation but also to respond to a number of questions aimed at assessing your understanding of the capital-budgeting process. This is a standard procedure for all new financial analysts at Caledonia, and it will serve to determine whether you are moved directly into the capital-budgeting analysis department or are provided with remedial training. The memorandum you received outlining your assignment follows:

> To: The New Financial Analysts
> From: Mr. V. Morrison, CEO, Caledonia Products
> Re: Capital-Budgeting Analysis

Provide an evaluation of two proposed projects, both with 5-year expected lives and identical initial outlays of $110,000. Both of these projects involve additions to Caledonia's highly successful Avalon product line, and as a result, the required rate of return on both projects has been established at 12 percent. The expected free cash flows from each project are as follows:

|  | PROJECT A | PROJECT B |
| --- | --- | --- |
| Initial outlay | −$110,000 | −$110,000 |
| Inflow year 1 | 20,000 | 40,000 |
| Inflow year 2 | 30,000 | 40,000 |
| Inflow year 3 | 40,000 | 40,000 |
| Inflow year 4 | 50,000 | 40,000 |
| Inflow year 5 | 70,000 | 40,000 |

In evaluating these projects, please respond to the following questions:

a. Why is the capital-budgeting process so important?
b. Why is it difficult to find exceptionally profitable projects?
c. What is the payback period on each project? If Caledonia imposes a 3-year maximum acceptable payback period, which of these projects should be accepted?
d. What are the criticisms of the payback period?
e. Determine the *NPV* for each of these projects. Should they be accepted?
f. Describe the logic behind the *NPV*.
g. Determine the *PI* for each of these projects. Should they be accepted?
h. Would you expect the *NPV* and *PI* methods to give consistent accept/reject decisions? Why or why not?
i. What would happen to the *NPV* and *PI* for each project if the required rate of return increased? If the required rate of return decreased?
j. Determine the *IRR* for each project. Should they be accepted?
k. How does a change in the required rate of return affect the project's internal rate of return?
l. What reinvestment rate assumptions are implicitly made by the *NPV* and *IRR* methods? Which one is better?

You have also been asked for your views on three unrelated sets of projects. Each set of projects involves two mutually exclusive projects. These projects follow.

m. Caledonia is considering two investments with 1-year lives. The more expensive of the two is the better and will produce more savings. Assume these projects are mutually exclusive and that the required rate of return is 10 percent. Given the following free cash flows:

|  | PROJECT A | PROJECT B |
| --- | --- | --- |
| Initial outlay | −$195,000 | −$1,200,000 |
| Inflow year 1 | 240,000 | 1,650,000 |

1. Calculate the *NPV* for each project.
2. Calculate the *PI* for each project.
3. Calculate the *IRR* for each project.
4. If there is no capital-rationing constraint, which project should be selected? If there is a capital-rationing constraint, how should the decision be made?

n. Caledonia is considering two additional mutually exclusive projects. The free cash flows associated with these projects are as follows:

|  | PROJECT A | PROJECT B |
| --- | --- | --- |
| Initial outlay | −$100,000 | −$100,000 |
| Inflow year 1 | 32,000 | 0 |
| Inflow year 2 | 32,000 | 0 |
| Inflow year 3 | 32,000 | 0 |
| Inflow year 4 | 32,000 | 0 |
| Inflow year 5 | 32,000 | 200,000 |

The required rate of return on these projects is 11 percent.

1. What is each project's payback period?
2. What is each project's *NPV*?
3. What is each project's *IRR*?
4. What has caused the ranking conflict?
5. Which project should be accepted? Why?

# Cash Flows and Other Topics in Capital Budgeting

## Learning Objectives

| | | |
|---|---|---|
| **1** | **Identify** guidelines by which we measure cash flows. | **Guidelines for Capital Budgeting** |
| **2** | **Explain** how a project's benefits and costs—that is, its free cash flows—are calculated. | **Calculating a Project's Free Cash Flows** |
| **3** | **Explain** the importance of options, or flexibility, in capital budgeting. | **Options in Capital Budgeting** |
| **4** | **Understand, measure, and adjust** for project risk. | **Risk and the investment Decisions** |

In 2001, when Toyota introduced the first-generation model of its gas-electric hybrid car, the Prius, it seemed more like a little science experiment than real competition for the auto industry. In fact, in 2004, General Motors vice chairman Bob Lutz dismissed hybrids as "an interesting curiosity." But that's all changed. As gas prices climbed to around $4 a gallon in 2008, suddenly the gas-electric hybrid car seemed to be the way to go. In fact, from its humble beginnings in 2001 through April 2012 Toyota sold a total of 4 million hybrids and today is selling them at a pace of over 1 million per year.

How did Toyota gain leadership in the gas-electric hybrid car market? It started with its capital-budgeting decision to enter the gas-electric hybrid car market with the Prius and a very large investment—in excess of $1 billion. This action vaulted Toyota into the lead in the hybrid car market and could leave Toyota in great shape for the future if ExxonMobil is right in its forecast that by 2040, hybrids and other advanced vehicles will account for nearly 50 percent of light-duty vehicles on the road, compared to only about 1 percent today.

Still, according to many analysts, the Prius is not yet a big money maker for Toyota. In fact, when the Prius first came out, Toyota had it priced so that it was losing about $3,000 on each car it sold. For the Prius to be profitable there needed to be enough in the way of sales to cover its fixed costs, and that has finally happened as sales on the Prius have soared.

Toyota's initial decision to introduce the Prius and enter the hybrid car market was a difficult one. Would it simply move Toyota customers from one Toyota car to another, or would it bring new customers to Toyota? Was this a chance to gain a foothold on the new technology of the future, or were hybrid cars simply a fad?

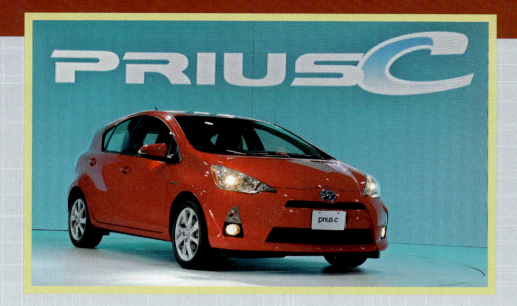

How did Toyota make the decision to go ahead with the Prius and the flexible-fuel car? It used the basic techniques described in the previous chapter; but before it could apply those techniques, Toyota had to come up with the cash-flow forecasts and adjust for the risk associated with the project. That's what we'll be looking at in this chapter.

# Guidelines for Capital Budgeting

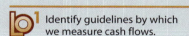

To evaluate investment proposals, we must first set guidelines by which we measure the value of each proposal. In effect, we are deciding what is and what isn't a relevant cash flow.

## Use Free Cash Flows Rather Than Accounting Profits

We use free cash flows, not accounting profits, as our measurement. The firm receives and is able to reinvest free cash flows, whereas accounting profits are shown when they are earned rather than when the money is actually in hand. Unfortunately, a firm's accounting profits and free cash flows may not be timed to occur together. For example, capital expenses, such as vehicles and plant and equipment, are depreciated over several years, with their annual depreciation subtracted from profits. Free cash flows correctly reflect the timing of benefits and costs—that is, when the money is received, when it can be reinvested, and when it must be paid out.

## Think Incrementally

Unfortunately, calculating free cash flows from a project may not be enough. Decision makers must ask, *What new free cash flows will the company as a whole receive if the company takes on a given project?* What if the company does not take on the project? Interestingly, we may find that not all cash flows a firm expects from an investment proposal are incremental in nature. When measuring free cash flows, however, the trick is to think incrementally. In doing so, we will see that only incremental after-tax free cash flows matter. As such, our guiding rule in deciding if a free cash flow is incremental is to look at the company with, versus without, the new project. As you will see in the upcoming sections, this may be easier said than done.

## Beware of Cash Flows Diverted from Existing Products

Assume for a moment that we are managers of a firm considering a new product line that might compete with one of our existing products and possibly reduce its sales. In determining the free cash flows associated with the proposed project, we should consider only the incremental sales brought to the company as a whole. New-product sales achieved at the cost

**LO 1** Identify guidelines by which we measure cash flows.

**REMEMBER YOUR PRINCIPLES**

**Principle** If we are to make intelligent capital-budgeting decisions, we must accurately measure the timing of a project's benefits and costs, that is, when we receive money and when it leaves our hands. **Principle 1: Cash Flow Is What Matters** speaks directly to this. Remember, it is cash inflows that can be reinvested and cash outflows that involve paying out money.

of losing sales of other products in our line are not considered a benefit. For example, when Quaker Oats introduced Cap'n Crunch's Cozmic Crunch, the product competed directly with the company's Cap'n Crunch and Crunch Berries cereals. (In fact, Cozmic Crunch was almost identical to Crunch Berries, with the shapes changed to stars and moons, along with a packet of orange space dust that turns milk green.) Quaker meant to target the market niche held by Post Fruity Pebbles, but there was no question that sales recorded by Cozmic Crunch bit into—literally cannibalized—Quaker's existing product line.

Remember that we are interested only in the sales dollars to the firm if the project is accepted, as opposed to what the sales dollars would be if the project were rejected. Just moving sales from one product line to a new product line does not bring anything new into the company. But if sales are captured from competitors or if sales that would have been lost to new competing products are retained, then these are relevant incremental free cash flows.

## Look for Incidental or Synergistic Effects

Although in some cases a new project may take sales away from a firm's current projects, in other cases a new effort might actually bring new sales to the existing line.

In April 2010, Apple introduced the first-generation iPad. To say the least, the iPad has been extremely successful with total sales since it was introduced easily topping the 100 million mark by the end of 2012. Without question, Apple has made a lot of money on sales of the iPad, but introducing the iPad has also resulted in increased sales of other Apple products. Impressed by the simplicity and elegance of the iPad, many PC users began making the switch to other Apple products. As a result, the introduction of the iPad not only generated iPad sales but also led to increased sales of Macs and iPhones as many new customers switched their user systems to exclusively Apple products. In addition, the ease of use of the iPad also convinced many corporate customers to give Apple products a second look. This is called a *synergistic* effect—the cash flow that comes from the sale of any Apple product that would not have occurred if a customer had not purchased an iPad. Synergistic effects are quite common in the business world.

If you owned a convenience store and were considering adding gas pumps, would you evaluate the project looking only at cash flows from the sale of gas? No. You would look at any new sales to any part of your business that the new gas pumps brought in. No doubt the additional traffic that the gas pumps bring in would increase your convenience-store sales. As such, these cash flows would be considered in evaluating whether or not to install the gas pumps. In effect, you should look at any change in cash flow to the company as a whole that results from the project being evaluated.

## Work in Working-Capital Requirements

Many times a new project involves an additional investment in working capital. This may take the form of new inventory to stock a sales outlet, an additional investment in accounts receivable resulting from additional credit sales, or an increased investment in cash to operate cash registers, and more. Working-capital requirements are considered a free cash flow even though they do not leave the company. Generally, working-capital requirements are tied up over the life of the project. When the project terminates, there is usually an offsetting cash inflow as the working capital is recovered, although this offset is not perfect because of the time value of money.

## Consider Incremental Expenses

Just as cash inflows from a new project are measured on an incremental basis, expenses, or cash outflows, should also be measured on an incremental basis. For example, if introducing a new product line necessitates training the sales staff, the after-tax cash flow associated with the training program must be considered a cash outflow and charged against the project. Likewise, if accepting a new project dictates that a production facility be reengineered, the cash flows associated with that capital investment should be charged against the project, and they will then be depreciated over the life of the project. Again, any incremental after-tax cash flow affecting the company as a whole is a relevant cash flow, whether it is flowing in or flowing out.

## Remember That Sunk Costs Are Not Incremental Cash Flows

Only cash flows that are affected by the decision making at the moment are relevant in capital budgeting. The manager asks two questions: (1) Will this cash flow occur if the project is accepted? (2) Will this cash flow occur if the project is rejected? Yes to the first question and no to the second equals an incremental cash flow. For example, let's assume you are considering introducing a new taste treat called Puddin' in a Shoe. You would like to do some test-marketing before production. If you are considering the decision to test-market and have not yet done so, the costs associated with the test-marketing are relevant cash flows. Conversely, if you have already test-marketed, the cash flows involved in test-marketing are no longer relevant to the project's evaluation. It's a matter of timing. Regardless of what you might decide about future production, the cash flows allocated to the marketing test have already occurred. Cash flows that have already taken place are often referred to as "sunk costs" because they have been sunk into the project and cannot be undone. As a rule, any cash flows that are not affected by the accept/reject criterion should not be included in capital-budgeting analysis.

## Account for Opportunity Costs

Now we will focus on the cash flows that are lost because a given project consumes scarce resources that would have produced cash flows if that project had been rejected. This is the opportunity cost of doing business. For example, a product consumes valuable floor space in a production facility. Although the cash flow is not obvious, the real question remains: What else could be done with this space? The space could have been rented out, or another product could have been stored there. The key point is that opportunity-cost cash flows should reflect the net cash flows that would have been received if the project under consideration were rejected. Again, we are analyzing the cash flows to the company as a whole, with or without the project.

## Decide If Overhead Costs Are Truly Incremental Cash Flows

Although we certainly want to include any incremental cash flows resulting in changes from overhead expenses such as utilities and salaries, we also want to make sure that these are truly incremental cash flows. Many times, overhead expenses—heat, light, rent—occur whether a given project is accepted or rejected. There is often not a single, specific project to which these expenses can be allocated. Thus, the question is not whether the project benefits from the overhead costs a firm spends but whether they are incremental cash flows associated with the project and relevant to capital budgeting.

## Ignore Interest Payments and Financing Flows

To evaluate new projects and determine cash flows, we must separate the investment decision from the financing decision. Interest payments and other financing cash flows that might result from raising funds to finance a project should not be considered incremental cash flows. If accepting a project means we have to raise new funds by issuing bonds, the interest charges associated with raising funds are not a relevant cash outflow. Why? Because when we discount the incremental cash flows back to the present at the required rate of return, we are implicitly accounting for the cost of raising funds to finance the new project. In essence, the required rate of return reflects the cost of the funds needed to support the project. Managers first determine the desirability of the project and then determine how best to finance it.

## Concept Check

1. What is an incremental cash flow? What is a sunk cost? Why must you account for opportunity costs?
2. If Ford introduces a new auto line, might some of the cash flows from that new car line be diverted from existing product lines? How should you deal with this?

## FINANCE AT WORK

### UNIVERSAL STUDIOS

A major capital-budgeting decision led Universal Studios to build its Islands of Adventure theme park. The purpose of this $2.6 billion investment by Universal was to get first crack at the tourist's dollar in Orlando, Florida. Although this capital-budgeting decision may, on the surface, seem like a relatively simple one, forecasting the expected cash flows associated with the theme park was, in fact, quite complicated.

To begin with, Universal was introducing a product that competes directly with itself. The original Universal Studios park features rides such as "Back to the Future," Jimmy Neutron's Nicktoon Blast," and "Men in Black Alien Attack." Were there enough tourist dollars to support both theme parks, or would the new Islands of Adventure park simply cannibalize ticket sales from the older Universal Studios park? In addition, what would happen if Disney countered with a new park of its own?

In the case of Universal's Islands of Adventure, we could ask what would happen to attendance at the original Universal Studios park if the new park were not opened versus what the attendance would be with the new park? In addition, would tourist traffic through the Islands of Adventure lead to addi-

tional sales and viewership of Comcast offerings and NBC Universal television and movies? Why do we care? Comcast owns 51 percent of NBC Universal, and Universal Parks and Resorts is owned by NBC Universal.

From Universal's point of view, the objective may have been threefold: to increase its share of the tourist market, to keep from losing market share as tourists look for the latest in technological rides and entertainment, and to promote NBC Universal's ventures such as television and movies. However, for companies in very competitive markets, the evolution and introduction of new products may serve more to preserve market share than to expand it. That explains Universal's proposed quarter of a billion dollar expansion of Harry Potter's Wizarding World to include the Gringotts Bank. After all, when Wizarding World first opened, attendance for the entire park climbed by 52 percent, and the park's hotels, dining, shopping, and all else in the park became more profitable. The bottom line here is that with respect to estimating cash flows, things are many times more complicated than they first appear. As such, we have to dig deep to understand how a firm's free cash flows are affected by the decision at hand.

---

**2** Explain how a project's benefits and costs—that is, its free cash flows—are calculated.

# Calculating a Project's Free Cash Flows

As we have explained, in measuring cash flows, we will focus our attention on the difference in the firm's after-tax free cash flows *with* versus *without* the project—the project's *free cash flows*. The worth of our decision depends on the accuracy of our cash flow estimates. For this reason, we first examined the question of which cash flows are relevant. Now we will see that, in general, a project's free cash flows will fall into one of three categories: (1) the initial outlay, (2) the annual free cash flows over the project's life, and (3) the terminal free cash flow. Once we have taken a look at these categories, we will take on the task of measuring these free cash flows.

## What Goes into the Initial Outlay

**initial outlay** the immediate cash outflow necessary to purchase the asset and put it in operating order.

The **initial outlay** is the *immediate cash outflow necessary to purchase the asset and put it in operating order*. This amount includes (1) the cost of purchasing the asset and getting it operational, including the purchase price, shipping and installation, and any training costs for employees who will be operating the equipment, and (2) any increases in working-capital requirements. The working capital includes any increases in current assets, less any increase in accounts payable. If we are considering a new sales outlet, there might be additional cash flows associated with making a net investment in working capital in the form of increased accounts receivable, inventory, and cash necessary to operate the outlet. Although these cash flows are not included in the cost of the asset or even shown as an expense on the income statement, they must be included in our analysis. The after-tax cost of expense items incurred as a result of the new investment must also be included as cash outflows—for example, any training expenses that would not have been incurred otherwise.

Finally, if the investment decision is a replacement decision, the cash inflow associated with the selling price of the old asset, in addition to any tax effects resulting from its sale, must be included. It should be stressed that the incremental nature of the cash flow is of great importance. In many cases, if the project is not accepted, then status quo for the firm will simply not continue. Thus, we must be realistic in estimating what the cash flows to the company would be if the new project were not accepted.

In a replacement decision, the initial outlay is equal to the cost of the new asset, less the amount we received from selling the old asset. Typically, when the old asset is sold there will be a gain or loss from the sale, which means we will have to pay taxes if there is a gain from the sale or a reduction of taxes if there is a loss. Thus the initial outlay is calculated as follows:

$$\frac{\text{Initial}}{\text{outlay}} = \frac{\text{cost of}}{\text{new asset}} - \frac{\text{sales price}}{\text{of the old asset}} +/- \frac{\text{taxes recovered or paid from a loss}}{\text{or gain on the sale of the old asset}}$$

So we need to state the sale of the old asset on an after-tax basis. When it comes to the taxes, there are three possible situations that can result:

1. The old asset is sold for a price above the depreciated value. Here the difference between the old machine's selling price and its depreciated value is considered a taxable gain and is taxed at the marginal corporate tax rate. If, for example, the old machine was originally purchased for $15,000, had a book value of $10,000, and was sold for $17,000, assuming the firm's marginal corporate tax rate is 34 percent, the taxes due from the gain would be ($17,000 − $10,000) × (0.34), or $2,380.

2. The old asset is sold for its depreciated value. In this case, no taxes result, because there is neither a gain nor a loss in the asset's sale.

3. The old asset is sold for less than its depreciated value. In this case, the difference between the depreciated book value and the salvage value of the asset is a taxable loss and can be used to offset capital gains and thus results in a tax savings. For example, if the depreciated book value of the asset is $10,000 and it is sold for $7,000, we have a $3,000 loss. Assuming the firm's marginal corporate tax rate is 34 percent, the cash inflow from the tax savings is ($10,000 − $7,000) × (0.34), or $1,020.

## What Goes into the Annual Free Cash Flows Over the Project's Life

Annual free cash flows come from operating cash flows (that is, what you've made as a result of taking on the project), changes in working capital, and any capital spending that might take place. In our calculations we'll begin with our pro forma statements and work from there. We will have to make adjustments for interest, depreciation, and working capital, along with any capital expenditures that might occur.

Before we look at the calculations, let's look at the types of adjustments that we're going to have to make to go from operating cash flows to free cash flows. To do this we'll have to make adjustments for:

♦ **Depreciation and taxes**  Depreciation is a non–cash-flow expense. It occurs because you bought a fixed asset (for example, you built a plant) in an earlier period, and now, through depreciation, you're expensing it over time—but depreciation does not involve a cash flow. That means the firm's net income understates cash flows by this amount. Therefore, we'll want to compensate for this by adding depreciation back into our measure of accounting income when calculating cash flows.

Although depreciation expense is a non-cash expense, it does affect cash flow because it is a tax-deductible expense. The higher the depreciation expense, the lower the firm's profits, which results in lower taxes.

There are a number of different methods for computing depreciation expense. For instance, we could use the Accelerated Cost Recovery System (ACRS) provided by the IRS. However, for our purposes, we will use a simplified straight-line method, where we calculate annual depreciation by taking the project's initial depreciable value and dividing by its depreciable life as follows:

$$\frac{\text{Annual depreciation using the}}{\text{simplified straight-line method}} = \frac{\text{initial depreciable value}}{\text{depreciable life}}$$

The initial depreciable value is equal to the cost of the asset plus any expenses necessary to get the new asset into operating order.

This is not how depreciation would actually be calculated. The reason we have simplified the calculation is to allow you to focus directly on what should and should not be included in the cash-flow calculations. Moreover, because the tax laws change rather frequently, we are more interested in recognizing the tax implications of depreciation than in understanding the specific depreciation provisions of the current tax laws.

◆ **Interest expenses**    There's no question that if you take on a new project, you'll have to pay for it somehow—either through internally generated cash or, say, by selling new stocks or bonds. In other words, there's a cost to that money. We recognize this principle when we discount future cash flows back to the present at the required rate of return. Remember, the project's required rate of return is the rate of return that it must earn to justify your taking on the project. It recognizes the risk of the project and the fact that there is an opportunity cost of money. If we discounted the future cash flows back to the present and also subtracted out interest expenses, then we would have double counted the cost of money—accounting for the cost of money once when we subtracted out interest expenses and once when we discounted the cash flows back to the present. Therefore, we want to make sure that cash flows are not lowered by financing costs such as interest payments. That means we'll want to make sure that financing flows (interest expense) are not included.

◆ **Changes in net working capital**    As we have explained, many projects require an increased investment in working capital. For example, some of the new sales may be credit sales resulting in an increased investment in accounts receivable. Also, in order to produce and sell the product, the firm may have to increase its investment in inventory. On the other hand, some of this increased working-capital investment may be financed by an increase in accounts payable. Because all these potential changes are changes in assets and liabilities, they don't affect accounting income. Thus, if this project brings with it a positive change in net working capital, then it means money is going to be tied up in increased working capital, and this would be a cash outflow. That means we'll have to make sure we account for any changes in working capital that might occur.

◆ **Changes in capital spending**    From an accounting perspective, the cash flow associated with the purchase of a fixed asset is not an expense. For example, when Marriott spends $50 million on building a new hotel resort, although there is a significant cash outflow, there is no accompanying expense. Instead, the $50 million cash outflow creates an annual depreciation expense over the life of the hotel. We'll want to make sure we include any changes in capital spending such as this in our cash-flow calculations.

## What Goes into the Terminal Cash Flow

The terminal cash flow is associated with the project's termination and includes the annual free cash flow and salvage value of the project plus or minus any taxable gains or losses associated with its sale. Under the current tax laws, in most cases there will be tax payments associated with the salvage value at termination. This is because the current laws allow all projects to be depreciated to zero. So, if a project has a book value of zero at termination and a positive salvage value, then that salvage value will be taxed. The tax effects associated with the salvage value of the project at termination are determined exactly like the tax effects on the sale of the old machine associated with the initial outlay. The salvage value proceeds are compared with the depreciated value, in this case zero, to determine the tax.

In addition to the salvage value, there may be a cash outlay associated with the project termination. For example, at the close of a strip-mining operation, the mine must be refilled in an ecologically acceptable manner.

Now let's put this all together and measure the project's free cash flows.

## Calculating the Free Cash Flows

Free cash-flow calculations can be broken down into three basic parts: cash flows from operations, cash flows associated with working-capital requirements, and capital-spending cash flows. Let's begin our discussion by looking at how to measure cash flows from operations and then move on to discuss measuring cash flows from working-capital requirements and capital spending.

**STEP 1**    *Measure the project's change in the firm's after-tax operating cash flows.* An easy way to calculate operating cash flows is to take the information provided on the firm's projected income statement and simply convert the accounting information into cash-flow information. To do this we take advantage of the fact that the difference between the change in sales and the change in costs should be equal to the change in earnings before interest and taxes (EBIT) plus depreciation.

Under this method, the calculation of a project's operating cash flow involves three steps. First, we determine the company's *earnings before interest and taxes (EBIT)* with and without this project. Second, we subtract out the change in taxes. Keep in mind that in calculating the change in taxes, we will ignore any interest expenses. Third, we adjust this value for the fact that depreciation, a non–cash-flow item, has been subtracted out in the calculation of EBIT. We do this by adding back depreciation. Thus, operating cash flows are calculated as follows:

Operating cash flows = change in earnings before interest and taxes (EBIT)
− change in taxes
+ change in depreciation

---

| EXAMPLE 11.1 | **Calculating the operating cash flows** |

Assume that a new project will annually generate additional revenues of $1,000,000 and additional fixed and variable costs of $500,000, while increasing depreciation by $150,000 per year. If the firm's marginal tax rate is 34 percent, what are the operating cash flows to the firm?

### STEP 1: FORMULATE A SOLUTION STRATEGY
The calculation of the operating cash flows based on the firm's earnings before interest and taxes (EBIT) is

EBIT = revenue − fixed and variable costs − depreciation

After determining the firm's EBIT, we subtract out the change in taxes. Finally, we adjust this value for the fact that depreciation, a non–cash-flow item, has been subtracted out in the calculation of EBIT. Thus, we add back depreciation to calculate the operating cash flows.

Operating cash flows = change in earnings before interest and taxes
− change in taxes
+ change in depreciation

### STEP 2: CRUNCH THE NUMBERS
Given this, the firm's net profit after tax, or net income, can be calculated as follows:

| | |
|---|---:|
| Revenue | $1,000,000 |
| − Fixed and variable costs | 500,000 |
| − Depreciation | 150,000 |
| = EBIT | $ 350,000 |
| − Taxes (34%) | 119,000 |
| = Net income | $ 231,000 |

The operating cash flows are calculated as follows:

$$\begin{aligned}
\text{Operating cash flows} &= \text{change in earnings before interest and taxes} \\
&\quad - \text{ change in taxes} \\
&\quad + \text{ change in depreciation} \\
&= \$350,000 - \$119,000 + \$150,000 = \$381,000
\end{aligned}$$

### STEP 3: ANALYZE YOUR RESULTS

By converting the firm's accounting information into cash flows, we are able to measure the exact timing of cash flows from operations. In this case it appears that the new project can annually generate $381,000 operating cash flows to the firm.

**STEP 2**    *Calculate the cash flows from the change in the firm's net working capital.* As we mentioned earlier in this chapter, many times a new project will involve additional investment in working capital—perhaps new inventory to stock a new sales outlet or simply additional investment in accounts receivable. There also may be some spontaneous short-term financing—for example, increases in accounts payable—that result from the new project. Thus, the change in net working capital is the additional investment in current assets minus any additional short-term liabilities that were generated.

**STEP 3**    *Calculate the cash flows from the change in the firm's capital spending.* Although there is generally a large cash outflow associated with a project's initial outlay, there may also be additional capital-spending requirements over the life of the project. For example, you may know ahead of time that the plant will need some minor retooling in the second year of the project in order to keep the project abreast of new technological changes that are expected to take place. In effect, we will look at the company with and without the new project, and any changes in capital spending that occur are relevant.

**STEP 4**    *Putting it together: calculating a project's free cash flows.* Thus, a project's free cash flows are:

$$\begin{aligned}
\text{Project's free cash flows} &= \text{change in earnings before interest and taxes (EBIT)} \\
&\quad - \text{ change in taxes} \\
&\quad + \text{ change in depreciation} \\
&\quad - \text{ change in net working capital} \\
&\quad - \text{ change in capital spending}
\end{aligned}$$

To estimate the changes in EBIT, taxes, depreciation, net working capital, and capital spending, we start with estimates of how many units we expect to sell, what the costs—both fixed and variable—will be, what the selling price will be, and what the required capital investment will be. From there we can put together a pro forma statement that should provide us with the data we need to estimate the project's free cash flows. However, you must keep in mind that our capital-budgeting decision will only be as good as our estimates of the costs and future demand associated with the project. In fact, most capital-budgeting decisions that turn out to be bad decisions are not so because of using a bad decision rule but because the estimates of future demand and costs were inaccurate. Let's look at an example.

---

**EXAMPLE 11.2**    **Calculating a project's free cash flows**

You are considering expanding your product line that currently consists of Lee's Press-on Nails to take advantage of the fitness craze. The new product you are considering introducing is Press-on Abs. You feel you can sell 100,000 of these per year for 4 years (after which time this project is expected to shut down because forecasters predict looking healthy will no longer be in vogue and looking like a couch potato will). The

Press-on Abs would sell for $6.00 each, with variable costs of $3.00 for each one produced. Annual fixed costs associated with production would be $90,000. In addition,
there would be a $200,000 initial capital expenditure associated with the purchase of new
production equipment. It is assumed that this initial expenditure will be depreciated, using the simplified straight-line method, down to zero over 4 years. The project will also
require a one-time initial investment of $30,000 in net working capital associated with
the inventory. Finally, assume that the firm's marginal tax rate is 34 percent. What are
the free cash flows to the firm?

### STEP 1: FORMULATE A SOLUTION STRATEGY

In general, a project's free cash flows will fall into one of three categories: (1) the initial
outlay, (2) the annual free cash flows over the project's life, and (3) the terminal cash
flow. Let's begin by calculating the initial outlay.

### STEP 2: CRUNCH THE NUMBERS

#### Initial Outlay

In this example, the initial outlay is the $200,000 initial capital expenditure plus the in-
vestment of $30,000 in net working capital, for a total of $230,000.

#### Annual Free Cash Flows

Table 11-1 calculates the annual change in earnings before interest and taxes. This calculation begins with the change in sales (Δ Sales) and subtracts the change in fixed and
variable costs in addition to the change in depreciation, to arrive at the change in earnings before interest and taxes (Δ EBIT). Depreciation is calculated using the simplified straight-line method, which is simply the depreciable value of the asset ($200,000)
divided by the asset's expected life of 4 years. Taxes are then calculated assuming a
34 percent marginal tax rate. Once we have calculated EBIT and taxes, we don't need
to go any further, because these are the only two values from the income statement that
we need. In addition, in this example there is not any annual increase in working capital
associated with the project under consideration. Also notice that we have ignored any
interest payments and financing flows that might have occurred. As mentioned earlier,
when we discount the free cash flows back to the present at the required rate of return,
we are implicitly accounting for the cost of the funds needed to support the project.

The project's annual change in operating cash flow is calculated in Table 11-2.
Remember: *The project's annual free cash flow is simply the change in operating cash flow less any
change in net working capital and less any change in capital spending.*

| TABLE 11-1  Calculating the Annual Change in Earnings Before Interest and Taxes for the Press-on Abs Project | |
|---|---|
| Δ Sales (100,000 units at $6.00/unit) | $ 600,000 |
| Less: Δ Variable costs (variable cost $3.00/unit) | $ 300,000 |
| Less: Δ Fixed costs | $   90,000 |
| Equals: EBITDA (assuming amortization is 0) | $ 210,000 |
| Less: Δ Depreciation ($200,000/4 years) | $   50,000 |
| Equals: Δ EBIT | $ 160,000 |
| Less: Δ Taxes: (taxed at 34%) | $   54,400 |
| Equals: Δ Net income | $ 105,600 |

| TABLE 11-2  Calculating the Annual Change in Operating Cash Flow, Press-on Abs Project | |
|---|---|
| Δ Earnings before interest and taxes (EBIT) | $160,000 |
| Minus: Δ Taxes | $ 54,400 |
| Plus: Δ Depreciation | $ 50,000 |
| Equals: Δ Operating cash flow | $155,600 |

### Terminal Cash Flow

For this project, the terminal cash flow is quite simple. The only unusual cash flow at the project's termination is the recapture of the net working capital associated with the project. In effect, the investment in inventory of $30,000 is liquidated when the project is shut down in 4 years

Keep in mind that in calculating free cash flow we subtract out the change in net working capital, but because the change in net working capital is negative (we are reducing our investment in inventory), we are subtracting a negative number, which has the effect of adding it back in. Thus, working capital was a negative cash flow when the project began and we invested in inventory, but at termination it becomes a positive offsetting cash flow when the inventory was liquidated. The calculation of the terminal free cash flow is illustrated in Table 11-3.

### STEP 3: ANALYZE YOUR RESULTS

In this example there are no changes in net working capital and capital spending over the life of the project. This is not the case for all projects that you will consider. For example, on a project where sales increase annually, it is likely that working capital will also increase each year to support a larger inventory and a higher level of accounts receivable. Similarly, on some projects the capital expenditures may be spread out over several years. The point here is that what we are trying to do is look at the firm with this project and without this project and measure the change in cash flows other than any interest payments and financing flows that might occur.

If we were to construct a free cash-flow diagram from this example (Figure 11-1), it would have an initial outlay of $230,000, the free cash flows during years 1 through 3 would be $155,600, and the free cash flow in the terminal year would be $185,600.

#### TABLE 11-3  Calculating the Terminal Free Cash Flow, Press-on Abs Project

| | |
|---|---|
| Δ Earnings before interest and taxes (EBIT) | $160,000 |
| Minus: Δ Taxes | $ 54,400 |
| Plus: Δ Depreciation | $ 50,000 |
| Minus: Δ Net working capital | ($ 30,000)* |
| Equals: Δ Free cash flow | $185,600 |

*Because the change in net working capital is negative (we are reducing our investment in inventory), we are subtracting a negative number, which has the effect of adding it back in.

#### FIGURE 11-1  Free Cash-Flow Diagram for Press-on Abs

| YEAR | 0 | 1 | 2 | 3 | 4 |
|---|---|---|---|---|---|
| Cash Flow | −$230,000 | 155,600 | 155,600 | 155,600 | 185,600 |

## A Comprehensive Example: Calculating Free Cash Flows

Now let's put what we know about capital budgeting together and look at a capital-budgeting decision for a firm in the 34 percent marginal tax bracket with a 15 percent required rate of return or cost of capital. The project we are considering involves the introduction of a new electric scooter line by Raymobile. Our first task is that of estimating cash flows, which is the focus of this section. This project is expected to last 5 years and then, because this is somewhat of a fad product, be terminated. Thus, our first task becomes that of estimating the initial outlay, the annual free cash flows, and the terminal free cash flow. Given the information in Table 11-4, we want to determine the free cash flows associated with the project. Once we have that, we can easily calculate the project's net present value, the profitability index, and the internal rate of return and apply the appropriate decision criteria.

## TABLE 11-4  Raymobile Scooter Line Capital-Budgeting Example

| Cost of new plant and equipment | $9,700,000 |
|---|---|
| Shipping and installation costs | $ 300,000 |
| Unit sales | |

| YEAR | UNITS SOLD |
|---|---|
| 1 | 50,000 |
| 2 | 100,000 |
| 3 | 100,000 |
| 4 | 70,000 |
| 5 | 50,000 |

| | |
|---|---|
| Sales price per unit | $150/unit in years 1 through 4, $130/unit in year 5 |
| Variable cost per unit | $80/unit |
| Annual fixed costs | $500,000 in years 1–5 |
| Working-capital requirements | There will be an initial working-capital requirement of $100,000 just to get production started. Then, for each year, the *total* investment in net working capital will be equal to 10 percent of the dollar value of sales for that year. Thus, the investment in working capital will increase during years 1 and 2, then decrease in year 4. Finally, all working capital will be liquidated at the termination of the project at the end of year 5. |
| The depreciation method | We use the simplified straight-line method over 5 years. It is assumed that the plant and equipment will have no salvage value after 5 years. Thus, annual depreciation is $2,000,000/year for 5 years. |

To determine the differential annual free cash flows, we first need to determine the annual change in operating cash flow. To do this we will take the change in EBIT, subtract out the change in taxes, and then add in the change in depreciation. This is shown in Section II of Table 11-5. We first determine what the change in sales revenue will be by multiplying the units sold times the sale price. From the change in sales revenue, we subtract out variable costs, which are $80 per unit. Then, the change in fixed costs is subtracted out, and the result is earnings before interest, taxes, depreciation, and amortization (EBITDA). Subtracting the change in depreciation and amortization, which in this case is assumed to be zero, from EBITDA then leaves us with the change in earnings before interest and taxes (EBIT). From the change in EBIT, we can then calculate the change in taxes, which are assumed to be 34 percent of EBIT.

Using the calculations provided in Section I of Table 11-5, we then calculate the operating cash flow in Section II of Table 11-5. As you recall, the operating cash flow is simply EBIT minus taxes, plus depreciation.

To calculate the annual free cash flows from this project, we subtract the change in net working capital and the change in capital spending from operating cash flow. Thus, the first step becomes determining the change in net working capital, which is shown in Section III of Table 11-5. The change in net working capital generally includes both increases in inventory and increases in accounts receivable that naturally occur as sales increase from the introduction of the new product line. Some of the increase

## CAN YOU DO IT?

### CALCULATING OPERATING CASH FLOWS

Assume that a new project will generate revenues of $300,000 annually, and the annual cash expenses, including both fixed and variable costs, will be $190,000 per year. Depreciation will be $20,000 per year. In addition, the firm's marginal tax rate is 40 percent. Calculate the operating cash flows.

(The solution can be found on page 357.)

## TABLE 11-5  Calculating the Free Cash Flow for Raymobile Scooters

| Year | 0 | 1 | 2 | 3 | 4 | 5 |
|---|---|---|---|---|---|---|
| **Section I. Calculate the Change in EBIT, Taxes, and Depreciation**<br>**(This Becomes an Input in the Calculation of Operating Cash Flow in Section II)** | | | | | | |
| Units sold | | 50,000 | 100,000 | 100,000 | 70,000 | 50,000 |
| Sales price | | $     150 | $     150 | $     150 | $     150 | $     130 |
| Sales revenue | | $7,500,000 | $15,000,000 | $15,000,000 | $10,500,000 | $6,500,000 |
| Less: Variable costs | | 4,000,000 | 8,000,000 | 8,000,000 | 5,600,000 | 4,000,000 |
| Less: Fixed costs | | 500,000 | 500,000 | 500,000 | 500,000 | 500,000 |
| Equals: EBITDA | | $3,000,000 | $ 6,500,000 | $ 6,500,000 | $ 4,400,000 | $2,000,000 |
| Less: Depreciation (amortization is assumed to be 0) | | 2,000,000 | 2,000,000 | 2,000,000 | 2,000,000 | 2,000,000 |
| Equals: EBIT | | $1,000,000 | $ 4,500,000 | $ 4,500,000 | $ 2,400,000 | 0 |
| Taxes (@34%) | | 340,000 | 1,530,000 | 1,530,000 | 816,000 | 0 |
| **Section II. Calculate Operating Cash Flow**<br>**(This Becomes an Input in the Calculation of Free Cash Flow in Section IV)** | | | | | | |
| **Operating cash flow:** | | | | | | |
| EBIT | | $1,000,000 | $ 4,500,000 | $ 4,500,000 | $ 2,400,000 | $     0 |
| Minus: Taxes | | 340,000 | 1,530,000 | 1,530,000 | 816,000 | 0 |
| Plus: Depreciation | | 2,000,000 | 2,000,000 | 2,000,000 | 2,000,000 | 2,000,000 |
| Equals: Operating cash flows | | $2,660,000 | $ 4,970,000 | $ 4,970,000 | $ 3,584,000 | $2,000,000 |
| **Section III. Calculate the Net Working Capital**<br>**(This Becomes an Input in the Calculation of Free Cash Flow in Section IV)** | | | | | | |
| **Change in net working capital:** | | | | | | |
| Revenue | | $7,500,000 | $15,000,000 | $15,000,000 | $10,500,000 | $6,500,000 |
| Initial working-capital requirement | $ 100,000 | | | | | |
| Net working-capital needs | | 750,000 | 1,500,000 | 1,500,000 | 1,050,000 | 650,000 |
| Liquidation of working capital | | | | | | 650,000 |
| Change in working capital | 100,000 | 650,000 | 750,000 | 0 | (450,000) | (1,050,000) |
| **Section IV. Calculate Free Cash Flow**<br>**(Using Information Calculated in Sections II and III, in Addition to the Change in Capital Spending)** | | | | | | |
| **Free cash flow:** | | | | | | |
| Operating cash flow | | $2,660,000 | $ 4,970,000 | $ 4,970,000 | $ 3,584,000 | $2,000,000 |
| Minus: Change in net working capital | $ 100,000 | 650,000 | 750,000 | 0 | (450,000) | (1,050,000) |
| Minus: Change in capital spending | 10,000,000 | 0 | 0 | 0 | 0 | 0 |
| Equals: Free cash flow | $(10,100,000) | $2,010,000 | $ 4,220,000 | $ 4,970,000 | $ 4,034,000 | $3,050,000 |

in accounts receivable may be offset by increases in accounts payable, but, in general, most new projects involve some type of increase in net working capital. In this example, there is an initial working capital requirement of $100,000. In addition, for each year the total investment in net working capital will be equal to 10 percent of sales for each year. Thus, the investment in working capital for year 1 is $750,000 (because sales are estimated to be $7,500,000). Working capital will already be at $100,000, so the change in net working capital will be $650,000. Net working capital will continue to increase during years 1 and 2, then decrease in year 4. Finally, all working capital is liquidated at the termination of the project at the end of year 5.

With the operating cash flow and the change in net working capital already calculated, the calculation of the project's free cash flow becomes easy. All that is missing is the change in capital spending, which in this example will simply be the $9,700,000 for plant and equipment plus the $300,000 for shipping and installation. Thus, the change in capital spending becomes $10,000,000. We then need merely to take operating cash flow and subtract from it both the change in net working capital and the change in capital spending. This is done in Section IV of Table 11-5 with the annual free cash flows given in the last row in that table. A free cash flow diagram for this project is provided in Figure 11-2.

## FIGURE 11-2  Free Cash-Flow Diagram for the Raymobile Scooter Line

| | | $r = 15\%$ | | | | |
|---|---|---|---|---|---|---|
| YEAR | 0 | 1 | 2 | 3 | 4 | 5 |
| Cash Flow | −$10,100,000 | 2,010,000 | 4,220,000 | 4,970,000 | 4,034,000 | 3,050,000 |

# DID YOU GET IT?
## CALCULATING OPERATING CASH FLOWS

You were asked to determine the operating cash flows for a project. Operating cash flows are calculated as:

Operating cash flows = change in earnings before interest and taxes (EBIT)
    − change in taxes
    + change in depreciation

**STEP 1  Calculate the change in EBIT**

| | |
|---|---|
| Revenue | $300,000 |
| −Cash fixed and variable expenses | 190,000 |
| −Depreciation | 20,000 |
| =EBIT | $ 90,000 |

**STEP 2  Calculate taxes by multiplying the increase in EBIT times the marginal tax rate of 40 percent**

| | |
|---|---|
| Change in EBIT | $90,000 |
| Times: Taxes (40%) | = $36,000 |

**STEP 3  Calculate operating cash flows**

Operating cash flows = change in earnings before interest and taxes (EBIT)
    − change in taxes
    + change in depreciation
    = $90,000 − $36,000 + $20,000 = $74,000

The operating cash flows of $74,000 then become an input to the calculation of the free cash flows.

# CAN YOU DO IT?
## CALCULATING FREE CASH FLOWS

Hurley's Hidden Snacks is introducing a new product and has an expected change in EBIT of $800,000. Hurley's Hidden Snacks has a 40 percent marginal tax rate. This project will also produce $100,000 of depreciation per year. In addition, this project will also cause the following changes in year 1:

| | WITHOUT THE PROJECT | WITH THE PROJECT |
|---|---|---|
| Accounts receivable | $35,000 | $63,000 |
| Inventory | 65,000 | 70,000 |
| Accounts payable | 70,000 | 90,000 |

What is the project's free cash flow in year 1?
(The solution can be found on page 360.)

## Concept Check

1. In general, a project's cash flows will fall into one of three categories. What are these categories?
2. What is a free cash flow? How do we calculate it?
3. Although depreciation is not a cash-flow item, it plays an important role in the calculation of cash flows. How does depreciation affect a project's cash flows?

 **3** Explain the importance of options, or flexibility, in capital budgeting.

# Options in Capital Budgeting

The use of discounted cash-flow decision criteria, such as the *NPV* method, provides an excellent framework within which to evaluate projects. However, what happens if the project being analyzed has the potential to be modified after some future uncertainty has been resolved? For example, if a project that had an expected life of 10 years turns out to be better than anticipated, it may be expanded or continued past 10 years, perhaps going on for 20 years. On the other hand, if its cash flows do not meet expectations, it may not last a full 10 years and be scaled back, abandoned, or sold. In addition, suppose the project were delayed for a year or two. This flexibility is something that the *NPV* and our other decision-making criteria have difficulty dealing with. In fact, the *NPV* may actually understate the value of the project if the future opportunities associated with modifying it have a positive value. It is this value of flexibility that we will be examining using options.

Three of the most common option types that can add value to a capital-budgeting project are (1) the option to delay a project until the future cash flows are more favorable—this option is common when the firm has exclusive rights, perhaps a patent, to a product or technology; (2) the option to expand a project, perhaps in size or even to develop new products that would not have otherwise been feasible; and (3) the option to abandon a project if the future cash flows fall short of expectations.

## The Option to Delay a Project

There is no question that the estimated cash flows associated with a project can change over time. In fact, as a result of changing expected cash flows, a project that currently has a negative net present value may have a positive net present value in the future. Let's take another look at the gas-electric hybrid car market we examined in the introduction to this chapter. This time, let's assume that you've developed a high-voltage, nickel-metal hydride battery that can be used to increase the mileage on hybrid cars to up to 150 miles per gallon. However, as you examine the costs of producing this new battery, you realize that it

---

## DID YOU GET IT?
### CALCULATING FREE CASH FLOWS

You were asked to determine the free cash flows in year 1 for a new product being introduced by Hurley's Hidden Snacks.

**STEP 1  Calculate the change in net working capital.**
The change in net working capital equals the increase in accounts receivable and inventory less the increase in accounts payable = $28,000 − $5,000 − $20,000 = $13,000.

**STEP 2  Calculate the change in free cash flows.**

Project's free cash flows = change in earnings before interest and taxes (EBIT)
- − change in taxes
- + change in depreciation
- − change in net working capital
- − change in capital spending

= $800,000 − ($800,000 × 0.40) + $100,000 − $13,000 − $0 = $567,000

The project's free cash flows represent the "Cash Flow Is What Matters" that we discussed in **Principle 1**.

is still relatively expensive to manufacture and that, given the costs, the market for a car using this battery is quite small right now. Does that mean that the rights to the high-voltage, nickel-metal hydride battery have no value? No, they have value because you may be able to improve on this technology in the future and make the battery even more efficient and less expensive. They also have value because oil prices might rise even further, which would lead to a bigger market for super–fuel-efficient cars. In effect, the ability to delay this project with the hope that technological and market conditions will change, making this project profitable, lends value to the project.

Another example of the option to delay a project until the future cash flows are more favorable involves a firm that owns the oil rights to some oil-rich land and is considering an oil-drilling project. Suppose after all of the costs and the expected oil output are considered, the project has a negative net present value. Does that mean the firm should give away its oil rights or that those oil rights have no value? Certainly not. There is a chance that in the future oil prices could rise to the point that this negative *NPV* project could become a positive *NPV* project. It is this ability to delay development that provides value. Thus, the value in this seemingly negative *NPV* project is provided by the option to delay it until the future cash flows are more favorable.

## The Option to Expand a Project

Just as we saw with the option to delay a project, the estimated cash flows associated with a project can change over time, making it valuable to expand a project. Again, this flexibility to adjust production to demand has value. For example, a firm might deliberately build a production plant with excess capacity so that if the product has more-than-anticipated demand, the firm can simply increase production. Alternatively, taking on this project might provide the firm with a foothold in a new industry and lead to other products that would not have otherwise been feasible. This reasoning has led many firms to expand into e-businesses, hoping to gain know-how and expertise that will lead to other profitable projects down the line. It also provides some of the rationale for research and development expenditures to explore new markets.

Let's go back to our example of the gas-electric hybrid car and examine the option to expand that project. One of the reasons that most of the major automobile firms are introducing gas-electric hybrid cars is that they feel if gas prices keep moving beyond the $2 to $3 per gallon price, these hybrids may become the future of the industry, and the only way to gain the know-how and expertise to produce a hybrid is to do it. As the cost of technology declines and the demand increases—perhaps pushed on by increases in gas prices—then the companies will be ready to expand into full-fledged production. This strategy becomes clear when you look at Honda, which first introduced the Insight in 2000, and Toyota, which introduced the Prius in 2001.

When hybrids were first introduced, analysts estimated that Honda was losing about $8,000 on each Insight it sold, whereas Toyota was losing about $3,000 per car, but both firms hoped to break even in a few years. Still, these projects made sense because they allowed these automakers to gain the technological and production expertise to profitably produce a gas-electric hybrid car. And, as mentioned in the chapter introduction, with predictions that hybrids will account for half of the light-duty vehicles on the road by 2040, it is a big market they're looking at. Moreover, the technology Honda and Toyota developed with the Insight and Prius may have profitable applications for other cars or in other areas. In effect, it is the option of expanding production in the future that brings value to this project.

## The Option to Abandon a Project

The option to abandon a project as the estimated cash flows associated with it change over time also has value. Again, it is this flexibility to adjust to new information that provides the value. For example, a project's sales in the first year or two might not live up to expectations, with the project being barely profitable. The firm might then decide to liquidate the project and sell the plant and all of the equipment. That liquidated value may be more than the value of keeping the project going.

Again, let's go back to our example of the gas-electric hybrid car and, this time, examine the option to abandon that project. If after a few years the cost of gas falls dramatically while the cost of technology remains high, the gas-electric hybrid car might not become profitable. At that point the manufacturer might decide to abandon the project and sell the technology, including all the patent rights to it. In effect, the original project, the gas-electric hybrid car, may not be of value, but the technology that has been developed might be. As a result, the value of abandoning the project and selling the technology might be more than the value of keeping the project running. Again, it is the value of flexibility associated with the possibility of modifying the project in the future—in this case abandoning the project— that can produce positive value.

### Options in Capital Budgeting: The Bottom Line

Because of the potential to be modified in the future after some future uncertainty has been resolved, we may find that a project with a negative net present value based upon its expected free cash flows is a "good" project and should be accepted. This demonstrates the value of options. In addition, we may find that a project with a positive net present value may be of more value if its acceptance is delayed. Options also explain the logic that drives firms to take on negative *NPV* projects that allow them to enter new markets. The option to abandon a project explains why firms hire employees on a temporary basis rather than permanently, why they lease rather than buy equipment, and why they enter into contracts with suppliers on an annual basis rather than long term.

### Concept Check

1. Give an example of an option to delay a project. Why might this be of value?
2. Give an example of an option to expand a project. Why might this be of value?
3. Give an example of an option to abandon a project. Why might this be of value?

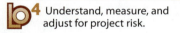
4 Understand, measure, and adjust for project risk.

# Risk and the Investment Decisions

Up to this point we have ignored risk in capital budgeting; that is, we have discounted expected cash flows back to the present and ignored any uncertainty that there might be surrounding that estimate. In reality, the future cash flows associated with the introduction of a new sales outlet or a new product are estimates of what is *expected* to happen in the future, not necessarily what will happen. For example, when Coca-Cola decided to replace Classic Coke with "New Coke," you can bet that the expected cash flows it based its decision on were nothing like the cash flows it realized. As a result, it didn't take Coca-Cola long to reintroduce Classic Coke. Other famous failures that didn't produce the cash flows that were expected include Bic disposable underwear, Thirsty Dog! beef-flavored bottled water for dogs, and Coors Rocky Mountain Spring Water. The cash flows we have discounted back to the present so far have only been our best estimate of the expected future cash flows. A cash-flow diagram based on the possible outcomes of an investment proposal rather than the expected values of these outcomes appears in Figure 11-3.

In this section, we assume that we do not know beforehand what cash flows will actually result from a new project. However, we do have expectations concerning the possible outcomes

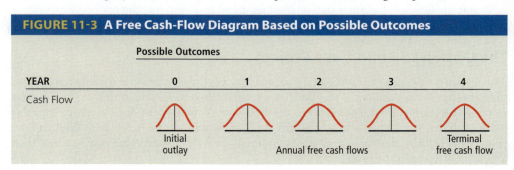

**FIGURE 11-3   A Free Cash-Flow Diagram Based on Possible Outcomes**

| | Possible Outcomes | | | | |
|---|---|---|---|---|---|
| YEAR | 0 | 1 | 2 | 3 | 4 |
| Cash Flow | Initial outlay | | Annual free cash flows | | Terminal free cash flow |

and are able to assign probabilities to these outcomes. Stated another way, although we do not know what the cash flows resulting from the acceptance of a new project will be, we can formulate the probability distributions from which the flows will be drawn. As we learned in Chapter 6, risk occurs when there is some question about the future outcome of an event.

In the remainder of this chapter, we assume that although future cash flows are not known with certainty, the probability distribution from which they are derived can be estimated. Also, because we have illustrated that the dispersion of possible outcomes reflects risk, we are prepared to use a measure of dispersion, or variability, later in the chapter when we quantify risk.

In the pages that follow, remember that there are only two basic issues that we address: (1) What is risk in terms of capital-budgeting decisions, and how should it be measured? and (2) How should risk be incorporated into a capital-budgeting analysis?

## What Measure of Risk Is Relevant in Capital Budgeting?

Before we begin our discussion of how to adjust for risk, it is important to determine just what type of risk we are to adjust for. In capital budgeting, a project's risk can be looked at on three levels. First, there is the **project standing alone risk**, which is a *project's risk ignoring the fact that much of this risk will be diversified away.* Second, we have the project's **contribution-to-firm risk**, which is the *amount of risk that the project contributes to the firm as a whole; this measure considers the fact that some of the project's risk will be diversified away as the project is combined with the firm's other projects and assets, but it ignores the effects of the diversification of the firm's shareholders.* Finally, there is **systematic risk**, which is the *risk of the project from the viewpoint of a well-diversified shareholder; this measure takes into account that some of a project's risk will be diversified away as the project is combined with the firm's other projects, and, in addition, some of the remaining risk will be diversified away by shareholders as they combine this stock with other stocks in their portfolios.* Graphically, this is shown in Figure 11-4.

Should we be interested in the project standing alone risk? The answer is no. Perhaps the easiest way to understand why not is to look at an example. Let's take the case of research and development projects at Johnson & Johnson. Each year Johnson & Johnson takes on hundreds of new R&D projects, knowing that they have only about a 10 percent probability of being successful. If they are successful, the profits can be enormous; if they fail, the investment is lost. If the company has only one project, and it is an R&D project, the company would have a 90 percent chance of failure. Thus, if we look at these R&D projects individually and measure their stand-alone risk, we would have to judge them to be enormously risky. However, if we

**project standing alone risk** a project's risk ignoring the fact that much of this risk will be diversified away.

**contribution-to-firm risk** the amount of risk that the project contributes to the firm as a whole; this measure considers the fact that some of the project's risk will be diversified away as the project is combined with the firm's other projects and assets but ignores the effects of diversification of the firm's shareholders.

**systematic risk** the risk of the project from the viewpoint of a well-diversified shareholder; this measure takes into account that some of a project's risk will be diversified away as the project is combined with the firm's other projects, and, in addition, some of the remaining risk will be diversified away by shareholders as they combine this stock with other stocks in their portfolios.

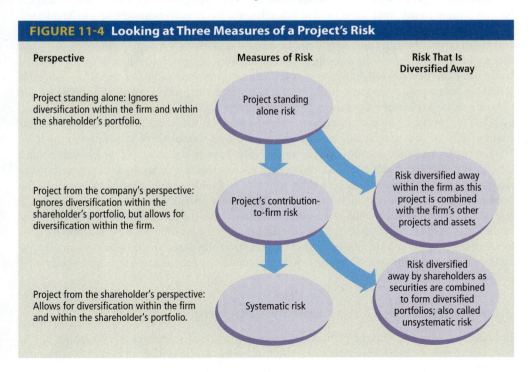

**FIGURE 11-4  Looking at Three Measures of a Project's Risk**

consider the effect of the diversification that comes about from taking on several hundred independent R&D projects a year, all with a 10 percent chance of success, we can see that each R&D project does not add much risk to Johnson & Johnson. In short, because much of a project's risk is diversified away within the firm, the project standing alone risk is an inappropriate measure of the meaningful level of risk of a capital-budgeting project.

Should we be interested in the project's contribution-to-firm risk? Once again, at least in theory, the answer is no, provided investors are well diversified and there are no bankruptcy costs. From our earlier discussion of risk in Chapter 6, we saw that as shareholders, if we combined an individual security with other securities to form a diversified portfolio, much of the risk of the individual security would be diversified away. In short, all that affects the shareholders is the systematic risk of the project and, as such, it is all that is theoretically relevant for capital budgeting.

## Measuring Risk for Capital-Budgeting Purposes with a Dose of Reality—Is Systematic Risk All There Is?

According to the capital asset pricing model (CAPM) we discussed in Chapter 6, systematic risk is the only relevant risk for capital-budgeting purposes. However, reality complicates this somewhat. In many instances a firm will have undiversified shareholders, including owners of small corporations. Because they are not diversified, for those shareholders the relevant measure of risk is the project's contribution-to-firm risk.

The possibility of bankruptcy also affects our view of what measure of risk is relevant. As you recall in developing the CAPM, we made the assumption that bankruptcy costs were zero. Because the project's contribution-to-firm risk reflects risk that the firm faces, that is, the risk that may lead to bankruptcy, this may be an appropriate measure of risk: Quite obviously, there is a cost associated with bankruptcy. First, if a firm fails, its assets, in general, cannot be sold for their true economic value. Moreover, the amount of money actually available for distribution to stockholders is further reduced by liquidation and legal fees that must be paid. Finally, the opportunity cost associated with the delays related to the legal process further reduces the funds available to the shareholder. Therefore, because costs are associated with bankruptcy, reducing the chance of a bankruptcy has a very real value associated with it.

The indirect costs of bankruptcy also affect other areas of the firm, including production, sales, and the quality and efficiency of management. For example, firms with a higher probability of bankruptcy may have a more difficult time recruiting and retaining quality managers because jobs with that firm are viewed as being less secure. Suppliers may be less willing to sell to the firm on credit. Finally, customers may lose confidence and fear that the firm is cutting corners in terms of quality and/or will not be around to honor a warranty or supply spare parts for products in the future. As a result, as the probability of bankruptcy increases, an eventual bankruptcy can become self-fulfilling as potential customers and suppliers flee. The end result is that because a project's contribution-to-firm risk affects the probability of bankruptcy for the firm, it may be a relevant risk measure for capital budgeting.

Finally, problems in measuring a project's systematic risk make its implementation extremely difficult. It is much easier talking about a project's systematic risk than measuring it.

Given all this, what risk measure do we use? The answer is that we will give consideration to both systematic risk and contribution-to-firm risk measures. We know in theory systematic risk is correct. We also know that bankruptcy costs and undiversified shareholders violate the assumptions of the theory, which makes the concept of a project's contribution-to-firm risk a relevant measure. Still, the concept of systematic risk holds value for capital-budgeting decisions because that is the risk that shareholders are compensated for assuming. Therefore, we will concern ourselves with both the project's contribution-to-firm risk and the project's systematic risk and not try to make any specific allocation of importance between the two for capital-budgeting purposes.

## Incorporating Risk into Capital Budgeting

Because different investment projects do in fact contain different levels of risk, let's now look at the risk-adjusted discount rate, which is based on the notion that investors require higher rates of return on more risky projects.

## Risk-Adjusted Discount Rates

The use of **risk-adjusted discount rates** is based on the concept that investors demand higher returns for more risky projects. This is the basic principle behind Principle 3 and the CAPM and is illustrated graphically in Figure 11-5.

As we know from **Principle 3**, the expected rate of return on any investment should include compensation for delaying consumption equal to the risk-free rate of return, plus compensation for any risk taken on. Under the risk-adjusted discount rate approach, if the risk associated with the investment is greater than the risk involved in a typical endeavor, the discount rate is adjusted upward to compensate for this added risk. Once the firm determines the appropriate required rate of return for a project with a given level of risk, the cash flows are discounted back to the present at the risk-adjusted discount rate. Then the normal capital-budgeting criteria are applied, except in the case of the *IRR*. For the *IRR*, the hurdle rate with which the project's *IRR* is compared now becomes the risk-adjusted discount rate. Expressed mathematically, the *NPV* using the risk-adjusted discount rate becomes

> **risk-adjusted discount rate** a method of risk adjustment when the risk associated with the investment is greater than the risk involved in a typical endeavor. Using this method, the discount rate is adjusted upward to compensate for this added risk.

> **REMEMBER YOUR PRINCIPLES**
>
> **Principle** All the methods used to compensate for risk in capital budgeting find their roots in **Principle 3: Risk Requires a Reward**. In fact, the risk-adjusted discount method puts this concept directly into play.

$$
\text{Risk-adjusted } NPV = \begin{bmatrix} \text{present value of all the} \\ \text{future annual free cash} \\ \text{flows discounted back} \\ \text{to present at the risk-adjusted} \\ \text{rate of return} \end{bmatrix} - \begin{bmatrix} \text{the initial cash outlay} \end{bmatrix}
$$

(11-1)

$$
= \frac{FCF_1}{(1 + k^*)^1} + \frac{FCF_2}{(1 + k^*)^2} + \cdots + \frac{FCF_n}{(1 + k^*)^n} - IO
$$

where $FCF_t$ = the annual free cash flow expected in time period $t$
$IO$ = the initial cash outlay
$k^*$ = the risk-adjusted discount rate
$n$ = the project's expected life

The logic behind the risk-adjusted discount rate stems from the idea that if the level of risk associated with a project is different from that of the typical project, then managers must incorporate the shareholders' probable reaction to this new endeavor into the decision-making process. For example, if the project has more risk than a typical project, then a higher required rate of return should apply. Otherwise, marginal projects will lower the firm's share price—that is, reduce shareholders' wealth. This will occur as the market raises its required rate of return on the firm to reflect the addition of the more risky project, because the incremental cash flows resulting from it might not be large enough to offset this risk. By the same logic, if the project has less than normal risk, a reduction in the required rate of return is appropriate. Thus, the risk-adjusted discount method attempts to apply more stringent standards—that is, require a higher rate of return—to projects that will increase the firm's risk level. This risk-adjusted financial decision rule can be summarized as follows:

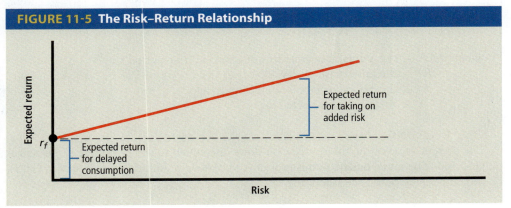

**FIGURE 11-5  The Risk–Return Relationship**

## FINANCIAL DECISION TOOLS

| Name of Tool | Formula | What It Tells You |
|---|---|---|
| Risk-adjusted net present value (NPV) | The present value of all the future annual free cash flows minus the initial cash outlay discounted back to present at the risk-adjusted discount rate:<br><br>$$= \frac{FCF_1}{(1 + k^*)^1} + \frac{FCF_2}{(1 + k^*)^2} + \cdots + \frac{FCF_n}{(1 + k^*)^n} - IO$$ | • What the NPV would be if the project's cash flows were discounted back to present at the appropriate (risk-adjusted) discount rate<br>• The amount of wealth that is created if the project is accepted<br>• If the risk-adjusted NPV is positive, then wealth is created and the project should be accepted. |

---

**EXAMPLE 11.3**   **Risk-adjusted discount rates**

A toy manufacturer is considering introducing a line of fishing equipment with an expected life of 5 years. In the past, the firm has been quite conservative in its investment in new products, sticking primarily to standard toys. In this context, the introduction of a line of fishing equipment is considered an abnormally risky project. Management thinks that the normal required rate of return for the firm of 10 percent is not sufficient. Instead, the minimum acceptable rate of return on this project should be 15 percent. The initial outlay would be $110,000, and the expected cash flows are as follows:

| YEAR | EXPECTED FREE CASH FLOW |
|---|---|
| 1 | $30,000 |
| 2 | 30,000 |
| 3 | 30,000 |
| 4 | 30,000 |
| 5 | 30,000 |

What is the NPV using the risk-adjusted discount rate? Should the project be accepted?

### STEP 1: FORMULATE A SOLUTION STRATEGY

The NPV using the risk-adjusted discount rate can be calculated using equation (11-1) as follows:

$$NPV = \left[ \begin{array}{l} \text{present value of all the} \\ \text{future annual free cash} \\ \text{flows discounted back} \\ \text{to present at the risk-adjusted} \\ \text{rate of return} \end{array} \right] - \left[ \text{the initial cash outlay} \right]$$

$$= \frac{FCF_1}{(1 + k^*)^1} + \frac{FCF_2}{(1 + k^*)^2} + \cdots + \frac{FCF_n}{(1 + k^*)^n} - IO$$

where $FCF_t$ = the annual free cash flow expected in time period $t$
$IO$ = the initial cash outlay
$k^*$ = the risk-adjusted discount rate
$n$ = the project's expected life

### STEP 2: CRUNCH THE NUMBERS

The present value of the future free cash flows discounted to the present at 15 percent is $100,560. The initial outlay on this project is $110,000. Substituting into equation (11-1), we compute the NPV issue as follows:

$$NPV = \begin{bmatrix} \text{present value of all the} \\ \text{future annual free cash} \\ \text{flows discounted back} \\ \text{to present at the risk-adjusted} \\ \text{rate of return} \end{bmatrix} - \begin{bmatrix} \text{the initial cash outlay} \end{bmatrix}$$

$$= \$100,560 - \$110,000 = -\$9,435$$

### STEP 3: ANALYZE YOUR RESULTS

The risk-adjusted *NPV* is −$9,435, thus the project should be rejected. If the normal required rate of return of 10 percent had been used as the discount rate, the project would have had a positive *NPV* of $3,724.

In practice, when the risk-adjusted discount rate is used, projects are generally grouped according to purpose, or risk class; then the discount rate preassigned to that purpose or risk class is used. For example, a firm with a required rate of return of 12 percent might use the following rate-of-return categorization:

| PROJECT | REQUIRED RATE OF RETURN (%) |
| --- | --- |
| Replacement decision | 12 |
| Modification or expansion of existing product line | 15 |
| Project unrelated to current operations | 18 |
| Research and development operations | 25 |

The purpose of this categorization of projects is to make their evaluation easier, but it also introduces a sense of arbitrariness into the calculations that makes the evaluation less meaningful. The trade-offs involved in the preceding classification are obvious: Time and effort are minimized but only at the cost of precision.

## Measuring a Project's Systematic Risk

When we initially talked about systematic risk or the beta, we were talking about measuring it for the entire firm. As you recall, although we could estimate a firm's beta using historical data, we did not have complete confidence in our results. As we will see, estimating the appropriate level of systematic risk for a single project is even more fraught with difficulties. To truly understand what it is we are trying to do and the difficulties we will encounter, let's step back a bit and examine systematic risk and the risk adjustment for a project.

What we are trying to do is use the CAPM to determine the level of risk and the appropriate risk–return trade-offs for a particular project. We then take the expected return on this project and compare it to the required return suggested by the CAPM to determine whether the project should be accepted. If the project appears to be a typical one for the firm, using the CAPM to determine the appropriate risk–return trade-offs and then judging the project against them may be a warranted approach. But if the project is not a typical project, what do we do? Historical data generally do not exist for a new project. In fact, for some capital investments—for example, a truck or a new building—historical data would not have much meaning. What we need to do is make the best of a bad situation. We either (1) fake it—that is, use historical accounting data, if available, to substitute for historical price data in estimating systematic risk—or (2) attempt to find a substitute firm in the same industry as the capital-budgeting project and use the substitute firm's estimated systematic risk as a proxy for the project's systematic risk.

## Using Accounting Data to Estimate a Project's Beta

When we are dealing with a project that is identical to the firm's other projects, we need only estimate the level of systematic risk for the firm and use that estimate as a proxy for the project's risk. Unfortunately, when projects are not typical of the firm, this approach does not work. For example, when Altria, which owns Philip Morris, the tobacco company, and Ste. Michelle Wine Estates, introduces a new dessert wine, this new product most likely carries with it a different level of systematic risk than what is typical for Altria as a whole.

To get a better approximation of the systematic risk level on this project, it would be great if we could estimate the level of systematic risk for the wine division and use that as a proxy for the project's systematic risk. Unfortunately, historical stock price data are available only for the company as a whole, and as you recall, historical stock return data are generally used to estimate a firm's beta. Thus, we are forced to use accounting return data rather than historical stock return data for the division to estimate the division's systematic risk. To estimate a project's beta using accounting data we need only run a time-series regression of the division's return on assets (net income/total assets) on the market index (the S&P 500). The regression coefficient from this equation would be the project's accounting beta and would serve as an approximation for the project's true beta, or measure of systematic risk. Alternatively, a multiple regression model based on accounting data could be developed to explain betas. The results of this model could then be applied to firms that are not publicly traded to estimate their betas.

How good is the accounting beta technique? It certainly is not as good as a direct calculation of the beta. In fact, the correlation between the accounting beta and the beta calculated on historical stock return data is only about 0.6. However, better luck has been experienced with multiple regression models used to predict betas. Unfortunately, in many cases there may not be any realistic alternative to the calculation of the accounting beta. Because adjusting for a project's risk is so important, the accounting beta method is much preferred to doing nothing.

## The Pure Play Method for Estimating Beta

**pure play method** a method for estimating a project's or division's beta that attempts to identify publicly traded firms engaged solely in the same business as the project or division.

Whereas the accounting beta method attempts to directly estimate a project's or division's beta, the **pure play method** attempts to identify publicly traded firms that are engaged solely in the same business as the project or division. Once the proxy or pure play firm is identified, its systematic risk is determined and then used as a proxy for the project's or division's level of systematic risk. What we are doing is *looking for a publicly traded firm with a project like ours and using that firm's required rate of return to judge our project*. In doing so we are presuming that the systematic risk and the capital structure of the proxy firm are identical to those of the project.

In using the pure play method it should be noted that a firm's capital structure is reflected in its beta. When the capital structure of the proxy firm is different from that of the project's firm, some adjustment must be made for this difference. Although not a perfect approach, it does provide some insights about the level of systematic risk a project might have.

## Examining a Project's Risk through Simulation

**simulation** a method for dealing with risk where the performance of the project under evaluation is estimated by randomly selecting observations from each of the distributions that affect the outcome of the project and continuing with this process until a representative record of the project's probable outcome is assembled.

Another method for evaluating risk in the investment decision is through the use of **simulation**. The risk-adjusted discount rate approach provided us with a single value for the risk-adjusted *NPV*, whereas a simulation approach gives us a probability distribution for the investment's *NPV* or *IRR*. Simulation *involves the process of imitating the performance of the project under evaluation. This is done by randomly selecting observations from each of the distributions that affect the outcome of the project and continuing with this process until a representative record of the project's probable outcome is assembled.*

The easiest way to develop an understanding of the computer simulation process is to follow through an example simulation for an investment project evaluation. Suppose a chemical producer is considering an extension to its processing plant. The simulation process is portrayed in Figure 11-6. First, the probability distributions are determined for all the factors that affect the project's returns. In this case, let us assume there are nine such variables:

1. Market size
2. Selling price
3. Market growth rate
4. Share of market (which results in physical sales volume)

## FIGURE 11-6  Capital-Budgeting Simulation

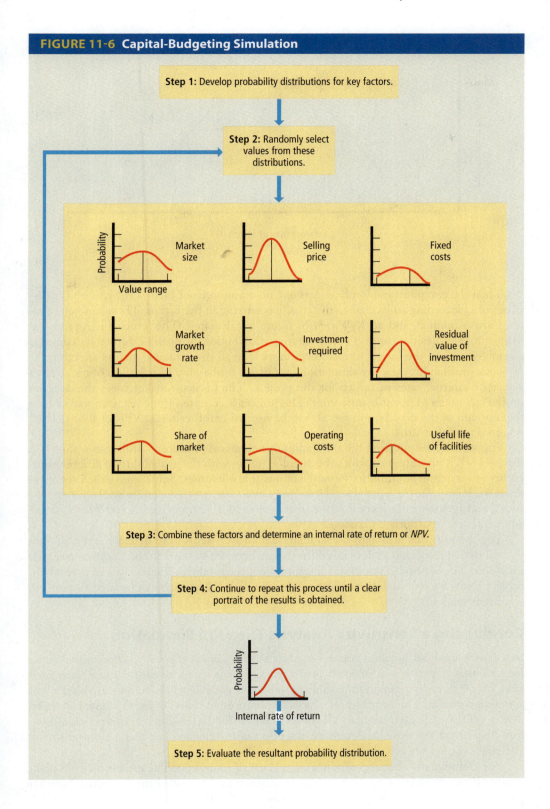

**Step 1:** Develop probability distributions for key factors.

**Step 2:** Randomly select values from these distributions.

Market size

Selling price

Fixed costs

Market growth rate

Investment required

Residual value of investment

Share of market

Operating costs

Useful life of facilities

**Step 3:** Combine these factors and determine an internal rate of return or *NPV*.

**Step 4:** Continue to repeat this process until a clear portrait of the results is obtained.

Internal rate of return

**Step 5:** Evaluate the resultant probability distribution.

5. Investment required
6. Residual value of investment
7. Operating costs
8. Fixed costs
9. Useful life of facilities

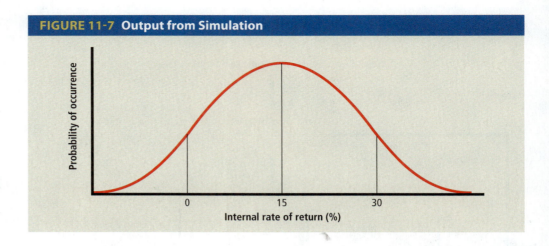

**FIGURE 11-7** Output from Simulation

Then the computer randomly selects one observation from each of the probability distributions, according to its chance of actually occurring in the future. These nine observations are combined, and an *NPV* or *IRR* figure is calculated. This process is repeated as many times as desired, until a representative distribution of possible future outcomes is assembled. Thus, the inputs to a simulation include all the principal factors affecting the project's profitability, and the simulation output is a probability distribution of net present values or internal rates of return for the project. The decision maker bases the decision on the full range of possible outcomes. The project is accepted if the decision maker feels that enough of the distribution lies above the normal cutoff criteria (*NPV* ≥ 0 or *IRR* ≥ required rate of return).

Suppose the output from the simulation of a chemical producer's project is as shown in Figure 11-7. This output provides the decision maker with the probability of different outcomes occurring in addition to the range of possible outcomes. Sometimes called **scenario analysis**, it *identifies the range of possible outcomes under the worst, best, and most likely cases*. The firm's management then examines the distribution to determine the project's level of risk and makes the appropriate decisions.

You'll notice that although the simulation approach helps us to determine the amount of total risk a project has, it does not differentiate between systematic and unsystematic risk. However, it does provide important insights about the total risk level of a given investment project. Now we will look briefly at how the simulation approach can be used to perform sensitivity analysis.

## Conducting a Sensitivity Analysis Through Simulation

**Sensitivity analysis** involves *determining how the distribution of possible net present values or internal rates of return for a particular project is affected by a change in one particular input variable*. This is done by changing the value of one input variable while holding all other input variables constant. The distribution of possible net present values or internal rates of return that is generated is then compared with the distribution of possible returns generated before the change was made to determine the effect of the change. For this reason sensitivity analysis is commonly called *what-if analysis*.

For example, the chemical producer that is considering a possible expansion to its plant may wish to determine the effect of a more pessimistic forecast of the anticipated market growth rate. After the more pessimistic forecast replaces the original forecast in the model, the simulation is rerun. The two outputs are then compared to determine how sensitive the results are to the revised estimate of the market growth rate.

**scenario analysis** a simulation approach for gauging a project's risk under the worst, best, and most likely outcomes. The firm's management examines the distribution of the outcomes to determine the project's level of risk and then makes the appropriate adjustment.

**sensitivity analysis** a method for dealing with risk where the change in the distribution of possible net present values or internal rates of return for a particular project resulting from a change in one particular input variable is calculated. This is done by changing the value of one input variable while holding all other input variables constant.

## Concept Check

1. Is a project's standing alone risk the appropriate level of risk for capital budgeting? Why or why not?
2. What problems are associated with using systematic risk as the measure for risk in capital budgeting?

3. What is the most commonly used method for incorporating risk into the capital-budgeting decision? How is this technique related to Principle 3?

4. Explain how simulations work.

5. What is a scenario analysis? What is a sensitivity analysis? When would you perform a sensitivity analysis?

# Chapter Summaries

## Identify guidelines by which we measure cash flows.  (pgs. 345–347)

**SUMMARY:** In this chapter, we examined the measurement of the incremental cash flows associated with a firm's investment proposals and methods used to evaluate those proposals. Relying on **Principle 1: Cash Flow Is What Matters** we focused only on the incremental, or differential, after-tax cash flows attributed to an investment proposal. Care is taken to beware of cash flows diverted from existing products, look for incidental or synergistic effects, consider working-capital requirements, consider incremental expenses, ignore sunk costs, account for opportunity costs, examine overhead costs carefully, and ignore interest payments and financing flows.

## Explain how a project's benefits and costs—that is, its free cash flows—are calculated.  (pgs. 348–358)

**SUMMARY:** To measure a project's benefits, we use the project's free cash flows:

Project's free cash flows = project's change in operating cash flows
       − change in net working capital
       − change in capital spending

We can rewrite this, inserting our calculation for the project's change in operating cash flows, to get

Project's free cash flows = change in earnings before interest and taxes
       − change in taxes
       + change in depreciation
       − change in net working capital
       − change in capital spending

**KEY TERMS**

**Initial outlay, page 348**  The immediate cash outflow necessary to purchase the asset and put it in operating order.

## Explain the importance of options, or flexibility, in capital budgeting.  (pgs. 358–360)

**SUMMARY:** There are several complications related to the capital-budgeting process. First, we examined capital rationing and the problems it can create by imposing a limit on the dollar size of the capital budget. Although capital rationing does not, in general, maximize shareholders' wealth, it does exist. The goal of maximizing shareholders' wealth remains, but it is now subject to a budget constraint.

## Understand, measure, and adjust for project risk.  (pgs. 360–369)

**SUMMARY:** Options, or flexibility, can make it worthwhile to pursue projects that would otherwise be rejected or make projects undertaken more valuable. Three of the most common types of options that can add value to a capital-budgeting project are (1) the option to delay a project until the

future cash flows are more favorable (this option is common when the firm has an exclusive right, perhaps a patent, to a product or technology); (2) the option to expand a project, perhaps in size or even to introduce new products that would not have otherwise been feasible; and (3) the option to abandon a project if its future cash flows fall short of expectations.

There are three types of capital-budgeting risk: the project standing alone risk, the project's contribution-to-firm risk, and the project's systematic risk. In theory, systematic risk is the appropriate risk measure, but bankruptcy costs and the issue of undiversified shareholders also give weight to considering a project's contribution-to-firm risk as the appropriate risk measure. Both measures of risk are valid, and we avoid making any specific allocation of the importance between the two.

The risk-adjusted discount rate relies on **Principle 3: Risk Requires a Reward** and involves an upward adjustment of the discount rate to compensate for risk. This method is based on the concept that investors demand higher returns for riskier projects. Thus, projects are evaluated using the appropriate, or risk-adjusted, discount rate.

The simulation method is used to provide information about the location and shape of the distribution of possible outcomes of the project. Decisions can be based directly on this method or used as an input to make decisions using the risk-adjusted discount rate method.

## KEY TERMS

**Project standing alone risk, page 361** A project's risk ignoring the fact that much of this risk will be diversified away.

**Contribution-to-firm risk, page 361** The amount of risk that the project contributes to the firm as a whole; this measure considers the fact that some of the project's risk will be diversified away as the project is combined with the firm's other projects and assets but ignores the effects of diversification of the firm's shareholders.

**Systematic risk, page 361** The risk of a project from the viewpoint of a well-diversified shareholder. This measure takes into account that some of the project's risk will be diversified away as the project is combined with the firm's other projects, and, in addition, some of the remaining risk will be diversified away by shareholders as they combine this stock with other stocks in their portfolios.

**Risk-adjusted discount rate, page 363** A method of risk adjustment when the risk associated with the investment is greater than the risk involved in a typical endeavor. Using this method, the discount rate is adjusted upward to compensate for this added risk.

**Pure play method, page 366** A method for estimating a project's or division's beta that

attempts to identify publicly traded firms engaged solely in the same business as the project or division.

**Simulation, page 366** A method for dealing with risk where the performance of the project under evaluation is estimated by randomly selecting observations from each of the distributions that affect the outcome of the project and continuing with this process until a representative record of the project's probable outcome is assembled.

**Scenario analysis, page 368** A simulation approach for gauging a project's risk under the worst, best, and most likely outcomes. The firm's management examines the distribution of the outcomes to determine the project's level of risk and then makes the appropriate adjustment.

**Sensitivity analysis, page 368** A method for dealing with risk where the change in the distribution of possible net present values or internal rates of return for a particular project resulting from a change in one particular input variable is calculated. This is done by changing the value of one input variable while holding all other input variables constant.

## KEY EQUATIONS

$$\text{Risk-adjusted } NPV = \begin{bmatrix} \text{present value of all the} \\ \text{future annual free cash} \\ \text{flows discounted back} \\ \text{to present at the risk-adjusted} \\ \text{rate of return} \end{bmatrix} - \begin{bmatrix} \text{the initial cash outlay} \end{bmatrix}$$

$$= \frac{FCF_1}{(1 + k^*)^1} + \frac{FCF_2}{(1 + k^*)^2} + \cdots + \frac{FCF_n}{(1 + k^*)^n} - IO$$

# Review Questions

All Review Questions are available in MyFinanceLab.

**11-1.** Why do we focus on cash flows rather than accounting profits in making our capital-budgeting decisions? Why are we interested only in incremental cash flows rather than total cash flows?

**11-2.** If depreciation is not a cash-flow expense, does it affect the level of cash flows from a project in any way? Why?

**11-3.** If a project requires an additional investment in working capital, how should this be treated when calculating the project's cash-flows?

**11-4.** How do sunk costs affect the determination of cash flows associated with an investment proposal?

**11-5.** In the preceding chapter we examined the payback period capital-budgeting criterion. Often this capital-budgeting criterion is used as a risk-screening device. Explain the rationale behind its use.

**11-6.** Use the concept of real options to explain why large restaurant chains often introduce new concept restaurants that have negative *NPV*s.

**11-7.** Explain how simulation works. What is the value in using a simulation approach?

# Study Problems

All Study Problems are available in MyFinanceLab.

**11-1.** (*Relevant cash flows*) Captins' Cereal is considering introducing a variation of its current breakfast cereal, Crunch Stuff. The new cereal will be similar to the old with the exception that it will contain sugarcoated marshmallows shaped in the form of stars and will be called Crunch Stuff n' Stars. It is estimated that the sales for the new cereal will be $25 million; however, 20 percent of those sales will be former Crunch Stuff customers who have switched to Crunch Stuff n' Stars but who would not have switched if the new product had not been introduced. What is the relevant sales level to consider when deciding whether to introduce Crunch Stuff n' Stars?

**11-2.** (*Consideration of sunk and opportunity costs*) Hewlett-Packard has designed a new type of printer that produces professional-quality photos. These new printers took 2 years to develop, with research and development running at $10 million after taxes over that period. Now all that's left is an investment of $22 million after taxes in new production equipment. It is expected that this new product line will bring in free cash flows of $5 million per year for each of the next 10 years. In addition, if Hewlett-Packard goes ahead with the new line of printers, the current production facility for the old printers that are to be replaced with this new line could be sold to a competitor, generating $3 million after taxes.

    a.  How should the $10 million of research and development be treated?
    b.  How should the $3 million from the sale of the existing production facility for the old printers be treated?
    c.  Given the information above, what are the cash flows associated with the new printers?

**11-3.** (*Capital gains tax*) The J. Harris Corporation is considering selling one of its old assembly machines. The machine, purchased for $30,000 5 years ago, had an expected life of 10 years and an expected salvage value of zero. Assume Harris uses simplified straight-line depreciation (depreciation of $3,000 per year) and could sell this old machine for $35,000. Also assume Harris has a 34 percent marginal tax rate.

    a.  What would be the taxes associated with this sale?
    b.  If the old machine were sold for $25,000, what would be the taxes associated with this sale?
    c.  If the old machine were sold for $15,000, what would be the taxes associated with this sale?
    d.  If the old machine were sold for $12,000, what would be the taxes associated with this sale?

**11-4.** (*Calculating free cash flows*) Racin' Scooters is introducing a new product and has an expected change in EBIT of $475,000. Racin' Scooters has a 34 percent marginal tax rate. The project will also produce $100,000 of depreciation per year. In addition, the project will also cause the following changes in year 1:

|  | WITHOUT THE PROJECT | WITH THE PROJECT |
| --- | :---: | :---: |
| Accounts receivable | $45,000 | $63,000 |
| Inventory | 65,000 | 80,000 |
| Accounts payable | 70,000 | 94,000 |

What is the project's free cash flow in year 1?

**11-5.** (*Calculating free cash flows*) Spartan Stores is expanding operations with the introduction of a new distribution center. Not only will sales increase but investment in inventory will decline due to increased efficiencies in getting inventory to showrooms. As a result of this new distribution center, Spartan expects a change in EBIT of $900,000. While inventory is expected to drop from $90,000 to $70,000, accounts receivables are expected to climb as a result of increased credit sales from $80,000 to $110,000. In addition, accounts payable are expected to increase from $65,000 to $80,000. This project will also produce $300,000 of depreciation per year, and Spartan Stores is in the 34 percent marginal tax rate. What is the project's free cash flow in year 1?

**11-6.** (*Calculating operating cash flows*) Assume that a new project will annually generate revenues of $2,000,000. Cash expenses including both fixed and variable costs will be $800,000, and depreciation will increase by $200,000 per year. In addition, let's assume that the firm's marginal tax rate is 34 percent. Calculate the operating cash flows.

**11-7.** (*Calculating free cash flows*) At present, Solartech Skateboards is considering expanding its product line to include gas-powered skateboards; however, it is questionable how well they will be received by skateboarders. While you feel there is a 60 percent chance you will sell 10,000 of these per year for 10 years (after which time this project is expected to shut down because solar-powered skateboards will become more popular), you also recognize that there is a 20 percent chance that you will only sell 3,000 and also a 20 percent chance you will sell 13,000. The gas skateboards would sell for $100 each and have a variable cost of $40 each. Regardless of how many you sell, the annual fixed costs associated with production would be $160,000. In addition, there would be a $1,000,000 initial expenditure associated with the purchase of new production equipment. It is assumed that this initial expenditure will be depreciated using the simplified straight-line method down to zero over 10 years. Because of the number of stores that will need inventory, the working-capital requirements are the same regardless of the level of sales, and this project will require a one-time initial investment of $50,000 in net working capital, and that working-capital investment will be recovered when the project is shut down. Finally, assume that the firm's marginal tax rate is 34 percent.

    a. What is the initial outlay associated with the project?

    b. What are the annual free cash flows associated with the project for years 1 through 9 under each sales forecast? What are the expected annual free cash flows for years 1 through 9?

    c. What is the terminal cash flow in year 10 (that is, what is the free cash flow in year 10 plus any additional cash flows associated with the termination of the project)?

    d. Using the expected free cash flows, what is the project's *NPV* given a 10 percent required rate of return? What would the project's *NPV* be if 10,000 skateboards were sold?

**11-8.** (*Calculating free cash flows*) You are considering new elliptical trainers and you feel you can sell 5,000 of these per year for 5 years (after which time this project is expected to shut down when it is learned that being fit is unhealthy). The elliptical trainers would sell for $1,000 each and have a variable cost of $500 each. The annual fixed costs associated with production would be $1,000,000. In addition, there would be a $5,000,000 initial expenditure associated with the purchase of new production equipment. It is assumed that this initial expenditure will be depreciated using the simplified straight-line method down to zero over 5 years. This project will also require a one-time initial investment of $1,000,000 in net working capital associated with inventory, and that working-capital investment will be recovered when the project is shut down. Finally, assume that the firm's marginal tax rate is 34 percent.

    a. What is the initial outlay associated with this project?

    b. What are the annual free cash flows associated with this project for years 1 through 4?

    c. What is the terminal cash flow in year 5 (that is, what is the free cash flow in year 5 plus any additional cash flows associated with the termination of the project)?

    d. What is the project's *NPV* given a 10 percent required rate of return?

**11-9.** (*New project analysis*) The Chung Chemical Corporation is considering the purchase of a chemical analysis machine. Although the machine being considered will result in an increase in earnings before interest and taxes of $35,000 per year, it has a purchase price of $100,000, and it would cost an additional $5,000 to properly install the machine. In addition, to properly operate the machine, inventory must be increased by $5,000. This machine has an expected life of 10 years, after which it will have no salvage value. Also, assume simplified straight-line depreciation and that this machine is being depreciated down to zero, a 34 percent marginal tax rate, and a required rate of return of 15 percent.

    a. What is the initial outlay associated with this project?

    b. What are the annual after-tax cash flows associated with this project for years 1 through 9?

   c. What is the terminal cash flow in year 10 (what is the annual after-tax cash flow in year 10 plus any additional cash flows associated with the termination of the project)?

   d. Should this machine be purchased?

**11-10.** (*New project analysis*) Raymobile Motors is considering the purchase of a new production machine for $500,000. The purchase of this machine will result in an increase in earnings before interest and taxes of $150,000 per year. To operate this machine properly, workers would have to go through a brief training session that would cost $25,000 after taxes. It would cost $5,000 to install the machine properly. Also, because the machine is extremely efficient, its purchase would necessitate an increase in inventory of $30,000. This machine has an expected life of 10 years, after which it will have no salvage value. Assume simplified straight-line depreciation and that this machine is being depreciated down to zero, a 34 percent marginal tax rate, and a required rate of return of 15 percent.

   a. What is the initial outlay associated with this project?

   b. What are the annual after-tax cash flows associated with this project for years 1 through 9?

   c. What is the terminal cash flow in year 10 (what is the annual after-tax cash flow in year 10 plus any additional cash flows associated with the termination of the project)?

   d. Should the machine be purchased?

**11-11.** (*New project analysis*) Garcia's Truckin' Inc. is considering the purchase of a new production machine for $200,000. The purchase of this machine will result in an increase in earnings before interest and taxes of $50,000 per year. To operate the machine properly, workers would have to go through a brief training session that would cost $5,000 after taxes. It would cost $5,000 to install the machine properly. Also, because this machine is extremely efficient, its purchase would necessitate an increase in inventory of $20,000. This machine has an expected life of 10 years, after which it will have no salvage value. Finally, to purchase the new machine, it appears that the firm would have to borrow $100,000 at 8 percent interest from its local bank, resulting in additional interest payments of $8,000 per year. Assume simplified straight-line depreciation and that the machine is being depreciated down to zero, a 34 percent marginal tax rate, and a required rate of return of 10 percent.

   a. What is the initial outlay associated with this project?

   b. What are the annual after-tax cash flows associated with this project for years 1 through 9?

   c. What is the terminal cash flow in year 10 (what is the annual after-tax cash flow in year 10 plus any additional cash flows associated with the termination of the project)?

   d. Should the machine be purchased?

**11-12.** (*Calculating free cash flows*) Vandelay Industries is considering a new project with a 4-year life with the following cost and revenue data. This project will require an investment of $140,000 in new equipment. This new equipment will be depreciated down to zero over 4 years using the simplified straight-line method and has no salvage value. This new project will generate additional sales revenue of $112,000 while additional operating costs, excluding depreciation, will be $68,000. Vandelay's marginal tax rate is 35 percent. What is the project's free cash flow in year 1?

**11-13.** (*Calculating free cash flows*) Doublemeat Palace is considering a new plant for a temporary customer, and its finance department has determined the following characteristics. The company owns much of the plant and equipment to be used for the product. This equipment was originally purchased for $90,000; however, if the project is not undertaken, this equipment will be sold for $50,000 after taxes; in addition, if the project is not accepted, the plant used for the project could be sold for $105,000 after taxes—the plant originally cost $40,000. The rest of the equipment will need to be purchased at a cost of $150,000. This new equipment will be depreciated by the straight-line method over the project's 3-year life, after which it will have zero salvage value. No change in net operating working capital would be required, and management expects revenues resulting from this new project to be $234,000 per year for 3 years, while increased operating expenses, excluding depreciation, are expected to be $82,000 per year over the project's 3-year life. The average tax rate is 25 percent and the marginal tax rate is 30 percent. The required rate of return for this project is 8 percent. What is the project's *NPV*?

**11-14.** (*Comprehensive problem*) Traid Winds Corporation, a firm in the 34 percent marginal tax bracket with a 15 percent required rate of return or cost of capital, is considering a new project. This project involves the introduction of a new product. The project is expected to last 5 years and then, because this is somewhat of a fad product, be terminated. Given the following information, determine the free cash flows associated with the project, the project's net present value, the profitability index, and the internal rate of return. Apply the appropriate decision criteria.

| Cost of new plant and equipment | $14,800,000 |
| Shipping and installation costs | $    200,000 |
| Unit sales | |

| YEAR | UNITS SOLD |
|---|---|
| 1 | 70,000 |
| 2 | 120,000 |
| 3 | 120,000 |
| 4 | 80,000 |
| 5 | 70,000 |

| | |
|---|---|
| Sales price per unit | $300/unit in years 1 through 4, $250/unit in year 5 |
| Variable cost per unit | $140/unit |
| Annual fixed costs | $700,000 per year in years 1–5 |
| Working-capital requirements | There will be an initial working-capital requirement of $200,000 just to get production started. For each year, the total investment in net working capital will be equal to 10 percent of the dollar value of sales for that year. Thus, the investment in working capital will increase during years 1 and 2, then decrease in year 4. Finally, all working capital is liquidated at the termination of the project at the end of year 5. |
| The depreciation method | Use the simplified straight-line method over 5 years. Assume that the plant and equipment will have no salvage value after 5 years. |

**11-15.** (*Comprehensive problem*) The Shome Corporation, a firm in the 34 percent marginal tax bracket with a 15 percent required rate of return or cost of capital, is considering a new project. The project involves the introduction of a new product. This project is expected to last 5 years and then, because this is somewhat of a fad product, be terminated. Given the following information, determine the free cash flows associated with the project, the project's net present value, the profitability index, and the internal rate of return. Apply the appropriate decision criteria.

| Cost of new plant and equipment | $6,900,000 |
| Shipping and installation costs | $  100,000 |
| Unit sales | |

| YEAR | UNITS SOLD |
|---|---|
| 1 | 80,000 |
| 2 | 100,000 |
| 3 | 120,000 |
| 4 | 70,000 |
| 5 | 70,000 |

| | |
|---|---|
| Sales price per unit | $250/unit in years 1 through 4, $200/unit in year 5 |
| Variable cost per unit | $130/units |
| Annual fixed costs | $300,000 per year in years 1–5 |
| Working-capital requirements | There will be an initial working-capital requirement of $100,000 just to get production started. For each year, the total investment in net working capital will be equal to 10 percent of the dollar value of sales for that year. Thus, the investment in working capital will increase during years 1 through 3, then decrease in year 4. Finally, all working capital is liquidated at the termination of the project at the end of year 5. |
| The depreciation method | Use the simplified straight-line method over 5 years. Assume that the plant and equipment will have no salvage value after 5 years. |

**11-16.** (*Real options*) Hurricane Katrina brought unprecedented destruction to New Orleans and the Mississippi gulf coast in 2005. Notably, the burgeoning casino gambling industry along the Mississippi coast was virtually wiped out overnight. GCC Corporation owns one of the oldest casinos in the Biloxi, Mississippi, area, and its casino was damaged but not destroyed by the tidal surge from the storm. The reason was that it had been located several blocks back from the beach on higher ground. However, since the competitor casinos were completely destroyed and will have to rebuild from scratch, GCC believes that it is likely to have a number of good opportunities. You have been hired to provide GCC with strategic advice. What have you learned about real options that will help you develop a strategy for GCC?

**11-17.** (*Real options and capital budgeting*) You have come up with a great idea for a Tex-Mex-Thai fusion restaurant. After doing a financial analysis of this venture, you estimate that the initial outlay will be $6 million. You also estimate that there is a 50 percent chance that this new restaurant will be well received and will produce annual cash flows of $800,000 per year forever (a perpetuity), while there is a 50 percent chance of it producing a cash flow of only $200,000 per year forever (a perpetuity) if it isn't received well.

    a.  What is the *NPV* of the restaurant if the required rate of return you use to discount the project cash flows is 10 percent?

    b.  What are the real options that this analysis may be ignoring?

    c.  Explain why the project may be worthwhile even though you have just estimated that its *NPV* is negative.

**11-18.** (*Real options and capital budgeting*) Go-Power Batteries has developed a high-voltage nickel-metal hydride battery that can be used to power a hybrid automobile. It can sell the technology immediately to Toyota for $10 million, or alternatively, Go-Power Batteries can invest $50 million in a plant and produce the batteries for itself and sell them. Unfortunately, given the current size of the market for hybrids, the present value of the cash flows from such a plant would be only $40 million, implying that the plant has a negative expected *NPV* of −$10 million. What are the real options that are being ignored in this analysis? Can you come up with a compelling reason why Go-Power should keep the technology rather than sell it to Toyota?

**11-19.** (*Risk-adjusted NPV*) The Hokie Corporation is considering two mutually exclusive projects. Both require an initial outlay of $10,000 and will operate for 5 years. Project A will produce expected cash flows of $5,000 per year for years 1 through 5, whereas project B will produce expected cash flows of $6,000 per year for years 1 through 5. Because project B is the riskier of the two projects, the management of Hokie Corporation has decided to apply a required rate of return of 15 percent to its evaluation but only a 12 percent required rate of return to project A. Determine each project's risk-adjusted net present value.

**11-20.** (*Risk-adjusted discount rates and risk classes*) The G. Wolfe Corporation is examining two capital-budgeting projects with 5-year lives. The first, project A, is a replacement project; the second, project B, is a project unrelated to current operations. The G. Wolfe Corporation uses the risk-adjusted discount rate method and groups projects according to purpose, and then it uses a required rate of return or discount rate that has been preassigned to that purpose or risk class. The expected cash flows for these projects are given here:

|                    | PROJECT A   | PROJECT B   |
|--------------------|-------------|-------------|
| Initial investment | −$250,000   | −$400,000   |
| Cash inflows:      |             |             |
| Year 1             | $130,000    | $135,000    |
| Year 2             | 40,000      | 135,000     |
| Year 3             | 50,000      | 135,000     |
| Year 4             | 90,000      | 135,000     |
| Year 5             | 130,000     | 135,000     |

The purpose/risk classes and preassigned required rates of return are as follows:

| PURPOSE | REQUIRED RATE OF RETURN |
|---|---|
| Replacement decision | 12% |
| Modification or expansion of existing product line | 15 |
| Project unrelated to current operations | 18 |
| Research and development operations | 20 |

Determine each project's risk-adjusted net present value.

# Mini Case

*This Mini Case is available in* MyFinanceLab.

It's been 2 months since you took a position as an assistant financial analyst at Caledonia Products. Although your boss has been pleased with your work, he is still a bit hesitant about unleashing you without supervision. Your next assignment involves both the calculation of the cash flows associated with a new investment under consideration and the evaluation of several mutually exclusive projects. Given your lack of tenure at Caledonia, you have been asked not only to provide a recommendation but also to respond to a number of questions aimed at judging your understanding of the capital-budgeting process. The memorandum you received outlining your assignment follows:

> To: The Assistant Financial Analyst
> From: Mr. V. Morrison, CEO, Caledonia Products
> Re: Cash Flow Analysis and Capital Rationing

We are considering the introduction of a new product. Currently we are in the 34 percent marginal tax bracket with a 15 percent required rate of return or cost of capital. This project is expected to last 5 years and then, because this is somewhat of a fad product, be terminated. The following information describes the new project:

| Cost of new plant and equipment | $7,900,000 |
|---|---|
| Shipping and installation costs | $ 100,000 |
| Unit sales | |

| YEAR | UNITS SOLD |
|---|---|
| 1 | 70,000 |
| 2 | 120,000 |
| 3 | 140,000 |
| 4 | 80,000 |
| 5 | 60,000 |

| | |
|---|---|
| Sales price per unit | $300/unit in years 1 through 4, $260/unit in year 5 |
| Variable cost per unit | $180/unit |
| Annual fixed costs | $200,000 per year in years 1–5 |
| Working-capital requirements | There will be an initial working-capital requirement of $100,000 just to get production started. For each year, the total investment in net working capital will be equal to 10 percent of the dollar value of sales for that year. Thus, the investment in working capital will increase during years 1 through 3, then decrease in year 4. Finally, all working capital is liquidated at the termination of the project at the end of year 5. |
| The depreciation method | Use the simplified straight-line method over 5 years. Assume that the plant and equipment will have no salvage value after 5 years. |

a. Should Caledonia focus on cash flows or accounting profits in making its capital-budgeting decisions? Should the company be interested in incremental cash flows, incremental profits, total free cash flows, or total profits?

b. How does depreciation affect free cash flows?

c. How do sunk costs affect the determination of cash flows?

d. What is the project's initial outlay?

e. What are the differential cash flows over the project's life?

f. What is the terminal cash flow?

g. Draw a cash-flow diagram for this project.

h. What is its net present value?

i. What is its internal rate of return?

j. Should the project be accepted? Why or why not?

k. In capital budgeting, risk can be measured from three perspectives. What are those three measures of a project's risk?

l. According to the CAPM, which measurement of a project's risk is relevant? What complications does reality introduce into the CAPM view of risk, and what does that mean for our view of the relevant measure of a project's risk?

m. Explain how simulation works. What is the value in using a simulation approach?

n. What is sensitivity analysis and what is its purpose?

## Appendix 11A

# The Modified Accelerated Cost of Recovery System

To simplify our computations we have used straight-line depreciation throughout this chapter. However, firms use accelerated depreciation for calculating their taxable income. In fact, the modified accelerated cost recovery system (MACRS) has been used since 1987. Under the MACRS the depreciation period is based on the asset depreciation range (ADR) system, which groups assets into classes by asset type and industry and then determines the actual number of years to be used in depreciating the asset. In addition, the MACRS restricts the amount of depreciation that may be taken in the year an asset is acquired or sold. These limitations have been called averaging conventions. The two primary conventions, or limitations, may be stated as follows:

1. *Half-Year Convention:* Personal property, such as machinery, is treated as having been placed in service or disposed of at the midpoint of the taxable year. Thus, a half-year of depreciation generally is allowed for the taxable year in which property is placed in service and in the final taxable year. As a result, a 3-year property class asset has a depreciation calculation that spans 4 years, with only a half a year's depreciation in the first and fourth years. In effect, it is assumed the asset is in service for 6 months during both the first and last year.

2. *Mid-Month Convention:* Real property, such as buildings, is treated as being placed in service or disposed of in the middle of the month. Accordingly, a half-month of depreciation is allowed for the month the property is placed in service and also for the final month of service.

Using the MACRS results in a different percentage of the asset being depreciated each year; these percentages are shown in Table 11A-1.

| TABLE 11A-1 | Percentages for Property Classes | | | | | |
|---|---|---|---|---|---|---|
| Recovery Year | 3-Year | 5-Year | 7-Year | 10-Year | 15-Year | 20-Year |
| 1 | 33.3% | 20.0% | 14.3% | 10.0% | 5.0% | 3.8% |
| 2 | 44.5 | 32.0 | 24.5 | 18.0 | 9.5 | 7.2 |
| 3 | 14.8 | 19.2 | 17.5 | 14.4 | 8.6 | 6.7 |
| 4 | 7.4 | 11.5 | 12.5 | 11.5 | 7.7 | 6.2 |
| 5 | | 11.5 | 8.9 | 9.2 | 6.9 | 5.7 |
| 6 | | 5.8 | 8.9 | 7.4 | 6.2 | 5.3 |
| 7 | | | 8.9 | 6.6 | 5.9 | 4.9 |
| 8 | | | 4.5 | 6.6 | 5.9 | 4.5 |
| 9 | | | | 6.5 | 5.9 | 4.5 |
| 10 | | | | 6.5 | 5.9 | 4.5 |
| 11 | | | | 3.3 | 5.9 | 4.5 |
| 12 | | | | | 5.9 | 4.5 |
| 13 | | | | | 5.9 | 4.5 |
| 14 | | | | | 5.9 | 4.5 |
| 15 | | | | | 5.9 | 4.5 |
| 16 | | | | | 3.0 | 4.5 |
| 17 | | | | | | 4.5 |
| 18 | | | | | | 4.5 |
| 19 | | | | | | 4.5 |
| 20 | | | | | | 4.5 |
| 21 | | | | | | 1.7 |
| Total | 100.0% | 100.0% | 100.0% | 100.0% | 100.0% | 100.0% |

## TABLE 11A-2  MACRS Demonstrated

| Year | Depreciation Percentage | Annual Depreciation |
|------|-------------------------|---------------------|
| 1 | 20.0% | $ 2,400 |
| 2 | 32.0 | 3,840 |
| 3 | 19.2 | 2,304 |
| 4 | 11.5 | 1,380 |
| 5 | 11.5 | 1,380 |
| 6 | 5.8 | 696 |
|   | 100.0% | $12,000 |

To demonstrate the use of the MACRS, assume that a piece of equipment costs $12,000 and has been assigned to a 5-year class. Using the percentages in Table 11A-1 for a 5-year class asset, the depreciation deductions would be calculated as shown in Table 11A-2.

Note that the averaging convention that allows for the half-year of depreciation in the first year results in a half-year of depreciation beyond the fifth year, or in year 6.

# What Does All This Mean?

Depreciation, while an expense, is not a cash-flow item. However, depreciation expense lowers the firm's taxable income, which in turn reduces the firm's tax liability and increases its cash flow. Throughout our calculations in Chapter 11 we used a simplified straight-line depreciation method to keep the calculations simple, but in reality you would use the MACRS method. The advantage of accelerated depreciation is that you end up with more depreciation expense (a non-cash item) in the earlier years and less depreciation expense in the latter years. As a result, you have less taxable profits in the early years and more taxable profits in the latter years. This reduces taxes in the earlier years when the present values are greatest, while increasing taxes in the latter years when the present values are smaller. In effect, the MACRS allows you to postpone paying taxes. Regardless of whether you use straight-line or accelerated depreciation (MACRS), the *total* depreciation is the same—it is just the timing of when the depreciation is expensed that changes.

Most corporations prepare two sets of books, one for calculating taxes for the IRS in which they use the MACRS, and one for their stockholders in which they use straight-line depreciation. For capital-budgeting purposes, only the set of books used to calculate taxes is relevant.

# Study Problems

*All Study Problems are available in* MyFinanceLab.

**11A-1.** (*Depreciation*) Compute the annual depreciation for an asset that costs $250,000 and is in the 5-year property class. Use the MACRS in your calculation.

**11A-2.** (*Depreciation*) The Mason Falls Mfg. Company just acquired a depreciable asset this year, costing $500,000. Furthermore, the asset falls into the 7-year property class using the MACRS.

    a.  Using the MACRS, compute the annual depreciation.

    b.  What assumption is being made about when the asset was bought within the year?

# 12

# Determining the Financing Mix

## Learning Objectives

**1** **Distinguish** between business and financial risk.

Understanding the Difference Between Business and Financial Risk

**2** **Use** break-even analysis.

Break-even Analysis

**3** **Understand** the relationships between operating, financial, and combined leverage.

Sources of Operating Leverage

**4** **Discuss** the concept of an optimal capital structure.

Capital Structure Theory

**5** **Use** the basic tools of capital structure management.

The Basic Tools of Capital Structure Management

What do telecom giant AT&T (T) and Heineken (HINKY.PK) (one of the world's largest brewers of beer) share in common? In the spring of 2012 they both borrowed a lot of money by issuing bonds in the public markets. AT&T raised $3 billion in April 2012 by issuing bonds while Heineken raised a paltry $750 million. The decision to issue debt was in both instances a choice made by the firm's respective management team and board of directors. Why corporate bonds; why not common or preferred stock? These are the questions we address in this chapter.

When a firm needs funds to support its investment plans, it typically raises them internally by reinvesting all or part of its earnings. This process of reinvesting firm earnings is tantamount to increasing the investment of the firm's common shareholders in the firm because the earnings represent what is left for the common stockholders after everyone else has been paid. However, occasionally firms find that they need to raise funds externally from the capital markets either because they do not have sufficient earnings to reinvest or they want to rebalance their capital structures. Historically, when firms tried to raise external sources of funds, they had to go to the public capital market where they sold bonds or stocks with the help of investment bankers to a diverse group of investors. However, today private equity firms are a growing source of external capital.

Earlier chapters allowed us to develop an understanding of how financial assets are valued in the marketplace. Drawing on the tenets of valuation theory, we presented various approaches to measuring the cost of funds to the business organization. This chapter presents concepts that relate to the valuation process and the cost of capital; it also discusses the crucial problem of planning the firm's financing mix.

The cost of capital provides a direct link between the formulation of the firm's asset structure and its financial structure. This is illustrated in Figure 12-1. Recall that the cost of capital is a basic input to the time-adjusted, capital-budgeting models. Therefore, it affects the capital-budgeting, or asset-selection, process. The cost of capital is affected, in turn, by the composition of the right-hand side of the firm's balance sheet—that is, its financial structure.

This chapter examines tools that can be useful aids to the financial manager in determining the firm's proper financial structure. First, we review the notion of risk from the perspective of the firm's shareholders as it relates to the potential volatility in shareholder earnings. Corporate CEOs and boards of directors are very sensitive to the earnings numbers they report to Wall Street, so it behooves the financial manager to understand fully how the firm's capital structure affects the variability of earnings.

**FIGURE 12-1** The Cost of Capital as a Link Between a Firm's Asset Structure and Financial Structure

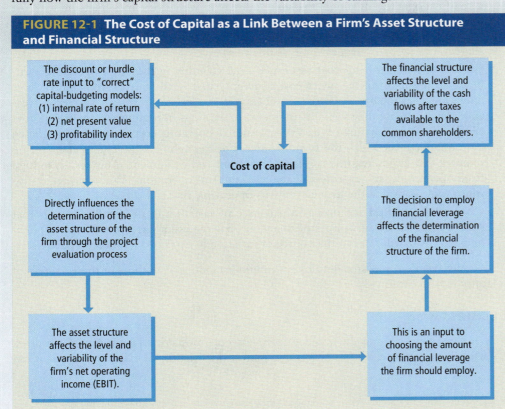

Next, we turn to a discussion of capital structure theory and the basic tools of capital structure management. Actual capital structure practices are also placed in perspective.

What is it about the nature of business that causes changes in sales revenues to translate into larger variations in net income and, finally, the earnings available to the common shareholders? It would be a good planning tool for management to be able to decompose such fluctuations into those policies associated with the operating side of the business and those policies associated with the financing side of the business.

If you understand the material and analytical processes in this chapter, you will be able to make positive contributions to company strategies that deal with the firm's financing mix. You will be able to formulate a defensible answer to the question: "Should we finance our next capital project with a new issue of bonds or a new issue of common stock?" You can also help a lot of firms avoid making serious financial errors, the consequences of which can last for many years.

**Distinguish between business and financial risk.**

# Understanding the Difference Between Business and Financial Risk

If investors are surprised by lower-than-expected corporate earnings, this can lead to a downward revision in their expectations of the firm's future prospects and, consequently, reduce the firm's common stock price. Thus, corporate executives and their boards of directors pay close attention to the earnings that they report to Wall Street. For this reason the financial analyst needs to understand the sources of volatility in firm earnings per share.

In this section we separate the variation in the firm's income stream into one of three sources:

1. **Choice of business line**—the variation in firm earnings that arises out of the natural volatility in revenues attributable to the industry in which it operates. For example, if the firm operates in a highly volatile industry in which revenues fluctuate with the business cycle, then the firm's earnings will be more volatile than another firm that operates in an industry that is less sensitive to the business cycle. We will refer to this source of variation in firm earnings as **business risk**.

2. **Choice of an operating cost structure**—the volatility in the firm's operating earnings that results from the firm's cost structure,[1] that is, the mix of fixed and variable operating costs the firm pays to do business. Greater fixed operating costs (versus variable costs) increase the variability in operating earnings in response to changes in revenues. The firm's mixture of fixed versus variable operating costs is largely determined by the industry in which the firm operates. For example, automobile manufacturing requires that large investments be made in plant and equipment. This results in high fixed operating costs regardless of the level of plant operations. We will refer to this source of variation in the firm earnings as **operating risk**.

3. **Choice of a capital structure**—the source of variation in the firm's earnings that results from its use of sources of financing that require a fixed return, such as debt financing. We will refer to this source of variation in earnings as **financial risk**.

We now spend some time developing an understanding of all three of these sources of volatility in firm earnings.

## Business Risk

The amount of business risk the firm decides to take on is most critical at the time the business is started. However, because business risk can affect the volatility of a firm's revenues, it can

**business risk** the risk of the firm's future earnings that is a direct result of the particular line of business chosen by the firm.

**operating risk** risk driven by the mix of fixed versus variable costs the firm incurs to do business.

**financial risk** risk driven by the presence of fixed finance costs in the firm's capital structure (as opposed to variable finance costs such as dividends declared and paid).

---

[1]Recall that the term EBIT is the acronym for earnings before interest and taxes. If what accountants call *other income* and *other expenses* are equal to zero, then EBIT is equal to net operating income. For our purposes we use these two terms interchangeably.

affect the firm's earnings per share. Thus, it behooves us to spend a little time discussing the sources of business risk. We identify four basic determinants of a firm's business risk:

1. **The stability of the domestic economy.**   Firms that operate in more volatile economies, such as those of developing nations, are subject to swings in revenue that is much more severe than those that operate within developed countries. For example, a chain of clothing stores operating within the United States faces a less volatile revenue stream than, say, a chain located in Nigeria or even Brazil.

2. **The exposure to, and stability of, foreign economies.**   In today's global economy, more and more firms produce and sell their products in multiple countries. This means that it is not only the natural volatility of the firm's home country that drives the volatility of the firm's revenues but also that of the countries in which its goods and services are produced and sold.

3. **Sensitivity to the business cycle.**   Some industries are more sensitive to the business cycle than others. For example, the sales of consumer durable goods such as automobiles, housing, and appliances tend to be more sensitive to swings in the business cycle than necessities such as food and clothing.

4. **Competitive pressures in the firm's industry.**   Here we refer to the forces of other firms within the firm's marketplace that provide the same (or close substitute) products and services. Greater competitive pressures will force the firm to make price concessions sooner and deeper than would otherwise be the case.

Although business risk is obviously a critical determinant of earnings volatility, for the balance of this chapter we will assume that the firm's business risk is fixed, or given. This will allow us to focus on operating and financial risks, over which managers have more control.

## Operating Risk

Operating risk increases when the firm incurs more fixed versus variable costs. Fixed costs do not vary with the firm's revenues, but variable costs, as the name implies, do rise and fall with revenues. A key tool for evaluating operating risk is break-even analysis. Therefore, we open our discussion of operating risk by defining the break-even chart.

## Concept Check

1. Why do managers care about the volatility of their firms' earnings?
2. What are the three determinants of the volatility of a firm's earnings?
3. Describe the sources of business risk.
4. What is the determinant of a firm's operating risk?

# Break-Even Analysis

 Use break-even analysis.

Both small and large organizations utilize the break-even analysis tool for two reasons: It is based on straightforward assumptions, and companies have found that the information gained from the break-even model is beneficial in decision-making situations. A break-even analysis is used to determine the **break-even quantity** of the firm's output. What is meant by the break-even quantity of output? It is that quantity of output, denominated in units, that results in operating income (or EBIT) equal to zero. In other words, a break-even analysis enables the analyst (1) to determine the quantity of output that must be sold to cover all operating costs, as distinct from financial costs and (2) to calculate the EBIT that will be achieved at various output levels.

**break-even quantity** the number of units a firm must sell before it starts to earn a profit.

## Essential Elements of the Break-Even Model

To implement the break-even model, we must separate the production costs of the company into two mutually exclusive categories: fixed costs and variable costs. You will recall from your study of basic economics that in the long run all costs are variable. The break-even analysis, therefore, is a short-run concept.

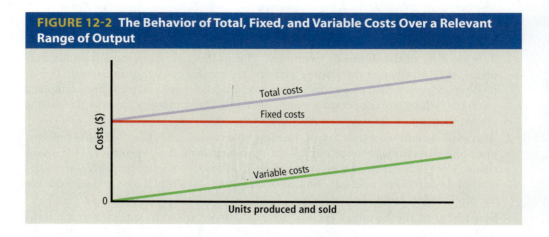

**FIGURE 12-2**  The Behavior of Total, Fixed, and Variable Costs Over a Relevant Range of Output

**Fixed Costs**    **Fixed costs**, also referred to as **indirect costs**, *do not vary with either the firm's sales or output.* As the production volume increases, the fixed cost *per unit* of product falls, because the firm's total fixed costs are spread over larger and larger quantities of output. Figure 12-2 graphs the behavior of total fixed costs with respect to the company's relevant range of units produced and sold. This total is shown to be unaffected by the quantity of product that is manufactured and sold. Over some other output range, the amount of total fixed costs might be higher or lower for the same company.

In a manufacturing setting, some specific examples of fixed costs are

1. Administrative salaries
2. Depreciation
3. Insurance
4. Lump sums spent on intermittent advertising programs
5. Property taxes
6. Rent

**fixed costs** costs that do not vary in total dollar amount as sales volume or quantity of output changes. Also called **indirect costs.**

**indirect costs** see **fixed costs.**

**Variable Costs**    **Variable costs** are sometimes referred to as **direct costs**. Variable costs *per unit vary as output changes.* Total variable costs are computed by taking the variable cost per unit and multiplying it by the total quantity produced and sold. The break-even model assumes proportionality between total variable costs and sales. Thus, if sales rise by 10 percent, it is assumed that variable costs will rise by 10 percent. Notice that if zero units of the product are manufactured, then variable costs are zero, but fixed costs are greater than zero. This implies that some contribution to the coverage of fixed costs occurs as long as the selling price per unit exceeds the variable costs per unit. This helps explain why some firms will operate a plant even when sales are temporarily depressed—that is, to try to cover fixed costs.

Some examples of variable costs include

1. Direct labor
2. Direct materials
3. Energy costs (fuel, electricity, natural gas) associated with production
4. Freight costs for products leaving the plant
5. Packaging
6. Sales commissions

**variable costs** expenses that vary in total as output changes. Also called **direct costs.**

**direct costs** see **variable costs.**

Figure 12-2 also graphs total costs with respect to the company's relevant range of output. Total cost is simply the sum of the firm's fixed and variable costs.

**More on the Behavior of Costs**    No one really believes that *all* costs behave as neatly as we have illustrated the fixed and variable costs in Figure 12-2. Nor does any law or accounting principle dictate that a certain element of the firm's total costs always will be classified as fixed or variable. This depends on each firm's specific circumstances. In

**FIGURE 12-3  Semivariable Cost Behavior Over a Relevant Range of Output**

one firm, energy costs may be predominantly fixed, whereas in another they may vary with output.[2]

Furthermore, some costs may be fixed for a while, then rise sharply to a higher level as a higher output is reached, remain fixed, and then rise again with further increases in production. Such costs may be termed either *semivariable* or *semifixed*. The label is your choice because both are used in practice. An example might be the salaries paid to production supervisors. Should output be cut back by 15 percent for a short period, the organization is not likely to lay off 15 percent of its supervisors. Similarly, the percentage commissions paid to salespeople are often incrementally stepped up the more they sell. This sort of cost behavior is shown in Figure 12-3.

To implement the break-even model and deal with such a complex cost structure, the financial manager must (1) identify the most relevant output range for planning purposes and then (2) approximate the cost effect of semivariable items over this range by segregating a portion of them to fixed costs and a portion to variable costs. In the actual business setting this procedure is not fun. It is not unusual for the analyst who deals with the figures to spend considerably more time allocating costs to fixed and variable categories than doing the actual break-even calculations.

**Total Revenue and Volume of Output**   Besides fixed and variable costs, the essential elements of the break-even model include total revenue from sales and volume of output. **Total revenue** means *total sales dollars* and is equal to the selling price per unit multiplied by the quantity sold. The **volume of output** refers to the *firm's level of operations* and may be *indicated either as a unit quantity or as sales dollars.*

**total revenue** total sales dollars.

**volume of output** the number of units produced and sold for a particular period of time.

## Finding the Break-Even Point

Finding the break-even point in terms of units of production can be accomplished in several ways. All approaches require the essential elements of the break-even model just described. The break-even model is a simple adaptation of the firm's income statement expressed in the following analytical format:

$$\text{Sales} - (\text{total variable cost} + \text{total fixed cost}) = \text{profit} \qquad (12\text{-}1)$$

On a units-of-production basis, it is necessary to introduce (1) the price at which each unit is sold and (2) the variable cost per unit of output. Because the profit item studied in a break-even analysis is EBIT, we use this acronym instead of the word *profit*. In terms of units, the income statement shown in equation (12-1) becomes the break-even model by setting EBIT equal to zero:

$$\left(\begin{array}{c}\text{Sales price}\\\text{per unit}\end{array}\right) \times \left(\begin{array}{c}\text{units}\\\text{sold}\end{array}\right) - \left[\left(\begin{array}{c}\text{variable cost}\\\text{per unit}\end{array}\right) \times \left(\begin{array}{c}\text{units}\\\text{sold}\end{array}\right) + \left(\begin{array}{c}\text{total fixed}\\\text{cost}\end{array}\right)\right] = \text{EBIT} = \$0 \quad (12\text{-}2)$$

---

[2]In a greenhouse operation, in which plants are grown (manufactured) under strictly controlled temperatures, heat costs will tend to be fixed whether the building is full or only half-full of seedlings. In a metal stamping operation, in which levers are being produced, there is no need to heat the plant to as high a temperature when the machines are stopped and the workers are not there. In this latter case, the heat costs will tend to be variable.

Our task now becomes finding the number of units that must be produced and sold in order to satisfy equation (12-2)—that is, to arrive at EBIT = $0. This can be done by simply solving equation (12-2) for the number of units sold that make EBIT = 0.

Specifically, the break-even number of units sold is found to equal:

$$\text{Break-even level of units} = \frac{\text{total fixed cost}}{\left(\dfrac{\text{sales price}}{\text{per unit}} - \dfrac{\text{variable cost}}{\text{per unit}}\right)} \qquad (12\text{-}3)$$

---

**EXAMPLE 12.1**    **Calculating the break-even level of units**

Even though Pierce Grain Company manufactures several different products, it has observed over a lengthy period that its product mix is rather constant. This allows management to conduct its financial planning by using a "normal" sales price per unit and a "normal" variable cost per unit. The "normal" sales price and variable cost per unit are calculated from the constant product mix. It is like assuming that the product mix is one big product. The selling price is $10 and the variable cost is $6. Total fixed costs for the firm are $100,000 per year. What is the break-even point in units produced and sold for the company during the coming year?

**STEP 1: FORMULATE A SOLUTION STRATEGY**

We are interested in knowing the number of the product mix Pierce Grain Company must sell before all its costs are covered. That is, EBIT (profit) will be equal to zero. Equation (12-3), which was derived from this general idea, is again shown below:

$$\text{Break-even} = \frac{\text{total fixed costs}}{(\text{sales price per unit} - \text{variable cost per unit})}$$

Comparing what we know from the question and this equation, we know:

1. Total fixed costs = $100,000
2. Sales prices per unit = $10
3. Variable cost per unit = $6

**STEP 2: CRUNCH THE NUMBERS**

Substituting this information into equation (12-3) yields:

$$\text{Break-even} = \frac{\$100,000}{(10 - 6)\ \$/\text{unit}}$$

Break-even = 25,000 units

**STEP 3: ANALYZE YOUR RESULTS**

Thus, Pierce Grain must sell 25,000 units in the coming year to cover only its fixed costs. In essence, after selling 25,000 units, Pierce Grain will have covered the costs it incurred to produce the 25,000 units and EBIT = 0.

$$\text{Break-even} = \frac{\text{total fixed costs}}{\left(1 - \dfrac{\text{variable costs}}{\text{revenues}}\right)}$$

---

## The Break-Even Point in Sales Dollars

For the multiproduct firm, it is convenient to compute the break-even point in terms of sales dollars rather than units sold. Sales, in effect, become a common denominator associated with

# CAN YOU DO IT?

## ANALYZING THE BREAK-EVEN SALES LEVEL

Creighton Manufacturing Company assembles brake controllers used to upgrade the brake systems of vintage automobiles that are being restored. The firm's revenues for the past year were $20 million, on which the firm had earnings before interest and taxes (EBIT) of $10 million. Fixed expenses were $2 million. Variable costs were of $8 million, or 40 percent of the firm's revenues. What do you estimate the firms break-even level of revenues to be based on its current cost structure?
(The solution can be found on page 388.)

a particular product mix. Furthermore, an outside analyst might not have access to internal unit cost data. He or she may, however, be able to obtain annual reports for the firm. If the analyst can separate the firm's total costs as identified from its annual reports into their fixed and variable components, he or she can calculate a general break-even point in sales dollars.

We illustrate this procedure using Pierce Grain Company's cost structure. Suppose that the reported financial information is arranged in the format shown in Table 12-1. If we are aware of the simple mathematical relationships on which cost-volume-profit analysis is based, we can use Table 12-1 to find the break-even point in sales dollars for Pierce Grain Company.

We can solve for the break-even level of revenues (as opposed to units sold) using equation (12-4) as follows:

$$\text{Break-even level of revenues} = \frac{\text{total fixed costs}}{\left(1 - \dfrac{\text{variable costs}}{\text{revenues}}\right)} \tag{12-4}$$

In the Pierce Grain Company example the ratio of the firm's variable costs ($180,000) to revenues ($300,000) is $180,000/$300,000, or 0.60, and is assumed to be constant for all revenue levels. Consequently, we can use equation (12-4) to solve for Pierce's break-even level of revenues as follows:

$$\text{Break-even level of revenues} = \frac{\$100,000}{\left(1 - \dfrac{\$180,000}{\$300,000}\right)} = \$250,000$$

**TABLE 12-1  Income Statement for Pierce Grain Company**

| | |
|---|---|
| Sales | $300,000 |
| Less: Total variable costs | 180,000 |
| Revenue before fixed costs | $120,000 |
| Less: Total fixed costs | 100,000 |
| EBIT | $ 20,000 |

## FINANCIAL DECISION TOOLS

| Name of Tool | Formula | What It Tells You |
|---|---|---|
| Break-even level of revenues | $\text{Break-even level of revenues} = \dfrac{\text{total fixed costs}}{\left(1 - \dfrac{\text{variable costs}}{\text{revenues}}\right)}$ | • The dollar amount of firm revenues needed for the firm to cover its fixed and variable costs<br>• To get break-even units divide break-even revenue level by the product price. |

## DID YOU GET IT?
### ANALYZING THE BREAK-EVEN SALES LEVEL

Creighton Manufacturing Company has fixed operating costs of $2 million and pays variable costs equal to $8 million/$20 million = 40 percent. Therefore, using equation (12-4), we can solve for the firm's break-even sales level as follows:

$$\text{Break-even level of revenues} = \frac{\$2,000,000}{\left(1 - \dfrac{\$8,000,000}{\$20,000,000}\right)} = \$3,333,333$$

## Concept Check

1. Distinguish among fixed costs, variable costs, and semivariable costs.
2. When is it useful or sometimes necessary to compute the break-even point in terms of sales dollars rather than units of output?

**3** Understand the relationship between operating leverage, financial leverage, and combined leverage.

**operating leverage** results from operating costs that are fixed and do not vary with the level of firm sales.

# Sources of Operating Leverage

When a firm has fixed operating costs, then it is subject to the effects of **operating leverage**. Moreover, the operating leverage increases the sensitivity of the firm's operating income to changes in sales.

For example, highly leveraged firms will see their incomes rise sharply when their sales rise. By contrast, firms with less leverage will see less-sharp rises in their incomes when their sales rise. To illustrate how this works, consider the Pierce Grain Company example. The firm's current sales are equal to $300,000, as found in Table 12-2. If Pierce's sales were to rise by 20 percent, up to $360,000, we calculate that the firm's EBIT would rise from $20,000 to $44,000. Note in the last column of Table 12-2 that we calculate the percent change in both revenues and EBIT. Revenues increase by just 20 percent, but the EBIT

| TABLE 12-2 How Operating Leverage Affects EBIT: An Increase in Pierce Grain Company's Sales | | | |
|---|---|---|---|
| Item | Base Sales Level, $t$ | Forecast Sales Level, $t + 1$ | Percentage Change |
| Sales | $300,000 | $360,000 | +20% |
| Less: Total variable costs | 180,000 | 216,000 | |
| Revenue before fixed costs | $120,000 | $144,000 | |
| Less: Total fixed costs | 100,000 | 100,000 | |
| EBIT | $ 20,000 | $ 44,000 | +120% |

## CAN YOU DO IT?
### ANALYZING THE EFFECTS OF OPERATING LEVERAGE

JGC Electronics operates in a very cyclical business environment such that it is not uncommon for the firm's sales to increase or decrease by 20 percent or more from year to year. Moreover, the firm has made a substantial investment in plant and equipment. The company's high fixed operating expenses associated with the plant and equipment make the firm's earnings before interest and taxes (EBIT) very sensitive to changes in revenues. In fact, if revenues were to rise by 20 percent, the firm's managers estimate that EBIT would rise by 40 percent. If JGC's revenues were to fall by 20 percent from their current level of $10 million, what percentage decline in EBIT would you anticipate for the firm?
(The solution can be found on page 389.)

increases by a whopping 120 percent. The reason for this difference is the effect of operating leverage. If Pierce had no operating leverage (that is, all of its operating costs were variable), then the increase in EBIT would have been 20 percent, just like revenues. Note also that if Pierce had experienced a 20 percent decline in revenues, it would have experienced a 120 percent decline in EBIT, as the numbers in Table 12-3 illustrate. Clearly, a higher operating leverage means higher volatility in EBIT!

So, what does this all mean for the management team at Pierce Grain? Is there something they can or should do in response to having high operating leverage? Yes, there is. Recognizing that firm operating earnings will be very sensitive to changes in firm revenues should make management very wary about using lots of financial leverage that carries with it fixed principal and interest payments. Moreover, with highly variable operating earnings, Pierce's management will probably want to hold a safety net of cash and marketable securities to help the firm weather any periods when revenue falls below the break-even level.

Before we complete this discussion of operating leverage and move on to the subject of financial leverage, ask yourself, "Which type of leverage is more under the control of management?" You will probably (and correctly) come to the conclusion that the firm's managers have less control over the operating cost structure and almost complete control over its financial structure. What the firm actually produces, for example, will determine to a significant degree the division between fixed and variable costs. However, there is more room for substitution among the various sources of financial capital than there is among the labor and real capital inputs that enable the firm to meet its production requirements. Thus, you can anticipate more arguments over the choice of the firm's financial structure than operating structure.

**TABLE 12-3  How Operating Leverage Affects EBIT: A Decrease in Pierce Grain Company's Sales**

| Item | Base Sales Level, $t$ | Forecast Sales Level, $t + 1$ | Percentage Change |
|------|-----------------------|-------------------------------|-------------------|
| Sales | $300,000 | $240,000 | −20% |
| Less: Total variable costs | 180,000 | 144,000 | |
| Revenue before fixed costs | $120,000 | $ 96,000 | |
| Less: Total fixed costs | 100,000 | 100,000 | |
| EBIT | $ 20,000 | $−4,000 | −120% |

## DID YOU GET IT?
### ANALYZING THE EFFECTS OF FINANCIAL LEVERAGE

Because JGC uses no financial leverage, there is *no* magnification effect of the percent change in EBIT on earnings per share. Therefore, a 20 percent increase in EBIT would lead to an equal 20 percent increase in the firm's earnings per share.

## Financial Leverage

**financial leverage** results from the firm's use of sources of financing that require a fixed rate of return. The primary example of such a form of financing is fixed interest rate debt whereby the firm must pay predetermined interest and principal on specified dates.

**Financial leverage** arises from *financing a portion of the firm's assets with securities bearing a fixed (limited) rate of return* in hopes of increasing the ultimate return to the common stockholders. The decision to use debt or preferred stock in the financial structure of the corporation means that those who own the common shares of the firm are exposed to financial risk. Any given level of variability in EBIT is magnified by the firm's use of financial leverage, and such additional variability is embodied in the variability of earnings available to the common stockholder and earnings per share.

Let's now focus on the responsiveness of the company's earnings per share to changes in its EBIT. (We are *not* saying that earnings per share is the appropriate criterion for all financing decisions. In fact, the weakness of such a contention is examined later. Rather, the use of financial leverage produces a certain type of *effect* on earnings per share.)

Let us assume that Pierce Grain Company is in the process of getting started as a going concern. The firm's potential owners have estimated that $200,000 is needed to purchase the necessary assets to conduct the business. Three possible financing plans have been identified for raising the $200,000; they are presented in Table 12-4. In plan A no financial risk is assumed: The entire $200,000 is raised by selling 2,000 common shares for $100 per share. In plan B a moderate amount of financial risk is assumed: 25 percent of the assets are financed with a debt issue that carries an 8 percent annual interest rate. Plan C would use the most financial leverage: 40 percent of the assets would be financed with a debt issue costing 8 percent.

Table 12-5 presents an analysis of the impact of financial leverage on earnings per share. If EBIT should increase from $20,000 to $40,000, then earnings per share would rise by 100 percent under plan A. The same change in EBIT would result in an earnings-per-share rise of 125 percent under plan B and 147 percent under plan C. In plans B and C, the 100 percent increase in EBIT (from $20,000 to $40,000) is magnified to a greater-than-100-percent

| TABLE 12-4 Possible Capital Structures for Pierce Grain Company | | | |
|---|---|---|---|
| **PLAN A: 0% DEBT** | | | |
| | | Total debt | $        0 |
| | | Common equity | 200,000[a] |
| Total assets | $200,000 | Total liabilities and equity | $200,000 |
| **PLAN B: 25% DEBT AT 8% INTEREST RATE** | | | |
| | | Total debt | $ 50,000 |
| | | Common equity | 150,000[b] |
| Total assets | $200,000 | Total liabilities and equity | $200,000 |
| **PLAN C: 40% DEBT AT 8% INTEREST RATE** | | | |
| | | Total debt | $ 80,000 |
| | | Common equity | 120,000[c] |
| Total assets | $200,000 | Total liabilities and equity | $200,000 |

[a]2,000 common shares outstanding.  [b]1,500 common shares outstanding.  [c]1,200 common shares outstanding.

**TABLE 12-5**  An Analysis of Financial Leverage at Different EBIT Levels: Pierce Grain Company

| (1) | (2) | (3) = (1) − (2) | (4) = (3) × 0.5 | (5) = (3) − (4) | (6) |
|---|---|---|---|---|---|
| EBIT | Interest | EBT | Taxes | Net Income to Common Shareholders | Earnings Per Share |
| **PLAN A: 0% DEBT; $200,000 COMMON EQUITY; 2,000 SHARES** | | | | | |
| $ 0 | $ 0 | $ 0 | $ 0 | $ 0 | $ 0 |
| 20,000 | 0 | 20,000 | 10,000 | 10,000 | 5.00 |
| 40,000 | 0 | 40,000 | 20,000 | 20,000 | 10.00 |
| 60,000 | 0 | 60,000 | 30,000 | 30,000 | 15.00 |
| 80,000 | 0 | 80,000 | 40,000 | 40,000 | 20.00 |
| **PLAN B: 25% DEBT; 8% INTEREST RATE; $150,000 COMMON EQUITY; 1,500 SHARES** | | | | | |
| $ 0 | $4,000 | $ (4,000) | $ (2,000)[a] | $ (2,000) | $ (1.33) |
| 20,000 | 4,000 | 16,000 | 8,000 | 8,000 | 5.33 |
| 40,000 | 4,000 | 36,000 | 18,000 | 18,000 | 12.00 |
| 60,000 | 4,000 | 56,000 | 28,000 | 28,000 | 18.67 |
| 80,000 | 4,000 | 76,000 | 38,000 | 38,000 | 25.33 |
| **PLAN C: 40% DEBT; 8% INTEREST RATE; $120,000 COMMON EQUITY; 1,200 SHARES** | | | | | |
| $ 0 | $6,400 | $ (6,400) | $ (3,200)[a] | $ (3,200) | $ (2.67) |
| 20,000 | 6,400 | 13,600 | 6,800 | 6,800 | 5.67 |
| 40,000 | 6,400 | 33,600 | 16,800 | 16,800 | 14.00 |
| 60,000 | 6,400 | 53,600 | 26,800 | 26,800 | 22.33 |
| 80,000 | 6,400 | 73,600 | 36,800 | 36,800 | 30.67 |

Plan A: 100% (EBIT, left) → 100% (EPS, right)
Plan B: 100% (EBIT, left) → 125% (EPS, right)
Plan C: 100% (EBIT, left) → 147% (EPS, right)

[a]The negative tax bill recognizes the credit arising from the carryback and carryforward provision of the tax code.

increase in earnings per share. The firm is employing financial leverage and exposing its owners to financial risk when the following situation exists:

$$\frac{\text{percentage change in earnings per share}}{\text{percentage change in EBIT}} > 1.00$$

As we have illustrated using the Pierce Grain Company example, the greater the firm's use of financial leverage, the greater will be the ratio of the percent change in earnings per share divided by the corresponding percent change in EBIT. To reiterate, this means that the use of financial leverage *magnifies* the effect of changes in EBIT on earnings per share. If, for example, the aforementioned ratio were 2, then a 20 percent change in EBIT (either positive or negative) would lead to a 40 percent change in earnings per share. For a firm that had even more financial leverage in its capital structure, the ratio might be 3, such that a 20 percent change in EBIT would lead to a 60 percent change in earnings per share.

## Combining Operating and Financial Leverage

Operating leverage causes changes in sales revenues to lead to even greater changes in EBIT. Additionally, changes in EBIT due to financial leverage translate into larger variations in both earnings per share (EPS) and the net income available to the common shareholders (NI), if the firm chooses to use financial leverage. It should be no surprise, then, to find out that combining operating and financial leverage causes rather large variations in earnings per share. This entire process is visually displayed in Figure 12-4.

Because the risk associated with possible earnings per share is affected by the use of **combined, or total, leverage**, it is useful to quantify the effect. To illustrate, we refer once more to Pierce Grain Company. The cost structure identified for Pierce Grain in our discussion of break-even analysis still holds. Furthermore, assume that plan B, which carried

**combined, or total, leverage** the result of the combined effects of both operating and financial leverage.

## CAN YOU DO IT?

### ANALYZING THE COMBINED EFFECTS OF OPERATING AND FINANCIAL LEVERAGE

Peterson Timber Company operates sawmills throughout the redwood areas of the Pacific Northwest. The firm's current level of revenues, EBIT, and earnings per share are $10 million, $4 million, and $1.00 per share, respectively. Peterson's CFO recently forecasted the firm's revenues and profits for next year and estimated that total revenues will grow to $12 million, EBIT will rise to $5.2 million, and earnings per share will be $1.60 a share. Analyze the effects of operating, financial, and combined leverage for Peterson. (The solution can be found on page 392.)

a 25 percent debt ratio, was chosen to finance the company's assets. Turn your attention to Table 12-6 to see how the effects of operating and financial leverage are combined.

In Table 12-6 an increase in output for Pierce Grain from 30,000 to 36,000 units is analyzed. This increase represents a 20 percent rise in sales revenues. From our earlier discussion of operating leverage and from the data in Table 12-6, we can see that this 20 percent increase in sales is magnified into a 120 percent rise in EBIT. Moreover, the 120 percent rise in EBIT induces a change in earnings per share and earnings available to the common shareholders of 150 percent. The upshot of the analysis is that the modest 20 percent rise in sales has been magnified to produce a 150 percent change in earnings per share.

Pierce Grain's use of both operating and financial leverage will cause any percentage change in sales (from the specific base level) to be magnified by a factor of 7.50 when the effect on earnings per share is computed. A 10 percent change in sales, for example, will result in a 75 percent change in earnings per share.

The total risk exposure the firm assumes can be managed by combining operating and financial leverage in different degrees. Knowing the various leverage measures will help you determine the proper level of overall risk that should be accepted. For example, if a high degree of business risk is inherent in the specific line of commercial activity, then a low amount of financial risk will minimize additional earnings fluctuations stemming from changes in the firm's sales. Conversely, the firm that by its very nature incurs a low level of

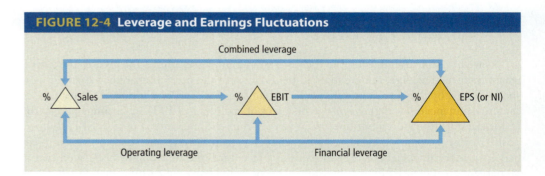

**FIGURE 12-4  Leverage and Earnings Fluctuations**

## DID YOU GET IT?

### ANALYZING THE COMBINED EFFECTS OF OPERATING AND FINANCIAL LEVERAGE

Peterson's CFO estimates that firm's revenues will increase by 20 percent, EBIT will increase by 30 percent, and earnings per share will rise 60 percent. Consequently, Peterson's operating leverage produces an increase in EBIT that is 1.5 times the 20 percent increase in sales, and an earnings per share increase by 60 percent, which is twice the percent change in EBIT that is 30 percent. Once again, we see that operating and financial leverage interact in a multiplicative fashion. That is, the percent increase in earnings per share is 2 times the increase in EBIT, which is 1.5 times the increase in sales. The net result is that the percent increase in earnings per share is equal to 1.5 × 2 = 3 times the percent increase in sales. Consequently, the 20 percent increase in sales results in a 3 × 20 percent = 60 percent increase in earnings per share.

**TABLE 12-6  The Combined-Leverage Effect on Pierce Grain Company's Earnings per Share**

| Item | Base Sales Level, $t$ | Forecast Sales Level, $t+1$ | Percentage Change |
|---|---|---|---|
| Sales | $300,000 | $360,000 | +20% |
| Less: Total variable costs | 180,000 | 216,000 | |
| Revenue before fixed costs | $120,000 | $144,000 | |
| Less: Total fixed costs | 100,000 | 100,000 | |
| EBIT | $ 20,000 | $ 44,000 | +120% |
| Less: Interest expense | 4,000 | 4,000 | |
| Earnings before taxes (EBT) | $ 16,000 | $ 40,000 | |
| Less: Taxes at 50% | 8,000 | 20,000 | |
| Net income | $  8,000 | $ 20,000 | +150% |
| Less: Preferred dividends | 0 | 0 | |
| Earnings available to common shareholders (EAC) | $  8,000 | $ 20,000 | +150% |
| Number of common shares | 1,500 | 1,500 | |
| Earnings per share (EPS) | $5.33 | $13.33 | +150% |

## FINANCE AT WORK

### WHEN FINANCIAL LEVERAGE PROVES TO BE TOO MUCH TO HANDLE

The financial crisis that began in 2007 and the ensuing economic slowdown had a heavy toll on U.S. automakers. General Motors (GM), once the largest automaker in the world, found itself drowning in more debt than it could afford. So, facing the prospect of not being able to honor its financial obligations the company approached its creditors with an offer to restructure its debt. The offer included the following for each dollar of debt owed: $0.08 in cash, $0.16 in unsecured debt, plus a 90% stake in the automaker. With about $28 billion in debt to

bondholders, the GM offer translated into $2.2 billion in cash and $4.3 billion in unsecured debt plus a stake in the restructured firm. Although the terms may sound extreme for the firm's bondholders, they were even harsher on the current stockholders, who went from owning 100% of the firm's equity down to only 10%! Of course, if the firm were to declare bankruptcy, the common stockholders would likely be wiped out completely.

Source: Reuters UK, http://uk.reuters.com/article/businessNews/idUKTRE52T6ZZ20090331, accessed April 2, 2009.

fixed operating costs might choose to use a high degree of financial leverage in the hope of increasing earnings per share and the rate of return on its common equity.

## Concept Check

1. When is operating leverage present in the firm's cost structure? What condition is necessary for operating leverage not to be present in the firm's cost structure?
2. What is the effect of operating leverage on the volatility of a firm's EBIT?
3. What creates financial leverage in a firm's capital structure?
4. How does financial leverage affect the volatility of firm earnings in response to changes in EBIT?
5. If the ratio of the percent change in earnings per share to the corresponding percent change in EBIT were 2, what percent change in earnings would you expect to follow a 15 percent decline in EBIT?
6. How do operating and financial leverage interact to affect the volatility of a firm's earnings per share?

# Capital Structure Theory

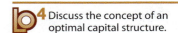
4 Discuss the concept of an optimal capital structure.

It is now time to consider the determination of the appropriate financing mix for the firm. A complete listing of the sources of financing a firm has used to finance its assets is found in the right-hand side of the firm's balance sheet. We will refer to this list of all sources of

**TABLE 12-7  Distinguishing Between a Firm's Financial Structure and Its Capital Structure**

| | | | | |
|---|---|---|---|---|
| Current assets | $ 100 | Accounts payable | $ 10 | |
| Fixed assets | 200 | Accrued expenses | 15 | |
| Total assets | $ 300 | Short-term debt | 50 | Financial structure |
| | | Current portion of long-term debt | 5 | |
| | | Current liabilities | $ 80 | |
| | | Long-term debt | 70 | |
| | | Preferred equity | 50 | Capital structure |
| | | Common equity | 100 | |
| | | Total liabilities and owners' equity | $300 | |

**financial structure** the mix of all sources of fundings that appears on the right-hand side of the balance sheet.

financing as the firm's **financial structure**. For example, in Table 12-7 we see a balance sheet for a firm that has $300 in assets that have been financed using a mixture of sources of financing that consists of $80 in current liabilities (debts that must be repaid within a period of 1 year or less), $70 in long-term debt, $50 in preferred stock, and finally $100 in common equity.

Note that some of the firm's current liabilities arise naturally as the firm carries out its day-to-day operations. We are referring to accounts payable and accrued expenses. For example, when the firm orders additional items of inventory its suppliers automatically extend credit to the firm, which appears on the balance sheet as accounts payable. Moreover, the firm accrues interest and other expenses continually over time but pays it only periodically (for example, semiannually). These accrued expenses then represent a liability of the firm that also arises naturally as the firm carries out its day-to-day business. Since accounts payable and accrued expense items arise automatically in response to the events that create them, these liabilities are not the ones we are directly concerned about in this chapter. Specifically, we are interested in that part of the firm's financial structure that requires the

**capital structure** the mix of interest-bearing short- and long-term debt plus equity funds used by the firm.

discretionary management by the firm. We refer to this as the firm's **capital structure**. In Table 12-7 the financial structure consists of all $300 of liabilities and owners' equity found on the right-hand side of the balance sheet, whereas the capital structure excludes accounts payable and accrued expenses and totals $275.

The relationship between a firm's financial structure and capital structure can be expressed in equation form as follows:

$$\text{Financial structure} = \begin{pmatrix} \text{non-interest-} \\ \text{bearing liabilities} \end{pmatrix} + \begin{pmatrix} \text{capital} \\ \text{structure} \end{pmatrix} \qquad (12\text{-}5)$$

| accounts payable accrued expenses | short-term debt long-term debt preferred stock common equity |
|---|---|

Note that we refer to accounts payable and accrued expenses as non-interest-bearing liabilities. The reason for this is that there is no explicit interest expense associated with these liabilities. An explicit interest expense would be something like the interest you pay on a bank loan. When a firm purchases items of inventory on credit, the credit terms simply say that the amount of the purchase must be paid within a specific time interval, such as 30 days. Consequently, the supplier is providing 30 days of credit to the firm without specifying a rate of interest. The supplier is aware of the fact that it is supplying credit and surely will incorporate some interest cost in the price terms for the items. The important point, however, is that this interest is hidden and not explicitly stated, so accounts payable and accrued expenses do not give rise to interest expense to the firm.

## CAUTIONARY TALE

### FORGETTING PRINCIPLE 3: RISK REQUIRES A REWARD

In 2008, we learned that when faced with a severe economic downturn, even the smartest of the Wall Street investment bankers can be done in. As 2008 dawned, there were five major independent investment banks. Now, there are only two (Goldman Sachs and Morgan Stanley). So what did the others in? The answer, very simply, is the excessive use of financial leverage.

Leverage can be a double-edged sword. In booming times, using leverage helped the investment banks increase their rates of return significantly. Of course, higher returns entail higher risk. And these banks—Bear Stearns, Lehman Brothers, and Merrill Lynch—were in effect exposing themselves to two types of risk: First, they were faced with the risk that their investments might not earn more than the costs to finance them. For example, if the rate of return the banks earned on their assets dropped below the rate they were paying for financing, then the shortfall in earnings came out of the stockholders' return. Second, the investment banks were borrowing funds using short-term loans called commercial paper and then investing this borrowed money in long-term investments. This meant that they continuously faced a refinancing risk as they needed to continually issue and re-issue commercial paper.

When the commercial paper market shut down as a result of the financial crisis in 2008, this left the investment banks without a source of financing, forcing them to sell their long-term investments at distressed prices. The result was that Bear Stearns, Lehman Brothers, and Merrill Lynch all found themselves unable to continue their operations. Merrill Lynch was bought by Bank of America, Bear Stearns was purchased by JPMorgan, and Lehman declared bankruptcy, and the British investment banking firm Barclays purchased many of its assets.

---

The design of a prudent capital structure requires that we address two questions:

1. **Debt maturity composition**—what mix of short-term and long-term debt should the firm use?
2. **Debt–equity composition**—what mix of debt and equity should the firm use?

**debt maturity composition** the mix of short- and long-term debt used by the firm.

**debt–equity composition** the mix of debt and equity used by the firm in its capital structure.

The primary influence on the debt maturity composition of the firm's capital structure (short- versus long-term debt) is the nature of the assets owned by the firm. Firms that are heavily committed to investments in fixed assets that are expected to produce cash flow over many years generally favor long-term debt to the extent that they borrow. Firms that tend to invest more heavily in assets that produce relatively short-lived cash flows tend to finance more heavily using short-term debt.

The focus of this chapter is on the debt-equity composition or what is usually called *capital structure management*. A firm's capital structure should mix the permanent sources of funds used by the firm in a manner that will maximize the company's common stock price or, put differently, *minimize the firm's composite cost of capital*. We can call this proper mix of fund sources the **optimal capital structure**.

Table 12-7 looks at equation (12-5) in terms of a balance sheet. It helps us visualize the overriding problem of capital structure management. The sources of funds that give rise to financing fixed costs (long-term debt and preferred equity) must be combined with common equity in the proportions most suitable to the investment marketplace. If that mix can be found, then holding all other factors constant, the firm's common stock price will be maximized.

**optimal capital structure** the capital structure that minimizes the firm's composite cost of capital (maximizes the common stock price) for raising a given amount of funds.

Obviously, taking on excessive financial risk can put the firm into bankruptcy proceedings. But using too little financial leverage results in an undervaluation of the firm's shares. The financial manager must know how to find the area of optimum financial leverage use—this will enhance share value, all other considerations being held constant.

The rest of this chapter covers three main areas. First, we briefly discuss the theory of capital structure. Second, we examine the basic tools of capital structure management. We conclude with a real-world look at actual capital structure management.

## A Quick Look at Capital Structure Theory

In this section of the chapter we address the theoretical underpinnings as to why a firm's capital structure is important to the firm's common stockholders. To do this we first discuss a world in which capital structure is unimportant—that is, where the particular mix of debt and equity in the firm's capital structure has no effect on the value of the firm or its cost of capital (Chapter 9). The reason we do this is to make it very clear why capital structure matters and to help us make prudent decisions about its composition. The heart of the argument about the importance of capital structure is found in the following question:

### Can the Firm Affect Its Overall Cost of Funds, Either Favorably or Unfavorably, by Varying the Mixture of Financing Sources Used?

This controversy has taken many elegant forms in the finance literature and tends to appeal more to academics than financial practitioners. To emphasize the ingredients of capital structure theory that have practical applications for business financial management, we will pursue an intuitive, or nonmathematical, approach to reach a better understanding of the underpinnings of this cost of capital, or capital structure, argument.

## The Importance of Capital Structure

It makes economic sense for the firm to strive to minimize the cost of using financial capital. Both capital costs and other costs, such as manufacturing costs, share a common characteristic in that they potentially reduce the size of the cash dividend that could be paid to common stockholders.

## Independence Position

Two Nobel Prize–winning financial economists, Franco Modigliani and Merton Miller (hereafter MM), analyzed the importance of the capital structure decision within the context of a very restrictive set of assumptions about the world in which businesses operate. Specifically, MM assumed that a firm's investment policies (that is, the set of investments it would undertake) and dividend policy (the amount of the firm's earnings paid to stockholders in dividends) were fixed such that they are not influenced by the firm's capital structure decision. They then demonstrated, under a set of assumptions, that the firm's capital structure mix did not affect the firm's cost of capital or the value of the firm's common equity. This position is sometimes referred to as capital structure independence since the value of the firm is independent of how it has been financed (that is, its capital structure). Some of the key assumptions underlying the MM independence proposition include the following:

1. Corporate income is not subject to taxation.
2. Capital structures consist only of stocks and bonds.
3. Investors make homogeneous forecasts of net operating income (what we earlier called EBIT).
4. Stocks and bonds are traded in perfect or efficient markets.

In this market setting, the answer to the question, "Can the firm affect its overall cost of funds, either favorably or unfavorably, by varying the mixture of financing sources used?" is no.

To summarize, the Modigliani and Miller hypothesis, or the MM view, puts forth that within the perfect economic world previously described, the total market value of the firm's outstanding securities will be *unaffected* by the manner in which the right-hand side of the balance sheet is arranged. This means the sum of the market value of outstanding common stock plus outstanding debt will always be the same regardless of how much or how little debt is actually used by the company. This MM view is sometimes called the *independence hypothesis*, as firm value is independent of capital structure design.

The crux of this position on financing choice is illustrated in Figure 12-5. Here the firm's asset mix (the left-hand side of the balance sheet) is held constant. All that is different is the way the assets are financed. Under financing mix A, the firm funds 30 percent of its assets with common stock and the other 70 percent with bonds. Under financing mix B, the firm reverses this mix and funds 70 percent of the assets with common stock and only 30 percent with bonds. From our earlier discussions we know that financing mix A is the more heavily leveraged plan.

Notice, however, that the size of the "pies" in Figure 12-5 are exactly the same. The pie represents firm value—the total market value of the firm's outstanding securities. Thus, the total firm value associated with financing mix A equals that associated with financing mix B. Firm value is *independent* of the actual financing mix that has been chosen.

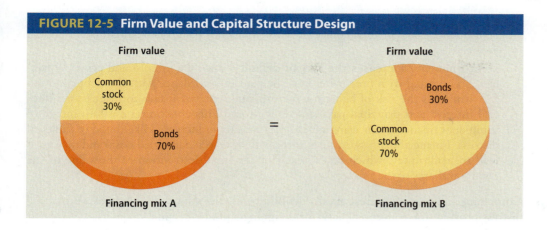

**FIGURE 12-5  Firm Value and Capital Structure Design**

This implication is taken further in Figure 12-6 where we see that the firm's overall cost of capital, $k_{wacc}$, is unaffected by an increased use of financial leverage. If more debt is used with a cost of $k_d$ in the capital structure, the cost of common equity, $k_{cs}$, will rise at the same rate additional earnings are generated. This will keep the composite cost of capital to the corporation unchanged. Furthermore, because the overall cost of capital does not change with leverage use, neither will the firm's common stock price.

The lesson of this view on financing choices is that debt financing is not as cheap as it first appears to be because the composite cost of funds or the firm's weighted average cost of capital is constant over the full range of financial leverage use. *The stark implication for financial officers is that one capital structure is just as good as any other.*

Recall, though, the strict assumptions used to define the economic world in which this theory was developed. We next turn to a market and legal environment that relaxes these extreme assumptions.

## The Moderate Position

We turn now to a more moderate description of the relationship between the firm's cost of capital and its capital structure that has wide appeal to both business practitioners and academics. This moderate view is based on the relaxation of two of the very restrictive assumptions underlying the MM independence theory:

1. **Interest expense is tax deductible**—when a firm incurs debt on which it pays interest that interest is tax deductible, which reduces the cost of debt to the firm by an amount

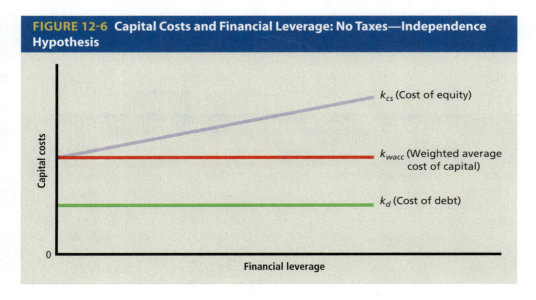

**FIGURE 12-6  Capital Costs and Financial Leverage: No Taxes—Independence Hypothesis**

equal to the reduced taxes the firm must pay. This constitutes an advantage of using debt financing rather than equity since the dividends paid to stockholders are not tax deductible.

2. **Debt financing increases the risk of default**—since the interest and principal payments associated with borrowing must be paid in accordance with the debt contract, the firm faces the risk of being forced into bankruptcy if it fails to meet its contractual interest and principal payment obligations. This constitutes a disadvantage of using debt financing, for using more debt leads to an increased likelihood of financial distress. Financial distress, in turn, forces the firm to incur added costs and may even lead to bankruptcy, which could result in the total destruction of the value of the common shares of the firm.

Combining the plus of interest tax deductibility with the minus of added risk of financial distress provides the conceptual basis for designing a prudent capital structure.

**The Benefits of Financial Leverage—Interest Tax Savings**    Table 12-8 illustrates this important element of the U.S. system of corporate taxation. We assume that Skip's Camper Manufacturing Company has an expected level of earnings before interest and taxes (EBIT) of $2 million and faces a corporate tax rate (made simple for example purposes) of 50 percent. Two financing plans are analyzed. The first is an unleveraged capital structure. The other assumes that Skip's Camper has $8 million of bonds outstanding that carry an interest rate of 6 percent per year.

Notice that if corporate income were *not* taxed, then earnings before taxes of $2 million per year could be paid to shareholders in the form of cash dividends or to bond investors in the form of interest payments, or any combination of the two. This means that the *sum* of the cash flows that Skip's Camper could pay to its contributors of debt or equity is *not* affected by its financing mix.

When corporate income is taxed by the government, and bond interest is a tax-deductible expense, the sum of the cash flows earned for all contributors of financial capital is affected by the firm's financing mix. Table 12-8 illustrates this point.

If Skip's Camper chooses the leveraged capital structure, the total payments to equity and debt holders will be $240,000 *greater* than under the all-common-equity capitalization. Where does this $240,000 come from? The answer is that the government's take, through taxes collected, is lower by that amount. This *difference, which flows to* Skip's Camper *security holders*, is called the **tax shield** on debt. In general, it may be calculated by equation (12-6), where $r_d$ is the interest rate paid or interest tax savings on the debt, $M$ is the principal amount of the debt, and $T_c$ is the firm's marginal tax rate:

**tax shield** the reduction in taxes due to the tax deductibility of interest expense.

$$\text{Tax shield} = r_d(M)(T_c) \tag{12-6}$$

The moderate position on the importance of capital structure presumes that the tax shield must have value in the marketplace. Accordingly, this tax benefit will increase the total market value of the firm's outstanding securities relative to the all-equity financing mix. Note that in this case financial leverage does affect firm value. Because the cost of capital is just the other side of the valuation coin, financial leverage also affects the firm's composite cost of capital. Can the firm increase firm value indefinitely and lower its cost of capital continuously by using more and more financial leverage? Common sense would tell us no!

| TABLE 12-8  Skip's Camper Cash Flows to All Investors—The Case of Taxes | Unleveraged Capital Structure | Leveraged Capital Structure |
| --- | --- | --- |
| Expected level of net operating income | $2,000,000 | $2,000,000 |
| Less: Interest expense | 0 | 480,000 |
| Earnings before taxes | $2,000,000 | $1,520,000 |
| Less: Taxes at 50% | 1,000,000 | 760,000 |
| Earnings available to common stockholders | $1,000,000 | $ 760,000 |
| Interest paid to creditors | 0 | 480,000 |
| Expected payments to all security holders | $1,000,000 | $1,240,000 |

So would most financial managers and academicians. The acknowledgment of bankruptcy costs provides one possible rationale.

**The Likelihood of Firm Failure**    The probability that the firm will be unable to meet the financial obligations identified in its debt contracts increases as more debt is employed. The highest costs would be incurred if the firm actually went into bankruptcy proceedings. Here, assets would be liquidated and often at distressed sale prices. If these assets do sell for something less than their perceived market values, both equity investors and debt holders could suffer losses. Other problems accompany bankruptcy proceedings. Additional lawyers and accountants have to be hired and paid. Managers must spend time preparing lengthy reports for those involved in the legal action. Moreover, all this distracts the firm's management from the efficient running of the business, and this causes missed opportunities and lost value.

Milder forms of financial distress also have their costs, as we have discussed. As the firm's financial condition weakens, creditors may take action to restrict normal business activity. Suppliers may not deliver materials on credit. Profitable capital investments may have to be forgone, and dividend payments may even be interrupted. At some point the expected cost of default will be large enough to outweigh the tax shield advantage of debt financing. The firm will turn to other sources of financing, mainly common equity (retained earnings).

**The Saucer-Shaped Cost-of-Capital Curve**    This moderate view of the relationship between financing mix and the firm's cost of capital is depicted in Figure 12-7. The result is a saucer-shaped (or U-shaped) weighted-average-cost-of-capital curve, $k_{wacc}$. The firm's average cost of equity, $k_{cs}$, is seen to rise as the firm uses more debt financing. For a while the firm can borrow funds at a relatively low after-tax cost of debt, $k_d$. Even though the cost of equity is rising, it does not rise at a fast enough rate to offset the use of the less-expensive debt financing. Thus, between points 0 and $A$ on the financial-leverage axis, the average cost of capital declines and stock price rises.

Eventually, however, the threat of financial distress causes the cost of debt to rise. In Figure 12-7 this increase in the cost of debt shows up in the after-tax average-cost-of-debt curve, $k_d$, at point $A$. Between points $A$ and $B$, mixing debt and equity funds produces an average cost of capital that is (relatively) flat. The firm's **optimal range of financial leverage** lies between points $A$ and $B$. *All capital structures between these two points are optimal because they produce the lowest composite cost of capital.* As we said earlier in this chapter, finding this optimal range of financing mixes is the objective of capital structure management.

**optimal range of financial leverage** the range of debt use in the firm's capital structure that yields the lowest overall cost of capital for the firm.

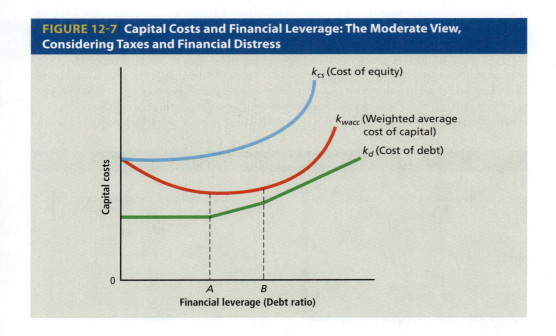

**FIGURE 12-7    Capital Costs and Financial Leverage: The Moderate View, Considering Taxes and Financial Distress**

**debt capacity** the maximum amount of debt that the firm can include in its capital structure and still maintain its current credit rating.

Point *B* signifies the firm's debt capacity. **Debt capacity** is the *maximum amount of debt the firm can include in its capital structure and still maintain its current credit rating*. Beyond point *B*, additional fixed-charge capital can be attracted only at very costly interest rates. At the same time, this excessive use of financial leverage would cause the firm's cost of equity to rise at a faster rate than it did previously. The composite cost of capital would then rise quite rapidly, and the firm's stock price would decline.

## Firm Value and Agency Costs

In Chapter 1 we mentioned the notion of agency problems. Recall that agency problems give rise to agency costs, which tend to occur in business organizations because the owners of the firm do not run the business, managers do. Thus, the firm's managers can properly be thought of as agents of the firm's stockholders. To ensure that agent-managers act in the stockholders' best interests requires that (1) they have proper incentives to do so and (2) their decisions are monitored. The incentives usually take the form of executive compensation plans and perquisites (or "perks" ). The perquisites, though, might be a bloated support staff, country club memberships, luxurious corporate planes, or other amenities. Monitoring this requires that certain costs be borne by the stockholders, such as (1) bonding the managers, (2) auditing financial statements, (3) structuring the organization in unique ways that limit managerial decisions, and (4) reviewing the costs and benefits of management perquisites. This list is indicative, not exhaustive. The main point is that monitoring costs are ultimately covered by the owners of the company—its common stockholders.

Capital structure management also gives rise to agency costs. Agency problems stem from conflicts of interest, and capital structure management gives rise to a natural conflict between stockholders and bondholders. For example, if acting in the stockholders' best interests causes managers to invest in extremely risky projects, existing investors in the firm's bonds could logically take a dim view of such an investment policy. This is because changing the risk structure of the firm's assets would change the business-risk exposure of the firm. This could lead to a downward revision of the bond rating the firm currently enjoys. A lowered bond rating, in turn, would lower the current market value of the firm's bonds. Clearly, bondholders would be unhappy with this result.

To reduce this conflict of interest, the creditors (bond investors) and stockholders may agree to include several protective covenants in the bond contract. These bond covenants were discussed in more detail in Chapter 7, but essentially they may be thought of as restrictions on managerial decision making. Typical covenants restrict the payment of cash dividends on common stock, limit the acquisition or sale of assets, or limit further debt financing. To make sure managers comply with the protective covenants means that monitoring costs are incurred. Like all monitoring costs, they are borne by common stockholders. Furthermore, like many costs, they involve the analysis of an important trade-off.

Figure 12-8 displays some of the trade-offs involved with the use of protective bond covenants. Note (in the left panel of Figure 12-8) that the firm might be able to sell bonds that carry no protective covenants only by incurring very high interest rates. With no protective covenants, there are no associated monitoring costs. Also, there are no lost operating efficiencies, such as being able to move quickly to acquire a particular company in the

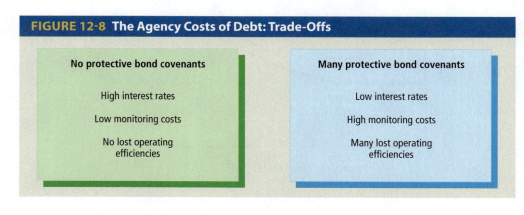

**FIGURE 12-8  The Agency Costs of Debt: Trade-Offs**

| No protective bond covenants | Many protective bond covenants |
|---|---|
| High interest rates | Low interest rates |
| Low monitoring costs | High monitoring costs |
| No lost operating efficiencies | Many lost operating efficiencies |

acquisitions market. Conversely, restrictive covenants could reduce the explicit cost of the debt contract, but this would involve incurring significant monitoring costs and losing some operating efficiencies (which also translates into higher costs). When the debt issue is first sold, then a trade-off will be made.

Next, we have to consider the presence of monitoring costs at low and higher levels of leverage. When the firm operates at a low debt-to-equity ratio, there is little need for creditors to insist on a long list of bond covenants. The financial risk is not sufficient to require that type of activity. The firm will likewise benefit from low explicit interest rates when leverage is low. When the debt-to-equity ratio is high, however, it is logical for creditors to demand a great deal of monitoring. This increase in agency costs will raise the implicit cost (the true total cost) of debt financing. It seems logical, then, to suggest that monitoring costs will rise as the firm's use of financial leverage increases. Just as the likelihood of firm failure (financial distress) raises a company's overall cost of capital ($k_{wacc}$), so do agency costs. On the other side of the coin, this means that total firm value (the total market value of the firm's securities) will be *lower* because of agency costs. Taken together, the agency costs and the costs associated with financial distress argue in favor of the concept of an *optimal* capital structure for the individual firm.

## Agency Costs, Free Cash Flow, and Capital Structure

In 1986, Professor Michael C. Jensen further extended the concept of agency costs into the area of capital structure management. The contribution revolves around a concept that Jensen labels "free cash flow," which he defines as follows:

> Free cash flow is cash flow in excess of that required to fund all projects that have positive net present values when discounted at the relevant cost of capital.[3]

Jensen then proposed that substantial free cash flow can lead to misbehavior by managers and poor decisions that are not in the best interests of the firm's common stockholders. In other words, managers have an incentive to hold onto the free cash flow and have "fun" with it, rather than "disgorge" it, say, in the form of higher cash dividend payments.

But all is not lost. This leads to what Jensen calls his "Control hypothesis" for using debt. This means that by leveraging up (taking on debt), the firm's shareholders will enjoy increased control over their management team. For example, if the firm issues new debt and uses the proceeds to retire outstanding common stock, then managers are obligated to pay out cash to service the debt—this simultaneously reduces the amount of free cash flow available to them to have fun with.

We can also refer to this motive for financial leverage use as the "threat hypothesis." Managers work under the threat of financial failure; therefore, according to the "free cash flow theory of capital structure," they work more efficiently. This is supposed to reduce the agency costs of free cash flow, which will in turn be recognized by the marketplace in the form of greater returns on the common stock.

Note that the free cash flow theory of capital structure does not give a theoretical solution to the question of just how much financial leverage is enough. Nor does it suggest how much leverage is too much. It is a way of thinking about why shareholders and their boards of directors might use more debt to control managerial behavior and decisions. The basic decision tools of capital structure management still have to be utilized. They are presented later in this chapter.

### REMEMBER YOUR PRINCIPLES

**P**rinciple  The discussions on agency costs, free cash flow, and the control hypothesis for debt creation return us to **Principle 5: Conflicts of Interest Cause Agency Problems.** The control hypothesis put forth by Jensen suggests that managers will work harder for shareholder interests when they have to "sweat it out" to meet contractual interest payments on debt securities. But we also learned that managers and bond investors can have a conflict that leads to agency costs associated with using debt capital. Thus, the theoretical benefits that flow from minimizing the agency costs of free cash flow by using more debt will cease when the rising agency costs of debt exactly offset those benefits. You can see how very difficult it is, then, for financial managers to identify precisely their true optimal capital structure.

---

[3]"Agency Costs of Free Cash Flow, Corporate Finance, and Takeovers" by Michael C. Jensen, from *American Economic Review* 76 (May 1986).

## Managerial Implications

Where does our examination of capital structure theory leave us? The upshot is that determining the firm's financing mix is centrally important to the financial manager because the firm's stockholders are affected by capital structure decisions. At the very least, and before bankruptcy costs and agency costs become detrimental, the tax shield effect will cause the shares of a leveraged firm to sell at a higher price than they would if the company had avoided debt financing. Because both the risk of failure and agency costs accompany the excessive use of leverage, the financial manager must exercise caution in the use of fixed-charge capital. This problem of searching for the optimal range of financial leverage is our next task.

You have now developed a workable knowledge of capital structure theory. This makes you better equipped to search for your firm's optimal capital structure. Several tools are available to help you in this search process and simultaneously help you make prudent financing choices. These tools are decision oriented. They help us answer the question, "The next time we need $20 million, should we issue common stock or sell long-term bonds?"

## Concept Check

1. What is the objective of capital structure management?
2. What is the basic controversy surrounding capital structure theory?
3. Explain the independence hypothesis as it relates to capital structure management.
4. Explain the moderate view of the relationship between a firm's financing mix and its average cost of capital.
5. How do agency costs and free cash flow relate to capital structure management?

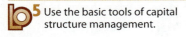 5 Use the basic tools of capital structure management.

# The Basic Tools of Capital Structure Management

We will review two basic tools that are commonly used in the evaluation of capital structure decisions. The first is the EBIT-EPS chart, which provides a way to visualize the effects of alternative capital structures on both the level and volatility of the firm's earnings per share (EPS). The second tool we review entails the analysis of the capital structures of comparable firms through the use of financial leverage ratios. Here we use ratios to standardize capital structure information as we did when we discussed financial ratios in Chapter 4 so that we can compare the capital structures of similar firms.

## EBIT-EPS Analysis

Before we launch into an analysis of the relationship between earnings per share (EPS) and EBIT for alternative capital structures, we need to remind ourselves why this is important. Specifically, in light of our discussions of capital structure theory you might ask, "Why should the firm's owners care about the effects of the capital structure on earnings per share (EPS)?" One possible response to this question is that corporate CEOs and boards of directors are very sensitive to the earnings numbers they report to Wall Street. The reason we offered earlier for this sensitivity relates to the perception of investors that the level of a firm's reported EPS signals important information about the firm's future prospects. For example, when a firm announces that its earnings will fall short of analyst expectations, this often triggers a revision in investor expectations regarding the future earnings prospects for the firm. This downward revision, in turn, results in a drop in the firm's stock price. Thus, corporate executives are very aware of the importance investors attach to earnings and take this information into account when considering the design of the firm's capital structure.

## EXAMPLE 12.2    EBIT-EPS analysis

Assume that plan B presented earlier in Table 12-4 is the existing capital structure for the Pierce Grain Company. Furthermore, the asset structure of the firm is such that EBIT is expected to be $20,000 per year for a very long time. A capital investment is available to Pierce Grain that will cost $50,000. Acquisition of this asset is expected to raise the projected EBIT level to $30,000 permanently. The firm can raise the needed cash by one of two ways:

1. Selling 500 shares of common stock at $100 each
2. Selling the new bonds that will net the firm $50,000 and carry an interest rate of 8.5 percent.

These capital structures and corresponding EPS amounts are summarized in Table 12-9.

At the projected EBIT level of $30,000 the EPS for the common stock and debt alternatives are $6.50 and $7.25, respectively. Both are considerably above the $5.33 that would occur if the new project were rejected and the new capital were not raised. Based on a criterion of selecting the financing plan that will provide the highest EPS, the bond alternative is favored. But what if the basic business risk to which the firm is exposed causes the EBIT to vary over a considerable range? Can we be sure that the bond alternative will always have the higher EPS associated with it?

### STEP 1: FORMULATE A SOLUTION STRATEGY

The best way to address this issue will be to use graphic analysis of earnings per share and earnings before interest and taxes for the proposed alternatives (that is, an EBIT-EPS chart). EBIT is plotted on the horizontal axis and EPS is plotted on the vertical axis. The intercepts on the horizontal (EBIT) axis represent the before-tax equivalent financing charges related to each plan. The straight lines for each plan tell us the EPS amounts that will occur at different EBIT amounts.

### STEP 2: CRUNCH THE NUMBERS

A review of the EBIT-EPS chart found in Figure 12-9 reveals that the answer to this question is no. That is, the bond alternative will *not* always have the higher EPS. Creating the

### TABLE 12-9  Analyzing Pierce Grain Company's Financing Choices

#### PART A: CAPITAL STRUCTURES

| Existing Capital Structure | | With New Common Stock Financing | | With New Debt Financing | |
|---|---|---|---|---|---|
| Long-term debt at 8% | $ 50,000 | Long-term debt at 8% | $ 50,000 | Long-term debt at 8% | $ 50,000 |
| Common stock | 150,000 | Common stock | 200,000 | Long-term debt at 8.5% | 50,000 |
| | | | | Common stock | 150,000 |
| Total liabilities and equity | $200,000 | Total liabilities and equity | $250,000 | Total liabilities and equity | $250,000 |
| Common shares outstanding | 1,500 | Common shares outstanding | 2,000 | Common shares outstanding | 1,500 |

#### PART B: PROJECTED EPS LEVELS

| | Existing Capital Structure | With New Common Stock Financing | With New Debt Financing |
|---|---|---|---|
| EBIT | $20,000 | $30,000 | $30,000 |
| Less: Interest expense | 4,000 | 4,000 | 8,250 |
| Earnings before taxes (EBT) | $16,000 | $26,000 | $21,750 |
| Less: Taxes at 50% | 8,000 | 13,000 | 10,875 |
| Net income | $ 8,000 | $13,000 | $10,875 |
| Less: Preferred dividends | 0 | 0 | 0 |
| Earnings available to common shareholders | $ 8,000 | $13,000 | $10,875 |
| EPS | $ 5.33 | $ 6.50 | $ 7.25 |

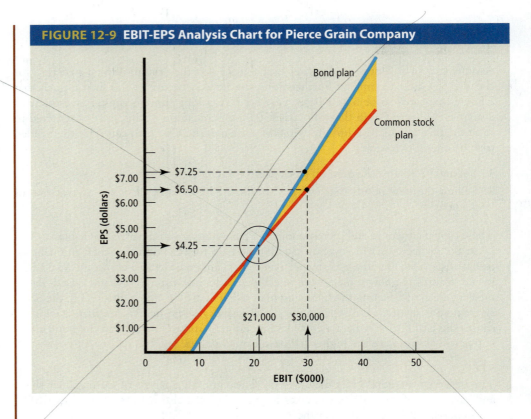

**FIGURE 12-9  EBIT-EPS Analysis Chart for Pierce Grain Company**

EBIT-EPS analysis chart allows the decision maker to visualize the impact of different financing plans on the EPS over a range of EBIT levels.

Note that using the data on the common stock plan at an EBIT of $4,000 this financing plan provides an EPS of zero. EPS is zero with the debt plan where EBIT is equal to $8,250. Note that $8,250 for the debt plan consists of the current interest expense of $4,000 plus the new interest cost of $4,250.

The bond plan financing option has a steeper slope than the common stock financing plan. This tells us that the bond plan's EPS is more sensitive to changes in EPS than the common stock financing plan. This is due to the financial leverage employed. Another observation is that the lines intersect. At that point, EPS is exactly the same for both financing plans. Above the intersection point, the EPS for the plan with greater leverage will exceed that for the plan with lesser leverage. The intersection point, circled in Figure 12-9, occurs at an EBIT level of $21,000. This intersection of the two capital structure options is at an EPS of $4.25. For all levels of EBIT above $21,000 the debt plan provides higher EPS, and for levels of EBIT below $21,000 the equity option offers the higher EPS.

### STEP 3: ANALYZE YOUR RESULTS

The EBIT-EPS analysis tells the analyst the level of EPS for a given EBIT. However, since the firm's EBIT is uncertain and can never be known with certainty in advance, the capital structure that produces the highest level of EPS cannot be known for certain.

**Computing Indifference Points**   The point of intersection in Figure 12-9 is called the **EBIT-EPS indifference point**. It identifies the *EBIT level at which the EPS will be the same regardless of the financing plan chosen by the financial manager*. This indifference point, sometimes called the break-even point, has major implications for financial planning. At EBIT amounts in excess of the EBIT indifference level, the more heavily leveraged financing plan will generate a higher EPS. At EBIT amounts below the EBIT indifference level, the

**EBIT-EPS indifference point** the level of earnings before interest and taxes (EBIT) that will equate earnings per share (EPS) between two different financing plans.

financing plan involving less leverage will generate a higher EPS. It is important, then, to know the EBIT indifference level.

We can find it graphically, as in Figure 12-9. At times it may be more efficient, though, to calculate the indifference point directly. This can be done by using the following equation:

$$\overset{\text{EPS: STOCK PLAN}}{\frac{(\text{EBIT} - I_s)(1 - T_c) - P}{S_s}} = \overset{\text{EPS: BOND PLAN}}{\frac{(\text{EBIT} - I_b)(1 - T_c) - P}{S_b}} \qquad (12\text{-}7)$$

where $S_s$ and $S_b$ are the numbers of common shares outstanding under the stock and bond plans, respectively; $I$ is interest expense; $T_c$ is the firm's income tax rate; and $P$ is preferred dividends paid. In the present case, $P$ is zero because there is no preferred stock outstanding. If preferred stock is associated with one of the financing alternatives, keep in mind that the preferred dividends, $P$, are not tax deductible. Equation (12-7) does take this fact into consideration.

For the present example, we calculate the indifference level of EBIT as

$$\frac{(\text{EBIT} - \$4,000)(1 - 0.5) - 0}{2,000} = \frac{(\text{EBIT} - \$8,250)(1 - 0.5) - 0}{1,500}$$

When the expression above is solved for EBIT, we obtain $21,000. If EBIT turns out to be $21,000, then EPS will be $4.25 under both plans.

**A Word of Caution**    Okay, now we know that using more financial leverage *may* provide higher firm earnings if EBIT is above the break-even point. But this is not all that we need to take away from this analysis. For example, assume that EBIT is expected to be above the break-even point 99.9 percent of the time for two alternative capital structure policies. Does this mean that we should automatically select the higher leverage option? The answer, as you might have suspected, is no, and here's the logic for this answer. The higher the firm's use of financial leverage, the steeper the slope of the EBIT-EPS line, which means the firm will experience larger swings in EPS for any given change in EBIT. CEOs and corporate boards care about these swings for the reason we noted earlier. That is, if the firm fails to meet its earnings expectations, investors may revise their expectations for the firm's future earnings prospects downward, at which point the share price might suffer. So, higher financial leverage increases the likelihood that an unanticipated swing in the firm's EBIT might have a very detrimental effect on the reported EPS, and this is a real source of concern.

How then are we to interpret and use the EBIT-EPS chart to analyze capital structure design issues? The answer, like many tools of financial analysis, entails the use of managerial judgment. The EBIT-EPS chart is simply a tool that can be used to learn about the consequences of using more or less financial leverage. The decision as to whether to use more or less financial leverage must be made after weighing all the factors that impinge on a firm's capital structure decision. For example, in the next section we look at the use of comparative financial ratios, which indicate the degree of similarity of the firm's capital structure to others in its same industry, or peer group.

## Comparative Leverage Ratios

In Chapter 4 we explored the overall usefulness of financial ratio analysis. Leverage ratios, one of the categories of financial ratios, are identified in that chapter. We emphasize here that the computation of leverage ratios is one of the basic tools of capital structure management.

Two types of leverage ratios must be computed when a financing decision faces the firm. We call these **balance-sheet leverage ratios** and **coverage ratios**. The firm's balance sheet supplies inputs for computing the balance-sheet leverage ratios. In various forms these balance-sheet metrics compare the firm's use of funds supplied by creditors with those supplied by owners.

**balance-sheet leverage ratios** ratios of a firm's use of financial leverage or debt capital to either the firm's total capital or equity. Since the needed information for computing these ratios is found in the balance sheet we refer to them as balance sheet leverage ratios.

**coverage ratios** ratios of the firm's earnings to the interest and principal related to a firm's borrowing.

Inputs to the coverage ratios generally come from the firm's income statement. At times the analyst may have to refer to balance-sheet information to construct some of these needed estimates. Regardless of the source of data, coverage ratios provide estimates of the firm's ability to service its financing contracts. High coverage ratios, compared with a standard, imply unused debt capacity.

In reality, we know that EBIT might be expected to vary over a considerable range of outcomes. For this reason the coverage ratios should be calculated several times, each at a different level of EBIT. If this is accomplished over all possible values of EBIT, a probability distribution for each coverage ratio can be constructed. This provides the financial manager with much more information than simply calculating the coverage ratios based on the expected value of EBIT.

## Industry Norms

The comparative leverage ratios have utility only if they can be compared with some standard. Generally, corporate financial analysts, investment bankers, commercial bank loan officers, and bond-rating agencies rely on industry classes to compute "normal" ratios. Although industry groupings may actually contain firms whose basic business-risk exposure differs widely, the practice is entrenched in American business behavior. At the very least, then, the financial officer must be interested in industry standards because almost everybody else is.

Capital structure ratios tend to differ among industry classes. For example, random samplings of the common equity ratios of large retail firms seem to differ statistically from those of major steel producers. The major steel producers use financial leverage to a lesser degree than do the large retail organizations. On the whole, firms operating in the *same* industry tend to exhibit capital structure ratios that cluster around a central value that we call a norm. The degree of business risk varies from industry to industry as well. As a consequence, the capital structure norms vary from industry to industry.

This is not to say that all companies in the industry will maintain leverage ratios "close" to the norm. For instance, firms that are very profitable might display high coverage ratios and high balance-sheet leverage ratios. The moderately profitable firm, though, might find such a posture unduly risky. Here the usefulness of industry-normal leverage ratios is clear. If the firm chooses to deviate substantially from the accepted values for the key ratios, it must have a sound reason.

## A Glance at Actual Capital Structure Management

We now examine some opinions and practices of financial executives that reinforce the importance of capital structure management. A survey of 392 corporate executives revealed the importance of a variety of factors that are believed to be either important or very important in deciding whether to use debt in their firm's capital structure.[4]

The 10 factors provide some practical guidance to the financial manager who is wrestling with capital structure design and management issues. Let's briefly consider each factor to see why it is relevant.

**Financial Flexibility**    When a firm needs to raise additional funds, its bargaining position is better if it has options or choices. For example, firms that have used very little debt in the past will find it easier to borrow or sell new shares of stock than firms that have borrowed heavily.

**Credit Rating**    Dropping a notch in the rating system leads to an increase in the firm's borrowing costs, so managers like to avoid this if at all possible.[5] Moreover, sometimes firms have contractual provisions inserted into some of their other debt agreements that require the firm to maintain a particular credit rating. For example,

---

[4]John Graham and Campbell Harvey, "How do CFOs make capital budgeting and capital structure decisions?," *Journal of Applied Corporate Finance*, Volume 15, Number 1, Spring 2002, 8–23.

[5]We discussed bond ratings in Chapter 7.

Enron's bankruptcy was triggered by the firm dropping one credit rating, which put the firm below investment-grade status. The firm had billions of dollars in outstanding debt that contained a covenant requiring them to maintain a BBB or higher rating.

**Insufficient Internal Funds**    It has long been known that firms tend to follow a priority list when raising new funds that has been referred to as a "pecking order." The order in which firms typically finance their operations begins with internally generated profits, followed by debt financing, and, finally, by issuing new equity.

**Level of Interest Rates**    Other things being the same, firms prefer to borrow when they feel interest rates are low relative to their expectations. For example, when interest rates are historically very low, a CFO may feel more inclined to enter into long-term debt agreements. However, there is little evidence that a CFO, or anyone for that matter, has any talent for knowing when rates are low and about to rise or high and about to fall. Nonetheless, all that is required for this factor to be considered important is a strong opinion about the future path of interest rates.

**Interest Tax Savings**    Interest expense, unlike dividends paid to shareholders, is a tax-deductible expense. This tax-savings feature serves as a subsidy to corporate borrowing and makes debt appear cheap relative to alternative sources of financing.

**Transaction Costs and Fees**    When a firm chooses between debt and equity, it faces very different costs of issuing the two types of securities. For example, debt holders receive interest and principal payments as prescribed in the debt contract (indenture). This type of security is relatively straightforward, and its value hinges on the creditworthiness of the firm. However, when a firm issues equity, there are no rules prescribing how much will be paid back to the buyers of the stock. This means that it can be much more costly to entice investors to become stockholders

## FINANCE AT WORK

### CAPITAL STRUCTURES AROUND THE WORLD

The use of debt financing by firms is influenced by many factors, and one of them apparently is the home country of the firm. To illustrate, consider the listing of median leverage ratios (total debt divided by the market value of the firm) by country provided below.*

| COUNTRY | LEVERAGE RATIO |
| --- | --- |
| South Korea | 70% |
| Pakistan | 49% |
| Brazil | 47% |
| Thailand | 46% |
| India | 40% |
| Japan | 33% |
| China | 33% |
| France | 28% |
| Belgium | 26% |
| Mexico | 26% |
| Chile | 21% |
| Germany | 17% |
| United Kingdom | 16% |
| United States | 16% |
| Greece | 10% |

The highest leverage ratio is observed in South Korea where the leverage ratio is close to 70%, while the lowest is only 10%, observed in Greece. The median leverage ratio in the United States is only 16%, which may seem quite low. However, this is the result of the fact that these ratios are based on the market values of the firms rather than their book value.

What kind of factors might encourage the use of debt in different countries? One factor that researchers found is that firms that operate in countries where the legal systems provide better protection for financial claimants tend to use less total debt, and the debt they use tends to be of a longer-term maturity. In addition, as you might expect, the tax policy of the country that the firm operates within also plays a role in the level of debt that a firm uses.

*The market value of the firm is defined to be the market value of common equity plus the book values of preferred stock and total debt.

Source: Joseph P. H. Fan, Sheridan Titman, and Garry J. Twite, "An International Comparison of Capital Structure and Debt Maturity Choices" (October 2008). AFA 2005 Philadelphia Meetings available at SSRN: http://ssrn.com/abstract=423483.

than to entice them to loan money to the firm. Thus, the differentially higher costs of issuing equity make it less attractive as a source of financing.

**Equity Undervaluation/Overvaluation**    Earlier we mentioned that CFOs often try to time their debt offerings to take advantage of abnormally low interest rates. The same holds true for equity offerings. For example, if the CFO thinks that the firm's shares of stock are undervalued, he or she will want to borrow money rather than sell new shares and risk the price of the shares falling further. Once again, there is no evidence that corporate executives are any better at forecasting their own share prices than they are at predicting the future of interest rates, but they only have to think they are good at it to believe it is an important factor.

**Comparable Firm Debt Levels**    Firms in similar businesses tend to have similar capital structures. This is made doubly important by virtue of the fact that lenders and credit-rating agencies often compare a firm's debt ratios to those of comparable firms when deciding credit terms and ratings.

**Bankruptcy/Distress Costs**    The more debt a firm has used in the past, the higher the likelihood is that the firm will at some point face financial distress and possibly fail. This risk forms the basis for the firm's credit rating.

**Customer/Supplier Discomfort**    An important source of financial distress brought on by the use of debt financing comes in the form of pressures from both the firm's customers (who fear that financial distress may interrupt their source of supply) and the firm's suppliers (who fear that financial distress may interrupt an important source of demand for their goods and services). The latter is compounded further if the supplier has provided the firm with trade credit, which is at risk if the firm fails.

After reading through the discussion of each of the 10 factors, you are probably beginning to think that capital structure management is more art than science. In other words, there simply is no magic formula that you can use to solve for the optimal capital structure. However, you should be gaining an appreciation for the basic considerations that go into the judgment call that the CFOs ultimately must make and that drives the capital structure of firms. Furthermore, selected comments from financial executives point to the widespread use of target debt ratios.

## Concept Check

1. Explain the meaning of the EBIT-EPS indifference point.
2. How are various leverage ratios and industry norms used in capital structure management?
3. Identify several factors that influence the decision to issue debt.
4. Why is capital structure design both an art and a science?

# Chapter Summaries

 **Distinguish between business and financial risk.** (pgs. 382–383)

**SUMMARY:** A firm's business risk arises out of the competitive environment in which the firm operates. The risk results in fluctuations in firm sales in response to changes in the overall economy and the conditions within the specific industry or industries in which the firm operates. Firms can make further choices that can amplify this volatility even more if, for example, they choose to purchase plant and equipment rather than rent it. In the former case, the firm will incur the fixed costs of the plant and equipment even if it produces nothing and this adds risk to the firm. Moreover, firms can choose to use sources of capital in their financial structure that entail a fixed financial obligation such as interest and principal payments on the debt. The effects of business, operating, and financial risk work in concert to determine the riskiness of the firm's future earnings streams.

**KEY TERMS**

**Business risk, page 382** The risk of the firm's future earnings that is a direct result of the particular line of business chosen by the firm.

**Operating risk, page 382** Risk driven by the mix of fixed versus variable costs the firm incurs to do business. For example, the greater the firm's fixed operating costs, other things remaining the same, the more volatile will be the firm's earnings in response to changes in firm sales.

**Financial risk, page 382** Risk driven by the presence of fixed finance costs in the firm's capital structure (as opposed to variable finance costs such as dividends declared and paid). The net effect of financial leverage (which corresponds to the firm's use of debt financing that entails the payment of predetermined interest and principal payments) is to make firm earnings more volatile.

---

## Use break-even analysis. (pgs. 383–388)

**SUMMARY:** A key number in any business's operations is the break-even quantity or sales level. Breakeven is key because it tells the firm's managers the minimum sales (dollars or units sold) that are needed to pay the firm's short-term liabilities.

**KEY TERMS**

**Break-even quantity, page 383** The number of units a firm must sell before it starts to earn a profit.

**Fixed costs, page 384** The expenses of the firm that do not vary with the level of firm sales. An example would be salaries paid to the firm's management team.

**Indirect costs, page 384** costs that do not vary in total dollar amount as sales volume or quantity of output changes.

**Variable costs, page 384** Expenses that move up and down with the level of firm sales.

**Direct costs, page 384** Expenses that vary in total as output changes.

**Total revenue, page 385** The total dollar sales for a particular period of time.

**Volume of output, page 385** The number of units produced and sold for a particular period of time.

**KEY EQUATION**

$$\text{Break-even level of revenues} = \frac{\text{total fixed costs}}{1 - \dfrac{\text{variable costs}}{\text{revenues}}}$$

---

## Understand the relationships between operating, financial, and combined leverage. (pgs. 388–393)

**SUMMARY:** The volatility of a firm's reported earnings over time is an important piece of information to investors and thus it is important that the firm's management understand what causes this volatility. It turns out that the volatility of earnings over time is largely driven by choices the firm's management has made. These choices relate to the type of business the firm runs; the operating decisions the firm has made, which, in turn, determine it's fixed versus operating costs; and financing decisions regarding the use of borrowed money. The combination of the firm's choice of type of business, operating models (fixed versus variable operating expenses), and financial risk (fixed versus variable financial expenses) dictates just how the firm's earnings will change in response to changing economic conditions. For example, should the economy swing into a period of rapid growth, then firms that sell products people want in periods of expansion (expensive cars, boats, and consumer durable goods) will experience an abnormally large upswing in sales. If these same firms were to experience a downturn in the economy their sales would drop disproportionately when compared to firms selling more essential goods and services such as food and clothing. The net result would be that the earnings of firms selling consumer durable and luxury goods will experience a large decline in earnings.

**KEY TERMS**

**Operating leverage, page 388** Results from operating costs that are fixed (rather than those that vary up and down with the level of output or sales).

**Financial leverage, page 390** Results from the firm's use of sources of financing that require a fixed rate of return. The primary example of such a form of financing is fixed interest rate debt whereby the firm must pay

pre-determined interest and principal on specified dates.

**Combined, or total, leverage, page 391** The result of the combined effects of both operating and financial leverage. Operating and financial leverage tend to magnify one another such that combining lots of operating and financial leverage will make the total leverage of the firm much greater.

 **4**   **Discuss the concept of an optimal capital structure.** (pgs. 393–402)

**SUMMARY:** A firm's capital structure is defined by the mix of sources of financing the firm has used to raise money in the past. The cost of each of the component sources then determines the overall cost of capital to the firm, which, in Chapter 9, we defined to be the weighted average cost of capital. The idea of an optimal capital structure is simply a particular mix of financing sources that results in the lowest possible weighted average cost of capital.

Many theories of capital structure have been developed that attempt to explain how a firm's cost of capital changes as the mix of financing sources is changed. Early theories used very restrictive sets of assumptions about investor behavior to argue that a firm's capital structure did not vary with the particular mix of financing sources the firm used. This result, however, ignored the tax bias built into the corporate tax code whereby the interest expense paid for debt is tax deductible to the corporation, whereas dividends paid to preferred or common stockholders are not tax deductible. This meant that using more debt was, other things being the same, advantageous to the firm. At this juncture it seemed that the best thing a firm could do with its capital structure was to borrow as much as it could. Alas, there are costs to becoming too highly leveraged. Having too much debt means that the firm could, in very bad economic circumstances, find itself unable to pay its interest and principle and default on its debt. The net result of such a default is that the firm's common stockholders would lose all they had invested in the firm, as the firm's creditors would take over in bankruptcy. Thus, most practicing managers believe that there is a trade-off between the "good" that comes with debt (tax deductibility of interest) and the "bad" (increasing risk of default), which forms the basis for believing there is indeed an optimal capital structure where these costs and benefits are just equal.

**KEY TERMS**

**Financial structure, page 394** The mix of all sources of funding that appears on the right-hand side of the firm's balance sheet.

**Capital structure, page 394** The mix of interest-bearing short- and long-term debt plus equity funds used by the firm.

**Debt maturity composition, page 395** The mix of short- and long-term debt used by the firm.

**Debt–equity composition, page 395** The mix of debt and equity used by the firm in its capital structure.

**Optimal capital structure, page 395** The capital structure that minimizes the firm's

composite cost of capital for raising a given amount of funds.

**Tax shield, page 398** The reduction in taxes due to the tax deductibility of interest expense.

**Optimal range of financial leverage, page 399** The range of debt use in the firm's capital structure that yields the lowest overall cost of capital for the firm.

**Debt capacity, page 400** The maximum amount of debt that a firm can include in its capital structure and still maintain its current credit rating.

 **5**   **Use the basic tools of capital structure management.** (pgs. 402–408)

**SUMMARY:** Although there are many theories concerning the existence of an optimal capital structure, it is difficult to analyze what this optimal structure might be. As a result, it is common practice for managers to begin their analysis of capital structure by looking at other firms and analyzing what they have done. In other words, they first emulate other, similar firms and then analyze the consequences of deviating from the practices of what they feel are comparable firms. Managers also analyze the effect of different capital structure choices on the volatility of the firm's reported earnings. The idea here is that using more debt results in more volatile firm earnings and investors typically dislike uncertainty.

## KEY TERMS

**EBIT-EPS indifference point, page 404** The level of earnings before interest and taxes (EBT) that will equate earnings per share (EPS) between two different financing plans.

**Balance-sheet leverage ratios, page 405** Ratios of a firm's use of financial leverage or debt capital to either the firm's

total capital or equity. Since the needed information for computing these ratios is found in the balance sheet we refer to them as balance sheet leverage ratios.

**Coverage ratios, page 405** Ratios of the firm's earnings to the interest and principal related to a firm's borrowing.

## KEY EQUATIONS

Earnings per share (Equity plan) = Earnings per share (Debt plan)

$$\frac{(EBIT - I_s)(1 - T_c)}{S_s} = \frac{(EBIT - I_b)(1 - T_c)}{S_b}$$

where

$$
\begin{aligned}
EBIT &= \text{earnings before interest and taxes} \\
I &= \text{interest expense} \\
T_c &= \text{tax rate} \\
S &= \text{number of common shares}
\end{aligned}
$$

and the $s$ and $b$ subscripts refer to the equity and bond or debt financing plan, respectively.

# Review Questions

*All Review Questions are available in* MyFinanceLab.

**12-1.** In the chapter introduction we learned that AT&T (T) borrowed $3 billion by issuing bonds in the public bond market. Although this may sound like a lot of money, AT&T owed almost $65 billion in corporate debt at the end of 2011. The company had over $270 billion in total assets in 2011. How much will the new bond issue increase AT&T's debt-to-total-assets ratio?

**12-2.** Distinguish between business risk and financial risk. What gives rise to, or causes, each type of risk?

**12-3.** Define the term *financial leverage*. Does the firm use financial leverage if preferred stock is present in its capital structure?

**12-4.** Define the term *operating leverage*. What type of effect occurs when the firm uses operating leverage?

**12-5.** A manager in your firm decides to employ a break-even analysis. Of what shortcomings should this manager be aware?

**12-6.** A break-even analysis assumes linear revenue and cost functions. In reality, these linear functions deviate over large output and sales levels. Why?

**12-7.** Define the following terms:
   a. Financial structure
   b. Capital structure
   c. Optimal capital structure
   d. Debt capacity

**12-8.** What is the primary weakness of using EBIT-EPS analysis as a financing decision tool?

**12-9.** What is the objective of capital structure management?

**12-10.** Why might firms whose sales levels change drastically over time choose to use debt only sparingly in their capital structures?

**12-11.** What does the term *independence hypothesis* mean as it applies to capital structure theory?

**12-12.** Many CFOs believe that the firm's composite cost of capital is saucer-shaped or U-shaped. What does this mean?

**12-13.** Define the EBIT-EPS indifference point.

**12-14.** Explain how industry norms might be used by the financial manager in the design of the company's financing mix.

# Study Problems

*All Study Problems are available in* MyFinanceLab.

**12-1.** (*Business and financial risk*) Which of the following sources of new earnings volatility represents the effect of business versus financial risk (discuss the rationale for your decisions):

    a. Amos Gooding Real Estate Company recently constructed a new office building and borrowed 100 percent of the money needed to fund the project.

    b. Clearing House Outsourcing has historically paid a printer to prepare all of its printed documents. However, last year the firm acquired its own printing press (paying cash).

    c. Smithers Enterprises has been a specialty retail shop that sold outdoor camping equipment. The firm recently decided to purchase a golf course.

**12-2.** (*Break-even analysis*) You have developed the following income statement for the Hugo Boss Corporation. It represents the most recent year's operations, which ended yesterday.

| | |
|---|---|
| Sales | $ 50,439,375 |
| Variable costs | (25,137,000) |
| Revenue before fixed costs | $ 25,302,375 |
| Fixed costs | (10,143,000) |
| EBIT | $ 15,159,375 |
| Interest expense | (1,488,375) |
| Earnings before taxes | $ 13,671,000 |
| Taxes at 50% | (6,835,500) |
| Net income | $  6,835,500 |

$$\frac{10143}{1-\left(\frac{25.137}{50434}\right)} = 20.221$$

$50439,375 \times 50\%$
$(25,137,000 \times 30\%)$
$= \triangle EBIT$

Your supervisor in the controller's office has just handed you a memorandum asking for written responses to the following questions:

    a. What is the firm's break-even point in sales dollars?

    b. If sales should increase by 30 percent, by what percent would earnings before taxes (and net income) increase?

**12-3.** (*Break-even point and selling price*) Parks Castings Inc. will manufacture and sell 200,000 units next year. Fixed costs will total $300,000, and variable costs will be 60 percent of sales.

    a. The firm wants to achieve a level of earnings before interest and taxes of $250,000. What selling price per unit is necessary to achieve this result?

    b. Set up an analytical income statement to verify your solution to part (a).

**12-4.** (*Break-even point and operating leverage*) Footwear Inc. manufactures a complete line of men's and women's dress shoes for independent merchants. The average selling price of its finished product is $85 per pair. The variable cost for this same pair of shoes is $58. Footwear Inc. incurs fixed costs of $170,000 per year.

    a. What is the break-even point in pairs of shoes for the company?

    b. What is the dollar sales volume the firm must achieve to reach the break-even point?

    c. What would be the firm's profit or loss at the following units of production sold: 7,000 pairs of shoes? 9,000 pairs of shoes? 15,000 pairs of shoes?

**12-5.** (*Operating leverage*) Rocky Mount Metals Company manufactures an assortment of wood-burning stoves. The average selling price for the various units is $500. The associated variable cost is $350 per unit. Fixed costs for the firm average $180,000 annually.

a. What is the break-even point in units for the company?
b. What is the dollar sales volume the firm must achieve to reach the break-even point?
c. What is the degree of operating leverage for a production and sales level of 5,000 units for the firm? (Calculate to three decimal places.)
d. What will be the projected effect on earnings before interest and taxes if the firm's sales level should increase by 20 percent from the volume noted in part (c)?

$$C = \frac{5000 \times (500-350)}{5000 \times (500-350)-180,000} = 1.316$$

**12-6.** (*Capital structure theory*) Match each of the following definitions to the appropriate terms:

| TERMS | DEFINITIONS |
|---|---|
| Independence theory—with corporate taxes | The cost of capital is unaffected by the firm's choice of debt and equity financing. |
| Independence theory—no taxes | The cost of capital decreases as the firm initially uses debt to substitute for equity financing but eventually begins to increase as extreme levels of debt are used. |
| Saucer-shaped cost of capital curve | The cost of capital decreases continuously as the firm increases its reliance on debt financing. |

**12-7.** (*Capital structure theory*) Which of the following statements most appropriately describes how agency costs affect a firm's choice of capital structure (explain)?

a. When firm owners borrow money they have an incentive to engage in excessive risk taking (that is, investing in very risky projects) since they are managing someone else's money.
b. When firms have very limited investment opportunities and little debt financing combined with healthy profits that provide them with free cash flow, their management team might squander the firm's earnings on questionable investments.

**12-8.** (*EBIT-EPS analysis*) Two inventive entrepreneurs have interested a group of venture capitalists in backing a new business project. The proposed plan would consist of a series of international retail outlets to distribute and service a full line of ingenious home garden tools. The stores would be located in high-traffic cities in Latin America such as Panama City, Bogotá, São Paulo, and Buenos Aires. Two financing plans have been proposed by the entrepreneurs. Plan A is an all common-equity structure. Five million dollars would be raised by selling 160,000 shares of common stock. Plan B would involve the use of long-term debt financing. Three million dollars would be raised by marketing bonds with an effective interest rate of 14 percent. Under the alternative, another $2 million would be raised by selling 64,000 shares of common stock. With both plans, $5 million is needed to launch the new firm's operations. The debt funds raised under plan B are considered to have no fixed maturity date, because this portion of financial leverage is thought to be a permanent part of the company's capital structure. The two promising entrepreneurs have decided to use a 35 percent tax rate in their analysis, and they have hired you on a consulting basis to do the following:

a. Find the EBIT indifference level associated with the two financing proposals.
b. Prepare income statements for the two plans that prove EPS will be the same regardless of the plan chosen at the EBIT level found in part (a).

**12-9.** (*EBIT-EPS analysis*) A group of retired college professors has decided to form a small manufacturing corporation. The company will produce a full line of traditional office furniture. Two financing plans have been proposed by the investors. Plan A is an all-common-equity alternative. Under this agreement, 1 million common shares will be sold to net the firm $20 per share. Plan B involves the use of financial leverage. A debt issue with a 20-year maturity period will be privately placed. The debt issue will carry an interest rate of 10 percent, and the principal borrowed will amount to $6 million. The corporate tax rate is 50 percent.

a.  Find the EBIT indifference level associated with the two financing proposals.
b.  Prepare an analytical income statement that proves EPS will be the same regardless of the plan chosen at the EBIT level found in part (a).
c.  Prepare an EBIT-EPS analysis chart for this situation.
d.  If a detailed financial analysis projects that long-term EBIT will always be close to $2.4 million annually, which plan will provide for the higher EPS?

**12-10.** (*Assessing leverage use*) Some financial data for three corporations are displayed here.

| MEASURE | FIRM A | FIRM B | FIRM C | INDUSTRY NORM |
|---|---|---|---|---|
| Debt ratio | 20% | 25% | 40% | 20% |
| Times interest covered | 8 times | 10 times | 7 times | 9 times |
| Price/earnings ratio | 9 times | 11 times | 6 times | 10 times |

a.  Which firm appears to be excessively leveraged?
b.  Which firm appears to be employing financial leverage to the most appropriate degree?
c.  What explanation can you provide for the higher price/earnings ratio enjoyed by firm B as compared with firm A?

# Mini Cases

*These Mini Cases are available in MyFinanceLab.*

**1.** Imagine that you were hired recently as a financial analyst for a relatively new, highly leveraged ski manufacturer located in the foothills of Colorado's Rocky Mountains. Your firm manufactures only one product, a state-of-the-art snow ski. The company has been operating up to this point without much quantitative knowledge of the business and financial risks it faces.

Ski season just ended, however, so the president of the company has started to focus more on the financial aspects of managing the business. He has set up a meeting for next week with the CFO, Maria Sanchez, to discuss matters such as the business and financial risks faced by the company.

Accordingly, Maria has asked you to prepare an analysis to assist her in her discussions with the president. As a first step in your work, you compiled the following information regarding the cost structure of the company:

| | |
|---|---|
| Output level | 80,000 units |
| Operating assets | $4,000,000 |
| Operating asset turnover | 8 times |
| Return on operating assets | 32% |
| Degree of operating leverage | 6 times |
| Interest expense | $600,000 |
| Tax rate | 35% |

As the next step, you need to determine the break-even point in units of output for the company. One of your strong points has been that you always prepare supporting work papers, which show how you arrived at your conclusions. You know Maria would like to see these work papers to facilitate her review of your work. Therefore, you will have the information you require to prepare an analytical income statement for the company. You are sure that Maria would also like to see this statement. In addition, you know that you need it to be able to answer the following questions. You also know Maria expects you to prepare, in a format that is presentable to the president, answers to the following questions to serve as a basis for her discussions with the president:

a.  What is the firm's break-even point in sales dollars?
b.  If sales should increase by 30 percent (as the president expects), by what percentage would EBT (earnings before taxes) and net income increase?
c.  Prepare another income statement, this time to verify the calculations from part (b).

**2.** Camping USA Inc. has been operating for only 2 years in the outskirts of Albuquerque, New Mexico, and is a new manufacturer of a top-of-the-line camping tent. You are starting an internship as assistant to the chief financial officer of the company, and the owner and CEO, Tom Charles, has decided that this is the right time to know more about the business and financial risks his company must deal with. For this, the CFO has asked you to prepare an analysis to support him in his next meeting with Tom Charles a week from today.

To make the required calculations, you have put together the following data regarding the cost structure of the company:

| | |
|---|---|
| Output level | 120,000 units |
| Operating assets | $6,000,000 |
| Operating asset turnover | 12 times |
| Return on operating assets | 48% |
| Degree of operating leverage | 10 times |
| Interest expense | $720,000 |
| Tax rate | 42% |

The CFO has instructed you to first determine the break-even point in units of output for the company. He requires that you prepare supporting documents, which demonstrate how you arrived at your conclusion and can facilitate his review of your work. Accordingly, you are required to have the information needed to prepare an analytical income statement for the company to be presented to the CFO. In a format that is acceptable for a meeting discussion with the CEO, you also need to prepare answers to the following questions:

a. What is the firm's break-even point in sales dollars?
b. If sales should increase by 40 percent, by what percentage would EBT (earnings before taxes) and net income increase?
c. Prepare another income statement, this time to verify the calculations from part (b).

$$DOL = \frac{\% \Delta EBIT}{\% \Delta Sale}$$

$$DFL = \frac{\% \Delta EPS}{\% \Delta EBIT}$$

$$DCL = DOL \times DFL = \frac{\% \Delta EPS}{\% Sales}$$

# 13

# Dividend Policy and Internal Financing

## Learning Objectives

| | |
|---|---|
| **1** **Describe** the trade-off between paying dividends and retaining (reinvesting) firm profits. | **Key Terms** |
| **2** **Does** dividend policy affect the company's stock price? | **Does a Dividend Policy Matter to Stockholders?** |
| **3** **Discuss** the constraints on dividend policy, commonly used dividend policies, and payment procedures. | **The Dividend Decision in Practice** |
| **4** **Describe** why firms sometimes pay noncash dividends. | **Stock Dividends and Stock Splits** |
| **5** **Distinguish** between the use of cash dividends and share repurchases. | **Stock Repurchases** |

Technology giant Apple (AAPL) launched a plan to pay a $2.65 fourth quarter cash dividend in addition to repurchasing $10 billion of its shares in March 2012. The combined effect of paying the dividends and repurchasing the shares is $45 billion! Interestingly, this is not Apple's first dividend payment. The firm paid dividends for 8 years, ending in 1995 when a worsening business outlook led the board to discontinue the dividend.[1] At least for the time being the dividend payment looks very secure as Apple expected to add some $35 billion to its cash holdings during 2011 even after paying dividends and repurchasing shares.

Why should an investor care about a firm's cash distributions? The answer, very simply, is that these cash distributions represent the *return on* the investment made by the stockholders. As such these distributions are tangible evidence of the value created by the firm for its owners. But not all companies distribute cash either as dividends or share repurchases. Apple, for example, did not distribute any cash during the early years of the company's life when it was growing rapidly and needed all its internally generated earnings to support its growth.

[1]Casey Newton, Apple to offer quarterly dividend, buy back shares, *SFGate*, March 20, 2012 (http://www.sfgate.com/cgi-bin/article.cgi?f=/ c/a/2012/03/19/BU201NN0EH.DTL&type=business).

Similarly, rapidly growing technology giant Google Inc. (GOOG) earned $9.8 billion from its operations in 2011 and had a cash plus marketable securities balance of over $44 billion but paid no cash dividends. So why did Google's stock price hover around $650 on March 26, 2012, if it was not distributing any cash? The answer is that it is the investor's expectation that at some point in the future the firm will begin distributing cash just as Apple has done. So it is the anticipated dividends and share repurchases that are the cash flow (Principle 1) that underlies stock valuation.

Because the goal of a firm should be to maximize the value of the firm's common stock, the success or failure of managerial decisions can be evaluated only in light of their impact on the price. We observed that the company's investment (Chapters 10 and 11) and financing decisions (Chapter 12) can increase the value of the firm. As we look at the firm's policies regarding dividends and internal financing (how much of the company's financing comes from cash flows generated internally), we return to the same basic question: Can managers influence the price of the firm's stock through its dividend policies? After addressing this important question, we then look at the practical side of the question: What practices do managers commonly follow when making decisions about paying or not paying a dividend to the firm's stockholders? We conclude with a discussion of the share repurchase decision. Firms have increasingly been repurchasing their shares of stock as an alternative to paying out cash dividends.

## Key Terms

 Describe the trade-off between paying dividends and retaining (reinvesting) firm profits.

Before taking up the particular issues relating to dividend policy, we must understand several key terms and interrelationships.

A firm's dividend policy includes two basic components. First, the **dividend payout ratio** indicates the *amount of dividends paid relative to the company's earnings*. For instance, if the dividend per share is $2, and the earnings per share are $4, the payout ratio is 50 percent ($2/$4). The second component is the stability of the dividends over time. As you will learn later in the chapter, dividend stability can be almost as important to the investor as the amount of dividends received.

**dividend payout ratio** the ratio of dividends paid per share divided by earnings per share.

In formulating a dividend policy, the financial manager faces trade-offs. Assuming that management has already decided how much to invest and has chosen its debt–equity mix for financing the firm's investments, the decision to pay a large dividend means simultaneously deciding to retain less of the firm's profits; this in turn results in a greater reliance on external equity financing. Conversely, given the firm's investment and financing decisions, a small dividend payment corresponds to high profit retention, making it less necessary to generate funds externally. These trade-offs, which are fundamental to our discussion, are illustrated in Figure 13-1.

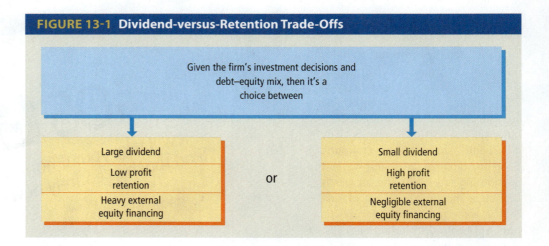

**FIGURE 13-1** Dividend-versus-Retention Trade-Offs

Given the firm's investment decisions and debt–equity mix, then it's a choice between

| Large dividend | or | Small dividend |
| --- | --- | --- |
| Low profit retention | | High profit retention |
| Heavy external equity financing | | Negligible external equity financing |

## Concept Check

1. Provide a financial executive with a useful definition of the term *dividend payout ratio*.
2. How does the firm's actual dividend policy affect its need for externally generated financial capital?

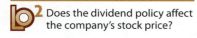
Does the dividend policy affect the company's stock price?

# Does Dividend Policy Matter to Stockholders?

What is a sound rationale or motivation for dividend payments? Put another way, given the firm's capital-budgeting and borrowing decisions, what is the effect of the firm's dividend policies on the stock price? *Does a high dividend payment decrease a stock's value, increase it, or make no real difference?*

At first glance, we might reasonably conclude that a firm's dividend policy is important. We have already (in Chapter 8) pointed out that the value of a stock is equal to the present value of its expected future dividends. Why else do so many companies pay dividends? Why are dividend announcements like the Apple announcement reported in the introduction to this chapter front-page news? How can we not conclude that dividend policies are important?

## Three Basic Views

Some would argue that the amount of a dividend is irrelevant and any time spent on the decision is a waste of energy. Others contend that a high dividend results in a high stock price. Still others take the view that dividends actually hurt the value of the dividend-paying stocks.

Before we delve into the various theories, or "views," on the dividend policy question, we need to be very careful about the conditions under which we pose the question. Specifically, we begin with the basic assumption that the firm plans to undertake all positive *NPV* investment opportunities *regardless* of whether it pays dividends or not. This is critical because if we allow the decision to pay a dividend to interfere with the firm's decision to undertake a good investment, then the policy obviously matters to the firm's stockholders. So, assuming that the firm will make the right set of investment decisions, why might the company's dividend policy matter?

**View 1: A Firm's Dividend Policy Is Irrelevant** Much of the controversy about the dividend issue is based in time-honored disagreements between the academic and professional communities. Experienced practitioners tend to believe that stock prices change as a result of dividend announcements and, therefore, see dividends as important. Professors often argue that the seemingly apparent relationship between dividends and stock prices may be an illusion.

The notion that dividends are not important rests on two preconditions. First, we must assume that the firm's investment and borrowing decisions have already been made and that these decisions will not be altered by the amount of any dividend payments. Second, **perfect capital markets** must exist, which means that *(1) investors can buy and sell stocks without incurring any transaction costs, such as brokerage commissions; (2) companies can issue stocks without any cost of doing so; (3) there are no corporate or personal taxes; (4) complete information about the firm is readily available; (5) there are no conflicts of interest between managers and stockholders; and (6) financial distress and bankruptcy costs are nonexistent.*

**perfect capital markets** markets in which information flows freely and market prices fully reflect all available information.

The first assumption—that the firm has already made its investment and financing decisions—simply keeps us from confusing the issues. We want to know the effect of dividend decisions on a stand-alone basis, without mixing in other decisions. The second assumption, that of perfect markets, also allows us to study the effect of dividend decisions in isolation, much as a physicist studies motion in a vacuum to avoid the influence of friction.

Given these assumptions, the effect of a dividend decision on share price may be stated unequivocally: *There is no relationship between dividend policy and stock value.* One dividend policy is as good as another. In the aggregate, investors are concerned only with *total* returns from investment decisions; they are indifferent to whether these returns come from capital gains or dividend income. They also recognize that the dividend decision is really a choice of financing strategy. That is, to finance growth, the firm (a) may choose to issue stock, allowing internally generated funds (profits) to be used to pay dividends; or (b) may use internally generated funds to finance its growth, paying less in dividends but not having to issue stock. In the first case, shareholders receive dividend income; in the second case, the value of their stocks should increase. Thus, the nature of the return is the only difference; total returns should be about the same.

**View 2: High Dividends Increase Stock Values**    The belief that a firm's dividend policy is unimportant implicitly assumes that an investor is indifferent about whether the increased income comes through capital gains (stock price increase) or comes through dividends. However, dividends are more predictable than capital gains. Managers can control dividends, but they cannot dictate the price of the stock. Investors are less certain of receiving income from capital gains than from dividends. The incremental risk associated with capital gains relative to dividend income implies a higher required rate for discounting a dollar of capital gains than for discounting a dollar of dividends. In other words, we would value a dollar of expected dividends more highly than a dollar of expected capital gains. We might, for example, require a 14 percent rate of return for a stock that pays its entire return from dividends, but a 20 percent return for a high-growth stock that pays no dividends. This view, which says *dividends are more certain than capital gains*, has been called the **bird-in-the-hand dividend theory**.

**bird-in-the-hand dividend theory** the view that dividends are more certain than capital gains and therefore more valuable.

The position that dividends are less risky than capital gains and should, therefore, be valued differently is not without its critics. If we hold to our basic decision not to let the firm's dividend policy influence its investment and capital-mix decisions, the company's operating cash flows, in both expected amount and variability, are unaffected by its dividend policy. Because the dividend policy has no impact on the volatility of the company's overall cash flows, it has no impact on the riskiness of the firm.

Increasing a firm's dividend does not reduce the basic riskiness of the stock; rather, if a dividend payment requires managers to issue new stock, it only transfers risk *and* ownership from the current owners to new owners. We would have to acknowledge that the current investors who receive the dividend trade an uncertain capital gain for a "safe" asset (the cash dividend). However, if risk reduction is the only goal, the investor could have kept the money in the bank and not bought the stock in the first place.

**View 3: Low Dividends Increase Stock Values**    The third view of how dividends affect stock price argues that dividends actually hurt the investors. This belief has largely been based on the difference in the tax treatment of dividends versus capital gains. Contrary to the perfect-markets assumption of no taxes, most investors do pay income taxes. For these taxpayers, the objective is to maximize the *after-tax* return on an investment relative to the risk assumed. This is done by *minimizing* the effective tax rate on the income and, whenever possible, by *deferring* the payment of taxes.

Like most tax code complexities, Congress over the years has changed whether capital gains are taxed at a lower or similar rate to "earned income." Think of a water faucet being randomly turned on and then off. From 1987 through 1992, no federal tax advantage was provided for capital gains income relative to dividend income. A revision in the tax code that took effect beginning in 1993 did provide a preference for capital gains income. Then the Taxpayer Relief Act of 1997 made the difference (preference) even more favorable for capital gains as opposed to cash dividend income. For some taxpayers, if a minimum holding period had been reached, the tax rate applied to capital gains was reduced to 20 percent from the previous level of 28 percent. But wait: In 2003, Congress again felt the need to change the tax code as it pertained to both dividend income and capital gains income. On May 28, President Bush signed into law the Jobs and Growth Tax Relief Reconciliation Act. Part of the impetus for this act was the recession that commenced in 2001 and the slow rate of job creation that followed that recession.

In a nutshell, this 2003 act lowered the top tax rate on dividend income to 15 percent from a previous top rate of 38.6 percent and also lowered the top rate paid on realized long-term capital gains to the same 15 percent from a previous 20 percent. For 2005-2012 the tax rate on both dividends and capital gains was 15 percent. However, as of 2012, dividends are taxed as ordinary income and capital gains are taxed at 20 percent.

Actually, a different benefit exists for capital gains returns relative to dividend income. Taxes on dividend income are paid when the dividend is received, whereas taxes on price appreciation (capital gains) are deferred until the stock is actually sold. Thus, when it comes to tax considerations, many investors prefer the retention of a firm's earnings—in expectation of a later capital gain—as opposed to the near-term payment of cash dividends. Again, if earnings are retained within the firm, hopefully the stock price increases, but the increase is not taxed until the stock is sold.

Although the majority of investors are subject to taxes, certain investment companies, trusts, and pension plans are not when it comes to their dividend income. Also, for tax purposes, a corporation can generally exclude 70 percent of the dividend income it receives from another corporation. In these cases, investors will prefer dividends over capital gains.

To summarize, when it comes to taxes, we want to maximize our *after*-tax return, as opposed to our *before*-tax return. Investors try to defer taxes whenever possible. Stocks that allow tax deferral (low dividends–high capital gains) will possibly sell at a premium relative to stocks that require current taxation (high dividends–low capital gains). This suggests that a policy of paying low or no dividends will result in a higher stock price. That is, high dividends hurt investors, whereas low dividends and high retention help investors. This is the logic of the advocates of the low-dividend policy. It does presume that the firm's management has a roster of positive net present value projects that will put the dollars retained to productive use. However, since 2003 the low tax rate on dividends challenges this logic.

## Making Sense of Dividend Policy Theory

We have now looked at three views on dividend policy. Which is right? The argument that dividends are irrelevant is difficult to refute, given the perfect-market assumptions. However, in the real world, it is not always easy to feel comfortable with such an argument. Conversely, the high-dividend philosophy, which measures risk by how we split the firm's cash flows between dividends and retained earnings, is not particularly appealing when studied carefully. The third view, which is essentially a tax argument against high dividends, is persuasive. Even today, although the preferential tax rate for capital gains is limited, the "deferral advantage" of capital gains is still alive and well. However, if low dividends are so advantageous and generous dividends are so hurtful, why do companies continue to pay dividends? It is difficult to believe that managers would forgo such an easy opportunity to benefit their stockholders. What are we missing?

The need to find the missing elements in our "dividend puzzle" has not been ignored. When we need to better understand an issue or phenomenon, we can either improve our thinking or gather more evidence about the topic. Scholars and practitioners have taken both approaches. Although no single definitive answer has yet been found that is acceptable to all, several plausible explanations have been developed. Some of the more popular explanations include (1) the residual dividend theory, (2) the clientele effect, (3) the information effect, (4) agency costs, and (5) the expectations theory.

**The Residual Dividend Theory**    In perfect markets, there are no costs to the firm when it issues new securities. However, in reality the process is quite expensive, and the flotation costs associated with a new offering may be as much as 20 percent of the dollar issue size. Thus, if managers choose to issue stock rather than retain profits to finance new investments, a larger amount of securities is required to finance the investment. For example, if $30 million is needed to finance the investment, more than $30 million will have to be issued to offset the flotation costs. This means, very simply, that new equity capital raised through the sale of common stock will be more expensive than capital raised via retained earnings.

In effect, flotation costs eliminate our indifference by using internal capital versus issuing new common stock. Given these costs, *dividends should be paid only if the firm's profits are not completely used for investment purposes*. That is, only "residual earnings" should be paid out. This policy is called the **residual dividend theory**.

Given the existence of flotation costs, the firm's dividend policy should therefore be as follows:

**residual dividend theory** a theory that a company's dividend payment should equal the cash left after financing all the investments that have positive net present values.

1. Accept an investment if the *NPV* is positive, that is, if the expected rate of return exceeds the cost of capital.

2. Finance the equity portion of new investments *first* by using internally generated funds. Only after this capital is fully utilized should the firm issue new common shares.

3. If any internally generated funds still remain after making all acceptable investments, pay dividends to the investors. However, if all of the internal capital is needed to finance acceptable investments, pay no dividends.

Thus, dividend policy is influenced by (1) the company's investment opportunities and (2) the availability of internally generated capital. Dividends are then paid *only* after all acceptable investments have been financed. According to this concept, a dividend policy is totally passive in nature and can't affect the market price of the common stock.

Now, let us consider a dose of corporate reality.

**The Clientele Effect**    What if the investors do not like the dividend policy chosen by managers? In perfect markets, in which we incur no costs when buying or selling stock, there is no problem. Investors can simply satisfy their personal income preferences by purchasing or selling securities when the dividends they receive do not satisfy their current needs. In other words, if an investor does not view the dividends received in any given year to be sufficient, he or she can simply sell a portion of stock, thereby "creating a dividend." In addition, if the dividend is larger than the investor desired, he or she can simply purchase stock with the "excess cash" created by the dividend.

However, once we remove the assumption of perfect markets, we find that buying or selling stock is not cost free. Brokerage fees are incurred, ranging from approximately 1 percent to 10 percent. Even more costly is the fact that the investor who buys the stock with cash received from a dividend will have to pay taxes before reinvesting the cash. And when a stock is bought or sold, it must first be reevaluated. This can be time-consuming and costly for investors. Finally, some institutional investors, such as investors in university endowment funds, are precluded from selling stock.

As a result of these considerations, investors may not be too inclined to buy stocks that require them to "create" a dividend stream more suitable to their purposes. Rather, if investors do in fact have a preference between dividends and capital gains, we could expect them to invest in firms that have a dividend policy consistent with these preferences. They would, in essence, "sort themselves out" by buying stocks that satisfy their preferences for dividends and capital gains. For example, individuals and institutions that need current income would be drawn to companies that have high dividend payouts. Other investors, such as wealthy individuals, would much prefer to avoid taxes by holding securities that offer no or small dividend income but large capital gains. In other words, there would be a **clientele effect**: *Firms draw a given clientele, depending upon their stated dividend policy.*

**clientele effect** the belief that individuals and institutions will invest in companies whose dividend payouts match their particular needs for current versus future cash flow. For example, those that need current income will invest in companies that have high dividend payouts.

The possibility that clienteles of investors exist might lead us to believe that the firm's dividend policy matters. However, unless there is a greater aggregate demand for a particular policy than the market can satisfy, one policy is as good as the other. The clientele effect only warns firms to avoid making capricious changes in their dividend policy. Moreover, given that the firm's investment decisions are already made, the level of the dividend is still unimportant. The change in the policy matters only when it requires clientele to shift to another company.

### The Information Effect

An investor in a world of perfect markets would argue with considerable persuasion that a firm's value is determined strictly by its investment and financing decisions and that its dividend policy has no impact on value. Yet we know from experience that a large, unexpected change in dividends can have a significant impact on the stock price. For instance, in November 1990, Occidental Petroleum cut its dividend from $2 to $1. In response, the firm's stock price went from about $32 to $17. How can we suggest that dividend policy matters little when we can cite numerous such examples?

Despite such "evidence," some experts claim we are not looking at the real cause and effect. It may be that investors use a change in dividend policy as a *signal* about the firm's financial condition, especially its earning power. Thus, a dividend increase that is larger than expected might signal to investors that managers expect significantly higher earnings in the future. Conversely, a dividend decrease, or even a less-than-expected increase, might signal that managers are forecasting less-favorable future earnings.

**information asymmetry** the notion that investors do not know as much about the firm's operations as the firm's management.

Likewise, some claim that managers frequently have inside information about the firm that cannot be made available to investors. This *difference in accessibility to information*, called **information asymmetry**, *they believe, can result in a lower or higher stock price than would otherwise occur.*

Dividends may, therefore, be important as a communication tool because managers may have no other credible way to inform investors about future earnings, or at least no convincing way that is less costly.

### Agency Costs

Conflicts often exist between stockholders and a firm's management. As a result, the stock price of a company owned by investors who are separate from management may be less than the stock price of a closely held firm. This potential difference in price is the *cost of the conflict to the owners*, which has come to be called **agency costs**.

**agency costs** the lost value a firm's security holders face where there are conflicts of interest between managers and the security holders.

Recognizing the possible problem, managers, acting independently or at the insistence of the firm's board of directors, frequently take action to minimize agency costs. Such action, which in itself is costly, includes auditing by independent accountants, assigning supervisory functions to the company's board of directors, creating covenants in lending agreements that restrict managerial powers, and providing incentive compensation plans for managers that help "bond" them with the owners.

A firm's dividend policy may be perceived by owners as a tool to minimize agency costs. Assuming that the payment of a dividend requires managers to issue stock to finance new investments, new investors will be attracted to the company only if they are convinced that the capital will be used profitably. Thus, the payment of dividends indirectly results in a closer monitoring of management's investment activities. In this case, dividends may make a meaningful contribution to the value of the firm.

### The Expectations Theory

A common thread through much of our discussion of dividend policy, particularly as it relates to information effects, is the word *expected*. We should not overlook the significance of this word when we are making any financial decision within the firm. *No matter what the decision area, how the market price responds to a firm's actions is not determined entirely by the action itself; it is also affected by investors' expectations about the ultimate decision to be made by management.* This concept or idea is called the **expectations theory**.

**expectations theory** the notion that investor reactions to a managerial decision are based on their *assessment* of the effect of the action on stock price. For example, the announcement of a higher dividend not only indicates that more cash will be received by investors this quarter but may also signal to investors that the firm's future prospects have improved.

For example, as the time approaches for managers to announce the amount of the firm's next dividend, investors form expectations about how much that dividend will be. These expectations are based on several factors related to the firm, such as past dividend decisions, current and expected earnings, investment strategies, and financing decisions. Investors also consider such things as the condition of the general economy, the strength or weakness of the industry at the time, and possible changes in government policies.

When the actual dividend decision is announced, the investor compares the actual decision with the expected decision. If the amount of the dividend is as expected, even if it represents an increase from prior years, the market price of the stock will remain unchanged. However, if the dividend is higher or lower than expected, investors will reassess their perceptions of the firm. In short, an actual decision about the firm's dividend policy is not likely to be terribly significant unless it departs from investors' expectations. But if there is a difference between actual and expected dividends, we will more than likely see a movement in the stock price.

## What Are We to Conclude?

A firm must develop a dividend policy regardless, so here are some of the things we have learned about the relevance of a firm's dividend policy.

1. As a firm's investment opportunities increase, its dividend payout ratio should decrease. In other words, an inverse relationship should exist between the amount of money a firm invests with expected rates of return that exceed the cost of capital (positive $NPV$s) and the dividends it remits investors. Because of flotation costs, internally generated equity financing is preferable to selling stock (in terms of the wealth of the current common shareholders).

2. The firm's dividend policy appears to be important; however, appearances can be deceptive. The real issue is the firm's *expected* earning power, and investors will use the dividend payment as a source of information about these earnings. The dividend may carry greater weight than a statement by management that earnings will be increasing or decreasing. (Actions speak louder than words.)

3. If dividends influence the stock price, this is probably based on the investor's desire to minimize or defer taxes and on the fact that dividends can minimize agency costs.

4. If the expectations theory has merit, which we believe it does, the firm should avoid surprising investors when it comes to its dividend decision.

5. The firm's dividend policy should effectively be treated as a *long-term residual*. Rather than project investment requirements for a single year, managers should anticipate financing needs for several years. If internal funds remain after the firm has undertaken all acceptable investments, dividends should be paid. Conversely, if over the long term the entire amount of internally generated capital is needed for reinvestment in the company, then no dividend should be paid.

In setting a firm's dividend policy, financial managers must work in the messy world of reality. This means that our theories do not provide an equation that perfectly explains the key relationships. However, they give us a more complete view of the world, which can only help us make better decisions.

## Concept Check

1. Summarize the position that a dividend policy may be irrelevant with regard to the firm's stock price.
2. What is meant by the bird-in-the-hand dividend theory?
3. Why are cash dividend payments thought to be more certain than capital gains?
4. How might personal taxes affect both the firm's dividend policy and its share price?
5. Distinguish between the residual dividend theory and the clientele effect.

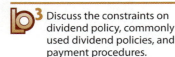

**3** Discuss the constraints on dividend policy, commonly used dividend policies, and payment procedures.

# The Dividend Decision in Practice

There are a number of practical considerations that will have an impact on a firm's decision to pay dividends. Some of the more obvious ones include the following.

## Legal Restrictions

Certain legal restrictions can limit the amount of dividends a firm may pay. These legal constraints fall into two categories. First, *statutory restrictions* may prevent a company from paying dividends. Although the specific limitations vary by state, generally a corporation may not pay a dividend (1) if the firm's liabilities exceed its assets, (2) if the amount of the dividend exceeds the firm's accumulated profits (retained earnings), and (3) if the dividend is being paid from capital invested in the firm.

The second type of legal restriction is unique to each firm and results from the restrictions in debt and preferred stock contracts. To minimize their risk, investors frequently impose restrictive provisions on managers as a condition to their investment in the company. These constraints might include the provision that dividends may not be declared before the debt is repaid. Also, the corporation might be required to maintain a given amount of working capital. Preferred stockholders might stipulate that common dividends may not be paid when any preferred dividends are delinquent.

## Liquidity Constraints

Contrary to popular opinion, the mere fact that a company shows a large amount of retained earnings in its balance sheet does not indicate that cash is available for the payment of dividends. The firm's liquid assets, including its cash, are basically independent of its retained earnings account. Generally, retained earnings are either reinvested in the company within a short period or used to pay maturing debt. Thus, a firm can be extremely profitable and still be *cash poor*. Because dividends are paid with cash, *and not with retained earnings*, the firm must have cash available for the dividends to be paid. Hence, the firm's liquidity position has a direct bearing on its ability to pay dividends.

## Earnings Predictability

A company's dividend payout ratio depends to some extent on the predictability of a firm's profits over time. If its earnings fluctuate significantly, the firm's managers know they cannot necessarily rely on internally generated funds to meet its future needs. As a result, when profits *are* realized, the firm is likely to retain larger amounts to ensure that money is available when needed. Conversely, a firm with a stable earnings trend will typically pay out a larger portion of its earnings in dividends. This company has less concern about the availability of profits to meet its future capital requirements.

## Maintaining Ownership Control

For many large corporations, control through the ownership of common stock is not an important issue. However, for many small and medium-sized companies, maintaining voting control is a high priority. If the current common stockholders are unable to participate in a new offering, issuing new stock is unattractive, in that the control of the current stockholder is diluted. The owners might prefer that managers finance new investments with debt and retained earnings rather than issue new common stock. This firm's growth is then constrained by the amount of debt capital available to it and by the company's ability to generate profits.

## Alternative Dividend Policies

Regardless of a firm's long-term dividend policy, most firms choose one of several year-to-year dividend payment patterns.

**constant dividend payout ratio** a dividend payment policy in which the percentage of earnings paid out in dividends is held constant. The dollar amount fluctuates from year to year as profits vary.

1. A **constant dividend payout ratio.** Under this policy, the *percentage of earnings paid out in dividends is held constant.* Although the dividend-to-earnings ratio is stable, the dollar amount of the dividend naturally fluctuates from year to year as profits vary.

2. **A stable dollar dividend per share.** This policy *maintains a relatively stable dollar dividend over time.* An increase in the dollar dividend usually does not occur until management is convinced that the higher dividend level can be maintained in the future. Conversely, a lower dollar dividend will not be paid until the evidence clearly indicates that a continuation of the current dividend cannot be supported.

3. **A small, regular dividend plus a year-end extra.** A corporation following this policy *pays a small, regular dollar dividend plus a year-end extra dividend in prosperous years.* The extra dividend is declared toward the end of the fiscal year after the company's profits for the period can be estimated. The objective is *to avoid the connotation of a permanent dividend being paid.* However, this purpose may be defeated if *recurring* extra dividends come to be expected by investors.

**stable dollar dividend per share** a dividend policy that maintains a relatively stable dollar dividend per share over time.

**small, regular dividend plus a year-end extra** a corporate policy of paying a small regular dollar dividend plus a year-end extra dividend in prosperous years to avoid the connotation of a permanent dividend.

## Dividend Payment Procedures

After the firm's dividend policy has been structured, several procedural details must be arranged. For instance, how frequently are dividend payments to be made? If a stockholder sells the shares during the year, who is entitled to the dividend? To answer these questions, we need to understand dividend payment procedures.

Generally, companies pay dividends quarterly. For example, on February 6, 2009, General Electric (GE) announced that it would pay a quarterly dividend of $0.31 per quarter to its shareholders for 2009. The annual dividend then would be $4 \times \$0.31 = \$1.24$ per share.

The final approval of a dividend payment comes from the company's board of directors. For example, the announcement or **declaration date** for General Electric's 2012 dividend was September 7, 2012, that holders of record as of September 24, 2012, would receive the dividend on the October 25, 2012, **payment date**. The **date of record**, September 24, 2012, designates when the stock transfer books are to be closed. Investors shown to own the stock on this date receive the dividend. If a notification of a transfer is recorded subsequent to September 24, the new owner is not entitled to the dividend. However, a problem could develop if the stock were sold on September 23, one day prior to the record date. Time would not permit the sale to be reflected on the stockholder list by the date of record. To address this problem, stock brokerage companies have uniformly terminated the right of ownership to the dividend two working days before the record date such that the **ex-dividend date** for the GE dividend is September 20 (note that in this instance September 24 was a Monday so the ex-dividend date was set two business days prior, which was September 20). The dividend declaration and payment process can be summarized as follows:

**declaration date** the date upon which a dividend is formally declared by the board of directors.

**payment date** the date on which the company mails a dividend check to each investor of record.

**date of record** the date at which the stock transfer books are to be closed for determining the investors to receive the next dividend payment.

**ex-dividend date** the date upon which stock brokerage companies have uniformly decided to terminate the right of ownership to the dividend, which is two days prior to the date of record.

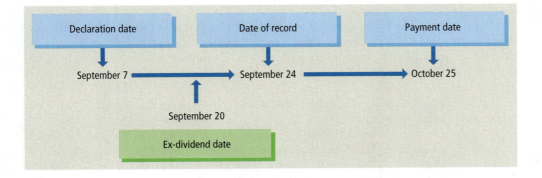

## Concept Check

1. Identify some practical considerations that affect a firm's payout policy.
2. Identify and explain three different dividend policies. (*Hint:* One of these is a constant dividend payout ratio.)
3. What is the typical frequency with which cash dividends are paid to investors?
4. Distinguish among the (a) declaration date, (b) date of record, and (c) ex-dividend date.

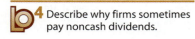

**4** Describe why firms sometimes pay noncash dividends.

**stock split** a stock dividend exceeding 25 percent of the number of shares currently outstanding.

**stock dividend** a distribution of shares of up to 25 percent of the number of shares currently outstanding, issued on a pro rata basis to the current stockholders.

# Stock Dividends and Stock Splits

A stock dividend entails the distribution of additional shares of stock in lieu of a cash payment. A stock split involves exchanging more (or less in the case of a "reverse" split) shares of stock for the firm's outstanding shares. In both cases the number of common shares outstanding changes but the firm's investments and future earnings prospects do not. In essence, the ownership pie is simply cut into more pieces (or fewer pieces in the case of a reverse split).

The only difference between a stock dividend and a stock split relates to their respective accounting treatments. Both represent a proportionate distribution of additional shares to the current stockholders. However, *for accounting purposes* the **stock split** has been defined as a *stock dividend exceeding 25 percent*. Thus, a **stock dividend** is conventionally defined as a *distribution of shares up to 25 percent of the number of shares currently outstanding*.

Although stock dividends and splits occur far less frequently than cash dividends, a significant number of companies choose to use these share distributions either with or in lieu of cash dividends. The extent of stock splits and stock dividends over the years can be made clear by a little price comparison. In 1926, a ticket to the movies cost 25¢—and even much less in the rural communities. At the same time, the average share price on the New York Stock Exchange was $35. Today, if we want to go to a new movie, we pay $7 or more. However, the average share price is still about $35. The relatively constant share price is the result of the shares being split over and over again. We can only conclude that investors apparently like it that way. But why do they, if no economic benefit results to the investor from doing so?

Proponents of stock dividends and splits frequently maintain that stockholders receive a key benefit because the price of the stock will not fall precisely in proportion to the share increase. For a two-for-one split, the price of the stock might not decrease a full 50 percent, so the stockholder is left with a higher total value. There are two reasons for this disequilibrium. First, many financial executives believe that an optimal price range exists. Within this range, the total market value of the common stockholders is thought to be maximized. As the price exceeds this range, fewer investors can purchase the stock, thereby restraining demand for the shares. Consequently, downward pressure is placed on its price. For example, Apple (AAPL) has engaged in multiple stock splits each time its share price rose above $100. It had 2-for-1 splits in 1987, 2000, and 2005. Rumors abounded in 2007 prior to the onset of the current recession that the company would split again as its stock price passed $160 in October of that year.

The second explanation relates to the *informational content* of the dividend-split announcement. Stock dividends and splits have generally been associated with companies with growing earnings. The announcement of a stock dividend or split has therefore been perceived as favorable news. The empirical evidence, however, fails to verify these conclusions. Most studies indicate that investors are perceptive in identifying the true meaning of such a distribution. If the stock dividend or split is not accompanied by a positive trend in earnings and increases in cash dividends, price increases surrounding the stock dividend or split are insignificant. Therefore, we should be suspicious of the assertion that a stock dividend or split can help increase investors' net worth.

A second reason for stock dividends or splits is the conservation of corporate cash. If a company is encountering cash problems, it may substitute a stock dividend for a cash dividend. However, as before, investors will probably look beyond the dividend to ascertain the underlying reason for conserving cash. If the stock dividend is an effort to conserve cash for attractive investment opportunities, shareholders might bid up the stock price. If the move to conserve cash relates to financial difficulties within the firm, the market price will most likely react adversely.

## Concept Check

1. What is the difference between a stock split and a stock dividend?
2. What managerial logic might lie behind a stock split or a stock dividend?

# Stock Repurchases

A **stock repurchase (stock buyback)** occurs when a *firm repurchases its own stock. This results in a reduction in the number of shares outstanding.* For well over three decades, corporations have been actively repurchasing their own equity securities. In the introduction we noted that Apple planned to repurchase up to $10 billion in company shares in March 2013. This new repurchase program follows the completion of a previous $40 billion in share repurchases. Note the use of the word *plan* in the announcement. This is important for it provides Apple leeway as to whether it carries out the planned repurchases in light of the uncertainties faced in the economic downturn that began with the financial crisis of 2007. However, uncertain economic times did not influence Walmart (WMT), which announced on June 5, 2009, that it planned to repurchase $15 billion of its shares. This follows a period of 5 years during which time the firm repurchased approximately $21 billion of shares.

Also, if you were to look at the balance sheet of almost any publicly held firm, you would see that the firm's treasury stock—the amount paid for repurchasing its own stock—is often-times severalfold the total amount originally invested by the stockholders. This situation is not unusual for many large companies. Several reasons have been given for stock repurchases. The benefits include:

**5** Distinguish between the use of cash dividends and share repurchases.

**stock repurchase (stock buyback)** the purchase of outstanding common stock by the issuing firm.

1. A means for providing an internal investment opportunity
2. An approach for modifying the firm's capital structure
3. A favorable impact on earnings per share
4. The elimination of a minority ownership group of stockholders
5. The minimization of the dilution in earnings per share associated with mergers
6. The reduction in the firm's costs associated with servicing small stockholders

Also, from the shareholders' perspective, a stock repurchase, as opposed to a cash dividend, has a potential tax advantage.

## A Share Repurchase as a Dividend Decision

Clearly, the payment of a common stock dividend is the conventional method for distributing a firm's profits to its owners. However, it need not be the only way. Another approach is to repurchase the firm's stock. The concept may best be explained by an example.

---

**EXAMPLE 13.1**      **Dividends vs. Share Repurchase**

Telink, Inc. is planning to pay $4 million ($4 per share) in dividends to its common stockholders. The following earnings and market price information is provided for Telink:

| | |
|---|---|
| Net income | $7,500,000 |
| Number of shares | 1,000,000 |
| Earnings per share | $7.50 |
| Price/earnings ratio | 8 |
| Expected market price per share after the dividend payment | $60 |

In a recent meeting, several board members, who are also major stockholders, questioned the need for the dividend payment. They maintained that they did not need the dividend income and suggested that the firm simply reinvest the earnings to fund future investments. In response to the question Telink's management argued that the firm's investment opportunities were not sufficiently profitable to justify retention of the income. Specifically, the required rate of return from the capital market was higher than the rate of return the firm thought it could earn by reinvesting the money in the firm.

As an alternative to paying dividends or reinvesting the earnings, the company's chief financial officer suggested that the firm repurchase company stock. This way the directors who did not want income from dividends could refrain from selling their shares and avoid current income.

To illustrate the effects of a share repurchase the company CFO suggested that the firm repurchase shares at a price of $64, which is the current market price plus the value of the proposed $4 dividend. He then said that the effect of the share repurchase would be the same as paying the dividend? Is this right?

### STEP 1: FORMULATE A SOLUTION STRATEGY

If a $4 dividend is paid then each shareholder will end up with a share of stock valued at $60 plus the dividend or a value of $64. The question then is, will the value of each share of stock be $64 if the share repurchase is carried out?

### STEP 2: CRUNCH THE NUMBERS

Note first that for $4 million the firm can repurchase 62,500 shares of stock at the $64 price ($4,000,000/$64). Now we can evaluate the price of the firm's shares after the repurchase by computing firm earnings per share:

$$\text{Earnings per share} = \text{net income/shares outstanding after the share repurchase}$$
$$= (\$7,500,000/(1,000,000 - 62,500)$$
$$= \$8 \text{ per share}$$

Next we compute the estimated share price per share using the price/earnings multiple of 8 times, that is

$$\text{Price per share} = \text{earnings per share} \times \text{price/earnings ratio}$$
$$= \$8.00 \times 8 \text{ times}$$
$$= \$64.00$$

### STEP 3: ANALYZE YOUR RESULTS

In the CFO's example Telink's stockholders are provided with the same $64.00 value whether a dividend is paid or shares are repurchased. Note, however, for the stockholders to be truly indifferent that the tax treatment of the $4 dividend must be the same as the $4 increase in the value of the firm's shares. This is not the case as the price appreciation realized by the stockholders that sell their shares may well be taxed at a lower capital gains tax rate than dividends, which are taxed as ordinary income. Moreover, if the stockholders do not sell into the repurchase there is no taxable event such that the gain in share price will be deferred until shares are actually sold.

## The Investor's Choice

Given the choice between a stock repurchase and a dividend payment, which should an investor prefer? If there are no taxes, no commissions when buying and selling stock, and no informational content assigned to a dividend, the investor should be indifferent with regard to the choices. For example, if the investor wants cash flow and the stock he owns does not pay a dividend, he can create a dividend by simply selling a portion of his shares. Note that these sales will not necessarily deplete the value of his investment as the value of the firm's shares should be growing because the firm's earnings are not being paid in dividends but are being reinvested.

There are certainly drawbacks related to repurchasing stock that investors should care about. First, the firm may have to pay too high a price for the repurchased stock, which is to the detriment of the remaining stockholders. If a relatively large number of shares are being bought, the price may be bid up too high, only to fall after the repurchase operation. Second, as a result of the repurchase, the market may perceive the riskiness of the corporation as increasing, which would lower the price/earnings ratio and the value of the stock.

## FINANCE AT WORK

### COMPANIES INCREASINGLY USE SHARE REPURCHASES TO DISTRIBUTE CASH TO THEIR STOCKHOLDERS

There has been a fundamental shift away from paying dividends and toward the buyback of company shares of stock. This change is at least partially due to changes in the U.S. tax code, which charges an additional 15% tax on dividends paid out to shareholders (before the Bush administration, this tax was as high as the graduated income tax—in some cases exceeding 35% on the federal level alone).

Evidence supporting the growth in share repurchases is found in the fact that the firms in the Standard & Poor's 500 repurchased $349 billion of their shares in 2005 alone. In fact, firms spent 73% more on buybacks than they did on dividends. On average, stock repurchases represented 61% of company earnings and dividends were only 32%. Clearly, there is a strong preference for share repurchases.*

Obviously firms are finding share repurchases a preferred way to distribute cash, but is this always best for the investor? Asked somewhat differently, are there reasons to prefer dividends over share repurchases? The answer is yes. For example, investors who need cash from their investments to live on may prefer dividends rather than being forced to sell shares and incur brokerage fees. Also, there's something comforting about receiving a regular check in the mail and not having to worry so much about fluctuations in the value of your shares from day to day.

Some companies now recognize the varied interests of their stockholders and attempt to blend share repurchases with cash dividends. For example, Home Depot has paid out about 65% of its earnings in a mix of share repurchases and dividend payments. For example, for the year ended January 29, 2006, the firm reported total net income of $5.838 billion, paid $0.857 billion in dividends, and repurchased $2.626 billion in company shares. This represents a total distribution of 59.7% of company earnings with 45% being distributed via share repurchase and 14.7% via dividends.**

*Matt Krantz, "More companies go for stock buybacks," *USA Today* (March 23, 2006).

**http://finance.yahoo.com/q/cf?s=HD&annual.

Source: Leslie Schism, "Many Companies Use Excess Cash to Repurchase Their Shares," September 2, 1993, the *Wall Street Journal,* Eastern edition.

## A Financing or Investment Decision?

Repurchasing stock when the firm has excess cash can be regarded as a dividend decision. However, a stock repurchase can also be viewed as a financing decision. By issuing debt and then repurchasing stock, a firm can immediately alter its debt–equity mix toward a higher proportion of debt. Essentially, rather than choose how to distribute cash to the stockholders, managers are using stock repurchases as a means to change the corporation's capital structure.

In addition to dividend and financing decisions, many managers consider a stock repurchase to be an investment decision. When equity prices are depressed in the marketplace, they may view the firm's own stock as being materially undervalued and therefore a good investment opportunity. Although this may be a wise move, the decision cannot and should not be viewed in the context of an investment decision. Buying its own stock cannot provide expected returns as other investments do. No company can survive, much less prosper, by investing only in its own stock.

## Practical Considerations—The Stock Repurchase Procedure

If management intends to repurchase a block of the firm's outstanding shares, it should make this information public. All investors should be given the opportunity to work with complete information. They should be told the purpose of the repurchase as well as the method to be used to acquire the stock.

Three methods for stock repurchase are available. First, the shares can be bought in the open market. Here the firm acquires the stock through a stockbroker at the going market price. This approach can put upward pressure on the stock price. Also, commissions must be paid to the stockbrokers as a fee for their services.

The second method is to make a tender offer to the firm's shareholders. A **tender offer** is a *formal offer by the company to buy a specified number of shares at a predetermined and stated price. The tender price is set above the current market price in order to attract sellers*. A tender offer is best when a relatively large number of shares are to be bought because the company's intentions are clearly known and each shareholder has the opportunity to sell the stock at the tendered price.

**tender offer** a formal offer by the company to buy a specified number of shares at a predetermined and stated price. The tender price is set above the current market price in order to attract sellers.

The third and final method for repurchasing stock entails the purchase of the stock from one or more major stockholders. These purchases are made on a negotiated basis. Care should be taken to ensure a fair and equitable price. Otherwise, the remaining stockholders may be hurt as a result of the sale.

## Concept Check

1. Identify three reasons why a firm might buy back its own common stock shares.
2. What financial relationships must hold for a stock repurchase to be a perfect substitute for a cash dividend payment to stockholders?
3. Within the context of a stock repurchase, what is meant by a tender offer?

# Chapter Summaries

 ### Describe the trade-off between paying dividends and retaining (reinvesting) firm profits. (pgs. 417–418)

**SUMMARY:** When firms decide to pay cash dividends this is a use of cash. That is, cash that otherwise would be sitting in a bank account or be invested in a short-term money market investment. For example, in the introduction we noted that Apple announced plans to pay out about $45 billion in dividends and stock repurchases during 2012. This means that this cash will not be available for Apple to reinvest in new projects.

**KEY TERM**

**Dividend payout ratio, page 417,** The ratio of dividends paid per share divided by earnings per share.

 ### Does dividend policy affect the company's stock price? (pgs. 418–423)

**SUMMARY:** A company's dividend decision has an immediate impact on the firm's financial mix. If the dividend payment is increased, fewer funds are available internally for financing investments. Consequently, if additional equity capital is needed, the company has to issue new common stock. In perfect markets, the choice between paying or not paying a dividend does not matter. However, when we realize that in the real world there are costs of issuing stock, we have a preference to use internal equity to finance our investment opportunities. Here the dividend decision is simply a residual factor, in which the dividend payment should equal the remaining internal capital after the firm finances all of its investments.

Other market imperfections that may cause a company's dividend policy to affect the firm's stock price include (1) the deferred tax benefit of capital gains, (2) agency costs, (3) the clientele effect, and (4) the informational content of a given policy. Other practical considerations that may affect a firm's dividend payment decision include

- Legal restrictions
- The firm's liquidity position
- The accessibility of capital markets to the company
- The stability of the firm's earnings
- The desire of investors to maintain control of the company

**KEY TERMS**

**Perfect capital markets, page 419** are markets in which information flows freely and market prices fully reflect all available information.

**Bird-in-the-hand dividend theory, page 419** The view that dividends are more certain than capital gains and therefore more valuable.

**Residual dividend theory, page 421** A theory that a company's dividend payment should equal the cash left after financing all the investments that have positive net present values.

**Clientele effect, page 422** The belief that individuals and institutions will invest in companies whose dividend payouts match their particular needs for current versus future cash flow. For example, those that need current income will invest in companies that have high dividend payouts.

**Information asymmetry, page 422** The notion that investors do not know as much about the firm's operations as the firm's management.

**Agency costs, page 422** The lost value a firm's security holders face where there are conflicts of interest between managers and the security holders.

**Expectations theory, page 422,** The notion that investor reactions to corporate actions is based on their *assessment* of the effect of the action on stock price which can incorporate their interpretation of what the action means. For example, the announcement of a higher dividend may signal to investors that the firm's future prospects have improved.

---

## Discuss the constraints on dividend policy, commonly used dividend policies, and payment procedures. (pgs. 424–425)

**SUMMARY:** Companies typically pay dividends on a quarterly basis. The final approval of a dividend payment comes from the board of directors. The critical dates in this process are as follows:

- Declaration date—the date when the dividend is formally declared by the board of directors
- Date of record—the date when the stock transfer books are closed to determine who owns the stock
- Ex-dividend date—two working days before the date of record, after which the right to receive the dividend no longer goes with the stock
- Payment date—the date the dividend check is mailed to the stockholders

In practice, managers have generally followed one of three dividend policies:

- A constant dividend payout ratio, whereby the percentage of dividends to earnings is held constant
- A stable dollar dividend per share, whereby a relatively stable dollar dividend is maintained over time
- A small, regular dividend plus a year-end extra, whereby the firm pays a small, regular dollar dividend plus a year-end extra dividend in prosperous years

Of the three dividend policies, the stable dollar dividend is by far the most common. The Jobs and Growth Tax Relief Reconciliation Act of 2003 reduced the top tax rate on dividend income to 15 percent and placed the top tax rate on realized long-term capital gains at this same 15 percent rate. This helped level the investment landscape for dividend income relative to qualifying capital gains. Taxes paid on capital gains, however, are still deferred until realized, but dividend income is taxed in the year that it is received by the investing taxpayer.

### KEY TERMS

**Constant dividend payout ratio, page 424** A dividend payment policy in which the percentage of earnings paid out in dividends is held constant. The dollar amount fluctuates from year to year as profits vary.

**Stable dollar dividend per share, page 425** A dividend policy that maintains a relatively stable dollar dividend per share over time.

**Small, regular dividend plus a year-end extra, page 425** a corporate policy of paying a small regular dollar dividend plus a year-end extra dividend in prosperous years to avoid the connotation of a permanent dividend.

**Declaration date, page 425** The date upon which a dividend is formally declared by the board of directors.

**Payment date, page 425** The date on which the company mails a dividend check to each investor of record.

**Date of record, page 425** The date at which the stock transfer books are to be closed for determining the investors to receive the next dividend payment.

**Ex-dividend date, page 425** The date upon which stock brokerage firms have uniformly decided to terminate the right of ownership to the dividend, which is two days prior to the date of record.

## Describe why firms sometimes pay noncash dividends. (pg. 426)

**SUMMARY:** Stock dividends and stock splits have been used by corporations either in lieu of or to supplement cash dividends. At present, no empirical evidence identifies a relationship between stock dividends and splits and the market price of the stock. Yet a stock dividend or split could conceivably be used to keep the stock price within an optimal trading range. Also, if investors perceive that the stock dividend contains favorable information about the firm's operations, the price of the stock could increase.

### KEY TERMS

**Stock split, page 426** a stock dividend exceeding 25 percent of the number of shares currently outstanding.

**Stock dividend, page 426** A distribution of shares of up to 25 percent of the number of shares currently outstanding, issued on a pro rata basis to the current stockholders.

## Distinguish between the use of cash dividends and share repurchases. (pgs. 427–430)

**SUMMARY:** As an alternative to paying a dividend, the firm can repurchase stock. In perfect markets, an investor would be indifferent between receiving a dividend or a share repurchase. The investor could simply create a dividend stream by selling stock when income is needed. If, however, market imperfections exist, the investor may have a preference for one of the two methods of distributing the corporate income.

A stock repurchase can also be viewed as a financing decision. By issuing debt and then repurchasing stock, a firm can immediately alter its debt–equity mix toward a higher proportion of debt.

Also, many managers consider a stock repurchase an investment decision—buying the stock when they believe it to be undervalued.

### KEY TERMS

**Stock repurchase (stock buyback), page 427** The purchase of outstanding common stock by the issuing firm.

# Review Questions

*All Review Questions are available in* MyFinanceLab.

**13-1.** What is meant by the term *dividend payout ratio*?

**13-2.** Explain the trade-off between retaining internally generated funds and paying cash dividends.

**13-3.** a. What is the *residual dividend theory*?
  b. Why is this theory operational only in the long term?

**13-4.** What legal restrictions may limit the amount of dividends to be paid?

**13-5.** In the introduction to the chapter we learned that Apple Computer (AAPL) recently reinstated the payment of cash dividends, which had been suspended since the 1990s. What are some reasons that might have influenced the firm's decision to begin paying dividends again?

**13-6.** How does a firm's liquidity position affect the payment of dividends?

**13-7.** How can ownership control constrain the growth of a firm?

**13-8.** Explain what a dividend's declaration date, date of record, and ex-dividend date are.

**13-9.** What are the advantages of a stock split or dividend over a cash dividend?

**13-10.** Why would a firm repurchase its own stock?

# Study Problems

*All Study Problems are available in* MyFinanceLab.

**13-1.** (*Dividend payout ratio*) Carson Electronics earned $2.4 million in net income last year and for the first time ever paid its common stockholders a cash dividend of $0.02 per share. The firm has 10 million shareholders. What was Carson's dividend payout ratio?

**13-2.** (*Dividend policy and the issue of new shares of common stock*) Your firm needs to raise $10 million to finance its capital expenditures for the coming year. The firm earned $4 million last year and will pay out half this amount in dividends. If the firm's CFO wants to finance new investments using no more than 40 percent debt financing, how much common stock will the firm have to issue to raise the needed $10 million?

---

**13-3.** (*Dividend policy and stock prices*) Explain in your own words the notion of a perfect capital market.

**13-4.** (*Dividend policy and stock prices*) The question as to whether dividend policy has an effect on share prices raises a question as to whether dividends paid out to stockholders are any more "certain" than the expected future dividends the stockholders hope to receive from the retention of firm earnings. This is known as the "bird-in-the-hand' theory of dividend policy. Do you agree with this theory? Explain.

**13-5.** (*Residual dividend policy*) FarmCo, Inc. follows a policy of paying out cash dividends equal to the residual amount that remains after funding 60 percent of its planned capital expenditures. The firm tries to maintain a 40 percent debt and 60 percent equity capital structure and does not plan on issuing more stock in the coming year. FarmCo's CFO has estimated that the firm will earn $12 million in the current year.

    a. If the firm maintains its target financing mix and does not issue any equity next year, what is the most it could spend on capital expenditures next year given its earnings estimate?

    b. If FarmCo's capital budget for next year is $10 million, how much will the firm pay in dividends and what is the resulting dividend payout percentage?

---

**13-6.** (*Legal restrictions on dividend payments*) Describe the types of limitations firms can face from legal restrictions on dividend payments.

**13-7.** (*Practical considerations in setting dividend policy*) The board of directors of Kensington Enterprises has decided to pay cash dividends totaling $5 million in the first quarter of the year. This payment represents the initiation of a cash dividend for the first time in company history, and your company CFO has asked you to look into any restrictions or constraints the firm might have in carrying out the plan. Write a brief report outlining the types of restrictions Kensington might face.

**13-8.** (*Dividend policies*) Final earnings estimates for Chilean Health Spa & Fitness Center have been prepared for the CFO of the company and are shown in the following table. The firm has 7,500,000 shares of common stock outstanding. As assistant to the CFO, you are asked to determine the yearly dividend per share to be paid depending on the following possible policies:

    a. A stable dollar dividend targeted at 40 percent of earnings over a 5-year period.

    b. A small, regular dividend of $0.60 per share plus a year-end extra when the profits in any year exceed $20,000,000. The year-end extra dividend will equal 50 percent of profits exceeding $20,000,000.

    c. A constant dividend payout ratio of 40 percent.

| YEAR | PROFITS AFTER TAXES |
|------|---------------------|
| 1 | $18,000,000 |
| 2 | 21,000,000 |
| 3 | 19,000,000 |
| 4 | 23,000,000 |
| 5 | 25,000,000 |

**13-9.** (*Constant dividend payout ratio policy*) The Patterson-Hale Trucking Company (PHT) needs to expand its fleet by 50 percent to meet the demands of two major contracts it just received to transport military equipment from manufacturing facilities scattered across the United States to various military bases. The cost of the expansion is estimated to be $14 million. PHT maintains a 30 percent debt ratio and pays out 50 percent of its earnings in common stock dividends each year.

    a. If PHT earns $4 million in 2013, how much common stock will the firm need to sell in order to maintain its target capital structure?

    b. If PHT wants to avoid selling any new stock but wants to maintain a constant dividend payout percentage of 50 percent, how much can the firm spend on new capital expenditures?

**13-10.** (*Constant dollar dividend payout policy*) Parker Prints is in negotiation with two of its largest customers to increase the firm's sales dramatically. The increase will require that Parker expand its production facilities at a cost of $30 million. Parker expects to pay out $8 million in dividends to its shareholders next year. Parker maintains a 40 percent debt ratio in its capital structure.

    a. If Parker earns $12 million in 2013, how much common stock will the firm need to sell in order to maintain its target capital structure?

    b. If Parker wants to avoid selling any new stock, how much can the firm spend on new capital expenditures?

**13-11.** (*Terminology*) Define each of the following dates and place them in their proper order with respect to the payment and receipt of cash dividends: date of record, ex-dividend date, declaration date, and payment date.

---

**13-12.** (*Stock dividends*) In the spring of 2014 the CFO of Placebo Pharmaceuticals, Inc. took a proposal to the firm's board of directors to distribute a noncash dividend to the firm's shareholders in the form of new shares of common stock. Specifically, the CFO proposed that the company pay 0.025 shares of stock to the holders of each share of common stock such that the holder of 1,000 shares of stock would receive an additional 25 shares of common stock.

    a. If Placebo had total net income for the year of $10,000,000 and 20,000,000 shares of common stock outstanding before the stock dividend, what are firm earnings per share?

    b. After paying the stock dividend, what is the firm's earnings per share?

    c. If you owned 1,000 shares of stock before the stock dividend, how many dollars of earnings did the firm earn on your 1,000 share investment? After the stock dividend is paid, how many dollars of earnings did the firm earn on your larger share holdings? What effect would you expect from the payment of the stock dividend on your total investment in the firm?

**13-13.** (*Stock splits and large stock dividends*) Marston Mfg. recently declared a 4-for-1 stock split for its common shares. Before the split the firm's share price had risen to $600 per share and the firm's CFO felt that this high stock price inhibited trading in the firm's shares. Prior to the split the firm had 10 million shares of stock outstanding and had net income of $40 million.

    a. Before the stock split what is Marston's earnings per share?

    b. Following the stock split, how many shares of common stock will Marston have outstanding?

    c. What are the firm's earnings per share after the stock split?

    d. If you owned 100 shares of stock before the split, how much are the total earnings for your shares? How much are the total earnings on your post-split shares?

    e. Were you better off financially as the holder of 100 shares of pre-split stock after the 4-for-1 split? Explain.

**13-14.** (*Stock splits*) The debt and equity section of the Robson Corporation balance sheet is shown here. The current market price of the common shares is $20. Reconstruct the financial statement assuming that (a) a 15 percent stock dividend is issued and (b) a 2-for-1 stock split is declared.

| Debt | $1,800,000 |
|---|---|
| Common equity | |
|   Par ($2; 100,000 shares) | 200,000 |
|   Paid-in capital | 400,000 |
|   Retained earnings | 900,000 |
| | $3,300,000 |

---

**13-15.** (*Repurchase of stock*) The Dunn Corporation is planning to pay dividends of $500,000. There are 250,000 shares outstanding, and earnings per share are $5. The stock should sell for $50 after the ex-dividend date. If, instead of paying a dividend, the firm decides to repurchase stock,

    a. What should be the repurchase price?

    b. How many shares should be repurchased?

    c. What if the repurchase price is set below or above your suggested price in part (a)?

    d. If you own 100 shares, would you prefer that the company pay the dividend or repurchase stock?

**13-16.** (*Stock repurchases and earnings per share*) CareMore, Inc. provides in-home medical assistance to the elderly and earned net income of $5 million that it plans to use to repurchase shares of the firm's common stock, which is currently selling for $50 a share. CareMore has 20 million shares of stock outstanding.

    a. What fraction of the firm's shares can the firm repurchase for $5 million?

    b. If the share repurchase has no impact on the firm's net income, what will be its earnings per share after the repurchase?

# Mini Case

*This Mini Case is available in* MyFinanceLab.

Assume that you write a column for a very widely followed financial blog titled, "Finance Questions: Ask the Expert." Your job is to field readers' questions that deal with finance. This week you are going to address two questions from your readers that have to do with dividends.

**Question 1:** I own 8 percent of the Standlee Corporation's 30,000 shares of common stock, which most recently traded for a price of $98 per share. The company has since declared its plans to engage in a two-for-one stock split.

    a. What will my financial position be after the stock split, compared to my current position? (*Hint*: Assume the stock price falls proportionately.)

    b. The executive vice-president in charge of finance believes the price will not fall in proportion to the size of the split and will only fall 45 percent because she thinks the pre-split price is above the optimal price range. If she is correct, what will be my net gain from the split?

**Question 2:** You are on the board of directors of the B. Phillips Corporation, and Phillips has announced its plan to pay dividends of $550,000. Presently there are 275,000 shares outstanding, and the earnings per share is $6. It looks to you like the stock should sell for $45 after the ex-dividend date. If instead of paying a dividend, the management decides to repurchase stock

    a. What should be the repurchase price that is equivalent to the proposed dividend? (*Hint*: Ignore any tax effects.)

    b. How many shares should the company repurchase?

    c. You want to look out for the small shareholders. If someone owns 100 shares, do you think he would prefer that the company pay the dividend or repurchase stock?

# Short-Term Financial Planning

## Learning Objectives

**Use** the percent of sales method to forecast the financing requirements of a firm.

**Financial Forecasting**

**Describe** the limitations of the percent of sales forecast method.

**Limitations of the Percent of Sales Forecasting Method**

**Prepare** a cash budget and use it to evaluate the amount and timing of a firm's financing needs.

**Constructing and Using a Cash Budget**

In the summer of 2012, the price of a gallon of diesel was over $4.00. If you were a financial manager in July 2012 working on the financial plans for the coming year at the United Parcel Service (UPS), the level of the price of fuel would be of great concern, given that fuel costs are a major component of the operating expenses of UPS. Clearly, having an estimate of future fuel costs is a critical variable in the financial forecast of UPS's future profitability. Yet there are countless examples of when our ability to predict the future is not very good.

If forecasting the future is so difficult and plans are built on forecasts, why do firms engage in planning efforts? Obviously, they do, but why? The answer, oddly enough, does not lie in the accuracy of the firm's projections, for planning offers its greatest value when the future is the most uncertain. The value of planning is derived out of the process itself. That is, by thinking about what the future might be like, the firm builds contingency plans that can improve its ability to respond to adverse events and take advantage of opportunities that arise.

Chapter 14 has two primary objectives:

◆ First, it will help you gain an appreciation for the role forecasting plays in the firm's financial planning process. Basically, forecasts of future sales revenues and their associated expenses give the firm the information it needs to project its future financing needs.

◆ Second, this chapter provides an overview of the basic elements of a financial plan: the cash budget, pro forma (planned) income statement, and pro forma balance sheet.

Pro forma financial statements are a very useful tool for analyzing the effects of the firm's forecasts and planned activities on its financial performance, as well as its needs for financing. In addition, pro forma statements can be used as a benchmark or standard to compare against actual operating results. Used in this way, pro forma statements are an instrument for monitoring and controlling the firm's progress throughout the planning period. For example, after the first energy crisis of the 1970s, the price of crude oil rose from $2.00 to more than $20.00 per barrel. Many thought that the price would rise above $50.00. Then in 1986, the price dropped to only $10.00 per barrel, and the $50.00 price looked like a foolish dream. However, in 2008, the price of a barrel of oil rose to $140.00 and then dropped below $90 in October 2012. What's next, will the price continue to rise or will it drop again as it did in an earlier crisis?

# Financial Forecasting

Use the percent of sales method to forecast the financing requirements of a firm.

Financial forecasting is the process of attempting to estimate a firm's future financing requirements. The basic steps involved in predicting those financing needs are the following:

**STEP 1**  Project the firm's sales revenues and expenses over the planning period.
**STEP 2**  Estimate the levels of investment in current and fixed assets that are needed to support the projected sales forecast.
**STEP 3**  Determine the firm's financing needs throughout the planning period that are required to fund its assets.

## The Sales Forecast

The key ingredient in the firm's planning process is the sales forecast. This projection is generally derived using information from a number of sources. At a minimum, the sales forecast for the coming year reflects (1) any past trend in sales that is expected to carry through into the new year and (2) the influence of any anticipated events that might materially affect that trend.[1] An example of the latter is the initiation of a major advertising campaign or a change in the firm's pricing policy.

## Forecasting Financial Variables

Traditional financial forecasting takes the sales forecast as a given and projects its impact on the firm's various expenses, assets, and liabilities. The most commonly used method for making these projections is the percent of sales method.

[1]A complete discussion of forecast methodologies is outside the scope of this book. The interested reader will find a large number of books on business forecasting with a simple Web search.

## The Percent of Sales Method of Financial Forecasting

**percent of sales method** a method of financial forecasting that involves estimating the level of an expense, asset, or liability for a future period as a percent of the sales forecast.

The **percent of sales method** involves *estimating the level of an expense, asset, or liability for a future period as a percentage of the sales forecast.* The percentage used can come from the most recent financial statement item as a percentage of current sales, from an average computed over several years, from the judgment of the analyst, or from some combination of these sources.

Table 14-1 presents a complete example that uses the percent of sales method of financial forecasting for Drew Inc. In this example each item in the firm's balance sheet that varies with sales is converted to a percentage of 2013 sales, which was $10 million. The forecast of the new balance for each item is then calculated by multiplying this percentage times the $12 million in projected sales for the 2014 planning period. This method offers a relatively low-cost and easy-to-use way to estimate the firm's future financing needs.

Note that in the example in Table 14-1, both current and fixed assets are assumed to vary with the level of sales. This means that the firm does not have sufficient productive capacity to absorb a projected increase in sales. Thus, if sales were to rise by $1, fixed assets would rise by $0.40, or 40 percent of the projected increase in sales. If instead the fixed assets the firm currently owns are sufficient to support the projected level of sales, then the assets will not be converted to a percentage of sales and will be projected to remain unchanged for the period being forecast.

Also, note that accounts payable and accrued expenses are the only liabilities allowed to vary with sales. Both these liability accounts might reasonably be expected to rise and fall with the level of firm sales, hence, the use of the percent of sales forecast. Because these two

**TABLE 14-1  Using the Percent of Sales Method to Forecast Drew Inc.'s Financing Requirements for 2014**

| | A | B | C | D | E | F | G | H | I |
|---|---|---|---|---|---|---|---|---|---|
| 1 | Drew Inc. | | | | | | Drew Inc. | | |
| 2 | Income Statement for 2013 | | | | | | Pro forma Income Statement for 2014 | | |
| 3 | | | | | % of 2013 Sales | | | Calculation | |
| 4 | | | | | | | Sales growth rate = | 20% | |
| 5 | Sales | | $ 10,000,000 | | | | Sales | $10 million x (1+.20) = | $ 12,000,000 |
| 6 | Net Income | | $ 500,000 | [$500,000/$10,000,000 = | 5.0% | | Net Income | $12 million x .05 = | $ 600,000 |
| 7 | | | | | | | | | |
| 8 | | | | | | | | | |
| 9 | | | | | | | | | |
| 10 | Drew Inc. | | | | | | Drew Inc. | | |
| 11 | Balance Sheet for 2013 | | | | | | Pro forma Balance Sheet for 2014 | | |
| 12 | | | | | % of 2013 Sales | | | Calculation | |
| 13 | | | | | | | | | |
| 14 | Current assets | | $ 2,000,000 | [$2m /$10m] = | 20.0% | | Current assets | .20 x$12m = | $ 2,400,000 |
| 15 | Net fixed assets | | 4,000,000 | [$4m /$10m] = | 40.0% | | Net fixed assets | .40 x$12m = | $ 4,800,000 |
| 16 | Total | | $ 6,000,000 | | | | Total | | $ 7,200,000 |
| 17 | | | | | | | | | |
| 18 | Accounts payable | | $ 1,000,000 | [$1m /$10 m] = | 10.0% | | Accounts payable | .10 x$12m = | $ 1,200,000 |
| 19 | Accrued expenses | | 1,000,000 | [$1m /$10m] = | 10.0% | | Accrued expenses | .10 x$12m = | 1,200,000 |
| 20 | Notes payable | | 500,000 | | NA* | | Notes payable | No change | 500,000 |
| 21 | Current Liabilities | | $ 2,500,000 | | | | Current Liabilities | | $ 2,900,000 |
| 22 | Long-term debt | | 2,000,000 | | NA* | | Long-term debt | No change | $ 2,000,000 |
| 23 | Total Liabilities | | $ 4,500,000 | | | | Total Liabilities | | $ 4,900,000 |
| 24 | Common stock (par) | | 100,000 | | NA* | | Common stock (par) | No change | 100,000 |
| 25 | Paid-in capital | | 200,000 | | NA* | | Paid-in capital | No change | 200,000 |
| 26 | Retained earnings | | 1,200,000 | | | | Retained earnings | Calculation¹ | 1,500,000 |
| 27 | Common Equity | | $ 1,500,000 | | | | Common Equity | | 1,800,000 |
| 28 | Total | | $ 6,000,000 | | | | Total Financing Provided | | $ 6,700,000 |
| 29 | | | | | | | Discretionary Financing Needed (Plug)* | | $ 500,000 |
| 30 | | | | | | | Total Financing Needed = Total Assets | | $ 7,200,000 |
| 31 | | | | | | | | | |
| 32 | *Not applicable. These account balances do not vary with sales. | | | | | | | | |
| 33 | ᵇProjected retained earnings for 2014 equals $1,500,000 which is equal to the 2013 level of retained earnings of $1,200,000 plus net income of $600,000 less common dividends | | | | | | | | |
| 34 | equal to 50% of projected net income or $300,000. | | | | | | | | |
| 35 | ᶜDiscretionary financing needed (DFN) for 2014 is a "plug figure" that equals the difference in the firm's projected total financing requirements or total assets equal to $7,200,000 | | | | | | | | |
| 36 | and total financing provided which is $6,700,000. In this scenario DFN is $500,000. | | | | | | | | |
| 37 | | | | | | | | | |
| 38 | | | | | | | | | |

categories of current liabilities normally vary directly with the level of sales, they are often referred to as sources of **spontaneous financing**. Included in spontaneous financing are *trade credit and other accounts payable that arise spontaneously in the firm's day-to-day operations.* Chapter 15, which discusses working-capital management, has more to say about these forms of financing. Notes payable, long-term debt, common stock, and paid-in capital are not assumed to vary directly with the level of firm sales. These sources of financing are termed **discretionary financing**, *which requires an explicit decision on the part of the firm's management every time funds are raised. An example is a bank note that requires that negotiations be undertaken and an agreement signed setting forth the terms and conditions for the financing.* Finally, note that the level of retained earnings does vary with estimated sales. The predicted change in the level of retained earnings equals the estimated after-tax profits (projected net income) equal to 5 percent of sales, or $600,000, less the common stock dividends of $300,000.

In the Drew Inc. example found in Table 14-1, we estimate that firm sales will increase from $10 million to $12 million, which will cause the firm's need for total assets to rise to $7.2 million. These assets will then be financed by $4.9 million in existing liabilities plus spontaneous liabilities; $1.8 million in owner funds, including an additional $300,000 in retained earnings from next year's sales; and finally, $500,000 in discretionary financing, which can be raised by issuing notes payable, selling bonds, offering an issue of stock, or some combination of these sources.

In summary, we can estimate the firm's discretionary financing needs (*DFN*), using the percent of sales method of financial forecasting, by following a four-step procedure:

**STEP 1** Convert each asset and liability account that varies directly with firm sales to a percentage of the current year's sales.

$$\frac{\text{Current assets}}{\text{sales}} = \frac{\$2M}{\$10M} = 0.2, \text{ or } 20\%$$

**STEP 2** Project the level of each asset and liability account in the balance sheet using its percentage of sales multiplied by projected sales or by leaving the account balance unchanged when the account does not vary with the level of sales.

$$\text{Projected current assets} = \text{projected sales} \times \frac{\text{current assets}}{\text{sales}} = \$12M \times 0.2 = \$2.4M$$

**STEP 3** Project the addition to retained earnings available to help finance the firm's operations. This equals projected net income for the period less planned common stock dividends.

$$\begin{aligned}\text{Projected addition} \atop \text{to retained earnings} &= \text{projected sales} \times \frac{\text{net income}}{\text{sales}} \times \left(1 - \frac{\text{cash dividends}}{\text{net income}}\right) \\ &= \$12M \times 0.05 \times (1 - 0.5) = \$300,000\end{aligned}$$

**STEP 4** Project the firm's *DFN* as the projected level of total assets less projected liabilities and owners' equity.

Discretionary financing needed
$$= \text{projected total assets} - \text{projected total liabilities} - \text{projected owners' equity}$$
$$= \$7.2M - \$4.9M - \$1.8M = \$500,000$$

## Analyzing the Effects of Profitability and Dividend Policy on *DFN*

Projecting discretionary financing needed, we can quickly and easily evaluate the sensitivity of our projected financing requirements to changes in key variables. For example, using the information from the preceding example, we evaluate the effect of net profit margins (*NPMs*) equal to 1 percent, 5 percent, and 10 percent in combination with dividend payout ratios of 30 percent, 50 percent, and 70 percent, as follows:

**Discretionary Financing Needed for Various Net Profit Margins and Dividend Payout Ratios**

| | DIVIDEND PAYOUT RATIOS = DIVIDENDS ÷ NET INCOME | | |
|---|---|---|---|
| NET PROFIT MARGIN | 30% | 50% | 70% |
| 1% | $716,000 | $740,000 | $764,000 |
| 5% | 380,000 | 500,000 | 620,000 |
| 10% | (40,000) | 200,000 | 440,000 |

If these *NPMs* are reasonable estimates of the possible ranges of values the firm might experience, and if the firm is considering dividend payouts ranging from 30 percent to 70 percent, then we estimate that the firm's financing requirements will range from ($40,000), which represents a surplus of $40,000, to a situation in which it would need to acquire $764,000. Lower *NPMs* mean higher funding requirements. Also, higher dividend payout percentages, other things remaining constant, lead to a need for more discretionary financing. This is a direct result of the fact that a high-dividend-paying firm retains less of its earnings.

## Analyzing the Effects of Sales Growth on a Firm's *DFN*

In Figure 14-1 we analyzed the *DFN* for Drew Inc., whose sales were expected to grow from $10 million to $12 million during the coming year. Recall that the 20 percent expected increase in sales led to an increase in the firm's needs for financing in the amount of $500,000. We referred to this added financing requirement as the firm's *DFN* because all these funds must be raised from sources, such as bank borrowing or a new equity issue, that require that management exercise its discretion in selecting the source. In this section we want to investigate how a firm's *DFN* varies with different rates of anticipated sales growth.

Table 14-2 expands on the financial forecast found in Table 14-1. Specifically, we use the same assumptions and prediction methods that underlie Table 14-1 but apply them to sales growth rates of 0 percent, 20 percent, and 40 percent. The *DFN* for these sales growth rates ranges from ($250,000) to $1,250,000. When *DFN* is negative, this means that the firm has more money than it needs to finance the assets used to generate the projected sales. Alternatively, when *DFN* is positive, this means that the firm must raise additional

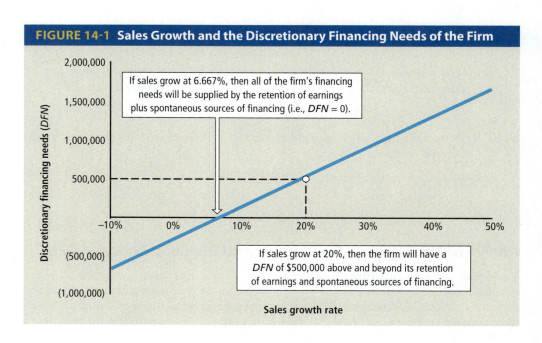

**FIGURE 14-1  Sales Growth and the Discretionary Financing Needs of the Firm**

If sales grow at 6.667%, then all of the firm's financing needs will be supplied by the retention of earnings plus spontaneous sources of financing (i.e., *DFN* = 0).

If sales grow at 20%, then the firm will have a *DFN* of $500,000 above and beyond its retention of earnings and spontaneous sources of financing.

Discretionary financing needs (*DFN*)

Sales growth rate

# CAN YOU DO IT?

## PERCENT OF SALES FORECASTING

The CFO for Madrigal Plumbing Supplies Inc. is developing financial plans for next year when he estimates that his sales will reach $10 million. During the 4 years the firm has been in business, its inventories have represented approximately 15 percent of its revenues. What would you estimate the firm's needs for inventories to be next year (using the percent of sales forecast method)? If Madrigal has economies of scale, would you expect its inventory needs to be more than, the same as, or less than the percent of sales forecast? (The solution can be found on page 442.)

**TABLE 14-2  Discretionary Financing Needs (*DFN*) and the Growth Rate in Sales**

| | A | B | C | D | E | F | G | H | I | J | K |
|---|---|---|---|---|---|---|---|---|---|---|---|
| 1 | Drew Inc. | | | | | | Drew Inc. | | | | |
| 2 | Income Statement for 2013 | | | | | | Pro forma Income Statement for 2014 | | | | |
| 3 | | | | | % of 2013 Sales | | | | | | |
| 4 | | | | | | | Alternative Growth Rates in Sales | | 0% | 20% | 40% |
| 5 | Sales | | $ 10,000,000 | | | | Sales | | $ 10,000,000 | $ 12,000,000 | $ 14,000,000 |
| 6 | Net Income | | $ 500,000 | [$500,000/$10,000,000 = | 5.0% | | Net Income | | $ 500,000 | $ 600,000 | $ 700,000 |
| 7 | | | | | | | | | | | |
| 8 | | | | | | | | | | | |
| 9 | Drew Inc. | | | | | | Drew Inc. | | | | |
| 10 | Balance Sheet for 2013 | | | | | | Pro forma Balance Sheet for 2014 | | | | |
| 11 | | | | | % of 2013 Sales | | | Calculation | | | |
| 12 | | | | | | | | | | | |
| 13 | Current assets | | $ 2,000,000 | [$2m /$10m] = | 20.0% | | Current assets | .20 x$12m = | $ 2,000,000 | $ 2,400,000 | $ 2,800,000 |
| 14 | Net fixed assets | | 4,000,000 | [$4m /$10m] = | 40.0% | | Net fixed assets | .40 x$12m = | 4,000,000 | $ 4,800,000 | $ 5,600,000 |
| 15 | Total | | $ 6,000,000 | | | | Total | | $ 6,000,000 | $ 7,200,000 | $ 8,400,000 |
| 16 | | | | | | | | | | | |
| 17 | Accounts payable | | $ 1,000,000 | [$1m /$10 m] = | 10.0% | | Accounts payable | .10 x$12m = | $ 1,000,000 | $ 1,200,000 | $ 1,400,000 |
| 18 | Accrued expenses | | 1,000,000 | [$1m /$10m] = | 10.0% | | Accrued expenses | .10 x$12m = | 1,000,000 | 1,200,000 | 1,400,000 |
| 19 | Notes payable | | 500,000 | | NA* | | Notes payable | No change | 500,000 | 500,000 | 500,000 |
| 20 | Current Liabilities | | $ 2,500,000 | | | | Current Liabilities | | $ 2,500,000 | $ 2,900,000 | $ 3,300,000 |
| 21 | Long-term debt | | 2,000,000 | | NA* | | Long-term debt | No change | 2,000,000 | 2,000,000 | 2,000,000 |
| 22 | Total Liabilities | | $ 4,500,000 | | | | Total Liabilities | | $ 4,500,000 | $ 4,900,000 | $ 5,300,000 |
| 23 | Common stock (par) | | 100,000 | | NA* | | Common stock (par) | No change | $ 100,000 | $ 100,000 | $ 100,000 |
| 24 | Paid-in capital | | 200,000 | | NA* | | Paid-in capital | No change | 200,000 | 200,000 | 200,000 |
| 25 | Retained earnings | | 1,200,000 | | | | Retained earnings | Calculation^b | 1,450,000 | 1,500,000 | 1,550,000 |
| 26 | Common Equity | | $ 1,500,000 | | | | Common Equity | | $ 1,750,000 | $ 1,800,000 | $ 1,850,000 |
| 27 | Total | | $ 6,000,000 | | | | Total Financing Provided | | $ 6,250,000 | $ 6,700,000 | $ 7,150,000 |
| 28 | | | | | | | Discretionary Financing Needed (Plug)* | | $ (250,000) | $ 500,000 | $ 1,250,000 |
| 29 | | | | | | | Total Financing Needed = Total Assets | | $ 6,000,000 | $ 7,200,000 | $ 8,400,000 |
| 30 | | | | | | | | | | | |
| 31 | | | | | | | | | | | |
| 32 | ^aNot applicable. These account balances do not vary with sales. | | | | | | | | | | |
| 33 | ^bProjected retained earnings for 2014 based on the 20% growth rate scenario is $1,500,000 and is calculated as follows:   The 2013 retained earnings of $1,200,000 added to 2014 projected net income of $600,000 less common dividends of $300,000. Note that dividends are assumed to be 50% or net income, so dividends vary across the three scenarios. | | | | | | | | | | |
| 34 | ^cDiscretionary financing needed (DFN) for 2014 and the 20% growth rate scenario is a "plug figure" that equals the difference in the firm's projected total financing requirements or total assets of $7,200,000 and total financing provided of $6,700,000. In this scenario DFN is $500,000. | | | | | | | | | | |

funds in this amount, by either borrowing or issuing stock. We can calculate *DFN* using the following relationship:

$$DFN = \frac{\text{predicted change}}{\text{in total assets}} - \frac{\text{predicted change}}{\text{in spontaneous liabilities}} - \frac{\text{predicted change}}{\text{in retained earnings}} \quad (14\text{-}1)$$

Notice that in defining *DFN* we consider only changes in spontaneous liabilities, which you will recall are those liabilities that arise more or less automatically in the course of doing business (examples include accrued expenses and accounts payable). In Table 14-1 the only liabilities that are allowed to change with sales are spontaneous liabilities, so we can calculate the change in spontaneous liabilities simply by comparing total liabilities at the current sales level with total liabilities for the predicted sales level.

# DID YOU GET IT?
## PERCENT OF SALES FORECASTING

Madrigal projects that its inventories will be 15 percent of revenues such that its projected inventory needs for next year will be the following:

$$0.15 \times \$10 \text{ million} = \$1,500,000$$

If Madrigal faces economies of scale, then its inventory needs will be less than the $1,500,000 predicted using the percent of sales method. When economies of scale are present, the firm's inventory needs do not increase proportionately with sales (nor do they decrease proportionately).

Equation (14-1) can be used to estimate the *DFN* numbers found in Table 14-2. For example, when sales are expected to grow at a rate of 10 percent (that is, *g* equals 10 percent), *DFN* can be calculated as follows:

$$DFN(g = 10\%) = (\$6,600,000 - \$6,000,000) - (\$4,700,000 - \$4,500,000)$$
$$- (\$1,475,000 - \$1,200,000) = \$125,000$$

**external financing needs** that portion of a firm's requirements for financing that exceeds its sources of internal financing (i.e., the retention of earnings) plus spontaneous sources of financing (e.g., trade credit).

Sometimes analysts prefer to calculate a firm's **external financing needs** (*EFN*), which include *all the firm's needs for financing beyond the funds provided internally through the retention of earnings*. Thus,

$$EFN = \text{predicted change in total assets} - \text{change in retained earnings} \quad (14\text{-}2)$$

For an anticipated growth in sales of 10 percent, *EFN* equals $325,000. The difference between *EFN* and *DFN* equals the $200,000 in added spontaneous financing that the firm anticipates receiving when its sales rise from $10 million to $11 million. We prefer to use the *DFN* concept because it focuses the analyst's attention on the amount of funds that the firm must actively seek to meet the firm's financing requirements.

Figure 14-1 contains a graphic representation of the relationship between growth rates for sales and *DFN*. The straight line in the graph depicts the level of *DFN* for each of the different rates of growth in firm sales. For example, if sales grow by 20 percent, then the firm projects a *DFN* of $500,000, which must be raised externally by

| FINANCIAL DECISION TOOLS | | |
|---|---|---|
| **Name of Tool** | **Formula** | **What It Tells You** |
| Percent of sales forecast of inventories | $\dfrac{\text{Inventory}}{\text{forecast}} = \dfrac{\text{sales}}{\text{forecast}} \times \dfrac{\text{inventories}}{\text{sales}}$ | • An estimate of inventories for a particular sales forecast and assuming the inventories to sales ratio is constant<br>• We can substitute any asset or liability for inventories in this equation so long as that asset or liability is expected to vary proportionately with sales. |
| Discretionary financing needed (*DFN*) | $DFN = \dfrac{\text{predicted change}}{\text{in total assets}} - \dfrac{\text{predicted change}}{\text{in spontaneous liabilities}} - \dfrac{\text{predicted change}}{\text{in retained earnings}}$ | • An estimate of the amount of new funding the firm's management must obtain from new sources that they must actively negotiate<br>• Spontaneous funding and retained earnings are passively raised as a result of the firm's ongoing operations. |

borrowing or a new equity offering. Note that when sales grow at 6.667 percent, the firm's *DFN* will be exactly zero. For firms that have limited sources of external financing or choose to grow through internal financing plus spontaneous financing, it is important that they be able to estimate the sales growth rate that they can "afford," which in this case is 6.667 percent.

## Concept Check

1. If we cannot predict the future perfectly, then why do firms engage in financial forecasting?

2. Why are sales forecasts so important to developing a firm's financial plans?

3. What is the percent of sales method of financial forecasting?

4. What are some examples of spontaneous and discretionary sources of financing?

5. What is the distinction between discretionary financing needs (*DFN*) and external financing needs (*EFN*)?

# Limitations of the Percent of Sales Forecasting Method

 Describe the limitations of the percent of sales forecast method.

The percent of sales method of financial forecasting provides reasonable estimates of a firm's financing requirements only when asset requirements and financing sources can be accurately forecast as a constant percent of sales. For example, predicting inventories for 2013 using the percent of sales method involves the following equation.

$$\text{Predicted inventories} \atop \text{for 2014} = \left( \frac{\text{inventories for 2013}}{\text{sales for 2013}} \right) \times \frac{\text{predicted sales}}{\text{for 2014}}$$

Figure 14-2A depicts this predictive relationship. Note that the percent of sales predictive model is simply a straight line that passes through the origin (that is, has a zero intercept). There are some fairly common instances in which this type of relationship fails to describe the relationship between an asset category and sales. Two such examples involve assets for which there are scale economies and assets that must be purchased in discrete quantities ("lumpy assets").

Economies of scale are sometimes realized from investing in certain types of assets. For example, a new computer system is likely to support a firm's operations over a wide range of firm sales. This means that these assets do not increase in direct proportion to sales. Figure 14-2B reflects one instance in which the firm realizes economies of scale from its investment in inventory. Note that inventories as a percentage of sales decline from 120 percent of sales, or $120 when sales are $100, to 30 percent of sales, or $300 when sales equal $1,000. This reflects the fact that there is a fixed component of inventories (in this case $100) that the firm must have on hand regardless of the level of sales, plus a variable

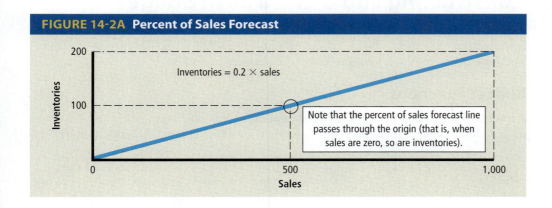

**FIGURE 14-2A  Percent of Sales Forecast**

Inventories = 0.2 × sales

Note that the percent of sales forecast line passes through the origin (that is, when sales are zero, so are inventories).

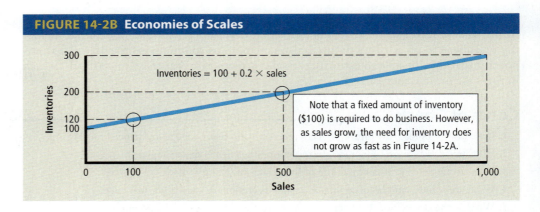

**FIGURE 14-2B  Economies of Scales**

Inventories = 100 + 0.2 × sales

Note that a fixed amount of inventory ($100) is required to do business. However, as sales grow, the need for inventory does not grow as fast as in Figure 14-2A.

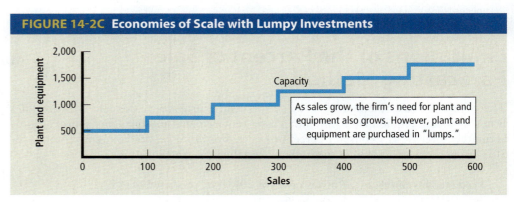

**FIGURE 14-2C  Economies of Scale with Lumpy Investments**

Capacity

As sales grow, the firm's need for plant and equipment also grows. However, plant and equipment are purchased in "lumps."

component (20 percent of sales). In this instance the predictive equation for inventories is as follows:

$$\text{Inventories}_t = a + b\, \text{sales}_t$$

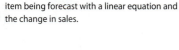

**intercept** the constant term in a linear equation. This is the value predicted in a linear equation for the item being forecast (e.g., operating expenses) where revenues are equal to zero.

**slope coefficient** the rate of change in the item being forecast with a linear equation and the change in sales.

In this example, $a$ (the **intercept**[2] of the inventories equation) is equal to 100 and $b$ (the **slope coefficient** in the equation) is 0.20.

Figure 14-2C is an example of *lumpy assets*, that is, assets that must be purchased in large, nondivisible components. For example, if the firm spends $500 on plant and equipment, it can produce up to $100 in sales per year. If it spends another $500 (for a total of $1,000), then it can support sales of $200 to $300 per year, and so forth. Note that when a block of assets is purchased, it creates excess capacity until sales grow to the point at which the capacity is fully used. The result is a step function like the one depicted in Figure 14-2C. Thus, if the firm does not expect sales to exceed the current capacity of its plant and equipment, there would be no projected need for added plant and equipment capacity.

 **3** Prepare a cash budget and use it to evaluate the amount and timing of a firm's financing needs.

# Constructing and Using a Cash Budget

The cash budget, like the pro forma income statement and pro forma balance sheet, is an essential tool of financial planning. The cash budget contains a detailed listing of planned cash inflows and outflows for each year of the planning period.

## Budget Functions

**budget** an itemized forecast of a company's expected revenues and expenses for a future period.

A **budget** is simply *a forecast of future events*. For example, students preparing for final exams make use of time budgets to help them allocate their limited preparation time among their

[2]Economies of scale are evidenced by the nonzero intercept value. However, scale economies can also result in nonlinear relationships between sales and a particular asset category. Later, when we discuss cash management, we will find that one popular cash management model predicts a nonlinear relationship between the optimal cash balance and the level of cash transactions.

## ETHICS IN FINANCIAL MANAGEMENT

### TO BRIBE OR NOT TO BRIBE

The pressure to "get the forecast right" can be tremendous, and these pressures can lead managers to engage in practices (especially in underdeveloped countries) of offering bribes and payoffs to public officials because they are considered the norm in business transactions. This raises a perplexing ethical question. If paying bribes is not considered unethical in a foreign country, should you consider it unethical to make these payments?

This situation provides an example of an ethical issue that gave rise to legislation. The Foreign Corrupt Practices Act of 1977 (as amended in the Omnibus Trade and Competitiveness Act of 1988) established criminal penalties for making payments to foreign officials, political parties, or candidates in order to obtain or retain business. Ethical problems are frequently areas

just outside the boundaries of current legislation and often lead to the passage of new legislation.

Consider the following question: If you were involved in negotiating an important business deal in a foreign country and the success or failure of the deal hinged on whether you paid a local government official to help you consummate the deal, would you authorize the payment? Assume that the form of the payment is such that you do not expect to be caught and punished; for example, your company agrees to purchase supplies from a family member of the government official at a price slightly above the competitive price. Can you see any pitfalls related to such a deal?

courses. Students also must budget their financial resources among competing uses, such as books, tuition, food, rent, clothes, and extracurricular activities.

Budgets perform three basic functions for a firm.

◆ First, they indicate the amount and timing of the firm's needs for future financing.
◆ Second, they provide the basis for taking corrective action in the event budgeted figures do not match actual or realized figures.
◆ Third, budgets provide the basis for performance evaluation and control. Plans are carried out by people, and budgets provide benchmarks that management can use to evaluate the performance of those responsible for carrying out those plans and, in turn, to control their actions.

## Concept Check

1. What, in words, is the fundamental relationship (equation) used in making percent of sales forecasts?

2. Under what circumstances does a firm violate the basic relationship underlying the percent of sales forecast method?

## The Cash Budget

The **cash budget** represents a *detailed plan of future cash flows* and is composed of four elements: cash receipts, cash disbursements, net change in cash for the period, and new financing needed.

**cash budget** a detailed plan of future cash flows. This budget is composed of four elements: cash receipts, cash disbursements, net change in cash for the period, and new financing needed.

---

**EXAMPLE 14.1**    **Constructing a cash budget**

To demonstrate the construction and use of the cash budget, consider Salco Furniture Company Inc., a regional distributor of household furniture. Salco is in the process of preparing a monthly cash budget for the upcoming 6 months (January through June 2014). The company's sales are highly seasonal, peaking in the months of March through May. Roughly 30 percent of Salco's sales are collected 1 month after the sale, 50 percent 2 months after the sale, and the remainder during the third month following the sale.

Salco attempts to pace its purchases with its forecast of future sales. Purchases generally equal 75 percent of sales and are made 2 months in advance of anticipated sales. Payments are made in the month following purchases. For example, June sales are estimated at $100,000; thus, April purchases are $0.75 \times \$100,000 = \$75,000$. Correspondingly, payments for purchases in May equal $75,000. Wages, salaries, rent, and other cash expenses are recorded in Table 14-3, which shows Salco's cash budget for the 6-month period ended in June 2011. Additional expenditures are recorded in the cash budget related to the purchase of equipment in the amount of $14,000 during February and the repayment of a $12,000 loan in May. In June, Salco will pay $7,500 interest on its $150,000 in long-term debt for the period of January to June 2011. Interest on the $12,000 short-term note repaid in May for the period January through May equals $600 and is paid in May.

Salco currently has a cash balance of $20,000 and wants to maintain a minimum balance of $10,000. Additional borrowing necessary to maintain that minimum balance is estimated in the final section of Table 14-3. Borrowing takes place at the beginning of the month in which the funds are needed. Interest on the borrowed funds equals 12 percent per annum, or 1 percent per month, and is paid in the month following the one in which funds are borrowed. Thus, interest on funds borrowed in January will be paid in February equal to 1 percent of the loan amount outstanding during January.

### STEP 1: FORMULATE A SOLUTION STRATEGY

Construct a cash budget that includes estimates of the firm's cash inflows and outflows for each of the next 6 months. This requires the preparation of estimates of monthly revenues and expenses, but this is not the end of the process. The analyst must then estimate when the revenues will actually be received (cash sales and collection of accounts receivable) as well as when the expenses will actually be paid. Once these estimates have been prepared, we can construct the cash budget and estimate the change in cash for the firm in each month of the forecast period.

### STEP 2: CRUNCH THE NUMBERS

Table 14-3 contains the monthly cash budget and all the supporting estimates that are required.

### STEP 3: ANALYZE YOUR RESULTS

The financing-needed line in Salco's cash budget determines that the firm's cumulative short-term borrowing will rise to $97,599 by May. However, this need for borrowing begins to subside in June and the firm is able to reduce its borrowing to $79,875. Note that the cash budget indicates not only the amount of financing needed during the period but also when the funds will be needed.

## ETHICS IN FINANCIAL MANAGEMENT

### BEING HONEST ABOUT THE UNCERTAINTY OF THE FUTURE

Put yourself in the shoes of Ben Tolbert, who is the CFO of Bonajet Enterprises. Ben's CEO is scheduled to meet with a group of outside analysts tomorrow to discuss the firm's financial forecast for the last quarter of the year. Ben's analysis suggests that there is a very real prospect that the coming quarter's results could be very disappointing. How would you handle Ben's dilemma?

As Ben looks over a draft of the report he must submit to the company CEO, he becomes increasingly concerned. Although the forecast is below initial expectations, this is not what worries Ben. The problem is that some of the basic assumptions underlying his prediction might not come true. If this is the case, then the company's performance for the last

quarter of the year will be dramatically below its annual forecast. The result would be a potentially severe reaction in the investment community, causing a downward adjustment of unknown proportions in the firm's stock price.

Bonajet's CEO is a no-nonsense guy who really doesn't like to see his CFO hedge his predictions, so Ben is under pressure to decide whether to ignore the downside prospects or make them known to his CEO. Complicating matters is the fact that the worst-case scenario would probably give rise to a reorganization of Bonajet that would lead to substantial layoffs of its workforce. Here is Ben's dilemma: what should he tell the CEO in their meeting tomorrow morning?

**TABLE 14-3  Salco Furniture Co. Inc. Cash Budget for 6 Months Ended June 30, 2014**

| | A | B October | C November | D December | E January | F February | G March | H April | I May | J June | K July | L August |
|---|---|---|---|---|---|---|---|---|---|---|---|---|
| 1 | | October | November | December | January | February | March | April | May | June | July | August |
| 2 | Worksheet | | | | | | | | | | | |
| 3 | Sales (forecasted) | 55,000 | 62,000 | 50,000 | 60,000 | 75,000 | 88,000 | 100,000 | 110,000 | 100,000 | 80,000 | 75,000 |
| 4 | Purchases (75% of sales in 2 months) | | | 56,250 | 66,000 | 75,000 | 82,500 | 75,000 | 60,000 | 56,250 | | |
| 5 | | | | | | | | | | | | |
| 6 | Cash Receipts | | | | | | | | | | | |
| 7 | Collections: | | | | | | | | | | | |
| 8 | First Month after sale (30%) | | | | 15,000 | 18,000 | 22,500 | 26,400 | 30,000 | 33,000 | | |
| 9 | Second Month after sale (50%) | | | | 31,000 | 25,000 | 30,000 | 37,500 | 44,000 | 50,000 | | |
| 10 | Third Month after sale (20%) | | | | 11,000 | 12,400 | 10,000 | 12,000 | 15,000 | 17,600 | | |
| 11 | Total Cash Receipts | | | | 57,000 | 55,400 | 62,500 | 75,900 | 89,000 | 100,600 | | |
| 12 | | | | | | | | | | | | |
| 13 | Cash Disbursements | | | | | | | | | | | |
| 14 | Payments (one-month lag of purchases from row 4) | | | | 56,250 | 66,000 | 75,000 | 82,500 | 75,000 | 60,000 | | |
| 15 | Wages and Salaries | | | | 3,000 | 10,000 | 7,000 | 8,000 | 6,000 | 4,000 | | |
| 16 | Rent | | | | 4,000 | 4,000 | 4,000 | 4,000 | 4,000 | 4,000 | | |
| 17 | Other Expenses | | | | 1,000 | 500 | 1,200 | 1,500 | 1,500 | 1,200 | | |
| 18 | Interest expense on existing debt[a] | | | | | | | | 600 | 7,500 | | |
| 19 | Taxes | | | | | | 4,460 | | | 5,200 | | |
| 20 | Purchase of Equipment | | | | 14,000 | | | | | | | |
| 21 | Loan Repayment[b] | | | | | | | | 12,000 | | | |
| 22 | Total Cash Disbursements | | | | 64,250 | 94,500 | 91,660 | 96,000 | 99,100 | 81,900 | | |
| 23 | | | | | | | | | | | | |
| 24 | Net Change in Cash for the Period | | | | (7,250) | (39,100) | (29,160) | (20,100) | (10,100) | 18,700 | | |
| 25 | Plus: Beginning cash balance | | | | 20,000 | 12,750 | 10,000 | 10,000 | 10,000 | 10,000 | | |
| 26 | Less: Interest on short-term borrowing | | | | 0 | 0 | (364) | (659) | (866) | (976) | | |
| 27 | Equals: Ending cash balance before short-term borrowing | | | | 12,750 | (26,350) | (19,524) | (10,759) | (966) | 27,724 | | |
| 28 | | | | | | | | | | | | |
| 29 | New Financing Needed[c] | | | | 0 | 36,350 | 29,524 | 20,759 | 10,966 | (17,724)[d] | | |
| 30 | Ending cash balance | | | | 12,750 | 10,000 | 10,000 | 10,000 | 10,000 | 10,000 | | |
| 31 | Cumulative borrowing | | | | 0 | 36,350 | 65,874 | 86,633 | 97,599 | 79,875 | | |
| 32 | | | | | | | | | | | | |
| 33 | | | | | | | | | | | | |

[a]An interest payment of $600 on the $12,000 loan is due in May, and an interest payment of $7500 on the $150,000 long-term debt is due in June.
[b]The principal amount of the $12,000 loan is also due in May.
[c]The amount of financing that is required to raise the firm's ending cash balance up to its $10,000 desired cash balance.
[d]Negative financing needed simply means the firm has excess cash that can be used to retire a part of its short-term borrowing from prior months.

## Concept Check

1. What is a cash budget?
2. How is a cash budget used in financial planning?

# Chapter Summaries

## Use the percent of sales method to forecast the financing requirements of a firm. (pgs. 437–443)

**SUMMARY:** The percent of sales method is commonly used to forecast a firm's assets, liabilities, and expenses. These forecasts are then used to prepare a financial plan that can be used to estimate the firm's future financing requirements. Developing a financial forecast can be viewed as a three step process:

**STEP 1**  Project the firm's sales revenues and expenses over the planning period.

**STEP 2**  Estimate the levels of investment in current and fixed assets that are needed to support the sales forecast.

**STEP 3**  Determine the firm's financing needs throughout the planning period that are required to fund its assets.

### KEY TERMS

**Percent of sales method, page 438**  A method of financial forecasting that involves estimating the level of an expense, asset, or liability for a future period as a percent of the sales forecast. For example, to estimate cost of goods sold for the current year the analyst might use the ratio of cost of goods sold for sales for last year multiplied by the sales forecast for the coming year.

**Spontaneous financing, page 439** The credit and other accounts payable that arise spontaneously in the course of the firm's day-to-day operations.

**Discretionary financing, page 439** Sources of financing that require an explicit decision on the part of the firm's management every time

funds are raised. Bank notes provide a typical example of this type of financing.

**External financing needs, page 442** That portion of a firm's financing requirements that exceeds its sources of internal financing (i.e., the retention of current earnings) plus spontaneous sources of financing (e.g., trade credit).

---

 **Describe the limitations of the percent of sales forecast method.**   (pgs. 443–444)

**SUMMARY:** The equation or model that underlies a percent of sales forecast is a straight line that passes through the intercept. Very simply, if we are forecasting a firm's inventory balance, then the percent of sales method will predict a zero inventory balance for a zero sales level. Although this may be roughly correct for some firms, it is often the case that the firm will plan on having inventory items in stock even when the sales level drops very low. For example, the firm might intend to keep 100,000 units in stock as a minimum regardless of the level of predicted sales (this recognizes the fact that forecasting is highly imperfect and also you can't sell anything if you do not have something to sell). Thus, the percent of sales method of forecasting is probably "roughly" correct for most things but is inherently inexact where the relationship between the item being forecast and sales is not linear or where there is some minimum level of the item the firm plans to have, regardless of the level of firm sales.

**KEY TERMS**

**Intercept, page 444** The constant term in a linear equation. This is the value predicted in a linear equation for the item being forecast (e.g., operating expenses) where revenues are equal to zero.

**Slope coefficient, page 444** The rate of change in the item being forecast with a linear equation and the change in sales.

---

 **Prepare a cash budget and use it to evaluate the amount and timing of a firm's financing needs.**   (pgs. 444–447)

**SUMMARY:** The cash budget, like the pro forma income statement and balance sheet, is an essential tool of financial planning. Specifically, the cash budget contains estimates of cash inflows and outflows organized by month, quarter, or year spanning the entire financial planning period. As such, the cash budget provides the firm's CFO and other financial analysts the opportunity to try to forecast the effect of their operating decisions on the firm's operations.

**KEY TERMS**

**Budget, page 444** An itemized forecast of a firm's expected revenues and expenses for a future period.

**Cash budget, page 445** A detailed plan of future cash flows. This budget is composed of

four elements: cash receipts, cash disbursements, net change in cash for the period, and new financing needed.

# Review Questions

*All Review Questions are available in* MyFinanceLab.

**14-1.** United Parcel Service (UPS) provides package delivery services throughout the United States and the world. Discuss the impact of seasonal variations in the delivery business for forecasting the firm's financing requirements.

**14-2.** Discuss the shortcomings of the percent of sales method of financial forecasting.

**14-3.** What would be the probable effect on a firm's cash position of the following events?

   a.  Rapidly rising sales

   b.  A delay in the payment of payables

c. A more liberal credit policy on sales (to the firm's customers)

d. Holding larger inventories

**14-4.** A cash budget is usually thought of as a means of planning for future financing needs. Why would a cash budget also be important for a firm that has excess cash on hand?

# Study Problems

*All Study Problems are available in* MyFinanceLab.

**14-1.** (*Financial forecasting*) Zapatera Enterprises is evaluating its financing requirements for the coming year. The firm has been in business for only 1 year, but its CFO predicts that the firm's operating expenses, current assets, net fixed assets, and current liabilities will remain at their current proportion of sales.

Last year Zapatera had $12 million in sales, and net income of $1.2 million. The firm anticipates that next year's sales will reach $15 million, with net income rising to $2 million. Given its present high rate of growth, the firm retains all its earnings to help defray the cost of new investments.

The firm's balance sheet for 2013 is found below:

**Zapatera Enterprises Inc.**

| BALANCE SHEET | | |
|---|---|---|
| | **12/31/2013** | **% OF SALES** |
| Current assets | $3,000,000 | 25% |
| Net fixed assets | 6,000,000 | 50% |
| Total | $9,000,000 | |
| **LIABILITIES AND OWNERS' EQUITY** | | |
| Accounts payable | $3,000,000 | 25% |
| Long-term debt | 2,000,000 | NA[a] |
| Total liabilities | $5,000,000 | |
| Common stock | 1,000,000 | NA |
| Paid-in capital | 1,800,000 | NA |
| Retained earnings | 1,200,000 | |
| Common equity | 4,000,000 | |
| Total | $9,000,000 | |

[a]Not applicable. This figure does not vary directly with sales and is assumed to remain constant for purposes of making next year's forecast of financing requirements.

Estimate Zapatera's financing requirements (that is, total assets) for 2014 and its discretionary financing needs (*DFN*).

**14-2.** (*Pro forma accounts receivable balance calculation*) On March 31, 2013, Mike's Bike Shop had outstanding accounts receivable of $17,500. Mike's sales are roughly evenly split between credit and cash sales, with the credit sales collected half in the month after the sale and the remainder 2 months after the sale. Historical and projected sales for the bike shop are given here:

| MONTH | SALES | MONTH | SALES |
|---|---|---|---|
| January | $15,000 | March | $25,000 |
| February | 20,000 | April (projected) | 30,000 |

a. Under these circumstances, what should the balance in accounts receivable be at the end of April?

b. How much cash did Mike's realize during April from sales and collections?

**14-3.** (*Financial forecasting*) Sambonoza Enterprises projects its sales next year to be $4 million and expects to earn 5 percent of that amount after taxes. The firm is currently in the process of projecting its financing needs and has made the following assumptions (projections):

1. Current assets will equal 20 percent of sales, and fixed assets will remain at their current level of $1 million.

2. Common equity is currently $0.8 million, and the firm pays out half its after-tax earnings in dividends.

3. The firm has short-term payables and trade credit that normally equal 10 percent of sales, and it has no long-term debt outstanding.

What are Sambonoza's financing needs for the coming year?

**14-4.** (*Financial forecasting—percent of sales*) Tulley Appliances Inc. projects next year's sales to be $20 million. Current sales are $15 million, based on current assets of $5 million and fixed assets of $5 million. The firm's net profit margin is 5 percent after taxes. Tulley forecasts that its current assets will rise in direct proportion to the increase in sales but that its fixed assets will increase by only $100,000. Currently, Tulley has $1.5 million in accounts payable (which vary directly with sales), $2 million in long-term debt (due in 10 years), and common equity (including $4 million in retained earnings) totaling $6.5 million. Tulley plans to pay $500,000 in common stock dividends next year.

    a. What are Tulley's total financing needs (that is, total assets) for the coming year?

    b. Given the firm's projections and dividend payments plans, what are its discretionary financing needs?

    c. Based on your projections, and assuming that the $100,000 expansion in fixed assets will occur, what is the largest increase in sales the firm can support without having to resort to the use of discretionary sources of financing?

**14-5.** (*Pro forma balance sheet construction*) Use the following industry-average ratios to construct a pro forma balance sheet for Phoebe's Cat Foods Inc.

| | |
|---|---|
| Total asset turnover | 1.5 times |
| Average collection period (assume 365-day year) | 15 days |
| Fixed asset turnover | 5 times |
| Inventory turnover (based on cost of goods sold) | 3 times |
| Current ratio | 2 times |
| Sales (all on credit) | $3.0 million |
| Cost of goods sold | 75% of sales |
| Debt ratio | 50% |

| | | | | |
|---|---|---|---|---|
| | | Current liabilities | | |
| Cash | | Long-term debt | | |
| Accounts receivable | | Common stock plus | | |
|   Net fixed assets | $_____ | Retained earnings | $_____ | |

**14-6.** (*Percent of sales forecasting*) Which of the following accounts would most likely vary directly with the level of a firm's sales? Discuss each briefly.

| | YES | NO | | YES | NO |
|---|---|---|---|---|---|
| Cash | ___ | ___ | Notes payable | ___ | ___ |
| Marketable securities | ___ | ___ | Plant and equipment | ___ | ___ |
| Accounts payable | ___ | ___ | Inventories | ___ | ___ |

**14-7.** (*Financial forecasting—percent of sales*) The balance sheet of the Boyd Trucking Company (BTC) follows:

**Boyd Trucking Company Balance Sheet, December 31, 2013 ($ Millions)**

| | | | |
|---|---|---|---|
| Current assets | $10 | Accounts payable | $ 5 |
| Net fixed assets | 15 | Notes payable | 0 |
|   Total | $25 | Bonds payable | 10 |
| | | Common equity | 10 |
| | |   Total | $25 |

BTC had sales for the year ended December 31, 2013, of $25 million. The firm follows a policy of paying all net earnings out to its common stockholders in cash dividends. Thus, BTC generates no funds from its earnings that can be used to expand its operations. (Assume that depreciation expense is just equal to the cost of replacing worn-out assets.)

   a. If BTC anticipates sales of $40 million during the coming year, develop a pro forma balance sheet for the firm on December 31, 2014. Assume that current assets vary as a percent of sales, net fixed assets remain unchanged, and accounts payable vary as a percent of sales. Use notes payable as a balancing entry.

   b. How much "new" financing will BTC need next year?

   c. What limitations does the percent of sales forecast method suffer from? Discuss briefly.

**14-8.** (*Financial forecasting—discretionary financing needs*) The most recent balance sheet for the Armadillo Dog Biscuit Co. Inc. is shown in the following table. The company is about to embark on an advertising campaign, which is expected to raise sales from the current level of $5 million to $7 million by the end of next year. The firm is currently operating at full capacity and will have to increase its investment in both current and fixed assets to support the projected level of new sales. In fact, the firm estimates that both categories of assets will rise in direct proportion to the projected increase in sales.

**Armadillo Dog Biscuit Co. Inc. ($ Millions)**

| | PRESENT LEVEL | PERCENT OF SALES | PROJECTED LEVEL |
|---|---|---|---|
| Current assets | $2.0 | 40% | 2.8 |
| Net fixed assets | 3.0 | 60% | 4.2 |
|   Total | $5.0 | | 7 |
| Accounts payable | $0.5 | 10% | 0.7 |
| Accrued expense | 0.5 | 10% | 0.7 |
| Notes payable | 0 | | |
| Current liabilities | $1.0 | | |
| Long-term debt | $2.0 | Nc | 2.0 |
| Common stock | 0.5 | NC | 0.5 |
| Retained earnings | 1.5 | 0.49 | 1.99 |
| Common equity | $2.0 | | 3.89 |
|   Total | $5.0 | | |

The firm's net profits were 6 percent of the current year's sales but are expected to rise to 7 percent of next year's sales. To help support its anticipated growth in asset needs next year, the firm has suspended plans to pay cash dividends to its stockholders. In past years a $1.50-per-share dividend has been paid annually. Armadillo's accounts payable and accrued expenses are expected to vary directly with sales. In addition, notes payable will be used to supply the funds needed to finance next year's operations that are not forthcoming from other sources.

   a. Fill in the table and project the firm's needs for discretionary financing. Use notes payable as the balancing entry for future discretionary financing needs.

   b. Compare Armadillo's current ratio and debt ratio (total liabilities ÷ total assets) before the growth in sales and after. What was the effect of the expanded sales on these two dimensions of Armadillo's financial condition?

   c. What difference, if any, would have resulted if Armadillo's sales had risen to $6 million in 1 year and $7 million only after 2 years? Discuss only; no calculations are required.

**14-9.** (*Forecasting discretionary financing needs*) Fishing Charter Inc. estimates that it invests $0.30 in assets for each dollar of new sales. However, $0.05 in profits are produced by each dollar of additional sales, of which $0.01 can be reinvested in the firm. If sales rise by $500,000 next year from their current level of $5 million, and the ratio of spontaneous liabilities to sales is 15 percent, what will be the firm's need for discretionary financing? (*Hint*: In this situation you do not know what the firm's existing level of assets is, nor do you know how those assets have been financed. Thus, you must estimate the change in financing needs and match this change with the expected changes in spontaneous liabilities, retained earnings, and other sources of discretionary financing.)

**14-10.** (*Forecasting net income*) In November of each year the CFO of Barker Electronics begins the financial forecasting process to determine the firm's projected needs for new financing during the coming year. Barker is a small electronics manufacturing company located in Moline, Illinois, which is best known as the home of the John Deere Company. The CFO begins the process with the most recent year's income statement, projects sales growth for the coming year, and then estimates net income and finally the additional earnings he can expect to retain and reinvest in the firm. The firm's income statement for 2010 follows (in $000):

Income Statement ($000)

|  | YEAR ENDED DECEMBER 31, 2010 |
| --- | --- |
| Sales | $ 1,500 |
| Cost of goods sold | (1,050) |
| Gross profit | $ 450 |
| Operating costs | (225) |
| Depreciation expense | (50) |
| Net operating profit | $ 175 |
| Interest expense | (10) |
| Earnings before taxes | $ 165 |
| Taxes | (58) |
| Net income | $ 107 |
| Dividends | $ 20 |
| Addition to retained earnings | $ 87 |

The electronics business has been growing rapidly over the past 18 months as the economy recovers, and the CFO estimates that sales will expand by 20 percent in the next year. In addition, he estimates the following relationships between each of the income statement expense items and sales:

| COGS/sales | 70% |
| --- | --- |
| Operating expenses/sales | 15% |
| Depreciation expense ($000) | $50 |
| Interest expense ($000) | $10 |
| Tax rate | 35% |

Note that for the coming year both depreciation expense and interest expense are projected to remain the same as in 2010.

   a. Estimate Barker's net income for 2011 and its addition to retained earnings under the assumption that the firm leaves its dividends paid at the 2010 level.
   b. Reevaluate Barker's net income and addition to retained earnings where sales grow at 40 percent over the coming year. However, this scenario requires the addition of new plant and equipment in the amount of $100,000, which increases annual depreciation to $58,000 per year, and interest expense rises to $15,000.

**14–11.** (*Misusing the percent of sales method*) The Caraway Seed Company has grown rapidly over the last decade and is trying to forecast the firm's inventory requirements for the next 5 years. Historical sales and inventories for the last 10 years are found below along with projected sales for the next 5 years.

| YEAR | SALES | INVENTORIES |
| --- | --- | --- |
| 2005 | $ 5,250,000 | $1,590,924 |
| 2006 | 6,200,000 | 1,724,221 |
| 2007 | 6,940,000 | 1,899,573 |
| 2008 | 5,650,000 | 1,530,054 |
| 2009 | 6,255,000 | 1,772,059 |
| 2010 | 7,100,000 | 1,919,042 |
| 2011 | 7,350,000 | 2,012,025 |
| 2012 | 8,010,000 | 2,006,023 |
| 2013 | 8,775,000 | 2,292,119 |
| 2014 | 10,390,000 | 2,537,486 |
| 2015 | 11,500,000 | |
| 2016 | 12,000,000 | |
| 2017 | 12,500,000 | |
| 2018 | 13,000,000 | |
| 2019 | 13,500,000 | |

a. Use the percent of sales method for forecasting Caraway's inventories for the next 5 years where the percent of sales is equal to the average of the percent of sales for the last 10 years.

b. The following graph includes a plot of the historical relationship between inventories and sales along with a line representing the percent of sales forecast. Analyze the forecast line compared to the plot of inventory and sales to see if you see any problems with the percent of sales forecast. Discuss.

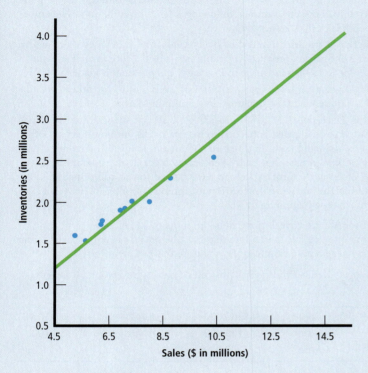

**14-12.** (*Forecasting inventories*) Findlay Instruments produces a complete line of medical instruments used by plastic surgeons and has experienced rapid growth over the past 5 years. In an effort to make more accurate predictions of its financing requirements, Findlay is currently attempting to construct a financial-planning model based on the percent of sales forecasting method. However, the firm's chief financial analyst (Sarah Macias) is concerned that the projections for inventories will be seriously in error. She recognizes that the firm has begun to accrue substantial economies of scale in its inventory investment and has documented this fact in the following data and calculations:

| YEAR | SALES ($000) | INVENTORY ($000) | % OF SALES |
|------|-------------|------------------|------------|
| 2006 | $15,000 | $1,150 | 7.67% |
| 2007 | 18,000 | 1,180 | 6.56% |
| 2008 | 17,500 | 1,175 | 6.71% |
| 2009 | 20,000 | 1,200 | 6.00% |
| 2010 | 25,000 | 1,250 | 5.00% |
| | | Average | 6.39% |

a. Plot Findlay's sales and inventories for the past 5 years. What is the relationship between these two variables?

b. Estimate firm inventories for 2011, when firm sales are projected to reach $30 million. Use the average percentage of sales for the past 5 years, the most recent percentage of sales, and your evaluation of the true relationship between the sales and inventories from part (a) to make three predictions.

**14-13.** (*Cash budget*) The Sharpe Corporation's projected sales for the first 8 months of 2014 follow on the next page:

| January | $190,000 | May | $300,000 |
|---------|----------|-----|----------|
| February | 120,000 | June | 270,000 |
| March | 135,000 | July | 225,000 |
| April | 240,000 | August | 150,000 |

Of Sharpe's sales, 10 percent is for cash, another 60 percent is collected in the month following the sales, and 30 percent is collected in the second month following sales. November and December sales for 2010 were $220,000 and $175,000, respectively.

Sharpe purchases its raw materials 2 months in advance of its sales. The purchases are equal to 60 percent of the final sales price of Sharpe's products. The supplier is paid 1 month after it makes a delivery. For example, purchases for April sales are made in February, and payment is made in March.

In addition, Sharpe pays $10,000 per month for rent and $20,000 each month for other expenditures. Tax prepayments of $22,500 are made each quarter, beginning in March.

The company's cash balance on December 31, 2013, was $22,000. This is the minimum balance the firm wants to maintain. Any borrowing that is needed to maintain this minimum is paid off in the subsequent month if there is sufficient cash. Interest on short-term loans (12 percent) is paid monthly. Borrowing to meet estimated monthly cash needs takes place at the beginning of the month. Thus, if in the month of April the firm expects to have a need for an additional $60,500, these funds would be borrowed at the beginning of April with interest of $605 (0.12 × 1/12 × $60,500) owed for April and paid at the beginning of May.

    a. Prepare a cash budget for Sharpe covering the first 7 months of 2014.
    b. Sharpe has $200,000 in notes payable due in July that must be repaid or renegotiated for an extension. Will the firm have ample cash to repay the notes?

**14-14.** (*Preparation of a cash budget*) Lewis Printing has projected its sales for the first 8 months of 2014 as follows:

| January | $100,000 | April | $300,000 | July | $200,000 |
|---------|----------|-------|----------|------|----------|
| February | 120,000 | May | 275,000 | August | 180,000 |
| March | 150,000 | June | 200,000 | | |

Lewis collects 20 percent of its sales in the month of the sale, 50 percent in the month following the sale, and the remaining 30 percent 2 months following the sale. During November and December of 2013, Lewis's sales were $220,000 and $175,000, respectively.

Lewis purchases raw materials 2 months in advance of its sales. These purchases are equal to 65 percent of its final sales. The supplier is paid 1 month after delivery. Thus, purchases for April sales are made in February and payment is made in March.

In addition, Lewis pays $10,000 per month for rent and $20,000 each month for other expenditures. Tax prepayments of $22,500 are made each quarter beginning in March. The company's cash balance as of December 31, 2013, was $28,000; a minimum balance of $25,000 must be maintained at all times to satisfy the firm's bank line of credit agreement. Lewis has arranged with its bank for short-term credit at an interest rate of 12 percent per annum (1 percent per month) to be paid monthly. Borrowing to meet estimated monthly cash needs takes place at the end of the month, and interest is not paid until the end of the following month. Consequently, if the firm needed to borrow $50,000 during April, then it would pay $500 ( = 0.01 × $50,000) in interest during May. Finally, Lewis follows a policy of repaying its outstanding short-term debt in any month in which its cash balance exceeds the minimum desired balance of $25,000.

    a. Lewis needs to know what its cash requirements will be for the next 6 months so that it can renegotiate the terms of its short-term credit agreement with its bank, if necessary. To evaluate this problem, the firm plans to evaluate the impact of a ±20 percent variation in its monthly sales efforts. Prepare a 6-month cash budget for Lewis and use it to evaluate the firm's cash needs.
    b. Lewis has a $20,000 note due in June. Will the firm have sufficient cash to repay the loan?

# Mini Case

*This Mini Case is available in* MyFinanceLab.

Phillips Petroleum is an integrated oil and gas company with headquarters in Bartlesville, Oklahoma, where it was founded in 1917. The company engages in petroleum exploration and production worldwide. In addition, it engages in natural gas gathering and processing, as well as petroleum refining and marketing primarily in the United States. The company has three operating groups: Exploration and Production, Gas and Gas Liquids, and Downstream Operations, which encompasses Petroleum Products and Chemicals.

In the mid-1980s, Phillips engaged in a major restructuring following two failed takeover attempts, one led by T. Boone Pickins and the other by Carl Ichan.[3] The restructuring resulted in a $4.5 billion plan to exchange a package of cash and debt securities for roughly half the company's shares and to sell $2 billion worth of assets. Phillips's long-term debt increased from $3.4 billion in late 1984 to a peak of $8.6 billion in April 1985.

During 1992, Phillips was able to strengthen its financial structure dramatically. Its subsidiary Phillips Gas Company completed an offering of $345 million of Series A 9.32% cumulative preferred stock. As a result of this action and prior years' debt reductions, the company lowered its long-term debt-to-capital ratio over the past 5 years from 75 percent to 55 percent. In addition, the firm refinanced over a billion dollars of its debt at reduced rates. A company spokesman said, "Our debt-to-capital ratio is still on the high side, and we'll keep working to bring it down. But the cost of debt is manageable, and we're beyond the point where debt overshadows everything else we do."[4]

Highlights of Phillips's financial condition from 1986 to 1992 are found in the accompanying table. These data reflect the company's financial restructuring following the downsizing and reorganization of Phillips's operations begun in the mid-1980s.

**Summary Financial Information for Phillips Petroleum Corporation: 1986 to 1992 (in Millions of Dollars Except for per Share Figures)**

|  | 1986 | 1987 | 1988 | 1989 | 1990 | 1991 | 1992 |
|---|---|---|---|---|---|---|---|
| Sales | $10,018.00 | $10,917.00 | $11,490.00 | $12,492.00 | $13,975.00 | $13,259.00 | $12,140.00 |
| Net income | 228.00 | 35.00 | 650.00 | 219.00 | 541.00 | 98.00 | 270.00 |
| EPS | 0.89 | 0.06 | 2.72 | 0.90 | 2.18 | 0.38 | 1.04 |
| Current assets | 2,802.00 | 2,855.00 | 3,062.00 | 2,876.00 | 3,322.00 | 2,459.00 | 2,349.00 |
| Total assets | 12,403.00 | 12,111.00 | 11,968.00 | 11,256.00 | 12,130.00 | 11,473.00 | 11,468.00 |
| Current liabilities | 2,234.00 | 2,402.00 | 2,468.00 | 2,706.00 | 2,910.00 | 2,503.00 | 2,517.00 |
| Long-term debt | 8,175.00 | 7,887.00 | 7,387.00 | 6,418.00 | 6,505.00 | 6,113.00 | 5,894.00 |
| Total liabilities | 10,409.00 | 10,289.00 | 9,855.00 | 9,124.00 | 9,411.00 | 8,716.00 | 8,411.00 |
| Preferred stock | 270.00 | 205.00 | 0.00 | 0.00 | 0.00 | 0.00 | 359.00 |
| Common equity | 1,724.00 | 1,617.00 | 2,113.00 | 2,132.00 | 2,719.00 | 2,757.00 | 2,698.00 |
| Dividends per share | 2.02 | 1.73 | 1.34 | 0.00 | 1.03 | 1.12 | 1.12 |

Source: Phillips annual reports for 1986 to 1992.

Phillips's managers are currently developing its financial plans for the next 5 years and want to develop a forecast of its financing requirements. As a first approximation, they have asked you to develop a model that can be used to make "ballpark" estimates of the firm's financing needs under the proviso that existing relationships found in the firm's financial statements remain the same over the period. Of particular interest is whether Phillips will be able to further reduce its reliance on debt financing. You may assume that Phillips's projected sales (in millions) for 1993 through 1997 are as follows: $13,000; $13,500; $14,000; $14,500; and $15,500.

   a. Project net income for 1993 to 1997 using the percent of sales method based on an average of this ratio for 1986 to 1992.
   b. Project total assets and current liabilities for 1993 to 1997 using the percent of sales method and your sales projections from part (a).
   c. Assuming that common equity increases only as a result of the retention of earnings and holding long-term debt and preferred stock equal to its 1992 balances, project Phillips's discretionary financing needs for 1993 to 1997. (*Hint*: Assume that total assets and current liabilities vary as a percentage of sales as per your answers to part (b). In addition, assume that Phillips plans to continue to pay its dividends of $1.12 per share in each of the next 5 years.)

[3]This discussion is based on a story in the *New York Times*, January 7, 1986.
[4]From *SEC Online*, 1992.

# 15

# Working-Capital Management

## Learning Objectives

**LO1** Describe the risk–return trade-off involved in managing working capital.

Managing Current Assets and Liabilities

**LO2** Describe the determinants of net working capital.

Determining the Appropriate Level of Working Capital

**LO3** Compute the firm's cash conversion cycle.

The Cash Conversion Cycle

**LO4** Estimate the cost of short-term credit.

Estimating the Cost of Short-Term Credit Using the Approximate Cost-of-Credit Formula

**LO5** Identify the primary sources of short-term credit.

Sources of Short-Term Credit

Early in its life as a publicly traded firm, the Dell Computer Corporation (DELL) experienced a period of declining sales that produced a serious cash shortfall. Moreover, the company realized that it had to accelerate its growth in order to move from the list of declining, second-tier manufacturers to the list of prospering, top-tier producers, and this required even more cash. The new Dell business model that emerged was designed to better manage the firm's working capital. Specifically, the model sought to lower inventory by 50 percent, improve lead time by 50 percent, reduce assembly costs by 30 percent, and reduce obsolete inventory by 75 percent.

The net result was that inventory dropped because Dell was aligning its inventory with sales and not holding inventories in anticipation of future sales. Furthermore, as its inventory disappeared, the company's profitability grew disproportionately because Dell avoided not only the carrying costs of holding inventories but also the losses associated with obsolete stock. Additionally, Dell was able to save money on purchasing components because the component prices were dropping 3 percent per month.

Because the firm's capital requirements to support its rapidly growing sales did not increase proportionately with sales, the company's financial needs were reduced. All this was brought about by better working-capital management.

Chapter 15 addresses two related topics: It introduces the principles involved in managing a firm's investment in working capital, and it presents a discussion of short-term financing. Traditionally, **working capital** is defined as the *firm's total investment in current assets*. **Net working capital**, on the other hand, is the *difference between the firm's current assets and its current liabilities*.

$$\text{Net working capital} = \text{currents assets} - \text{current liabilities}$$

$$(15\text{-}1)$$

Throughout this chapter, the term *working capital* refers to net working capital. In managing the firm's net working capital, we are also *managing the firm's liquidity*. This entails managing two related aspects of the firm's operations: (1) its investment in current assets, and (2) its use of short-term or current liabilities.

Short-term sources of financing include all forms of financing that have maturities of 1 year or less—that is, current liabilities. There are two major issues involved in analyzing a firm's use of short-term financing: (1) How much short-term financing should the firm use? and (2) What specific sources of short-term financing should the firm select? We use the hedging principle of working-capital management to address the first of these questions. We then address the second issue by considering three basic factors: (1) the effective cost of credit, (2) the availability of credit in the amount needed and for the period that financing is required, and (3) the influence of the use of a particular credit source on the cost and availability of other sources of financing.

## Managing Current Assets and Liabilities

A firm's current assets consist of cash and marketable securities, accounts receivable, inventories, and other assets that the firm's managers expect to be converted to cash within a period of a year or less. Consequently, firms that choose to hold more current assets are, in general, more liquid than firms that do not. Similarly, current liabilities are liabilities that are payable in 1 year or less. Examples include accounts and notes payable.

### The Risk–Return Trade-Off

Actually, firms that want to reduce their risk of illiquidity by holding more current assets do so by investing in larger cash and marketable securities balances. Holding larger cash and marketable securities balances has an unfortunate consequence, however. Because investments in cash and marketable securities earn relatively modest returns when compared with the firm's other investments, the firm that holds larger investments in these assets will reduce its overall rate of return. Thus, the increased liquidity must be traded off against the firm's reduction in return on investment. Managing this trade-off is an important theme of working-capital management.

The firm's use of current versus long-term debt also involves a risk–return trade-off. *Other things remaining the same, the greater the firm's reliance on short-term debt or current liabilities in financing its assets, the greater the risk of illiquidity.* However, the use of

 Describe the risk–return trade-off involved in managing working capital.

**working capital** a concept traditionally defined as a firm's investment in current assets.

**net working capital** the difference between the firm's current assets and its current liabilities.

current liabilities offers some very real advantages in that they can be less costly than long-term financing, and they provide the firm with a flexible means of financing its fluctuating needs for assets. However, if for some reason the firm has problems raising short-term funds or it should need funds for longer than expected, it can get into real trouble. Thus, a firm can reduce its risk of illiquidity through the use of long-term debt at the expense of a reduction in its return on invested funds. Once again we see that the risk–return trade-off involves an increased risk of illiquidity versus increased profitability.

## The Advantages of Current Liabilities: Return

**Flexibility**    Current liabilities offer the firm a flexible source of financing. They can be used to match the timing of a firm's needs for short-term financing. If, for example, a firm needs funds for a 3-month period during each year to finance a seasonal expansion in inventories, then a 3-month loan can provide substantial cost savings over a long-term loan (even if the interest rate on short-term financing should be higher). The use of long-term debt in this situation involves borrowing for the entire year rather than for the period when the funds are needed, which increases the amount of interest the firm must pay. This brings us to the second advantage generally associated with the use of short-term financing.

**Interest Cost**    In general, interest rates on short-term debt are lower than on long-term debt for a given borrower. This relationship was introduced in Chapter 2 and is referred to as the term structure of interest rates. For a given firm, the term structure might appear as follows.

| LOAN MATURITY | INTEREST RATE |
| --- | --- |
| 3 months | 4.00% |
| 6 months | 4.60 |
| 1 year | 5.30 |
| 3 years | 5.90 |
| 5 years | 6.75 |
| 10 years | 7.50 |
| 30 years | 8.25 |

Note that this term structure reflects the rates of interest applicable to a given borrower at a particular time. It would not, for example, describe the rates of interest available to another borrower or even those applicable to the same borrower at a different time.

## The Disadvantages of Current Liabilities: Risk

The use of current liabilities, or short-term debt, as opposed to long-term debt subjects the firm to a greater risk of illiquidity for two reasons. First, short-term debt, because of its very nature, must be repaid or rolled over more often, so it increases the possibility that the firm's financial condition might deteriorate to a point at which the needed funds might not be available.[1]

A second disadvantage of short-term debt is the uncertainty of interest costs from year to year. For example, a firm borrowing during a 6-month period each year to finance a seasonal expansion in current assets might incur a different rate of interest each year. This rate reflects the current rate of interest at the time of the loan, as well as the lender's perception of the firm's riskiness. If fixed-rate, long-term debt were used, the interest cost would be stable for the entire period of the loan agreement.

## Concept Check

1. How does investing more heavily in current assets (while not increasing the firm's current liabilities) decrease both the firm's risk and its expected return on its investment?

2. How does the use of current liabilities enhance profitability and also increase the firm's risk of default on its financial obligations?

[1]The dangers of such a policy are readily apparent in the experiences of firms that have been forced into bankruptcy. Penn Central, for example, went bankrupt when it had $80 million in short-term debt that it was unable to finance (roll over).

# Determining the Appropriate Level of Working Capital

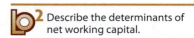
**2** Describe the determinants of net working capital.

Managing the firm's net working capital (its liquidity) involves interrelated decisions regarding its investments in current assets and use of current liabilities. Fortunately, a guiding principle exists that can be used as a benchmark for the firm's working-capital policies: the hedging principle, or principle of self-liquidating debt. This principle provides a guide to the maintenance of a level of liquidity sufficient for the firm to meet its maturing obligations on time.[2]

In Chapter 12 we discussed the firm's financing decision in terms of the choice between debt and equity sources of financing. There is, however, yet another critical dimension of the firm's financing decision. This relates to the maturity structure of the firm's debt. How should the decision be made about whether to use short-term (current) debt or longer-maturity debt? This is one of the fundamental questions addressed in this chapter and one that is critically important to the financial success of the firm.

## The Hedging Principles

Very simply, the **hedging principle**, or **principle of self-liquidating debt**, involves *matching the cash-flow-generating characteristics of an asset with the maturity of the source of financing used to fund its acquisition*. For example, a seasonal expansion in inventories, according to the hedging principle, should be financed with a short-term loan or current liability. The rationale underlying the rule is straightforward. The funds are needed for a limited period, and when that time has passed, the cash needed to repay the loan will be generated by the sale of the extra inventory items. Obtaining the needed funds from a long-term source (longer than 1 year) would mean that the firm would still have the funds after the inventories they helped finance had been sold. In this case the firm would have "excess" liquidity, which it would either hold in cash or invest in low-yield marketable securities until the seasonal increase in inventories occurs again and the funds are needed. The result of all this would be lower profits.

Consider an example in which a firm purchases a new conveyor belt system, which is expected to produce cash savings to the firm by eliminating the need for two employees and, consequently, their salaries. This amounts to an annual savings of $24,000. The conveyor belt costs $250,000 to install and will last 20 years. If the firm chooses to finance this asset with a 1-year note, then it will not be able to repay the loan from the $24,000 cash-flow-generated by the asset. In accordance with the hedging principle, the firm should finance the asset with a source of financing that more nearly matches the expected life and cash-flow-generating characteristics of the asset. In this case, a 15- to 20-year loan would be more appropriate.

## Permanent and Temporary Assets

The notion of the hedging principle (matching the maturities of cash inflows and cash outflows) can be most easily understood when we think in terms of the distinction between permanent and temporary investments in assets, as opposed to the more traditional fixed and current asset categories. **Permanent investments** in an asset are *investments that the firm expects to hold for a period longer than 1 year*. Note that we are referring to the period the firm plans to hold an investment, not the useful life of the asset. For example, permanent investments are made in the firm's minimum level of current assets, as well as in its fixed assets. **Temporary investments**, by contrast, consist of *current assets that will be liquidated and not replaced within the current year*. Thus, some part of the firm's current assets is permanent and the remainder is temporary. For example, a seasonal increase in level of inventories is

**hedging principle (principle of self-liquidating debt)** a working-capital management policy which states that the cash-flow-generating characteristics of a firm's investments should be matched with the cash-flow requirements of the firm's sources of financing. Very simply, short-lived assets should be financed with short-term sources of financing while long-lived assets should be financed with long-term sources of financing.

**permanent investment** investments that the firm expects to hold longer than 1 year. The firm makes permanent investments in fixed and current assets.

**temporary investments** a firm's investments in current assets that will be liquidated and not replaced within a period of 1 year or less. Examples include seasonal expansions in inventories and accounts receivable.

[2]A value-maximizing approach to the management of the firm's liquidity involves assessing the value of the benefits derived from increasing the firm's investment in liquid assets and weighing them against the added costs to the firm's owners resulting from investing in low-yield current assets. Unfortunately, the benefits derived from increased liquidity relate to the expected costs of bankruptcy to the firm's owners, and these costs are very difficult to measure. Thus, a "valuation" approach to liquidity management exists only in the theoretical realm.

a temporary investment: the buildup in inventories that will be eliminated when no longer needed. In contrast, the buildup in inventories to meet a long-term increasing sales trend is a permanent investment.

## Temporary, Permanent, and Spontaneous Sources of Financing

Because total assets must always equal the sum of temporary, permanent, and spontaneous sources of financing, the hedging approach provides the financial manager with the basis for determining the sources of financing to use at any point.

What constitutes a temporary, permanent, or spontaneous source of financing? Temporary sources of financing consist of current liabilities. Short-term notes payable are the most common example of a temporary source of financing. Examples of notes payable include unsecured bank loans, commercial paper, and loans secured by accounts receivable and inventories. Permanent sources of financing include intermediate-term loans, long-term debt, preferred stock, and common equity.

**trade credit** credit made available by a firm's suppliers in conjunction with the acquisition of materials. Trade credit appears on the balance sheet as accounts payable.

Spontaneous sources of financing consist of trade credit and other accounts payable that arise *spontaneously* in the firm's day-to-day operations. For example, as the firm acquires materials for its inventories, **trade credit** is often *made available spontaneously or on demand from the firm's suppliers when it orders its supplies or more inventory of products to sell. Trade credit appears on the firm's balance sheet as accounts payable*, and the size of the accounts-payable balance varies directly with the firm's purchases of inventory items. In turn, inventory purchases are related to anticipated sales. Thus, part of the financing needed by the firm is spontaneously provided in the form of trade credit.

In addition to trade credit, wages and salaries payable, accrued interest, and accrued taxes also provide valuable sources of spontaneous financing. These expenses accrue throughout the period until they are paid. For example, if a firm has a wage expense of $10,000 a week and pays its employees monthly, then its employees effectively provide financing equal to $10,000 by the end of the first week following a payday, $20,000 by the end of the second week, and so forth, until the workers are paid. Because these expenses generally arise in direct conjunction with the firm's ongoing operations, they, too, are referred to as spontaneous.

## The Hedging Principle: A Graphic Illustration

The hedging principle can now be stated very succinctly: *Asset needs of the firm not financed by spontaneous sources should be financed in accordance with this rule: Permanent-asset investments are financed with permanent sources, and temporary investments are financed with temporary sources.*

## CAUTIONARY TALE

### FORGETTING PRINCIPLE 3: RISK REQUIRES A REWARD

An important rule of thumb for financing a firm's assets is something called the hedging principle. Very simply, this principle suggests that the firm's long-term asset investments should be matched with long-term sources of financing such as long-term debt or equity. Similarly, the firm's temporary or short-term assets can be financed using short-term sources of financing. In fact, this principle has been summed up in the maxim "never finance long-term investments using short-term sources of financing."

When firms violate this basic principle, the immediate effect may actually be positive as the firm utilizes lower-cost short-term debt to finance its long-term investments. However, at some point, the music stops and the financing merry-go-round stops. This is exactly what happened with many of the nation's banks during the financial crisis that began in 2007. These firms used short-term borrowing to finance their long-term investments. Moreover, these investments were heavily concentrated in loans and other securities that were tied to real estate. When problems developed in the real estate market that raised concerns about the value of these investments, the firms that were making these investments quickly found that they could no longer get favorable terms on their short-term borrowing.

The important lesson learned here is that matching up the maturity of the sources of financing with the type of investments being financed can be important to your financial health.

**FIGURE 15-1  The Hedging Principle Illustrated**

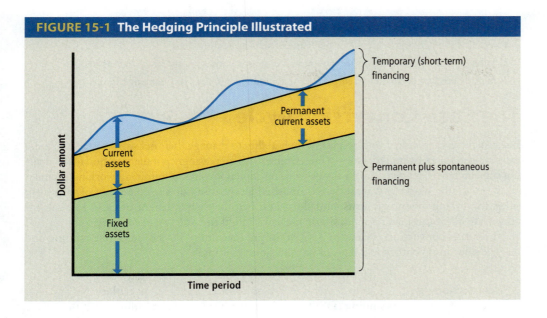

The hedging principle is depicted in Figure 15-1 and described in Table 15-1. Total assets are broken down into temporary- and permanent-asset investment categories. The firm's permanent investment in assets is financed by the use of permanent sources of financing (intermediate- and long-term debt, preferred stock, and common equity) or spontaneous sources (trade credit and other accounts payable). For illustration purposes, spontaneous sources of financing are treated as if their amount were fixed. In practice, of course, spontaneous sources of financing fluctuate with the firm's purchases and its expenditures for wages, salaries, taxes, and other items that are paid on a delayed basis. Its temporary investment in assets is financed with temporary (short-term) debt.

**TABLE 15-1  The Hedging Principle Applied to Working-Capital Management**

A firm's asset needs that are not financed by spontaneous sources of financing should be financed in accordance with the following "matching rule" —permanent-asset investments are financed with permanent sources, and temporary-asset investments are financed with temporary sources of financing.

| Classification of a Firm's Investments in Assets | Definitions and Examples | Classification of a Firm's Sources of Financing | Definitions and Examples |
|---|---|---|---|
| Temporary investments | *Definition*: Current assets that will be liquidated and not replaced within the year.<br><br>*Examples*: Seasonal expansions in inventories and accounts receivable. | Spontaneous financing | *Definition*: Financing that arises more or less automatically in response to the purchase of an asset.<br><br>*Examples*: Trade credit that accompanies the purchase of inventories and other types of accounts payable created by the purchase of services (for example, wages payable). |
| | | Temporary financing | *Definition*: Current liabilities other than spontaneous sources of financing.<br><br>*Examples*: Notes payable and revolving credit agreements that must be repaid in a period less than 1 year. |
| Permanent investments | *Definition*: Current and long-term asset investments that the firm expects to hold for a period longer than 1 year.<br><br>*Examples*: Minimum levels of inventory and accounts receivable the firm maintains throughout the year as well as its investments in plant and equipment. | Permanent financing | *Definition*: Long-term liabilities not due and payable within the year and equity financing.<br><br>*Examples*: Term loans, notes, and bonds as well as preferred and common equity. |

## Concept Check

1. What is the hedging principle or principle of self-liquidating debt?
2. What are some examples of permanent and temporary investments in current assets?
3. Is trade credit a permanent, temporary, or spontaneous source of financing? Explain.

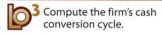 **3** Compute the firm's cash conversion cycle.

# The Cash Conversion Cycle

Because firms vary widely with respect to their ability to manage their net working capital, there exists a need for an overall measure of effectiveness. An increasingly popular method for evaluating the efficient management of a firm's working capital involves minimizing working capital.

Minimizing working capital is accomplished by speeding up the collection of cash from sales, increasing inventory turns, and slowing down the disbursement of cash. We can incorporate all of these factors in a single measure called the *cash conversion cycle*.

The cash conversion cycle, or CCC, is simply the sum of days of sales outstanding and days of sales in inventory less days of payables outstanding:

$$
\begin{array}{c}
\text{Cash} \\
\text{conversion} \\
\text{cycle (CCC)}
\end{array}
=
\begin{array}{c}
\text{days of} \\
\text{sales} \\
\text{outstanding (DSO)}
\end{array}
+
\begin{array}{c}
\text{days of} \\
\text{sales in} \\
\text{inventory (DSI)}
\end{array}
-
\begin{array}{c}
\text{days of} \\
\text{payables} \\
\text{outstanding (DPO)}
\end{array}
$$

We calculate days of sales outstanding as follows:

$$
\begin{array}{c}
\text{Days of} \\
\text{sales} \\
\text{outstanding (DSO)}
\end{array}
=
\frac{\text{accounts receivable}}{\text{sales}/365}
\tag{15-2}
$$

Recall from Chapter 4 that DSO can also be thought of as the average age of the firm's accounts receivable or the average collection period.

Days of sales in inventory is defined as follows:

$$
\begin{array}{c}
\text{Days of} \\
\text{sales} \\
\text{in inventory (DSI)}
\end{array}
=
\frac{\text{inventories}}{\text{cost of goods sold}/365}
\tag{15-3}
$$

Note that DSI can also be thought of as the average age of the firm's inventory, that is, the average number of days that a dollar of inventory is held by the firm.

Days of payables outstanding is defined as follows:

$$
\begin{array}{c}
\text{Days of} \\
\text{payables} \\
\text{outstanding (DPO)}
\end{array}
=
\frac{\text{accounts payable}}{\text{cost of goods sold}/365}
\tag{15-4}
$$

This ratio indicates the average age, in days, of the firm's accounts payable.

To illustrate the use of the CCC metric, consider Dell Computer Corporation. In 1989 Dell was a fledgling start-up whose CCC was 121.88 days. By 1998, Dell had reduced this number to −5.6 days. (See Table 15-2.) How, you might ask, does a firm reduce its CCC below zero? The answer is through very aggressive management of its working capital. As Table 15-2 indicates, Dell achieved this phenomenal reduction in CCC primarily through very effective management of inventories (days of sales in inventories dropped from 37.36

## CAN YOU DO IT?

### COMPUTING THE CASH CONVERSION CYCLE

Harrison Electronics is evaluating its cash conversion cycle and has estimated each of its components as follows:
- Days of sales outstanding (DSO) = 38 days
- Days of sales in inventory (DSI) = 41 days
- Days of payables outstanding (DPO) = 30 days

What is the firm's cash conversion cycle?

(The solution can be found on page 463.)

**TABLE 15-2  The Determinants of Dell Computer Corporation's Cash Conversion Cycle for 1995–2005**

Cash conversion cycle (CCC)  =  days of sales outstanding (DSO)  +  days of sales in inventory (DSI)  −  days of payables outstanding (DPO)

| | 1995 | 1996 | 1997 | 1998 | 1999 | 2000 | 2001 | 2002 | 2003 | 2004 | 2005 |
|---|---|---|---|---|---|---|---|---|---|---|---|
| Days of sales outstanding (DSO) | 50.04 | 42.48 | 44.00 | 49.64 | 38.69 | 33.14 | 26.57 | 26.66 | 32.01 | 32.74 | 35.59 |
| Days of sales in inventory (DSI) | 37.36 | 15.15 | 8.92 | 7.10 | 7.17 | 5.79 | 3.99 | 9.22 | 7.75 | 4.20 | 4.65 |
| Days of payables outstanding (DPO) | 40.58 | 62.79 | 62.87 | 62.34 | 64.92 | 62.07 | 72.87 | 75.79 | 79.41 | 81.46 | 79.41 |
| Cash conversion cycle (CCC) | 46.81 | (5.15) | (9.96) | (5.60) | (19.06) | (23.14) | (42.30) | (39.90) | (39.64) | (44.51) | (39.17) |

in 1995 to 4.65 in 2005) and more favorable trade credit payment practices (days of payables outstanding increased from 40.58 in 1995 to 81.46 in 2004). Specifically, Dell, a direct marketer of personal computers, does not build a computer until an order is received. It purchases its supplies using trade credit. This business model results in minimal investment in inventories. Dell has obviously improved its working-capital management practices, as evidenced in Figure 15-2, where we compare Dell with Apple. Obviously, both firms follow

**FIGURE 15-2  Cash Conversion Cycles for Apple and Dell: 1995–2005**

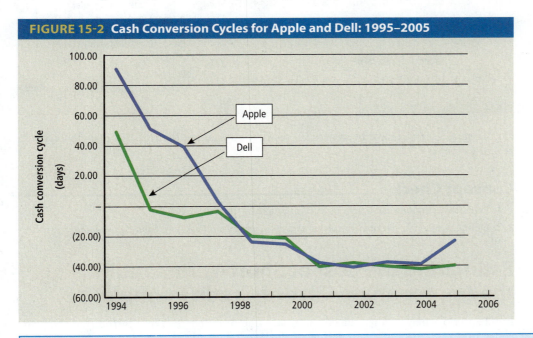

# DID YOU GET IT?
## COMPUTING THE CASH CONVERSION CYCLE

The cash conversion cycle (CCC) is calculated as follows:

$$
\begin{pmatrix} \text{Cash} \\ \text{conversion} \\ \text{cycle (CCC)} \end{pmatrix} = \begin{pmatrix} \text{days of} \\ \text{sales outstanding} \\ \text{(DSO)} \end{pmatrix} + \begin{pmatrix} \text{days of} \\ \text{sales in inventory} \\ \text{(DSI)} \end{pmatrix} - \begin{pmatrix} \text{days of payables} \\ \text{outstanding} \\ \text{(DPO)} \end{pmatrix}
$$

Substituting the following:
   Days sales outstanding (DSO) = 38 days
   Days sales in inventory (DSI) = 41 days
   Days of payables outstanding (DPO) = 30 days
What is the firm's cash conversion cycle?

   Cash conversion cycle (CCC) = 38 days + 41 days − 30 days = 49 days

We calculate the CCC to be 49 days. Harrison can reduce its cash conversion cycle by reducing DSO (for example, offering a cash discount for early payment or simply reducing the firm's credit terms) and DSI (for example, reducing the amount of inventory the firm carries), or by seeking better credit terms that increase its DPO.

## FINANCIAL DECISION TOOLS

| Name of Tool | Formula | | | What It Tells You |
|---|---|---|---|---|
| Cash conversion cycle (CCC) | days of sales outstanding (DSO) | + days of sales in inventory (DSI) | + days of payables outstanding (DPO) | • The number of days that it takes for cash to cycle through the firm<br>• The shorter the cycle, the less money the firm has tied up in working capital |
| Days of sales outstanding (DSO) | $\dfrac{\text{accounts receivable}}{\text{sales/365 days}}$ | | | • The average number of days until credit sales are collected<br>• The lower the number is, the less money the firm has tied up in accounts receivable at any time |
| Days of sales in inventory (DSI) | $\dfrac{\text{inventories}}{\text{cost of goods sold/365 days}}$ | | | • The number of days that an item sits in inventory before being sold<br>• The lower the number, the smaller is the firm's investment in inventories |
| Days of payables outstanding (DPO) | $\dfrac{\text{accounts payable}}{\text{cost of goods sold/365 days}}$ | | | • The number of days that the firm takes to pay its trade credit<br>• The higher the number, the lower is the firm's need for cash to support its investment in current assets |

similar strategies and have been very successful in managing their cash conversion cycle in recent years.

## Concept Check

1. What three actions can a firm take to minimize its net working capital?
2. Define *days of sales outstanding*, *days of sales in inventory*, and *days of payables outstanding*.

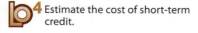 4 Estimate the cost of short-term credit.

# Estimating the Cost of Short-Term Credit Using the Approximate Cost-of-Credit Formula

In Chapter 5 when we introduced the time value of money, we first introduced the principles that underlie the computation of the cost of credit. However, we repeat much of that discussion in this chapter because it is critical to gaining an understanding of how to estimate the cost of short-term credit.

The procedure for estimating the cost of short-term credit is a very simple one and relies on the basic interest equation:

$$\text{Interest} = \text{principal} \times \text{rate} \times \text{time} \tag{15-5}$$

where *interest* is the dollar amount paid by a borrower to a lender in return for the use of the *principal* amount of a loan for a fraction of a year (represented by *time*). For example, a 6-month loan for $1,000 at 8 percent interest would require an interest payment of $40.

$$\text{Interest} = \$1,000 \times 0.08 \times \frac{1}{2} = \$40$$

We use this basic relationship to solve for the cost of a source of short-term financing or the annual percentage rate (*APR*) when the interest amount, the principal sum, and the time period for financing are known. Thus, solving the basic interest equation for *APR* produces[3]

$$APR = \frac{\text{interest}}{\text{principal} \times \text{time}} \tag{15-6}$$

[3]For ease of computation, we assume a 30-day month and 360-day year in this chapter.

or

$$APR = \frac{interest}{principal} \times \frac{1}{time} \qquad (15\text{-}7)$$

This equation, called the *APR* calculation, is clarified by the following example.

---

**EXAMPLE 15.1**   **Estimating the cost of short-term credit**

The SKC Corporation plans to borrow $1,000 for a 90-day period. At maturity the firm will repay the $1,000 principal amount plus $30 interest. The effective annual rate of interest for the loan can be estimated using the APR equation, as follows:

**STEP 1: FORMULATE A SOLUTION STRATEGY**
The cost of short-term credit is estimated using the annual percentage rate (*APR*) formula, which represents the ratio of interest to principal multiplied by the annualized time period fraction of the debt, that is,

$$APR = \frac{interest}{principal} \times \frac{1}{time}$$

Note that interest, in the *APR* equation above, is the product of the principal, interest rate, and time. In this example, the interest payment is adjusted to match the time period of less than 1 year. With the following equation, an annualized interest rate is adjusted so that payments match the time period of the debt,

$$Interest = principal \times rate \times time$$

**STEP 2: CRUNCH THE NUMBERS**
Substituting the characteristics of SKC Corporation's short-term credit, we get the following:

$$APR = \frac{\$30}{\$1,000} \times \frac{1}{90/360}$$

$$= 0.03 \times \frac{360}{90} = 0.12 = 12\%$$

**STEP 3: ANALYZE YOUR RESULTS**
Because SKC Corporation's bondholders require a $30 payment of interest over the 90-day time period for the principal amount of $1,000, the effective cost of borrowing short-term credit is equated by annualizing the bondholders' required rate of return of 3 percent ($30/$1,000) over the four quarters in the year. The effective annual cost of funds provided by the loan is, therefore, 12 percent.

---

The simple *APR* calculation does not consider compound interest. To account for the influence of compounding, we can use the following equation:

$$APY = \left(1 + \frac{i}{m}\right)^m - 1 \qquad (15\text{-}8)$$

where *APY* is the annual percentage yield, $i$ is the nominal rate of interest per year (12 percent in the previous example), and $m$ is the number of compounding periods within a year [$m = 1/time = 1/(90/360) = 4$ in the preceding example]. Thus, the *APY* on the loan in the example problem, considering compounding, is

$$APY = \left(1 + \frac{0.12}{4}\right)^4 - 1 = 0.126 = 12.6\%$$

Compounding effectively raises the cost of short-term credit. Because the differences between *APR* and *APY* are usually small, we use the simple interest values of *APR* to compute the cost of short-term credit.

## CAN YOU DO IT?

### THE APPROXIMATE COST OF SHORT-TERM CREDIT

Hempstead Electric buys its wiring materials in bulk directly from Hamilton Wire and Cable Company. Hamilton offers credit terms that involve a cash discount of 3 percent if payment is received in 30 days. Otherwise, the full amount is due in 90 days. What is the approximate cost of credit to Hempstead if it exceeds 30 days and passes up the cash discount? (The solution can be found below.)

### FINANCIAL DECISION TOOLS

| Name of Tool | Formula | What It Tells You |
|---|---|---|
| Annual percentage rate (APR) | $$\frac{interest}{principal \times time}$$ Interest = dollar interest expense<br>Principal = face amount of credit extended<br>Time = the fraction of time for which credit is extended (e.g., 0.5 for a six-month loan) | • An estimate of the approximate annual cost of short-term credit that does not consider the effects of compounding |
| Annual percentage yield (APY) | $$\left(1 + \frac{\text{nominal rate of interest }(i)}{\text{number of compounding periods per year }(m)}\right)^m - 1$$ | • The compounded annual rate of interest<br>• The cost of short-term (less than one year) credit |

## Concept Check

1. What is the fundamental interest equation that underlies the calculation of the approximate cost-of-credit formula?
2. What is the annual percentage yield (*APY*) and how does it differ from the annual percentage rate (*APR*)?

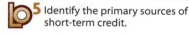 **5** Identify the primary sources of short-term credit.

# Sources of Short-Term Credit

Short-term credit sources can be classified into two basic groups: unsecured and secured. **Unsecured loans** include all those *sources that have as their security only the lender's faith in the ability of the borrower to repay the funds when due.* The major sources of unsecured short-term credit include accrued wages and taxes, trade credit, unsecured bank loans, and commercial paper. A **secured loan** involves the *pledge of specific assets as collateral in the event the borrower defaults in payment of principal or interest.* Commercial banks, finance companies, and factors are the primary suppliers of secured credit. The principal sources of collateral include accounts receivable and inventories.

**unsecured loans** all sources of credit that have as their security only the lender's ability to repay the funds when due.

**secured loans** sources of credit that require security in the form of pledged assets. In the event the borrower defaults in payment of principal or interest, the lender can seize the pledged assets and sell them to settle the debt.

## DID YOU GET IT?

### THE APPROXIMATE COST OF SHORT-TERM CREDIT

If Hempstead chooses to pass up the cash discount, then the cost of credit will reflect the loss of the 3 percent discount so that the firm can use the principal amount of the purchases (that is, 97 percent of each dollar of wire purchased) for a period of 60 days (the difference in the discount period of 30 days and the end of the credit period of 90 days). The *APR* is calculated as follows using equation (15-6):

$$APR = \frac{interest}{principal \times time} = \frac{0.03}{0.97 \times \frac{60}{360}} = 0.1856, \text{ or } 18.56\%$$

# FINANCE AT WORK

## MANAGING WORKING CAPITAL BY TRIMMING RECEIVABLES

LaFarge Corporation is located in Reston, Virginia, and operates in the building materials industry. Last year LaFarge was able to dramatically improve its management of accounts receivable. This improvement is reflected in a decrease in the days of sales outstanding ratio (*DSO*); that is,

$$DSO = \frac{\text{accounts receivable}}{\text{sales}/365}$$

After reviewing this formula, you may recall that we referred to *DSO* in Chapter 4 as the average collection period. The company's success is due in large part to the fact that it ties incentive pay to the return on net assets (*RONA*) as defined here:

$$RONA = \frac{\text{earnings before interest and taxes}}{\text{net assets}}$$

Note that improvements in accounts-receivable management that result in a decrease in *DSO* also lead to a reduction in the firm's net assets and a corresponding increase in *RONA*. Of course, this presumes that the reduction in *DSO* does not have an adverse impact on the firm's revenues and, consequently, earnings.

### How Did They Do It?

Pete Sacripanti, vice president and controller of LaFarge's Calgary-based construction materials business, credits the firm's improved collections to 12 fundamental steps:[a]

1. **Focusing on customers and collections,** which involves all layers of management and is not just a finance responsibility.
2. **Building a base of preferred customers** that confers a competitive advantage.
3. **Delineating clear ownership of customer accounts** among the sales staff, which prevents passing the buck on delinquent accounts.
4. **Fixing clear guidelines** that govern LaFarge's commitments and responsibilities to customers.
5. **Articulating standard sales terms and conditions,** stipulating terms that are negotiable and those that are never negotiable.
6. **Establishing monthly collection targets by salesperson and division,** with collection targets based on the prior month's sales plus past-due accounts.

7. **Training salespeople on customer profitability,** with particular attention to (1) the link between past-due accounts and increased risk of bad debt write-offs, (2) the volume of business required to recover the cost of bad debts, and (3) higher borrowing costs for the company.
8. **Engaging in regular (weekly) credit and collection meetings** with the sales team, the credit manager, and the general manager.
9. **Encouraging constant "in-your-face" executive management,** featuring weekly status updates of collections by salespeople, including key account information.
10. **Facilitating collections through advance phone calls** to establish expected payment amount and availability and to provide a courier to pick up the payments.
11. **Developing collection skills,** including partial holdback releases; offsetting balances owed for services or equipment; use of construction liens, guarantees, letters of credit, and payment bonds; negotiation techniques for securing extras in lieu of write-offs; and better knowledge of the company's products, its industry, and its customers.
12. **Developing unique value** by building stronger relationships with customers, such as air-miles loyalty programs, engineered solutions, quality assurance, and new-product development.

The key thing to note in this list is that each item represents a managerial action aimed at improving the firm's success in collecting its receivables. The *DSO* metric captures the success of these actions, but it is these 12 steps that actually brought about the improvements.

### Measuring Success

LaFarge engaged in a 3-year program aimed at reducing its investment in working capital. The success of the program is most clearly evident in the company's western Canadian construction-materials operation based in Calgary. This unit slashed its working capital by 38 percent to around $36 million while increasing sales by 10 percent to $425 million. The effect on *RONA* was dramatic because the firm simultaneously increased earnings (the numerator of the ratio) and decreased net assets (the denominator).

[a]Based on "Dollars in the Details: The 1999 Working Capital Survey" by S. L. Mintz, CFO.com, July 1, 1999.

## Unsecured Sources: Accrued Wages and Taxes

Because most businesses pay their employees only periodically (weekly, biweekly, or monthly), firms accrue a wages-payable account that is, in essence, a loan from their employees. For example, if the wage expense for the Appleton Manufacturing Company is $450,000 per week and it pays its employees monthly, then by the end of a 4-week month the firm will owe its employees $1.8 million in wages for services they have already performed during the month. Consequently, the employees finance their own efforts by waiting a full month for payment.

Similarly, firms generally make quarterly income tax payments for their estimated quarterly tax liability. This means that the firm has the use of the tax money it owes based on its

## CAN YOU DO IT?

## THE COST OF SHORT-TERM CREDIT (CONSIDERING COMPOUNDING EFFECTS)

Re-evaluate the cost of short-term credit for Hempstead using the annual percentage yield (*APY*), which incorporates compound interest.
(The solution can be found on page 469.)

quarterly profits through the end of the quarter. In addition, the firm pays sales taxes and withholding (income) taxes for its employees on a deferred basis. The longer the period that the firm holds the tax payments, the greater the amount of financing they provide for the firm.

Note that these sources of financing *rise and fall spontaneously* with the level of the firm's sales. That is, as the firm's sales increase, so do its labor expenses, sales taxes collected, and income tax. Consequently, these accrued expense items provide the firm with automatic, or spontaneous, sources of financing.

### Unsecured Sources: Trade Credit

Trade credit provides one of the most flexible sources of short-term financing available to the firm. We previously noted that trade credit is a primary source of spontaneous, or on-demand, financing. That is, trade credit arises spontaneously with the firm's purchases. To arrange for credit, the firm need only place an order with one of its suppliers. The supplier checks the firm's credit and, if it is good, sends the merchandise. The purchasing firm then pays for the goods in accordance with the supplier's credit terms.

**Credit Terms and Cash Discounts**   Very often the credit terms offered with trade credit involve a cash discount for early payment. For example, a supplier might offer terms of 2/10, net 30, which means that a 2 percent discount is offered if payment is made within 10 days or the full amount is due in 30 days. Thus, a 2 percent penalty is involved for not paying within 10 days, or for delaying payment from the tenth to the thirtieth day (that is, for 20 days). The effective annual cost of not taking the cash discount can be quite severe. Using a $1 invoice amount, the effective cost of passing up the discount period using the preceding credit terms and our *APR* equation can be estimated.

$$APR = \frac{\$0.02}{\$0.98} \times \frac{1}{20/360} = 0.3673 = 36.73\%$$

Note that the 2 percent cash discount is the *interest* cost of extending the payment period an *additional* 20 days. Note also that the principal amount of the credit is $0.98. This amount constitutes the full principal amount as of the tenth day of the credit period, after which time the cash discount is lost. The effective cost of passing up the 2 percent discount for 20 days is quite expensive: 36.73 percent. Furthermore, once the discount period has passed, there is no reason to pay before the final due date (the thirtieth day). Table 15-3 lists the effective annual cost of a number of alternative credit terms. Note that the cost of trade credit varies directly with the size of the cash discount and inversely with the length of time between the end of the discount period and the final due date.

**TABLE 15-3**  The Rates of Interest on Selected Trade Credit Terms

| Credit Terms | Effective Rates |
|---|---|
| 2/10, net 60 | 14.69% |
| 2/10, net 90 | 9.18 |
| 3/20, net 60 | 27.84 |
| 6/10, net 90 | 28.72 |

## DID YOU GET IT?

### THE COST OF SHORT-TERM CREDIT (CONSIDERING COMPOUNDING EFFECTS)

Using equation (15-8) we can estimate the cost of short-term credit to Hempstead as follows:

$$APY = \left(1 + \frac{i}{m}\right)^m - 1 = \left(1 + \frac{0.18}{6}\right)^6 - 1 = 0.1941, \text{ or } 19.41\%$$

where *i* is the nominal annual rate of interest. That is, the cash discount is 3 percent and this gets Hempstead an added 60 days or 1/6th of a year. Therefore, the nominal rate of interest for a year is 6 × 0.03, or 18 percent. Considering the effects of compound interest, the cost of short-term credit from deferring payment to Hamilton for wiring until the end of the 90-day credit period is 19.41 percent.

**The Stretching of Trade Credit**   Some firms that use trade credit engage in a practice called *stretching of trade accounts*. This practice involves delaying payments beyond the prescribed credit period. For example, a firm might purchase materials under credit terms of 3/10, net 60; however, when faced with a shortage of cash, the firm might delay payment until the eightieth day. Continued violation of trade terms can eventually lead to a loss of credit. However, for short periods, and at infrequent intervals, stretching offers the firm an emergency source of short-term credit.

**The Advantages of Trade Credit**   As a source of short-term financing, trade credit has a number of advantages. First, trade credit is conveniently obtained as a normal part of the firm's operations. Second, no formal agreements are generally involved in extending credit. Furthermore, the amount of credit extended expands and contracts with the needs of the firm; this is why it is classified as a spontaneous, or on-demand, source of financing.

## Unsecured Sources: Bank Credit

Commercial banks provide unsecured short-term credit in two basic forms: lines of credit and transaction loans (notes payable). Maturities of both types of loans are usually 1 year or less, with rates of interest depending on the creditworthiness of the borrower and the level of interest rates in the economy as a whole.

**Line of Credit**   A **line of credit** is *generally an informal agreement or understanding between the borrower and the bank about the maximum amount of credit that the bank will provide the borrower at any one time.* Under this type of agreement there is *no legal commitment on the part of the bank to provide the credit.* In a **revolving credit agreement**, which is a variant of this form of financing, a *legal obligation is involved.* The line of credit agreement generally covers a period of 1 year corresponding to the borrower's *fiscal* year. Thus, if the borrower is on a July 31 fiscal year, its lines of credit are based on the same annual period.

Lines of credit generally do not involve fixed rates of interest; instead they state that credit will be extended at $\frac{1}{2}$ *percent over prime* or some other spread over the bank's prime rate.[4] Furthermore, the agreement usually does not spell out the specific use that will be made of the funds beyond a general statement, such as *for working-capital purposes.*

Lines of credit usually require that the borrower maintain a *minimum balance in the bank throughout the loan period,* called a **compensating balance**. This required balance (which can be stated as a percentage of the line of credit or the loan amount) increases the effective cost of the loan to the borrower unless a deposit balance equal to or greater than this balance requirement is maintained in the bank.

The effective cost of short-term bank credit can be estimated using the *APR* equation. Consider the following example.

**line of credit** generally an informal agreement or understanding between a borrower and a bank as to the maximum amount of credit the bank will provide the borrower at any one time. Under this type of agreement there is no "legal" commitment on the part of the bank to provide the stated credit.

**revolving credit agreement** an understanding between the borrower and the bank as to the amount of credit the bank will be legally obligated to provide the borrower.

**compensating balance** a balance of a given amount that the firm maintains in its demand deposit account. It may be required by either a formal or an informal agreement with the firm's commercial bank. Such balances are usually required by the bank (1) on the unused portion of a loan commitment, (2) on the unpaid portion of an outstanding loan, or (3) in exchange for certain services provided by the bank, such as check-clearing or credit information. These balances raise the effective rate of interest paid on borrowed funds.

---

[4]The *prime rate of interest* is the rate that a bank charges its most creditworthy borrowers.

### EXAMPLE 15.2    Calculating the effective annual cost of short-term bank credit

M&M Beverage Company has a $300,000 line of credit that requires a compensating balance equal to 20 percent of the loan amount. The rate paid on the loan is 10 percent per annum; $200,000 is borrowed for a 6-month period deposit with the lending bank. The dollar cost of the loan includes the interest expense and the opportunity cost of maintaining an idle cash balance equal to the 20 percent compensating balance. To accommodate the cost of the compensating-balance requirement, assume that the added funds will have to be borrowed and simply left idle in the firm's checking accounts.

#### STEP 1: FORMULATE A SOLUTION STRATEGY

The amount actually borrowed ($B$) will be larger than the $200,000 needed. In fact, the needed $200,000 will constitute 80 percent of the total borrowed funds because of the 20 percent compensating-balance requirement; hence,

$$0.80B = \$200,000, \text{ such that } B = \$250,000$$

Thus, interest is paid on a $250,000 loan, of which only $200,000 is available for use by the firm.[5]

$$\begin{aligned} \text{Interest} &= \text{principal} \times \text{rate} \times \text{time} \\ &= \$250,000 \times 0.10 \times (180/360) = \$12,500 \end{aligned}$$

Note that we use the $250,000 as the principal when calculating the interest payment. The reason is that the firm must borrow the 20 percent compensating balance of $50,000 that is left idle in the firm's checking account.

The effective annual cost of credit, therefore, is calculated using the APR formula:

$$APR = \frac{\text{interest}}{\text{principal}} \times \frac{1}{\text{time}}$$

#### STEP 2: CRUNCH THE NUMBERS

Substituting the characteristics of M&M Beverage Company's bank loan into the *APR* equation above, we get the following:

$$APR = \frac{\$12,500}{\$200,000} \times \frac{1}{180/360} = 0.125 = 12.5\%$$

Note that we use $200,000 as the principal when calculating the annual percentage rate. This amount represents the available portion of the loan, or the effective portion; therefore, we use it to calculate effective annual cost.

#### STEP 3: ANALYZE YOUR RESULTS

In the M&M Beverage Company example, the loan required the payment of principal ($250,000), which includes the 20 percent compensatory balance, plus interest ($12,500), a 10 percent rate, at the end of the 6-month loan period. The effective annual cost of credit was calculated using the ratio of interest ($12,500) to effective principal amount ($200,000). When annualized, this ratio produced an effective annual cost of bank credit of 12.5 percent.

Frequently, bank loans will be made on a discount basis. That is, the loan interest will be deducted from the loan amount before the funds are transferred to the borrower. Extending the M&M Beverage Company example to consider discounted interest involves reducing the effective loan proceeds ($200,000) in the previous example by the amount of interest for the full 6 months ($12,500). The effective rate of interest on the loan is now:

---

[5]The same answer would have been obtained by assuming a total loan of $200,000, of which only 80 percent, or $160,000, was available for use by the firm; that is,

$$APR = \frac{\$10,000}{\$160,000} \times \frac{1}{180/360} = 12.5\%$$

Interest is now calculated on the $200,000 loan amount $\left( \$10,000 = \$200,000 \times 0.10 \times \frac{1}{2} \right)$

$$APR = \frac{\$12,500}{\$200,000 - \$12,500} \times \frac{1}{(180/360)} = 0.1333 = 13.33\%$$

The effect of discounting interest was to raise the cost of the loan from 12.5 percent to 13.33 percent. This results from the fact that the firm pays interest on the same amount of funds as before ($250,000); however, this time it gets the use of $12,500 less, or $200,000 − $12,500 = $187,500.[6]

**Transaction Loans**   Still another form of unsecured short-term bank credit can be obtained in the form of a **transaction loan**. Here the loan is *made for a specific purpose*. This is the type of loan that most individuals associate with bank credit and is obtained by signing a promissory note.

> **transaction loan** a loan where the proceeds are designated for a specific purpose—for example, a bank loan used to finance the acquisition of a piece of equipment.

An unsecured transaction loan is very similar to a line of credit with regard to its cost, term to maturity, and compensating-balance requirements. In both instances commercial banks often require that the borrower *clean up* its short-term loans for a 30- to 45-day period during the year. This means, very simply, that the borrower must be free of any bank debt for the stated period. The purpose of such a requirement is to ensure that the borrower is not using short-term bank credit to finance a part of its permanent needs for funds.

## Unsecured Sources: Commercial Paper

Only the largest and most creditworthy companies are able to use **commercial paper**, which is simply a *short-term promise to pay that is sold in the market for short-term debt securities*.

> **commercial paper** short-term unsecured promissory notes sold by large businesses in order to raise cash. Unlike most other money-market instruments, commercial paper has no developed secondary market.

The maturity of the credit source is generally 6 months or less, although some issues carry 270-day maturities. The interest rate on commercial paper is generally slightly lower ($\frac{1}{2}$ to 1 percent) than the prime rate on commercial bank loans. Also, the interest is usually discounted, although sometimes interest-bearing commercial paper is available.

New issues of commercial paper are either directly placed (sold by the issuing firm directly to the investing public) or dealer placed. A dealer placement involves the use of a commercial paper dealer, who sells the issue for the issuing firm. Many major finance companies, such as General Motors Acceptance Corporation, place their commercial paper directly. The volume of direct versus dealer placements is roughly 4 to 1 in favor of direct placements. Dealers are used primarily by industrial firms that either make only infrequent use of the commercial paper market or, owing to their small size, would have difficulty placing the issue without the help of a dealer.

### Commercial Paper as a Source of Short-Term Credit   Several advantages accrue to the user of commercial paper.

1. **Interest rate.**   Commercial paper rates are generally lower than rates on bank loans and comparable sources of short-term financing.
2. **Compensating-balance requirement.**   No minimum balance requirements are associated with commercial paper. However, issuing firms usually find it desirable to maintain line-of-credit agreements sufficient to back up their short-term financing

---

[6]If M&M needs the use of a full $200,000, then it will have to borrow more than $250,000 to cover both the compensating-balance requirement *and* the discounted interest. In fact, the firm will have to borrow some amount B such that

$$B - 0.2B - \left(0.10 \times \frac{1}{2}\right)B = \$200,000$$

$$0.75B = \$200,000$$

$$B = \frac{\$200,000}{0.75} = \$266,667$$

The cost of credit remains the same at 13.33 percent, as we see here:

$$APR = \frac{\$13,333}{\$266,667 - \$53,333 - \$13,333} \times \frac{1}{180/360}$$

$$= 0.1333 = 13.33\%$$

needs in the event that a new issue of commercial paper cannot be sold or an outstanding issue cannot be repaid when due.

3. **Amount of credit.**   Commercial paper offers the firm with very large credit needs a single source for all its short-term financing. Because of loan amount restrictions placed on the banks by the regulatory authorities, obtaining the necessary funds from a commercial bank might require borrowing from a number of institutions.[7]

4. **Prestige.**   Because it is widely recognized that only the most creditworthy borrowers have access to the commercial paper market, its use signifies a firm's credit status.

Using commercial paper for short-term financing, however, involves a very important risk. The commercial paper market is highly impersonal and denies even the most creditworthy borrower any flexibility in terms of repayment. When bank credit is used, the borrower has someone with whom he or she can work out any temporary difficulties that might be encountered in meeting a loan deadline. This flexibility simply does not exist for the user of commercial paper.

**Estimating the Cost of Using Commercial Paper**   The cost of commercial paper can be estimated using the simple, effective cost-of-credit equation (*APR*). The key points to remember are that commercial paper interest is usually discounted and that if a dealer is used to place the issue, a fee is charged. Even if a dealer is not used, the issuing firm will incur costs associated with preparing and placing the issue, and these costs must be included in estimating the cost of this credit.

---

**EXAMPLE 15.3**   **Calculating the effective cost of credit**

The EPG Manufacturing Company uses commercial paper regularly to support its needs for short-term financing. The firm plans to sell $100 million in 270-day-maturity paper, on which it expects to pay discounted interest at a rate of 12 percent per annum ($9 million). In addition, EPG expects to incur a cost of approximately $100,000 in dealer placement fees and other expenses of issuing the paper. What is the effective cost of credit to EPG?

**STEP 1: FORMULATE A SOLUTION STRATEGY**
EPG's effective cost of credit can be determined using the annual percentage rate formula. By identifying each of the variables and plugging them into the *APR* equation, the following calculation is generated:

$$APR = \frac{\text{interest}}{\text{principal}} \times \frac{1}{\text{time}} \tag{15-7}$$

where interest is calculated using the formula

interest = (principal × rate × time) + financing fees

In this example, interest will represent the interest itself plus any other financing fees. The principal is the total cash received from financing, less any interest costs. Finally, the time period is over 270 days.

**STEP 2: CRUNCH THE NUMBERS**
Substituting the characteristics of EPG's commercial paper financing strategy into equation (15-7) we get the following:

$$APR = \frac{\$9,000,000 + \$100,000}{\$100,000,000 - \$100,000 - \$9,000,000} \times \frac{1}{270/360}$$

$$= 0.1335 = 13.35\%$$

---

[7]Member banks of the Federal Reserve System are limited to 10 percent of their total capital, surplus, and undivided profits when making loans to a single borrower. Thus, when a corporate borrower's needs for financing are very large, it may have to deal with a group of participating banks to raise the needed funds.

where the interest cost is calculated as $100,000,000 \times 0.12 \times (270/360) = $9,000,000$ plus the $100,000 dealer placement fee. Thus, the effective cost of credit to EPG is 13.35 percent.

### STEP 3: ANALYZE YOUR RESULTS

It appears that at the 12 percent discount rate, the commercial paper sale will only return $89,900,000 in cash financing, after the $100,000 of dealer placement fees are included. This means that $9.1 million is the interest cost of financing $89.9 million. In this case, the interest represents 13.35 percent of the total cash received, which therefore represents the effective cost of credit.

## Secured Sources: Accounts-Receivable Loans

Secured sources of short-term credit have certain assets of the firm pledged as collateral to secure the loan. Upon default of the loan agreement, the lender has first claim to the pledged assets in addition to its claim as a general creditor of the firm. Hence, the secured credit agreement offers an added margin of safety to the lender.

Generally, a firm's receivables are among its most liquid assets. For this reason they are considered by many lenders to be prime collateral for a secured loan. Two basic procedures can be used in arranging for financing based on receivables: pledging and factoring.

**Pledging Accounts Receivable**    Under the **pledging accounts receivable** arrangement, the *borrower simply pledges accounts receivable as collateral for a loan obtained from either a commercial bank or a finance company*. The amount of the loan is stated as a percentage of the face value of the receivables pledged. If the firm provides the lender with a *general line* on its receivables, then all of the borrower's accounts are pledged as security for the loan. This method of pledging is simple and inexpensive. However, because the lender has no control over the quality of the receivables being pledged, it will set the maximum loan at a relatively low percentage of the total face value of the accounts, generally ranging downward from a maximum of around 75 percent.

> **pledging accounts receivable** a loan the firm obtains from a commercial bank or a finance company using its accounts receivable as collateral.

Still another approach to pledging involves the borrower presenting specific invoices to the lender as collateral for a loan. This method is somewhat more expensive because the lender must assess the creditworthiness of each individual account pledged; however, given this added knowledge, the lender should be willing to increase the loan as a percentage of the face value of the invoices. In this case the loan might reach as high as 85 or 90 percent of the face value of the pledged receivables.

*Credit Terms*    Accounts-receivable loans generally carry an interest rate that is 2 to 5 percent higher than the bank's prime lending rate. Finance companies charge an even higher rate. In addition, the lender usually charges a handling fee stated as a percentage of the face value of the receivables processed, which may be as much as 1 to 2 percent of the face value.

---

| **EXAMPLE 15.4** | **Calculating the annual percentage rate of short-term lender credit** |

The A. B. Good Company sells electrical supplies to building contractors on terms of net 60. The firm's average monthly sales are $100,000; thus, given the firm's 2-month credit terms, its average receivables balance is $200,000. The firm pledges all of its receivables to a local bank, which in turn advances up to 70 percent of the face value of the receivables at 3 percent over prime and charges a 1 percent processing fee on all receivables pledged. A. B. Good follows a practice of borrowing the maximum amount possible, and the current prime rate is 10 percent. What is the *APR* of using this source of financing for a full year?

## STEP 1: FORMULATE A SOLUTION STRATEGY

In this example, the same annual percentage rate formula is used. However, the key is identifying the correct characteristics to use as variables in the equation:

$$\text{Annual percentage rate} = \frac{\text{interest}}{\text{principal}} \times \frac{1}{\text{time}} \tag{15-7}$$

Note that we can calculate interest by adding the interest expense plus the annual processing fee. The principal will be represented by the actual amount of credit extended. Finally, our time period should be over the full year:

$$APR = \frac{\text{interest expense} + \text{processing fee}}{\text{credit extended}} \times \frac{1}{\text{time}}$$

## STEP 2: CRUNCH THE NUMBERS

Once we substitute the correct variables from above into the equation, we get the following result:

$$APR = \frac{\$18,200 + \$12,000}{\$140,000} \times \frac{1}{360/360} = 0.2157 = 21.57\%$$

where the total dollar cost of the loan consists of both the annual interest expense ($0.13 \times 0.70 \times \$200,000 = \$18,200$) and the annual processing fee ($0.01 \times \$100,000 \times 12$ months $= \$12,000$). The amount of credit extended is $0.70 \times \$200,000 = \$140,000$. Note that the processing charge applies to all receivables pledged. Thus, the A. B. Good Company pledges $100,000 each month, or $1,200,000 during the year, on which a 1 percent fee must be paid, for a total annual charge of $12,000.

## STEP 3: ANALYZE YOUR RESULTS

It appears that A. B. Good Company's lender charges a rate of about 14 percent (13 percent interest and 1 percent annual processing fee) for the 70 percent of receivables for which they give a receivables advance. In this example the effective *APR* is actually more than this charge of 14 percent, because of the discounted amount of the receivables advance. Since only 70 percent of the receivables are actually credited, the effective *APR* is increased to account for the 30 percent of receivables for which no advance is given.

One more point: The lender, in addition to making advances or loans, may be providing certain credit services to the borrower. For example, the lender may provide billing and collection services. The value of these services should be considered in computing the cost of credit. In the preceding example, A. B. Good Company may save $10,000 per year in credit department expenses by pledging all of its accounts and letting the lender provide those services. In this case, the cost of short-term credit is only:

$$APR = \frac{\$18,200 + \$12,000 - \$10,000}{\$140,000} \times \frac{1}{360/360} = 0.1443 = 14.43\%$$

***The Advantages and Disadvantages of Pledging***  The primary advantage of pledging as a source of short-term credit is the flexibility it provides the borrower. Financing is available on a continuous basis. The new accounts created through credit sales provide the collateral for the financing of new production. Furthermore, the lender may provide credit services that eliminate or at least reduce the need for similar services within the firm. The primary disadvantage associated with this method of financing is its cost, which can be relatively high compared with other sources of short-term credit, owing to the level of the interest rate charged on loans and the processing fee on pledged accounts.

**Factoring Accounts Receivable**    **Factoring accounts receivable** involves the *outright sale of a firm's accounts to a financial institution called a factor*. A **factor** is *a firm that acquires the receivables of other firms*. The factoring institution might be a commercial finance company that engages solely in the factoring of receivables (known as an *old-line factor*) or it might be a commercial bank. The factor, in turn, bears the risk of collection and, for a fee, services the accounts. The fee is stated as a percentage of the face value of all receivables factored (usually 1 to 3 percent).

The factor firm typically does *not* make payment for factored accounts until the accounts have been collected or the credit terms have been met. Should the firm wish to receive immediate payment for its factored accounts, it can borrow from the factor, using the factored accounts as collateral. The maximum loan the firm can obtain is equal to the face value of its factored accounts less the factor's fee (1 to 3 percent) less a reserve (6 to 10 percent) less the interest on the loan. For example, if $100,000 in receivables is factored, carrying 60-day credit terms, a 2 percent factor's fee, a 6 percent reserve, and interest at 1 percent per month on advances, then the maximum loan or advance the firm can receive is computed as follows:

| | |
|---|---|
| Face amount of receivables factored | $100,000 |
| Less: Fee (0.02 × $100,000) | (2,000) |
| Reserve (0.06 × $100,000) | (6,000) |
| Interest (0.01 × $92,000 × 2 months) | (1,840) |
| Maximum advance | $ 90,160 |

Note that interest is discounted and calculated based on a maximum amount of funds available for advance ($92,000 = $100,000 − $2,000 − $6,000). Thus, the effective cost of credit can be calculated as follows:

$$APR = \frac{\$1,840 + \$2,000}{\$90,160} \times \frac{1}{60/360}$$
$$= 0.2555 = 25.55\%$$

## Secured Sources: Inventory Loans

**Inventory loans**, or *loans secured by inventories*, provide a second source of security for short-term credit. The amount of the loan that can be obtained depends on both the marketability and perishability of the inventory. Some items, such as raw materials (grains, oil, lumber, and chemicals), are excellent sources of collateral, because they can easily be liquidated. Other items, such as work-in-process inventories, provide very poor collateral because of their lack of marketability.

There are several methods by which inventory can be used to secure short-term financing. These include a floating, or blanket, lien, a chattel mortgage, a field-warehouse receipt, and a terminal-warehouse receipt.

Under a **floating lien agreement**, *the borrower gives the lender a lien against all of its inventories*. This provides the simplest but least secure form of inventory collateral. The borrowing firm maintains full control of the inventories and continues to sell and replace them as it sees fit. Obviously, this lack of control over the collateral greatly dilutes the value of this type of security to the lender.

Under a **chattel mortgage agreement**, *the inventory is identified* (by serial number or otherwise) *in the security agreement, and the borrower retains title to the inventory but cannot sell the items without the lender's consent.*

Under a **field-warehouse agreement**, *inventories used as collateral are physically separated from the firm's other inventories and are placed under the control of a third-party field-warehousing firm.*

**factoring accounts receivable** the outright sale of a firm's accounts receivable to another party (the factor) without recourse. The factor, in turn, bears the risk of collection.

**factor** a firm that, in acquiring the receivables of other firms, bears the risk of collection and, for a fee, services the accounts.

**inventory loans** loans secured by inventories. Examples include floating or blanket lien agreements, chattel mortgage agreements, field-warehouse receipt loans, and terminal-warehouse receipt loans.

**floating lien agreement** an agreement, generally associated with a loan, whereby the borrower gives the lender a lien against all its inventory.

**chattel mortgage agreement** a loan agreement in which the lender can increase his or her security interest by having specific items of inventory identified in the loan agreement. The borrower retains title to the inventory but cannot sell the items without the lender's consent.

**field-warehouse agreement** a security agreement in which inventories pledged as collateral are physically separated from the firm's other inventories and placed under the control of a third-party field-warehousing firm.

**terminal-warehouse agreement** a security agreement in which the inventories pledged as collateral are transported to a public warehouse that is physically removed from the borrower's premises. This is the safest (though costly) form of financing secured by inventory.

A **terminal-warehouse agreement** differs from a field-warehouse agreement in only one respect. Here *the inventories pledged as collateral are transported to a public warehouse that is physically removed from the borrower's premises.* The lender has an added degree of safety or security because the inventory is totally removed from the borrower's control. Once again the cost of this type of arrangement is increased because the warehouse firm must be paid by the borrower; in addition, the inventory must be transported to and, eventually, from the public warehouse.

## Concept Check

1. What are some examples of unsecured and secured sources of short-term credit?
2. What is the difference between a line of credit and a revolving credit agreement?
3. What are the types of credit agreements a firm can get that are secured by its accounts receivable as collateral?
4. What are some examples of loans secured by a firm's inventories?

# Chapter Summaries

## Describe the risk-return trade-off involved in managing working capital.
(pgs. 457–458)

**SUMMARY:** Working-capital management involves managing the firm's liquidity, which in turn involves managing (1) the firm's investment in current assets and (2) its use of current liabilities. Each of these problems involves risk–return trade-offs. Investing in current assets reduces the firm's risk of illiquidity at the expense of lowering its overall rate of return on its investment in assets. By contrast, the use of long-term sources of financing enhances the firm's liquidity while reducing its rate of return on assets.

### KEY TERMS

**Working capital, page 457** A concept traditionally defined as a firm's investment in current assets.

**Net working capital, page 457** The difference between the firm's current assets and its current liabilities.

### KEY EQUATION

Net working capital = current assets − current liabilities

## Describe the determinants of net working capital. (pgs. 459–462)

**SUMMARY:** A firm's net working capital is determined by its need for current assets and the sources of financing it uses to acquire them. In deciding on the sources of financing, it is important to note that the firm gets some financing automatically from the firm's suppliers in the form of accounts payable. However, the firm typically needs more financing, which can come in the form of short- (less than 1 year) or long-term financing. Using short-term sources is often cheaper than long-term sources but adds risk as the firm is faced with a near-term maturity that must be repaid. The hedging principle, or principle of self-liquidating debt, offers the financial manager one tool for resolving this financing problem. Basically, this methodology requires that the firm match up the maturities of its liabilities with the maturity of its asset needs. For example, if the firm has a seasonal and temporary need to raise its inventories and accounts receivable (for example, a retailer at Christmas) then short-term financing is appropriate. However, if the firm has a more permanent need to increase its current assets, then long-term financing should be used.

## KEY TERMS

**Hedging principle (principle of self-liquidating debt), page 459** A working-capital management policy which states that the cash-flow-generating characteristics of a firm's investments should be matched with the cash-flow requirements of the firm's sources of financing. Very simply, short-lived assets should be financed with short-term sources of financing while long-lived assets should be financed with long-term sources of financing.

**Permanent investment, page 459** Investments that the firm expects to hold longer than 1 year. The firm makes permanent investments in fixed and current assets.

**Temporary investments, page 459** A firm's investments in current assets that will be liquidated and not replaced within a period of 1 year or less. Examples include seasonal expansions in inventories and accounts receivable.

**Trade credit, page 460** Credit made available by a firm's suppliers in conjunction with the acquisition of materials. Trade credit appears on the balance sheet as accounts payable.

---

## Compute the firm's cash conversion cycle. (pgs. 462–464)

**SUMMARY:** The cash conversion cycle is a key measure of how efficiently the firm is in managing its net working capital. Specifically, the cash conversion cycle equals the number of days it takes to collect on credit sales, plus the number of days items are in inventory, less the number of days that payables are outstanding. The importance of the length of the conversion cycle is that this is the number of days that the firm has money tied up in inventories and accounts receivable. The longer is this period, other things being the same, the more money the firm must invest in current assets.

## KEY EQUATIONS

$$\text{Cash conversion cycle (CCC)} = \text{days of sales outstanding (DSO)} + \text{days of sales in inventory (DSI)} - \text{days of payables outstanding (DPO)}$$

$$\text{Days of sales outstanding (DSO)} = \frac{\text{accounts receivable}}{\text{sales}/365}$$

$$\text{Days of sales in inventory (DSI)} = \frac{\text{inventories}}{\text{cost of goods sold}/365}$$

$$\text{Days of payables outstanding (DPO)} = \frac{\text{accounts payable}}{\text{cost of goods sold}/365}$$

---

## Estimate the cost of short-term credit. (pgs. 464–466)

**SUMMARY:** The key consideration in selecting a source of short-term financing is the effective cost of credit. Since short-term credit is, by definition, extended for a period less than 1 year, the analyst must adjust the interest paid for the term of the financing (less than 1 year) in order to compute an annual rate of interest. The adjustment can assume simple interest (that is, not compounded) to compute the annual percentage rate (*APR*) or the adjustment can account for compound interest, in which case we compute the annual percentage yield (*APY*).

**KEY EQUATIONS**

$$\text{Interest} = \text{principal} \times \text{rate} \times \text{time}$$

$$\begin{array}{c}\text{Annual percentage} \\ \text{rate } (APR)\end{array} = \frac{\text{interest}}{\text{principal} \times \text{time}}$$

$$\begin{array}{c}\text{Annual percentage} \\ \text{rate } (APR)\end{array} = \frac{\text{interest}}{\text{principal}} \times \frac{1}{\text{time}}$$

$$\begin{array}{c}\text{Annual percentage} \\ \text{yield } (APY)\end{array} = \left(1 + \frac{i}{m}\right)^m - 1$$

 **5**  **Identify the primary sources of short-term credit.**  (pgs. 466–476)

**SUMMARY:** The various sources of short-term credit can be categorized into two groups: unsecured and secured. Unsecured credit offers no specific assets as security for the loan agreement. The primary sources include trade credit, lines of credit, unsecured transaction loans from commercial banks, and commercial paper. Secured credit is generally provided to business firms by commercial banks, finance companies, and factors. The most popular sources of security involve the use of accounts receivable and inventories. Loans secured by accounts receivable include pledging agreements, in which a firm pledges its receivables as security for a loan, and factoring agreements, in which the firm sells the receivables to a factor. In a pledging arrangement, the lender retains the right of recourse in the event of default, whereas in factoring, a lender is generally without recourse. Loans secured by inventories can be made using one of several types of security arrangements. Among the most widely used are the floating lien, chattel mortgage, field-warehouse agreement, and terminal-warehouse agreement. The form of agreement used depends on the type of inventories pledged as collateral and the degree of control the lender wishes to exercise over the collateral.

**KEY TERMS**

**Unsecured loans, page 466** All sources of credit that have as their security only the lender's faith in the borrower's ability to repay the funds when due.

**Secured loans, page 466** Sources of credit that require security in the form of pledged assets. In the event the borrower defaults in payment of principal or interest, the lender can seize the pledged assets and sell them to settle the debt.

**Line of credit, page 469** Generally an informal agreement or understanding between a borrower and a bank as to the maximum amount of credit the bank will provide the borrower at any one time. Under this type of agreement there is no "legal" commitment on the part of the bank to provide the stated credit.

**Revolving credit agreement, page 469** An understanding between the borrower and the bank as to the amount of credit the bank will be legally obligated to provide the borrower.

**Compensating balance, page 469** A balance of a given amount that the firm maintains in its demand deposit account. It may be required by either a formal or an informal agreement with the firm's commercial bank. Such balances are usually required by the bank (1) on the unused portion of a loan commitment, (2) on the unpaid portion of an outstanding loan, or (3) in

exchange for certain services provided by the bank, such as check-clearing or credit information. These balances raise the effective rate of interest paid on borrowed funds.

**Transaction loan, page 471** A loan where the proceeds are designated for a specific purpose—for example, a bank loan used to finance the acquisition of a piece of equipment.

**Commercial paper, page 471** Short-term unsecured promissory notes sold by large businesses in order to raise cash. Unlike most other money-market instruments, commercial paper has no developed secondary market.

**Pledging accounts receivable, page 473** A loan the firm obtains from a commercial bank or a finance company using its accounts receivable as collateral.

**Factoring accounts receivable, page 475** The outright sale of a firm's accounts receivable to another party (the factor) without recourse. The factor, in turn, bears the risk of collection.

**Factor, page 475** A firm that, in acquiring the receivables of other firms, bears the risk of collection and, for a fee, services the accounts.

**Inventory loans, page 475** Loans secured by inventories. Examples include floating or blanket lien agreements, chattel mortgage agreements, field-warehouse receipt loans, and terminal-warehouse receipt loans.

**Floating lien agreement, page 475** An agreement, generally associated with a loan, whereby the borrower gives the lender a lien against all its inventory.

**Chattel mortgage agreement, page 475** A loan agreement in which the lender can increase his or her security interest by having specific items of inventory identified in the loan agreement. The borrower retains title to the inventory but cannot sell the items without the lender's consent.

**Field-warehouse agreement, page 475** A security agreement in which inventories pledged as collateral are physically separated from the firm's other inventories and placed under the control of a third-party field-warehousing firm.

**Terminal-warehouse agreement, page 476** A security agreement in which the inventories pledged as collateral are transported to a public warehouse that is physically removed from the borrower's premises. This is the safest (though costly) form of financing secured by inventory.

# Review Questions

*All Review Questions are available in* MyFinanceLab.

**15-1.** Dell Computer Corporation (DELL) has long been recognized for its innovative approach to managing its working capital. Describe how Dell pioneered the management of net working capital to free up resources in the firm.

**15-2.** Define and contrast the terms *working capital* and *net working capital*.

**15-3.** Discuss the risk–return relationship involved in the firm's asset-investment decisions as that relationship pertains to its working-capital management.

**15-4.** What advantages and disadvantages are generally associated with the use of short-term debt? Discuss.

**15-5.** Explain what is meant by the statement "The use of current liabilities as opposed to long-term debt subjects the firm to a greater risk of illiquidity."

**15-6.** Define the hedging principle. How can this principle be used in the management of working capital?

**15-7.** Define the following terms:
   a. Permanent asset investments
   b. Temporary asset investments
   c. Permanent sources of financing
   d. Temporary sources of financing
   e. Spontaneous sources of financing

**15-8.** How can the formula "interest = principle × rate × time" be used to estimate the cost of short-term credit?

**15-9.** How can we accommodate the effects of compounding in our calculation of the effective cost of short-term credit?

**15-10.** There are three major sources of unsecured short-term credit other than accrued wages and taxes. List and discuss the distinguishing characteristics of each.

**15-11.** What is meant by the following trade credit terms: 2/10, net 30? 4/20, net 60? 3/15, net 45?

**15-12.** Define the following:
   a. Line of credit
   b. Commercial paper
   c. Compensating balance
   d. Prime rate

# Study Problems

*All Study Problems are available in* MyFinanceLab.

**15-1.** (*Risk–return trade-off*) The Carton Packing Company (CPC) is located in rapidly growing Austin, Texas. To meet its need for funds to finance its growing assets the firm has reinvested earnings and borrowed using short-term bank notes. Balance sheets for the last 5 years are found below:

**Carton Packing Company Balance Sheets**

|  | 2010 | 2011 | 2012 | 2013 | 2014 |
|---|---|---|---|---|---|
| Current assets | $100 | $130 | $160 | $190 | $220 |
| Fixed assets | 250 | 270 | 290 | 310 | 330 |
| Total | $350 | $400 | $450 | $500 | $550 |
| Current liabilities | $ 50 | $ 90 | $130 | $170 | $210 |
| Long-term liabilities | 100 | 100 | 100 | 100 | 100 |
| Owners' equity | 200 | 210 | 220 | 230 | 240 |
| Total | $350 | $400 | $450 | $500 | $550 |

a. Compute CPC's current ratio (current assets divided by current liabilities) and the firm's debt ratio (current plus long-term liabilities divided by total assets) for the 5-year period found above. Describe the firm's risk using both the current ratio and debt ratio.

b. Alter the financial statements above such that current liabilities remain constant at $50 and long-term liabilities increase in the amount needed to meet the firm's financing requirements. Compute CPC's current ratio (current assets divided by current liabilities) and the firm's debt ratio (current plus long-term liabilities divided by total assets) using the revised financial statements you have prepared for the 5-year period 2010–2014. Describe the firm's risk using both the current ratio and debt ratio.

c. Which of the financing plans is more risky? Why?

**15-2.** (*Hedging principle*) A popular theory for managing risk to the firm that arises out of its management of working capital (that is, current assets and current liabilities) involves following something called the principle of self-liquidating debt. How would this principle be applied in each of the following situations? Explain your responses to each alternative.

a. Longleaf Homes owns a chain of senior housing complexes in the Seattle, Washington, area. The firm is presently debating whether it should borrow short or long term to raise $10 million in needed funds. The funds are to be used to expand the firm's care facilities, which are expected to last 20 years.

b. Arrow Chemicals needs $5 million to purchase inventory to support its growing sales volume. Arrow does not expect the need for additional inventory to diminish in the future.

c. Blocker Building Materials, Inc. is reviewing its plans for the coming year and expects that during the months of November through January it will need an additional $5 million to finance the seasonal expansion in inventories and receivables.

**15-3.** (*Cash conversion cycle*) Sims Electric Corp. has been striving for the last 5 years to improve its management of working capital. Historical data for the firm's sales, accounts receivable, inventories, and accounts payable follow:

**Sims Electric Corp. Financial Data**

|  | JAN-10 | JAN-11 | JAN-12 | JAN-13 | JAN-14 |
|---|---|---|---|---|---|
| Sales—Net | 2,873 | 3,475 | 5,296 | 7,759 | 12,327 |
| Receivables | 411 | 538 | 726 | 903 | 1,486 |
| Accounts payable | 283 | 447 | 466 | 1,040 | 1,643 |
| Inventories | 220 | 293 | 429 | 251 | 233 |

a. Calculate Sims' days of sales outstanding and days of sales in inventory for each of the 5 years. What has Sims accomplished in its attempts to better manage its investments in accounts receivable and inventory?

b. Calculate Sims' cash conversion cycle for each of the 5 years. Evaluate Sims' overall management of its working capital.

**15-4.** (*Estimating the cost of bank credit*) Paymaster Enterprises has arranged to finance its seasonal working-capital needs with a short-term bank loan. The loan will carry a rate of 12 percent per annum with interest paid in advance (discounted). In addition, Paymaster must maintain a minimum demand deposit with the bank of 10 percent of the loan balance throughout the term of the loan. If Paymaster plans to borrow $100,000 for a period of 3 months, what is the cost of the bank loan?

**15-5.** (*Cost of short-term financing*) The R. Morin Construction Company needs to borrow $100,000 to help finance the cost of a new $150,000 hydraulic crane used in the firm's commercial construction business. The crane will pay for itself in 1 year, and the firm is considering the following alternatives for financing its purchase:

**Alternative A**—The firm's bank has agreed to lend the $100,000 at a rate of 14 percent. Interest would be discounted and a 15 percent compensating balance would be required. However, the compensating-balance requirement would not be binding on R. Morin because the firm normally maintains a minimum demand deposit (checking account) balance of $25,000 in the bank.

**Alternative B**—The equipment dealer has agreed to finance the equipment with a 1-year loan. The $100,000 loan would require payment of principal and interest totaling $116,300.

a.  Which alternative should R. Morin select?
b.  If the bank's compensating-balance requirement were to necessitate idle demand deposits equal to 15 percent of the loan, what effect would this have on the cost of the bank loan alternative?

**15-6.** (*Cost of secured short-term credit*) The Sean-Janeow Import Co. needs $500,000 for the 3-month period ending September 30, 2013. The firm has explored two possible sources of credit.

a.  S-J has arranged with its bank for a $500,000 loan secured by its accounts receivable. The bank has agreed to advance S-J 80 percent of the value of its pledged receivables at a rate of 11 percent plus a 1 percent fee based on all receivables pledged. S-J's receivables average a total of $1 million year-round.
b.  An insurance company has agreed to lend the $500,000 at a rate of 9 percent per annum, using a loan secured by S-J's inventory of salad oil. A field-warehouse agreement would be used, which would cost S-J $2,000 a month. Which source of credit should S-J select? Explain.

**15-7.** (*Cost of short-term financing*) You plan to borrow $20,000 from the bank to pay for inventories for a gift shop you have just opened. The bank offers to lend you the money at 10 percent annual interest for the 6 months the funds will be needed.

a.  Calculate the effective rate of interest on the loan.
b.  In addition, the bank requires you to maintain a 15 percent compensating balance in the bank. Because you are just opening your business, you do not have a demand deposit account at the bank that can be used to meet the compensating-balance requirement. This means that you will have to put up 15 percent of the loan amount from your own personal money (which you had planned to use to help finance the business) in a checking account. What is the cost of the loan now?
c.  In addition to the compensating-balance requirement in part (b), you are told that interest will be discounted. What is the effective rate of interest on the loan now?

**15-8.** (*Estimating the cost of commercial paper*) On February 3, 2012, the Burlington Western Company plans a commercial paper issue of $20 million. The firm has never used commercial paper before but has been assured by the firm placing the issue that it will have no difficulty raising the funds. The commercial paper will carry a 270-day maturity and require interest based on a rate of 11 percent per annum. In addition, the firm will have to pay fees totaling $200,000 to bring the issue to market and place it. What is the effective cost of the commercial paper to Burlington Western?

**15-9.** (*Cost of trade credit*) Calculate the effective cost of the following trade credit terms when payment is made on the net due date:

a.  2/10, net 30
b.  3/15, net 30
c.  3/15, net 45
d.  2/15, net 60

**15-10.** (*Annual percentage yield*) Compute the cost of the trade credit terms in problem 15-3 using the compounding formula, or effective annual rate.

**15-11.** (*Cost of short-term bank loan*) On July 1, 2013, the Southwest Forging Corporation arranged for a line of credit with the First National Bank of Dallas. The terms of the agreement call for a $100,000 maximum loan with interest set at 1 percent over prime. In addition, the firm has to maintain a 20 percent compensating balance in its demand deposit account throughout the year. The prime rate is currently 12 percent.

    a. If Southwest normally maintains a $20,000 to $30,000 balance in its checking account with FNB of Dallas, what is the effective cost of credit under the line-of-credit agreement when the maximum loan amount is used for a full year?

    b. Recompute the effective cost of credit if the firm borrows the compensating balance and the maximum possible amount under the loan agreement. Again, assume the full amount of the loan is outstanding for a whole year.

**15-12.** (*Cost of commercial paper*) Tri-State Enterprises plans to issue commercial paper for the first time in the firm's 35-year history. The firm plans to issue $500,000 in 180-day maturity notes. The paper will carry a 10 1/2 percent rate with discounted interest and will cost Tri-State $12,000 (paid in advance) to issue.

    a. What is the effective cost of credit to Tri-State?

    b. What other factors should the company consider in analyzing whether to issue the commercial paper?

**15-13.** (*Cost of accounts receivable*) Johnson Enterprises Inc. is involved in the manufacture and sale of electronic components used in small AM/FM radios. The firm needs $300,000 to finance an anticipated expansion in receivables due to increased sales. Johnson's credit terms are net 60, and its average monthly credit sales are $200,000. In general, the firm's customers pay within the credit period; thus, the firm's average accounts-receivable balance is $400,000. Chuck Idol, Johnson's comptroller, approached the firm's bank with a request for a loan for the $300,000 using the firm's accounts receivable as collateral. The bank offered to make a loan at a rate of 2 percent over prime plus a 1 percent processing charge on all receivables pledged ($200,000 per month). Furthermore, the bank agreed to lend up to 75 percent of the face value of the receivables pledged.

    a. Estimate the cost of the receivables loan to Johnson when the firm borrows the $300,000. The prime rate is currently 11 percent.

    b. Idol also requested a line of credit for $300,000 from the bank. The bank agreed to grant the necessary line of credit at a rate of 3 percent over prime and required a 15 percent compensating balance. Johnson currently maintains an average demand deposit of $80,000. Estimate the cost of the line of credit to Johnson.

    c. Which source of credit should Johnson select? Why?

**15-14.** (*Cost of factoring*) MDM Inc. is considering factoring its receivables. The firm has credit sales of $400,000 per month and has an average receivables balance of $800,000 with 60-day credit terms.

    The factor has offered to extend credit equal to 90 percent of the receivables factored less interest on the loan at the rate of 1.5 percent per month. The 10 percent difference in the advance and the face value of all receivables factored consists of a 1 percent factoring fee plus a 9 percent reserve, which the factor maintains. In addition, if MDM Inc. decides to factor its receivables, it will sell them all so that it can reduce its credit department costs by $1,500 a month.

    a. What is the cost of borrowing the maximum amount of credit available to MDM Inc. through the factoring agreement?

    b. What considerations other than cost should be accounted for by MDM Inc. in determining whether to enter the factoring agreement?

**15-15.** (*Cost of factoring*) A factor has agreed to lend the JVC Corporation working capital on the following terms: JVC's receivables average $100,000 per month and have a 90-day average collection period. (Note that JVC's credit terms call for payment in 90 days, and accounts receivable average $300,000 because of the 90-day average collection period.) The factor will charge 12 percent interest on any advance (1 percent per month paid in advance) and a 2 percent processing fee on all receivables factored and will maintain a 20 percent reserve. If JVC undertakes the loan, it will reduce its own credit department expenses by $2,000 per month. What is the annual effective rate of interest to JVC on the factoring arrangement? Assume that the maximum advance is taken.

**15-16.** (*Cost of a short-term bank loan*) Jimmy Hale is the owner and operator of the grain elevator in Brownfield, Texas, where he has lived for most of his 62 years. The rains during the spring have been the best in a decade, and Mr. Hale is expecting a bumper wheat crop. This prompted him to rethink his current financing sources. He now believes he will need an additional $240,000 for the 3-month period ending with the close of the harvest season. After meeting with his banker, Mr. Hale is puzzling over what the additional financing will actually cost. The banker quoted him a rate of 1 percent over prime (which is currently 7 percent) and also requested that the firm increase its current bank balance of $4,000 up to 20 percent of the loan.

a.  If interest and principal are all repaid at the end of the 3-month loan term, what is the annual percentage rate on the loan offer made by Mr. Hale's bank?

b.  If the bank were to lower the rate to prime if interest is discounted, should Mr. Hale accept this alternative?

---

**15-17.** (*Terminology*) Identify each of the following sources of short-term credit in terms of whether they are secured (include some type of collateral) or are unsecured:

- ◆ Line of credit
- ◆ Pledging of accounts receivable
- ◆ Trade credit
- ◆ Factoring of accounts receivable
- ◆ Inventory loans
- ◆ Commercial paper

# 16

# International Business Finance

## Learning Objectives

| | | |
|---|---|---|
| 1 | **Discuss** the internationalization of business. | **The Globalization of Product and Financial Markets** |
| 2 | **Explain** why foreign exchange rates in two different countries must be in line with each other. | **Foreign Exchange Markets and Currency Exchange Rates** |
| 3 | **Discuss** the concept of interest rate parity. | **Interest Rate Parity** |
| 4 | **Explain** the purchasing-power parity theory and the law of one price. | **Purchasing-Power Parity and the Law of One Price** |
| 5 | **Discuss** the risks that are unique to the capital-budgeting analysis of direct foreign investment. | **Capital Budgeting for Direct Foreign Investment** |

It is generally easier for firms to expand the market for their products rather than develop new products, which is why most large companies look for new markets around the world. That's certainly been the direction that McDonald's (MCD) has taken in recent years. Today, McDonald's operates more than 33,000 restaurants in over 123 countries. The busiest McDonald's restaurant in the world is not in America but thousands of miles away in Pushkin Square in Moscow, Russia. The store serves 40,000 customers a day, even more than it did on its opening day, January 31, 1990. The menu is essentially the same as in the United States, with the addition of cabbage pie among other traditional Russian food items.

Was this an expensive venture? It certainly was. In fact, the food plants that McDonald's built to supply burgers, fries, and everything else sold there cost more than $60 million. In addition to the costs, there are a number of other factors that make opening an outlet outside of the United States both different and challenging. First, in order to keep the quality consistent with what is served at any McDonald's anywhere else in the world, McDonald's spent 6 years putting together a supply chain that would provide the necessary raw materials McDonald's demands. On top of that, there are risks associated with the Russian economy and its currency that are well beyond the scope of the risk exposures in the United States.

These risks all materialized in 1998 when the Russian economy, along with its currency, the ruble, tanked. In the summer of 1998, the Russian economy spun out of control, and in August the entire banking system failed, resulting in a catastrophic decline in the value of the ruble. Because McDonald's sells its Russian burgers for rubles, when it came time to trade the rubles for U.S. dollars, McDonald's Russian outlets were not worth

nearly as much as they were the year before. In spite of all this, the Moscow McDonald's has proven to be enormously successful since it opened. In fact, by 2012 there were 314 McDonald's restaurants in Russia with plans to open 40 to 45 new locations each year. It all goes to show that not all new investment opportunities require new products; introducing existing products to new international markets can be equally or even more profitable.

This chapter highlights the complications that an international business faces when it deals in multiple currencies. Effective strategies for reducing foreign exchange risk are discussed. Working-capital management and capital structure decisions in the international context are also covered.

## The Globalization of Product and Financial Markets

 Discuss the internationalization of business.

To say the least, the market for most products crosses many borders. In fact, some industries and states are highly dependent on the international economy. For example, the electronic consumer products and automobile industries are widely considered to be global industries. Ohio ranks fourth in the United States in terms of manufactured exports, and more than half of Ohio workers are employed by firms that depend to some extent on exports.

There has also been a rise in the global level of international portfolio and direct investment. Both direct and portfolio investments in the United States have been increasing faster than U.S. investment overseas. **Direct foreign investment (DFI)** occurs when the **multinational corporation (MNC)**, *a corporation with holdings and/or operations in more than one country*, has control over the investment, such as when it builds an offshore manufacturing facility. *Portfolio investment* involves financial assets with maturities greater than 1 year, such as the purchase of foreign stocks and bonds.

A major reason for direct foreign investment by U.S. companies is the high rates of return obtainable from these investments. And the amount of U.S. direct foreign investment (DFI) abroad is large and growing. Significant amounts of the total assets, sales, and profits of American MNCs are attributable to foreign investments and foreign operations. Direct foreign investment is not limited to American firms. Many European and Japanese firms have operations abroad, too. During the past decade, these firms have been increasing their sales and setting up production facilities abroad, especially in the United States.

Capital flows (portfolio investment) between countries have also been increasing. Many firms, investment companies, and individuals invest in the capital markets in foreign countries. The motivation is twofold: to obtain returns higher than those obtainable in the domestic capital markets and to reduce portfolio risk through international diversification. The increase in world trade and investment activity is reflected in the recent globalization of financial markets. The **Eurodollar** market is now larger than any domestic financial market, and U.S. companies are increasingly turning to this market for funds. Even companies and public entities that have no overseas presence are beginning to rely on this market for financing.

**direct foreign investment (DFI)** a company from one country making a physical investment, such as building a factory, in another country.

**multinational corporation (MNC)** a corporation with holdings and/or operations in more than one country.

**Eurodollars** U.S. dollars held by foreign (often European) banks and financial institutions outside the United States, and often as a result of payments to foreign companies for goods or services.

In addition, most national financial markets are becoming more integrated with global markets because of the rapid increase in the volume of interest rate and currency swaps. (We will discuss currency swaps later in the chapter.) Because of the widespread availability of these swaps, the currency denomination and the source country of financing for many globally integrated companies are dictated by accessibility and relative-cost considerations, regardless of the currency ultimately needed by the firm. Even a *purely domestic firm* that buys all its inputs and sells all its output in its home country is not immune to foreign competition, nor can it totally ignore the workings of the international financial markets.

## Concept Check

**1.** Why do U.S. companies invest overseas?

**2** Explain why foreign exchange rates in two different countries must be in line with each other.

**foreign exchange (FX) market** the market in which the currencies of various countries is traded.

# Foreign Exchange Markets and Currency Exchange Rates

The **foreign exchange (FX) market** is by far the world's largest financial market, with daily trading volumes of more than $4 trillion. Trading in this market is dominated by a few key currencies including the U.S. dollar, the British pound sterling, the Japanese yen, and the euro. The FX market is an over-the-counter market with participants (buyers and sellers) located in major commercial and investment banks around the world. Table 16-1 lists the top 10 currencies traded in the FX market.

Some of the major participants in foreign exchange trading include the following:

◆ *Importers and exporters of goods and services.* For example, when a U.S. importer purchases goods from a Japanese manufacturer and pays using Japanese yen, the importer will need to convert dollars to yen in the FX market. Similarly, if an exporter is paid in a foreign firm's domestic currency, it will enter the FX market to convert the payment to its home currency.

◆ *Investors and portfolio managers who purchase foreign stocks and bonds.* Investors who acquire the shares of foreign companies that are traded on a foreign exchange need foreign currency to complete the transaction.

◆ *Currency traders who make a market in one or more foreign currencies.* Currency traders buy and sell different currencies, hoping to make money from their trades.

| TABLE 16-1  The Market for Foreign Exchange: Most Traded Currencies | |
|---|---|
| **Currency** | **Percentage Shares of Average Daily Turnover** |
| U.S. dollar | 84.9 |
| Euro | 39.1 |
| Japanese yen | 19.0 |
| Pound sterling | 12.9 |
| Australian dollar | 7.6 |
| Swiss franc | 6.4 |
| Canadian dollar | 5.3 |
| Hong Kong dollar | 2.4 |
| Swedish krona | 2.2 |
| New Zealand dollar | 1.6 |
| Other | 18.6 |
| Total | 200.0 |

Note: The total is 200% since trading volume includes one trade for buying and one for selling on each transaction, such that volume is double-counted.

Source: Triennial Central Bank Survey (December 2011), Bank for International Settlements.

## Foreign Exchange Rates

An **exchange rate** is simply the price of one currency stated in terms of another. For example, if the exchange rate of U.S. dollars for British pounds was 2 to 1, this means that it would take $2.00 to purchase 1 pound.

**exchange rate** the price of one currency stated in terms of another.

**Reading Exchange Rate Quotes**    Table 16-2 shows the exchange rates from June 14, 2012, which are available online at *The Wall Street Journal Online, reuters.com, xe.com,* and *The Financial Times Online.* In fact, *The Financial Times Online* even provides a Currencies Macromap that displays a map of the world with a color-coded view of the performance of the different world currencies relative to a currency of your choice.[1] The first column of Table 16-2 gives the number of dollars it takes to purchase one unit of foreign currency. Because the exchange rate is expressed in U.S. dollars, it is referred to as a **direct quote.** Given the figures in Table 16-2, we can see that it took $1.5562 to buy 1 British pound (£1), $1.0518 to buy 1 Swiss franc, and $1.2633 to buy 1 euro. Conversely, an **indirect quote** indicates the number of foreign currency units it takes to purchase one American dollar. The second column shows the indirect exchange rate.

**direct quote** the exchange rate that indicates the number of units of the home currency required to buy one unit of a foreign currency.

**indirect quote** the exchange rate that expresses the number of units of foreign currency that can be bought for one unit of home currency.

We can further illustrate the use of direct and indirect quotes with a simple example. Suppose you want to compute the indirect quote from the direct quote for pounds given in column 1 of Table 16-2. The direct quote for the British pound is $1.5562. The related indirect quotes are calculated as the reciprocal of the direct quote as follows:

$$\text{Indirect quote} = \frac{1}{\text{direct quote}} \qquad\qquad (16\text{-}1)$$

Thus,

$$\frac{1}{1.5562} = £0.6426$$

Notice that the indirect quote is identical to that shown in the second column of Table 16-2.

---

**EXAMPLE 16.1**    **Computing an exchange amount using a direct quote**

An American business must pay 1,000 euros to a German firm on June 14, 2012. Using the information in Table 16-2, how many dollars will be required for this transaction?

**STEP 1: FORMULATE A SOLUTION STRATEGY**
The dollar amount required for this transaction can be computed using the following equation:

$$\text{Amount in dollars} = \frac{\text{dollar amount}}{\text{foreign currency}} \times €1{,}000$$

Note that after finding the direct quote you must then multiply the amount by the amount of foreign currency required for the transaction in order to obtain the required dollar amount.

**STEP 2: CRUNCH THE NUMBERS**
Substituting into the equation we compute the dollar amount required as follows:

$$\text{Amount in dollars} = \frac{\$1.2633}{€} \times €1{,}000 = \$1{,}263.30$$

**STEP 3: ANALYZE YOUR RESULTS**
For the American business to pay the German firm €1,000, it will require $1,263.30 to complete the transaction.

---

[1]To view the Currencies Macromap, go to http://markets.ft.com/research/Markets/Currencies and click on Currencies Macromap.

| TABLE 16-2  Foreign Exchange Rates (June 14, 2012) | | |
|---|---|---|
| | **U.S.-Dollar Foreign Exchange Rates in Late New York Trading** | |
| **Country/currency** | **U.S. $ Equivalent** | **Trading and Currency Per U.S. $** |
| **Americas** | | |
| Brazil real | 0.4864 | 2.056 |
| Canada dollar | 0.9777 | 1.0228 |
| Colombia peso | 0.0005577 | 1793.08 |
| Mexico peso | 0.0719 | 13.9004 |
| Venezuela b. fuerte | 0.22988506 | 4.35 |
| **Asia-Pacific** | | |
| Australian dollar | 1.0025 | 0.9975 |
| 1-mos forward | 0.99965778 | 1 |
| 3-mos forward | 0.99432028 | 1.01 |
| 6-mos forward | 0.98759862 | 1.01 |
| China yuan | 0.1569 | 6.372 |
| Hong Kong dollar | 0.1289 | 7.7588 |
| India rupee | 0.01795 | 55.69495 |
| Japan yen | 0.01260199 | 79.35 |
| 1-mos forward | 0.01260671 | 79.32 |
| 3-mos forward | 0.01261797 | 79.25 |
| 6-mos forward | 0.0126379 | 79.13 |
| New Zealand dollar | 0.7826 | 1.2778 |
| Pakistan rupee | 0.0106 | 94.355 |
| South Korea won | 0.0008587 | 1164.55 |
| **Europe** | | |
| Euro area euro | 1.2633 | 0.7916 |
| Norway krone | 0.1683 | 5.942 |
| Russia rubleá | 0.03078 | 32.484 |
| Sweden krona | 0.1427 | 7.0092 |
| Switzerland franc | 1.0518 | 0.9508 |
| 1-mos forward | 1.0524 | 0.9502 |
| 3-mos forward | 1.0543 | 0.9485 |
| 6-mos forward | 1.0574 | 0.9457 |
| Turkey lira | 0.5509 | 1.8152 |
| UK pound | 1.5562 | 0.6426 |
| 1-mos forward | 1.556 | 0.6427 |
| 3-mos forward | 1.5556 | 0.6429 |
| 6-mos forward | 1.5551 | 0.643 |
| **Middle East/Africa** | | |
| Egypt pound | 0.1653 | 6.0488 |
| Israel shekel | 0.2587 | 3.8655 |
| Saudi Arabia riyal | 0.2667 | 3.7502 |
| South Africa rand | 0.1194 | 8.3751 |
| UAE dirham | 0.2723 | 3.6724 |

Note: Slight rounding error explains the fact that the numbers in the "U.S. $ Equivalent" column do not always equal the inverse of the numbers in the "Currency per U.S. $" column.

Source: Data from Reuters and *Wall Street Journal Online*, June 14, 2012.

## Exchange Rates and Arbitrage

The foreign exchange quotes in two different countries must be in line with each other. If the exchange rate quotations between the London and New York spot exchange markets were *out of line*, then an *enterprising trader could make a profit by buying in the market where the currency was cheaper and selling it in the other*. Such a buy-and-sell strategy would involve a zero net investment of funds and no risk bearing, yet it would provide a sure profit. A person executing this strategy is called an **arbitrageur**, and the process of buying and selling in more than one market to make a riskless profit is called arbitrage. Spot exchange markets are efficient in the sense that arbitrage opportunities do not persist for any length of time. That is, the exchange rates between two different markets are quickly brought *in line*, aided by the arbitrage process. **Arbitrage** *eliminates exchange rate differentials across the markets for a single currency*, as in the preceding example for the New York and London quotes.

**arbitrageur** an individual involved in the process of buying and selling in more than one market to make a riskless profit.

**arbitrage** trading to eliminate exchange rate differentials across the markets for a single currency.

Suppose that you could buy a UK pound for $1.5400 in London rather than the $1.5562 quoted in New York in Table 16-2. If you simultaneously bought a pound in London for $1.54 and sold it in New York for $1.5562, you would have (1) taken a zero net investment position because you bought £1 and sold £1, (2) locked in a sure profit of $0.0162 on every pound you bought and sold *no matter which way* the pound subsequently moves, and (3) set in motion the forces that will eliminate the different quotes in New York and London. As others in the marketplace learn of your transaction, they will attempt to make the same transaction. The increased demand to buy pounds in London will lead to a higher quote there, and the increased supply of pounds will lead to a lower quote in New York. The workings of the market will produce a new spot rate that lies between $1.54 and $1.5562 and is the same in New York and in London.

## Asked and Bid Rates

Two types of rates are quoted in the spot exchange market: the asked and the bid rates. The **asked rate** is the *rate the bank or the foreign exchange trader "asks" the customer to pay in home currency for foreign currency when the bank is selling and the customer is buying*. The asked rate is also known as the *selling rate* or the *offer rate*. The **bid rate** is *the rate at which the bank buys the foreign currency from the customer by paying in home currency*. The bid rate is also known as the *buying rate*. As you would expect, the asking price is greater than the bid price. Note that Table 16-2 contains only the selling, offer, or asked rates, not the buying rate.

**asked rate** the rate the bank or the foreign exchange trader "asks" the customer to pay when the bank is selling and the customer is buying. The asked rate is also known as the selling rate or the offer rate.

**bid rate** the rate at which the bank buys the foreign currency from the customer. The bid rate is also known as the buying rate.

The bank sells a unit of foreign currency for more than it pays for it. Therefore, the direct asked quote ($/FC) is greater than the direct bid quote. *The difference between the asked quote and the bid quote* is known as the **bid-asked spread**. When there is a large volume of transactions and the trading is continuous, the spread is small and can be less than 1 percent (0.01) for the major currencies. The spread is much higher for infrequently traded currencies. The spread exists to compensate the banks for holding the risky foreign currency and for providing the service of converting currencies.

**bid-asked spread** the difference between the asked quote and the bid quote.

## Cross Rates

A **cross rate** is the exchange rate between two foreign currencies, neither of which is the currency of the domestic country. Some cross rates are given in Table 16-3. The following example illustrates how two cross rates can be used to derive a third cross rate.

**cross rate** the exchange rate between two foreign currencies, neither of which is the currency of the domestic country.

## CAN YOU DO IT?

### USING THE SPOT RATE TO CALCULATE A FOREIGN CURRENCY PAYMENT

An American business must pay the equivalent of $10,000 in United Arab Emirates (UAE) dirhams to a firm in Dubai on June 14, 2012. Using the information in Table 16-2, how many dirhams will the firm in Dubai receive?
(The solution can be found on page 491.)

**TABLE 16-3  Key Currency Cross Rates, Thursday, June 14, 2012**

|             | Dollar  | Euro     | Pound    | SFranc  | Peso    | Yen     | CdnDlr  |
|-------------|---------|----------|----------|---------|---------|---------|---------|
| **Canada**      | 1.0228  | 1.2920   | 1.5916   | 1.0757  | 0.0736  | 0.0129  | ...     |
| **Japan**       | 79.3526 | 100.2426 | 123.4896 | 83.4613 | 5.7086  | ...     | 77.5860 |
| **Mexico**      | 13.9004 | 17.5598  | 21.6320  | 14.6202 | ...     | 0.1752  | 13.5910 |
| **Switzerland** | 0.9508  | 1.2011   | 1.4796   | ...     | 0.0684  | 0.0120  | 0.9296  |
| **U.K.**        | 0.6426  | 0.8117   | ...      | 0.6759  | 0.0462  | 0.0081  | 0.6283  |
| **Euro**        | 0.7916  | ...      | 1.2319   | 0.8326  | 0.0569  | 0.0100  | 0.7740  |
| **U.S.**        | ...     | 1.2633   | 1.5562   | 1.0518  | 0.0719  | 0.0126  | 0.9777  |

Source: Data from Reuters and *Wall Street Journal Online*, June 14, 2012, wsj.com.

---

**EXAMPLE 16.2**  **Calculating the Canadian dollar/Swiss franc exchange rate**

Calculate the Canadian dollar/Swiss franc and Swiss Franc/Canadian dollar exchange rates using the cross-rates listed in columns 2 and 4 of Table 16-3.

### STEP 1: FORMULATE A SOLUTION STRATEGY

Columns 2 and 4 of Table 16-3 provide the Canadian dollar/euro and euro/Swiss Franc rates, which can be used to determine the Canadian dollar/Swiss franc and Swiss franc/Canadian dollar exchange rates as follows:

$$\frac{\text{Canadian \$}}{\text{€}} \times \frac{\text{€}}{\text{Swiss franc}} = \frac{\text{Canadian \$}}{\text{Swiss franc}}$$

Since the Swiss franc/Canadian dollar is reciprocal of this, it can then be calculated as the reciprocal of the direct quote.

### STEP 2: CRUNCH THE NUMBERS

Substituting into the equation we compute the euro/pound exchange rate:

$$\frac{\text{Canadian \$}}{\text{€}} \times \frac{\text{€}}{\text{Swiss franc}} = 1.2920 \times 0.8326 = \frac{1.0757 \text{ Canadian \$}}{\text{Swiss franc}}$$

Thus, the Swiss Franc/Canadian dollar exchange rate is:

$$\frac{1}{1.0757} = \frac{0.9296 \text{ Swiss francs}}{\text{Canadian \$}}$$

### STEP 3: ANALYZE YOUR RESULTS

The Canadian dollar/Swiss franc exchange rate is 1.0757 Canadian dollars per Swiss franc, and the Swiss franc/Canadian dollar exchange rate is 0.9296 Swiss francs per Canadian dollar. You'll notice that these rates are the same exchange rates as those given in Table 16-3 under Key Currency Cross Rates.

## Types of Foreign Exchange Transactions

**spot exchange rate** an exchange rate for a transaction that calls for immediate delivery.

**forward exchange rate** an exchange rate for a transaction that calls for delivery in the future.

**delivery date** the date on which the actual payment of one currency in exchange for another takes place in a foreign exchange transaction.

Thus far, the exchange rates and transactions we have discussed are those meant for immediate delivery. This type of exchange rate is called a **spot exchange rate**. Another type of transaction carried out in the foreign exchange markets is known as a **forward exchange rate**, which is an exchange rate agreed upon today but which calls for delivery of currency at the agreed rate at some future date.

The actual payment of one currency in exchange for the other takes place on a future date called the **delivery date**, and the agreement that captures the terms of both the rate

## DID YOU GET IT?

### USING THE SPOT RATE TO CALCULATE A FOREIGN CURRENCY PAYMENT

On page 489 you were asked to determine how much an American firm had to pay a firm in Dubai in the United Arab Emirates to receive an equivalent of $10,000 in dirhams.

3.6724 dirhams/$ $\times$ $10,000 = 36,724 dirhams

Any time money changes hands internationally, there is a transaction in the foreign currency markets. Interestingly, the dollar is the most frequently traded currency, accounting for over 42.5 percent of total trading volume, with the euro coming in second with a 19.6 percent share.

and delivery is called a futures contract or **forward exchange contract.**[2] For example, a forward contract agreed upon on March 1 would specify the exchange rate and might call for delivery on March 31. Note that the forward rate is not necessarily the same as the spot rate that will exist in the future—in fact, no one knows exactly what the exchange rate will be in the future. These contracts can be used to manage a firm's exchange rate risk (the risk that tomorrow's exchange rate will differ from today's rate) and are usually quoted for periods of between 30 days and 1 year. A contract for any intermediate date can be obtained, usually with the payment of a small premium.

Forward rates, like spot rates, are quoted in both direct and indirect form. The direct quotes are the dollar/foreign currency rate, and the indirect quotes are the foreign currency/dollar rate, similar to the spot exchange quotes. The direct quotes for the 30-day and 90-day forward contracts on pounds, yen, Australian dollars, and Swiss Francs are given in column 1 of Table 16-2. As with spot rates, the indirect quotes for forward contracts are reciprocals of the direct quotes. The indirect quotes are indicated in column 2 of Table 16-2.

In Table 16-2 the 1-month forward quote for pounds is $1.556 per pound. This means that the bank is contractually bound to deliver £1 at this price, and the buyer of the contract is legally obligated to buy it at this price in 30 days. Therefore, this is the price the customer must pay regardless of the actual spot rate prevailing in 30 days. If the spot price of the pound is less than $1.556, then the customer pays *more* than the spot price. If the spot price is greater than $1.556, then the customer pays *less* than the spot price.

*The forward rate is often quoted at a premium or a discount from the existing spot rate.* For example, the 30-day forward rate for the pound may be quoted as a $0.0002 discount ($1.556 forward rate – $1.5562 spot rate). If the forward rate for the British pound is greater than the spot rate, it is said to be selling at a premium relative to the dollar, and the dollar is said to be selling at a discount to the British pound. This premium or discount is also called the **forward-spot differential**.

Notationally, the relationship may be written

$$F - S = \text{premium } (F > S) \text{ or discount } (S > F)$$

where $F$ = the forward rate, direct quote
$S$ = the spot rate, direct quote

The premium or discount can also be expressed as an annual percentage rate, computed as follows:

$$\frac{F - S}{S} \times \frac{12}{n} \times 100 = \text{annualized percentage}$$

premium $(F > S)$ or discount $(S > F)$ $\qquad\qquad$ (16-2)

where $n$ = the number of months on the forward contract.

> **forward exchange contract** an agreement between two parties to exchange one currency for another on a future date.

> **forward-spot differential** the premium or discount between forward and spot currency exchange rates.

---

[2]These contracts are very similar, with one major difference being that futures contracts are exchange traded, while forward contracts are traded on the over-the-counter market.

### EXAMPLE 16.3 | Computing the percent-per-annum discount

Using the information from Table 16-1, calculate the percent-per-annum discount on the 90-day or 3-month pound.

#### STEP 1: FORMULATE A SOLUTION STRATEGY

First, we have to identify $F$ (the 3-month forward rate), $S$ (the spot rate), and $n$ (the number of months on the forward contract):

$$F = 1.5556, \ S = 1.5562, \ n = 3 \text{ months}$$

Next, because $S$ is greater than $F$, we compute the annualized percentage discount using equation (16-2):

$$\frac{F - S}{S} \times \frac{12}{n} \times 100 = \text{annualized percentage} \tag{16-2}$$

#### STEP 2: CRUNCH THE NUMBERS

When we substitute into the equation, we get

$$\text{Annualized percentage} = \frac{1.5556 - 1.5562}{1.5562} \times \frac{12 \text{ months}}{3 \text{ months}} \times 100 = -0.1542\%$$

#### STEP 3: ANALYZE YOUR RESULTS

The percent-per-annum premium is negative on the 90-day pound at −0.1542%.

## Exchange Rate Risk

The concept of exchange rate risk applies to all types of international business. The measurement of these risks, and the type of risk, differ among businesses. Let us see how exchange rate risk affects international trade contracts, international portfolio investments, and direct foreign investments.

**Exchange Rate Risk in International Trade Contracts**   The idea of exchange rate risk in trade contracts is illustrated in the following situations.

*Case I* An American automobile distributor agrees to buy a car from the manufacturer in Detroit. The distributor agrees to pay $25,000 on delivery of the car, which is expected to be 30 days from today. The car is delivered on the 30th day and the distributor pays $25,000. Notice that from the day this contract was written until the day the car was delivered, the buyer knew the *exact dollar amount* of the liability. There was, in other words, *no uncertainty* about the value of the contract.

*Case II* An American automobile distributor enters into a contract with a British supplier to buy a car from Britain for £16,065. The amount is payable upon the delivery of the

### CAN YOU DO IT?

#### COMPUTING A PERCENT-PER-ANNUM PREMIUM

Using the information in Table 16-2, compute the percent-per-annum premium on the 90-day (3 month) yen.
(The solution can be found on page 493.)

car, 30 days from today. Unfortunately, the exchange rate between British pounds and U.S. dollars may change in the next 30 days. In effect, the American firm is not certain what its future dollar outflow will be 30 days hence. That is, the *dollar value of the contract is uncertain*.

These two examples help illustrate the idea of foreign exchange risk in international trade contracts. In the domestic trade contract (Case I), the exact dollar amount of the future dollar payment is known today with certainty. In the case of the international trade contract (Case II), in which the *contract is written in the foreign currency*, the exact dollar amount of the contract is not known. The variability of the exchange rate causes variability in the future cash flow of the firm.

Exchange rate risk exists when the contract is written in terms of the foreign currency, or *denominated* in foreign currency. There is no direct exchange rate risk if the international trade contract is written in terms of the domestic currency. That is, in Case II, if the contract were written in dollars, the American importer would face *no* direct exchange rate risk. With the contract written in dollars, the British exporter would bear *all* of the exchange rate risk because the British exporter's future pound receipts would be uncertain. That is, the British exporter would receive payment in dollars, which would have to be converted into pounds at an unknown (as of today) future pound/dollar exchange rate. In international trade contracts of this type, at least one of the two parties to the contract *always* bears the exchange rate risk.

Certain types of international trade contracts are denominated in a third currency that is different from either the importer's or the exporter's domestic currency. In Case II, the contract might have been denominated in, say, the Hong Kong dollar. With a Hong Kong dollar contract, both the importer and exporter would be subject to exchange rate risk.

Exchange rate risk is not limited to the two-party trade contracts; it exists also in foreign portfolio investments and direct foreign investments.

**Exchange Rate Risk in Foreign Portfolio Investments**   Let us look at an example of exchange rate risk in the context of portfolio investments. An American investor buys a Hong Kong security. The exact return on the investment in the security is unknown. Thus, the security is a risky investment. The investment return in the holding period of, say, 3 months stated in HK$ could be anything from −2 to +8 percent. In addition, the U.S. dollar/HK$ exchange rate may depreciate by, say, 4 percent or appreciate by 6 percent during the 3-month period. The return to the American investor in U.S. dollars will, therefore, be in the range of −6 to +14 percent. Hence, the exchange rate fluctuations may increase the riskiness of the investments.

## DID YOU GET IT?
### COMPUTING A PERCENT-PER-ANNUM PREMIUM

Compute the percent-per-annum premium on the 90-day yen.

**STEP 1** Identify $F$, $S$, and $n$.

$F = \$0.01261797/¥$, $S = \$0.01260199/¥$, and $n = 3$ months

**STEP 2**  Because $F$ is greater than $S$, we compute the annualized percentage premium:

$$\frac{0.01261797 - 0.01260199}{0.01260199} \times \frac{12 \text{ months}}{3 \text{ months}} \times 100 = 0.5072\%$$

The percent-per-annum premium on the 90-day yen is 0.5072 percent.

**Exchange Rate Risk in Direct Foreign Investment**  The exchange rate risk of a direct foreign investment (DFI) is more complicated. In a DFI, the parent company invests in assets denominated in a foreign currency. That is, the balance sheet and the income statement of the subsidiary are written in terms of the foreign currency. The parent company, if based in the United States, receives the repatriated (or converted) profit stream from the subsidiary in dollars. Thus, the exchange rate risk concept applies to fluctuations in the dollar value of the assets located abroad as well as to the fluctuations in the home currency–denominated profit stream. Moreover, exchange risk not only affects immediate profits but may also affect the future profit stream as well.

Although exchange rate risk can be a serious complication in international business activity, remember the principle of the risk–return trade-off: Traders and corporations find numerous reasons why the returns from international transactions outweigh the risks.

## Concept Check

1. What is a spot transaction? What is a direct quote? An indirect quote?
2. Who is an arbitrageur? How does an arbitrageur make money?
3. What is a forward exchange rate?
4. Describe exchange rate risk in direct foreign investment.

 **3** Discuss the concept of interest rate parity.

# Interest Rate Parity

Interest rates can vary dramatically from country to country. For example, in mid-2012 the 1-year interest rate in the United States was approximately 0.87 percent, while in Turkey it was 7.98 percent. The concepts of interest rate parity and purchasing-power parity, which we will introduce shortly, provide the basis for understanding how prices and rates of interest across different countries are related to one another.

**interest rate parity (IRP) theory** a theory that states that (except for the effects of small transaction costs) the forward premium or discount should be equal and opposite in size to the difference in the national interest rates for securities of the same maturity.

**Interest rate parity (IRP) theory** can be used to relate differences in the interest rates in two countries to the ratios of spot and forward exchange rates of the two countries' currencies. Specifically, the interest parity condition can be stated as follows:

$$\frac{\text{Difference in}}{\text{interest rates}} = \frac{\text{ratio of the}}{\text{forward and spot rates}}$$

$$\frac{\left(1 + \begin{array}{c}\text{domestic} \\ \text{rate of interest}\end{array}\right)}{\left(1 + \begin{array}{c}\text{foreign} \\ \text{rate of interest}\end{array}\right)} = \left(\frac{\text{forward exchange rate}}{\text{spot exchange rate}}\right) \tag{16-3}$$

This equation can be rearranged such that,

$$\left(1 + \begin{array}{c}\text{domestic} \\ \text{rate of interest}\end{array}\right) = \left(\frac{\text{forward exchange rate}}{\text{spot exchange rate}}\right)\left(1 + \begin{array}{c}\text{foreign} \\ \text{rate of interest}\end{array}\right) \tag{16-3a}$$

To illustrate how this equation is applied, consider the following situation. Suppose that the 6-month risk-free rate of interest in the United States was 2 percent. On that date the spot exchange rate between the U.S. dollar and the Japanese yen ($/¥) was 0.010798 and the forward exchange rate for 6 months hence was 0.010803. According to interest rate parity, what would you expect the 6-month risk-free rate of interest to be in Japan? Substituting into equation (16-3a) we calculate the following:

$$\left(1 + \frac{\text{U.S. 6-month risk-free}}{\text{rate of interest}}\right) = \left(\frac{\text{forward exchange rate}}{\text{spot exchange rate}}\right)\left(1 + \frac{\text{Japanese 6-month risk-free}}{\text{rate of interest}}\right)$$

$$(1 + 0.02) = \left(\frac{0.010803}{0.010798}\right)\left(1 + \frac{\text{Japanese 6-month risk-free}}{\text{rate of interest}}\right)$$

$$(1 + 0.02) = 1.000463\left(1 + \frac{\text{Japanese 6-month risk-free}}{\text{rate of interest}}\right)$$

Thus, the Japanese 6-month risk-free rate of interest = 0.019528, or 1.9528 percent.

What this means is that you get the same total return whether you change your dollars to yen and invest in the risk-free rate in Japan and then convert them back to dollars or simply invest your dollars in the U.S. risk-free rate of interest. For example, if you started with $100 and converted it to yen at the spot rate of 0.010798 $/¥, you'd have 9,260.97 yen; if you invested those yen at 1.9528 percent, after 6 months you'd have ¥9,441.82. Converting this back to dollars at the forward rate you end up with $102.00, the same as you would have if you had invested your dollars at the U.S. 6-month rate of 2 percent.

## Concept Check

1. In simple terms, what does the interest rate parity theory mean?

# Purchasing-Power Parity and the Law of One Price

 **4** Explain the purchasing-power parity theory and the law of one price.

**purchasing-power parity (PPP)** a theory that states that exchange rates adjust so that identical goods cost the same amount regardless of where in the world they are purchased.

According to the theory of **purchasing-power parity (PPP)**, exchange rates adjust so that identical goods cost the same amount regardless of where in the world they are purchased. For example, if an Apple iPad costs $399 in the United States and €319.20 in France, according to the purchasing-power parity theory, the spot exchange rate should be $1.25 per euro ($399/€319.20). Thus, if you would like to buy a new iPad, you could either buy it for $399 in the United States or trade in your $399 for €319.20 and buy your iPad in France—either way it costs you the same amount. Stated formally,

$$\frac{\text{Spot exchange}}{\text{rate for euros (\$/€)}} \times \frac{\text{French price of}}{\text{an iPad}} = \frac{\text{U.S. price of}}{\text{an iPad}}$$

More generally, the spot exchange rate for the foreign country (in this case the spot exchange rate for euros) should be equal to the ratio of the price of the good in the home country ($P_h$) to the price of the same good in the foreign country ($P_f$), that is,

$$\text{Spot exchange rate} = \frac{P_h}{P_f}$$

Thus, as we just showed, the spot exchange rate of $/€ should be the following:

$$\text{Spot exchange rate} = \frac{P_h}{P_f} = \frac{\$399}{€319.20} = \$1.25/€$$

**law of one price** an economic principle that states that a good or service cannot sell for different prices in the same market. Applied to international markets, this law states that the same goods should sell for the same price in different countries after making adjustment for the exchange rate between the two currencies.

Therefore, PPP implies that if a new Callaway RAZR Fit golf club cost €320 in France, it should cost €320 × 1.25 = $400 in the United States where the $/€ exchange rate is 1.25.

Underlying the PPP relationship is a fundamental economic principle called the **law of one price**. Applied to international trade, this law states that the same goods should sell for the same price in different countries after making adjustment for the exchange rate between the two currencies. The idea is that the worth of a good does not depend on where it is bought or sold. Thus, in the long run, exchange rates should adjust so that the purchasing power of each currency is the same. As a result, exchange rates should reflect the international differences in inflation rates with currencies with high rates of inflation experiencing declines in the value of their currency.

There are enough obvious exceptions to the concept of purchasing-power parity that it may, at first glance, seem difficult to accept. To illustrate differences in purchasing power across countries, the *Economist* publishes what it calls its Big Mac Index, which compares the price of a Big Mac in different countries. In 2012, a Big Mac cost $4.20 in the United States; and, given the then-existing exchange rates, it cost an equivalent of $2.11 in the Ukraine, $2.12 in Hong Kong, $2.44 in China, $6.79 in Norway, and $6.81 in Switzerland. Why aren't these prices the same? First, tax differences between countries can be one cause. In addition, labor costs and the rental cost of the McDonald's outlets may differ across countries.

So, does this mean that PPP does not hold? Well it clearly does not hold for what economists call nontraded goods, like restaurant meals and haircuts. As we all know, for these goods, purchasing-power parity does not hold even within the United States—indeed, a Big Mac does not sell for the same price in Des Moines as it does in Los Angeles. However, for goods that can be very cheaply shipped between countries, like expensive gold jewelry, we expect PPP to hold relatively closely.

Clearly, a dollar doesn't go very far in Switzerland and Norway, but you get a lot for a dollar in Asian countries like China, Thailand, and Malaysia. Why does this matter? When the world is going through economic problems, as it has recently, a strong exchange rate (that is, one whose domestic currency buys relatively more units of foreign currency) makes it difficult to sell goods abroad and makes foreign goods look less expensive. On the other hand, a country with a weak exchange rate (that is, one whose domestic currency buys relatively fewer units of foreign currency), like China, has an easier time selling goods abroad (because its goods are less expensive abroad). However, the weak exchange rate made it more difficult for Chinese consumers to buy pricey imports over cheaper Chinese-produced goods.

## The International Fisher Effect

According to the domestic Fisher effect, nominal interest rates reflect the expected inflation rate, a real rate of interest and the product of the real rate of interest and the inflation rate. In other words,

$$\frac{\text{Nominal}}{\text{interest rate}} = \frac{\text{expected}}{\text{inflation rate}} + \frac{\text{real rate}}{\text{of interest}} + \left(\frac{\text{expected}}{\text{inflation rate}} \times \frac{\text{real rate}}{\text{of interest}}\right) \quad (16\text{-}4)$$

Although there is mixed empirical support for the international Fisher effect, it is widely thought that, for the major industrial countries, the real rate of interest is about 3 percent when a long-term period is considered. Thus, if the expected inflation rate was 2 percent in Britain and 4 percent in Japan, the interest rates in Britain and Japan would be 0.02 + 0.03 + 0.0006, or 5.06, percent and 0.04 + 0.03 + 0.0012, or 7.12 percent, respectively.

In effect, the international Fisher effect states that the real interest rate should be the same all over the world, with the difference in nominal or stated interest rates simply resulting from the differences in expected inflation rates. As we look at interest rates around the world, this tells us that we should not necessarily send our money to a bank account in the country with the highest interest rates. That course of action might only result in sending our money to a bank in the country with the highest expected level of inflation.

## Concept Check _____

1. What does the law of one price say?
2. What is the international Fisher effect?

# Capital Budgeting for Direct Foreign Investment

**5** Discuss the risks that are unique to the capital-budgeting analysis of direct foreign investment.

Today, there is no ducking the global markets, and it is common for U.S. firms to open manufacturing and sales operations abroad. In fact, in 2011 Yum! Brands (the parent company of KFC, Pizza Hut, and Taco Bell) invested over half a billion dollars to purchase the Chinese hot pot chain Little Sheep. Direct foreign investment occurs when a company from one country makes a physical investment, perhaps building a factory in another country. Examples of such a direct foreign investment include Yum! Brands' store in Dubai and Dell Computer Corporation's (DELL) construction of offshore manufacturing facilities in China, India, and Mexico.

Many European and Japanese firms, like their American counterparts, have operations abroad as well. During the last decade, these firms have been increasing their sales and setting up production facilities abroad, especially in the United States. A major reason for direct foreign investment by U.S. companies is the prospect of higher rates of return from these investments. As you know from **Principle 3: Risk Requires a Reward**, while there may be higher expected rates of return with many foreign investments, many of them also come with increased risk.

The method used by multinational corporations to evaluate foreign investments is very similar to the method used to evaluate capital-budgeting decisions in a domestic context—but with some additional considerations. When corporations invest abroad they generally set up a subsidiary in the country in which they are investing. Funds then are transferred back, or repatriated, to the parent firm in its home country through dividends, royalties, and management fees, with both the dividends and royalties subject to taxation in both the foreign and home countries. Moreover, many countries restrict the flow of funds back to the home country. As a result, there is often a difference between the cash flows that a project produces and the cash flows that can be repatriated to its parent country. To evaluate these investment projects, firms discount *the cash flows that are expected to be repatriated to the parent firm*. As we know from **Principle 1: Cash Flow Is What Matters**, we are only interested in the cash flows that we expect the subsidiary to return to the parent company. In most cases, the timing is crucial. If your project generates cash flows in 2015 that cannot be repatriated until 2018, the cash flows must be discounted from the 2018 date when the cash will be actually received. Once the cash flows are estimated, they must be discounted back to present at the appropriate discount rate or required rate of return, with both the discount rate and the cash flows being measured in the same currency. Thus, if the discount rate is based on dollar-based interest rates, the cash flows must also be measured in dollars.

## Foreign Investment Risks

Risk in domestic capital budgeting arises from two sources: (1) business risk related to the specific attributes of the product or service being provided and the uncertainty associated with that market, and (2) financial risk, which is the risk imposed on the investment as a result of how the project is financed. The foreign direct investment opportunity includes both these sources of risk, plus political risk and exchange rate risk. Since business and finance risk have been discussed at some length in previous chapters, let us consider the risks that are unique to international investing.

**Political Risk**   Political risk can arise if the foreign subsidiary conducts its business in a politically unstable country. A change in a country's political environment frequently brings a change in policies with respect to businesses—and especially with respect to foreign businesses. An extreme change in policy might involve nationalization or even outright expropriation (government seizure) of certain businesses. For example, in 2007 Venezuela nationalized the country's largest telecommunications company, several electrical companies, and four lucrative oil projects that were owned by ExxonMobil, Chevron, and ConocoPhillips. These are the political risks of conducting business abroad. Some examples of political risk are as follows:

1. Expropriation of plants and equipment without compensation
2. Expropriation with minimal compensation that is below actual market value
3. Nonconvertibility of the subsidiary's foreign earnings into the parent's currency—the problem of blocked funds
4. Substantial changes in tax rates
5. Governmental controls in the foreign country regarding the sale price of certain products, wages and compensation paid to personnel, the hiring of personnel, transfer payments made to the parent, and local borrowing
6. Requirements regarding the local ownership of the business

All of these controls and governmental actions put the cash flows of the investment to the parent company at risk. Thus, these risks must be considered before making the foreign investment decision. For example, the MNC might decide against investing in countries with risks of types 1 and 2 as mentioned above, whereas other risks can be borne—provided that the returns from the foreign investments are high enough to compensate for them. It should be noted that although an MNC cannot protect itself against all foreign political risks, insurance against some types of political risks can be purchased from private insurance companies or from the U.S. government's Overseas Private Investment Corporation.

**Exchange Rate Risk**   Exchange rate risk is the risk that the value of a firm's operations and investments will be adversely affected by changes in exchange rates. For example, if U.S. dollars must be converted into euros before making an investment in Germany, an adverse change in the value of the dollar with respect to the euro will affect the total gain or loss on the investment when the money is converted back to dollars.

## Concept Check

1. Define the types of risk that are commonly referred to as political risk, and give some examples of them.
2. What is exchange rate risk? Why would a multinational firm be concerned about it?

# Chapter Summaries

 **Discuss the internationalization of business.** (pgs. 485–486)

**SUMMARY:** The growth of our global economy, the increasing number of multinational corporations, and the increase in foreign trade itself underscore the importance of the study of international finance. In addition, capital flows (portfolio investment) between countries has been increasing in order to obtain higher returns and reduce portfolio risk through international diversification.

**KEY TERMS**

**Direct foreign investment (DFI), page 485**   A company from one country making a physical investment such as building a factory in another country.

**Multinational corporation (MNC), page 485**   A corporation with holdings and/or operations in more than one country.

**Eurodollars, page 485**   U.S. dollars held by foreign (often European) banks and financial institutions outside the United States, and often as a result of payments to foreign companies for goods or services.

## Explain why foreign exchange rates in two different countries must be in line with each other.  (pgs. 486–494)

**SUMMARY:** The foreign exchange (FX) market is where one currency is traded for another. This is by far the largest financial market in the world, with a daily trading volume of more than $4 trillion. Trading is dominated by a few key currencies, including the U.S. dollar, the British pound sterling, the Japanese yen, and the euro. The FX market is an over-the-counter market rather than a single exchange location like the New York Stock Exchange where buyers and sellers get together. This means that market participants (buyers and sellers) are located in major commercial and investment banks around the world.

### KEY TERMS

**Foreign exchange (FX) market, page 486**  The market in which the currencies of various countries is traded.

**Exchange rate, page 487**  The price of one currency stated in terms of another.

**Direct quote, page 487**  The exchange rate that indicates the number of units of the home currency required to buy one unit of a foreign currency.

**Indirect quote, page 487**  The exchange rate that expresses the number of units of foreign currency that can be bought for one unit of home currency.

**Arbitrageur, page 489**  An individual involved in the process of buying and selling in more than one market to make a riskless profit.

**Arbitrage, page 489**  Trading to eliminate exchange rate differentials across the markets for a single currency.

**Asked rate, page 489**  The rate the bank or the foreign exchange trader "asks" the customer to pay when the bank is selling and the customer is buying. The asked rate is also known as the selling rate or the offer rate.

**Bid rate, page 489**  The rate at which the bank buys the foreign currency from the customer. The bid rate is also known as the buying rate.

**Bid-asked spread, page 489**  The difference between the asked quote and the bid quote.

**Cross rate, page 489**  The exchange rate between two foreign currencies, neither of which is the currency of the domestic country.

**Spot exchange rate, page 490**  An exchange rate for a transaction that calls for immediate delivery.

**Forward exchange rate, page 490**  An exchange rate for a transaction that calls for delivery in the future.

**Delivery date, page 490**  The date on which the actual payment of one currency in exchange for another takes place in a foreign exchange transaction.

**Forward exchange contract, page 491**  An agreement between two parties to exchange one currency for another on a future date.

**Forward-spot differential, page 491**  The premium or discount between forward and spot currency exchange rates.

### KEY EQUATIONS

$$\text{Indirect quote} = \frac{1}{\text{direct quote}}$$

$$F - S = \begin{cases} \text{Premium if } F > S \\ \text{Discount if } F < S \end{cases}$$

$$\frac{F - S}{S} \times \frac{12}{n} \times 100 = \text{annualized percentage}$$

where $n =$ the number of months of the forward contract

## Discuss the concept of interest rate parity.  (pgs. 494–495)

**SUMMARY:**  The forward exchange market provides a valuable service by quoting rates for the delivery of foreign currencies in the future. The foreign currency is said to sell at a discount relative to the spot rate when the forward rate is lower than the spot rate. It is said to sell at a premium relative to the spot rate when the forward rate is higher than the spot rate. According to the interest rate parity theory, these premiums and discounts depend solely on the differences in the levels of the interest rates of countries.

**KEY TERM**

**Interest rate parity (IRP) theory, page 494**
A theory that states that (except for the effects of small transaction costs) the forward premium or discount should be equal and opposite in size to the difference in the national interest rates for securities of the same maturity.

**KEY EQUATIONS**

$$\left(1 + \frac{\text{domestic}}{\text{rate of interest}}\right) = \left(\frac{\text{forward exchange rate}}{\text{spot exchange rate}}\right)\left(1 + \frac{\text{foreign}}{\text{rate of interest}}\right)$$

$$\frac{\text{Nominal rate}}{\text{of interest}} = \frac{\text{expected rate}}{\text{of inflation}} + \frac{\text{real rate}}{\text{of interest}} + \left(\frac{\text{expected rate}}{\text{of inflation}}\right)\left(\frac{\text{real rate}}{\text{of return}}\right)$$

---

 **4 Explain the purchasing-power parity theory and the law of one price.** (pgs. 495–496)

**SUMMARY:** According to the purchasing-power parity (PPP) theory, in the long run, exchange rates adjust so that the purchasing power of each currency is the same. Thus, exchange rate changes tend to reflect international differences in inflation rates. As a result, countries with high rates of inflation tend to experience declines in the value of their currency. Underlying the PPP relationship is the law of one price. This law is actually a proposition that in competitive markets in which there are no transportation costs or barriers to trade, the same goods sold in different countries sell for the same price if all of the different prices are expressed in terms of the same currency.

**KEY TERMS**

**Purchasing-power parity (PPP), page 495** A theory that states that exchange rates adjust so that identical goods cost the same amount regardless of where in the world they are purchased.

**Law of one price, page 495** An economic principle that states that a good or service cannot sell for different prices in the same market. Applied to international markets, this law states that the same goods should sell for the same price in different countries after making adjustment for the exchange rate between the two currencies.

---

 **5 Discuss the risks that are unique to the capital-budgeting analysis of direct foreign investment.** (pgs. 497–498)

**SUMMARY:** The complexities encountered in the direct foreign investment decision include the usual sources of risk—business and financial—faced by domestic investments, plus additional risks associated with political considerations and fluctuating exchange rates. Political risk is caused by differences in political climates, institutions, and processes between the home country and abroad. Under these conditions, the estimation of future cash flows and the choice of the proper discount rates are more complicated than for the domestic investment situation.

# Review Questions

*All Review Questions are available in* MyFinanceLab.

**16-1.** What additional factors are encountered in international as compared with domestic financial management? Discuss each briefly.

**16-2.** What different types of businesses operate in the international environment? Why are the techniques and strategies available to these firms different?

**16-3.** What is meant by arbitrage profits?

**16-4.** What are the markets and mechanics involved in generating simple arbitrage profits?

**16-5.** How do purchasing-power parity, interest rate parity, and the Fisher effect explain the relationships among the current spot rate, the future spot rate, and the forward rate?

**16-6.** What is meant by (a) exchange risk and (b) political risk?

**16-7.** In the New York exchange market, the forward rate for the Indian currency, the rupee, is not quoted. If you were exposed to exchange risk in rupees, how could you hedge your position?

**16-8.** What risks are associated with direct foreign investment? How do these risks differ from those encountered in domestic investment?

**16-9.** Are the inputs more complicated to a direct foreign investment than those to the domestic investment problem? If so, why?

# Study Problems

*All Study Problems are available in* MyFinanceLab.

The data for Study Problems 16-1 through 16-5 are given in the following table:

| COUNTRY | CONTRACT | $/FOREIGN CURRENCY |
|---|---|---|
| Canada—dollar | Spot | 0.8437 |
| | 30-day | 0.8417 |
| | 90-day | 0.8395 |
| Japan—yen | Spot | 0.004684 |
| | 30-day | 0.004717 |
| | 90-day | 0.004781 |
| Switzerland—franc | Spot | 0.5139 |
| | 30-day | 0.5169 |
| | 90-day | 0.5315 |

**16-1.** (*Spot exchange rates*) An American business needs to pay (a) 10,000 Canadian dollars, (b) 2 million yen, and (c) 50,000 Swiss francs to businesses abroad. What are the dollar payments to the respective countries?

**16-2.** (*Spot exchange rates*) An American business pays $10,000, $15,000, and $20,000 to suppliers in, respectively, Japan, Switzerland, and Canada. How much, in local currencies, do the suppliers receive?

**16-3.** (*Indirect quotes*) Compute the indirect quote for the spot and forward Canadian dollar, yen, and Swiss franc contracts.

**16-4.** (*Exchange rate arbitrage*) You own $10,000. The dollar rate in Tokyo is 216.6743. The yen rate in New York is given in the preceding table. Are arbitrage profits possible? Set up an arbitrage scheme with your capital. What is the gain (loss) in dollars?

**16-5.** (*Cross rates*) Compute the Canadian dollar/yen and the yen/Swiss franc spot rate from the data in the preceding table.

**16-6.** (*Spot exchange rate*) If one euro buys 1.32 U.S. dollars, how many euros can you purchase for 3 U.S. dollars?

**16-7.** (*Spot exchange rate*) Suppose the exchange rate between U.S. dollars and Japanese yen is $1 US = ¥79.1 JPY, and the exchange rate between the U.S. dollar and the British pound is $1 US = £0.64 GBP. What is the cross rate of Japanese yen to British pounds? (In other words, how many yen are needed to purchase 1 pound?)

**16-8.** (*Spot exchange rate*) Suppose 1 year ago, Miller Company had inventory in Britain valued at 1.5 million Swiss francs. The exchange rate for dollars to Swiss francs was 1 franc = 1.15 dollars. Today, the exchange rate is 1 Swiss franc = 1.06 U.S. dollars. The inventory in Switzerland is still valued at 1.5 million francs. What is the U.S. dollar gain or loss in inventory value as a result of the change in exchange rates?

**16-9.** (*Cross rates*) This morning, you noticed the following information in your financial newspaper:

    1 British po3und = 103.25 yen (JPY)
    1 U.S. dollar = 81.23 yen
    1 U.S. dollar = 0.77 euros

Given this information, how many euros did the newspaper likely state could be converted from 1 British pound?

**16-10.** (*Interest rate parity*) Suppose 90-day investments in Europe have a 5 percent annualized return and a 1.25 percent quarterly (90-day) return. In the United States, 90-day investments of similar risk have a 7 percent annualized return and a 1.75 percent quarterly return. In to-day's 90-day forward market, 1 euro equals $1.32. If interest rate parity holds, what is the spot exchange rate ($/€)?

**16-11.** (*Purchasing-power parity*) A McDonald's Big Mac costs 2.44 yuan in China, but costs $4.20 in the United States. Assuming that purchasing-power parity (PPP) holds, how many Chinese yuan are required to purchase 1 U.S. dollar?

# Mini Case

*This Mini Case is available in* MyFinanceLab.

For your job as the business reporter for a local newspaper, you are asked to put together a series of articles on multinational finance and the international currency markets for your readers. Much recent local press coverage has been given to losses in the foreign exchange markets by JGAR, a local firm that is the subsidiary of Daedlufetarg, a large German manufacturing firm.

Your editor would like you to address several specific questions dealing with multinational finance. Prepare a response to the following memorandum from your editor:

> To: Business Reporter
> From: Perry White, Editor, *Daily Planet*
> Re: Upcoming Series on Multinational Finance

In your upcoming series on multinational finance, I would like to make sure you cover several specific points. Before you begin this assignment, I want to make sure we are all reading from the same script because accuracy has always been the cornerstone of the *Daily Planet*. I'd like a response to the following questions before we proceed:

    a. What new problems and factors are encountered in international, as opposed to domestic, financial management?
    b. What does the term *arbitrage profits* mean?
    c. What can a firm do to reduce exchange risk?
    d. What are the differences among a forward contract, a futures contract, and options?

Use the following data in your responses to the remaining questions:

**Selling Quotes for Foreign Currencies in New York**

| COUNTRY—CURRENCY | CONTRACT | $/FOREIGN |
| --- | --- | --- |
| Canada—dollar | Spot | 0.8450 |
|  | 30-day | 0.8415 |
|  | 90-day | 0.8390 |
| Japan—yen | Spot | 0.004700 |
|  | 30-day | 0.004750 |
|  | 90-day | 0.004820 |
| Switzerland—franc | Spot | 0.5150 |
|  | 30-day | 0.5182 |
|  | 90-day | 0.5328 |

e. An American business needs to pay (a) 15,000 Canadian dollars, (b) 1.5 million yen, and (c) 55,000 Swiss francs to businesses abroad. What are the dollar payments to the respective countries?

f. An American business pays $20,000, $5,000, and $15,000 to suppliers in, respectively, Japan, Switzerland, and Canada. How much, in local currencies, do the suppliers receive?

g. Compute the indirect quote for the spot and forward Canadian dollar contract.

h. You own $10,000. The dollar rate in Tokyo is 216.6752. The yen rate in New York is given in the preceding table. Are arbitrage profits possible? Set up an arbitrage scheme with your capital. What is the gain (loss) in dollars?

i. Compute the Canadian dollar/yen spot rate from the data in the preceding table.

# Glossary

**accounting book value**—the value of an asset as shown on a firm's balance sheet. It represents the depreciated historical cost of the asset rather than its current market value or replacement cost.

**accounts payable (trade credit)**—credit provided by suppliers when a firm purchases inventory on credit.

**accounts receivable**—money owed by customers who purchased goods or services from the firm on credit.

**accounts receivable turnover ratio**—a firm's credit sales divided by its accounts receivable. This ratio expresses how often accounts receivable are "rolled over" during a year.

**accrual basis accounting**—a method of accounting whereby revenue is recorded when it is earned, whether or not the revenue has been received in cash. Likewise, expenses are recorded when they are incurred, even if the money has not actually been paid out.

**accrued expenses**—expenses that have been incurred but not yet paid in cash.

**accumulated depreciation**—the sum of all depreciation taken over the entire life of a depreciable asset.

**acid-test (quick) ratio**—the sum of firm's cash and accounts receivable divided by its current liabilities. This ratio is a more stringent measure of liquidity than the current ratio because it excludes inventories and other current assets (those that are least liquid) from the numerator.

**agency costs**—the lost value a firm's security holders face where there are conflicts of interest between managers and the security holders.

**agency problem**—problems and conflicts resulting from the separation of the management and ownership of the firm.

**amortized loan**—a loan that is paid off in equal periodic payments.

**angel investor**—a wealthy private investor who provides capital for a business start-up.

**annuity**—a series of equal dollar payments made for a specified number of years.

**annuity due**—an annuity in which the payments occur at the beginning of each period.

**annuity future value factor**—the value of $\left[ \dfrac{(1 + r)^n - 1}{r} \right]$ used as a multiplier to calculate the future value of an annuity.

**annuity present value factor**—the value of $\left[ \dfrac{1 - (1 + r)^{-n}}{r} \right]$ used as a multiplier to calculate the present value of an annuity.

**anticipatory buying**—buying in anticipation of a price increase to secure goods at a lower cost.

**arbitrage**—trading to eliminate exchange rate differentials across the markets for a single currency.

**arbitrageur**—an individual involved in the process of buying and selling in more than one market to make a riskless profit.

**asked rate**—the rate the bank or the foreign exchange trader "asks" the customer to pay when the bank is selling and the customer is buying. The asked rate is also known as the selling rate or the offer rate.

**asset allocation**—identifying and selecting the asset classes appropriate for a specific investment portfolio and determining the proportions of those assets within the portfolio.

**asset management**—how efficiently management is using the firm's assets to generate sales.

**average tax rate**—the tax rate on average that a company pays on its total taxable income.

**balance sheet**—a statement that shows a firm's assets, liabilities, and shareholder equity at a given point in time. It is a snapshot of the firm's financial position on a particular date.

**balance-sheet leverage ratios**—ratios of a firm's use of financial leverage or debt capital to either the firm's total capital or equity. Since the needed information for computing these ratios is found in the balance sheet we refer to them as balance sheet leverage ratios.

**behavioral finance**—the field of study examining when investors act rationally or irrationally when making investment decisions.

**beta**—the relationship between an investment's returns and the market's returns. This is a measure of the investment's nondiversifiable risk.

**bid-asked spread**—the difference between the asked quote and the bid quote.

**bid rate**—the rate at which the bank buys the foreign currency from the customer. The bid rate is also known as the buying rate.

**bird-in-the-hand dividend theory**—the view that dividends are more certain than capital gains and therefore more valuable.

**bond**—a long-term (10-year or more) promissory note issued by the borrower, promising to pay the owner of the security a predetermined, fixed amount of interest each year.

**book value**—(1) the value of an asset as shown on the firm's balance sheet. It represents the historical cost of the asset rather than its current market value or replacement cost. (2) The depreciated value of a company's assets (original cost less accumulated depreciation) less outstanding liabilities.

**break-even quantity**—the number of units a firm must sell before it starts to earn a profit.

**budget**—an itemized forecast of a company's expected revenues and expenses for a future period.

**business risk**—the risk of the firm's future earnings that is a direct result of the particular line of business chosen by the firm.

**call protection period**—a prespecified time period during which a company cannot recall a bond.

**call provision**—a provision that entitles the corporation to repurchase its preferred stock from investors at stated prices over specified periods.

**callable bond (redeemable bond)**—an option available to a company issuing a bond whereby the issuer can call (redeem) the bond before it matures. This is usually done if interest rates decline below what the firm is paying on the bond.

**capital asset pricing model (CAPM)**—an equation stating that the expected rate of return on an investment (in this case a stock) is a function of (1) the risk-free rate, (2) the investment's systematic risk, and (3) the expected risk premium for the market portfolio of all risky securities.

**capital budgeting**—the decision-making process with respect to investment in fixed assets.

**capital gains**—gains from selling any asset that is not part of the ordinary operations.

**capital markets**—all institutions and procedures that facilitate transactions in long-term financial instruments.

**capital rationing**—placing a limit on the dollar size of the capital budget.

**capital structure**—the mix of long-term sources of funds used by the firm. This is also called the firm's capitalization. The relative total (percentage) of each type of fund is emphasized.

**capital structure decision**—the decision-making process with funding choices and the mix of long-term sources of funds.

**cash**—cash on hand, demand deposits, and short-term marketable securities that can quickly be converted into cash.

**cash basis accounting**—a method of accounting whereby revenue is recorded when physical cash is actually received. Likewise, expenses are recorded when physical cash is paid out.

**cash budget**—a detailed plan of future cash flows. This budget is composed of four elements: cash receipts, cash disbursements, net change in cash for the period, and new financing needed.

**characteristic line**—the line of "best fit" through a series of returns for a firm's stock relative to the market's returns. The slope of the line, frequently called beta, represents the average movement of the firm's stock returns in response to a movement in the market's returns.

**chattel mortgage agreement**—a loan agreement in which the lender can increase his or her security interest by having specific items of inventory identified in the loan agreement. The borrower retains title to the inventory but cannot sell the items without the lender's consent.

**clientele effect**—the belief that individuals and institutions will invest in companies whose dividend payouts match their particular needs for current versus future cash flow. For example, those that need current income will invest in companies that have high dividend payouts.

**combined, or total, leverage**—the result of the combined effects of both operating and financial leverage.

**commercial paper**—short-term unsecured promissory notes sold by large businesses in order to raise cash. Unlike most other money-market instruments, commercial paper has no developed secondary market.

**common-sized balance sheet**—a balance sheet in which a firm's assets and sources of debt and equity are expressed as a percentage of its total assets.

**common-sized income statement**—an income statement in which a firm's expenses and profits are expressed as a percentage of its sales.

**common stock**—shares that represent ownership in a corporation.

**common stockholders**—investors who own the firm's common stock. Common stockholders are the residual owners of the firm.

**company-unique risk**—see unsystematic risk.

**compensating balance**—a balance of a given amount that the firm maintains in its demand deposit account. It may be required by either a formal or an informal agreement with the firm's commercial bank. Such balances are usually required by the bank (1) on the unused portion of a loan commitment, (2) on the unpaid portion of an outstanding loan, or (3) in exchange for certain services provided by the bank, such as check-clearing or credit information. These balances raise the effective rate of interest paid on borrowed funds.

**compound annuity**—depositing an equal sum of money at the end of each year for a certain number of years and allowing it to grow.

**compound interest**—the situation in which interest paid on an investment during the first period is added to the principal. During the second period, interest is earned on the original principal plus the interest earned during the first period.

**constant dividend payout ratio**—a dividend payment policy in which the percentage of earnings paid out in dividends is held constant. The dollar amount fluctuates from year to year as profits vary.

**contribution-to-firm risk**—the amount of risk that the project contributes to the firm as a whole; this measure considers the fact that some of the project's risk will be diversified away as the project is combined with the firm's other projects and assets but ignores the effects of diversification of the firm's shareholders.

**convertible bond**—a debt security that can be converted into a firm's stock at a pre-specified price.

**convertible preferred stock**—preferred shares that can be converted into a pre-determined number of shares of common stock, if investors so choose.

**corporation**—an entity that legally functions separate and apart from its owners.

**cost of common equity**—the rate of return that must be earned on the common stockholders' investment in order to satisfy their required rate of return.

**cost of debt**—the rate that has to be received from an investment in order to achieve the required rate of return for the creditors.

**cost of goods sold**—the cost of producing or acquiring a product or service to be sold in the ordinary course of business.

**cost of preferred equity**—the rate of return that must be earned on the preferred stock-

holders' investment in order to satisfy their required rate of return.

**coupon interest rate**—the interest rate contractually owed on a bond as a percent of its par value.

**coverage ratios**—ratios of the firm's earnings to the interest and principal related to a firm's borrowing.

**credit scoring**—the numerical evaluation of credit applicants where the score is evaluated relative to a predetermined standard.

**cross rate**—the exchange rate between two foreign currencies, neither of which is the currency of the domestic country.

**cumulative feature**—a requirement that all past, unpaid preferred stock dividends be paid before any common stock dividends are declared.

**cumulative voting**—voting in which each share of stock allows the shareholder a number of votes equal to the number of directors being elected. The shareholder can then cast all of his or her votes for a single candidate or split them among the various candidates.

**current assets (gross working capital)**—current assets consist primarily of cash, marketable securities, accounts receivable, inventories, and other current assets.

**current debt (short-term liabilities)**—debt due to be paid within 12 months.

**current ratio**—the firm's current assets divided by its current liabilities. This ratio indicates a company's degree of liquidity by comparing its current assets to its current liabilities.

**current yield**—the ratio of a bond's annual interest payment to its market price.

**date of record**—the date at which the stock transfer books are to be closed for determining the investors to receive the next dividend payment.

**days in inventory**—inventory divided by daily cost of goods sold. This ratio measures the number of days a firm's inventories are held on average before being sold; it also indicates the quality of the inventory.

**days in receivables (average collection period)**—a firm's accounts receivable divided by the company's average daily *credit* sales (annual credit sales ÷ 365). This ratio expresses how many days on average it takes to collect receivables.

**debenture**—any unsecured long-term debt.

**debt**—liabilities consisting of such sources as credit extended by suppliers or a loan from a bank.

**debt capacity**—the maximum amount of debt that the firm can include in its capital structure and still maintain its current credit rating.

**debt–equity composition**—the mix of debt and equity used by the firm in its capital structure.

**debt maturity composition**—the mix of short- and long-term debt used by the firm.

**debt ratio**—a firm's total liabilities divided by its total assets. This ratio measures the extent to which a firm has been financed with debt.

**declaration date**—the date upon which a dividend is formally declared by the board of directors.

**default-risk premium**—the additional return required by investors to compensate them for the risk of default. It is calculated as the difference in rates between a U.S. Treasury bond and a corporate bond of the same maturity and marketability.

**delivery date**—the date on which the actual payment of one currency in exchange for another takes place in a foreign exchange transaction.

**delivery-time stock**—the inventory needed between the order date and the receipt of the inventory ordered.

**depreciation expense**—a noncash expense to allocate the cost of depreciable assets, such as plant and equipment, over the life of the asset.

**direct costs**—see **variable costs**.

**direct foreign investment (DFI)**—a company from one country making a physical investment, such as building a factory, in another country.

**direct quote**—the exchange rate that indicates the number of units of the home currency required to buy one unit of a foreign currency.

**direct sale**—the sale of securities by a corporation to the investing public without the services of an investment-banking firm.

**discount bond**—a bond that sells at a discount, or below par value.

**discounted payback period**—the number of years it takes to recapture a project's initial outlay from the discounted free cash flows.

**discretionary financing**—sources of financing that require an explicit decision on the part of the firm's management every time funds are raised. Bank notes provide a typical example of this type of financing.

**diversifiable risk**—see unsystematic risk.

**dividend-payout ratio**—dividends as a percentage of earnings.

**dividends per share**—the amount of dividends a firm pays for each share outstanding.

**divisional WACC**—the cost of capital for a specific business unit or division.

**Dutch auction**—a method of issuing securities (common stock) by which investors place bids indicating how many shares they are willing to buy and at what price. The price the stock is then sold for becomes the lowest price at which the issuing company can sell all the available shares.

**earnings before taxes (taxable income)**—operating income minus interest expense.

**earnings per share**—net income on a per share basis.

**EBIT-EPS indifference point**—the level of earnings before interest and taxes (EBIT) that will equate earnings per share (EPS) between two different financing plans.

**economic value added**—measures a company's economic profits, as compared to its accounting profits, by including not only interest expense as a cost but also the shareholders' required rate of return on their investment.

**effective annual rate (EAR)**—the annual compound rate that produces the same return as the nominal, or quoted, rate when something is compounded on a nonannual basis. In effect, the EAR provides the true rate of return.

**efficient market**—market where the values of all securities fully recognize all available public information.

**equity**—stockholders' investment in the firm and the cumulative profits retained in the business up to the date of the balance sheet.

**equivalent annual annuity (*EAA*)**—an annuity cash flow that yields the same present value as the project's *NPV*.

**Eurobond**—a bond issued in a country different from the one in which the currency of the bond is denominated; for example, a bond issued in Europe or Asia by an American company that pays interest and principal to the lender in U.S. dollars.

**Eurodollars**—U.S. dollars hold by foreign (often European) banks and financial institutions outside the United States, and often as a result of payments to foreign companies for good or services.

**exchange rate**—the price of one currency stated in terms of another.

**ex-dividend date**—the date upon which stock brokerage companies have uniformly decided to terminate the right of ownership to the dividend, which is two days prior to the date of record.

**expectations theory**—the notion that investor reactions to a managerial decision are based on their *assessment* of the effect of the action on stock price. For example, the announcement of a higher dividend not only indicates that more cash will be received by investors this quarter but may also signal to investors that the firm's future prospects have improved.

**expected rate of return**—The rate of return investors expect to receive on an investment by paying the current market price of the security.

**external financing needs**—that portion of a firm's requirements for financing that exceeds its sources of internal financing (i.e., the retention of earnings) plus spontaneous sources of financing (e.g., trade credit).

**factor**—a firm that, in acquiring the receivables of other firms, bears the risk of collection and, for a fee, services the accounts.

**factoring accounts receivable**—the outright sale of a firm's accounts receivable to another party (the factor) without recourse. The factor, in turn, bears the risk of collection.

**fair value**—the present value of an asset's expected future cash flows.

**field-warehouse agreement**—a security agreement in which inventories pledged as collateral are physically separated from the firm's other inventories and placed under the control of a third-party field-warehousing firm.

**financial leverage**—results from the firm's use of sources of financing that require a fixed rate of return. The primary example of such a form of financing is fixed interest rate debt whereby the firm must pay predetermined interest and principal on specified dates.

**financial markets**—those institutions and procedures that facilitate transactions in all types of financial claims.

**financial policy**—the firm's policies regarding the sources of financing it plans to use and the particular mix (proportions) in which they will be used.

**financial ratios**—accounting data restated in relative terms in order to help people identify some of the financial strengths and weaknesses of a company.

**financial risk**—risk driven by the presence of fixed finance costs in the firm's capital structure (as opposed to variable finance costs such as dividends declared and paid).

**financial structure**—the mix of all sources of fundings that appears on the right-hand side of the balance sheet.

**financing cash flows**—the amount of cash received from or distributed to the firm's investors, usually in the form of interest, dividends, issuance of debt, or issuance or repurchase of stocks.

**finished-goods inventory**—goods on which the production has been completed but that are not yet sold.

**fixed asset turnover**—a firm's sales divided by its net fixed assets. This ratio indicates how efficiently the firm is using its fixed assets.

**fixed assets**—assets such as equipment, buildings, and land.

**fixed costs**—costs that do not vary in total dollar amount as sales volume or quantity of output changes. Also called **indirect costs.**

**fixed-rate bond**—a bond that pays a fixed amount of interest to the investor each year.

**float**—the length of time from when a check is written until the actual recipient can draw upon the funds.

**floating lien agreement**—an agreement, generally associated with a loan, whereby the borrower gives the lender a lien against all its inventory.

**flotation costs**—the costs incurred by the firm when it issues securities to raise funds.

**foreign exchange (FX) market**—the market in which the currencies of various countries are traded.

**Form 10-K**—an annual report required by the Securities and Exchange Commission (SEC) that provides such information as the firm's history, audited financial statements, management's analysis of the company's performance, and executive compensation.

**forward exchange contract**—an agreement between two parties to exchange one currency for another on a future date.

**forward exchange rate**—an exchange rate for a transaction that calls for delivery in the future.

**forward-spot differential**—the premium or discount between forward and spot currency exchange rates.

**free cash flows**—the amount of cash available from operations after the firm pays for the investments it has made in operating working capital and fixed assets. This cash is available to distribute to the firm's creditors and owners.

**future value**—the amount to which your investment will grow, or a future dollar amount.

**future value factor**—the value of $(1 + r)^n$ used as a multiple to calculate an amount's future value.

**futures markets**—markets where you can buy or sell something at a future date.

**general partnership**—a partnership in which all partners are fully liable for the indebtedness incurred by the partnership.

**Generally Accepted Accounting Principles (GAAP)**—rule-based set of accounting principles, standards, and procedures that companies use to compile their financial statements. These principles are issued by the Financial Accounting Standards Board.

**gross fixed assets**—the original cost of a firm's fixed assets.

**gross profit**—sales or revenue minus the cost of goods sold.

**gross profit margin**—gross profit divided by net sales. It is a ratio denoting the gross profit earned by the firm as a percentage of its net sales.

**hedging principle (principle of self-liquidating debt)**—a working-capital management policy which states that the cash-flow-generating characteristics of a firm's investments should be matched with the cash-flow requirements of the firm's sources of financing. Very simply, short-lived assets should be financed with short-term sources of financing while long-lived assets should be financed with long-term sources of financing.

**high-yield bond**—see junk bond.

**holding-period return (historical or realized rate of return)**—the rate of return earned on an investment, which equals the dollar gain divided by the amount invested.

**income statement (profit and loss statement)**—a basic accounting statement that measures the results of a firm's operations over a specified period, commonly 1 year. The bottom line of the income statement, net profits (net income), shows the profit or loss for the period that is available for a company's owners (shareholders).

**incremental cash flow**—the difference between the cash flows a company will produce both with and without the investment it is thinking about making.

**indenture**—the legal agreement between the firm issuing bonds and the bond trustee who represents the bondholders, providing the specific terms of the loan agreement.

**indirect costs**—see **fixed costs**.

**indirect quote**—the exchange rate that expresses the number of units of foreign currency that can be bought for one unit of home currency.

**inflation premium**—a premium to compensate for anticipated inflation that is equal to the price change expected to occur over the life of the bond or investment instrument.

**information asymmetry**—the notion that investors do not know as much about the firm's operations as the firm's management.

**initial outlay**—the immediate cash outflow necessary to purchase the asset and put it in operating order.

**initial public offering, IPO**—the first time a company issues its stock to the public.

**insolvency**—the inability to meet interest payments or to repay debt at maturity.

**intercept**—the constant term in a linear equation. This is the value predicted in a linear equation for the item being forecast (e.g., operating expenses) where revenues are equal to zero.

**interest rate parity (IRP) theory**—a theory that states that (except for the effects of small transaction costs) the forward premium or discount should be equal and opposite in size to the difference in the national interest rates for securities of the same maturity.

**interest rate risk**—the variability in a bond's value caused by changing interest rates.

**internal growth**—a firm's growth rate resulting from reinvesting the company's profits rather than distributing them as dividends. The growth rate is a function of the amount retained and the return earned on the retained funds.

**internal rate of return (_IRR_)**—the rate of return that the project earns. For computational purposes, the internal rate of return is defined as the discount rate that equates the present value of the project's free cash flows with the project's initial cash outlay.

**International Financial Reporting Standards (IFRS)**—a principle-based set of international accounting standards stating how particular types of transactions and other events should be reported in financial statements. The principles are issued by the International Accounting Standards Board.

**intrinsic, or economic, value**—the present value of an asset's expected future cash flows. This value is the amount the investor considers to be fair value, given the amount, timing, and riskiness of future cash flows.

**inventories**—raw materials, work in progress, and finished goods held by the firm for eventual sale.

**inventory loans**—loans secured by inventories. Examples include floating or blanket lien agreements, chattel mortgage agreements, field-warehouse receipt loans, and terminal-warehouse receipt loans.

**inventory management**—the control of assets used in the production process or produced to be sold in the normal course of the firm's operations.

**inventory turnover**—a firm's cost of goods sold divided by its inventory. This ratio measures the number of times a firm's inventories are sold and replaced during the year, that is, the relative liquidity of the inventories.

**investment banker**—a financial specialist who underwrites and distributes new securities and advises corporate clients about raising new funds.

**junk bond**—any bond rated BB or below.

**just-in-time inventory control system**—a production and management system in which inventory is cut down to a minimum through adjustments to the time and physical distance between the various production operations. Under this system the firm keeps a minimum level of inventory on hand, relying upon suppliers to furnish parts "just in time" for them to be assembled.

**law of one price**—an economic principle that states that a good or service cannot sell for different prices in the same market. Applied to international markets, this law states that the same goods should sell for the same price in different countries after making adjustment for the exchange rate between the two currencies.

**limited liability**—a protective provision whereby the investor is not liable for more than the amount he or she has invested in the firm.

**limited liability company (LLC)**—a cross between a partnership and a corporation under which the owners retain limited liability but the company is run and is taxed like a partnership.

**limited partnership**—a partnership in which one or more of the partners has limited liability, restricted to the amount of capital he or she invests in the partnership.

**line of credit**—generally an informal agreement or understanding between a borrower and a bank as to the maximum amount of credit the bank will provide the borrower at any one time. Under this type of agreement there is no "legal" commitment on the part of the bank to provide the stated credit.

**liquidation value**—the dollar sum that could be realized if an asset were sold.

**liquidity**—the ability to convert an asset into cash quickly without a significant loss of its value.

**liquidity preference theory**—the theory that the shape of the term structure of interest rates is determined by an investor's additional required interest rate in compensation for additional risks.

**liquidity-risk premium**—the additional return required by investors for securities that cannot be quickly converted into cash at a reasonably predictable price.

**long-term debt**—loans from banks or other sources that lend money for longer than 12 months.

**majority voting**—voting in which each share of stock allows the shareholder one vote

and each position on the board of directors is voted on separately. As a result, a majority of shares has the power to elect the entire board of directors.

**marginal tax rate**—the tax rate that would be applied to the next dollar of income.

**market risk**—see systematic risk.

**market segmentation theory**—the theory that the shape of the term structure of interest rates implies that the rate of interest for a particular maturity is determined solely by demand and supply for a given maturity. This rate is independent of the demand and supply for securities having different maturities.

**market value**—the value observed in the marketplace.

**marketable securities**—security investments (financial assets) the firm can quickly convert to cash balances. Also known as near cash or near-cash assets.

**maturity**—the length of time until the bond issuer returns the par value to the bondholder and terminates the bond.

**maturity-risk premium**—the additional return required by investors in longer-term securities to compensate them for the greater risk of price fluctuations on those securities caused by interest rate changes.

**modified internal rate of return (MIRR)**—the discount rate that equates the present value of the project's future free cash flows with the terminal value of the cash inflows.

**money market**—all institutions and procedures that facilitate transactions for short-term instruments issued by borrowers with very high credit ratings.

**mortgage**—a loan to finance real estate where the lender has first claim on the property in the event the borrower is unable to repay the loan.

**mortgage bond**—a bond secured by a lien on real property.

**multinational corporation (MNC)**—a corporation with holdings and/or operations in more than one country.

**mutually exclusive projects**—projects that, if undertaken, would serve the same purpose. Thus, accepting one will necessarily mean rejecting the others.

**net fixed assets**—gross fixed assets minus the accumulated depreciation taken over the life of the assets.

**net income (net profit, or earnings available to common stockholders)**—the earnings available to the firm's common and preferred stockholders.

**net present value (NPV)**—the present value of an investment's annual free cash flows less the investment's initial outlay.

**net present value profile**—a graph showing how a project's *NPV* changes as the discount rate changes.

**net profit margin**—net income divided by sales. A ratio that measures the net income of the firm as a percent of sales.

**net working capital**—the difference between the firm's current assets and its current liabilities.

**nominal (or quoted) rate of interest**—the interest rate paid on debt securities without an adjustment for any loss in purchasing power.

**nondiversifiable risk**—see systematic risk.

**operating expenses**—marketing and selling expenses, general and administrative expenses, and depreciation expense.

**operating income (earnings before interest and taxes)**—sales less the cost of goods sold less operating expenses.

**operating leverage**—results from operating costs that are fixed and do not vary with the level of firm sales.

**operating profit margin**—a firm's operating profits divided by sales. This ratio serves as an overall measure of operating effectiveness.

**operating return on assets (OROA)**—the ratio of a firm's operating profits divided by its total assets. This ratio indicates the rate of return being earned on the firm's assets.

**operating risk**—risk driven by the mix of fixed versus variable costs the firm incurs to do business.

**operations management**—how effectively management is performing in the day-to-day operations in terms of how well management is generating revenues and controlling costs and expenses; in other words, how well is the firm managing the activities that directly affect the income statement?

**opportunity cost**—the cost of making a choice defined in terms of the next best alternative that is foregone.

**opportunity cost of funds**—the next-best rate of return available to the investor for a given level of risk.

**optimal capital structure**—the capital structure that minimizes the firm's composite cost of capital (maximizes the common stock price) for raising a given amount of funds.

**optimal range of financial leverage**—the range of debt use in the firm's capital structure that yields the lowest overall cost of capital for the firm.

**order point problem**—determining how low inventory should be depleted before it is reordered.

**order quantity problem**—determining the optimal order size for an inventory item given its usage, carrying costs, and ordering costs.

**ordinary annuity**—an annuity where the cash flows occur at the end of each period.

**organized security exchanges**—formal organizations that facilitate the trading of securities.

**other current assets**—other short-term assets that will benefit future time periods, such as prepaid expenses.

**over-the-counter markets**—all security markets except organized exchanges. The money market is an over-the-counter market. Most corporate bonds also are traded in the over-the-counter market.

**paid-in capital**—the amount a company receives above par value from selling stock to investors.

**par value**—for a bond, par value is the stated amount that the firm is to repay when the bond comes due (matures); for a stock, par value is the arbitrary value a firm assigns to each share of stock when issued to investors. Any amount received from the stock sale that is above par value is paid-in-capital.

**partnership**—an association of two or more individuals joining together as co-owners to operate a business for profit.

**payable-through draft (PTD)**—a legal instrument that has the physical appearance of an ordinary check but is not drawn on a bank. A payable-through draft is drawn on and paid by the issuing firm. The bank serves as a collection point and passes the draft on to the firm.

**payback period**—the number of years it takes to recapture a project's initial outlay.

**payment date**—the date on which the company mails a dividend check to each investor of record.

**percent of sales method**—a method of financial forecasting that involves estimating the level of an expense, asset, or liability for a future period as a percent of the sales forecast.

**perfect capital markets**—markets in which information flows freely and market prices fully reflect all available information.

**permanent investment**—investments that the firm expects to hold longer than 1 year. The firm makes permanent investments in fixed and current assets.

**perpetuity**—an annuity with an infinite life.

**pledging accounts receivable**—a loan the firm obtains from a commercial bank or a finance company using its accounts receivable as collateral.

**portfolio beta**—the relationship between a portfolio's returns and the market returns.

It is a measure of the portfolio's nondiversifiable risk.

**preemptive right**—the right entitling the common shareholder to maintain his or her proportionate share of ownership in the firm.

**preferred stock**—a hybrid security with characteristics of both common stock and bonds. Preferred stock is similar to common stock in that it has no fixed maturity date, the nonpayment of dividends does not bring on bankruptcy, and dividends are not deductible for tax purposes. Preferred stock is similar to bonds in that dividends are limited in amount.

**preferred stockholders**—stockholders who have claims on the firm's income and assets after creditors, but before common stockholders.

**premium bond**—a bond that is selling above its par value.

**present value**—the value in today's dollars of a future payment discounted back to present at the required rate of return.

**present value factor**—the value of $1/(1 + r)^n$ used as a multiplier to calculate an amount's present value.

**price/book ratio**—the market value of a share of the firm's stock divided by the book value per share of the firm's reported equity in the balance sheet. Indicates the market price placed on $1 of capital that was invested by shareholders.

**price/earnings ratio**—the price the market places on $1 of a firm's earnings. For example, if a firm has an earnings per share of $2, and a stock price of $30 per share, its price/earnings ratio is 15. ($30 ÷ $2).

**primary market**—a market in which securities are offered for the first time for sale to potential investors.

**private placement**—a security offering limited to a small number of potential investors.

**privileged subscription**—the process of marketing a new security issue to a select group of investors.

**profitability index (PI) or benefit–cost ratio**—the ratio of the present value of an investment's future free cash flows to the investment's initial outlay.

**profit margins**—financial ratios (sometimes simply referred to as margins) that reflect the level of the firm's profits relative to its sales. Examples include the gross profit margin (gross profit divided by sales), operating profit margin (operating income divided by sales), and the net profit margin (net income ÷ sales).

**profit-retention rate**—the company's percentage of profits retained.

**project standing alone risk**—a project's risk ignoring the fact that much of this risk will be diversified away.

**protective provisions**—provisions for preferred stock that protect the investor's interest. The provisions generally allow for voting in the event of nonpayment of dividends, or they restrict the payment of common stock dividends if sinking-fund payments are not met or if the firm is in financial difficulty.

**proxy**—a means of voting in which a designated party is provided with the temporary power of attorney to vote for the signee at the corporation's annual meeting.

**proxy fight**—a battle between rival groups for proxy votes in order to control the decisions made in a stockholders' meeting.

**public offering**—a security offering where all investors have the opportunity to acquire a portion of the financial claims being sold.

**purchasing-power parity (PPP)**—a theory that states that exchange rates adjust so that identical goods cost the same amount regardless of where in the world they are purchased.

**pure play method**—a method for estimating a project's or division's beta that attempts to identify publicly traded firms engaged solely in the same business as the project or division.

**raw-materials inventory**—the basic materials purchased from other firms to be used in the firm's production operations.

**real rate of interest**—the nominal (quoted) rate of interest less any loss in purchasing power of the dollar during the time of the investment.

**real risk-free interest rate**—the required rate of return on a fixed-income security that has no risk in an economic environment of zero inflation.

**required rate of return**—minimum rate of return necessary to attract an investor to purchase or hold a security.

**residual dividend theory**—a theory that a company's dividend payment should equal the cash left after financing all the investments that have positive net present values.

**retained earnings**—cumulative profits retained in a business up to the date of the balance sheet.

**return on equity**—a firm's net income divided by its common book equity. This ratio is the accounting rate of return earned on the common stockholders' investment.

**revolving credit agreement**—an understanding between the borrower and the bank as to the amount of credit the bank will be legally obligated to provide the borrower.

**right**—a certificate issued to common stock-holders giving them an option to purchase a stated number of new shares at a specified price during a 2- to 10-week period.

**risk**—potential variability in future cash flows.

**risk-adjusted discount rate**—a method of risk adjustment when the risk associated with the investment is greater than the risk involved in a typical endeavor. Using this method, the discount rate is adjusted upward to compensate for this added risk.

**risk-free rate of return**—the rate of return on risk-free investments. The interest rates on short-term U.S. government securities are commonly used to measure this rate.

**risk premium**—the additional return expected for assuming risk.

**safety stock**—inventory held to accommodate any unusually large and unexpected usage during delivery time.

**scenario analysis**—a simulation approach for gauging a project's risk under the worst, best, and most likely outcomes. The firm's management examines the distribution of the outcomes to determine the project's level of risk and then makes the appropriate adjustment.

**S-corporation**—a corporation that, because of specific qualifications, is taxed as though it were a partnership.

**seasoned equity offering, SEO**—the sale of additional stock by a company whose shares are already publicly traded.

**secondary market**—a market in which currently outstanding securities are traded.

**secured loans**—sources of credit that require security in the form of pledged assets. In the event the borrower defaults in payment of principal or interest, the lender can seize the pledged assets and sell them to settle the debt.

**security market line**—the return line that reflects the attitudes of investors regarding the minimum acceptable return for a given level of systematic risk associated with a security.

**semivariable costs**—costs composed of a mixture of fixed and variable components.

**sensitivity analysis**—a method for dealing with risk where the change in the distribution of possible net present values or internal rates of return for a particular project resulting from a change in one particular input variable is calculated. This is done by changing the value of one input variable while holding all other input variables constant.

**short-term notes (debt)**—amounts borrowed from lenders, mostly financial institutions such as banks, where the loan is to be repaid within 12 months.

**simple interest**—if you only earned interest on your initial investment, it would be referred to as simple interest.

**simulation**—a method for dealing with risk where the performance of the project under evaluation is estimated by randomly selecting observations from each of the distributions that affect the outcome of the project and continuing with this process until a representative record of the project's probable outcome is assembled.

**sinking-fund provision**—a protective provision that requires the firm periodically to set aside an amount of money for the retirement of its preferred stock. This money is then used to purchase the preferred stock in the open market or through the use of the call provision, whichever method is cheaper.

**slope coefficient**—the rate of change in the item being forecast with a linear equation and the change in sales.

**small, regular dividend plus a year-end extra**—a corporate policy of paying a small regular dollar dividend plus a year-end extra dividend in prosperous years to avoid the connotation of a permanent dividend.

**sole proprietorship**—a business owned by a single individual.

**spontaneous financing**—the trade credit and other accounts payable that arise spontaneously in the firm's day-to-day operations.

**spot exchange rate**—an exchange rate for a transaction that calls for immediate delivery.

**spot market**—cash market.

**stable dollar dividend per share**—a dividend policy that maintains a relatively stable dollar dividend per share over time.

**standard deviation**—a statistical measure of the spread of a probability distribution calculated by squaring the difference between each outcome and its expected value, weighting each value by its probability, summing over all possible outcomes, and taking the square root of this sum.

**statement of cash flows**—a statement that shows how changes in balance sheet accounts and income affect cash and cash equivalents, and breaks the analysis down to operating, investing, and financing activities.

**stock dividend**—a distribution of shares of up to 25 percent of the number of shares currently outstanding, issued on a pro rata basis to the current stockholders.

**stock repurchase (stock buyback)**—the purchase of outstanding common stock by the issuing firm.

**stock split**—a stock dividend exceeding 25 percent of the number of shares currently outstanding.

**subordinated debenture**—a debenture that is subordinated to other debentures in terms of its payments in case of insolvency.

**syndicate**—a group of investment bankers who contractually assist in the buying and selling of a new security issue.

**systematic risk**—(1) the risk related to an investment return that cannot be eliminated through diversification. Systematic risk results from factors that affect all stocks. Also called market risk or nondiversifiable risk. (2) The risk of a project from the viewpoint of a well-diversified shareholder. This measure takes into account that some of the project's risk will be diversified away as the project is combined with the firm's other projects, and, in addition, some of the remaining risk will be diversified away by shareholders as they combine this stock with other stocks in their portfolios.

**tax shield**—the reduction in taxes due to the tax deductibility of interest expense.

**taxable income**—gross income from all sources, except for allowable exclusions, less any tax-deductible expenses.

**temporary investments**—a firm's investments in current assets that will be liquidated and not replaced within a period of 1 year or less. Examples include seasonal expansions in inventories and accounts receivable.

**tender offer**—a formal offer by the company to buy a specified number of shares at a predetermined and stated price. The tender price is set above the current market price in order to attract sellers.

**term structure of interest rates**—the relationship between interest rates and the term to maturity, where the risk of default is held constant.

**terminal-warehouse agreement**—a security agreement in which the inventories pledged as collateral are transported to a public warehouse that is physically removed from the borrower's premises. This is the safest (though costly) form of financing secured by inventory.

**terms of sale**—the credit terms identifying the possible discount for early payment.

**times interest earned**—a firm's operating profits divided by interest expense. This ratio measures a firm's ability to meet its interest payments from its annual operating earnings.

**total asset turnover**—a firm's sales divided by its total assets. This ratio is an overall measure of asset efficiency based on the relation between a firm's sales and the total assets.

**total revenue**—total sales dollars.

**trade credit**—credit made available by a firm's suppliers in conjunction with the acquisition of materials. Trade credit appears on the balance sheet as accounts payable.

**transaction loan**—a loan where the proceeds are designated for a specific purpose—for example, a bank loan used to finance the acquisition of a piece of equipment.

**treasury stock**—the firm's stock that has been issued and then repurchased by the firm.

**unbiased expectations theory**—the theory that the shape of the term structure of interest rates is determined by an investor's expectations about future interest rates.

**underwriter's spread**—the difference between the price the corporation raising money gets and the public offering price of a security.

**underwriting**—the purchase and subsequent resale of a new security issue. The risk of selling the new issue at a satisfactory (profitable) price is assumed (underwritten) by the investment banker.

**unsecured loans**—all sources of credit that have as their security only the lender's faith in the borrower's ability to repay the funds when due.

**unsystematic risk**—the risk related to an investment return that can be eliminated through diversification. Unsystematic risk is the result of factors that are unique to the particular firm. Also called company-unique risk or diversifiable risk.

**variable costs**—expenses that vary in total as output changes. Also called **direct costs**.

**venture capitalist**—an investment firm (or individual investor) that provides money to business start-ups.

**volume of output**—the number of units produced and sold for a particular period of time.

**weighted average cost of capital**—an average of the individual costs of financing used by the firm. A firm's weighted cost of capital is a function of (1) the individual costs of capital, and (2) the capital structure mix.

**working capital**—a concept traditionally defined as a firm's investment in current assets.

**working capital management**—the management of the firm's current assets and short-term financing.

**work-in-process inventory**—partially finished goods requiring additional work before they become finished goods.

**yield to maturity**—the rate of return a bondholder will receive if the bond is held to maturity.

**zero balance accounts (ZBA)**—a cash management tool that permits centralized control over cash outflow while maintaining divisional disbursing authority. Objectives are (1) to achieve better control over cash payments; (2) to reduce excess cash balances held in regional banks for disbursing purposes; and (3) to increase disbursing float.

**zero coupon bond**—a bond issued at a substantial discount from its $1,000 face value and that pays little or no interest.

# Indexes